MARKETING RESEARCH in a
MARKETING ENVIRONMENT

Third Edition

THE IRWIN SERIES IN MARKETING
(Gilbert A. Churchill, Jr.; Consulting Editor; **University of Wisconsin, Madison**)

MARKETING RESEARCH MARKETING ENVIRONMENT

Third Edition

WILLIAM R. DILLON
University of South Carolina

THOMAS J. MADDEN
University of South Carolina

NEIL H. FIRTLE
Leggett Lustig Firtle, Inc.

IRWIN

Burr Ridge, Illinois
Boston, Massachusetts
Sydney, Australia

This symbol indicates that the paper in this book is made of recycled paper. Its fiber content exceeds the recommended minimum of 50% waste paper fibers as specified by the EPA.

Executive editor: *Rob Zwettler*
Senior developmental editor: *Andy Winston*
Project editor: *Jean Lou Hess*
Production manager: *Ann Cassady*
Designer: *Jeanne M. Rivera*
Art manager: *Kim Meriwether*
Photo research coordinator: *Patricia A. Seefelt*
Compositor: *Weimer Graphics, Inc.*
Typeface: *10/12 Electra*
Printer: *R. R. Donnelley & Sons Company*

Library of Congress Cataloging-in-Publication Data

Dillon, William R.
    Marketing research in a marketing environment/William R.
Dillon, Thomas J. Madden, Neil H. Firtle.—3rd ed.
        p.   cm.
    Includes bibliographical references and index.
    ISBN 0-256-10517-0   ISBN 0-256-10829-3 (International ed.)
    1. Marketing research.   I. Madden, Thomas J.   II. Firtle, Neil H.
III. Title.
HF5415.2.D54 1994
    658.8'3—dc20   93–24883

Printed in the United States of America
1 2 3 4 5 6 7 8 9 0   DOC   0 9 8 7 6 5 4 3

To Jennifer: the most enjoyable bundle of end benefits a father could experience

—

To my parents: Thomas J. Madden and Winifred K. Madden

—

To Maureen: a friend, colleague, and wife

Preface

The preface to the first edition of *Marketing Research in a Marketing Environment* declared our primary motivation for writing another marketing research text: to bridge the gap between the theory and practice of marketing research. The second, and now the third, edition continue this approach by again emphasizing the problem-oriented nature of marketing research and by discussing and illustrating how marketing research is actually implemented by professional marketing researchers. Key features in *Marketing Research in a Marketing Environment* include:

- *Involving the reader in the marketing research community.* This community is discussed in terms of its principal parties and primary activities. The reader gains an appreciation for the primary players who conduct marketing research and their respective responsibilities.
- *Developing a framework that places marketing research within the well-known product life cycle.* Cross-classifying specific marketing research activities according to the marketing research stage and the focus of the research helps the student understand the problem-oriented nature of marketing research.
- *Introducing the reader to traditional content areas by discussing prototypical marketing research proposals.* Real-world marketing research proposals provide much of the motivation for the material presented in this book. The project proposals used throughout the book have been derived from actual marketing research projects. Though brand and research supplier names have been

changed to ensure confidentiality, the illustrative proposals convey the essence of how marketing research is conducted in the real world.
- *Building on the secondary sources of information available.* In recent years the ability to locate and obtain secondary sources of market research information has been revolutionized by online computer-assisted data search technology. Scanner services are changing the face of commercial marketing research.
- *Introducing the reader to current sources of purchase and media data.* Syndicated sources of purchase and media data continue to be an important source of information that can be used to solve many marketing-related problems.
- *Involving the reader in a variety of marketing research studies.* The tools and techniques of marketing research take on greater meaning when discussed and illustrated in the context of real-world applications. The Case Studies at the end of each of the seven parts in this text use real-world vignettes to demonstrate the important role that marketing research plays in providing relevant answers to marketing-related problems. In addition, data sets are provided for two cases, as well as for several illustrative examples introduced throughout the text.
- *Reinforcing the major concepts introduced throughout the book.* Throughout each chapter marginal definitions are used to highlight

key principles, and case studies and end-of-chapter questions ask the student to apply them. Further reinforcement is provided by learning objectives at the beginning of each chapter and by key concepts at the close.

We earnestly feel that these features represent a major step toward conveying the essence of marketing research.

Marketing Research in a Marketing Environment, third edition, is divided into seven major parts. The book introduces the practice of marketing research through a scenario that describes the job search activities of a recent undergraduate marketing major and her discussions with the members of a marketing research department. This material sets the stage for the ensuing discussion in Part I and will interest the many students who are looking forward to a business-related career.

Part I, Marketing Research Environments, consists of two chapters. In Chapter 1, we describe the elements of marketing research environments and discuss the role and activities of marketing researchers. Chapter 2 discusses the necessary steps in designing a marketing research project.

Part II, Acquiring Data: An Overview, considers tools and techniques that can be used to obtain the market information necessary to answer marketing-related questions. In Chapter 3, we describe secondary information from the perspectives of both traditional and newer online computer-assisted technologies. This material is up to date and is not covered in many current textbooks. Syndicated sources of information on purchase and media behavior are described in Chapter 4. The major suppliers of this sort of information are discussed and attention is focused on the new technology (i.e., scanner services) that is changing the face of marketing research. Chapter 5 discusses techniques and issues of qualitative interviewing methods. In Chapter 6, we provide a comprehensive treatment of survey interviewing methods, including the increasingly popular method of mall intercepts. Chapter 7 follows with a discussion of

the issue of causality and, in particular, experimental research methods. All the experimental designs presented are discussed in the context of real-world marketing research studies to increase the relevance and understanding of this subject matter.

Part III, Sampling Theory and Practices, consists of two chapters. Chapter 8 presents the fundamentals of sampling. Further details on drawing probability samples are provided in Chapter 9. (For the reader not needing technical details on the procedures for drawing probability samples, Chapter 8 will suffice.)

Part IV, Measurement, Scaling, and Questionnaire Design, covers both theoretical and practical issues related to what to ask and how to ask it. Chapter 10 discusses the basic concepts of measurement and provides a discussion of the primary measurement scales used in marketing research. In Chapter 11, we provide a treatment of attitude scales and the concepts of reliability and validity. The final chapter in this part, Chapter 12, presents a comprehensive treatment of the issues that should be considered when designing a questionnaire. In Chapter 13, we discuss issues related to processing the data; in essence, these procedures prepare the data for analysis.

Part V, Data Processing and Analysis, considers the tools and techniques of analysis. Chapter 14 offers a discussion of techniques that can be used to give the researcher an initial glimpse of the data. The next two chapters describe techniques that can be used to uncover and test hypotheses concerning a single variable or the relationships between two or more variables. Chapter 15 discusses hypothesis testing and is followed by two appendices that deal with Analysis of Variance. Chapter 16 discusses measures of association and regression analysis. A brief treatment of some popular multivariate data analysis procedures is presented in the appendices to this chapter. In all instances the discussion includes many examples and is directed to the unsophisticated reader.

Part VI, Applications, presents details on how several different types of marketing research studies are typically conducted. Specifically, Chapter 17 considers what are commonly referred to as *market studies*, Chapter 18 considers *concept and product studies*, Chapter 19 considers *package and name studies*, Chapter 20 considers *advertising testing studies*, and Chapter 21 considers *test market studies*, including *simulated/pre-test markets*. These applications are discussed in separate chapters for three reasons. First, these studies typify the practice of marketing research. Second, they provide a vehicle for illustrating how the concepts, tools, and techniques from the first five parts of the book can be used to solve real-world, marketing-related problems. Third, they provide exemplary material on which to build class projects. The final chapter in this part of the book, Chapter 22, discusses *marketing decision support systems*. With the recent advances in computer PC-based technology, marketing professionals are beginning to rely on marketing decision support systems with greater regularity and frequency. Although this trend is likely to increase in the future, marketing decision support systems receive only minimal coverage in many current textbooks. As part of our coverage of marketing decision support systems, an appendix to Chapter 22 discusses forecasting techniques.

Part VII, Report Preparation and Ethical Issues, consists of two chapters in which we present topics central to the successful practice marketing research, but not part of the research process. Chapter 23 presents the suggestions of practicing marketing researchers for writing and orally presenting the results of a research project. Chapter 24, a new chapter, explores the foundations of ethical research practices as well as current dilemmas facing research professionals.

Supplements

We have prepared all of the supplements that accompany this textbook. In doing so, we have attempted to provide elements and features of value to the inexperienced as well as experienced instructor.

Instructor's Manual

- *Learning objectives.* The learning objectives that appear at the beginning of each chapter are reproduced.
- *Key terms and concepts.* The key terms and concepts that appear throughout the textbook are reproduced.
- *Lecture notes.* A detailed outline of each chapter is provided.
- *Transparency masters.* Key exhibits, tables, and figures appearing in the textbook are reproduced as $8^{1}/_{2} \times 11$ transparency masters. Transparency masters are also provided for supplemental material not appearing in the textbook. The suggested spot for use of each of these is designed within the teaching suggestions.
- *Teaching suggestions.* These hints and ideas indicate how the authors would organize and present the material appearing in each chapter. Suggestions for where to integrate the transparency masters are also provided.
- *Author comments.* These describe the author's rationale for the major topics presented in each chapter.
- *Answers to end-of-chapter problems.* Detailed answers to every question are provided.
- *Case notes.* For instructors who decide to use any or all of the case studies appearing in the text, a detailed set of case notes is provided.

Test Bank

The test bank contains over 1,000 questions, categorized by chapter. In addition to correct answers, page references are provided.

CompuTest

All questions appearing in the test bank are reproduced in Irwin's CompuTest test-generation system, for use with the IBM PC and compatible computers. The test-generation system provides the following features:

1. Individual test items can be added or deleted.
2. Individual test items can be edited.
3. A shuffle option is provided that allows different versions of the same examination.
4. Ample documentation.

Software

A unique set of contemporary interactive software programs are available to adopters. The software is pedagogical in nature and designed to enhance students' understanding of the concepts and techniques discussed throughout the textbook. Six individual modules are available:

1. The SAMPLE module demonstrates selected concepts related to drawing simple and stratified samples.
2. The SCALE module takes students through various types of monadic and comparative rating scales. Asking students to rate a set of brands on different types of scales enables them to gain an appreciation for the issues involved in selecting a rating instrument.
3. The ACA module illustrates how conjoint analysis works in an interactive PC environment. The module utilizes the Adaptive Conjoint Analysis (ACA) system developed by Richard Johnson of Sawtooth Software, Inc.
4. The QUADMAP module is a system for analyzing top-box importance ratings along with top-box ratings of a brand on a number of salient attributes. This type of analysis is referred to as *quadrant analysis* and is discussed in Chapter 14.
5. The ASCID module is a marketing decision support system for perceptual mapping. A unique feature of this system is the ability to position new objects in an existing perceptual space.
6. The FORCAST module is designed to demonstrate how the more popular forecasting techniques work.

7. The MARITZSTATS module is an interactive statistical analysis system for testing hypotheses concerning means and proportions for one or multiple independent/dependent samples. It also includes an option for determining sample sizes.

Color Transparencies

There are 75 acetates, many of which include material and sources that do not appear in the textbook.

Videos

Focus group sessions are featured; they provide real life experiences.

Acknowledgments

In writing this textbook we have benefited greatly from the comments, suggestions, help, and last but not least, sympathy of many. The review process has been rigorous and constructive. The content of the textbook has been greatly influenced by the hundreds of comments and suggestions made by the reviewers. We gratefully acknowledge the help of the following reviewers:

David Andrus
Kansas State University

Joan M. Baumer
North Carolina State University

Richard Beltramini
Arizona State University

Norman Bruvold
University of Cincinnati

Lee Cooper
University of California at Los Angeles

Forrest S. Carter
Michigan State University

Melvin Crask
University of Georgia

Richard Davis
California State University—Chico

Dale Duhan
Michigan State University

Elizabeth Ensley
Oregon State University

Lawrence Feick
University of Pittsburgh

Susan Higgins
Texas Christian University

Roy Howell
Texas Tech University

Rajshekhar Javalgi
Cleveland State University

Masaaki Kotabe
University of Missouri—Columbia

Michael Loizides
Hampton University

Gary McCain
Boise State University

Kent Nakamoto
The University of Arizona

Nicholas Nugent
Boston College

Lawrence Patterson
Southwest Texas State University

Pradeep A. Rau
Kent State University

Arno Rethans
California State University—Chico

Marsha Richins
Louisiana State University

Sandra Schmidt
University of Virginia

Richard Skinner
Kent State University

Gail Tom
California State University—Sacramento

David J. Urban
Virginia Commonwealth University

Louis Volpp
California State University—Fresno

Gary Young
University of Massachusetts at Boston

As with the first two editions, our task in this revision was made easier by the thoughtful and penetrating reviews we received. We gratefully acknowledge the following reviewers:

Frank Carmone, Jr.
Florida International University

Elizabeth Ferrell
University of Alabama

Robert T. Fisher
University of Colorado

Donald Fuller
University of Central Florida

John Gwin
University of Virginia

Brian McCue
Fontbonne College

Other individuals also deserve thanks. Nancy Podolak, the consummate administrative assistant, had the unenviable task of typing the first edition. Her professionalism and skills allowed the manuscript to be finished on schedule in spite of an exceedingly long first draft. JoAnn Woo provided expert programming skills in connection with the software modules. Needless to say, without her help the software programs would not have been completed. Beth Schwartz provided administrative assistance on the first edition and supervised the most difficult task of securing all of the permissions. Her perseverance and detective work is greatly appreciated. We were fortunate to be able to call on the expertise of Sal M. Meringolo, Chief, Humanities and Social Sciences Department, Penn State University, who prepared most of Chapter 3. Finally, Robert Johnson of Sawtooth Software, Inc., graciously provided the ACA software module.

The authors have greatly benefited from the help and suggestions of members of the business community. In particular, special thanks go to Lisa Myer of CLT Research Associates; Jerry Leighton and Jeff Starr of CRC Information, Inc.; Steve Wilson, Bill Moults, and Ron Tatham of Burke Marketing Services, Inc.; Jody Bernstein of

Millward Brown, Inc.; Andy Boes of LINK Resources; Narendra Mulani of IRI; and Mark Arkin of S. B. Thomas, Inc.

Several members of the academic community deserve acknowledgment. Thanks are especially due Professors Gloria Thomas, Steve Schnaars, and Leon Schiffman of Baruch College and Professors Donald G. Frederick, Subhash Sharma, and Terry Shimp of the University of South Carolina. Second, while all the names are too numerous to mention, some other influential and helpful people have been David Brinberg now at VIP, Rajiv Grover at the University of Pittsburgh and Ajith Kumar now at Arizona State University.

The third edition could not have been completed without the help, sympathy, and hard work of others. Rob Zwettler, our editor, provided critical guidance and support to the project. It was nurtured by Andy Winston, the developmental editor assigned to this project. All of us want to extend our heartfelt gratitude to Andy for the professional treatment we received. Throughout the project he provided insightful comments and an uncanny ability to bring to the forefront the salient content areas in need of attention.

This project began in 1983 while two of the authors were at the University of Massachusetts. In addition, both of these authors started their careers at that institution and since most of our professional development took place at the University of Massachusetts, we would be remiss not to acknowledge our gratitude.

The third edition was completed at the University of South Carolina. We wish to thank Jennie Symrl and Edie Beaver, the marketing department secretaries, for their hard work and assistance in putting together the third edition. Their ability to quickly decipher our handwriting and their talents for getting things done on time is most appreciated. Finally, we would like to thank our marketing department colleagues and in particular our program director, Donald Frederick, for his support and assistance.

William R. Dillon
Thomas J. Madden
Neil H. Firtle

Brief Contents

Contents

Part III
SAMPLING THEORY AND PRACTICES

Part IV
MEASUREMENT, SCALING, AND QUESTIONNAIRE DESIGN

Chapter 10
Concepts of Measurement and Measurement Scales
285

Chapter 11
Attitude Scaling and Concepts in Reliability and Validity
313

Chapter 12
Questionnaire Design Including International Considerations
330

Part VI
APPLICATIONS

Chapter 17
Strategic Market Studies
Positioning, Segmentation, and Structuring
533

Chapter 18
Concept and Product Testing
558

MARKETING RESEARCH ENVIRONMENTS

In Part I we focus on the environment of marketing research and its role in the planning process. Our objective is to have you appreciate the environment in which marketing research takes place and the steps involved in planning and designing a marketing research study.

Chapter 1 defines marketing research and discusses its role in developing effective marketing strategy. A framework for understanding marketing research environments is presented. Our discussion centers on the three principal components of such an environment: internal parties (in-house marketing research department), external parties that interface with in-house personnel, and facilitating external parties. These components are discussed in the context of the research cycle (in its relationship with the product life cycle).

After showing what happens when marketing research is not well planned, Chapter 2 defines each step in a research project. Most important, we introduce the elements of a marketing research proposal. This book uses prototypical marketing research proposals throughout as a framework for introducing, discussing, and illustrating the various concepts, techniques, and principles that make up what is the essence of marketing research.

Marketing Research Environments

- Define marketing research.
- Analyze the role of research in marketing strategy.
- Describe the characteristics of marketing research environments.
- Explain the relationship between members of the marketing and research departments.
- Identify six principal parties outside the organization that play a crucial role in defining marketing research activities.
- Describe the relationship between the research and product life cycles.

INTRODUCTION

This chapter begins our introduction to the theory and practice of marketing research. We want you to appreciate the role marketing research plays in developing effective marketing strategies and to understand the structure of the industry. The position that we will unequivocally take is that decisions on product positioning, price, promotion, and distribution for a brand or service should be based on intelligent, carefully conceived, and properly conducted marketing research.

An essential ingredient in developing effective marketing strategy is a thorough understanding of consumers' needs and wants. An important role of marketing research is to provide such information and to help management and engineering think explicitly about who their customers are and what product features are most important in specific contexts. In other words, marketing research can help to identify segments of the population that, for a variety of reasons, demand different product specifications. In discussing the concept of *customer driven engineering* (CDE), authors Hauser and Klein introduce Fred, a prototypical automobile commuter.

> Fred leaves early each morning by automobile to his workplace. The approximate driving time is one hour. He usually picks up coffee and a doughnut on route, which he eats while driving. Fred pays particular attention to the traffic reports, and he consults his maps if an alternative route is suggested. Whenever possible Fred

utilizes the exact change lanes on the tollway, and consequently he likes to be able to easily access the correct change with his left hand.[1]

There are several obvious product features that would be attractive to Fred; for example, a place to put his coffee and doughnut without fear of mess or spilling, one or more map pockets, and a coin storage tray on the left corner of the dashboard. Among the less obvious but potentially equally important product features are good gas economy, dependability, quick dealer service, good visibility for changing lanes, good acceleration for merging, comfortable and roomy front seats, a smooth ride that doesn't spill coffee, seats that won't wrinkle his suit, and an effective heating and air conditioning system that will do the job for the one-hour trip to and from the office.

Effective marketing research can ensure that Fred gets what he wants in a way that is profitable for the manufacturer. As we discuss in this and following chapters, market research should be undertaken throughout the life cycle of the product. Typically, it begins with focus groups and surveys of consumer perceptions that are slanted toward identifying the customer attributes that are important to different target segments. (Though Fred may not value a roof rack, especially if it means he must give up something important like roomy front seats, another segment of the driving population may value a roof rack more than the product features that are most attractive to Fred.) Analysis of customer preferences for specific combinations of product features can provide priorities for concept and product design. When a product is launched it should be tracked in order to determine early customer feedback. Analysis of in-home use of a product should be undertaken to identify product improvements, and periodic customer input can provide solutions to problems before they damage the company's or product's image. For established products, segmentation and repositioning research frequently point to ways of revitalizing the product by identifying new users and/or uses.

It is important to understand that marketing research is an ongoing, continual process; a more formal discussion of what marketing research is all about is provided.

UNDERSTANDING MARKETING RESEARCH

In 1986 the board of directors of the American Marketing Association endorsed the following definition of marketing research:

Marketing research is the function that links the consumer, customer, and public to the marketer through information—information used to identify and define marketing opportunities and problems; generate, refine, identify and evaluate marketing actions; monitor marketing performance; and improve understanding of marketing as a process. Marketing research specifies the information required to address these issues; designs

---

[1]This scenario and discussion is taken from the work of John Hauser and Robert Klein, "Without good Research, Quality Is a Shot in the Dark," *Marketing News* 22 (January 4, 1988), pp. 1–2.

the method for collecting information; manages and implements the data collection process; analyzes the results; and communicates the findings and their implications.[2]

Put simply, **marketing research** helps the marketing manager to make better informed and less risky marketing decisions. Accordingly, the information obtained through marketing research must be objective, impartial, current, translatable, and relevant. Marketing research involves the systematic gathering, recording, processing, and analyzing of marketing data, which—when interpreted—will help the marketing manager uncover opportunities and reduce the risks in decision making.

marketing research
Activities involving the systematic gathering, recording, processing, and analyzing of marketing data.

Marketing Research Information

The information collected by conducting marketing research is used to (1) identify and define marketing opportunities and problems; (2) generate, refine, and evaluate marketing actions; (3) monitor marketing performance; and (4) improve the understanding of marketing as a process.

Marketing research can help the marketing manager to[3]

1. *Learn the values of the high-profit customers.* In the sales of many products and services, the '80/20 Rule' applies—20 percent of the customers generate 80 percent of the profits. Marketing research can help the manager identify which customers are its best, or "core," customers and understand the values and perceptions that distinguish these customers from others. Marketing research information can help in designing marketing strategies to better satisfy these customers and strengthen their ties to the company.

2. *Analyze customer purchase patterns.* Evaluating the sales of individual products and services should not be undertaken in a vacuum. Marketing research information can help the marketing manager to understand purchasing patterns. For example, a particular product or service may not be profitable but may be valued by many of the firm's core customers. This product or service may in fact form a strong bond between those customers and the company.

3. *Continually monitor customers.* The behavior of customers changes over time. Companies use marketing research information to stay one step ahead of their core customers. Marketing research information can contribute to the development of institutionalized systems and practices that virtually eliminate production defects and service breakdowns.

4. *Develop product strategy.* Marketing managers must be concerned not only with how to market a product or service but also with whether the product or service should be marketed in the first place. Marketing research information provides a framework for analyzing the potential profitability of new products or services before a decision to launch is made.

---

[2]"AMA Board Approves New Marketing Definition," *Marketing News*, March 1, 1985, pp. 1, 14.

[3]Adapted from Robert S. Duboff, "Bottom Line Marketing," *Mercer Management Quarterly* volume 8, no. 1 (Spring 1992), pp. 5–7.

Marketing Research Activities

At the heart of marketing research is the collection and dissemination of information. The practice of marketing research involves a number of activities. Specifically, marketing researchers, in cooperation with marketing managers, perform and/or supervise the following activities:

1. *Define the research problem.* Perhaps the most important responsibility of marketing researchers is to ensure that the problem facing the company is accurately and precisely defined. Symptoms, for example, declining sales or market share, are not problems. Problem formulation is discussed in Chapter 2. The nature of the problem facing the firm will determine the type of study to conduct. Various types of marketing research studies are discussed in Chapters 17 through 22.

2. *Specify the information required.* Having defined the problem the marketing researcher must determine what kind of information will best meet the research objectives. The marketing researcher may decide to use information that has been already collected by the firm or information that is in the public domain. This kind of information is called secondary data. The marketing researcher can decide to collect data from the firm's customers. This kind of information is called primary data. Secondary information sources are discussed in Chapters 3 and 4.

3. *Design the method for collecting the needed information.* There are a variety of ways for collecting marketing research information. For example, information obtained from customers of a firm can be collected via a mail, telephone, or personal interview. Some marketing research firms maintain consumer panels, consisting of individuals who have agreed to provide purchasing and media viewing behavior. Chapters 5 through 7 provide details on various aspects of collecting marketing research information.

4. *Decide on the sampling design.* The marketing researcher must determine the qualifications for being in a study. The sampling design must result in the proper sample of respondents being selected. A variety of different sampling designs are open to researchers. Sampling issues are discussed in Chapters 8 and 9.

5. *Design the questionnaire.* The marketing researcher generally has the primary responsibility for constructing the data collection instrument. The instrument must be designed to be easily administered and understood by the respondent. Chapters 10 through 12 present material on measurement issues and questionnaire construction.

6. *Manage and implement the data collection.* An important activity that the marketing researcher is responsible for is the overseeing of the data collection process. Among other things, the marketing researcher must provide instructions for training interviewers and procedures for controlling the quality of the interviewing. Fielding the questionnaire and preparing the

information collected for analysis are discussed in Chapters 13 and 14, respectively.

7. *Analyze and interpret the results.* The marketing researcher has the primary responsibility for analyzing the information that has been collected and for interpreting the results. The analysis plan follows closely from the research objective of the study. Approaches for analyzing marketing research data are discussed in Chapters 15 and 16.

8. *Communicate the findings and implications.* The results of a marketing research study must be disseminated. The marketing researcher is responsible for providing a written report and generally an oral presentation to management. Chapter 23 provides tips for presenting the results of a marketing research study.

In performing and/or supervising these activities, marketing managers must adhere to ethical standards. Ethical issues surrounding the collection and use of marketing research information are discussed in Chapter 24.

MARKETING RESEARCH AND STRATEGY CONSIDERATIONS

Regardless of the primary objective of a business, satisfactory profits must be obtained if the business is to remain financially viable in the long run. It should be clear that marketing research plays a vital role in ensuring that satisfactory profits are achieved because it is through marketing research that a business comes to understand which goods and services will satisfy consumers' needs and wants. It is no surprise that most of the leading consumer package goods companies have sophisticated marketing research departments. The Procter & Gamble Company is a good case in point. Over the years the research teams at Procter & Gamble have been successful in identifying needs and relevant **end benefits** (those product features, both tangible and intangible, that satisfy consumers' needs and wants) and manufacturing appropriate products. Many of Procter & Gamble's products have developed tremendous loyalty in the marketplace and, although introduced decades ago, still maintain category leadership. For example, Ivory Soap was introduced in 1879, Tide in 1947, and Crest in 1966.

end benefits
Product features that satisfy consumers' needs and wants.

It is important to realize that the role of marketing research is not simply to point out product-related problems, but rather to provide a unified framework for ensuring that the voice of the consumer is deployed throughout strategy development.

Custom Driven Engineering (CDE). Producing high-quality products is frequently the primary objective of engineers and designers. Historically, most engineers and quality control managers defined quality in terms of "number of defects," or "conformance to specifications." This definition often misses the mark because it does not consider exactly whose specifications are being met. Today, some companies rely on marketing research to define exactly what quality means. For example, a procedure called Quality Function Deployment (QFD), recently imported from Japan, has been implemented

EXHIBIT 1–1
———
Information
Provided by
Marketing Research
and Engineering in
Customer Driven
Engineering

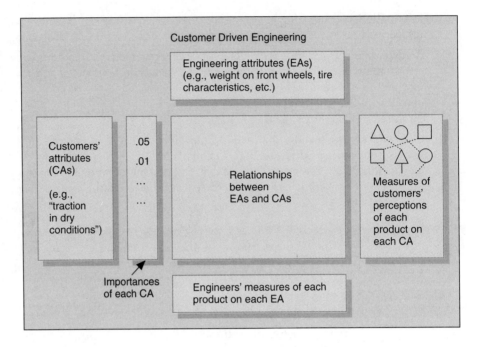

by such American companies as Ford, General Motors, Digital Equipment, Hewlett-Packard, and Polaroid. QFD is a simple concept: In order to assure that customers perceive their products to be of high quality, manufacturers must deploy the voice of the customer throughout the design, engineering, manufacturing, and distribution processes.

Customer Driven Engineering (CDE) is a market research and measurement model that attempts to incorporate these processes. According to Hauser and Klein[4] CDE defines quality in terms of "conformance to *customer* specifications." The essence of CDE is shown in Exhibit 1–1. At the heart of the CDE procedure is the recognition of the relationship between customer attributes (CAs) and engineering attributes (EAs). The rows of the CDE matrix are the CAs. CAs will rarely be expressed in units that are consistent with the way people in engineering and quality control talk about product features. CAs are defined in the customer's language, that is, roomy seats, quick acceleration as opposed to, say, millimeters and seconds. These CAs usually are grouped into higher level bundles, for example, *comfort*, which may be reflected by product features such as roominess of the front seat or leg room, that managers can easily understand and act on. The columns of the CDE matrix are EAs. The EAs, which represent physical characteristics, usually can be grouped together to identify subsystem design or manufacturing responsibility. The challenge of CDE is to link the EAs with the CAs. For example, the size of random access memory (RAM), the speed at which the machine processes input information (megahertz), and number of weight states, all have causal impacts on customers' perceptions of speed of cursor movement, speed of file

———

[4]Hauser and Klein, "Without Good Research."

recovery, and effective speed of an application of a desktop computer. These EA–CA linkages specify the amount by which changes in one or more EAs produce changes in the CAs.

Marketing research plays an extremely instrumental role in strategy development. The information collected through marketing research can provide valuable information on (1) changes in the firm's environment, (2) changes in competitive offerings, (3) changes in the firm's customer base, and (4) reactions to new products or product modifications. Consider, for example, the case of an established brand that has reached market maturity and is facing stagnant sales and decreasing profit margins. One strategy would be to spruce up the brand, reformulate the ingredients, add "new" to the packaging, and launch it as a "new and improved" product. An alternative strategy, one that requires careful monitoring of category movement and consumers' attitudes and lifestyles, would be to define a new role for the established brand in the marketplace. This latter strategy is called **repositioning.** The potential rewards of repositioning a stagnant brand can be great. Let's look at one successful repositioning strategy.

> repositioning
> *A strategy that defines a new role (new users or uses) for an aging product in the marketplace.*

Gatorade. Before The Quaker Oats Company acquired Gatorade, it was promoted by portraying users as competitive athletes, adult men, teens, and caricatures of athletes, with no message on the uses of this product or under which circumstances and occasions it was supposed to be used (see Exhibit 1–2). However, when Quaker's marketing research managers took a look at the marketing research on Gatorade, they found that its main users were men, aged 19–44, who understood the product, had a good perception of what it did, and knew when to drink it and how to use it.[5]

Based on marketing research, Gatorade has adopted a focused positioning strategy directed toward physical-activity enthusiasts as a drink that would quench their thirst and replenish the minerals they had lost during exercise better than other beverages did. Since 1987 there have been refinements. Users are now portrayed as accomplished but not professional athletes, and the ads have added a fun component by showing that people can enjoy Gatorade together. In addition they have attempted to emphasize the thirst-quenching benefits associated with this product (see Exhibit 1–2).

In looking at growth opportunities, which are limited because of the narrow positioning with respect to users and usage occasions, Quaker is examining opportunities consistent with the product's image. Tracking of consumer attitudes and usage behavior indicates that mothers with active children constitute a large segment that can be targeted separately and that Gatorade can be marketed year-round.

Sometimes the financial viability of an entire company depends on understanding trends in the marketplace and developing positioning strategies that will appeal to a changing marketplace. For example, General Motors has embarked on a major repositioning campaign for its mid- to late-1990s North American product line.[6] The general strategy is to sacrifice models that blur the distinctive images

---

[5]The repositioning of Gatorade is discussed in L. Dykstra, "Quaker Looks to Expand Market for Gatorade," *Marketing News* 22 (January 4, 1988), p. 38.

[6]This material is adapted from Phil Frame, "Olds Goal: Young and Stylish," *Automotive News,* May 11, 1992, pp. 2, 42.

EXHIBIT 1–2   Gatorade Advertisement

Source: The Quaker Oats Co.

across marketing divisions and that compete too closely with other GM vehicles. Oldsmobile, one of GM's most foundering divisions, will get the biggest makeover, positioned to appeal to younger and more style-conscious buyers. Other product changes being considered include replacing the Cadillac Allante with a domestic car, dropping the Oldsmobile Ninety Eight, and dropping the Buick Skylark (see Exhibit 1–3).

Exhibit 1–3 shows that Oldsmobile would have to shift the most dramatically from its current position on the GM perceptual map. A **perceptual map** positions products spatially. Note that GM product lines are positioned relative to two dimensions (the *x* axis and the *y* axis), which in this case correspond to price (high versus low) and styling (conservative versus expressive). These dimensions are presumed to be evaluative in the sense that they are important to the consumer when making a selection of a particular product from the competitive set. According to the map, the strategy for Oldsmobile is to move to a more expressive and higher priced position, thus distancing itself from Buick. We will have more to say about

perceptual maps
Spatial representations that show the relative positions of a set of products on a set of evaluative dimensions.

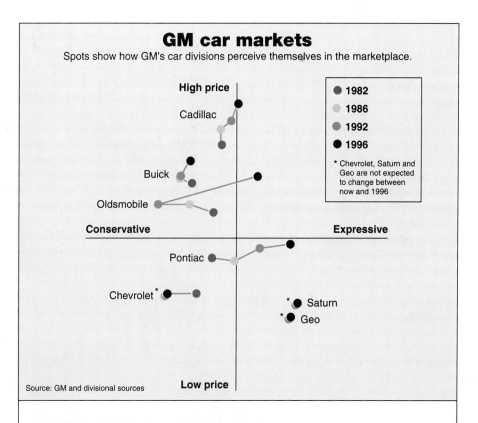

GM car markets

Spots show how GM's car divisions perceive themselves in the marketplace.

High price

Cadillac

	1982
	1986
	1992
	1996

Buick

Oldsmobile

Conservative   **Expressive**

Pontiac

Chevrolet *

Saturn

Geo

* Chevrolet, Saturn and Geo are not expected to change between now and 1996

Source: GM and divisional sources   **Low price**

Source: Phil Frame, "Olds Goal: Young and Stylish," *Automotive News,* May 11, 1992, p. 2.

Other Changes

Buick
   Buick will continue to be positioned as a conservative automobile, appealing to wealthy, older people. The Regal, Skylark, and Roadmaster are in danger. The Park Avenue will continue as Buick's flagship.

Chevrolet
   Chevrolet's positioning will not undergo radical changes, appealing to value-conscious customers. The Caprice, however, is likely to be dropped.

Pontiac
   Pontiac's image will be more expressive and sporty. The four-door Grand Prix and the LeMans will likely be dropped.

Cadillac
   The plan for Cadillac is to make the product line slightly more upscaled and more highly styled, sporty, and sleeker. The Allante will be dropped.

Saturn
   The Saturn will remain unchanged.

EXHIBIT 1–3
—
GM Positioning Strategy

perceptual maps in later chapters. As can be seen from this simple illustration, perceptual maps convey a lot of useful information on the perceived similarities and differences among a set of products.

MARKETING RESEARCH ENVIRONMENTS

Exhibit 1–4 diagrams the principal organizations that make up the marketing research community, separated into principal internal, principal external, and facilitating external parties. The internal parties are persons and departments that are part of a firm's organizational structure. These include the marketing researcher, the marketing manager; the research and development department (R&D); and management information services (MIS), which includes marketing decision support systems (MDSS).

The principal external parties are organizations and individuals outside of the firm that are hired to provide marketing research functions and that interact directly with principal internal parties within the firm. These include various types of suppliers and advertising agencies. Suppliers and ad agencies subcontract marketing research activities to local field services, tabulation houses, and independent consultants; these are all referred to as facilitating external parties.

EXHIBIT 1–4

Overview of
Marketing Research
Environments

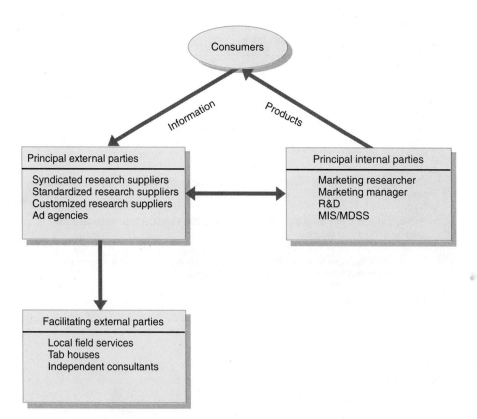

Exhibit 1–4 gives us a way to describe the interrelationships among these parties and the basic marketing research functions they provide.

Principal Internal Parties

Let us begin with the marketing research department. Marketing research is a staff function, similar to legal, personnel, and accounting functions. Thus, the marketing researcher does not have the power to dictate or control line function activities. Put simply, the marketing researcher's role is to advise. Accordingly, compelling arguments presented persuasively are the marketing researcher's most important weapons.

At the head of the marketing research department is the director of marketing research, who reports directly to the vice president of marketing services. Reporting to the director of marketing research are a number of group managers, often titled associate directors. Associate directors or group managers are responsible for overseeing the marketing research activities for specific groups of products, say, carbonated soft drinks or health-care products. Under each associate director or group manager is a marketing research manager who oversees the senior and junior research analysts who are assigned to particular products and/or services (see Exhibit 1–5).

Marketing research budgets are controlled by marketing managers. Consequently they must approve the study. When the manager identifies a possible reason for initiating a study, the manager will contact the marketing research department. The product or service category or the nature of the problem determines which marketing researcher is assigned to the project. Once a marketing researcher has been assigned, the marketing manager and the researcher then operate as a team, although the marketing researcher is primarily responsible for designing the research.

The marketing researcher must understand the environment in the industry and how the marketing manager views the problem that he or she is facing. Knowing the industry environment and viewing the problem from the marketing manager's perspective are critical to identifying the key variables that the marketing research manager should focus on. Also, a knowledge of the corporate culture is important since it determines how decisions are made. Such knowledge can increase the chance that research results are accepted and correctly implemented.

Both the marketing manager and the marketing researcher interface with the *R&D department* and the *MIS/MDSS department*. R&D provides technological support and advice and plays an instrumental role in product design decisions. MIS/MDSS provide computer-based technology—databases and software—enabling the marketing manager and marketing researcher to access information needed for strategic and tactical decisions.

Principal External Parties

Four principal parties outside the organization play an important role in shaping marketing research activities: (1) syndicated research suppliers, (2) standardized

EXHIBIT 1–5   Organization Chart for a Corporate Marketing Research Department

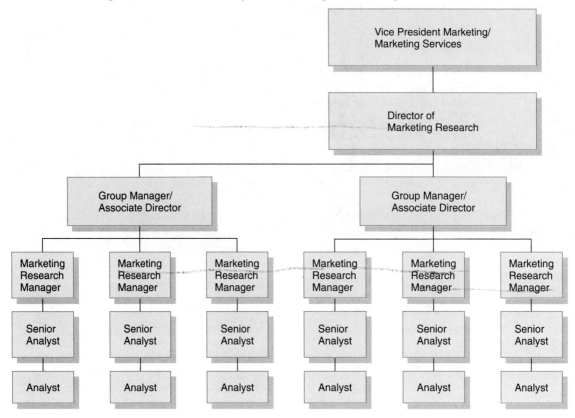

research suppliers, (3) customized research suppliers, and (4) advertising agencies. The first three parties are commonly referred to as marketing research suppliers and are distinguished by the unique nature of the services they provide. These parties interface with the marketing manager and the marketing researcher and provide services that cannot be found within the organization.

marketing research suppliers
Independent companies that execute marketing research studies.

Marketing Research Suppliers. The main business of **marketing research suppliers** is research—they are the primary data gatherers and analysts who execute marketing research studies. There are literally thousands of marketing research suppliers, ranging from small one- or two-person firms to extremely large multinational corporations. Table 1–1 gives worldwide and U.S. marketing research revenues for the top 50 marketing research suppliers for 1992. Leading the field is Nielsen, with estimated total (U.S. and worldwide) revenues of $1,307.9 million. A distant second is IMS International, Inc., with estimated revenues of $586.0 million.

TABLE 1–1   Top 50 Research Organizations

Rank 1992	Rank 1991	Organization	Total Research Revenues* (millions)	Percent Change from 1991**	Percent of Revenues from Outside United States
1	1	Nielsen	$1,307.9	9.7%	61.0%***
2	2	IMS International	586.0	15.1	65.0***
3	3	Information Resources Inc.	276.4	24.1	12.6
4	4	The Arbitron Co.	178.0***	−5.2	
5	5	Westat Inc.	113.7	30.3	
6	10	Walsh/PMSI	87.3	26.7	36.0
7	6	Maritz Marketing Research Inc.	69.7	16.9	
8	8	The NPD Group	57.1	17.0	23.0
9	7	The M/A/R/C Group	53.9	−4.0	
10	9	NFO Research Inc.	47.1	5.2	
11	11	Elrick & Lavidge Inc.	46.8	6.4	
12	12	Market Facts Inc.	40.7	2.6	
13	14	Walker Group	38.7	18.9	1.5
14	13	MRB Group	34.1	−8.7	
15	15	MAI Information Group	31.9	−1.0	
16	16	Intersearch Corp.	30.1	6.4	
17	21	The BASES Group	28.0	23.3	3.5
18	18	The National Research Group Inc.	27.5	10.0	15.0
19	22	Abt Associates Inc.	27.2	20.9	
20	25	Millward Brown Inc.	25.1	27.4	
21	17	Burke Marketing Research	24.4	1.2	
22	20	Louis Harris and Associates Inc.	24.1	5.7	70.0***
23	19	Chilton Research Services	23.8	1.3	
24	23	Research International USA	22.9	8.0	26.0
25	24	Starch INRA Hooper Inc.	22.8	8.0	3.5
26	26	J.D. Power & Associates	20.9	16.1	
27	—	Yankelovich Partners	19.9	13.1	7.5
28	29	Creative & Response Research Svcs.	18.6	22.8	
29	27	ASI Market Research	17.4	1.8	
30	32	Decision Research Corp.	17.0	21.4	
31	30	Custom Research Inc.	16.2	8.7	
32	28	M.O.R.-PACE	15.0	0.0	11.0
33	33	Data Development Corp.	14.8	13.6	
34	37	The Wirthlin Group	13.6	37.3	
35	31	National Analysts	13.2	−9.0	
36	36	Lieberman Research West Inc.	13.2	21.9	4.0
37	34	Total Research Corp.	11.9	−1.0	20.0
38	42	ICR Survey Research Group	10.9	27.7	
39	43	MSW-McCollum Spielman Worldwide	10.6	25.5	5.0
40	35	Strategic Research & Consulting	10.5	−14.0	
41	46	Market Strategies Inc.	10.5	43.8	
42	40	Guideline Research Corp.	10.4	13.0	
43	47	Research Data Analysis Inc.	10.3	51.7	
44	41	Response Analysis Corp.	10.3	17.2	
45	38	Conway/Milliken & Assocs.	9.0	−8.5	
46	—	Market Decisions	8.9	21.4	
47	39	The Vanderveer Group	7.7	−16.3	
48	—	Shifrin Research Inc.	7.6	21.6	
49	45	Newman-Stein Inc.	7.4	−7.5	
50	—	Gordon S. Black Corp.	7.4	3.2	
		Subtotal, Top 50	$3,538.4	11.1%	36.3%
		All other (109 CASRO member companies not included in Top 50)****	337.6	5.5	
		Total (159 organizations)	$3,876.0	10.7%	

*Total revenues that include nonresearch activities for some companies are significantly higher. This information is given in the individual comany profiles in the main article.

**Rate of growth from year to year has been adjusted so as not to include revenue gains from acquisition. See company profiles for explanation.

***Estimate.

****Total revenues of 109 survey research firms—beyond those listed in Top 50—that provide financial information, on a confidential basis, to the Council of American Survey Research Organizations (CASRO).

Source: *Marketing News*, June 7, 1993, p. H4.

The reasons for using outside research services are simple: Compared with internal providers, marketing research suppliers

1. Provide economies of scale by offering specialized services that could be provided internally only at considerable cost.
2. Are less subject to internal politics.
3. Provide greater flexibility in terms of scheduling.

full-service supplier
A marketing research company that can and usually does carry out all aspects of a research project.

There are two basic types of suppliers. A **full-service supplier** can carry out all aspects of a research project: questionnaire design, preparation and production, interviewing, research design, data processing, and analysis and interpretation. A **limited-service supplier** specializes in one or more marketing research activities and may not offer the full range of marketing research services.

limited-service supplier
A marketing research company that specializes in one or more marketing research activities.

Marketing research suppliers provide three broad categories of service: (1) syndicated research services, (2) standardized research services, and (3) customized research services.

syndicated research service
A marketing research company that provides information from common pools of data.

1. **Syndicated research services.** Companies that provide information from common pools of data to different clients are in the syndicated research service business. For example, you are probably familiar with A. C. Nielsen's television viewing service, which estimates audience share of prime-time programming. Suppliers who offer syndicated research services tend to be among the largest in the marketing research business. All four of the top marketing research suppliers listed in Table 1–1 provide mainly syndicated services. Details on most of the major syndicated research services will be provided in Chapter 4.

standardized research service
A marketing research company that uses the same research design for different clients.

2. **Standardized research services.** Standardized research is research conducted for different clients using the same research design. Advertising testing techniques, for example, are frequently standardized so that the results from one study can be compared with those obtained in another study. Such comparability across studies generally leads to the development of "norms," which then provide the basis for evaluating a particular study versus the average of many studies.

customized research service
A marketing research company that provides one-of-a-kind studies.

3. **Customized research services.** Almost all marketing research suppliers offer tailor-made, one-of-a-kind studies for particular clients. Customized marketing research studies probably constitute the largest number of studies conducted, but not the most significant in terms of dollar billings. Among the major marketing research suppliers offering customized research services are Westat, Inc., The M/A/R/C Group, Maritz Marketing Research, Inc., The NPD Group, and Burke Marketing Research.

Advertising Agencies. The marketing manager and marketing researcher often work with the **advertising agency** that currently handles the firm's account (or a particular brand of the firm). There must be coordination between the research activities for a product or service and current and future advertising campaigns. Some advertising agencies maintain their own marketing research departments, although the emphasis placed on marketing research varies greatly. In most instances, the agency's marketing researcher acts as an internal consultant.

Facilitating External Parties

Marketing research suppliers and ad agencies subcontract with a number of other types of companies who perform many of the activities necessary to implement and complete a marketing research study. These companies facilitate the research function. Among the more important facilitators are (1) field services, (2) tabulation houses, and (3) independent consultants.

Local Field Services. **Field services** are firms that are hired to collect data, that is, administer interviews. These firms are dispersed in communities throughout the United States. A field service can be a single proprietorship where the owner acts in the capacity of field supervisor. This person hires interviewers from the pool of available interviewers in the area based on who will be interviewed, the type of interview, and the number of interviews to complete. The field supervisor assembles the interviewers, briefs them, and coordinates their efforts while in the field. Most field service firms are freelance and frequently do work for more than one marketing research supplier.

The director of field services at the marketing research supplier selects the field service to use. Some of the largest marketing research suppliers have their own field services, especially in the areas of central-location telephone interviewing and mall-intercept personal interviewing.

Tabulation Houses. **Tab (tabulation) houses** are firms dedicated to statistical analysis and computation. Tab houses are responsible for ensuring that the data collected are coded properly and can be transferred onto magnetic tape or diskette. They also provide specialized programming assistance and have libraries of statistical software programs for performing statistical analysis and generating cross tabulations of data. Selection of a tab house is based primarily on cost and turnaround. The marketing research supplier selected to execute the research generally decides on which tab house to use.

Independent Consultants. **Independent consultants** are individuals with unique and specialized marketing research skills. The sponsoring firm or the marketing research supplier hires independent consultants to assist them on specific research projects. These marketing research professionals could be academicians from universities or business schools.

Current Trends

Some restructuring of the industry is changing established practices. On the corporate side, mergers and acquisitions coupled with the impact of new technologies, especially in the area of syndicated services, have created considerable turmoil. The trend has also been away from large advertising marketing re-

---

advertising agency
A firm whose primary responsibility is to create and develop effective communication material and, in the course of such activities, interact with the client's marketing research department and/or provide marketing research support.

field services
Marketing research companies that specialize in activities involved in collecting data.

tab house
A marketing research company that specializes in tabulating and analyzing marketing research data.

independent consultants
Individuals with specialized skills that assist marketing research companies on specific projects.

*From the World
of Research*
—
1-1

The Mystique Is Gone

The fizz is gone.

In February, Source Perrier S.A. voluntarily recalled Perrier worldwide after traces of benzene, a suspected carcinogen, were found in some bottles. By mid-July, the water was again available throughout most of the United States. But the protracted absence unleashed competitive forces that have broken the once-invincible import's stranglehold over the U.S. imported bottled water market.

Today, Perrier is a brand in deep water. Evian has replaced it as the top-selling imported bottled water, with Perrier's sales at just 60 percent of its pre-recall levels. The brand's plight would probably be less severe, marketing experts say, had it not been for the evasiveness and strategic blunders of Perrier officials on both sides of the Atlantic.

Perrier officials in the United States vow the brand will regain 85 percent of its sales by the end of 1991, a goal critics say is wishful thinking. Its share of the imported bottled water market has sunk to 20.7 percent from 44.8 percent. And the brand's sales plunged 42 percent this year to $60 million. Perrier Group of America expects to report a sales gain for this year of 3.7 percent to $630 million, but that is largely because of the strong performance of such domestic brands as Calistoga and Poland Spring.

A host of rival brands—Saratoga, LaCroix, Quibell—have reaped minor windfalls in the aftermath of the contamination debacle. But the biggest winner is BSN S.A.'s Evian, a nonsparkling water. The aggressive marketing and advertising campaign Evian has waged since Perrier's recall has been so successful that "it's unlikely that Perrier will recover its number-one imported position in the near term," says Michael Bellas, president of Beverage Marketing Corp., a consulting firm.

search departments. Agency marketing research departments have been downsized, and fewer resources are being devoted to supporting marketing research activities.[7] Agency marketing researchers more and more service their own creative groups' needs rather than their clients' needs. Finally, on the supplier side, there seems to be a growing distinction between marketing research suppliers that provide custom research services and those providing technology-based market information systems.

THE RESEARCH CYCLE

The research needs and activities of a company change over time, especially as its product line matures and grows. Frequently, changes in the competitive environment influence, and sometimes even dictate, the types of research studies that must be implemented. A rather extreme example of this is described in From the World of Research 1–1. The woes of Perrier, as described in a 1990 *Wall Street Journal* article, illustrate the worst-case scenario of a successful, established brand being thrown into a state of shock. As described in the box, Perrier's current market condition was precipitated by, but not completely due to, the fear of benzene. Competitive forces were bound to surface eventually. But without the contami-

---

[7]William D. Neal, "Researchers Can Have a Say in Their Destiny," *Marketing News*, November 4, 1990, p. 4.

Perrier distributors say the brand has been especially unsuccessful in staging a comeback in bars and restaurants, which formerly accounted for about 35 percent of its sales. And Perrier Group of America has resorted to unprecedented discounting this holiday season, which risks cheapening the brand's image.

It isn't the fear of benzene that has led many former loyalists to eschew the water. (Memory of the incident has all but faded, Perrier research confirms.) Rather, the contamination crisis exposed a fundamental flaw: Consumers tended to pick Perrier out of inertia and a perceived lack of alternatives, not any true product preference.

Photography by Jack Holtel.

Source: Alix M. Freedman, *The Wall Street Journal*, December 12, 1990, p. B1. Reprinted by permission of *THE WALL STREET JOURNAL*, © 1990 Dow Jones & Company, Inc. All Rights Reserved Worldwide.

nation crisis, Perrier's loss of market share probably would not have been as quick or as severe.

Perrier's research needs are now very different from when the water was first distributed in the United States. This section deals with that subject: the changing configuration of research needs that brands face as they or their markets mature.

Most of you are probably familiar with the *product life cycle* concept. The product life cycle divides a product's evolution by sales patterns over time into four stages: *introduction, growth, maturity, decline*. Although a product's research needs are cyclical as well, the idea of a *research life cycle* is not so widely recognized.

Research results from the need to anticipate, understand, or respond to changes in the marketplace. The **research cycle** acknowledges the fact that as products move through their life cycle they have unique research needs.

Exhibit 1–6 depicts this relationship. Note that the product follows a sales pattern over time from introduction through growth and maturity to decline. Prior to the introduction stage comes a precommercialization period, though it is not specifically included as one of the four life-cycle stages. Over the course of the cycle, the marketing research needs of the product change correspondingly. The research cycle, which can be divided into prelaunch, rollout, and established markets, recognizes such changes and specifically matches research activities to the unique needs of a product during each stage in its life cycle.

research cycle *Acknowledges that specific kinds of research projects are conducted as a product moves through its life cycle.*

EXHIBIT 1–6   Interface between Product and Research Life Cycles

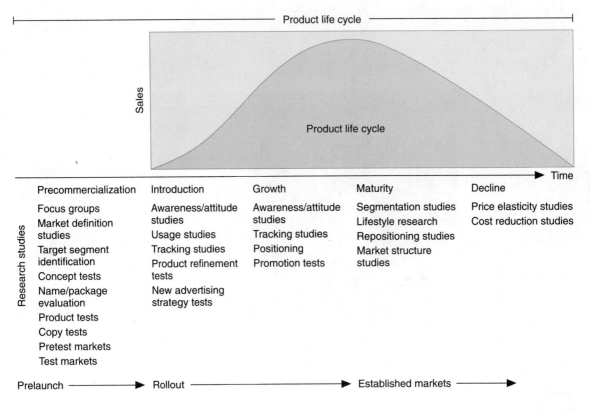

Precommercialization	Introduction	Growth	Maturity	Decline
Focus groups	Awareness/attitude studies	Awareness/attitude studies	Segmentation studies	Price elasticity studies
Market definition studies	Usage studies	Tracking studies	Lifestyle research	Cost reduction studies
Target segment identification	Tracking studies	Positioning	Repositioning studies	
Concept tests	Product refinement tests	Promotion tests	Market structure studies	
Name/package evaluation	New advertising strategy tests			
Product tests				
Copy tests				
Pretest markets				
Test markets				

Prelaunch ⟶ Rollout ⟶ Established markets ⟶

Prelaunch Stage

prelaunch phase
That stage in the research life cycle characterized by research activities aimed at assisting the marketing manager in developing and introducing new and improved products that are likely to be successful in the marketplace.

The **prelaunch phase** of the research life cycle is characterized by research activities aimed at assisting the marketing manager in developing and introducing (i.e., rolling out) new and improved products that can compete successfully in the marketplace. For many firms, the development and successful rollout of new products and services are essential for the continued financial health of the organization. All the marketing research activities undertaken in the prelaunch stage are designed to ensure that a national rollout, if undertaken, will be successful in matching or exceeding management's performance objectives.

The different types of research activities undertaken in the prelaunch phase of the research life cycle include concept testing, product testing, name testing, package testing, and test marketing. We briefly describe each of these activities in the following sections.

Concept Testing. **Concept tests** provide a system for shaping, defining, and formulating ideas to arrive at a basic concept for a product that has greater potential for market acceptance. Generally, concept tests are conducted to assess the relative appeal of ideas or alternative product positionings that aim the product at different target segments by highlighting particular product features that are most desired by given segments of the population.

concept tests
Tests conducted to assess the relative appeal of ideas or alternative product positionings that aim the product at different target segments.

Concept tests can also be used later in the prelaunch phase to estimate ultimate consumer demand for the basic product concept before introduction. A concept test at this stage would expose respondents to a positioning concept statement, which lists all the product's end benefits as well as various secondary features. A statement of this sort is much longer than a core idea concept, generally several paragraphs long.

Chapter 18 is devoted to concept testing. There we discuss and illustrate the different types of concept testing studies that are implemented at different stages of the research life cycle.

Product Testing.   **Product tests** attempt to answer one of the most basic questions relating to ultimate market acceptance of a product: "How does this product perform?" There is no better way to answer this question than to experience and use the product under real-life conditions. From product testing we learn what product is most acceptable to consumers. Product testing is particularly important in the consumer package goods industries (food, health and beauty aids, household products) where physical product improvements can quickly affect market shares in a product category and where production/distribution of product prototypes is economically feasible.

product tests
Tests that assess the product's ability to deliver promised end benefits.

Performance of the product during the test can be evaluated in terms of different criteria. For example, performance can be evaluated in isolation, without reference to other brands. Alternatively, performance can be judged relative to competitive brands, or against their advertising claims, or possibly against formula variations. Chapter 18 presents further details on product testing procedures.

Name Testing.   Names are important because they convey information. Product names have both denotative and connotative meaning. Denotative meaning refers to the literal, explicit meaning of a term. For example, the term *mustang* literally refers to a wild untamed horse. Connotative meaning refers to the associations that the name provokes beyond its literal, explicit meaning. In other words, the image that is called up by the term is its connotative meaning. For example, to some consumers a product branded with the name *mustang* may conjure up images of power or strength.

Names serve two basic functions: (1) to identify the product to the consumer, retailer, distributor, and manufacturer and (2) to differentiate the product from competitive products while conveying physical (i.e., tangible) and emotional (i.e., intangible) benefits. **Name tests** attempt to assess how well a particular name serves these as well as other functions (see Exhibit 3–6). Name-testing procedures are described in further detail in Chapter 19.

name tests
Tests that are aimed at assessing the information that a name conveys.

Package Testing.   The package design is one of a product's most important marketing elements. Do packaging and point-of-purchase displays make a difference? Consider the influence that packaging and point-of-purchase displays have had on the success of such brands as L'eggs hosiery, Lite beer from Miller, Diet Rite Cola, O'Grady's, Janitor in a Drum, and Early Times Bourbon, and you'll agree that there is more to the product than its physical properties.

package tests
Tests that are aimed at assessing the benefits that a package provides.

Package tests are designed to assess the benefits a package provides. A package serves several basic functions. Besides containing, protecting, and dispensing the product, the package

1. Provides point-of-purchase (e.g., in-store displays) advertising.
2. Serves as an attention-getting device.
3. Presents information about directions, ingredients, and potential cautions.
4. Promises physical (i.e., tangible) and emotional (e.g., intangible) end benefits.
5. Encourages purchase.

Various approaches to package testing are discussed and illustrated in Chapter 19.

Test Markets. Before national rollout, a test market study is generally conducted to assess how the new product or service is likely to fare under realistic conditions. The primary objective of a test market is to obtain an accurate forecast of first-year volume if the new product or service was indeed rolled out nationally.

Test marketing studies take one of three basic approaches—simulated/pretest, standard, or control. Each of these approaches is discussed and illustrated in Chapter 21.

Rollout

rollout phase
That stage of the research cycle that provides information about product/market activities in the introduction and growth stages of a product's life cycle.

In the **rollout phase** of the research life cycle, the chief purpose of marketing research is to provide information about what is going on in the marketplace. Throughout this phase, research studies that track consumer awareness levels and attitudes, and trial and repeat purchase, are extremely important. As rollout progresses, tracking of consumer perceptions and usage becomes more important.

Market tracking and positioning studies are two research activities undertaken in the rollout phase of the research life cycle.

market tracking
Tests designed to determine where a firm stands compared with competition.

Market Tracking. **Market tracking** provides a means for determining where a firm stands compared with competition. Tracking serves two basic objectives. The first objective is monitoring the marketplace. Tracking studies are often the principal source of data about category and brand-use patterns, demographic characteristics of users, consumer attitudes and predispositions, and brand awareness levels. Market tracking is relatively undisruptive; that is, the test is conducted under normal market conditions with current marketing budgets in place.

The second objective is assessment. Monitoring the marketplace yields information on real-world performance, and thereby provides managers with information that allows them to evaluate the results of their decisions. The strategic assessment that market tracking affords allows managers to set or develop measurable objectives. In other words, tracking provides realistic benchmarks by which the performance of real-world marketing campaigns can be evaluated. Market tracking as well as other advertising testing studies are discussed in Chapter 20.

Positioning Studies.   **Product positioning studies** provide "pictures" or maps of the competitive structure among particular products or brands or services. Positioning maps provide management with a consumer perspective on competition in the marketplace and presumably reflect how the market evaluates a particular set of brands or products.

product positioning studies
Studies that provide pictures or maps of the competitive structure among particular products or brands or services.

Besides providing a structure of competitive relationships, product maps are used to

1. Develop and evaluate strategic plans.
2. Track market changes.
3. Investigate the relationship between the firm's actions and their market consequences.
4. Position or reposition a brand to appeal to specific consumers.

Product maps are constructed from consumers' perceptual beliefs. These beliefs are elicited by asking a sample of consumers to rate a set of products or brands based on the degree to which each brand or product provides a predetermined set of end benefits. In practice, consumers are asked to rate or rank a set of products or brands on a number of product attributes or descriptive statements concerning how each brand or product performs.

Perceptual ratings provide a means of identifying the primary dimensions on which brand or product evaluations are made. Statistical analysis procedures are used to identify the relevant evaluative dimensions. Typically, dimensions represent broader and perhaps more abstract evaluations. For example, *efficacy* (effectiveness) and *mildness* are two broad conceptual end benefits that consumers look for in laundry powders. There are, however, a number of specific product attributes that relate to these two broad conceptual and benefit categories:

Efficacy	Mildness
Strong, powerful	Gentle to natural fibers
Gets out dirt	Won't harm colors
Removes stains	Won't harm synthetics
Good for grease, oil	

Exhibit 1–7 presents a hypothetical perceptual map for several varieties of laundry detergent. Note that the various brands are positioned on "effectiveness" and on "mildness." In the perceptual space, All and Bold are perceived to be more similar to each other than either one is to Ajax. Therefore, the implication is that these two brands compete more fiercely against each other because they offer the consumer the same end benefits. Further details on developing and using perceptual maps are provided in Chapter 17.

EXHIBIT 1–7

—

Laundry Detergent
Perceptual Map

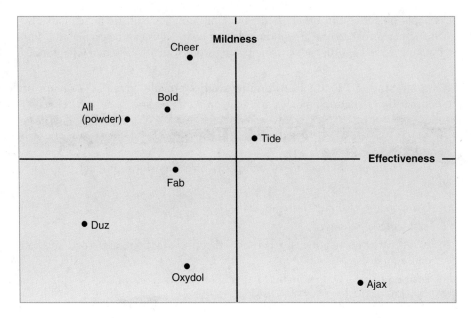

Established Markets

established markets
phase
*That stage of the re-
search cycle that provides
information that man-
agers can use to strategically manage products in
the mature and decline
stages of the product life
cycle.*

In the **established markets phase** of the research life cycle, the primary function of research activities is to provide information that managers can use to strategically manage the product. Research focuses on new ways to build interest in the product, on identifying new segments of customers, and on developing effective ways to become more competitive. The accent is firmly on competition. The growing intensity of competition in most businesses makes predicting the reactions of competitors to a firm's own marketing program extremely urgent. Research activities undertaken in established markets include, among others, market structure studies and market segmentation studies.

Market Structure Studies. An essential ingredient in designing successful marketing strategies is a thorough understanding of the structure of markets and the patterns of competition within the markets. It is difficult to conceive of a situation where decisions concerning the marketing-mix elements (i.e., product design, price, advertising, and distribution) would be made without first acquiring an understanding of the competitive arena.

market structure studies
*Studies that seek to de-
fine the competitive relationships within a
product/service market.*

Market structure studies seek to define the competitive relationships within a product/service market. Perceptual product maps, discussed earlier, identify a product's competitors and define the boundaries of a market. However, perceptual product maps do *not* specify the *extent* of competition among a set of products or brands. Market structure studies do just that by measuring the degree to which one competitive product might substitute for another.

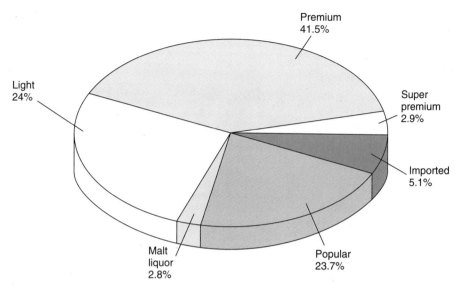

EXHIBIT 1–8
—
Segments in the Beer
Industry

Source: Adapted from "Beer Trends: Market Breakdown by Product," in *Beverage Industry Annual Manual 1989* (Cleveland: Edge, 1989), pp. 38–47.

The objective in market structure analysis is to determine the degree of substitutability among a set of products or brands. Obviously, before the extent of competitiveness among a set of products or brands can be determined, the relevant product market must be defined. Hence, most market structure analysis techniques define product market boundaries and measure the degree of substitutability among the brands making up the product market. Various aspects of market structure analysis will be discussed and illustrated in Chapter 17.

Market Segmentation Studies. The term *market segment* simply refers to subgroups of consumers that respond to a given marketing mix strategy in a similar manner. More specifically, segments consist of subgroups of consumers who exhibit differing sensitivities to some marketing mix element.

The beer market is a good example of a market that over time has become increasingly segmented. As Exhibit 1–8 reveals, the beer market is now made up of super premiums, premiums, low-price populars, imports, lights/low calorie, and malts. More recent entries include dry beer and low-alcohol and nonalcohol brands. Brand proliferation is presumably a direct result of recognizing the distinctive desires of beer customers with respect to taste and lifestyle.

Market segmentation studies provide guidelines for a firm's marketing strategy and resource allocation among markets and products and, consequently, influence all marketing tactical plans and programs. By recognizing consumer heterogeneity, a firm can increase its profitability by segmenting its market.

Initially the contribution of segmentation analysis to marketing planning was to provide a framework for the analysis of existing data. Today its role has

market segmentation studies
Studies that provide guidelines for a firm's resource allocations among markets and products.

*From the World
of Research*

1–2

Hitting the Bull's-Eye

Brand	Heavy User Profile	Life-Style and Media Profile	Top Three Stores
Peter Pan Peanut Butter	Households with kids headed by 18- to 54-year-olds, in suburban and rural areas	— Heavy video renters — Go to theme parks — Below-average TV viewers — Above-average radio listeners	Foodtown Super Market 3350 Hempstead Turnpike Levittown, NY Pathmark Supermarket 3635 Hempstead Turnpike Levittown, NY King Kullen Market 598 Stewart Ave. Bethpage, NY
Stouffers Red Box Frozen Entrees	Households headed by people 55 and older, and upscale suburban households headed by 35- to 54-year-olds	— Go to gambling casinos — Give parties — Involved in public activities — Travel frequently — Heavy newspaper readers — Above-average TV viewers	Dan's Supreme Super Market 69–62 188th St. Flushing, NY Food Emporium Madison Ave. & 74th St. NYC Waldbaum Super Market 196–35 Horace Harding Blvd. Flushing, NY
Coors Light Beer	Head of household, 21–34, middle to upper income, suburban and urban	— Belong to a health club — Buy rock music — Travel by plane — Give parties, cookouts — Rent videos — Heavy TV sports viewers	Food Emporium 1498 York Ave. NYC Food Emporium First Ave. & 72nd St. NYC Gristedes Supermarket 350 E. 86th St. NYC

Sources: Spectra Marketing Systems, with data from Information Resources, Inc., Simmons Market Research Bureau, Claritas Corp., and *Progressive Grocer.* Adapted from *The Wall Street Journal*, March 18, 1991.

expanded to provide a basis for identifying the data needed for strategy development and implementation. Segmentation research is used to answer a wide variety of questions concerning market response to a firm's marketing strategies, including product or price changes, new product offerings, and the selection of target markets. Typical management questions that guide market segmentation studies include

1. How do the evaluations of a set of new product concepts vary by different respondent groups—men versus women, users versus nonusers of the company's brand, light versus heavy users, and so on?

2. Are there different promotion-sensitive segments for a new product concept? If so, how do they differ with respect to product use, concept evaluations, attitudes, and demographic and psychographic profiles?

3. How do the target markets for a new product concept differ regarding the end benefits sought, product use characteristics, and other background characteristics?

From these management questions we see that there is an intimate relationship between product positioning and segmentation analysis. Effectively positioning a product for a specific target—consumers who share certain characteristics such as similar reactions to price, promotion, and the like—presumes that these subgroups of consumers have actually been identified, that is, that the market has been segmented. In fact, it is reasonable to suggest that in order to develop effective marketing strategies, managers should apply the concept of segmentation in all activities.

Marketers are using segmentation analysis rather effectively. In particular, marketers can now target a product's best customers and the stores where they're most likely to shop. From the World of Research 1–2 presents an analysis of three products' best targets in the New York area. Chapter 17 provides additional details and illustrations of market segmentation studies.

SUMMARY

We introduced several concepts basic to marketing research. Our main focus was that marketing research provides information that helps the marketing manager and product engineers to think explicitly about who their customers are and what product features are most important. The formal definition of marketing research that we used emphasizes that marketing research links the consumer and marketer through information. We outlined the environment in which marketing research takes place and the principal parties that conduct marketing research activities.

This chapter also described the concept of a research life cycle and specifically the notion that the research needs of a product or service change over time. The discussion centered on different types of marketing research studies undertaken in the prelaunch, rollout, and established markets phases of the research life cycle.

KEY CONCEPTS

marketing research

end benefits

marketing research suppliers

advertising agencies

local field services

consultants

standardized research services

customized research services

syndicated data companies

tab houses

research life cycle

concept tests

name tests

market tracking

market structuring

product life cycle

product tests

package tests

positioning

segmentation

REVIEW QUESTIONS

1. Describe the set of end benefits relevant to a student who is considering the following purchase decisions:

   a. Purchasing a PC for college use.

   b. Choosing a vacation site for spring break.

   c. Renting an apartment for the school year.

   Relate each end benefit identified to one or more product features.

2. In explaining why large firms with experienced managers often "miss the boat" on new opportunities, former General Electric executive John B. McKitterick made the following comment:

   So the principal task of management function in following the marketing concept is not so much to be skillful in making the customer do what suits the interests of the business as to be skillful in conceiving and then making the business do what suits the interests of the customer.[8]

   The sentiments voiced by Mr. McKitterick embody what has been labeled the *marketing concept*. Discuss how marketing research relates to the marketing concept.

3. If companies have in-house marketing research departments, how can they justify going outside to hire marketing research expertise?

4. List the primary functions of each of the internal and external parties involved in the marketing research function.

5. Define the interface between the product life cycle and the research life cycle.

---

[8]John B. McKitterick, "What Is the Marketing Concept?" *The Frontiers of Marketing Thought and Action* (Chicago: American Marketing Association, 1957), pp. 71–82.

Planning a Research Project

— Discuss the marketing planning process.

— Explain how potential problems and opportunities are identified and defined.

— Describe the steps in the course of a research project.

— Delineate the key elements of a marketing research proposal.

INTRODUCTION

By all accounts new products continue to be rolled out at a feverish pace. Although in 1991 there was a 3 percent decline in the number of new product introductions from the record level set in 1990, consumers were still bombarded with more than 15,000 new product introductions. And in 1992, the number of new product introductions increased by 3.1 percent, bringing the total back to the record level set in 1990.[1] In spite of the enormous amount of resources devoted to new product development activities and introduction, estimates of new product failure rates continue to be alarmingly high, however, with some estimates as high as 86 percent. Adding to the disappointment is the rather lackluster profit performance of brands that continue to be promoted and maintained. The "hot competition" that exists in many categories, for example, healthy frozen foods, has brought with it large commitments of advertising dollars and other marketing-related expenditures with apparently small returns.[2]

Previous success in rolling out new products is also not a guarantee of future successes. Take, for example, the case of 7UP Gold.[3] The Seven-Up Co. had been very successful with the launch of Cherry 7UP. So in 1988 the Seven-Up management team decided to launch another new variety, 7UP Gold. Unfortunately, Seven-Up's sure-fire strategy (see From the World of Research 2–1) wasn't so sure-fire after all, and this product has been written off by the company. The image problems of 7UP Gold should have been identified long

---

[1] *Marketing News*, January 18, 1993, p. 1

[2] Gebriella Stern, "Makers of 'Healthy' Frozen Foods Watch Profits Melt as Competition Gets Hotter," *The Wall Street Journal*, February 6, 1992, pp. B1, B6.

[3] The following discussion is based on D. C. McGill, "7UP Gold: The Failure of a Can't-Lose Plan," *New York Times*, February 11, 1989, pp. 17, 26.

From the World of Research

—

2–1

Market Share Estimates, 1988 Carbonated Soft Drinks, 1988*

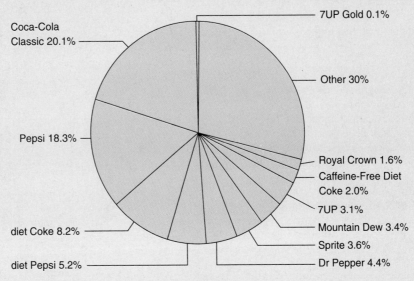

Coca-Cola Classic 20.1%

7UP Gold 0.1%

Other 30%

Pepsi 18.3%

Royal Crown 1.6%

Caffeine-Free Diet Coke 2.0%

7UP 3.1%

Mountain Dew 3.4%

Sprite 3.6%

Dr Pepper 4.4%

diet Coke 8.2%

diet Pepsi 5.2%

Source: Maxwell Consumer Reports, *New York Times*, February 11, 1989, p. B6.

*This discussion is based on D. C. McGill, "7UP Gold: The Failure of a Can't-Lose Plan," *New York Times*, February 11, 1989, pp. 17, 26.

before the product was rolled out. Apparently, the research conducted by Seven-Up concentrated on taste alone, ignoring the fit of this product with the parent brand The research conductedby Seven-Up undoubtedly indicated that 7UP Gold had a taste that people liked but failed to investigate whether people could understand the total concept of a brownish-colored, caffeinated 7UP variety. The research problem was poorly formulated.

Successful products come about from understanding consumer decision making and through careful planning based on solid research. This chapter discusses both these issues with particular emphasis on developing the stages in planning a marketing research study. Because every marketing research problem is in some way unique, the steps undertaken in planning a particular research study will vary. However, there is a sequence of stages called the **research process** that provides a general framework to follow when designing and implementing a research study (see Exhibit 2–1). The remainder of this chapter is devoted to overviewing this process. The chapter concludes with a discussion of marketing research proposals and illustrates how firms may request competitive bids from suppliers for conducting specific types of studies.

research process
Sequence of stages that provides a general framework to follow when implementing a marketing research study.

STAGE 1: FORMULATE THE PROBLEM

The research problem can come about from a desire to either (1) solve a current problem (e.g., decreasing market share) or (2) pursue an opportunity (e.g., the growth of convenience-oriented microwavable products). Precise definition of the

Filled with optimism after their success in rolling out Cherry 7UP, the Seven-Up Co.'s management decided to roll out another new product, 7UP Gold, in the spring of 1988. Seven-Up's executives, along with Seven-Up's bottlers and distributors, thought they would have another hit because they followed what seemed to them a sure-fire strategy: Test the flavor to make sure people like it, sell it under the brand name of an established brand, and back it with $10 million in advertising.

Unfortunately, for Seven-Up, this strategy didn't work. Since its introduction, 7UP Gold has captured only one-tenth of 1 percent of the market, and it has been written off by the company.

What was the reason for this failure? Probably several factors. First, the company that established its product as the "Un-Cola" gave 7UP Gold a brownish hue. Second, in contrast to its advertising, which emphasized the end benefit of a caffeine-free beverage, 7UP Gold did contain caffeine. Finally, partly because of the success of Cherry 7UP, the company rolled out 7UP Gold without extensive test marketing.

The general consensus among Seven-Up executives, bottlers, and distributors is that 7UP Gold was simply misunderstood by consumers. Consumers perceive Seven-Up products as clear, clean, and crisp beverages that have no caffeine. The name Gold was selected because of its connotation of high quality; in addition, 7UP Gold had a distinctive flavor that tasted like ginger ale with a cinnamon-apple overtone and a caffeine kick, a situation that is similar to Dr Pepper and Mountain Dew, which do not fit into an established category, and it needed a name that did not attempt to define the taste. Unfortunately, a dark-colored, caffeinated Seven-Up did not fit the usual Seven-Up image, and it was something consumers could not understand.

problem aids in understanding the information that will be needed and helps in formulating research objectives. If the problem is well formulated and the objectives of the research are precisely defined, then the likelihood of designing a research study that will provide the necessary information in an efficient manner is greatly increased. The end result of **problem formulation** should be a precise statement of the objectives of the research to be conducted and a set of research questions.

There are two fundamental components in formulating a problem. The first is the **research objective.** Ideally, this is a short, perhaps even a single-sentence, description of the purpose of the marketing research effort, which provides the focus of everything that is to follow. The second component is made up of a set of **research questions** that immediately flow from the research objective and that will be answered by the research to be conducted. It is important to emphasize that symptoms of the problem (e.g., declining sales) should not be confused with what the problem actually is (i.e., the reasons sales are declining).

Research objectives and questions evolve from a process of give and take by the marketing researcher and the client/decision maker. It is important to understand the relationships between these two parties.

problem formulation
A precise statement of the objectives of the research to be conducted.

research objective
A short description of the marketing research effort that provides the focus of the marketing research activities to follow.

research questions
A list of questions that follows from the research objective that will be answered by the study.

Researcher and Client

To accurately formulate the problem, marketing researchers must understand their role and relationships to their client. Of course, there must be good communication between the researcher and the client. To understand the nature of the

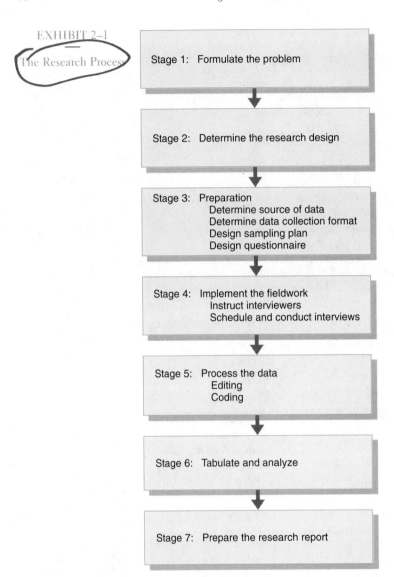

EXHIBIT 2–1
The Research Process

Stage 1: Formulate the problem

Stage 2: Determine the research design

Stage 3: Preparation
Determine source of data
Determine data collection format
Design sampling plan
Design questionnaire

Stage 4: Implement the fieldwork
Instruct interviewers
Schedule and conduct interviews

Stage 5: Process the data
Editing
Coding

Stage 6: Tabulate and analyze

Stage 7: Prepare the research report

decisions managers face and what they hope to learn from the research is essential. However, to properly diagnose the problem, the researcher cannot solely rely on the information provided by the client since the client may tend to be myopic, may misunderstand or misinterpret the situation, and may not disclose all relevant information.

The marketing researcher, like the doctor, is responsible for an accurate diagnosis. Again like the doctor, the marketing researcher cannot fulfill his [her] responsibility without some help from the client. It is with respect to this issue that one of the most frequent and crucial errors made in marketing research occurs. When the research director allows the project to be based on the client's request for specific information he

[she] not only allows the client to diagnose the cause of the problem but to specify a prescription for the cure as well. The doctor's responsibility is to cure the patient; the marketing researcher's responsibility is to solve the client's problem. In each case the cure may or may not have any relationship to the information presented by the patient.[4]

The situation is somewhat complicated by the fact that generally the client controls the research budget. Political conflicts are, unfortunately, a reality of the workplace. The marketing researcher must fight against doing "politically correct" research and research designed to justify decisions or programs that have been previously implemented.

It is often useful to ask the client for a tentative problem definition statement. If the client has difficulty in formulating a tentative problem definition statement, the marketing researcher can assist the process by asking questions: What is the basic problem here? Why do you feel that a research study should be implemented? In many instances the tentative problem statement may be too broad for a single study; for example, how can profitability be improved? Of course, problems that are broadly framed can be attacked through a series of marketing research projects. In any event, the tentative problem definition statement and the information provided by clients are only the first step in formulating the problem.

Once a tentative problem definition statement has been framed, the marketing researcher would—as a first step—ask more detailed questions of the client/decision maker. Such questions could include the following categories:

1. Available knowledge—What do we know?
2. Anticipated actions—How will the results of this study be used?
3. Alternative scenarios—If the results indicate outcome X as opposed to outcome Y, how will this influence your decision?
4. Actionable information—What type of information will allow you to take action?

Exhibit 2–2 presents two examples of how the research objective and the set of research questions can be framed in particular problem settings. In problem setting A, the research questions recognize the competitive aspects of the category. At issue is not only the likely volume and market share of the new product but also its effects on existing products. The research questions also consider the questions of whether the market is segmented with respect to consumer preferences and end benefits sought. Similarly, in problem setting B, the research questions recognize that perceptions of service delivery can vary by the meal occasion.

From Exhibit 2–2 we see that research questions are often posed in terms of hypotheses. For example, is speed of delivery or price more important in the decision to use an overnight carrier? In essence, relevant forms of research questions include: Who . . . ?, What . . . ?, Why . . . ?, When . . . ?, Where . . . ?, and How . . . ? These types of questions can be put into perspective through situation analysis.

---

[4]Robert W. Joselyn, *Designing the Marketing Research Project* (New York: Petrocelli/Charter, 1977), pp. 25–26.

Problem Setting A: A Consumer Package Goods Firm

Project:	A major package goods firm is deciding on whether to continue development of a new "hard candy" product. The new product is a line extension offering a distinctive new ingredient that should be attractive to at least some category users. Brand managers want to collect information on the likely success of the new product.
Research Objective:	To determine the likely market success of a new "hard candy" product containing ingredient X and its relation to existing products.
Possible Research Questions:	1. What volume and market share will the new product achieve when it is rolled out nationally? 2. What trial rate can be expected? 3. Will the new product cannibalize existing products in our line? 4. Which existing products does the new product draw its share from? 5. Are there segments of consumers who have a greater likelihood of trying the new product? 6. Are there segments of consumers who are particularly attracted to the new ingredient?

Problem Setting B: A Fast Food Chain

Project:	The corporate management of a national fast food chain wanted to determine whether customer perceptions of service are uniform across their franchises. The parent corporation has followed a policy of minimizing variation in services provided. The intent of management is to assess whether customer perceptions of services is consistent with corporate standards.
Research Objective:	To evaluate customers' perceptions of the services provided by franchise operators and to identify areas that need attention.
Possible Research Questions:	1. What is the relevant set of service features that franchises should be evaluated on? 2. What is the perceived value of each service feature? 3. Do perceptions of services vary by meal? 4. Does the value of a service feature vary by meal? 5. Are there regional differences across franchises in terms of services provided? 6. What factors contribute to any differences that are observed?

Situation Analysis

The essence of **situation analysis** is taking stock of where you've been, where you are, and where you are likely to end up, if you follow existing plans and if current trends continue. The organization's past and current marketing programs, the state of the market and current competition, and consumer reaction to these factors all play a vital role in helping the researcher and manager both recognize potential opportunities and problems and develop appropriate new strategies. Situation analysis involves scanning (1) the general environment, (2) the firm's product markets, (3) the firm's customers, and (4) the firm's marketing programs.

The General Environment. The first step in situation analysis is to understand the environment. The environment includes the general state of the economy, the economic situation of the industry, and the condition of the company in that industry. Industries and particular sectors of the economy face different economic conditions. Industries and particular sectors of the economy must identify economic, political, and governmental forces that influence business practices and how these forces are likely to change in the near and distant future. Understanding such factors is instrumental in identifying market and product opportunities and/or potential problems.

Take, for example, the pharmaceutical industry. Over the last few years, this industry has experienced several important environmental changes. Today, this industry faces global competition as well as increasing consolidation, exemplified by the merger of such companies as Smith-Kline with Beecham. One important component in this industry is the ethical drugs category. With the rise in medical expenses, governments (worldwide) are speeding the pace at which pharmaceutical companies can bring prescription drugs to the over-the-counter market. And, not surprisingly, it is the over-the-counter market in ethical drugs that is experiencing the most profound changes in composition. This over $10 billion market is and will continue to be the site of increasing competition from both pharmaceutical and consumer package good firms alike.

A comparative analysis of the position of a company within its industry can often be revealing. Consider the situation of DuPont corporation, whose corporate slogan is "better living through chemistry." Unfortunately, the pharmaceutical division of DuPont has experienced limited success in penetrating several of the pharmaceutical markets. Indeed, this over $1 billion business unit has over the last few years accounted for just 4 percent of corporate revenues, but has typically consumed over 20 percent of the total research and development budget of the corporation.

Product Markets. Understanding competitive product markets is perhaps the most fundamental issue facing a firm. Assessing the strengths and weaknesses of the array of competing products in the markets that a firm serves is an important step in clarifying the problem.

Product markets need to be understood in terms of some basic and fundamental indicators. Among other things, the product markets that a firm serves should be evaluated in terms of (1) product types, varieties, and brands; (2) sales volume and trends; (3) growth rate; (4) market share; (5) competitive vulnerability; and (6) rate of return on investment.

Consider, for example, the analgesics market, which represents an important component of the over-the-counter ethical drug category. Over the last few years this market has had annual sales of more than $2.5 billion. This category is expected to undergo spectacular growth of more than 30 percent per annum. Exhibit 2–3 presents information on the analgesics product market. Part a of the exhibit divides the category into its basic components. Aspirin, acetaminophen, and ibuprofen are the three major types of pain relievers. Ibuprofen is the newcomer and

EXHIBIT 2–3   The Analgesics Product Market

Part a. Basic Components

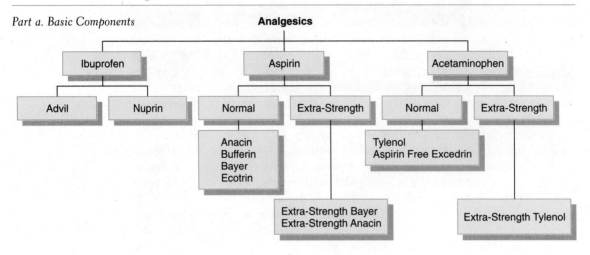

Part b. Perceptual Map

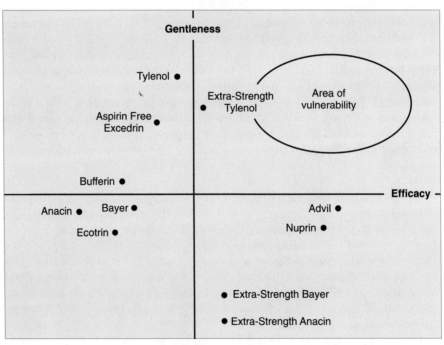

has been growing at a double-digit rate since its introduction. Aspirin and aceta-minophen brands have experienced little growth in recent years. The market has been for some time dominated by Tylenol, an acetaminophen product. (Average market shares over the last few years are presented in Exhibit 2–4.) The tendency has been for companies to launch new brands of ibuprofen pain relievers rather than pure-line extensions.

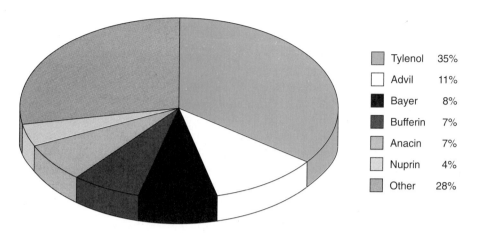

EXHIBIT 2–4
—
Average Market
Shares of Major
Analgesic Brands

Tylenol	35%
Advil	11%
Bayer	8%
Bufferin	7%
Anacin	7%
Nuprin	4%
Other	28%

Customer Markets. In addition to its product markets, a firm must also understand the customers that it currently serves as well as the customers that it wishes to serve. *Customer markets* refer to subgroups of customers that desire the same set of end benefits in the products they purchase.

Evaluating a firm's customer markets amounts to doing a sort of customer audit. Among other things, this means that customer markets should be evaluated in terms of (1) demographic factors, for example, age, gender, income, and education; (2) lifestyle patterns, for example, interests, opinions, and activities; (3) usage patterns and behaviors, for example, what products are being used, who is using the product, in what usage contexts, and frequency of use; (4) preferences for specific end benefits, for example, what is more important, price or quality; and (5) price sensitivity, for example, how deal-prone our customers are.

For analgesics, the customer markets can be understood by examining usage patterns and preferences for specific end benefits. Exhibit 2–3, part b shows a product market for analgesics. This perceptual map (recall we discussed perceptual maps in Chapter 1) positions the major brands of analgesics in terms of gentleness and efficacy. In other words, perceptions of gentleness and efficacy are the salient dimensions that differentiate brands and customers place different importance on each of these factors. The acetaminophen compounds are more gentle than their aspirin and ibuprofen competitors and are accordingly positioned on the north side in the map. Since Tylenol has maintained its dominant position in this category, it is safe to conclude that there are a large number of customers that are concerned with gentleness. However, Advil and Nuprin have made inroads, primarily by appealing to customers who want fast and effective pain relief.

Marketing Programs. Situation analysis of marketing programs should include assessment of a variety of past and current strategic elements. Among other things, (1) advertising and promotional programs; (2) pricing practices, and (3) relationships with dealers, wholesalers, and retailers should be evaluated.

DuPont's primary strength lies in its ability to bring new technological breakthroughs to market. Products such as Lycra Spandex fiber and Teflon nonstick resins have provided innovations in the apparel and cooking utensil markets. The success of ibuprofen products is a clear sign that technologically advanced new drugs can gain significant market share in the over-the-counter analgesics category. The market appears vulnerable to new products that can deliver on gentleness while at the same time being effective in relieving pain, thus occupying a position in the upper northeast region of the map shown in Exhibit 2–3, part b. However, DuPont has been primarily a supplier of input materials and, consequently, has had relatively limited experience in consumer marketing. DuPont's marketing programs in the pharmaceutical arenas must be refined to effectively communicate with the end user, especially if the over-the-counter ethical drug market is to be entered.

STAGE 2: DETERMINE THE RESEARCH DESIGN

Having formulated the problem, the researcher must determine an appropriate research design. The choice of an appropriate research design will depend on (1) the value of the information provided by alternative courses of action and (2) the requirements of the research objective and research questions.

Valuing Alternative Courses of Action

As part of determining the appropriate research design the researcher must identify alternative courses of action and evaluate the information that each alternative course of action would provide. Faced with a particular research question, there will likely be several different options that the researcher can follow. In addition to recognizing the options that are available, the researcher must be able to value the information provided in relation to the cost of obtaining it.

As an example, consider the decision to introduce a new product.[5] There are several research options available to the researcher. One option, of course, is to roll the new product out without extensive testing. However, as we have seen in the case of 7UP Gold, this can be extremely risky. The brand manager responsible for the new product may be considering the following two-phase approach:

- Phase 1. On the basis of a pretest-market study, make a go/no-go decision concerning the new product on the basis of its estimated market share and/ or volume.
- Phase 2. If the phase 1 decision is to go, then initiate a test-market study, and use the volume projection to make a final decision as to whether the new product should be launched nationally.

The brand manager responsible for this new product presented this test strategy to the marketing researcher assigned to this category. Being experienced in test-market studies, the researcher knew that considerable amounts of resources would be needed. Test-market studies involve introducing the new product in selected

---

[5]The material following is adapted from G. L. Urban, G. M. Katz, T. E. Hatch, and A. J. Silk, "The ASSESSOR Pre-Test Market Evaluation Systems," *Interfaces*, December 1983, pp. 55–56.

geographical markets to evaluate sales; such studies typically cost millions of dollars. Similar to test-market studies, pretest-market studies are designed to weed out product failures prior to test marketing and are considerably less expensive than test-market studies because they do not involve actually introducing the product in specific geographical markets. The researcher also knew, however, that without test-marketing programs the risk of product failure would be much greater.

The researcher thought that, if the various alternatives could in some way be valued, a more intelligent decision could be made concerning what test-marketing programs to implement, if any. The researcher decided to do some detective work. Based on internal secondary data on previous new-product launches, the researcher learned that profits from new products having been subjected to both a pretest-market and a test-market study averaged about $28.5 million dollars. For new products that were launched without conducting a pretest-market or a test-market study, profits were considerably lower, averaging about $16.75 million dollars.

Based on this information, the researcher concluded that the value of implementing both a pretest-market and a test-market study is approximately $11.75 million dollars.

$$\$28.5 - \$16.75 = \$11.75$$

From previous new-product launches, the researcher also determined that profits for new products launched with only a pretest-market study averaged about $20 million dollars. Comparing this profit level to those obtained without initiating any test-marketing program, the researcher valued a pretest-market study at $3.25 million dollars.

$$\$20.0 - \$16.75 = \$3.25$$

For those new products launched solely on the basis of test-market results (i.e., without any pretest-market study), profits averaged about $25.25 million dollars. Thus, the researcher valued the information provided by test-market studies at $8.5 million dollars.

$$\$25.25 - \$16.75 = \$8.5$$

Thus, the researcher concluded that the available evidence clearly supports initiating test marketing programs. However, the researcher wondered about the wisdom of conducting both types of tests: Should a test-market study be initiated given that a pretest-market study has already been performed? Yes, since the incremental profit contributed from conducting a test-market study after a pretest-market study has been performed is $5.25 million.

$$\$8.5 - \$3.25 = \$5.25$$

This simple example illustrates how a researcher might handle a difficult and complex question. Remember, the purpose of marketing research is to provide managers with information that reduces their uncertainty about the outcomes of specific courses of action. Marketing research, however, involves the commitment of resources, both labor and dollars. The actual value of information depends on three factors: (1) the likelihood of making a correct decision on the basis of the information collected, (2) the relative profitability of the alternative decisions, and (3) the cost of acquiring the information.

Research Objective Requirements

As we discussed earlier, problem formulation is important because it determines the information that will be needed. Information needs determine the objectives of the research and, in large measure, what kind of research design is most appropriate. The way the problem is formulated with respect to the research objective and accompanying research questions places certain demands on the research design.

In certain instances, the research problem to be solved is rather broad or vague. In such cases, the research designs must be flexible to permit the researcher to exercise judgment concerning possible areas and tactics of investigation. For example, although the Campbell Soup Company has tried to convince consumers that "soup is good food," increasing numbers of consumers have been shunning canned soup because of its high sodium content. More frustrating, however, is the fact that Campbell has had a low-sodium line on the market for years, but consumers have been unmoved.[6] In addressing the problem of why low-sodium soups have not had greater market penetration, the marketing researcher will probably have to conduct research that will give some ideas about and insights into the problem. One way to proceed is to interview small groups of soup consumers to find out about their experiences with, and reactions to, low-sodium soups. When the researcher knows relatively little about the issue being investigated, *exploratory research designs* are most appropriate. **Exploratory research designs** provide the marketing researcher with ideas and insights about a broad or relatively vague problem. Such designs allow a more precise statement of the problem to be formulated, which in turn will allow causal or descriptive research designs to be used.

In certain instances, the research problem to be solved is more specific in the sense that the marketing researcher and client/decision maker are aware of those factors that may be contributing to the problem. In such instances, the research design must allow the researcher to focus on specific aspects of the product or on the relationship between those factors thought to be contributing to the problem. For example, having determined that soup consumers believe low-sodium soups are not much different from soups having normal sodium content, Campbell might initiate a study to develop demographic and lifestyle profiles of those people who are currently buying low-sodium and health-conscious products and their perceptions of the benefits offered by such products with particular emphasis on why a low-sodium appeal is more believable in certain product categories. When the researcher knows something about the problem being addressed, *descriptive re-*

exploratory research designs
Research designs that provide the marketing manager with ideas and insights about broad and/or vague research problems.

---

[6]Kathleen Deveny and Richard Gibson, "Food Giants Hope New 'Healthy' Soups Will Be Ingredients of Financial Success," *The Wall Street Journal*, September 4, 1991, p. B1.

search designs are often employed. **Descriptive research designs** generally involve attempts to determine the frequency with which something happens or the extent to which two or more variables are related.

Finally, in certain instances, the research problem to be solved is clearly and specifically identified. In such instances, the research design must allow the researcher to assess the exact relationship between factors thought to contribute to the problem. For example, having determined that soup consumers are confused about what low sodium actually means, Campbell might initiate a study to determine which of two advertisements produce greater change in consumers' understanding of the benefits of specific levels of sodium and their perceptions of products with different sodium levels. The purpose of this study is to test the informational effect of the two advertisements with a view toward determining which advertisement is superior. When the researcher wants to test specific hypotheses about those factors thought to contribute to the problem being investigated, *causal research designs* are often employed. **Causal research designs** generally involve attempts to determine the extent to which changes in one variable cause changes in some other variable. Experimental designs, which are the subject of Chapter 8, are frequently used when the objective of the research is to assess cause-and-effect relationships among variables.

descriptive research designs
Research designs that attempt to determine the frequency with which something happens or the extent to which two or more variables are related.

causal research designs
Research designs that attempt to determine the extent to which changes in one variable cause changes in another variable.

STAGE 3: PREPARATION

The preparation stage of the research process entails a number of activities. The researcher must (1) identify who will supply the information (the source), (2) determine how the needed information will be obtained, (3) design the sampling plan, and (4) design the data collection instrument. All of these activities precede going into the field.

Determine Source of Data

The first question facing the researcher is whether the problem at hand will require *secondary data sources* or *primary data sources* of information.

Secondary data sources already exist and can be found in libraries or other public institutions. The government represents a large depository of information that can be accessed to solve marketing research problems. One government agency that recently updated its information is the Census Bureau, which completed the 1990 U.S. Census. Another source of secondary information can be found within the firm itself. Accounting, sales, and other departments within the firm can provide valuable information that can be accessed to solve marketing research problems. Marketing research suppliers who offer syndicated services are also sources of secondary data. Chapters 4 and 5 provide additional details on sources of secondary and syndicated data.

secondary data sources
Data that already exists and can be found in libraries or other public institutions or found within the firm itself.

More often than not, the research problem being investigated will require information that is not readily available, or if available, the information is not in a suitable form. In such instances, the researcher will have to collect the necessary information directly. **Primary data** are information that has been collected specifically for the research problem at hand. For example, though some kinds of secondary information, such as income and population changes, may be useful to the marketing researcher in attempting to forecast first-year volume for a new-product introduction, primary data on how well the new product will sell in specific geographical regions are necessary in order to accurately predict what first-year volume would be if the new product were rolled out nationally. The need to collect primary data brings with it a number of accompanying activities. Many of the remaining chapters are devoted to issues and practices surrounding primary data collection.

Determine Data Collection Method

If the decision is to collect primary data, then the researcher will need to determine the appropriate method of collecting the data. Primary data can be collected through such *qualitative interviewing techniques* as direct observation, in-depth interviews, or focus group interviews. Alternatively, the researcher can use *survey interviewing methods*, which usually involve the use of a structured questionnaire. Qualitative data collection methods are relatively unstructured forms of interviewing and generally involve small numbers of respondents. In contrast, more structured interviewing formats (e.g., having an individual fill out a questionnaire) are generally used in survey research involving larger numbers of respondents where the objectives of the research require that survey results be projectable to the wider population.

Design Sampling Plan

There are three basic steps in designing a sampling plan. First, the researcher must precisely define who should participate in the study. Second, the researcher must devise a method for identifying and reaching those eligible to participate in the study. And third, the researcher must determine how many respondents to include.

The term **sample** is used to denote the particular subset of the population that has been selected to participate in the study. The sample can consist of individuals, households, firms, homeowners, doctors, weightlifters, or any other segment of the population. However, determining who is eligible to participate in the study at hand may not be as clear-cut as it might first appear.

Consider the case of a manufacturer of rug-cleaning products who is contemplating marketing a new line of rug-cleaning products designed specifically for households with dogs and cats. In designing a study, say, to investigate the viability of this concept, the researcher will have to decide the type of household to include in the sample. Should it be made up of households that have carpets? Or perhaps the sample should be restricted to households with carpets and a dog or cat, or to households with carpets and pets *and* who have had their carpets cleaned within the last 18 months. The decision as to which sample of households to include is determined by the objectives of the study; so again it is important that the problem be precisely defined.

The researcher must devise a way to identify those who are eligible to participate in a study. This can be accomplished in a variety of ways. For example, mailing lists or telephone directories are two vehicles for identifying and reaching sample prospects. The way in which the researcher goes about identifying the sample has important consequences for the representativeness of the information obtained. When mailing lists and telephone directories are used, for example, the sample selected may not be representative of the population as a whole since only those individuals whose names appear in the mailing list or those whose phone numbers are listed in the directory can be included in the sample. A sampling plan is used to ensure that a *representative* sample of the target population is obtained. We discuss various sampling designs in Chapter 9.

The final step in designing the sampling plan is to determine the size of the sample, that is, how many individuals, households, institutions, and so on, to sample. The size of the sample is influenced by several factors.

Obviously, the amount of dollars allocated to the research study at hand plays an important role. The length of the interview and the type of interviewing method used also play a role since the cost of collecting data will be greater the longer the interview, with costs varying depending on whether a mail, telephone, or personal interview is used. Finally, the research objectives influence what sample size will be representative. Sampling issues are discussed in Chapters 9 and 10.

Design Questionnaire

The final activity before entering the field to collect the necessary information is to design the questionnaire. The form of the questionnaire depends on the decisions that have been made up to this point. The nature of the problem and the data collection method, along with the chosen sampling design, all influence how the questionnaire will be structured and the format of the questions asked. For example, a questionnaire can be administered with the aid of a computer, by means of a telephone, and with or without the presence of an interviewer. The target sample of respondents may be adults between the ages of 18 and 54, or children 12 years of age. Researchers must take into account these considerations, as well as others, when designing the questionnaire. Questionnaire design considerations are discussed in Chapter 11.

STAGE 4: IMPLEMENT THE FIELDWORK

Implementing and completing the fieldwork involves a number of activities. As we discussed in Chapter 1, local field service firms handle the day-to-day activities for collecting the data. These firms are hired by marketing research suppliers to collect the needed information. Usually, the marketing research supplier has a "field department" that is responsible for coordinating and overseeing the activities of the local field services being used. The following briefly describes some of the activities that are necessary in fielding a study. Additional details are presented in Chapter 13.

Instruct Interviewers

Before the data can be collected, the interviewers must be properly acquainted with various aspects of the study. Field instructions are prepared by the research supplier and sent to the local field services. These instructions generally provide details on how the questionnaire should be administered and often provide instructions on a question-by-question basis.

Schedule and Conduct Interviews

The field department also prepares another set of instructions, this time covering how the fieldwork should be organized and controlled. These instructions typically go to interviewing supervisors and, among other things, provide guidance concerning (1) how to screen respondents, (2) sample quotas, and (3) when and where the sample should be selected. For example, if the plan is to intercept individuals while they are shopping at local malls, the instructions would cover which malls are to be used, how many individuals are to be intercepted at each mall, and where in the mall prospective respondents are to be intercepted.

STAGE 5: PROCESS THE DATA

There are two necessary and important functions that must be performed before data collected in the field can be analyzed. These include (1) check-in and editing and (2) coding and transcription. The following briefly describes each of these functions. Further details will be presented in Chapter 13.

Editing

After a completed questionnaire is received from the field, it must be inspected to determine whether it is acceptable for use in the study. A number of problems can cause a completed questionnaire to be excluded, for example, (1) portions of the questionnaire, or key questions, may be left unanswered, (2) questions may have been answered improperly, or (3) the questionnaire may have been completed by someone who should have been excluded from participating.

editing
Refers to evaluating the accuracy and precision of the questionnaires.

The **editing** process involves reviewing completed questionnaires for maximum accuracy and precision. Response consistency and accuracy are the primary concerns. When two answers are inconsistent—for example, the respondent indicates no familiarity with the test brand, but also indicates that the brand was purchased on the last shopping trip—it may be possible to determine which, if either, of the responses is correct by examining other responses. When this is not possible, both answers are usually discarded.

With respect to accuracy, the person responsible for editing concentrates on signs of interviewer bias or cheating, for example, common patterns of responses across different questionnaires for the same interviewer. In addition to these concerns, editing is also concerned with (1) response legibility, (2) response clarity, and (3) response completeness.

Coding

Coding involves (1) assigning numerical values (codes) to represent a specific response to a specific question and (2) designating the location of all responses appearing in the data file. Assigning numerical codes to each answer provided by a respondent is necessary so that the data collected can be analyzed by a computer.

A data file contains the coded responses of all the respondents who have participated in the survey. For example, consider the following question: Which of the following categories best describes your total household income before taxes in 1992:

Less than $10,000	1
$10,000–$14,999	2
$15,000–$24,999	3
$25,000 or more	4

Codes

In the data field, a response of "less than $10,000" would be represented by a "1." In order for a computer to be able to properly read the data, the computer must be told where in the data file each answer resides. This involves specifying the row and column position(s) of each question in the data file. Data files are stored on magnetic tape or disk. Details on coding questionnaires and related data file issues are discussed in Chapter 13.

STAGE 6: TABULATE AND ANALYZE

The penultimate phase of the research process involves what can generally be referred to as *tabulation and data analysis*. Here, interest centers on reporting and interpreting relationships among the key questions that respondents have answered. As we indicated in Chapter 1, a tabulation house is generally responsible for analyzing the data, although the marketing researcher and supplier bear the responsibility for interpretation.

One basic component of the analysis phase is the tabulation plan. A **tabulation plan** refers to the orderly arrangement of the data in a table or other summary format by counting the frequency of responses to each question. For example, the researcher may wish to tabulate responses to the question dealing with how many units of a brand have been purchased by each respondent by the income of the respondent. The researcher, in consultation with the supplier, generally specifies what tables will be run. Chapters 13 and 14 provide details on various aspects of tabulating the data.

In addition, the researcher may also wish to perform other types of analyses. These analyses would allow the researcher to form specific conclusions about the research problem at hand that cannot be easily gleaned from a simple tabulation of the data. For example, the researcher may wish to test specific hypotheses about the relationships among key variables. Statistical analysis procedures are discussed in Chapters 15 through 17.

coding
Assigning numerical values to represent specific responses to specific questions.

tabulation plan
Orderly arrangement of data in a table or other summary format.

STAGE 7: PREPARE THE RESEARCH REPORT

The results of marketing research must be effectively communicated to management. Presenting the results of a marketing research study to management generally involves a formal written research report as well as an oral presentation. Needless to say, the report and presentation are extremely important. First, they are important because the results of marketing research are often intangible. After the study has been completed and a decision is made, there is very little physical evidence of the resources such as time, money, and effort that went into the project. Thus, the written report and oral presentation represent one physical source of "documentation."

Second, and perhaps more important, the written report and oral presentation are typically the only aspects of a study that many marketing executives are exposed to. Consequently, the overall evaluation of the research project rests on how well this information is communicated.

Finally, the quality of the written report and oral presentation ultimately reflects favorably or unfavorably upon the research supplier who conducted the study and ultimately determines whether that particular supplier will be used in the future. Chapter 23 provides several suggestions and guidelines for preparing written reports and oral presentations. Some guidelines to consider are: (1) think of your audience, (2) be concise yet complete, and (3) understand the results and draw appropriate conclusions.

RESEARCH PROPOSALS

Two formal documents are used to summarize the marketing research planning process. The first is called a *request for proposal.* In response to the request for proposal, a formal *research proposal* is prepared.

RFPs

RFPs
Documents inviting research suppliers to submit research proposals.

Requests for Proposals (RFPs) are written documents that formally invite marketing research suppliers to submit a formal research proposal describing how the research study should be conducted. RFPs are prepared by corporate marketing research departments. The usual practice is to distribute the RFP to suppliers that have been used by the firm in the past. RFPs should present pertinent information regarding (1) background of the marketing problem, (2) objectives of the research, (3) sample design considerations, (4) timing, and (5) selection criteria and criteria weights. Exhibit 2–5 presents a typical RFP.

Rarely will the corporate marketing research department disclose the budget it has allocated to the project. However, the RFP should contain sufficient information to allow suppliers to set a reasonable price for conducting the study. Typically, given the objectives of the study and information on the sampling design, suppliers can accurately price the study.

The solicitation of research proposals should meet ethical standards regarding (1) proposal content, (2) conditions governing submission, and (3) ownership rights.

EXHIBIT 2–5

Request for Proposal

Background:	Our low-salt and unsalted crackers now account for 7.2 percent of total cracker sales, providing $119.3 million in sales and 88.6 million pounds in volume in 1992. The low-salt and unsalted crackers vary in importance to the parent brand. Our established entry into the low-salt and unsalted category now accounts for 23 percent of total brand volume, while our most recent entry accounts for 9 percent of total brand volume. However, with the recent success of our low-salt crackers, competitive entries have begun to appear. In order to continue to build our low-salt cracker business and to effectively defend these brands against new competitive entries, a better understanding of consumers' usage of low-salt and unsalted crackers and their attitudes is needed.
Objective:	The objective of this research is to better understand the overall dynamics (i.e., behavioral and attitudinal) of the low-salt/unsalted cracker market. More specifically, the research will help answer the following key marketing questions:

— What are the behavioral (purchase and usage) dynamics within the low salt/unsalted cracker market?

— What is the attitudinal framework for low-salt/unsalted products?

— What demographic and attitudinal factors are best associated with product usage?

Sampling Frame:	Minimum sample of 150 users (past 3 months) of each of the following low-salt/unsalted brands:

Krispy (unsalted tops).

Premium (both low-salt and unsalted tops).

Ritz.

Town House.

Wheat Thins.

Zestas (unsalted tops).

Timing Selection Criteria:	The study should be completed within 20 weeks of its starting point. Proposals submitted will be evaluated according to the following criteria:

Supplier skills/expertise	30
Comprehensiveness	25
Technical competency	30
Cost	15

The Council of American Survey Research Organizations (CASRO) has provided ethical guidelines for the solicitation of proposals (see Exhibit 2–6 on page 48).

Finally, as mentioned above, the RFP should also include a statement concerning the criteria on which the various proposals will be evaluated, along with the weights associated with each criterion. For example, Exhibit 2–5 indicates that 30 percent of the evaluation will be based on the expertise of the supplier in conducting market studies, 25 percent on the comprehensiveness of the proposal's content, 30 percent on the technical competency of the proposal, and 15 percent on the cost component.

A. Proposal content.

Research firms that are asked to submit cost estimates should be given a complete set of specifications (written, if possible) covering the following items where applicable or known:
a. Tasks to be performed by the client and by the contractor.
b. Description of questionnaire (or questionnaires) by (1) number of questions, by type of question—i.e., open-ended, single response closed-end, multiple response closed-end, etc.; or (2) duration of interview in minutes plus number of open-ended questions.
c. Estimated incidence (percent) and description of incidence groups.
d. Sample design and universe.
e. Household selection/respondent selection.
f. Percent of data entry that will be verified.
g. Type of edit/clean utilized, i.e., clean to questionnaire versus machine clean.
h. Number of banners and banner points for tabulation.
i. Number of cross tabs.
j. Total copies of reports and/or tabs.
k. Special hand tabs required.

B. Conditions governing submission of proposals.

Proposals are prepared in response to a client request, entirely at the expense of the research company.

These should be submitted to the requesting client only. If that client does not authorize the work, the proposal may be submitted to other prospective clients, unless so doing would reveal confidential information.

C. Ownership rights related to proposals.

Absent a contrary agreement between the prospective contractor and the prospective client:
Proposals prepared at the expense of a prospective contractor.
a. Such proposals are the property of the company that prepared them, and they may not be used by a prospective client in any way to its benefit without the permission of the prospective contractor.
b. Any part of proposal content, including questions or a questionnaire (which is constructed by the prospective contractor), are the property of the research company that prepared them.
c. Proposals prepared wholly or in substantial part at the expense of a prospective client are the property of the company that has requested and paid for them, and they are considered to be "reports."

The Research Proposal

research proposal
Document that describes the marketing problem, the purpose of the study, and the research methodology.

A **research proposal** is a formal written document that describes the marketing problem, the purpose of the study, and provides a somewhat detailed outline of the research methodology. The form and length of research proposals vary greatly. Some research proposals are over 20 pages, and others are as short as a single page. Exhibit 2–7 presents a research proposal written in response to the RFP shown in Exhibit 2–5.

Though the exact form of the proposal is also variable, most research proposals contain the following elements.

Background and Problem/Opportunity Definition. A research proposal should provide relevant background for the proposed study. Specifically, the proposal

Category:	Low-salt crackers
Project:	Market study
Objectives:	In order to continue to build low-salt/unsalted cracker business and to effectively defend these brands against new competitive entries, a better understanding of consumers' usage of low-salt/unsalted crackers and their attitudes toward low-salt/unsalted crackers is needed.
Research Method:	A two-phase research study (screening and follow-up) will be conducted among households who are members of the supplier's mail panel.
Screening Phase:	In order to address the marketing questions outlined above, it will be necessary to obtain a basic sample of low-salt/unsalted cracker users and readable samples (N = 150 in follow-up phase) for each of the brands of interest.
Sampling Frame:	Screening questionnaires will be mailed to a nationally balanced sample of 36,000 panel member households. Within each household, men and women, age 18 or older, will complete the questionnaire. Returns are expected from 25,200 individuals, which is a response rate of 70 percent. A random sample of 2,000 of these respondents will be fully processed in the second phase of the study.
Follow-Up Phase:	In the follow-up phase, an extensive self-administered survey will be mailed to individuals having certain characteristics (i.e., category/ specific brand usage) as identified in the screening phase.
Analysis:	Analysis will include standard cross-tabular analyses plus a number of multivariate statistical techniques (specifically a segmentation analysis) in order to help answer key research questions. For example,
	1. What is the underlying need structure within the low-salt cracker market? 2. How is the market segmented in terms of usage dynamics? 3. What are the (particular brand's) strengths and weaknesses among its franchise?
Action Standard:	Not applicable.
Cost:	The cost for conducting the study as specified within this proposal will be $121,500 ± 10% ($28,500 for screener and $93,000 for follow-up). This cost includes sample selection, questionnaire production, first-class postage (out and back), reminder postcards (follow-up study only), respondent incentives (follow-up study only), data processing (up to 12 cards and 6 open ends), four banners of tabulations at the follow-up phase, all necessary multivariate statistical analyses, and one presentation or report.
Timing:	Scheduling for the study will be as follows:

	Weeks Elapsed (from start of field, August 3)
Screeners returned	4
Phase I data available	7
Phase II commences	8
Phase II data collection ends	12
Phase II data available	16
Draft presentation available	20

EXHIBIT 2–7
—
Marketing Research Project Proposal

should precisely define the problem at hand. In the research proposal shown in Exhibit 2–7, for example, the background indicates that although the firm's low-salt and unsalted crackers have been successful, they are likely to face increasing competitive pressures in the near future.

In general, a useful starting point is to define why the research is being undertaken, what the study is designed to measure, and how the information will be used.

Objectives. A research proposal should provide a clear explanation of the study's objectives and value. For example, in the research proposal shown in Exhibit 2–7, the stated objectives are to investigate consumers' usage of and attitudes toward low-salt and unsalted crackers.

Research Method. Choice of the appropriate research methodology involves important and interdependent decisions. Major decisions include

- Selection of the sample—who and how many respondents to include.
- Selection of the data collection method—whether to use primary or secondary data; whether to conduct mail, telephone, or personal interviews.
- Evaluation of the design—how the research methodology being proposed is going to be implemented and how it will meet the objectives of the study.

In Exhibit 2–7 the proposed research design methodology involves a two-phase screening and follow-up procedure that utilizes the supplier's mail panel. Note that the research proposal is rather specific concerning the approach to be used and the anticipated completion rates. Consequently, the client knows exactly what will be done and what they are getting for their money.

Information to Be Obtained. The research proposal must express crucial decisions relating to

- Measurement content—what should be measured.
- Measurement technique—how we should measure it.

Note that the measurement content and technique to be used in the low-salt/unsalted cracker market study are both defined precisely in Exhibit 2–7. Cracker usage information and purchase dynamics will be measured, as well as the importance attached to brand-related end benefits for specific usage situations. Where appropriate, the research proposal specifies the type of measurement scales to be used.

Analysis. The analysis section of the research proposal provides a description of how the data collected will be analyzed. It can contain a description of the tabulation plans, indicating the scope and nature of the cross tabulations to be run, for example, usage by age. In addition, it must also describe whether other types of statistical analyses will be performed. For example, in the research proposal described in Exhibit 2–7, the supplier has indicated that a segmentation analysis will be performed.

Action Standard.   The **action standard** for the research proposal clearly defines the performance criterion to be applied. How the research results are judged is ultimately tied to the study's purpose and objectives, and it also influences the choice of an analysis technique. Action standards provide an *a priori* means for evaluating survey results. When action standards are used, the interpretation of the data is less subject to political pressure. Note that in the project proposal shown in Exhibit 2–7, no action standards are specified. Market studies typically do not lend themselves to explicit performance criteria since the objective of such studies is to describe competitive relationships, as opposed to judging the superiority of one brand over another.

action standard
Statement in the research proposal that clearly defines the performance criterion to be applied to the results of the study.

If we were considering a project proposal for, say, a concept test concerning new snack food ideas, an appropriate action standard might be:

> Those concepts that have been selected by at least one-third of the respondents will be singled out for further testing.

Cost and Timing.   A research proposal will include a statement of the estimated project cost and a schedule that outlines deadlines for various aspects of the project. Exhibit 2–7 indicates that the data collected will be available to the client 16 weeks from August 3, the beginning of the field operation, and will cost $121,500, plus or minus the customary 10 percent contingency factor.

SUMMARY

The research process provides a general framework to follow when designing and implementing a research study. In this chapter we have explained each stage in the research process. Each stage was described in terms of a number of research activities that must be completed. In addition, we also considered how firms request competitive bids from marketing research suppliers for conducting specific types of studies. In response to requests for proposals, suppliers prepare formal written documents outlining how the research study would be conducted. Each major component of the marketing research proposal was explained and illustrated.

KEY CONCEPTS

research process
problem formulation
research objective
research questions
situation analysis

exploratory research designs
descriptive research designs
causal research designs

sources of data
sampling plan
questionnaire design
instructing interviewers
editing

coding
tabulating and analysis
report writing
research proposal
request for proposals

REVIEW QUESTIONS

1. Suppose that the pharmaceutical division of DuPont is considering entering the over-the-counter antacid ethical drug category.

   a. Perform a situational analysis of this category, concentrating on product markets and customer markets. The discussion can be brief. Focus on the competitive environment and the apparent end benefits that are important. (*The Wall Street Journal* may prove useful; you may want to check *Consumer Reports* as well. Your local drug store and supermarket can provide valuable information.)

   b. On the basis of the information collected in 1a, prepare a diagram of this product market and a perceptual map (see Exhibit 2–3).

   c. If DuPont is to enter this category, formulate a problem statement.

2. Develop a research objective and set of research questions for a study to revive 7UP Gold.

3. Discuss the differences between exploratory, descriptive, and causal research designs, and give specific illustrations of the type of research objectives and accompanying set of research questions that are consistent with each design.

4. For each stage in the research process, develop a set of questions that a researcher should attempt to answer.

CASE STUDIES FOR
PART I

CASE 1:
NBC Drops Shows Older Audiences Favor

By Kevin Goldman

The NBC network, after two years of double-digit declines in ratings and a troublesome trend toward an older audience, is embarking on major changes to attract the younger viewers advertisers seek most.

NBC, which lost its No. 1 position to CBS this season after six consecutive years on top, has unceremoniously jettisoned two of its reliable one-hour dramas. "In the Heat of the Night," starring ol' Archie Bunker-actor Carroll O'Connor, and "Matlock," starring silver-haired Andy Griffith. Both shows continue to perform respectably, running No. 2 in their time slots. Both do especially well among adults over age 55: "Matlock" ranks No. 3, and "Heat" is No. 5 when compared with all prime-time programs.

That, it turns out, is the problem. The two series perform far worse among the under-50 crowd that is the most coveted target for sponsors: "Heat" runs 65th and "Matlock" ranks 83rd among all prime-time shows this season. In their place, NBC is likely to try new shows with younger appeal.

"NBC is conforming to the preferences of the advertising community instead of trying to change the world," says Jerome Dominus, senior vice president at ad agency J. Walter Thompson. News Corp.'s Fox network "has made a fortune saying they aren't interested in people 50-plus. NBC is learning from this."

In some ways NBC is a victim of its own success. Instead of developing new hits, it stayed with some programs perhaps longer than it should have. That let it continue to win the household ratings race, but NBC

also began losing the more important, younger demographic race as its audience aged with its shows.

Now the median age of the NBC viewer is 42 years old—up from age 39 just two TV seasons ago. At ABC, by contrast, the median viewer age is 36 years old, and at Fox it's only 28. Only CBS's median age is older—44 years old. Overall, 44 percent of all NBC viewers have passed age 50, up by one percentage point in three years.

The NBC network, owned by General Electric Co., acknowledges it is in a period of transition and must shed some veteran shows. The two cancellations are only part of the major restructuring of NBC's once potent prime-time line-up. In September, NBC will lose "The Cosby Show," whose final episode will be taped this evening in the Astoria, Queens, section of New York. NBC also is losing the once-popular "Night Court." And "The Golden Girls" will return with a new format and without co-star Bea Arthur.

Further, its Thursday schedule is besieged by unprecedented competition from its three major rivals. "Cheers" has shown signs of erosion, and "L.A. Law" is having creative difficulties, recently dismissing its executive producer and bringing back co-creator Steven Bochco.

NBC originally had added the two older-skewing series to offer up the audience to those sponsors that wanted to reach the over-50 set. The two canceled shows were quickly snatched up by rivals, with Capital Cities/ABC Inc.'s ABC network acquiring "Matlock" and CBS Inc.'s CBS network buying "In the Heat of the Night," for much the same reason.

"We realize the strategic importance to attract an older audience at least one night of the week," says Larry Hyams, ABC's director of audience research.

Ultimately, NBC told the producers of "In the Heat of the Night" that it needed to move "onward and upward and thanks for the four years," says Edward B. Gradinger, president of MGM Worldwide Television

Source: *The Wall Street Journal*, March 6, 1992, p. B4. Reprinted with permission.

Group, a unit of MGM-Pathe Communications Co. "They're going to try to be more like Fox and ABC."

"I would call this a rather dramatic move on their part," says David F. Poltrack, a CBS senior vice president. "Older viewers are a very important part of the prime-time audience, and it's one we'll continue to appeal to."

NBC executives say they aren't looking to make a dramatic right-turn in the schedule. Rather, "we're trying to gradually transition an increasingly older-skewing schedule into one that features younger shows with overall younger demographics, which is more consistent to what advertisers are buying," says Perry Simon, NBC's No. 2 programming executive.

"We have no intention of turning into a kiddie network," he adds, citing "I'll Fly Away" and "Reasonable Doubts," two dramas that premiered last September, as "serious" shows that have broad appeal.

NBC's hopes to snare a younger audience rest on its still unfolding development season. Top candidates include a spinoff of Bill Cosby's show starting his wise cracking but earnest TV son, Malcolm Jamal-Warner. New versions of "Route 66" and "Journey to the Center of the Earth" are due, as are "Rise and Shine," a situation comedy from the off-center creators of "Northern Exposure," and comedies from Marcy Carsey and Tom Werner, the producers of "The Cosby Show" starring Robert Townsend, as well as a new show from the "Cheers" team.

Bill Croasdale, president of national broadcasting at Western International Media, characterizes NBC's move as "smart," but adds ominously, "The mystery is how good the replacement shows will be."

Case Questions

1. Define the research problem NBC is facing.
2. Develop the research objective(s) and set of research questions that should guide the research conducted by NBC.

CASE 2:
Redesign Boosts Rold Gold Sales

Frito Lay assigned Apple Designsource, a New York City–based marketing design firm, to create packaging for Rold Gold Pretzels that would help position it as a

Source: *Snack Food*, May 1991, p. 22. Reprinted with permission.

new and revitalized product in the East. This is where approximately 50 percent of all pretzels are consumed.

"Having recently reformulated and improved the product, we now needed our packaging to communicate to the shopper that this was the best pretzel on the market today," explains Walt Root, senior product manager for new business development at Frito Lay. "We wanted an exciting look that would be both eye-catching to the purchaser and appealing to the ultimate user."

Without a real need to retain brand equity, since Rold Gold's market share in the nation's pretzel belt was small, the design firm overhauled the graphics, changed the colors and greatly expanded the size of the window.

It is the window, according to the company's market research, that helps generate appetite appeal and plays a huge role within the pretzel category.

"You usually can't go this far (with a packaging redesign), but we had no recognition in this area and so were pretty much given a license to start a new brand," adds Lee Peterson, senior creative service manager at Frito Lay. "Our previous packaging was very simple and offered little shelf impact. With the new packaging, however, the pretzels flew off the shelf."

The new packaging displays the brand name, in bold yellow letters, on a black diamond background. The product designator lies at the base of the diamond (a band of red for Thins, purple for Sticks, light blue for Tiny Twists, dark blue for Rods, and green for Bavarian). The top and the bottom of the package are in light blue.

"We gave the package greater shelf impact and made it more masculine by adding a shape—a diamond—and a color—black—that males generally respond to," says Barry Seeling, president of Apple Designsource. "To emphasize the product's healthy, wholesome image, wheat stalks curl around the logo and a burst, with the trademark, 'Low Fat Snack, Baked and Crispy,' appears near the bottom of the package," he adds.

The new packaging scored an immediate hit. *Several months after its introduction, and without any increased advertising spending, Rold Gold has shown a sales increase in the heartland of well over 50 percent.*

Case Questions

1. Newly redesigned Rold Gold pretzels has been reintroduced and is apparently doing well. What problems and/or opportunities will Rold Gold likely face

in the near future? Develop a list of research questions that will guide future research efforts.

2. On the basis of the research questions identified in question 1, determine what research studies Frito Lay should consider doing for Rold Gold pretzels.

CASE 3:
Food Giants Hope New 'Healthy' Soups Will Be Ingredients of Financial Success

By Kathleen Deveny and Richard Gibson

On a shelf above the desk of Robert Bernstock, vice president of Campbell Soup Co., sits a symbol of one of the most pressing challenges now facing the nation's largest soup maker. It is a can of Healthy Choice soup, made by archrival ConAgra Inc.

Mr. Bernstock will attempt to squash that challenge when Campbell soon announces a new line of more healthful soups—the company's most important product launch in recent years. Called Healthy Request, the soups promise to be lower in fat, sodium, and cholesterol than Campbell's regular fare.

The Healthy Request launch, coming later this week, takes place at a time when Campbell is feeling the heat. David W. Johnson, who became Campbell's chief executive last year, has cut costs and pumped up earnings. But Campbell still counts on soup for half its profits, and U.S. per capita soup consumption has stalled at about 43 bowls a year. While the company still controls two-thirds of the $2.6 billion soup market, competitors have nibbled away at its dominance. Worse yet, for all of Campbell's efforts to convince consumers that "soup is good food," increasing numbers are shunning canned soup because of its high sodium content.

"We're very much trying to retain the loyalty of our customers," says Anthony Adams, Campbell's vice president of marketing research. "Healthy Request gets us out in front of their needs and out in front of the competition."

But Campbell's lead in healthy soups could be fleeting. ConAgra is about to roll out 10 low-sodium soups under its powerful Healthy Choice brand. Other brands, including Progresso, Lipton, and Weight Watchers, are also cooking up healthier recipes of their own.

Source: *The Wall Street Journal*, September 4, 1991, p. B1. Reprinted with permission.

The contest between Campbell and ConAgra, however, promises to be the most bitter. Although it has no experience selling soup, ConAgra is nearly three times Campbell's size, with $19.5 billion in revenues. The two companies have long been rivals in the supermarket freezer case, where ConAgra's Banquet and Healthy Choice entrees compete with Campbell's Swanson and Le Menu lines. ConAgra has fared especially well recently: Since their introduction two years ago, Healthy Choice frozen dinners have scorched competitors, including Campbell.

Now ConAgra has similar aspirations in soup. "We breathe life into the markets we enter," boasts Charles D. Weil, president of ConAgra Frozen Foods, the unit launching Healthy Choice soup. "If we didn't think we could do a sizable [soup] business over time, we wouldn't be entering the market."

Critics have already begun sniping about just how wholesome the new soups are. And it's uncertain whether consumers will find them as pleasing to their taste buds as the salt-laden stuff they grew up on. Campbell's has had a very low-sodium line on the market for years, but consumers have been unmoved.

For the company that prevails, the prize is potentially large. The wholesome varieties may eventually account for 30 percent of the total soup market, by Campbell's estimate. Though consumers have largely ignored low-salt soups up to now, many would devour them if they tasted better, says Mona Doyle, president of Consumer Network Inc., which polls consumers nationally. To ballyhoo their shaped-up soups, the two marketers together are expected to pour as much as $20 million in print and television advertising.

The fight between the two food giants has already gotten nasty. They tangled in court last year when ConAgra tried to block Campbell's use of the word "healthy" on its label. In March, Campbell won the right to keep the word on its new soups but can't use the Healthy Request brand on other food products without ConAgra's consent.

Case Questions

1. On the basis of the material provided, what would you say were the research objectives and set of research questions facing the Campbell Soup Co. prior to introducing the Healthy Request product line?

2. Discuss what research projects should have been undertaken by the Campbell Soup Co. prior to the

introduction of the Healthy Request products, and relate each of these projects to the research objectives and research questions developed in question 1.

3. Discuss the product and research life cycles that Healthy Request will likely face.

CASE 4:
Novel Microwave Dinners Are Tasty—And Likely to Fail without a Quick Fix

Most of the thousands of food products introduced this year will flop. Many deserve to. They're misconceived, poorly marketed, me-too items that offer consumers little new.

Every so often, though, one emerges that's innovative and tastes better than the competition. And even then, the chances of survival are slim.

Hidden Valley frozen microwave entrees seem to be such a product. Slipped into test markets early this year by HVR Co., a unit of Clorox Co., the food takes novel advantage of microwave oven technology. Instead of simply thawing and reheating precooked fare, Hidden Valley turns the appliance into a steamer. Consumers must add water—a paper measuring cup is included—but the result is crisp vegetables, al dente pasta, tasty meats, and flavorful sauces. Moreover, cooking time is shortened.

Yet the line is limping along in test markets and seems unlikely to make it without changes. "None of them is setting the world on fire," says Ed Snaza, head buyer at Country Club Markets in suburban Minneapolis. "They're slow," agrees Tim Heyman, head grocery perishable buyer for Wetterau, Inc.'s Pittsburgh division. Hidden Valley's other test markets are Indianapolis and Ft. Wayne, Indiana, where grocers report mixed results.

The tale of why this promising product is going awry could be textbook material for marketers everywhere. Consider:

Wrong Category. Few areas are as crowded, or costly to enter, as frozen foods. Spurred by the microwave-cooking phenomenon, heat-and-eat foods quickly be-

came a $4 billion-a-year market, although it seems to be slowing; tonnage grew only 4 percent last year, the National Frozen Food Association says.

"There's too much new stuff coming out," says Doug Kleven, explaining why the Lunds, Inc., store he manages in Minneapolis's lake district carries only 3 of Hidden Valley's 10 entrees. Besides the usual array of meat-and-macaroni dishes, the store's freezers are packed with exotic eating alternatives, from Howlin' Coyote black bean chili to Vietnamese egg rolls.

Wrong Product. Growth in frozen foods is in the low-fat, low-calorie end, as illustrated by the impressive debut of ConAgra's Healthy Choice line. "Anything that has 'light' on it seems to do very well," says Roger Robbe, corporate director of frozen foods and dairy for Super Valu Stores, Inc., a big Minnesota-based food distributor.

But while Kraft recently augmented its frozen lineup with Eating Right lower-calorie entrees, Hidden Valley opted for flavor. Several of its entrees even contain butter. Its macaroni and cheese, which comes with cubes of cheddar, contains 572 calories; the lowest-calorie item is seafood scampi, at 310 calories, and grocers say it's the most popular. By comparison, Healthy Choice entrees top out at 280 calories.

Wrong Turf. Frozen meals are a veritable Muscle Beach patrolled by four giants: ConAgra, the Kraft General Foods unit of Philip Morris Cos., Nestle S.A.'s Stouffer unit, and Campbell Soup Co. They leave little room for interlopers.

A recent survey of Minneapolis and St. Paul supermarkets found graphic evidence of that. Often the Hidden Valley line was lost amid rows of Big Four fare. Of the 350 frozen-food shelves in one Rainbow Foods store in St. Paul, Hidden Valley had just two. Stouffer, on the other hand, had 28, ConAgra 25, Campbell 24, and Kraft 19.

Wrong Brand Name. For most people Hidden Valley means salad dressing mixes, not frozen foods. Moreover, the competition vastly outspends Hidden Valley to build brand identity. (The Clorox name doesn't appear anywhere on the entrees' packages.)

Wrong Packaging. Alongside its competition, Hidden Valley's package appears to be smaller and to contain less food. Grocery-trade sources say the size was partly intended to make better use of limited freezer space, and Hidden Valley officials say the package size and shape are vital to the steaming technology. Still, Mr. Heyman of Wetterau thinks the package is deter-

Source: Richard Gibson, *The Wall Street Journal*, July 12, 1991, p. B1. Reprinted by permission of *The Wall Street Journal*, © 1991 Dow Jones & Company, Inc. All Rights Reserved Worldwide.

ring sales. Also, because consumers add 2.5 ounces of water to each package, the presteamed weight on the label is less than its rivals' weight.

Wrong Advantage. Shopping pulse taker Mona Doyle, president of Consumer Network, Inc., applauds Hidden Valley's use of steam cooking as a "right-on approach" that should attract buyers. But she worries that requiring consumers to add water and stir the cooked ingredients may be asking too much.

"This doesn't sound like it's totally mindless," she says. "If they're otherwise engaged and tired, people wouldn't want to bring very much to it."

Despite the hurdles, Hidden Valley entrees may still make it. Wetterau's Mr. Heyman says the company re-cently held a "brainstorming" session about what it should do. (He suggested reshaping the package and cutting the price.) Once the consumer gets the product home, "she'll understand it's a good value," he believes.

Case Question

1. As Hidden Valley's experiences indicate, the frozen food category is extremely competitive. Based on the information provided in the case as well as other information about the frozen food category (e.g., look at the success of ConAgra's Healthy Choice product line), perform a situation analysis.

EXHIBIT 1   Acquiring Market Research Information

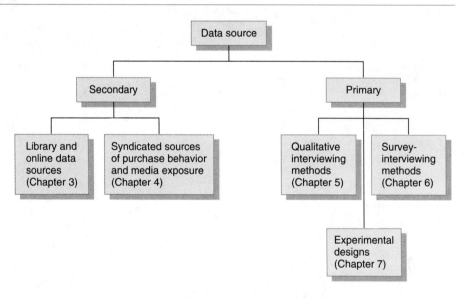

ACQUIRING DATA: AN OVERVIEW

In Part II we introduce, discuss, illustrate, and whenever possible critically compare approaches and procedures for acquiring informative marketing research data. Our objective is to thoroughly expose you to the principal sources of marketing research data and the variety of ways in which such data can be collected. The discussion is comprehensive, focusing on technologically based methods of accessing and collecting data as well as on traditional approaches.

Exhibit 1 outlines the general areas that will be considered. Note that a variety of data sources and collection methods are available. The first distinction is between secondary sources (that already exist) and primary sources (that require data collection). Acquisition of secondary market information is easier than ever: Chapter 3 familiarizes you with online databases, and Chapter 4 is a comprehensive treatment of syndicated sources of purchase behavior and media exposure information. Chapter 5 presents commonly used qualitative interviewing techniques. The remaining two chapters focus attention on procedures for collecting primary research information. Chapter 6 considers the major interviewing methods, and Chapter 7 discusses experimental designs that can be used to assess both cause and effect relationships.

Secondary Information
*The Major Access Tools**

— Understand the distinction between primary and secondary sources of marketing information.

— Explain how to evaluate secondary information.

— Introduce traditional sources of secondary market data.

— Describe online databases.

— Explain the role of database vendors who serve as information providers.

— Describe how online databases are accessed.

— Illustrate the unique features and capabilities of online databases.

— Describe CD-ROM databases.

INTRODUCTION

Faced with a marketing-related problem or potential opportunity, the marketing manager wants to obtain information that increases the likelihood of choosing the best course of action. However, before spending time, money, and effort to collect data, the researcher needs to determine whether useful information already exists and, if so, how to access it. Existing sources of useful market data are more widespread than you might expect and should be considered first.

This chapter discusses sources of already-existing market research information. Specifically, we focus on library and other traditional sources of secondary data. We attempt to integrate the traditional print sources with computerized databases. Without a doubt, one of the most dramatic developments of the last decade is *the information revolution*—a term used to describe the rapid progress in computerizing information. The application of computerized information to marketing research is relatively new; nevertheless, it has already had a substantial impact on the ways in which market information is disseminated to business. One analyst has predicted that mergers between "companies holding large databases and supplying secondary data reports . . .

---

*This chapter was prepared by Salvatore M. Meringolo, Chief of the Humanities and Social Sciences Department, Pennsylvania State University Libraries.

and the more traditional market research companies will be frequent enough to cause dramatic changes in the structure of the commercial marketing research industry estimated to be worth over $3 billion in worldwide billings."[1] Although this chapter includes the traditional bibliographic essay on printed marketing research tools, it concentrates on the size, scope, and use of interactive databases. We also introduce the mechanics of accessing online databases, and we offer some examples illustrating their use in marketing research.

PRIMARY VERSUS SECONDARY DATA

primary data
Data collected for a specific research need; they are customized and require specialized collection procedures.

At the broadest level, information sources that are available to the marketing researcher can be classified as primary or secondary. **Primary data** are collected for a specific research need; in this sense they are customized and require, in most cases, specialized data-collection procedures. Interviewing methods and experimental designs used for collecting primary data are discussed in Chapters 5, 6, and 7. **Secondary data** involve already-published data collected for purposes other than the specific research need at hand. **Internal secondary data** are available within the organization—for example, accounting records, management decision support systems, or sales records. **External secondary data** are available outside the organization from two main sources: library and other public sources and syndicated services that involve data collected under standardized procedures intended to serve the needs of an array of clients. Syndicated services will be discussed in detail in Chapter 4.

secondary data
Already published data collected for purposes other than the specific research need at hand.

internal secondary data
Data available within the organization—for example, accounting records, management decision support systems, and sales records.

For example, if Firm A conducts a survey to determine a demographic or psychographic profile of purchasers of solar heating equipment, it is collecting *primary data*. Firm B might query its sales force to get this same consumer information, rather than conduct a survey; in this case, the information is considered *internal secondary data*. It is secondary because it is a by-product of another activity (selling), and it is internal because the data are derived from existing information within Firm B. Alternatively, Firm C might conduct a search for external secondary data with regard to these same consumers. A consumer market study conducted by the U.S. Department of Energy and utilized by this firm would be considered *external secondary data* because the data were gathered for another purpose by an external agency—a government department needing to know—and describe the extent to which government policy has influenced the use of an alternative energy source.

external secondary data
Data available outside the organization from libraries and syndicated services.

With these examples in mind, let's draw some conclusions about the characteristics of primary and secondary data.

1. Primary data are gathered for a specific purpose and conform to the objective of a particular research design.
2. Because gathering primary data requires specialized expertise (e.g., survey design and administration), it can be both expensive and time-consuming.

---

[1]Council of American Survey Research Organizations (CASRO), 1991.

3. Because secondary data already have been collected and may be published, their acquisition is relatively inexpensive; they frequently can be located quickly using appropriate printed reference tools or the newer information technologies.

4. The examination of available secondary data is a prerequisite to the collection of primary data; indeed, it can help the researcher to define the parameters of the primary research. For example, national consumption patterns of a product collected by a trade association (secondary data) may provide useful benchmarks against which a firm's sales (primary data) can be measured.

5. The examination of secondary data can be of critical importance in strategic marketing planning because it may alert management to future threats or opportunities in the marketplace.

EVALUATING SECONDARY INFORMATION

The quality of the information that is used in solving a marketing-related problem should be determined, regardless of how the data were obtained. Researchers should especially examine external secondary information because the data were collected for a purpose other than the current one by someone outside the organization. Information obtained from secondary sources is not all equally reliable and/or valid. Secondary information can be misleading, and the data must be evaluated carefully regarding its recency and credibility.

When evaluating secondary information, you should consider the source of the data, the measures used, the time period in which the data were collected, and the appropriateness of the analyses. The user of secondary information should routinely ask the following general questions:[2]

1. *What was the purpose of the study?* A fundamental question concerns why the information was collected in the first place. Rarely are data collected without some intent. The intent of the study ultimately determines the degree of precision, the types of scales used, and the method of data collection. Consider the Consumer Price Index (CPI), which is calculated monthly by the U.S. Bureau of Labor Statistics. The CPI measures price movements in the United States; it is based on 400 items of consumption. The index for each item is based on the average price paid for each item by a sample of wage earners and clerical workers during some key year. Specifically, the index represents an average for a family of four, living in an urban area, with the following description: father, 38 years of age; mother, not employed outside the home; boy, 13 years of age; girl, 8 years of age. The index, therefore, clearly is not representative of the expenditures of most families. When using this index we must ask whether expenditure patterns for the group of respondents that we are interested in are different from those used to define the index. In addition, because the index is only a rough barometer

---

[2]The following material was adopted from David W. Stewart, *Secondary Research: Information Sources and Methods* (Beverly Hills, Calif.: Sage Publications, 1984), pp. 23–33.

of what is happening to purchasing power, we must question its usefulness in making specific decisions that may require a high degree of precision.

2. *Who collected the information?* Because secondary information is collected by someone outside the organization, a natural question concerns the expertise and credibility of the source. Organizations that provide secondary information vary with respect to their technical competence, resources, and overall quality. First, we can learn about the reputation of various sources of secondary information by contacting clients and others who have used the information provided by the source. Second, we can investigate how the data were obtained and the training and expertise present in the organization supplying the information.

3. *What information was collected?* You should always identify what information was actually collected by the organization supplying the data. In particular, it is important to identify (1) what was measured—for example, were fares or riders counted in a study on mass transit use? (2) in what context were the data collected—were all the leading brands included in the taste study? (3) what was the relationship between what was measured and the event of interest—were self-report data used to infer actual behavior? (4) how were the data classified—were the data broken down by uses and markets, or were they simply aggregated?

4. *When was the information collected?* The time period in which secondary information was collected plays an integral role in how the data should be interpreted. Factors that are present at the time the data were collected may influence the results. For example, information on world affairs and, specifically, attitudes toward Russia should be examined when interpreting tracking data on the U.S. sales and consumer attitudes toward Russian imports such as Stolichnaya vodka. Time may influence the definition measures, change the measurement instrument, or render the information obsolete.

5. *How was the information obtained?* An essential ingredient in evaluating the quality of secondary information is the methodology employed to collect the data. For example, the size and nature of the target sample, the response rate obtained, the questionnaire used, the experimental procedures employed (if any), the interview procedure followed, and the analytical method used should be examined in detail in order to adequately evaluate the quality of the data collection. When evaluating the procedure employed in collecting data, the critical issue is one of bias; that is, was there anything in the collection procedure that could potentially lead to a particular result, that could produce results that could not be generalized to the target population, or that could invalidate the results?

6. *Is the information consistent with other information?* In principle, two or more independent sources of secondary information should agree. When you are evaluating secondary information, a good strategy is to attempt to find multiple sources of the data and then to compare their conclusions. When differences exist, you should try to find the reasons for such differences and you should eventually determine which source is more reliable.

However, this may be difficult or even impossible to do, depending on the amount of disclosure concerning the collection procedure.

Exhibit 3–1 presents a flowchart indicating the various decisions that need to be made when using secondary data. The flowchart is divided into two main sections: one examines the applicability of secondary data to the objectives of the research project; the other examines the accuracy of the data.

EXHIBIT 3–1   Evaluating Secondary Data

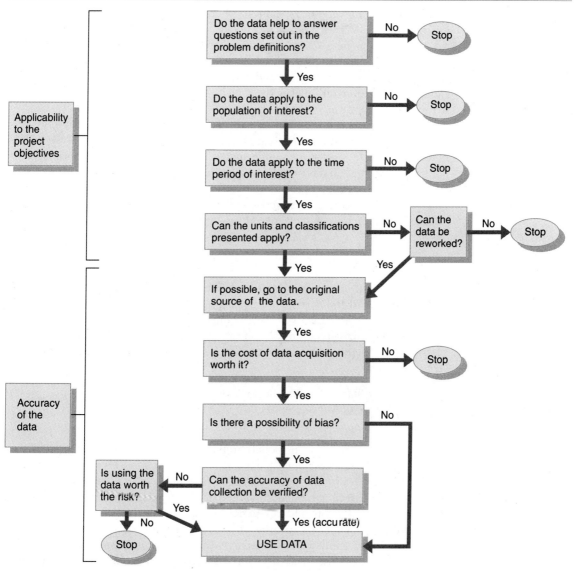

Source: Robert W. Joselyn, *Designing the Marketing Research* (New York: Petrocelli/Charter, 1977), p. 15.

TRADITIONAL SOURCES OF SECONDARY MARKET DATA

Secondary market data are produced by many organizations, including federal, state, and local governments, quasi-governmental organizations, trade associations, nonprofit enterprises (such as research institutes and universities), commercial publishers, investment brokerage houses, and professional market research firms. Organizations such as the U.S. Bureau of the Census, the National Sporting Goods Manufacturers Association, *Sales and Marketing Management*, Smith-Barney, and Frost & Sullivan are all representative examples of secondary market data producers.

The first prerequisite for locating appropriate secondary data is intellectual curiosity. You should never begin a half-hearted search with the assumption that what is being sought is so unique that no one else has ever bothered to collect it and publish it. On the contrary, assume there are corollary secondary data that should help provide definition and scope for the primary research effort. This game of "trivial pursuit" makes the search for published secondary market information both interesting and challenging.

Since the number of potentially useful print sources is considerable, we will concentrate on an important group of reference works that lead the researcher to other appropriate secondary source materials. These tools consist primarily of guides, handbooks, directories, indexes, and compilations that help the novice researcher move into a complex maze of secondary source documents. It is important to be familiar with these reference works, most of which can be located in large research libraries or specialized business libraries.

Preliminary Concept: Industrial Classification

The arrangement of secondary market data in many standard reference works utilizes the Standard Industrial Classification (SIC) scheme. Therefore, one prerequisite for the researcher is to become familiar with this hierarchical structure that is used for organizing product and industry data. In addition to understanding this classification scheme, the researcher must know how to locate an SIC for a product or industry.

> – *Standard Industrial Classification Manual*, rev. ed.
> U.S. Office of Management and Budget
> Washington, D.C.: Government Printing Office, 1987

As is pointed out in the introduction to the Manual, "Standard Industrial Classification (SIC) was developed for use in the classification of establishments by type of activity in which they are engaged." The purpose of the classification is to facilitate the collection, tabulation, presentation, and analysis of these data. It also promotes the uniformity and comparability of data collected not only by federal and state government but also by private organizations. Thus every industry is assigned an SIC number by the federal government and all of the firms in an industry will report their activity (i.e., sales and employment) according to their number.

The SIC makes it possible for researchers to collect and disseminate industry data on a two-digit, three-digit, or four-digit level, with each level being more specific than the preceding one. For example:

Major group 20—Food and Kindred Products

    Industry group 202–Dairy Products

        Industry number 2021—Creamery Butter
                    2022—Cheese

Thus, the two-digit, major group 20 includes the establishments engaged in the manufacture or processing of foods and beverages. The three-digit, industry group 202 includes firms that manufacture or process dairy products, and the four-digit industry number 2022 represents only establishments engaged in the processing of cheese. The four-digit level is usually the most descriptive, and it is as detailed as the SIC Manual gets. However, you will encounter other reference works that extend the classification to as many as seven digits in order to more precisely identify and classify product-level information (i.e., cheese dips). Therefore, locating the appropriate SIC numbers in the SIC Manual is a prerequisite to locating secondary information in many standard business directories, periodical indexes, and statistical compilations.

Guides to Business Information Sources

One of the best places to begin searching for secondary source information is in a guide to business information sources. Because the vast array of business reference sources are impossible to document in a single chapter, descriptive guides will explain the reference capability of these various sources. A guide can help the researcher to identify the important standard or recurring information sources on a specific subject. For example, in attempting to locate information about a specific industry, a guide may help to identify the major statistical information sources, the pertinent trade associations, and the trade journals or directories. Some useful business information guides include

- *Business Information, How to Find It, How to Use It*, 2nd ed.
  Michael R. Lavin
  Phoenix, Ariz.: Oryx Press, 1992
- *Business Information Sources*, rev. ed.
  Lorna M. Daniells
  Berkeley, Calif.: University of California Press, 1985
- *Encyclopedia of Business Information Sources*, 9th ed.
  James Way, editor
  Detroit: Gale Research Company, 1993
- *Information Sourcebook for Marketing and Strategic Planners*
  Van Mayros and D. Michael Werner
  Radnor, Pa.: Chilton Book Company, 1983

If a guidebook fails to produce useful sources of information, this may indicate that the research strategy needs to uncover information of a one-time, nonstandard nature or that you need to turn to primary sources.

Directories

Because the pursuit of secondary market research frequently involves the identification of individuals or organizations that gather pertinent information, it may be necessary to use directories. One tool that is indispensable because it serves as an index to over 10,000 published directories is

- *Directories in Print*, 10th ed.
  Cecilia Ann Marlow, editor
  Detroit: Gale Research Company, 1992

Trade associations frequently are the most accurate, up-to-date source of information regarding specific industries. Two directories that receive heavy use and can assist you in the identification of over 20,000 trade associations are

- *Encyclopedia of Associations*, 27th ed.
  Karin Koek et al., editors
  Detroit: Gale Research Company, 1993
- *National Trade and Professional Association of the United States*, 28th ed.
  John J. Russell et al., editors
  Washington, D.C.: Columbia Books, Inc., 1993

Data on the most specialized of products (e.g., tempered glass) are frequently collected by a trade association. Since these data may not be widely disseminated, a researcher may need to contact an association directly for information.

Indexes to Business Literature

Marketing information must be as current as possible in order to be useful to the researcher. Significant shifts can and do occur in the marketplace, and these swings must be accurately reflected in your research. The business periodical literature is a critical current information resource. Indexes are useful because they help the researcher identify journal articles on a specific subject in any of hundreds of different periodical publications. Thus a researcher might use an index to locate survey data on supermarket shoppers contained in a pertinent trade journal article. The major business indexes, which differ in scope, retrospectiveness, frequency of update, and format, are

- *Business Index*
  Menlo Park, Calif.: Information Access Company, 1979 to present
- *Business Periodical Index*
  New York: H. W. Wilson Company, 1958 to present
- *F & S Index: Europe*
  Cleveland: Predicasts, Inc., 1980 to present

- *F & S Index: International*
  Cleveland: Predicasts, Inc., 1969 to present
- *F & S Index: United States*
  Cleveland: Predicasts, Inc., 1964 to present
- *Journal of Marketing* (Every issue contains the section "Marketing Abstracts")
  Chicago: American Marketing Association, 1936 to present
- *Topicator: Classified Article Guide to the Advertising/Communications/ Marketing Periodical Press*
  Florissant, Colo.: Topicator

Indexes to Newspapers

Newspapers are also important sources of business/market information, but many local newspapers are not indexed in traditional indexes. Three major newspaper indexes provide subject indexing and are regularly updated:

- *National Newspaper Index*
  Menlo Park, Calif.: Information Access Company, 1979 to present (Indexes five newspapers: The *New York Times, The Wall Street Journal, Christian Science Monitor, Los Angeles Times*, and *Washington Post*)
- *The New York Times Index*
  New York: The New York Times Company, 1851 to present
- *The Wall Street Journal Index*
  New York: Dow Jones & Company, Inc., 1958 to present

Although these indexes are still useful, developments in the new information technologies address the historically poor access to information from our cities' important newspapers. For example, Vu/Text is a database vendor that provides online search and access to the contents of many major-market newspapers, such as the *Philadelphia Inquirer*. The new CD-ROM technology, which we will discuss at the end of this chapter, has made possible the introduction of Newspaper Abstracts Ondisc, produced by UMI. This database, which is available in many research libraries, contains abstracts and indexing from 1987 to the present for the *New York Times, The Wall Street Journal*, the *Christian Science Monitor*, the *Los Angeles Times*, the *Chicago Tribune*, the *Boston Globe*, and the *Atlanta Constitution*.

Because the market researcher frequently attempts to identify particular statistical series, these indexes are extremely important tools. They provide detailed subject indexing of statistical contents of thousands of publications produced by government, trade, and commercial organizations and are updated regularly.

- *American Statistics Index: A Comprehensive Guide to the Statistical Publications of the U.S. Government*
  Bethesda, Md.: Congressional Information Service, 1973 to present

- *Indexes to International Statistics: A Guide to the Statistical Publications of International Intergovernmental Organizations*
  Bethesda, Md.: Congressional Information Service, 1983 to present
- *Statistical Reference Index: A Selective Guide to American Statistical Publications from Private Organizations and State Government Sources*
  Bethesda, Md.: Congressional Information Service, 1980 to present

Indexes to Specialized Business Information Services

Apart from the marketing information gathered from trade associations, business periodicals, government documents, and assorted other publishers of statistical information, commercial market research reports and investment brokerage house reports are two additional important bodies of literature that are now indexed by subject. Firms such as Frost & Sullivan, Business Communications Company, and Predicasts regularly publish market surveys on various products and industries. Although these reports can be expensive ($1,000 is not uncommon), they may represent a low-cost alternative to primary research. One source that provides subject indexing of marketing research studies is

- *Findex, The Directory of Market Research Reports, Studies, and Surveys*
  Bethesda, Md., NSA Directories, 1979 to present

Other important sources of marketing information are the reports of investment brokerage houses such as Bear Stearns, Inc., and Kidder, Peabody & Company, Inc. The company and industry reports are prepared for these firms by expert professionals and can, for example, be a source of information on market share or industry trends and forecasts. One index to these reports is

- *CIRR/Corporate and Industry Research Reports Index*
  Eastchester, N.Y.: J. A. Micropublishing, Inc., 1982 to present

This index serves as a guide to a microfiche collection of these reports; reports are also available from J. A. Micropublishing.

Statistical Compilations

Unlike the statistical indexes that direct the researcher to specific statistical publications, the statistical compilation actually reprints the data extracted from numerous secondary source documents. One can save considerable research time if the needed data can be located in one of the following sourcebooks:

- Predicasts *Basebook*
  Cleveland: Predicasts, 1974 to present (Time series statistics on the U.S. economy, industries, products, and services)
- Predicasts *Forecasts*
  Cleveland: Predicasts 1960 to present (Statistical forecasts on products, industries, services, and the U.S. economy)

- Standard & Poor's *Statistical Service*
  New York: Standard & Poor's Corporation, monthly (A current source for basic statistics on the U.S. economy, financial markets, and basic industries)
- *County and City Data Book*
  U.S. Bureau of the Census
  Washington, D.C.: Government Printing Office, irregular (Repackages census data relating to counties and cities)
- *State and Metropolitan Area Data Book*
  U.S. Bureau of the Census
  Washington, D.C.: Government Printing Office, irregular (Repackages census data relating to states and metropolitan statistical areas)
- *Statistical Abstract of the United States*
  U.S. Bureau of the Census
  Washington, D.C.: Government Printing Office, annual (An essential compilation of social, political, and economic data from a variety of public and private sources)

Census-Based Statistical Extrapolations

Because of their completeness and level of detail, the various censuses conducted by the U.S. Bureau of the Census form the statistical foundation for much of the extrapolation done on the U.S. population and economic activity. The various major components of the census series are

- U.S. Bureau of the Census
  Census of Housing (published every 10 years)
  Census of Population (published every 10 years)
  Census of Agriculture (published every 5 years)
  Census of Construction Industries (published every 5 years)
  Census of Manufacturers (published every 5 years)
  Census of Retail Trade (published every 5 years)
  Census of Service Industries (published every 5 years)
  Census of Transportation (published every 5 years)
  Census of Wholesale Trade (published every 5 years)
  County Business Patterns (published annually)

Two of the most useful compendia of consumer market data that extrapolate U.S. census figures are the *Sourcebook of Demographics and Buying Power* and the *Survey of Buying Power*.

- *Sourcebook of Demographics and Buying Power for Every Zip Code in the USA*
  Arlington, Va.: CACI, 1984 to present

This source is unique because of the work that CACI has done in developing demographic data for zip code areas. In addition to supplying a population and socioeconomic profile for each zip code, CACI has also calculated buying power,

TABLE 3–1   Example of Zip Code Area Analysis

NORTH CAROLINA   SOCIOECONOMIC PROFILE
C   CACI's 1988 Sourcebook of Demographics and Buying Power for Every Zip Code in the USA

ZIP CODE #	POST OFFICE NAME	MEDIAN HOUSEHOLD INCOME 1980	1988	1993	% ANNUAL GROWTH RATE 80-88	NAT'L CENTILE 1988	CENTILE WITHIN STATE 1988	AVG. HSHLD. INCOME 1988	AVG. HSHLD. SIZE 1988	AVG. FAMILY INCOME 1988	AVG. FAMILY SIZE 1988	# FAMILIES 1988	PER CAPITA INCOME 1988	% POP. IN POVERTY 1980	% POP. IN GROUP QTRS. 1980	MEDIAN YEARS OF EDUC. 1980	% COLLEGE GRADS 1980	% WHITE COLLAR 1980	% WOMEN IN LABOR FORCE 1980	AVG. TRAVEL MINS. TO WORK 1980	% UNEMPLOYED 1980	EMPLOYMENT/POP. RATIO (%) 1980
28396	WAGRAM	12458	18611	20771	5.1	24	28	22107	3.0	24098	3.5	654	7096	24.0	2.7	11.5	8.8	33.9	55.1	23.4	12.0	53.1
28397	WAKULLA	11875	19583	23333	6.5	30	35	21444	3.6	22440	3.9	41	5949	24.8	0.0	10.6	6.2	14.9	52.2	32.3	9.8	51.1
28398	WARSAW	10926	18119	18132	6.5	21	23	22447	2.8	25213	3.4	1721	7875	23.0	0.5	12.1	12.6	35.5	48.8	22.1	4.7	59.9
28399	WHITE OAK	10101	15177	16809	5.2	9	5	16956	2.9	19017	3.4	374	5746	21.6	0.0	10.7	6.4	19.1	43.2	30.1	4.8	48.6
28401	WILMINGTON	8847	13704	15290	5.6	4	1	18339	2.4	21282	3.0	6380	7540	28.9	2.2	11.5	8.7	39.2	47.8	21.6	9.1	49.6
28402	WILMINGTON	0	0	0	0.0	0	0	0	32.0	0	32.0	1	165	0.0	98.4	14.4	28.0	0.0	0.0	11.4	0.0	86.0
28403	WILMINGTON	17163	26543	29159	5.6	72	87	30236	2.5	34472	3.0	14715	11724	9.7	1.9	12.7	22.1	56.9	51.1	21.5	6.0	59.8
28404	WILMINGTON	15000	23226	27500	5.6	55	65	25402	2.9	27394	3.3	117	8728	17.8	0.0	11.3	3.2	30.8	46.4	27.7	8.6	56.0
28405	WILMINGTON	18148	27725	30227	5.4	76	90	29862	2.9	31991	3.2	8291	10243	12.1	1.9	12.4	12.5	50.9	51.7	23.7	7.7	60.1
28420	ASH	11524	19035	22145	6.5	27	31	22633	2.8	25116	3.2	1059	8090	24.5	0.0	11.3	5.8	32.9	40.7	30.5	8.9	47.3
28421	ATKINSON	10921	16458	18453	5.3	13	11	19926	2.7	21595	3.3	374	7381	18.8	0.0	12.0	6.1	23.6	47.0	37.3	4.9	52.6
28422	BOLIVIA	14089	23029	26541	6.3	54	64	25307	2.8	27926	3.2	1174	9150	18.5	0.4	12.0	7.9	36.6	40.9	28.5	8.1	49.4
28423	BOLTON	12311	20093	22218	6.3	34	38	24306	3.2	26591	3.6	626	7640	28.5	0.7	11.0	4.0	20.9	40.1	33.7	7.2	53.2
28424	BRUNSWICK	12438	20204	21809	6.3	34	39	24593	2.6	27866	3.1	157	9151	18.6	3.1	12.1	11.3	50.6	52.5	20.7	8.0	55.8
28425	BURGAW	12981	18840	20808	4.8	25	30	22188	2.7	25430	3.2	1794	7825	20.7	3.9	11.6	8.4	40.5	47.8	27.3	7.4	52.3
28428	CAROLINA BEACH	13161	19935	21396	5.3	32	37	23409	2.4	26243	2.8	857	9371	10.7	3.1	12.3	9.0	45.6	46.3	23.3	6.4	54.7
28429	CASTLE HAYNE	17613	26888	29206	5.4	73	88	28138	2.8	30684	3.2	1686	9913	11.7	1.1	12.1	5.1	42.7	57.7	23.5	8.0	60.0
28430	CERRO GORDO	9462	14915	16486	5.9	8	5	19750	2.8	21755	3.3	507	6963	30.1	0.0	10.9	5.0	33.6	52.0	27.0	4.4	53.6
28431	CHADBOURN	9602	15226	16843	5.9	9	6	19282	2.7	22165	3.2	2045	7049	30.4	0.0	10.7	6.7	33.1	45.0	24.6	7.5	52.4
28432	CLARENDON	9703	15430	16929	6.0	10	7	19569	2.8	21752	3.2	460	7078	27.5	0.0	9.9	3.4	28.7	41.7	27.7	4.3	55.2

#	POST OFFICE NAME	County FIPS CODE (SEE APPDX.)	1988 POP.	1988 AGE DISTRIBUTION (%)										MEDIAN AGE			RACE (%)					
																	WHITE			BLACK		
				0–4	5–11	12–17	18–24	25–34	35–44	45–54	55–64	65–74	75+	1980	1988	1993	1980	1988	1993	1980	1988	1993
28396	WAGRAM	165	2536	9.2	12.3	11.4	11.7	16.2	14.8	7.7	7.1	5.5	4.2	26.3	28.5	29.3	44.9	42.1	39.4	45.1	47.6	50.0
28397	WAKULLA	155	167	11.4	14.4	12.0	13.8	16.2	12.6	8.4	6.0	4.2	1.8	22.9	24.3	25.2	5.7	5.4	4.9	3.5	3.6	3.8
28398	WARSAW	061	6379	9.6	11.6	9.9	11.5	15.4	12.8	8.7	8.5	6.9	5.0	28.7	29.5	30.3	51.3	48.4	45.5	48.3	51.3	54.2
28399	WHITE OAK	017	1395	9.2	11.2	10.8	12.9	14.8	13.6	9.0	6.6	6.9	5.2	28.1	29.0	29.5	53.2	50.3	47.4	46.7	49.6	52.5
28401	WILMINGTON	129	23857	7.7	9.9	8.5	11.4	16.5	13.1	7.8	8.8	9.2	7.0	30.5	33.1	33.9	48.8	49.4	49.2	50.7	50.1	50.1
28402	WILMINGTON	129	185	0.0	0.0	0.0	56.8	28.6	10.8	1.6	0.5	0.0	0.0	22.9	24.7	25.3	89.0	89.2	89.8	7.1	7.6	7.5
28403	WILMINGTON	129	51649	6.4	8.8	8.6	11.9	16.9	15.1	11.0	9.7	7.2	4.4	30.6	33.7	35.2	89.7	89.2	88.4	9.5	10.0	10.7
28404	WILMINGTON	019	416	8.7	12.0	10.3	12.5	16.8	14.2	10.1	7.2	4.3	3.1	26.4	28.6	29.6	70.1	67.8	65.1	28.9	31.3	33.7
28405	WILMINGTON	129	29249	7.1	10.4	10.6	11.9	16.0	17.0	10.7	7.7	5.2	3.3	28.6	31.1	32.5	78.3	77.4	76.2	21.0	21.8	23.0
28420	ASH	019	3626	8.2	10.9	9.7	11.3	15.4	12.6	9.5	9.5	8.0	4.9	30.1	31.3	32.1	69.7	67.5	65.1	29.4	31.6	34.1
28421	ATKINSON	141	1369	9.5	11.8	10.6	10.4	13.7	11.9	9.0	8.4	8.4	6.4	31.0	30.1	30.3	51.4	48.4	45.4	48.5	51.6	54.5
28422	BOLIVIA	019	4063	8.0	11.1	10.2	11.0	14.9	13.3	9.7	9.0	8.0	4.7	30.2	31.5	32.1	74.1	72.3	70.2	25.3	27.1	29.1
28423	BOLTON	047	2390	9.5	11.8	11.0	12.6	14.8	12.6	9.5	7.4	6.7	4.4	27.4	28.5	28.9	32.2	30.0	27.9	46.3	48.1	49.9
28424	BRUNSWICK	047	563	7.6	9.9	9.2	10.8	15.5	14.2	10.5	8.9	7.3	5.9	30.9	33.1	34.1	68.5	66.3	63.7	30.9	33.2	35.8
28425	BURGAW	141	6579	7.5	9.9	9.8	10.7	15.1	13.5	9.8	9.3	8.0	6.4	31.4	33.0	33.7	59.3	56.4	53.6	40.5	43.3	46.2
28428	CAROLINA BEACH	129	2858	5.8	8.0	7.8	10.5	15.6	14.5	10.9	9.8	10.0	7.0	33.9	36.9	37.9	97.6	97.4	97.2	1.2	1.3	1.5
28429	CASTLE HAYNE	129	5812	7.3	10.2	10.2	11.2	16.3	16.3	11.0	8.8	5.7	3.1	29.1	31.7	33.3	78.9	76.5	74.1	20.3	22.7	25.1
28430	CERRO GORDO	047	1792	9.1	11.3	9.6	11.2	14.6	13.3	10.4	9.0	7.0	4.5	30.4	30.7	31.4	78.6	76.7	74.7	21.3	23.1	25.1
28431	CHADBOURN	047	7179	9.6	11.7	9.2	10.9	15.8	12.2	9.5	8.6	7.4	5.1	29.3	30.1	31.1	69.6	67.1	64.5	29.4	31.9	34.4
28432	CLARENDON	047	1568	8.6	10.7	9.3	11.7	14.6	13.4	12.1	8.3	7.0	4.3	30.4	31.3	32.3	88.7	87.4	66.1	11.0	12.2	13.5

TABLE 3–2   Example of Reports in the *Survey of Buying Power*

New York

Population*

METRO AREA County City	Total Population (thousands)	% of U.S.	Median Age of Pop.	% of Population by Age Group				Households (thousands)
				18–24 Years	25–34 Years	35–49 Years	50 & Over	
ALBANY-SCHENECTADY- TROY	879.9	.3510	34.1	11.5	16.6	21.2	27.2	338.0
Albany	293.1	.1169	34.0	13.3	16.7	20.8	27.6	116.0
— Albany	101.3	.0404	31.4	20.1	18.4	17.3	26.1	42.2
Greene	45.1	.0180	35.7	9.6	16.1	20.8	30.1	16.7
Montgomery	51.9	.0207	36.8	8.3	14.3	19.4	33.1	20.2
Rennselaer	154.6	.0617	32.9	12.7	16.6	20.5	26.1	57.7
— Troy	54.3	.0216	29.8	19.9	17.9	15.7	25.0	20.8
Saratoga	185.9	.0742	32.8	10.3	17.6	23.4	22.8	68.2
Schenectady	149.3	.0595	35.7	9.8	16.1	20.7	30.4	59.2
— Schenectady	65.6	.0262	32.9	12.7	18.9	17.3	28.7	27.8
SUBURBAN TOTAL	658.7	.2628	35.1	9.3	16.0	22.7	27.5	247.2
BINGHAMTON	264.4	.1054	34.0	11.0	16.5	20.1	28.2	100.6
Broome	211.8	.0844	34.2	11.7	16.5	19.7	29.0	81.7
— Binghamton	52.9	.0211	34.5	13.7	16.9	17.4	31.7	22.6
Tioga	52.2	.0210	33.0	8.2	16.7	21.5	25.1	18.9
SUBURBAN TOTAL	211.5	.0843	33.8	10.3	16.6	20.7	27.3	78.0
BUFFALO	966.3	.3852	34.8	10.5	16.3	20.1	29.7	376.1
Erie	966.3	.3852	34.8	10.5	16.3	20.1	29.7	376.1
— Buffalo	327.4	.1305	32.2	12.5	18.2	17.6	27.2	136.1
SUBURBAN TOTAL	638.9	.2547	36.5	9.5	15.3	21.4	30.8	240.0

*All data are based on *Sales & Marketing Management* estimates, December 31, 1990.

which it calls the *purchasing potential index*. This score for each zip code area measures the likelihood that households will exhibit specific purchasing patterns, when compared with the U.S. average. The purchasing potential index in the *Sourcebook* is based on a national score of 100. An index score of 105 for apparel means that consumers in that zip code area have a 5 percent greater capacity to purchase apparel than the U.S. average, while a score of 85 would indicate 15 percent less potential to purchase apparel.[3] Table 3–1 provides an example of the variety of zip code area analysis available for selected areas in North Carolina.

The statistical extrapolation considered by many marketing practitioners to be the most important single sourcebook for the marketing researcher is

— *Survey of Buying Power*
   New York: *Sales and Marketing Management*, annual in two parts

---

[3]This definition was taken from the *Sourcebook of Demographics and Buying Power for Every Zip Code in the USA* (Arlington, Va.: CACI, 1986).

TABLE 3–2   *(concluded)*

Effective Buying Income

					Retail Sales by Store Group				
Total EBI ($000)	Median Hsld. EBI	Buying Power Index	Total Retail Sales ($000)	Food ($000)	Eating, Drinking Places ($000)	General Mdse. ($000)	Furniture/ Furnish. Appliance ($000)	Automotive ($000)	Drug ($000)
13,612,194	30,420	.3816	7,045,006	1,539,547	663,119	842,591	372,380	1,577,469	251,632
4,875,168	31,029	.1451	3,136,897	565,279	317,651	481,435	209,586	750,590	100,707
1,484,343	23,181	.0482	1,141,631	167,060	129,477	197,257	56,343	302,906	37,968
547,441	24,074	.0165	303,378	88,449	22,738	23,063	9,567	61,049	12,211
669,613	25,062	.0188	311,405	93,803	21,413	31,959	7,145	46,619	18,130
2,201,583	29,079	.0579	849,624	249,174	81,321	60,559	28,147	170,664	41,771
676,229	22,053	.0198	349,284	103,314	47,677	24,887	19,199	43,878	25,390
2,921,803	34,136	.0782	1,299,958	274,885	135,461	113,225	52,127	338,321	32,873
2,396,586	30,466	.0651	1,143,744	267,957	84,535	132,350	65,808	210,226	47,940
922,293	23,985	.0265	486,243	133,804	44,334	32,316	28,738	121,231	24,526
10,529,329	33,286	.2871	1,968,059	402,534	184,343	263,497	96,456	418,051	89,198
4,041,791	30,046	.1116	1,732,885	342,163	170,359	254,937	93,362	333,087	80,620
3,222,537	29,378	.0918	541,436	116,166	55,006	66,833	41,829	102,731	28,043
748,263	22,201	.0239	235,174	60,371	13,984	8,560	3,094	84,964	8,578
819,254	33,371	.0198	1,426,623	286,368	129,337	196,664	54,627	315,320	61,155
3,293,528	32,531	.0877	6,781,443	1,611,814	710,071	758,104	369,250	1,406,349	336,787
13,697,931	28,022	.3854	6,781,443	1,611,814	710,071	758,104	369,250	1,406,349	336,787
13,697,931	19,227	.3854	1,554,462	499,801	222,825	97,446	69,604	203,234	107,205
3,867,145	19,227	.1072	1,554,462	499,801	222,825	97,446	69,604	203,234	107,205
9,830,786	32,845	.2782	5,226,981	1,112,013	487,246	660,658	299,646	1,203,115	229,582

The *Survey of Buying Power* is published annually in two parts, in July and in October. It is most valuable for its current population and income analysis of metropolitan statistical areas, counties, and states, as well as population and income projections for these same geographic areas. Specifically, it includes, for each geographical area, population and other characteristics, total retail sales, effective buying income, and the **buying power index (BPI)**. Table 3–2 illustrates these reports for several New York cities.[4]

The BPI is a weighted index that converts three basic elements—population, effective buying income (EBI equals gross income available after taxes to purchase goods and services), and retail sales—into a measurement of a market's ability to buy, and is expressed as a percentage of the U.S. potential. It is calculated by

buying power index (BPI)
A weighted index that converts three basic elements—population, effective buying income, and retail sales—into a measurement of a market's ability to buy, expressed as a percentage of U.S. potential.

[4]The definitions were taken from *Sales and Marketing Management's Survey of Buying Power*, July 27, 1987, pp. C–3, 4, A–5, A–6.

giving weights of 0.5 to the particular market's percent of U.S. EBI, 0.3 to its percent of U.S. retail sales, and 0.2 to its percent of U.S. population.

$$\text{BPI} = \underset{(\text{EBI \%})}{0.5} + \underset{(\text{Retail sales \%})}{0.3} + \underset{(\text{Population \%})}{0.2}$$

The BPI is probably one of the *Survey of Buying Power's* most widely used single market measures. Because it is broadly based, it is most useful in estimating the potential for mass products sold at popular prices. The less a product's mass-market appeal, the greater the need for a BPI that is refined by more defining or discriminating factors, such as social class, income, age, or gender. Appendix 3A provides an example of a customized BPI.

International Sources

Continuing globalization and searches for opportunities in new markets will require marketing researchers and managers to develop information on relevant overseas economies. There are a fairly large number of sources on international activity. Appendix 3B provides details on a relatively large number of available sources.

Other Sources

Three other basic sources of standardized market research information provide standardized data covering either product usage, media habits, and social trends, or consumer values and lifestyles.

- *The Study of Media and Markets*
  New York: Simmons Market Research Bureau, Inc.
  Simmons Market Research Bureau (SMRB) is one of the most widely used sources of product usage and media audience data. SMRB produces a wealth of market information; data are available for 750 product/service categories, 3,500 brands, and numerous media audiences (print and broadcast). SMRB data can provide useful information in developing category and brand target segments and identifying the media that reach them. Many reference libraries have made SMRB volumes available, and SMRB data can be accessed through vendors that provide time-sharing services.
- *Yankelovich Monitor*
  New York: Yankelovich, Skelly, and White, 1970 to present, annual
  The *Yankelovich Monitor* is a research service that tracks over 40 social trends and provides information about their shifts in size and direction and the resulting market implications. Social trend information as reported by the *Yankelovich Monitor* has proven useful in identifying likely shifts in demand for various product categories. One example is the U.S. shift to "white" liquors (e.g., vodka and gin) from "brown" (e.g., Scotch or blended whiskies).
- SRI Values and Lifestyles (VALS)
  Menlo Park, Calif.: SRI International
  VALS is a research service that tracks marketing-relevant shifts in the beliefs, values, and lifestyles of a sample of the U.S. population. The VALS system

divides the population into segments consisting of three major groups of consumers, which in turn are divided into nine specific segments. Tracking the shifts in the values and behavior of these segments can help researchers understand a target segment.

THE NEW AGE OF INFORMATION

With the rapid development of online information databases, the researcher can ✓ frequently monitor developments without ever leaving the office. Gathering secondary data, which once required trips to a large research library and countless telephone calls to potential information sources, may now be accomplished with a fraction of that effort. Indeed, thousands of new documents are becoming available every day; the data that could not be located one month ago may suddenly appear in the public domain.

Millions of pieces of potentially useful information are floating about the information environment. To get some notion of the magnitude and development of on-line databases, consider the following: In 1968 there were fewer than 250,000 items in bibliographic databases (one category of online databases). By 1980 this number was estimated to have grown to 75 million items in over 600 databases. Another source indicates that through 1987 the on-line database industry had grown to 3,699 databases compiled by 1,685 different producers. Assuming a constant rate of growth, we could estimate that we now have on-line access to approximately 450 million discrete pieces of information available for problem solving.

A number of factors have contributed to this explosive growth in online information systems:

1. Publishers and other data compilers are now using computers as their primary production technology—witness the almost-extinct practice of manual typesetting in the newspaper industry. Thus, editing and publishing tomorrow's edition of the *New York Times* automatically adds hundreds of new stories to the on-line *New York Times* database.

2. Companies referred to as *on-line vendors* serve as information supermarkets and provide easy access to hundreds of databases. These vendors greatly simplify the search process because they generally provide uniform search commands and protocols for each of the databases mounted on their computer. Thus, you could gain access to the online *New York Times* or the on-line version of *Business Week* and numerous other publications through Mead Data Central's Nexis services.

3. Telecommunications networks now provide low-cost access to remote databases with send or receive speeds of typically up to 2,400 characters per second.

4. Perhaps the most important element in on-line database expansion has been the market penetration of personal computers. Until a significant number of potential users were able to interact with remote databases, the market for on-line services was quite limited, mainly to research institutes and corporate libraries. The personal computer outfitted for communications and in

the possession of thousands of information seekers has radically expanded the potential market. A current marketing strategy for database producers and on-line vendors is to reach the end-user market, the information consumer, rather than relying solely on intermediaries such as librarians and information specialists.

Fundamentals of accessing on-line databases are illustrated in Appendix 3C.

ON-LINE DATABASE SERVICES

We should be aware of a number of aspects concerning on-line database services. These include database varieties, directories, and vendors.

Database Varieties

The information represented in the hundreds of databases varies from discipline to discipline. Beyond subject matter, databases may differ in scope, geographic and chronological coverage, and the frequency with which they are updated. Databases also differ according to the type of information that they contain. These varieties may be categorized into several types.

- Bibliographic databases contain citations to journal articles, government documents, technical reports, market-research studies, newspaper articles, dissertations, patents, and so on. Frequently, they provide summaries or abstracts of the cited material.
- Numeric databases contain original survey information such as time-series data. An example would be the sales data of sporting goods during the past 20 years.
- Directory databases are made up of information about individuals, organizations, and services. Using a directory database you could, for example, generate a list of business establishments in a given geographic area that have incorporated within the last two years.
- Full-text databases are perhaps the variety of on-line databases that will experience the most rapid growth during the next decade. As the name implies, such databases contain the complete text of the source documents that make up the database. An example of a full-text database is the New York Times Information Bank, which provides the complete text of each issue of the *New York Times*.

Directories of Databases

Among the numerous on-line database source listings are three directories that are particularly useful because they are updated periodically:

1. *Directory of On-Line Databases* (Santa Monica, Calif.: Cuadra Associates, Inc., 1979 to present).

2. *North American Online Director*, 2nd ed. (New York: R. R. Bowker, 1987).
3. *Information Industry Directory*, 13th ed. (Detroit: Gale Research, 1993).

Information specialists who work with on-line services in large libraries or corporate information centers are good sources of direction in the use of directories.

Vendors

On-line vendors or gateways are intermediaries that generally mount numerous databases produced by many different organizations. They can supply descriptive and cost information on many of these databases. The advantages of accessing a database through an on-line vendor rather than directly through the producer are

1. One contract with a vendor can usually provide access to many different databases.
2. A vendor's on-line database index may help the researcher pinpoint the database(s) most appropriate for a specific search.
3. Search protocol is generally standardized across all of the databases on the vendor's system, which simplifies the research process.
4. One contract simplifies billing for the use of various databases with one periodic invoice.

There are hundreds of on-line vendors. The larger ones are described in Exhibit 3–2 with respect to the market served and growth rates in the 1980s. Appendix 3C describes an on-line search.

Before selecting a vendor as a database supplier, you should examine the descriptions of the databases distributed, understand the charges or fee structures, verify that the vendor's system will support communications with your terminal or personal computer, inquire about the availability of database documentation (a detailed description of database content and record structure), and determine the level of user support that the vendor is willing to provide (e.g., on-site system training).

The cost of an on-line search varies according to the database selected, the amount of online time used, and the volume of information retrieved. For example, a 10-minute search of ABI/Inform, a bibliographic database, retrieving 20 abstracted journal citations, would cost approximately $30.

CD-ROM DATA FILES

Up to now, we have discussed on-line information retrieval systems that are accessed using a telecommunications link between the user and a mainframe computer. Yet, local microcomputer-driven databases are proliferating with developments in optical disc technology. A 5-inch disc read by a laser beam, known as CD-ROM (compact-disc-read-only memory), is having a profound impact on the information industry. A number of on-line, mainframe databases are now being converted to this microcomputer-based technology, which preserves many of the

EXHIBIT 3–2   Growth of On-line Services

Company	Service	Market	1988–89	1985–89
Prodigy Information Service	Prodigy (households)	General Interest	700.0%	—
Accu-Weather	Accu-Data	News	47.1%	—
Business Wire	Business Wire	News	40.4%	150.0%
Comtex Scientific	Newsgrid/OTC NewsAlert	News	38.9%	212.5%
TWA/Northwest Airlines	PARS	Airline	37.2%	133.7%
TRW	Credit Data Service	Credit	36.7%	167.8%
Information America	Information America	Sci/Tech/Prof	35.5%	—
Data Transmission Network	Agricultural Service	Business/Financial	33.9%	874.8%
General Electric	GEnie	General Interest	32.7%	8788.9%
OCLC	OCLC	Sci/Tech/Prof	30.5%	61.9%
American Airlines	SABRE	Airline	28.2%	100.4%
Western Union	Easylink	General Interest	25.0%	96.5%
Maxwell Communications	Maxwell Online	Sci/Tech/Prof	23.9%	—
Dow Jones	Capital Markets Report	Business/Financial	22.2%	307.4%
Telerate	Telerate	Business/Financial	20.5%	148.7%
Reuters/Real-time	Monitor	Business/Financial	19.6%	227.4%
Quantum Computer Services	Quantum Link/PC Link, etc.	General Interest	19.0%	—
Knight-Ridder	Dialog Info Services	Sci/Tech/Prof	18.6%	64.3%
PRC Realty	Mult. Listing Service	Sci/Tech/Prof	17.9%	79.2%
Knight-Ridder	K-R Financial Info	Business/Financial	16.8%	167.4%
Knight-Ridder	VU/TEXT	Sci/Tech/Prof	16.7%	197.9%
Datatek	Datatimes	Sci/Tech/Prof	14.7%	290.9%
British Telecom	Dialcom	General Interest	14.3%	113.3%
CompuServe	CompuServe Info Service	General Interest	12.7%	112.7%
Dow Jones	Prof. Investor's Report	Business/Financial	12.6%	—
Info Globe	Info Globe	Sci/Tech/Prof	9.9%	94.2%
Mead Data Central	LEXIS, NEXIS, MEDIS	Sci/Tech/Prof	9.7%	28.0%
NewsNet	NewsNet	News	8.8%	68.2%
Equifax	Credit Bureau Inc.	Credit	7.0%	44.6%
ADP	Financial Info Service/FS Partner	Business/Financial	6.9%	12.7%
General Videotex	Delphi	General Interest	6.7%	236.8%
Dow Jones	Dow Jones News/Retrieval	Business/Financial	6.5%	40.4%
FastFinder	FastFinder	Sci/Tech/Prof	5.3%	—
Delta	Datas Link	Airline	4.8%	—
Dun & Bradstreet	DunSprint	Credit	4.0%	119.8%
Texas Air	System 1 Direct Access	Airline	3.3%	—
United Airlines	Apollo	Airline	1.9%	66.7%
BusinessWire	Sports Wire	News	1.2%	—
BusinessWire	Entertainment Wire	News	0.0%	—
BusinessWire	Analyst Wire	News	0.0%	—

useful search features of the on-line versions, such as the use of differentiating or grouping commands (see Appendix 3C at the end of the chapter for further explanation). As research libraries acquire these products, they are able to eliminate the fees previously associated with on-line database research. Once the CD-ROM is purchased, it can be used on an unlimited number of databases without incurring additional access fees.

EXHIBIT 3–3
———
Number of North
American CD-ROM
Titles by Market

| | | | | | Growth | |
Market	1990	1989	1988	1987	1989–90	1987–90
Industry-specific	141	54	35	19	161.1%	642.1%
Health care	101	40	26	16	152.5%	531.3%
Reference*	98	40	28	11	145.0%	790.9%
Professional	95	43	33	26	120.9%	265.4%
Science/technical	66	33	27	14	100.0%	371.4%
Business/financial	47	15	11	3	213.3%	1466.7%
Marketing	31	16	10	4	93.8%	675.0%
Government	21	11	9	4	90.9%	425.0%
Total	600	252	179	97	138.1%	518.6%

*Reference is a new classification made up primarily of titles classified last year as general interest and library-oriented professional titles. Some general interest titles were reclassified as noninformation and don't appear in these statistics.

Source: Julie B. Schwerin, *Optical Publishing Industry Assessment 1990 Edition,* produced by InfoTech, based in Pittsfield, Vermont, and published by the Optical Publishing Association in Dublin, Ohio.

EXHIBIT 3–4
———
Average Price of a
CD-ROM by Market

| | | | | | Change | |
Market	1990	1989	1988	1987	1989–90	1987–90
Business/financial	$5,172	$4,599	$3,605	$2,382	12.5%	117.2%
Government	3,724	5,041	3,441	5,432	−26.1%	−31.4%
Marketing	2,576	2,110	2,177	3,025	22.1%	−14.8%
Science/technical	1,941	1,425	1,735	1,473	36.2%	31.8%
Professional	1,849	1,645	1,518	1,188	12.4%	55.7%
Health care	1,142	1,159	1,552	2,487	−1.5%	−54.1%
Industry-specific	1,075	2,118	2,128	3,123	−49.3%	−65.6%
Reference	815	783	1,062	1,081	4.1%	−24.6%
Average price	1,708	1,736	1,829	2,067	−1.6%	−17.4%

A number of CD-ROM products currently available are useful in marketing research. Exhibit 3–3 displays the number of CD-ROM titles by various markets. Note that marketing-oriented CD-ROM titles have grown from 4 in 1987 to 31 in 1990, a 675 percent increase. Exhibit 3–4 provides the average price for a CD-ROM for the same time period as Exhibit 3–3.

To illustrate the potential of CD-ROM databases, consider the plight of a group of financial advisors who are considering starting their own financial services business. It occurs to them that there may be different segments of customers who need financial advice. As a preliminary step in their investigation, they decide to check the business periodical literature for articles that may have been written on

EXHIBIT 3–5

—

Sample Result of a
Search Procedure

```
ProQuest    ABI/Inform                    Jan 1988–Feb 1992
              Search Terms                   Item Count

(01):  segmentation → SEGMENTATION            794
(02):  financial → FINANCIAL                 34888
(03):  (01) pre/1 (02)                           3
Search results in 3 item(s).


92-02724
Title:    Positioning Professional Services:
          Segmenting the Financial Services Market
Authors:  McAlexander, James H.; Schouten, John W.; Scammon, Debra L.
Journal:  Journal of Professional Services Marketing Vol: 7 Iss: 2
          Date: 1991 pp: 149+166 Jrnl Code: JPF ISSN: 0748-4623
Terms:    Market segmentation; Financial services; Market
          positioning; Target markets; Surveys; Characteristics; US
Codes:    8100 (Financial services industry); 7100 (Market research);
          9190 (United States)
```

Abstract: Market segmentation and positioning allow marketers to differentiate themselves from competitors in a way that is valued by customers and that results in competitive advantage. Through an analysis of the financial services market, a segmentation and positioning strategy is developed based on the proposition that consumers employ many kinds of professional service providers to compensate for an inability or unwillingness to perform certain tasks. The selection and use of financial advisers varies considerably from segment to segment. Knowledgeable, intrinsically motivated consumers appear to have little interest in comprehensive services from a financial planner. The selection and use of financial advisers varies considerably from segment to segment. Knowledgeable consumers who are not intrinsically motivated are a potential target for comprehensive financial services. Less knowledgeable but intrinsically motivated consumers also represent a viable target, but they will respond to different appeals. Such consumers are good candidates for comprehensive financial planning services as well. References. Charts.

```
92-02607
Title:    Applying Latent Trait Analysis in the Evaluation of
          Prospects for Cross-Selling of Financial Services
Authors:  Kamakura, Wagner A.; Ramaswami, Sridhar N.; Srivastava,
          Rajendra K.
Journal:  International Journal of Research in Marketing Vol: 8 Iss: 4
          Date: Nov 1991 pp: 329-349 Jrnl Code: IJR ISSN: 0167-8116
Terms:    Market research; Studies; Financial services; Cross
          selling; Consumer behavior; Mathematical models
Codes:    7100 (Market research); 8100 (Financial services industry);
          9130
Use + and − for Next and Previous Items.
                    F4=Output F1=Help F2=Commands
```

segmenting the financial services market. They use the bibliographic database, ABI/Inform Ondisc Availability from University Microfilms International (UMI). This CD-ROM database accesses periodicals from a variety of databases from January 1988 to February 1992. Exhibit 3–5 presents the search procedures and sample results of this exercise.

SUMMARY

Applying appropriate secondary market research can be critically important to overall research success. New information technologies are revolutionizing the researcher's acquisition of secondary-source market information. Because many college, university, and corporate libraries provide a computer search service and maintain contracts with some of the vendors mentioned in this study, you might inquire about a firsthand demonstration of an interactive, on-line database search. Although the cost of these services may make a database search impractical for an undergraduate research assignment, access to new CD-ROM databases that are available in many libraries may make computerized secondary-source research possible at no expense to the end user.

Although there has been an explosive growth in on-line databases, considerable information may still have to be gathered through a traditional manual search. Traditional "print" tools remain indispensible to the gathering of secondary-source materials.

KEY CONCEPTS

primary data

secondary data

evaluating secondary data

effective buying income

buying power index

customized buying power index

directories

indexes to business literature

indexes to statistical information

statistical compilations

on-line databases

CD-ROM databases

REVIEW QUESTIONS

1. Discuss the role that secondary information plays in the research process?

2. Describe a situation in which it could be useful to employ both primary and secondary research. When is primary data preferred?

3. Visit your library and examine the SIC Manual. Select an SIC number that represents an industry of interest to you, and identify three standard business reference works that use SIC numbers to organize their information.

4. As a marketing manager for a consumer product manufacturer, how might the *Survey of Buying Power* be used to help develop marketing strategy?

5. What are the advantages of using a bibliographic database to locate journal articles compared with a traditional periodical index, such as the *Business Periodical Index*?

HOW TO CONSTRUCT A CUSTOM BPI

The Buying Power Index, or BPI, was patented by *Sales & Marketing Management* and has been a part of the *Survey of Buying Power* for more than 30 years, providing marketers with a standardized measurement of the relative buying power of states, metros, counties, and cities. The BPI listed in the *Survey*'s data sections is a general indicator constructed from data on total population, total effective buying income (EBI), and total retail sales—the three basic categories of statistics covered by the *Survey*.

For those who need to define their markets more specifically, however, it is possible to construct a customized version of the BPI, using any of the subclassifications of statistics in the *Survey*'s three basic data fields. By selecting a demographic component (population), an economic component (income), and a distribution component (retail sales), you can use the formula outlined below to convert data from individual markets into a custom BPI for your product or service.

For our purposes, we will label these three BPI components as follows: Demographic = A; Economic = B; and Distribution = C. Looking at each of these areas individually, here's how you might go about selecting them:

A. *Demographic.* First of all, you'll need to isolate the population or household-related factor that best describes your "ideal" consumer. For example, if you're selling video games, the 18-and-under age segment is a better indicator of market potential than total population. On the other hand, if your product is media-oriented (magazines, mail-order catalogs, etc.), you may want to use household counts as your demographic component.

B. *Economic.* The next step involves selecting the income group(s) best suited to your product. Here, the *Survey* offers you five basic ranges of household incomes, and you can easily combine two or more groups to achieve a broader spectrum of potential. For example, if you're selling a premium-priced product, you might select households with incomes of $35,000 and above.

C. *Distribution.* Isolating a particular store group that parallels your preferred channel of distribution is the final step in the preliminary selection process. If you're selling beer, for example, you may want to combine Eating & Drinking Place sales and Food Store sales, since these are the two largest markets for your product. On the other hand, if you're selling shampoo, Drugstores and General Merchandise stores (which includes department stores and discount stores) would be a better distribution-related indicator.

Source: *Sales & Marketing Management*, August 19, 1991, p. A–15.

Once these three factors have been selected, you can then compute your custom BPI by following this simple four-step process:

Step 1. For each market (region, state, metro, county, etc.), you'll first need to compare local activity with that for the United States as a whole, producing a ratio for each of the three BPI factors (A-B-C). In this example, the demographic component A would be calculated as follows:

$$\frac{\text{Market's Population under 18}}{\text{U.S. Population under 18}} = A\%$$

Next, using households with EBIs of $35,000 and above as the economic factor B, we compare the market with the appropriate U.S. total:

$$\frac{\text{Market's Households with EBIs \$35,000 +}}{\text{U.S. Households with EBIs \$35,000+}} = B\%$$

And finally, we calculate the distribution component C by constructing a ratio of local Food Store sales to U.S. Food Store sales:

$$\frac{\text{Market's Food Store Sales}}{\text{U.S. Food Store Sales}} = C\%$$

Step 2. Armed with these percentages (A-B-C), we are now ready to assign weights to the demographic, economic, and distribution-related components, according to their perceived importance in the selling process. In all cases, the assigned weights should be expressed in decimals (50% = 0.5, 30% = 0.3, etc.).

Since income is often cited as the most important indicator of potential purchasing power, your weighting of these factors might look something like this:

Factor A (demographic)—0.2 (20%)

Factor B (economic)—0.5 (50%)

Factor C (distribution)—0.3 (30%)

Step 3. Multiplying each component ratio (A-B-C) by its appropriate weight and adding the resulting totals will then give you the BPI for a particular market:

$$(0.2 \times A\%) + (0.5 \times B\%) + (0.3 \times C\%) = BPI$$

The fractional figure you arrive at can then be used as a relative indicator to compare the potential buying power of this market with that for the United States as a whole (U.S. = 100.00).*

Step 4. Repeat this same procedure for each targeted market, compiling a list of markets ranked according to their BPIs. If your particular product warrants the construction of a BPI with only two factors (or possibly four or five), remember that the same principles apply in terms of weighting the various components. In other words, the percentages should still total 100 percent, regardless of the number of BPI components.

---

*Note: If you're selling your product in a limited number of markets, you may want to substitute the combined total of these markets for the U.S. totals in your calculations. In such a case, your BPI of 100.00 would represent the total of these markets only.

SOURCES OF SECONDARY DATA FOR INTERNATIONAL MARKETING RESEARCH

1. Information available from international agencies
   a. The United Nations. United Nations publications can be obtained from:
   United Nations Publications
   Room CD2-853
   New York, NY 10017
      i. United Nations Bibliographic Information System (UNBIS)
      (This database consists of the *United Nations Documents Index* for coverage of the organization's own documentation network and the current bibliographical information for books produced by specialized agencies, commercial publishers, governments, or other institutions.)
      ii. *Bibliography on Transnational Corporations*
      (A computer-produced listing of 4,200 bibliographic items, with subject index.)
      iii. *World Economic Survey*
      (A comprehensive survey of world economic conditions with emphasis on international trade, payments, and production.)
      iv. *Handbook of International Trade and Development Statistics*
      (A major source of world economic data. Includes information on population, manpower, agriculture, manufacturing, mining, construction, trade, transport, communications, balance of payments, consumption, wages, prices, health, and education.)
      v. *Economic Survey of Europe*
      (Annual survey analyzing the development of the European economy and world economic changes having an important bearing upon economic policies in Eastern and Western Europe.)
      vi. *Economic Bulletin for Asia and the Pacific*
      (Review concerning agriculture, industry, transportation, trade, and balance of payments.)
      vii. *Economic Survey of Latin America and the Caribbean*
      (Information about regional and internal economic developments in Latin America.)
   b. Organization for Economic Cooperation and Development. OECD publications can be obtained from:
   OECD Publications Office, Suite 1305
   1750 Pennsylvania Avenue, N.W.
   Washington, D.C. 20006
      i. *OECD Economic Surveys*
      (Each title in this series of economic studies is a booklet published

annually. Each booklet has information concerning recent trends of demand and output, prices and wages, foreign trade and payments, economic policy, and prospects and conclusions in an individual member country.)

    ii. OECD Economic Outlook

(Semiannual survey of economic trends and prospects in the 21 member countries given in two volumes, imports and exports. The survey gives the quantity and value of international trade for 272 commodity categories and examines the current situation and prospects regarding demand and output, employment, costs and prices, and foreign trade for the OECD as a whole.)

    iii. Monthly Statistics of Foreign Trade

(This bulletin is intended to serve as a timely source of statistical data on the foreign trade by OECD member countries. The data cover not only overall trade by countries, but also a number of seasonally adjusted series, volume and average value indices, and trade by SITC sections.)

  c. International Monetary Fund (IMF). IMF publications can be obtained from:

International Monetary Fund
Washington, D.C. 20431

    i. International Financial Statistics

(Monthly publication that provides data for 104 countries on exchange rates, balance of payments, international reserves, money supply, price, interest rates, and other financial information.)

  d. The World Bank. World Bank publications can be obtained from:

The World Bank
1818 H Street, N.W.
Washington, D.C. 20433

    i. World Bank Atlas

(Annual publication that includes information such as population, gross domestic product, and average growth rates for every country in the world.)

    ii. World Bank: Annual Report

(Report containing information on developing countries around the world.)

2. Information available from U.S. government sources

  a. U.S. Department of Commerce. The following publications can be obtained through either:

U.S. Department of Commerce
Publications Sales Branch
Room 1617
Washington, D.C. 20230

or from a state's International Trade Administration Office, which is run by the Department of Commerce.

    i. Commerce Information Management System (CIMS)
(This database includes all information previously found in such publications as *Global Market Surveys, Country Market Surveys, Trade Lists,* and *Market Share Reports.* The database permits search for information on particular countries, industries, and products and can provide a listing of potential buyers, distributors, and agents for different industries in selected countries.)

    ii. Foreign Trade Reports, FT-410
(Monthly publication that provides a statistical record of all U.S. exports by product and country of destination.)

    iii. Business America
(Monthly magazine that covers domestic and international news.)

    iv. Overseas Business Report
(Report compiled for a particular country that includes information on the best markets, industry trends, local regulations, investment alternatives, labor, and taxation.)

    v. Export Promotion Calendar
(Calendar prepared quarterly that lists all upcoming trade shows overseas by product category, country, and date.)

3. Information available from commercial publishers
   a. Reference material
    i. International Market Information System
(A computer bank containing import data on more than 1,900 products from 133 countries; prepared at Georgia State University in Atlanta.)

    ii. Inter-Trade Center File of Information Services
(A computer data bank of sources of information related to international trade from the World Trade Center in New York.)

    iii. Sources of European Economic Information
(A publication that describes nearly 2,000 statistical bulletins, yearbooks, directories, and reports for 17 European countries.)

    iv. Business International Weekly Report
(Weekly publication that reports on events and topics of interest to managers of worldwide operations. It is published by Business International Corporation of New York.)

    v. Doing Business in . . . Series
(A series of books published by Business International Corporation that explores doing business in particular countries.)

    vi. Encyclopedia of Geographic Information Sources
(Published by Gale Research of Detroit.)

    vii. European Markets: A Guide to Company and Industry Information Sources
(Guide available from Washington Researchers of Washington, D.C.)

    viii. Exporter's Encyclopedia
        (Published annually by Dun & Bradstreet International in New York. It is supplemented by twice-monthly bulletins and newsletters.)
    ix. Reference Book for World Traders
        (Covers information necessary for planning exports to and imports from all foreign countries. It is available from Croner Publications, Inc., of New York.)
    x. World Advertising Expenditures
        (Published by Starch INRA Hooper Group of Companies of New York.)
    xi. Business Publications Rates and Data USA and International
        (Listings of domestic and international publications and their rates in order to help potential exporters find marketing and advertising representation.)

b. Magazines and newspapers
    i. The *Wall Street Journal*
    ii. The *Asian Wall Street Journal*
    iii. The *New York Times*
    iv. European Marketing and Research, the Netherlands
    v. Financial Times, England
    vi. Nihom Keizai Shimbum, Japan
    vii. Frankfurter Algemeine, Germany
    viii. Business Week
    ix. Advertising Age
    x. Marketing News
    xi. Fortune
    xii. Forbes

ACCESSING ON-LINE DATABASES: THE MECHANICS

To understand how to use on-line databases, you need to be familiar with the system that is required as well as the fundamentals of online searching.

Required System

To use an on-line database, you first need a device that will support data communications. Thus, the prerequisite is access to a "dumb" terminal equipped for communication (with an acoustical coupler) or a personal computer that includes a modem and appropriate communications software.

The second requirement is a telephone through which the data stream flows from the host computer to your local terminal. The host computer may be hundreds or thousands of miles away. Significant economies can be achieved by using a telecommunications network that provides local nodes in cities throughout the world (e.g., Telenet or Tymnet). In this way a marketing researcher in New York is able to dial the local number of a telecommunications network and thereby log on to a computer in California relatively inexpensively.

Once the researcher has established the capability to transmit and receive information, the next task is to identify the host computer(s) containing the database(s) and the information that is needed for the market research problem at hand.

Fundamentals of On-line Searching

Although there are variations in search procedure from system to system or from vendor to vendor, one common theme in most of these systems is the use of the Boolean operators: *And, Or,* and *Not*. These system commands help the researcher link ideas together in different relationships.

The "And" search command requires that each term in the search statement exist in a record before it is retrieved. A simple field search performed in one bibliographic database using the "And" operator might be described as a *search for documents relating to market data (and) personal computers*. This command would retrieve a set of references in which both personal computers and market data are discussed.

The "Or" search command requires that any of the terms used in a search statement exist in a document before it is retrieved. For example, the search for *documents dealing with personal computers (or) microcomputers* would result in a set of documents dealing with either personal computers or microcomputers.

The "Not" command makes it possible to eliminate an idea or concept represented by a word or phrase from the search result set. For example, a search for *documents dealing with personal computers (not) minicomputers* would eliminate from the set of documents those personal computer references that discuss minicomputers.

These Boolean commands are best illustrated with the use of a diagram. Exhibit 3C–1 illustrates the search for *all documents containing market data that are related to personal computers or home computers, but not minicomputers.* The result is the shaded area, which represents all of the documents dealing with market data and personal or home computers, but eliminates those that deal also with minicomputers.

Note that although these three Boolean operators are basic search commands in most online systems, they represent a small percentage of the search options

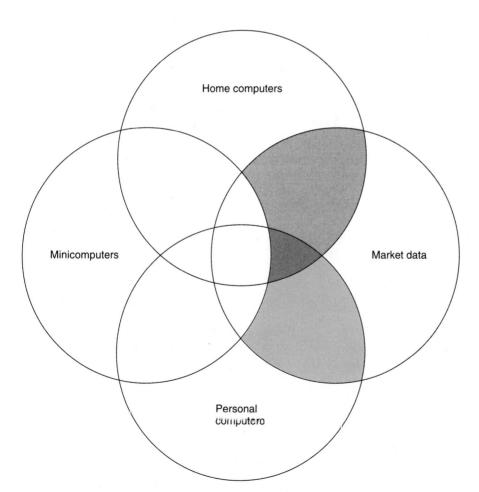

EXHIBIT 3C–2   Consumer Demographic Analysis Prepared for an Automobile Leasing Company

---

```
File 575: D&B-Donnelley Demographics-11+91 (Copr. 1990 DMIS)
** FILE575: 1991 Estimates and 1996 projections now available
```

Set	Items	Description
?s ALO50000 99999		[The searcher(s) asks for communities with a median household income (AL =) between $50,000 and $99,999.]
S1 2648 AL = 50000:99999		[The system responds with set 1. There are 2,648 communities in the United States that meet this requirement.]
?s VN = 13.0:16.1		[The searcher(s) asks for communities that have a median educational level between 13 and 16 years (VN =).]
S2 4523 VN = 13.0:16.1		[The system responds with set 2. There are 4,523 communities that meet this requirement.]
?s LA = 75:99		[The searcher(s) ask for communities with a socioeconomic status indicator (SESI) between 75 and 99 (the average for the U.S. is 53)].
S3 4152 LA=75:99		[The system responds with set 3. There are 4,152 communities that meet this requirement.]
?ss st = ny or st = nj or st = ct		[The searcher(s) ask for all communities in New York (NY), New Jersey (NJ), and Connecticut (CT)(ST =).]
S4 2939 ST=NY (NEW YORK)		
S5 1111 ST=NJ (NEW JERSEY)		
S6 432 ST=CT (CONNECTICUT)		
S7 4482 ST=NY OR ST=NJ OR ST=CT		[The system responds with set 7, which is the resultant combination of sets 5, 6, and 7. There are 4,482 communities in this tri-state region.]
?ss s1 and s2 and s3 and s7	2648 S1	
	4523 S2	
	4152 S3	
	4482 S7	[The searcher(s) now asks that all of the above demographic requirements be applied simultaneously.]
S8 501 S1 and S2 and S3 and S7		[The system responds with set 8. There are 501 communities in the database that meet all of the above requirements.]
?t 8/5/1		

Note: This database utilizes codes to represent search concepts. Thus, the searcher uses the code AL when specifying household incomes; GA for population in managerial positions; GB for population in professional positions; and so on.

that are available to the researcher.[1] Understanding and using these basic search commands, however, allow us to examine more closely a few considerations of the application of online databases to the market research function.

The example illustrates the effective use of secondary market information that is available on the Dialog system. In the interactive online environment, numerous vendors offer hundreds of databases that may be used in the search for relevant secondary market research information.

---

[1]The database vendors (such as Dialog) generally provide manuals and training for the use of system commands. There are also a number of books on this subject, such as C. C. Chen and S. Schweizer, *Online Bibliographic Searching: A Learning Manual* (New York: Neal-Schumen Publishers, 1981), or C. L. Borgman et al., *Effective Online Searching* (New York: Marcel Dekker, 1984).

Consumer Demographics   An automobile leasing company that specializes in exotic for-eign cars is considering a local media advertising campaign in the tristate region—New York, New Jersey, and Connecticut. Past company records indicate that the target markets are communities with median household incomes in excess of $50,000, median education of at least one year in college, and high socioeconomic status.

EXAMPLE

Database	Donnelley Demographics
Availability	Dialog Information Retrieval Service
Type	Numeric
Description	Donnelley Marketing Information Services produces a database of selected demo-graphic information from the 1990 census that is enhanced with current and five-year projections for some data series. Arranged by a variety of geographic subdivi-sions, the database contains information on demographic characteristics and is reloaded annually.

Exhibit 3C–2 presents the search procedure that would be executed on the Dialog system.

Syndicated Sources of Purchase Behavior and Media Exposure Information

— Explain the general characteristics, advantages, disadvantages, and uses of diary panels.
— Describe the leading diary panel services covering purchase and media panels.
— Explain the general characteristics and advantages of store audits.
— Illustrate the increasing importance of electronic scanner services.
— Explain the general characteristics, advantages, disadvantages, uses of electronic scanner services, and single source information.

INTRODUCTION

Having exhausted the available print tools for gathering secondary market information as well as the newer computerized online and offline secondary sources, the marketing manager may want to consult a marketing research supplier. As we discussed in Chapter 1, many of these suppliers sell data and reports on specialized topics to client companies. The information collected by these suppliers is offered on a **syndicated service** basis—common pools of data and reports are sold to different client companies. The data are collected by researchers on a regular basis who use standardized procedures; it is then "syndicated" to various users. Because the service is supplied to a number of clients simultaneously, syndicated services frequently are less expensive than collecting the necessary data on your own.

Unlike the secondary data discussed in Chapter 3, the information provided by syndicated sources has been collected to aid specific businesses that have specific needs. The data and reports supplied to client companies generally are personalized to fit the specific needs of each client. For example, reports can be organized on the basis of the client's sales territories and the unit of reporting will be changed from ounces to pounds for a specific client. Most information from syndicated sources can be applied to consumer package goods. The competitive nature of this industry requires that firms have in-depth and timely information about purchase behavior and media exposure. Such information is invaluable in determining where a particular brand or product category is headed and then deciding the appropriate strategy to employ to solve a particular problem.

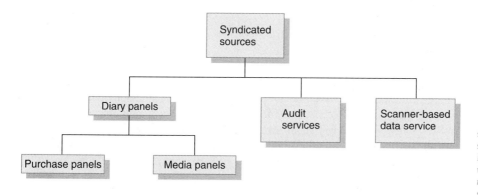

EXHIBIT 4–1
—
Typology of
Syndicated Sources
of Purchase Behavior
and Media Exposure
Data

syndicated research services
Market research suppliers who collect data on a regular basis with standardized procedures. The data are sold to different clients.

mail diary services
General term for services involving a sample of respondents who have agreed to provide information such as media exposure and purchase behavior on a regular basis over an extended period of time.

Chapter 4 is a comprehensive treatment of the syndicated sources of data on purchase behavior and media exposure. Exhibit 4–1 provides the framework for our discussion. We open with a discussion of **mail diary services,** which involve a sample of respondents who have agreed to provide information such as media exposure and purchase behavior on a regular basis over an extended period of time. Then we shift to the leading available retail, wholesale, and warehouse audit survey services, as well as the custom audit services that usually involve measurement of new-product movement in test markets and controlled store tests. Finally, we look at computerized electronic scanner systems that are revolutionizing marketing research and have proven to be formidable competition for traditional audit survey services.

Several comments on suppliers are in order. First, several factors influence the choice of a particular syndicated service. Aside from the characteristics and quality of the information supplied, the reputation, technical competence, experience, and personnel employed by the research supplier will be important. Second, the information presented in this chapter is not an endorsement or advertisement. Many marketing research suppliers provide information on purchase behavior and media exposure. We cannot discuss all of them. For the most part, the information we present is taken from promotional material supplied to client companies by the marketing research suppliers.

DIARY PANELS

A **diary panel** is a special kind of mail diary service. Diary panels involve samples of households that have agreed to provide specific information regularly over an extended period of time. For this reason, they frequently are referred to as "continuous" panels. Although traditional diary panels still are very important for clothing, home durables, and other product categories in which the Universal Product Code (UPC) is not well entrenched, for consumer package goods the trend is to use electronic scanner services.

diary panels
Samples of households that have agreed to provide specific information regularly over an extended period of time. Respondents in a diary panel are asked to record specific behaviors as they occur, as opposed to merely responding to a series of questions.

General Characteristics

Diary panels are maintained by commercial marketing research suppliers. Respondents are asked to *record* specific behaviors as they occur, rather than to merely respond to a series of questions. As a syndicated service, the same diary panel data are sold to a number of clients, although the analysis and presentation of the data usually are personalized to meet the client's needs.

Diary panels can be classified by the type of information that is recorded—either purchase behavior data or media exposure data. For most traditional diary panels, respondents are asked to use a self-administered questionnaire called a *diary* to record specific information periodically; for media panels electronic devices automatically record viewing patterns, supplementing a diary. Typically, the diary that contains the self-recorded data is returned to the sponsoring supplier every one to four weeks.

Comparative Evaluation

Because the data in diary panels are recorded at the time of purchase as opposed to being retrospectively reported by the respondent as in other types of surveys, these panels have the potential to be more accurate. Although purchase data reported in surveys are fairly accurate for estimating relative magnitudes of the quantities of brands purchased, recall data about purchase behavior tend to either overestimate, for nationally advertised brands, or underestimate, for sensitive expenditure categories such as liquor or cigarettes and for local or chain brands, the "true" national aggregate purchase data.[1] In addition to typical response biasing factors—forgetting, ambiguous questions, reporting errors—the lack of accuracy in recall surveys of purchase behavior is due to the problems inherent in any effort to measure purchase behavior. These include mistaken identification of a brand that is possibly due to similar packaging designs, lack of brand awareness, lack of knowledge of purchases made by other household members, and so on.[2]

Diary panels suffer from three primary practical weaknesses.

1. *Representativeness.* Despite extensive recruitment efforts, most diary panels underrepresent minority groups and people who have low education levels. For example, panel companies still report that blacks are underrepresented in their panels.[3] Also, turnover among members of a household can seriously affect the representativeness of the panel.

---

[1]See, for example, L. Drayton, "Bias Arising in Wording Consumer Questionnaires," *Journal of Marketing*, October 1954, pp. 140–45; J. Lansing, G. Ginsburger, and K. Braaten, *An Investigation of Response Error* (Urbana: University of Illinois, Bureau of Economics and Business Research, 1961); and J. Metz, *Accuracy of Responses Obtained in a Milk Consumption Study* (Ithaca, N.Y.: Cornell University, 1956).

[2]See, for example, J. H. Parfitt, "A Comparison of Purchase Recall with Diary Panel Records," *Journal of Advertising Research*, September 1967, pp. 16–31; S. Sudman, "On the Accuracy of Recording of Consumer Panels I," *Journal of Marketing Research*, May 1964, pp. 14–20; S. Sudman, "On the Accuracy of Recording of Consumer Panels: II," *Journal of Marketing Research*, August 1964, pp. 69–83; S. Sudman and M. Bradburn, *Response Effects in Surveys* (Chicago: Aldine Publishing Co., 1974); and S. Sudman and R. Ferber, *Consumer Panels* (Chicago: American Marketing Association, 1978).

[3]Telephone conversations with account executives at Market Facts, NFO Research, and the NPD Group, May 1989.

2. *Maturation.* Over time the average age of the panel increases, and so the panel must be "rolled over," which means that younger members are added periodically.

3. *Response Biases.* Knowing that their purchases are being scrutinized, panel members may behave differently than they would otherwise. In addition, recording errors are possible because the panel member is responsible for entering the purchase or media data by hand.

Uses

The two types of diary panels are diary purchase panels and diary media (TV and radio) panels. Diary media panels, such as the Nielsen ratings of TV shows, have been used primarily for establishing advertising rates (by radio and TV networks), for selecting the appropriate media program or time to air a commercial, and for establishing demographic profiles of viewer or listener subgroups. Diary purchase panels traditionally have been used in forecasting the sales level or market share of new products, for identifying trends and establishing demographic profiles of specific user groups, for evaluating test markets and controlled stores tests, for testing different advertising campaigns, and for estimating brand switching and trier-repeat purchases. Exhibit 4–2 (see page 98) illustrates several ways diary panel data can be used to solve marketing problems.

Diary Purchase Panels. Our description of diary purchase panel services is at best a snapshot of a feature-length movie. Diary panel companies provide many services covering many product categories. Two of the larger diary purchase panels are National Family Opinion (NFO) and National Purchase Diary Panel (NPD).

The NFO panel contains more than 400,000 households selected to be a representative sample of the United States. NFO also maintains an Hispanic Panel consisting of more than 16,000 households recruited from the country's most heavily Hispanic populated areas. The following list describes some of the product categories, sizes, and periodicity of the NFO panels. The beverage panel uses a diary format, while the remaining studies ask consumers to report in retrospect about purchases rather than to record the purchase when it was made.

— *SIP (Share of Intake Panel).* Diary purchase panel that reports quarterly on beverage consumption.

— *CARS (Carpet and Rug Study).* Tracking survey that profiles carpet purchasers and reports on extensive purchase details.

— *NFO Travels America.* Pleasure travel monitor with national- and state-level focus.

Special-purpose panel members are recruited from NFO's entire mail panel sample to make available special panels of households such as

— *The Mover Panel.* Households that have recently made a residential move.

— *The Baby Panel.* Households with new babies and expectant mothers.

— *50 Plus Panel.* Households with members 50 years of age or older.

EXHIBIT 4–2
—
Using Diary Panel
Data to Solve
Marketing-Related
Problems

How Loyal Are My Brand's Buyers vis-à-vis My Main Competitor?
Of next 3 purchases same brand was bought

	My brand	Competitor
0 of 3 times	25%	17%
1 of 3 times	33	24
2 of 3 times	21	24
All 3 times	21	35

The competitor has much higher loyalty among his buyers than my brand does.

Marketing Implication:
Efforts directed toward extending usage among existing buyers should increase loyalty.
Options include in/on-pack coupons, in-pack contests, premiums available for several proofs-of-purchase, etc.

How Does My Brand's Demographic Profile Compare to Other Brands?
Am I Reaching My Target Audience?

Income	Total category	Distribution of volume		
		Brand A	Brand B	Brand C
Under $10,000	21%	32	14	16
$10,000-20,000	31	29	31	32
$20,000 +	48	39	55	52

Relative to both the category and competition, Brand A is not doing well among upper income households.

Marketing Implication:
Advertising should be retargeted or revamped to reach the proper audience.

Should I Promote My Brand Using a Coupon or Free Sample?

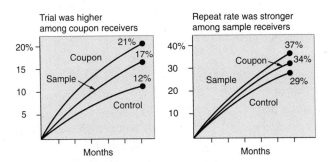

Both promotions encouraged more purchasing, with the stronger trial/weaker repeat for coupon receivers resulting in as much sales as the free sample.

Marketing Implication:
Since the sample cost three times as much, the coupon was chosen.

Source: National Purchase Diary Panel, used with permission.

As with any panel, response bias can be a problem. NFO reports a dropout rate for panel members of between 30 and 40 percent. The information obtained is often used to analyze brand-switching patterns and to track trial and repeat purchase levels. Exhibit 4–3 shows an example of an NFO purchase record.

National Purchase Diary Panel operates a variety of consumer panels that address the various marketing research needs of its clients.[4]

— *National purchase panels.* Using a monthly diary, NPD collects continuous purchase data from a national panel of households. NPD guarantees monthly *returns* from 14,500 national panel members. Three different data collection vehicles are used: The N1 and N2 diaries are *each* completed by a minimum of 6,500 *family* households per month, and the NF diary is completed by a minimum of 1,500 *nonfamily* households per month. The use of multiple data-collection vehicles gives NPD flexibility in tailoring sample sizes to meet the requirements of clients. For example, categories with low penetration (such as in-home blood pressure kits as opposed to shampoos) can be included in all three diaries, whereas categories with high penetration and short purchase cycles, dominated by national brands, may appear in only one or two of the three national diaries. Manufacturers use these data to track and analyze consumer purchases of both established brands and new-product introductions.

— *National CREST panel.* This panel of 12,800 national households completes the Eating Habit Study diary for two weeks during each quarter of the year. The syndicated CREST Report (Consumer Report on Eating Share Trends), which is based on these data, has become the primary source of consumer information for the food service industry.

— *National NET panel.* This household panel is a subset of the CREST panel, and its members complete a daily meal diary for a two-week period each year. The syndicated NET (National Eating Trends) service uses this database to provide continuous tracking of in-home food and beverage preparation and consumption patterns.

— *Local market purchase panels.* Using a monthly diary, NPD collects continuous purchase data from 35,000 households in 35 test-market areas across the country. These data are used for tracking new-product performance and for evaluating consumer promotional plans.

Diary Media Panels. *Nielsen Television Index* (NTI) is perhaps the most famous of A. C. Nielsen's varied services. As a system for estimating national television audiences, NTI produces a "rating" and corresponding share estimate. A **rating** is the percent of all households that have at least one television set tuned to a program for at least 6 out of every 15 minutes that the program is telecast. **Share** is the percent of households that have a television set tuned to a specific program at a specific time.

rating
The percent of all households that have at least one television set viewing a program for at least 6 minutes out of every 15 minutes that the program is telecast.

---

[4]The following panel descriptions were supplied by Rita E. Turgeon, vice president, The NPD Group.

EXHIBIT 4–3 NFO Purchase Record

Monday, February 10 thru Sunday, February 23

☐ NONE RECEIVED

COUPONS RECEIVED

DATE REC'D	FOR WHICH OF THE DAIRY PRODUCTS? Please write in.	BRAND NAME:	HOW RECEIVED? ✓ OR WRITE IN: By Mail	From Ad	From Pkg.	From Friend	Other
____	____	____	☐	☐	☐	☐	____
____	____	____	☐	☐	☐	☐	____
____	____	____	☐	☐	☐	☐	____
____	____	____	☐	☐	☐	☐	____

☐ NONE RECEIVED

SAMPLES RECEIVED

DATE REC'D	FOR WHICH OF THE DAIRY PRODUCTS? Please write in.	BRAND NAME:	HOW RECEIVED? ✓ OR WRITE IN: By Mail	From Ad	From Pkg.	From Friend	Left at Door	Other
____	____	____	☐	☐	☐	☐	☐	____
____	____	____	☐	☐	☐	☐	☐	____
____	____	____	☐	☐	☐	☐	☐	____
____	____	____	☐	☐	☐	☐	☐	____

☐ NONE BOUGHT

☐ COFFEE

DATE BOUGHT	Copy complete BRAND NAME from package	TYPE: (✓) ONE		Is it Decaf-feinated?		IF INSTANT, does label say "freeze-dried"?		IF GROUND COFFEE, Check (✓) to indicate TYPE OF GRIND					SIZE:	NUMBER BOUGHT	TOTAL PRICE PAID	HOW MUCH DID YOU PAY? Don't include taxes. WAS THIS A SPECIAL PRICE OFFER?							TOTAL AMOUNT SAVED (if any)—value of special offer, cents off, value of coupon, etc.	WHERE BOUGHT?		
																		IF YES, DESCRIBE OFFER:								
		Instant	Ground	YES	NO	YES	NO	Regu-lar	Drip	Fine	Elec-tric	Other	# lbs. or # of oz.			YES	NO	Coupon Used	Cents Off	Combina-tion deal	Store Special	Other - describe		Super-market	Inde-pend-ent Grocery	Other-describe
____	____	☐	☐	☐	☐	☐	☐	☐	☐	☐	☐	☐	____	____	____	☐	☐	☐	☐	☐	☐	____	____	☐	☐	____
____	____	☐	☐	☐	☐	☐	☐	☐	☐	☐	☐	☐	____	____	____	☐	☐	☐	☐	☐	☐	____	____	☐	☐	____
____	____	☐	☐	☐	☐	☐	☐	☐	☐	☐	☐	☐	____	____	____	☐	☐	☐	☐	☐	☐	____	____	☐	☐	____
____	____	☐	☐	☐	☐	☐	☐	☐	☐	☐	☐	☐	____	____	____	☐	☐	☐	☐	☐	☐	____	____	☐	☐	____
____	____	☐	☐	☐	☐	☐	☐	☐	☐	☐	☐	☐	____	____	____	☐	☐	☐	☐	☐	☐	____	____	☐	☐	____

☐ NONE BOUGHT

☐ JAM, JELLY, PRESERVES, FLAVORED REFRIGERATED SPREADS, MARMALADE, FRUIT BUTTER, ect.

DATE BOUGHT	Copy complete BRAND NAME from package	KIND OF PRODUCT (jam, jelly, preserves, flavored refrigerated spread, marmalade, fruit butter, etc.)	FLAVOR (copy from the label-such as "raisin cinnamon", "grape", "strawberry", "fruit-nut", etc.)	TYPE OF PACKAGE			SIZE:	NUMBER BOUGHT	TOTAL PRICE PAID	HOW MUCH DID YOU PAY? Don't include taxes. WAS THIS A SPECIAL PRICE OFFER?							TOTAL AMOUNT SAVED (if any)—value of special offer, cents off, value of coupon, etc.	WHERE BOUGHT?		
												IF YES, DESCRIBE OFFER:								
				Jar	Tub	Other	# lbs. or # of oz.			YES	NO	Coupon Used	Cents Off	Combina-tion deal	Store Special	Other - describe		Super-market	Inde-pend-ent Grocery	Other-describe
____	____	____	____	☐	☐	☐	____	____	____	☐	☐	☐	☐	☐	☐	____	____	☐	☐	____
____	____	____	____	☐	☐	☐	____	____	____	☐	☐	☐	☐	☐	☐	____	____	☐	☐	____
____	____	____	____	☐	☐	☐	____	____	____	☐	☐	☐	☐	☐	☐	____	____	☐	☐	____
____	____	____	____	☐	☐	☐	____	____	____	☐	☐	☐	☐	☐	☐	____	____	☐	☐	____

Source: National Family Opinion, used with permission.

In 1987 Nielsen changed its measurement process to incorporate the use of "people meters." These devices were more accurate measuring audiences than the previous method of diary recording. The institution of this method delivered lower audience ratings than the prior method and, initially, was widely criticized by TV network executives whose job it was to explain the lower ratings to advertising buyers. Exhibit 4–4 describes the measurement process.

share
The percent of households with a television set on who are tuned to a specific program at a specific time.

The NTI panel consists of approximately 2,000 households, matched according to United States' national statistics, that have agreed to use an electronic device, called a *people meter*, attached to their television sets. The people meter continuously monitors and records television viewing in terms of when the set was turned on, what channels were viewed, how long the channels were tuned in, and who in the household was watching it. The data are stored in the people meter (see Exhibit 4–5) and later are transmitted via telephone lines to a central processing facility. From the World of Research 4–1 (see pages 104–105) discusses a potential rival to Nielsen's people meter.

The viewing and audience-characteristics data are combined to produce a report entitled **NTI-NAD (Nielsen Television Index, National Audience Demographics)**, which is used to help companies decide which television programs are the best vehicles for their commercials. The NTI-NAD report gives ratings broken down by the following demographics:

NTI-NAD (Nielsen Television Index, National Audience Demographics) A report combining viewing and audience characteristics used to identify a program (or programs) that will potentially reach the most appropriate and largest target audience.

- Households.
- Women employed outside the home.
- Women 18+, 12–24, 18–34, 18–49, 25–54, 35–64, and 55+ age groups.
- Men 18+, 18–34, 18–49, 25–54, 35–65, and 55+ age groups.
- Teenagers.
- Children aged 2 and older, and aged 6 to 11.

As indicated, Nielsen NTI-NAD data are used by media planners to analyze alternative network programs. First, programs reaching the largest number of

EXHIBIT 4–4

—

NTI Measurement Process

The Nielsen people meter electronically stores half-minute by half-minute records of TV receiver tunings and audience data entries in NTI sample households. Each TV set in a household is equipped with a Nielsen people meter, which consists of an on-set unit and a remote control unit. Each member of the household is assigned buttons (one on the set-top unit and a corresponding one on the remote control) that he or she can use to enter their viewing status. (The name, age, and gender of each household member, as well as other demographic information on the household, is collected by periodic personal interviews conducted by Nielsen. The name of each household member is indicated above his or her people-meter button.)

Tuning records from the people meter are automatically transmitted by phone to a central computer. These data records are inherently free of response error because they require no effort, recall, or reply from persons in the NTI sample concerning dial settings, station call letters, programs, and the like.

Source: A. C. Nielsen, used with permission (1987–1988 NTI Reference Supplement).

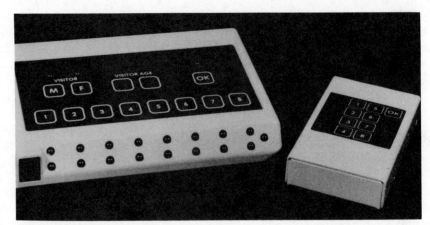

Courtesy of Nielsen Media Research.

The Nielsen people meter is the result of years of development to produce a device to collect persons' viewing data electronically.

The Nielsen people meter (shown above) is a small unit (7″ × 4¾″ × 1¼″) placed on top of or beside the television set. Eight sets of red and green lights on the front are used to indicate if selected people are in the viewing audience (green) or not (red). Each set of lights is assigned to a household family member who can indicate their presence as a viewer by pushing their assigned button on top of the meter, changing their light from red (all red lights are on and flashing when the set is turned on) to green.

Several light sets/buttons are allocated for visitor use. Visitors must also indicate their sex and age using buttons designed for that purpose.

The Nielsen people-meter unit also includes a remote box so that entries can be made from across the room.

Data entered into the Nielsen people meter is stored in a Nielsen Storage Instantaneous Audiometer (SIA) System, which is polled periodically using telephone lines.

target audiences are identified using the NTI-NAD reports. Next, the cost efficiency of each program is calculated. Cost efficiency represents a television program's ability to deliver the largest target audience at the smallest cost. A **cost-per-thousand (CPM)** calculation is computed by taking

CPM (cost-per-thousand)
Cost-efficiency calculation that represents a television program's ability to deliver the largest target audience at the smallest cost.

$$CPM = \frac{\text{Cost of a commercial}}{\text{Number of target audiences delivered}}$$

Arbitron maintains both national and regional radio and TV diary panels. Prospective panel members are drawn primarily from lists that are maintained by Metro-Mail of households with listed telephone numbers. Exhibit 4–6 provides a summary of Arbitron's TV diary panel.

The diary data that cover radio listening are used to evaluate advertising alternatives (stations and programs) by estimating in each area the listening audience for 15-minute blocks of time. A description of Arbitron's radio diary panel is provided in From the World of Research 4–2 (see pages 108–109), including an example of the diary page.

EXHIBIT 4–6
—
Arbitron's Television
Diary

Arbitron uses one-week family diaries in about 209 ADI markets to gather household and demographic viewing data for the television local market reports. The ADI (area of dominant influence) is a geographic sales and marketing area design created by Arbitron in 1965. It has since become the industry standard for the marketing and selling of most advertised products that are being sold today. Metropolitan areas are included within the ADI. The diary is still the most economically feasible measurement method available to produce local ratings.

Diaries are furnished for each television set in the home. Diary pages are ruled and printed to provide spaces for viewing entries during any quarter-hour between 6 A.M. and 2 A.M. each day. Columns provide station call letters, channel number, and program title, as well as for the identity of each family member viewing.

Homes are computer-selected to be in the diary sample, based on lists that are supplied to Arbitron by the Metromail company. Both listed and unlisted telephone homes are used in the sample.

Letters are sent to each listed home in the sample informing them of their selection by computer. The letter is followed by a telephone call requesting household members' cooperation. Unlisted homes are mailed a confirmation letter after they have been contacted.

Diaries are mailed to all eligible households in the sample with a small cash incentive to stimulate cooperation. Both black and Hispanic households receive increased cash premiums and additional follow-up telephone calls. Hispanic homes are mailed bilingual diaries.

During the course of an average sweep period, Arbitron tabulates approximately 105,000 diaries on a national basis. Over a four-week period, individual markets may have anywhere from 250 (in small markets) to over 1,600 diaries tabulated for their ADI.

Source: "The Arbitron Television Book," 1990.

The age and gender makeup of each audience also is available so that key evaluative measures can be calculated based on audience profiles. The TV diary panel is supplemented with a sample of households that have agreed to attach an electronic meter to their television sets. Meters automatically record viewing patterns in all of Arbitron's major markets. Telephone lines transmit the electronic data to Arbitron's central-processing facility. Panel members are "rolled out" every five years.

Arbitron also produces custom reports for clients. Typically, these are based on an interactive computer-based system called **Arbitron Information on Demand (AID).**[5]

- **Radio and Television AID** can analyze any station's audience by selected demographics, specific geography, or nonstandard time periods. Subscribers use AID to select the audience estimates that best meet their needs.

- **Target AID** can categorize audiences by lifestyle, purchasing habits, and economic standing, allowing advertisers to choose the stations that deliver their target audience.

- **Product Target AID** is a microcomputer that categories television viewers by their purchasing patterns. *Arbitrends* delivers radio and television audience estimates directly to stations' and agencies' microcomputers. Radio Arbitrends updates radio listening information and selected markets each month and helps stations to interpret and use these data.

Arbitron Information on Demand (AID)
An interactive computer-based system that provides the basis for Arbitron custom reports for clients.

Radio and Television AID
Analysis of a station's audience by selected demographics, specific geography, or nonstandard time periods.

Target AID
Categorization of audiences by lifestyle, purchasing habits, and economic standing.

Product Target AID
A microcomputer that categorizes television viewers by their purchasing patterns.

---

[5]The following material was taken directly from *Arbitron Ratings Today*, supplied by Shelly Cagner, administrative assistant in communications.

Nielsen Rival to Unveil New "Peoplemeter"

Television executives have complained ever since A. C. Nielsen Co. switched to push-button "peoplemeters" in 1987 that dictate how some $15 billion in national advertising is spent each year. Now Nielsen rival Arbitron Co. thinks it has found a better mousetrap to measure the TV ratings.

TV brass have griped that peoplemeters require too much effort from viewers, who must punch in and out whenever they turn on the set or leave or re-enter the room. They've blamed the dreaded device for plunging ratings for children's cartoons and sliding ratings elsewhere, insisting Nielsen families keep watching but tire of all the button-pushing.

Arbitron's device is a computerized contraption that won't require any button-pushing at all. Next Tuesday, the company is set to unveil plans for what it calls a portable, personal, passive peoplemeter.

The new device, though it won't be introduced commercially for a few years, may well re-ignite the debate over the accuracy of TV ratings. It also could put new pressure on Nielsen, the pre-eminent ratings agency, to accelerate efforts to introduce a passive peoplemeter of its own. Moreover, it's already drawing fire from some of the same TV executives who blasted the Nielsen peoplemeter.

The Arbitron device's design isn't final, but it will be small enough to be carried or worn by each member of a household, perhaps in beeper, pin, or pendant form. More importantly, it would use a computer chip to measure both TV viewing and radio listening by a single consumer—offering advertisers, for the first time, an intimate peek into someone's combined media habits. Radio ratings today rely mostly on hand-scrawled diaries.

The new gadget would pick up audio signals encoded in the programs being watched or listened to, eliminating the risk that a lazy viewer would slack off and ignore punching in. Another prime advantage: It could stay with the roving viewer to measure radio habits in the car, TV habits at the local bar, and other out-of-home viewing that the peoplemeter fails to pick up.

Arbitron, a unit of Ceridian Corp., is likely to use the new meter for some of the 210 local TV markets and 260 radio markets in which it produces local ratings. Officials at Arbitron declined to discuss the device.

The plan for a better mousetrap is already meeting with a mixed reception. It's "the Buck Rogers approach to media," says a critical Nicholas Schiavone, vice president of media and marketing research for the NBC network. He favors simpler TV-set meters, which he contends are more accurate and reliable, and says Arbitron may "once again be making an act of faith in technology, which is unwarranted."

"The fact that one has to wear [the new Arbitron meter] makes it a highly active device," not a passive one, he adds.

A passive peoplemeter "isn't inherently going to be a better measurement system," says David Poltrack, a senior vice president at the CBS network. But, he adds, "if it can increase the level and quality of cooperation, then it is certainly a step forward. If it just replaces one technology with another, then it is only going to raise the costs of measurement."

The TV industry has been on a quest for years for a so-called passive system that would require little or no effort on the part of the person whose viewing habits are being measured. The goal is so elusive that TV executives occasionally joke about wishing they could implant computer chips under viewers' skin to ensure an absolutely accurate and complete measurement of who watches what and when.

"I have no doubt that it can be done. This is America," says Alan Wurtzel, senior vice president at the ABC network.

In the early 1980s, Nielsen experimented with giving viewers rings to wear, which picked up frequencies from the TV set. But half the participants lost them. Watches have been tried as well, but viewers refused to wear them.

In the late 1980s, R. D. Percy Co. developed a passive meter that relied on infrared sensors to tell whether viewers were actually sitting in front of a TV set that was on, but there were doubts about its reliability, the industry didn't support it, and Percy went out of business.

"The technology has been around," says Jack Loftus, a spokesman for Nielsen. "The single greatest issue is getting people to cooperate." Nielsen could likely match Arbitron's new system "tomorrow, but we think it raises even more significant cooperation issues," he says.

Nielsen, a unit of Dun & Bradstreet Corp., holds an unchallenged monopoly on the national TV ratings that guide network ad spending. Arbitron tried to start a rival service but spent millions, ran two years behind schedule, and abruptly pulled the plug last September.

But Nielsen holds only a slight edge in intensive competition with Arbitron for market-by-market local ratings, which affect some $15 billion in local TV advertising. Most markets continue to rely on handwritten diaries for TV and radio ratings alike. Arbitron and Nielsen both use TV-set meters, which don't require much viewer effort, in the two dozen or so biggest markets.

Those meters, however, can't give advertisers what they want most: breakdowns by age and sex. That's the advantage of peoplemeters, which Nielsen uses in 4,000 homes for national TV ratings and which Arbitron uses in six markets for some local ratings.

Nielsen is developing its own passive system, still several years away from implementation, which uses computer imaging to compare the viewers that are in front of a TV set with stored images of household members to identify who is watching at a particular time. But the system doesn't work well in areas such as patios and rooms with lots of windows. Critics also question whether people will allow it to be installed in bedrooms and bathrooms (one million homes have bathroom TV sets), where the system's quasi-picture-taking element could be seen as an invasion of privacy.

The Arbitron County
Coverage Report
Report that measures au-
diences in every county in
the continental United
States.

Arbitron Marketing
Research
A customized research
service offered by
Arbitron.

— **The Arbitron County Coverage Report** measures audiences in every county in the continental United States; it is conducted every year in television and every two years in radio.

— **Arbitron Marketing Research** produces special-audience surveys conducted by telephone, personal interviews, and direct mailings to meet specific research needs expressed by clients.

AUDIT SERVICES

Many marketing decisions are ultimately based on how much product has sold. Audits indicate what is happening in the marketplace not only for a given marketer, but also for the competition.

General Characteristics

audit
A formal examination
and verification of how
much of a product has
sold at the store level.

Audits are offered by commercial marketing research suppliers as part of their syndicated-services portfolio. As the name implies, an **audit** involves a formal examination and verification of how much of a product has sold at the store level. Participating operators (such as retail chains, health and beauty-aid rack operators, frozen food warehouses), who have agreed to open up their doors or records so that audits can be performed, receive basic reports and a cash payment. Again, like diary panels, audit services face stiff competition from electronic scanning syndicated services.

Comparative Evaluation

Audits provide relatively precise information on the movement of many different products. Because most consumer products are not sold directly to consumers, but to retailers, wholesalers, and distributors, a national consumer goods manufacturer does not have information on current sales at the retail level. Even though information about factory shipments is known, warehouse inventories may be building as a result of limited retail sales, and the consumer goods manufacturer has no knowledge of the situation. Eventually, the consumer goods manufacturer finds out, but this is probably too late for him or her to develop corrective strategies to stimulate retail sales. Even when information about sales at the retail level is available, similar data for competitive products are rarely known. By reporting on these kinds of data, audit services provide a very important function.

One problem endemic to conventional auditing services involves limited or incomplete coverage. Not all areas or operators are included in the audit. Even though the operators included in the audit typically account for more than 80 percent of the volume in the area, if a product tends to do better or worse in areas not included or with operators not included, then, as an absolute measure, the information reported in the audit can be misleading. In general, national data on market share are quite accurate, but the accuracy of regional breakdowns can be much lower. Another practical weakness involves the issue of the timeliness of the information. There is typically a two-month gap between the audit cycle's completion and the publication of basic reports. Finally, there can be a problem in match-ing data on different types of competitive activity—for example, in matching advertising expenditures with the audit volume and share data because the former information usually is purchased from additional commercial sources and then integrated into basic reports.

Uses

Because varied sales data are provided by retail, wholesale, and custom audits, this service is particularly valuable for researchers when they develop marketing strate-gies. Among the many uses of audit services are (1) measuring consumer sales rela-tive to competition; (2) monitoring the full range of competitive activities; (3) identifying where new products are appearing and the volume of sales in each geo-graphical location; (4) measuring the competitive impact of private brands; (5) ana-lyzing and correcting distribution problems, if they exist; (6) developing advertising allocation schedules based on actual sales volume in a market; and (7) developing sales potentials for specific markets (category and brand development indexes).

Syndicated Audit Services. Retail audits involve in-store measurement of prod-uct-category movement. Periodically, auditors appear at participating stores and record such information as beginning inventory, ending inventory, receipts, prices, deals, local advertising, and displays. Retail sales figures are computed by taking

$$\text{Opening inventory} + \text{Receipts} - \text{Ending inventory} = \text{Retail sales}$$

The largest retail audit service for consumer packaged goods is the *Nielsen Retail Index*.[6] By using this service, consumer responsiveness to products within the food, drug/health and beauty-aid, and alcoholic beverage industries is mea-sured at the actual point of sale on a bimonthly basis.

Nielsen divides the country into strata, which are based on geography, popula-tion, and store type and size characteristics. Outlets are then probabilistically drawn from each stratum. Over 76,000 separate audits are made annually in 11,350+ separate retail outlets. Nielsen employs more than 600 full-time field representatives to gather the new data. These field representatives are college-educated, well-trained professionals who have an average of approximately eight years in-field experience. The data provide information on a wide range of marketing variables and are typically provided on a bimonthly basis. Nielsen data are used to

- Measure sales relative to competitors.
- Measure sell-in to the retailer.
- Evaluate a brand's in-store position.
- Analyze and correct distribution problems.
- Evaluate pricing and promotion strategies.

---

[6]The following discussion is based on material provided by the A. C. Nielsen Company.

A Day in the Life of an Arbitron Diary

There are more than a half billion radios in the United States today. The Arbitron radio diary must go wherever people listen to radio. Statistics show that 75 percent of all radio listening takes place away from home. Fifty-eight percent of adult listeners listen to a radio at their office, and 90 percent listen while in their cars or trucks. Wherever they are, participants jot down what station they tune in, how long they listen, and where they listen.

Arbitron's centralized Interview Center places more than 5 million phone calls annually. Interviewers speak with potential diarykeepers to collect demographic information and determine their eligibility to participate in an Arbitron survey. On the average, 79 percent of those asked consent to filling out a radio diary.

Once participants are selected, coded address labels are mass produced and placed on each diary. When the diaries are returned to Arbitron, these codes are helpful in sorting diaries and as a data-entry reference. The "radio diary package" consists of one diary for each member of the household over the age of 12, a letter thanking the participants in advance of the survey, and a cash premium for each participant. Each diary is stamped and preaddressed for quick, effortless return to Arbitron. A bilingual Hispanic radio diary package is also prepared for certain markets.

At the end of the survey week, Arbitron survey participants check that all the appropriate information is included and simply seal the self-closing, prestamped diary and drop it in the nearest postal box. Arbitron diaries arrive by the crateful to the company's Beltsville, Maryland, facility, where they are hand sorted by county and predesignated market groups. Errors or clarifications are clearly marked in red ink by the Arbitron editors so the data entry specialists can note any adjustment or correction made to the diary to ensure that only the correct information is entered into the system. At the data-entry level, those diaries that are now considered suitable for tabulation (roughly 85 percent) are keyed into the system to be processed by Arbitron's mainframe computer that generates the final Local Market Report.

Once Arbitron's computer produces a master copy of each Local Market Report, the copies are sent to printers for mass production. Arbitron's mailing center coordinates orders and packs the Local Market Reports for shipping to subscribers.

Source: The Pulse of Radio, January 29, 1990.

- Track advertising effects.
- Monitor competitors' marketing efforts.
- Analyze the effect of marketing variables by store type.
- Analyze sales and marketing effects by territory.

Exhibit 4–7 displays Nielsen Retail Index data for brands of muffin mixes, showing market share and percent change from the previous year for Betty Crocker, Duncan Hines, and all other brands for the bimonthly periods.

Other prominent national auditing firms include *Audits and Surveys* and *IMS.* Audits and Surveys provides the National Total-Market Audit, which not only provides data on some of the packaged goods categories covered by Nielsen, but also

	Time		Station			Place			
Monday									
			Call letters or station name	Check (✓) one		Check (✓) one			
	Start	Stop	*Don't know? Use program name or dial setting.*	AM	FM	At home	In a car	At work	Other place
→ Early morning (from 5 A.M.)									
→ Midday									
→ Late afternoon									
→ Night (to 5 A.M. Tuesday)									

If you didn't hear a radio today, please check here. ☐

allows for tracking of product movement in the automotive, sporting goods, photography, home-improvement, and quite a few other industries. IMS provides audits of pharmaceutical products based on purchase invoices to both drugstores and hospitals.

Custom Audit Services Research suppliers who provide these services offer two basic types of studies that depend solely on the level of control desired by the client. The highest level of control is known as a controlled store test. In **controlled store testing** (also known as minimarket testing), the supplier takes over warehousing and distribution of the test product as well as total control of test variables (such as pricing, maintenance of out-of-stocks, display setup, couponing) within the market under examination—in addition to the basic task of measuring

controlled store testing Audit in which the supplier takes over warehousing and distribution of test product as well as total control of test variables within the market under examination—in addition to the basic task of measuring product sales.

EXHIBIT 4–7   Nielsen Retail Index Data for Brands of Muffin Mix

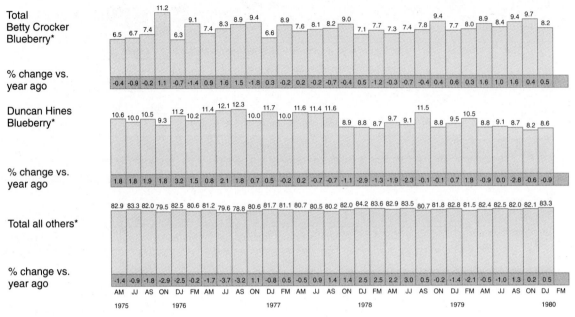

*Market share of muffin mixes over a five-year period (equivalent 24-unit-case basis × 1,000).

Source: A. C. Nielsen, used with permission.

product sales. On the other hand, **store audits** represent the lowest level of control because suppliers do nothing to alter the test environment; they only measure product sales.

Costs for conducting these studies vary widely, depending on the test design. In designing custom audits, remember that costs vary based on degree of control, number of items in product category, number of stores, and length of time.

Some leading suppliers who have this research expertise include

- – Audits and Surveys.
- – Burgoyne.
- – Ehrhart-Babic Associates.

SINGLE-SOURCE SERVICES

With the advent of the universal product code (UPC) it became possible to record (through electronic optical checkout devices) information about *actual* purchase behavior as opposed to human reported behavior from a diary. In the late 1970s, single-source services were developed to integrate store sales tracking, purchasing behavior of individual households, monitoring of advertising/promotion, and in-store variables into one unified system. They help marketers understand not only *what* is being purchased, but also *why* it is being purchased.

General Characteristics

Since 1979 scanner data field services have rapidly expanded, although development has varied by geography and merchandising chain. By 1988 the estimated number of stores participating in scanner services was over 10,000, covering almost 60 percent of **all commodity volume (ACV)**. The major reasons for the increase in stores that participate in scanner services are gains in labor productivity, tighter inventory control, and most important, greater sophistication on the part of retailers when trying to maximize profitability per selling footage of shelf space.

> **all commodity volume (ACV)**
> *Expressed as a percentage, this index gives the relative penetration that a product has in a particular geographic area; that is, it reflects the percentage of retail outlets in a geographic area that stock a given item—it is a common index of distribution intensity.*

Commercial marketing research suppliers offer single-source services on a syndicated or national custom (test-market) basis. The two basic services offered by these companies are: volume (sales) tracking and household purchasing behavior. Sales tracking services usually provide information about purchases by brand, size, price, and flavor or formulation based on sales data collected from the checkout scanner tapes. The information is collected from a sample of supermarkets that use electronic scanning systems. Household purchasing behavior is collected with the help of scanner "panels." Scanner panel members are given plastic identification cards that they use whenever they make purchases in participating supermarkets. Specially equipped scanners read the identification cards and automatically record these purchases along with the identification number of the panel member. The specially designed scanner records identification numbers when purchases are made, and an analysis of purchase behavior by demographic characteristics can be performed. Thus, scanner panels provide an opportunity for researchers to conduct fairly controlled experiments in a relatively natural environment. Controlled experiments (experimental designs) are discussed in Chapter 7.

Comparative Evaluation

Single-source services provide a number of attractive features. Compared with in-store audit services, electronic scanner tracking services have five principal advantages:

1. *Accuracy.* Volume tracking via electronic scanner systems provides increased accuracy with respect to product movement and price information, and it eliminates the possibility that breakage or pilferage losses are counted as sales. In addition, direct-store-delivered items such as soft drinks and cookies can be tracked more accurately.

2. *Time.* Volume tracking via electronic scanner systems provides much shorter turnaround time because the information is collected automatically. In addition, there is greater currency since scanner tapes are collected weekly as opposed to bimonthly (usually the case with in-store audits).

3. *Cost.* Volume tracking via electronic scanner systems is less expensive than nationally projectable volume tracking services.

4. *Experimental control.* Because of the ability to target alternative advertising-copy executions and media plans into specific homes, an extremely controlled testing environment is possible (for test-marketing applications only).

5. *Analytical capabilities.* Because demographic information about the panel is available, analyses of purchases by demographic characteristic of the consumer are possible. In addition, causal analysis is possible in light of the highly controlled and monitored testing environment (see Chapter 7).

Compared with in-store audits, electronic scanner tracking services have two principal disadvantages:

1. *Representativeness.* Volume tracking via electronic scanner systems may not produce projectable volume and share estimates because only the larger supermarkets have scanner capability, and, typically, the store samples have poor drugstore coverage. However, since a large proportion of food manufacturers' sales come from large supermarket chains that have these capabilities, the sample inadequacy is often overlooked.

2. *Quality of data.* Volume tracking via electronic scanner systems is highly dependent upon the ability of the checkout clerk to use the equipment correctly. Errors in recording can occur if clerks do not properly scan all of the purchases: For example, a clerk may use the register and ring up a heavy item to avoid lifting it. In the case of scanning multipackage purchases (different flavors) of the same product, the clerk may simply scan only one package and then ring in the number of purchases, which incorrectly records the transaction as consisting of several packages of only one flavor.

Uses

Single-source services provide a rich source of data that can be used when researchers develop marketing strategy. Among the primary uses of national tracking via electronic scanner systems are sales, market share, retail price, distribution, and modeling. Because of the quantity of data available about purchase behavior and panel characteristics and the highly controlled and monitored nature of the environment, single-source facilities in test markets have been used in a variety of marketing research projects. For example, they have been used in (1) new-product test markets, (2) product-repositioning studies, (3) copy-execution studies, (4) advertising-expenditure level (high, low) analysis studies, (5) advertising/promotion mix analysis, and (6) resizing (up, down) investigations.

Exhibit 4–8 provides a synopsis of the services supplied by Information Resource's InfoScan and Nielsen's Scantract.

EXHIBIT 4–8
—
Single-Source
Services

Information Resources Incorporated (IRI): InfoScan

InfoScan collects and integrates four types of data in a unique way to maximize the usable information and provide compatible cross referencing. With it, manufacturers can monitor the activity of (1) a specific UPC, a brand, a segment, or a category or (2) for a store, a chain, a market, a region, or the total United States.

— *Retail store sales*—InfoScan collects scanner-based movement data from thousands of retail grocery stores, convenience stores, drugstores, and mass merchandisers throughout the United States.

— *Consumer purchases*—Collection and reporting of individual household scanner purchase data for all UPC products allows tracking and customized analysis of purchase dynamics within and across categories. InfoScan panelists are provided with an easy-to-use identification card that is presented to the cashier so that data can be recorded and integrated at checkout.

— *Trade and consumer promotion*—IRI's own field staff provides weekly monitoring for all UPCs in each InfoScan store and market. Users can then match causal data, including all in-store merchandising conditions (price reductions, features, and displays) plus couponing activity, to their retail and consumer data.

— *Television viewing*—Each household monitored for television viewing is also an InfoScan Household Panel participant. Television advertising effectiveness can be determined by linking household television viewing back to actual consumer purchasing of the advertised brand.

Nielsen: ScanTrack

Each week, over 3,000 scanner-equipped stores, in a scientifically designed national sample of more than 800 organizations, give a completed record of their sales. These records provide the sales of any product that bears a Universal Product Code (UPC) symbol.

— *The National Service*—Panelists use a hand-held scanner to record all of their purchases, regardless of which store they shopped in—whether it was a major grocery chain, an independent supermarket, a mass merchandiser, or even a department store.

Panelists in the largest media markets are also metered for television viewing. Using a system developed by Nielsen Media Research to aid in developing television audience ratings, they identify individual commercials and match the programs consumers watch to the commercials they are exposed to. Linking this to their purchasing behavior provides the key to evaluating the effectiveness of TV advertising. Coupled with ScanTrack reports and other market-level economic and environmental information, a complete picture of what households buy and the impact on product sales of television, coupons, retail features, displays, and other marketing stimuli is provided.

— *The Local Service*—In key major markets across the country, Nielsen has local market panels of households who record their purchasing by presenting an ID card at the cash register of participating supermarkets. These supermarkets are spread across the United States to maximize the representativeness of the sample and are included in the ScanTrack Store Sample to ensure compatibility with the ScanTrack sales reports.

Since Nielsen monitors all in-store activity, in-market coupon activity, and television impressions, it becomes possible to look at the impact various marketing programs have on product sales. Which chain's displays and features were more successful in attracting buyers to a brand or in generating incremental volume? Did the coupon program really pay out? Did heavy buyers respond like light buyers or like new-brand buyers? Both services offer the ability to tie specific consumer response directly to individual activities.

Material summarized from Nielsen brochure.

SUMMARY

The marketing researcher who needs standard or customized data available from syndicated services has a choice of many different kinds of information from three basic sources: diary panels, audit services, and single-source services. The research project will determine which source provides the most appropriate data. Each type of syndicated service has advantages and disadvantages, which are related to representativeness of the sample, accuracy, quality and quantity of data, and so forth.

KEY CONCEPTS

syndicated research services

mail diary services

diary panels

rating

share

NTI-NAD (Nielsen Television Index, National Audience Demographics)

CPM (cost per thousand)

Arbitron Information on Demand (AID)

Radio and Television AID

Target AID

Product Target AID

The Arbitron County Coverage Report

Arbitron Marketing Research

audit

controlled store testing

store audits

all commodity volume (ACV)

REVIEW QUESTIONS

1. What are the advantages of syndicated services?
2. What factors should a marketing manager consider if he or she wanted to assess the quality of syndicated data?
3. Should scanner services replace diary panels?

4. How would a marketing manager use a store audit?
5. What is the major advantage of single source data compared to the other forms of syndicated data services?

Qualitative Interviewing Methods

— Describe what is meant by qualitative research.

— Discuss the primary methods of observational study.

— Explain the major uses of and implementation of issues regarding using focus groups and depth interviews.

— Describe and illustrate projective techniques.

INTRODUCTION

If existing secondary and syndicated sources of market research information are not sufficient to solve the marketing problem at hand, the researcher will probably have to collect primary data. In this chapter and the next we shift our attention to examining procedures and methods that can be used to acquire such data. Because this is primary research such alternatives usually involve conducting an interview. In certain circumstances the interview is highly structured. **Structured interviews** are purposely standardized so that each respondent is exposed to the same questionnaire and questioning process. This means that the interviewer cannot alter the interview by (1) adding or deleting questions, (2) changing the sequence of the questions, or (3) changing the wording of the questions.

Using standardized procedures may not be useful in cases in which the respondent's feelings and beliefs are not well developed and, consequently, are not well known. On occasion the researcher may wish to use a procedure less structured. For example, exploratory research designs are typically used when the purpose of the research is to gain insights about a broad or vague problem. In this instance, the researcher may want the flexibility of being able to ask questions in different orders, to change the wording of specific questions for different respondents, or to be able to probe respondents to clarify certain answers to questions.

The focus group interview and the depth interview discussed in this chapter use a relatively **unstructured interview** format.

All of the interviewing techniques discussed in this chapter fall under the general umbrella of **qualitative research methods.** Qualitative research methods can be distinguished from **quantitative research methods** in that they generally involve one or more of the following characteristics.

1. Small numbers of respondents.
2. Unstructured formats.
3. Indirect measurement of respondents' feelings and beliefs.
4. Direct observation.

FOCUS GROUPS

The **focus group interview** is one of the most frequently used data-collection methods in marketing research. Focus groups provide a unique opportunity to experience the market firsthand. The basic purpose of a focus group interview is to listen to a group of individuals, who belong to the appropriate target market, talk about an important marketing issue in order to learn something from the group discussion. Who is using focus groups? Almost every *Forbes* 500 company including General Motors, AT&T, and Xerox.[1] Exhibit 5–1 presents a case study of the use of focus groups by the Buick division of General Motors in developing the Regal two-door, six-passenger coupe introduced in 1987.

Procedure

Focus groups usually involve anywhere from 6 to 12 people, prerecruited to meet defined characteristics—for example, age, gender, use of certain products, and frequency of product use—who meet with a moderator to discuss a subject for anywhere from one to two hours. In some instances the representatives of the sponsoring firm view the session through one-way mirrors or on closed-circuit television. In general, the more emotional or complicated the subject, the smaller the group. Typically, if industrial or professional people are used, the size of the group is usually seven or eight.

Focus groups are conducted in commercial research facilities. The focus group room should provide a relaxed and comfortable setting (typically the room looks like a boardroom, although it can also look like an ordinary living room). In some facilities, one wall of the room is a mirror, which actually is a one-way glass with an observation room behind it. The room also has microphones feeding into both the observation room and a tape recorder. A videotape camera also may be used to record the session.

The number of focus groups that should be conducted on a single subject depends on several factors.[2]

1. Number of distinct market segments represented in the firm's target market.
2. Geographical scope of the firm's market area.
3. Importance of management's decision resulting from the research.

---

[1]Jeffery A. Trachtenberg, "Listening, the Old-Fashioned Way," *Forbes*, October 5, 1987, p. 202.

[2]Joe L. Welch, "Researching Marketing Problems and Opportunities with Focus Groups," *Industrial Marketing Management* 14, 1985, pp. 246–47.

EXHIBIT 5–1
—
The Example of the
Use of Focus Groups

The Buick division of General Motors used focus groups to help develop the Regal two-door, six-passenger coupe introduced in 1987. The effort began more than three years prior to introducing the car, when Buick held about 20 focus groups across the country and asked what features customers wanted in a new car. Who were the customers? Those wealthy enough to afford a $14,000 price tag; at this time the price was about $1,000 to $2,000 more than the average new car, which meant annual incomes of $40,000 or above. All the participants, gathered in every major geographical region of the country, had purchased new cars within the past four years.

What these groups indicated was that the customers wanted a legitimate back seat, at least 20 miles per gallon gas consumption, and 0-to-60 miles-per-hour acceleration in 11 seconds or less. They also wanted a stylish car, but they didn't want it to look like it just landed from outer space.

After Buick engineers created clay models of the car and mockups of the interior, the company went back to yet another focus group of target buyers. What the customers didn't like were the oversized bumper and the severe slope of the hood. What they did like was the four-wheel independent suspension.

Focus groups also helped to refine the advertising campaign for the Regal. Participants were first asked which competing cars most resembled the Buick in terms of image and features. The answer was Oldsmobile, a sister General Motors division. In response, Buick was repositioned above Oldsmobile by focusing on comfort and luxury features such as full six-passenger seating, wood-grain instrument panels, velour-type fabrics, and special stereo systems.

Source: Jeffery A. Trachtenberg, "Listening the Old-Fashioned Way," *Forbes,* October 5, 1987, p. 202; photo courtesy of Buick Motor Division.

4. Number of potential participants in a given geographical market area.
5. Number of new ideas generated by each successive group; additional focus groups should be conducted until the moderator can anticipate what is going to be said.

Focus groups have been conducted with all types of respondents—women, children (six or older), and professionals. At a given focus group session it is preferable to recruit participants who have similar backgrounds and experiences. If prospective participants are too different, their diverse backgrounds can lead to arguments, and important trends and patterns can be overlooked. For this and other issues relating to complete coverage of the primary target segments for a product or service, it is a common practice to commission more than one focus group for any given topic.

Focus group participants are recruited; that is, they usually are chosen by a field service that also usually provides the physical facility. Participants are paid from $30 (say, in the case of office workers) to as much as $150 (say, in the case of respondents who have professional degrees). Identifying and recruiting the appropriate participants for focus groups is perhaps the most important and difficult task because it will have great influence on the quality and quantity of the responses. Obviously, disastrous results can occur if the wrong people are recruited. Clear and specific profiles must be given to field services regarding the type of people that should be recruited. Table 5–1 outlines seven important rules for recruiting focus group participants. Exhibit 5–2 describes an unethical focus group recruiting procedure.

A focus group is led by a moderator. The moderator plays much the same role as a therapist does in group therapy. Similar to the therapist, the focus group moderator wants members of the group to discuss a certain set of topics within a certain time period, although not in any particular order. It is the moderator's responsibility to ensure that every member of the focus group participates in the discussion. Also the moderator should not allow one or two strong personalities to dominate the discussion. The role of the moderator is not to lead or direct the

---

TABLE 5–1

Seven Rules in Recruiting Focus Group Participants

1. Specifically define the characteristics of people who will be included in the groups.
2. If you are conducting an industrial focus group, develop screening questions that probe into all aspects of the respondents' job functions. Do not depend on titles or other ambiguous definitions of your responsibilities.
3. If you are conducting an industrial focus group, provide the research company with the names of specific companies and employees, when possible. If specific categories of companies are needed, a list of qualified companies is critical.
4. Ask multiple questions about a single variable to validate the accuracy of answers. Therefore, if you want to recruit personal computer users, do not simply ask for the brand and model of personal computers they use. In addition, ask them to describe the machine and its function; this will ensure that they are referring to the appropriate equipment.
5. Require that recruiters provide completed screener questionnaires at the end of each day. Check them carefully to ensure that appropriate people were recruited from appropriate companies. When in doubt, make a follow-up call to confirm the participant.
6. Do not accept respondents who have participated in a focus group during the previous year.
7. Have each participant arrive 15 minutes early to complete a prediscussion questionnaire. This will provide additional background information on each respondent, will reconfirm their suitability for the discussion, and will help the company collect useful factual information.

Source: Joe L. Welch, "Research Marketing Problems and Opportunities with Focus Groups," *Industrial Marketing Management* 14, 1985, p. 248.

EXHIBIT 5–2

Ethical Standards
for Focus Group
Recruitment

Ethical Considerations

A sell group is similar in composition to a focus group. However, the purpose of a sell group is to get a set of people together (e.g., doctors, lawyers, engineers, etc.) to make a sales pitch. It is unethical to recruit people under the disguise that the purpose of the meeting is to conduct a focus group, when in fact the purpose is to sell.

Focus Groups Disguised as Sales Pitch
To the editor: June 2, 1988

It has recently come to my attention that certain ethical drug companies and their marketing research consultants are engaged in a practice which, if true, represents a serious breach of professional ethics.

It seems that otherwise reputable research companies have hired former drug salespeople as "focus group moderators" to conduct group detailing and sales promotion sessions among physicians, under the guise of conducting market research focus groups. The purpose of such sessions is to brief the physicians on the client's product and manipulate the "discussion" in such a way as to positively affect their attitudes toward the product.

These "focus groups" are then followed up by a direct sales effort on the part of the client company, involving a letter and personal call to those physicians who participated in the "focus group."

Because none of the physicians know the true nature of the "focus group," they are unwitting participants. Since this practice is a gross misuse of legitimate market research and violates basic ethical principles by which researchers ought to feel guided, I feel a personal responsibility as a qualitative research consultant to expose this practice and call for its condemnation in the strongest terms.

As with the unscrupulous telemarketer who conducts sales campaigns under the guise of conducting a survey, AMA members who are engaging in this practice should be put on notice that their behavior and continued AMA membership are not compatible.

Not only do ethical considerations warrant the halting of this practice, but so does enlightened self-interest. Such behavior can only sully the profession's reputation and discredit all practitioners of the discipline. We all stand to be "tarred by the same brush" unless we, as a profession, expose those amongst us who threaten our integrity.

While any commercial practitioner will understand that the realities of the marketplace often present situations that are often in an ethical gray area and call for a rational and balanced judgment, the amount of money alleged to be involved in such "focus group" projects has clearly prompted those firms involved to abandon any pretense of professional integrity to pursue the lure of substantial financial gain.

Not that I am opposed to people making money, but let them do so openly and honestly, and not by a subterfuge that cheapens us all.

I call on all concerned professionals to demand an investigation and, if these allegations prove true, to cleanse our house.

Timm R. Sweeney, President
Sweeney International Ltd.
Brookfield, Conn.

Source: *Marketing News,* August 29, 1988, p. 4.

group discussion, but rather to keep it focused on the topic of interest. Ideally, the moderator should say as little as possible. As the abridged transcript of a focus group interview conducted for an AT&T military residence project shown in Exhibit 5–3 indicates, the moderator speaks informally and conversationally to the focus group participants and does not work from a formal prepared outline.

The process of obtaining focus group members is facilitated by using a screening questionnaire. The screening questionnaire clearly sets forth the qualifications that a person must possess in order to be in the focus group. Once the group meets, the flow of the interview is usually from a general discussion of the product category to a discussion of a specific product or specific characteristic of a product. A **discussion guide** establishes the plan of the focus group interview, including the topics that will be covered and sometimes the time allocated to each topic. The discussion guide is not a questionnaire; it simply provides an agenda for the group session that is flexible enough to be altered as the group discussion progresses.

EXHIBIT 5–3
—
Focus Group
Transcript

Group II 6:30 P.M.

Moderator:	I'd like to go around the room first and hear a little bit about you. My name is Donna. I'd like to hear your names, what you do in the military, rank or specialty you have, and a little about your long-distance telephone usage. If you don't mind, tell me the size of your bill, the number of calls you make, whether they are made to family or friends or to clients because of a side business you have, and the places you call. This is so we can get an idea whether you call Alaska once a month, or whether you make smaller calls. And do you place them during particular times of the day, or on days you're off work, and the brand of long distance you use. Who would like to start?
Respondent:	I'm a First Class Mate. I call my father once a week for maybe an hour. Sometimes I call my sister in Las Vegas, Nevada. My wife takes care of all the bills. My father was in an accident, is still recuperating.
Moderator:	So you call and kind of check on him once a week?
Respondent:	Yes.
Moderator:	If your wife takes care of the bills, do you know how much you spend on long distance?
Respondent:	I think the maximum has been about $49. It could be less than that. We call around 8:30–9:00 at night.
Moderator:	O.K. Curtis?
Respondent (Curtis):	I'm in the Navy. Some of the phone calls are made more or less, well a lot are long-distance calls when I go overseas. I was in Canada and my father was in the hospital. My wife calls a lot to Virginia to her parents, maybe once a week. I call North Carolina, relatives there. I call Florida sometimes.
Moderator:	About how many long-distance calls do you think your household makes every month in the United States?
Respondent (Curtis):	At least five.
Moderator:	Do you know what your average bill is?
Respondent (Curtis):	50-some dollars.
Moderator:	What brand of long distance do you use?
Respondent (Curtis):	AT&T. We just had Tel-something
Moderator:	Telamco? It's what I saw today written on something downstairs.
Respondent (Curtis):	Yes, I think that's it.
Moderator:	Thank you, Curtis.

Exhibit 5–4 provides an overview of the procedures involved in conducting a focus group.

Advantages and Disadvantages

On the negative side, focus groups are not intended to provide hard and fast conclusions and should not be used to try to answer questions that begin, "How many . . .?" The results from focus groups cannot be projected to the wider population at large and, consequently, they are not a substitute for quantitative studies.

On the positive side, focus groups have several important advantages.

1. Focus groups allow the client to get a firsthand, close-up picture of the target market.

2. Focus groups can provide more complex answers about a set of relevant issues than can a structured questionnaire.

3. Focus groups are fast. Completion of three or four geographically dispersed focus groups, along with final reports, can be accomplished in four to five weeks.

4. Focus groups are, relative to quantitative studies, inexpensive. In general, a one-group study costs approximately $3,000–$4,000, $5,000–$6,000 for two groups, and $10,000–$12,000 for four groups. Costs will vary according to the length of the interview and the target population.

5. Focus groups are flexible.

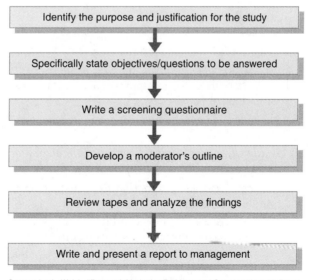

EXHIBIT 5–4
—
Focus Group
Procedure

Source: Joe L. Welch, "Research Marketing Problems and Opportunities with Focus Groups," *Industrial Marketing Management* 14, 1985, p. 247.

Uses

Focus group interviews are typically the first step in the research process for many types of marketing problems. Because they are used in the early, exploratory stages of the research process, their primary usefulness is not in providing precise quantitative information but rather in providing qualitative, descriptive information that bridges the gap between the firm (and its products) and the consumer. The following applications and examples briefly describe a number of uses, from generating ideas for advertising to seeking explanation of survey results.[3]

- *New products screening.* Products in concept or prototype stage are presented to potential user groups. Group technique is preferred due to need for depth of response, need to view prototype or imagine concept, and confidentiality. Works best when design personnel are present.

   Example: The reduction of the number of electric telephone concepts from six to three for a quantitative test.

- *Identification of attitudes underlying purchase of established products.* Focus group interviews conducted to explore reasons for purchase/nonpurchase among users/nonusers in effort to tailor marketing strategy.

   Example: The study conducted to identify the reasons for the falling sales of a firm's pre-fab houses.

- *Evaluation of advertising concepts.* Ad concepts at idea, storyboard, or animatic stage are presented to consumer groups for evaluation. Works best with presence of creative personnel.

   Example: Evaluation of potentially humorous animatics for commercial development.

- *Prequantitative issue and language identification.* Prior to conducting a quantitative study, salient issues and the language of the consumer are explored through groups.

   Example: The identification of language used by teenagers to describe shopping for fashionable clothing.

- *Packaging and/or name screening.* Responses to package and/or name alternatives probed, with emphasis on emotional reactions to packages and connotations of names.

   Example: The selection of a new name for a home test kit from six alternatives.

- *Acquisition of general background information on a product or service.* Used by ad agencies when pursuing an account or searching for creative ideas.

   Example: An ad agency that needed to know something about spackling products in a hurry.

- *Idea generation.* Groups conducted among consumers or management personnel to generate new product ideas.

   Example: The determination of a list of banking services to be presented to a consumer group.

---

[3]Material in this section was provided by Burke Institute.

Focus groups are being used more often in the industrial sector, and several differences should be kept in mind when researchers conduct industrial focus groups. Table 5–2 summarizes these factors.

Although focus groups have many valid uses, they can be used in an unethical manner. Focus groups should not be used to serve a client's hidden agenda. Exhibit 5–5 presents several illustrations of unethical focus groups.

ONE-ON-ONE/DEPTH INTERVIEWS

The **depth interview**, often referred to as a **"one-on-one,"** is frequently used to uncover underlying motivations, prejudices, attitudes toward sensitive issues, and so forth. Depth interviews are like long psychoanalytic sessions in which free association and hidden sources of feelings are discussed, generally through a question guide or agenda administered by a highly skilled interviewer.

depth interview ("one-on-one")
Sessions in which free association and hidden sources of feelings are discussed, generally through a very loose, unstructured question guide, administered by a highly skilled interviewer. It attempts to uncover underlying motivations, prejudices, attitudes toward sensitive issues, etc.

---

1. Moderator is likely to know very little about many industrial products; therefore, moderators must be briefed for longer period of time and in more detail.
2. Participants are almost always recruited from a list. Recruiters need very detailed information about industrial respondents. Frequently, the recruiter will need a list of firms that are involved in the product area.
3. Recognize that direct competitors may be participating in the client's focus group.
4. Technical and engineering participants frequently need a longer period of time to become comfortable with the interviewing process.
5. Props or stimuli may be difficult to use with industrial products; videotape is often a good substitute.
6. Many industrial clients have never before been involved in focus groups, so don't take anything for granted.

TABLE 5–2
—
Factors Influencing the Use of Focus Groups in Industrial Settings

Source: "In-Depth Data: Using Focus Groups to Study Industrial Markets," *Business Marketing,* November 1987.

Focus groups have many valid uses, but they can be used in an unethical manner to serve a client's hidden agenda. The following types of focus groups are considered unethical.

Sell groups: Focus groups that attempt to get a set of people together (doctors, lawyers, engineers, etc.) to make a sales pitch.

Prayer groups: These are usually political and designed to get consumers to say what the client wants to hear.

Tour groups: Focus groups that are commissioned for the sole purpose of getting the client and/or marketing researcher to visit an attractive location.

T-groups: Here the client wants to generalize from a percentage of the respondents liking the product to national market share.

Right-to-life groups: Here the clients keep changing moderators and groups of people until they find a group that is in favor of the idea.

Ethnic groups: Here the client limits the type of people eligible for the focus group so that they will fit specific notions of product users.

EXHIBIT 5–5
—
Ethical Standards for the Use of Focus Groups

Source: Adapted from Alexa Smith, "Focus Groups Being Subverted by Clients," *Marketing News,* June 8, 1984, p. 7.

EXHIBIT 5–6
—
Laddering Interview

Interviewer:	You indicated that you would be more likely to drink a wine cooler at a party on the weekend with friends. Why is that?
Respondent:	Well, wine coolers have *less alcohol* than a mixed drink and because they are so *filling* I tend to drink fewer and more slowly.
Interviewer:	What is the benefit of having less alcohol when you are around your friends?
Respondent:	I never really have thought about it. I don't know.
Interviewer:	Try to think about it in relation to the party situation. When was the last time you had a wine cooler in this party-with-friends situation?
Respondent:	Last weekend.
Interviewer:	Okay, why coolers last weekend?
Respondent:	Well, I knew I would be drinking a long time and I *didn't want to get wasted.*
Interviewer:	Why was it important not to get wasted at the party last weekend?
Respondent:	When I'm at a party I like to *socialize,* talk to my friends, and hopefully make some new friends. If I get wasted, I'm afraid I'd make an ass of myself and people won't invite me next time. It's important for me to be *part of the group.*

The summary ladder is

V sense of belonging
(part of the group)

C socialize

C avoid getting drunk
(wasted)

A less alcohol/filling

Depth interviews can prove most useful if the marketing research issue under study deals with (1) a confidential, emotionally charged, or embarrassing matter; (2) a behavior for which socially acceptable norms exist and the need to conform in group discussions influences responses; (3) a complex behavioral or decision-making process that requires a detailed idiosyncratic, step-by-step description; and (4) when group interviews are difficult to schedule for the target population, for example, doctors and other professionals. Depth interviews also are useful for studying routine or ritualistic behaviors. They have been used in brand-name research to understand consumers' perceptions and responses to names,[4] and other commercial applications have included copy and concept evaluations, wherein respondents are queried concerning what they recall or what they feel after listening to an advertisement.

The depth interviewer must strictly follow certain rules. The interviewer should (1) avoid appearing superior or condescending and use familiar words; (2) ask questions indirectly and informatively; (3) remain detached and objective, letting the respondent first describe brand and product category thoughts—for example, feelings about the current brand most often used and the product category in general—before asking "why" questions; (4) not accept "yes" or "no" answers; (5)

---

[4]M. Z. Knox, "In-Depth Interviews Can Reveal 'What's In A Name'," *Marketing News,* January 3, 1986, p. 4.

EXHIBIT 5–7   Focus Groups versus One-on-One Interviews

Factor	Focus Groups	One-on-One Interviews
Value of interaction	Use when interactions of participants will spark new thought (Example: physicians discussing treatment procedures)	Use when interactions are limited or appear to be nonproductive (Example: preschool children discussing new cereal product)
Sensitivity of subject matter	Use when subject matter is such that participants will not withhold information or temper remarks (Example: do-it-yourself mechanics discussing auto parts)	Use when subject matter is so sensitive that few respondents would speak openly in group setting (Example: research on selling strategies of competitive insurance agents)
Cost and timing	Use when turnaround critical and need to economize present	Use when turnaround not critical and budget will permit high costs of execution and reporting
Depth of information per respondent	Assumes most respondents can say all that they know in 8–12 minutes (Example: group conducted among women on use of prepared cake mixes)	Permits greater depth of response per individual; use when subject matter complex and participants very knowledgeable (Example: interviewing CPAs on tax preparation)
Logistics	Assumes that an acceptable number of respondents can be assembled in one location	Use when respondents are geographically dispersed and travel costs prohibitive

Source: The Burke Institute.

probe for all details and underlying feelings; and (6) encourage the respondent to talk freely while keeping the conversation on-target.

One example of the use of depth interviewing is a technique called *laddering*, which is based on means end theory.[5] Depth interviews, with frequent probing, are used to determine linkages between attributes (A), consequences (C), and values (V). Exhibit 5–6 provides an example of a laddering interview with the resulting ladder.[6] When analyzed across respondents, these laddering techniques can provide valuable information for the development of advertising strategy by identifying the linkages between attributes and consequences on the one hand and the values that a person (or group of people) wishes to achieve.

Depth interviews attempt to uncover content and intensity of respondents' feelings and motivations beyond the rationalized overt responses to structured questions. Because tape recordings are usually used, depth interviews take a long time to complete, transcribe, and read, and they must be analyzed by either an experienced practitioner who knows the technique and the product category under study or a psychology specialist. Exhibit 5–7 (see page 126) discusses factors affecting the choice of focus groups versus one-on-one (depth) interviews.

projective techniques *A class of techniques that presume that respondents cannot or will not communicate their feelings and beliefs directly; provides a structured question format in which respondents can respond indirectly by projecting their own feelings and beliefs into the situation while they interpret the behavior of others.*

---

[5]J. Gutman, "A Means End Chain Model Based on Consumer Categorization Process," *Journal of Marketing* 46, no. 2 (1982), pp. 60–72.

[6]T. J. Reynolds and J. Gutman, "Laddering Theory, Method, Analysis and Interpretation," *Journal of Advertising Research*, February/March 1988, p. 16.

PROJECTIVE TECHNIQUES

word association
Projective technique whereby respondents are presented with a list of words, one at a time, and asked to indicate what word comes immediately to mind.

In certain situations it may be beneficial for researchers to obtain information on respondents' feelings and beliefs indirectly. **Projective techniques,** taken from clinical psychology, exemplify this type of survey-interviewing method. Projective techniques presume respondents cannot or will not communicate their feelings and beliefs directly. Instead, respondents are allowed to respond indirectly by projecting their own feelings and/or beliefs into the situation as they interpret the behavior of others. Among the more frequently used projective techniques are

1. **Word association.** We are all probably familiar with word association tests, in which respondents are presented with a list of words, one at a time, and asked to indicate what word comes immediately to mind. The respondent's response and the time it takes to respond are recorded and analyzed according to the frequency with which a response is given, the amount of time elapsed, and the number of respondents unable to respond within the time allowed. Elapsed time is important because a hesitation could indicate that the respondent was searching for a "socially acceptable" response.

sentence completion
Projective technique whereby respondents are asked to complete a number of incomplete sentences with the first word or phrase that comes to mind.

2. **Sentence completion.** Similar to word association, sentence completion tests are based on free association. The respondent is asked to complete a number of incomplete sentences with the first word or phrase that comes to mind. Responses are then analyzed for content.

unfinished scenario story completion
Projective technique whereby respondents complete the end of a story or supply the motive for why one or more actors in a story behaved as they did.

3. **Unfinished scenario story completion.** When the unfinished scenario story completion technique is used respondents are asked to complete the end of a story or supply the motive for why one or more actors in a story behaved as they did.

third person/role playing
Projective technique that presents respondents with a verbal or visual situation and asks them to relate the feelings and beliefs of a third person to the situation, rather than to directly express their own feelings and beliefs about the situation.

4. **Third person/role playing.** The third person and role playing technique presents respondents with a verbal or visual situation in which they are asked to relate the feelings and beliefs of a third person—for example, a friend, a neighbor, or a "typical" person—to the situation, rather than to directly express their own feelings and beliefs about the situation. It is hoped that the respondent will reveal personal feelings and beliefs while describing the reactions of a third party. A popular version of the third person technique presents the respondent with a description of a shopping list and asks for a characterization of the purchaser.[7]

cartoon completion test
Protective technique that presents respondents with a cartoon of a particular situation and asks them to suggest the dialogue that one cartoon character might make in response to the comments of another cartoon character.

5. **Cartoon completion test.** A cartoon completion test presents respondents with a cartoon of a particular situation and asks them to suggest the dialogue that one cartoon character might make in response to the comment(s) of another cartoon character.

Exhibit 5–8 illustrates each of these projective techniques.

Like depth interviews, projective techniques require a highly skilled interviewer, and they must be analyzed and interpreted by experienced professionals. Not surprisingly, the cost per interview is high compared with other types of

---

[7]Maison Haire, "Projective Techniques in Marketing Research," *Journal of Marketing,* April 1950, pp. 649–56.

EXHIBIT 5–8

Examples of
Projective
Techniques

Word association: Subjects are asked to respond to a list of words, read to them one at a time, with the first word that comes to mind. The words of interest (in this case, methods of conducting banking transactions) are dispersed throughout the list to disguise the purpose of the study.

Stimulus Word	*Response*
Mechanic	_____
Bank teller*	_____
Dry cleaner	_____
House	_____
Automatic teller machine*	_____
Automobile	_____
Waiter	_____
Bank by phone*	_____

Sentence completion: Subjects are asked to complete a sentence with the first thought(s) that comes to mind.

a. What I like most about automatic teller machines is _____

_____

b. People that use automatic teller machines are _____

_____

c. Automatic teller machines may be convenient, but they _____

_____

Unfinished scenario technique: Subjects are asked to complete an unfinished scenario with what they think is happening.

Bill had just received a large commission check and because he was out of town was going to deposit it in an automatic teller machine because _____, but his friend told him that he should _____, because _____.

Cartoon completion: Subjects are asked to fill in the response to a character in a cartoon setting.

survey-interviewing methods. As a result, projective techniques usually are not used extensively in commercial marketing research, except for word association, which is frequently used in brand-name studies.

OBSERVATIONAL METHODS

At the broadest level, methods of data collection can be distinguished according to whether they involve asking the respondent to retrospectively report on some behavior or whether they directly or indirectly, by human or mechanical methods, observe the behavior under study. The choice between human or mechanical measurement generally depends on which is easier to use in a given research situation. The advantage of human observation is its ability to provide additional insights into what is being observed. **Observational methods** can be particularly important research tools, especially in situations in which the respondent is either unable or unwilling to report past behavior, or in cross-cultural research, where it is likely that respondents from different cultures may be asked imperfectly translated questions about concepts that may not exist and where the language of the questionnaire may generate systematic bias. In many instances it is the most accurate way to measure overt behavior. However, observational methods cannot be used to measure variables that are directly unobservable, such as thoughts and feelings, and this type of research can be extremely costly.

observational methods
Observation of behavior, directly or indirectly, by human or mechanical methods.

Naturalistic Inquiry

As we discuss in Chapter 7, in a laboratory experiment behaviors are usually taken out of their usual context and placed in controlled settings for observation. For example, in a study of consumer decision making, respondents might be placed in a laboratory environment and exposed to different types of information about a set of competitive brands, and the researcher might measure behavioral and attitudinal responses, for example, intentions to purchase or brand evaluations. The working premise is that responses to the information in the laboratory will reflect how the individual will respond in the marketplace; in other words, these relationships can be taken out of their natural and complex environments, and there is consistency between what is observed in the laboratory and what will take place outside it, in a natural context.

In contrast, methods falling under the umbrella of naturalistic inquiry demand a natural setting because it is believed that the behaviors under study take their meaning as much from the context in which the behavior takes place as they do from the behavior itself. Observations are inevitably time- and context-dependent. It is not possible to understand a behavior out of its relationship to the time and context that spawned, harbored, and supported it.[8]

---

[8]Yvonna S. Lincoln and Egon G. Guba, *Naturalistic Inquiry* (Beverly Hills, Calif.: Sage Publications, 1985).

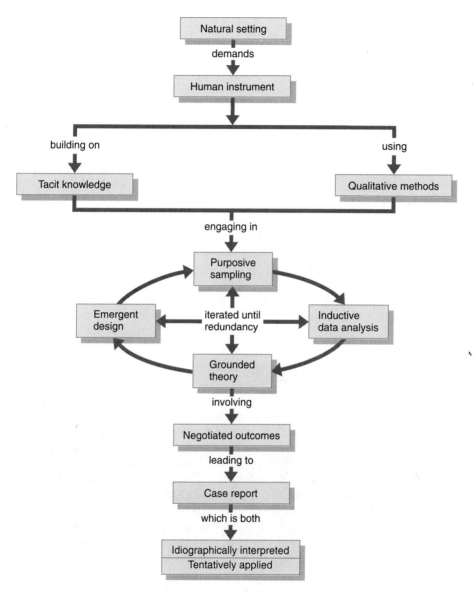

EXHIBIT 5–9

The Flow of
Naturalistic Inquiry

Source: Yvonna S. Lincoln and Egon G. Guba, *Naturalistic Inquiry* (Beverly Hills, Calif.: Sage Publications, 1985), p. 188.

Even though naturalistic studies are almost impossible to design in any definite way prior to conducting the study, they do have a pattern of flow (see Exhibit 5–9) and a number of distinguishing characteristics.[9]

---

[9]Ibid, Chapter 9.

1. *Natural setting.* In naturalistic inquiry, research must be conducted in situ— that is, in a natural setting because behaviors take their meaning as much from their context as they do from themselves.

2. *The human as an instrument.* In naturalistic inquiry, the researcher is the data collection instrument because he or she interprets what is being observed. The researcher cannot, and should not, be separated from the behavior being studied. The researcher is qualified as the instrument of choice for the following reasons: (1) the researcher is responsive, (2) the researcher is adaptable, (3) the researcher is capable of understanding the entire environment, (4) the researcher can process data as soon as it becomes available, (5) the researcher can summarize data and feed it back to the respondent for clarification, and (5) the researcher can handle atypical responses.

3. *Tacit knowledge.* Tacit knowledge allows us to recognize faces, to comprehend metaphors, and to know ourselves. Take, for example, nonverbal cues. Nonverbal cues provide information without the receiver or sender necessarily knowing that he or she is giving off useful information. Actors convey tacitly as much as they do through overt verbal communication. When Dustin Hoffman prepared for his role in the hit movie *Tootsie,* he worked for hours to evoke just the right gestures and movements that would characterize him as a woman, rather than a man.

4. *Qualitative methods.* Naturalistic inquiry emphasizes qualitative research methods because they are more consistent with viewing the researcher as the instrument.

5. *Purposive sampling.* In contrast to conventional research methods, naturalistic inquiry does not seek to select a representative sample so that results can be generalized to the wider population. Naturalistic inquiry typically utilizes maximum variation sampling. The objective of maximum variation sampling is to detail the many specifics that give the context its unique flavor as opposed to focusing on similarities that can be developed into generalizations. If the researcher follows maximum variation sampling, it also means that (1) the sample cannot be drawn in advance, (2) each successive sampling unit must be chosen so as to extend the information already obtained, and (3) the sampling is terminated when no new information is forthcoming from new sampled units.

6. *Inductive data analysis.* Inductive data analysis is defined as the process of making sense of field data. The researcher does not work with any preexisting theory or predetermined set of variables; these are expected to emerge from the field inquiry. Content analysis, which aims at uncovering embedded information and making it explicit, is very similar to inductive data analysis.

7. *Ground theory.* Naturalistic inquiry is consistent with the notion that theory follows from data rather than preceding it. In other words, theory is discovered empirically.

8. *Case report.* The case report is the preferred way of reporting on inquiry. Put simply, a case report is a snapshot of life, or an episode.[10]

Naturalistic inquiry has been used by academic researchers in the study of consumption behaviors.[11] In the commercial arena, a special form of naturalistic inquiry, called **ethnography,** which means the study of cultures, has been used by advertising agencies for some time. For example, Young & Rubicam (Y&R) has used ethnography to peer more deeply into people's lives to create ads that are consistent with reality; it has helped them to come up with new product ideas as well.[12] Y&R has observed in people's homes such things as how parents and kids interact, which brand-name products are in the refrigerator, and how a home is decorated. One of Y&R's ethnography projects dealt with what they labeled the "new traditional woman." They found that new traditional women are not what one might think of as the stereotypic housewife or the stereotypic executive. New traditional women typically have left the work force to care for their families. They view caring for their families as extremely important, yet they will eventually return to the work force. From the World of Research 5–1 (see page 132) describes the use of ethnographic procedures by advertising agencies.

ethnography
The study of cultures.

"Garbology"

Checking the garbage cans of households and recording the goods consumed, as evinced by the discarded cans, bottles, and wrappers, is an indirect and unobtrusive observational research method for the study of product consumption. It is an indirect method because the researcher does not actually observe the consumption taking place, but rather takes the discarded can, bottle, and so forth, as prima facie evidence of the consumption. The same can be said of pantry audits (going through a kitchen and recording what is on the shelves) and the Nielsen TV rating system discussed in Chapter 4, because what is on the shelf may not be actually consumed, and, similarly, there is no guarantee that the program the TV set is tuned to is actually the one that was being watched.

The notion of using samples of garbage as indicators of consumption is not new. It was used by Charles Parlin in the early 1900s to prove to the Campbell Soup Company that, contrary to their assumption, wealthy people who usually had household help did not use canned soup, whereas blue-collar families did.[13]

Garbage analysis begins with the collection of a household's garbage, which is usually done by the local sanitation department at periodic intervals, for example,

---

[10]Ibid.

[11]See, for example, Russell W. Belk, John F. Sherry, and Melanie Wallendorf, "A Naturalistic Inquiry into Buyer and Seller Behavior at a Swap Meet," *Journal of Consumer Research*, March 14, 1988, pp. 449–70.

[12]Ronald Alsop, "People Watchers Seek Clues to Consumers' True Behavior," *The Wall Street Journal*, September 4, 1986.

[13]Kenneth Hollander, "Audacious Audi Ad Echoes Parlin's Iconoclasm," *Marketing News* 11, January 27, 1978.

You Are What You Buy

The scene: the kitchen of Elizabeth Makkay, shopper and mother of three in Putnam Valley, N.Y. For nearly two hours, consumer snoop Allison Cohen has probed the depths of Makkay's shopping psyche—and the contents of her cabinets, refrigerator, and medicine chest. Her mission: to categorize consumers' shopping styles and determine their response to a new line of products called President's Choice. Video camera rolling, she spots a preponderance of store-brand and discounted merchandise. But, oh, what's this? A bag of President's Choice "Decadent" cookies, a jar of President's Choice peanut butter, and a bottle of President's Choice barbecue sauce. Cohen has seen Makkay's type before. "Definitely shopping involved," she declares. "A terrific candidate for 'The Price Is Right'."

Call them the Margaret Meads of Madison Avenue. Cohen is among a new breed of advertising professionals known in the trade as "ethnographers." Adapted from the anthropological practice of recording human culture, ethnography emphasizes observing consumers in their natural habitat—and incorporating those observations into advertising. Ally & Gargano, where Cohen is a senior vice president, used the technique to devise an advertising strategy for Tampax tampons and Swiss chocolates. Grey Advertising used it to see how consumers feel about shortening. One product-development firm has even used ethnographic techniques to correlate customers' buying preferences with levels of self-esteem. Despite its popularity, some advertising professionals view the idea of anthropologic-style snooping with considerable distaste. "Ick," says Andy Berlin, managing director of Goodby, Berlin & Silverstein in San Francisco. "It seems kind of creepy for the people who do ads to go into people's homes and see what's under their sinks. It's commercial spying."

The linkage of anthropology and advertising may strike some people as unsavory. Yet Peter Kim, director of research and consumer behavior for J. Walter Thompson, believes the fields are closely allied. "Brands are much akin to the role of myth in traditional societies," he says. "Choosing a brand becomes a way for one group of consumers to differentiate themselves from another." With that in mind, strategic planners are placing a little less emphasis on quantitative market research and more on such ethereal concepts as how consumers "bond" with corn flakes. Says Barbara Feigin, an executive vice president at Grey Advertising in New York: "You want people to feel that the brand understands them—where they live, not just in their minds, but in their hearts and their guts."

twice a week. The usual procedure for analysis is as follows.[14] Each household's garbage is placed in specially marked plastic bags and then transported to a central facility where sorting takes place. The content of each bag is recorded by experienced sorters by noting the respondent code, the census location of the household, the data, and the names of the sorters. Each bag is weighed and the content is

---

[14]For discussion of the procedures used in garbage analysis see Joseph A. Cote, James McCullough, and Michael Reilly, "Effects of Unexpected Situations on Behavior-Intention Differences: A Garbology Analysis," *Journal of Consumer Research*, September 12, 1985, pp. 188–94; and Melanie Wallendorf and Michael D. Reilly, "Ethnic Migration, Assimilation, and Consumption," *Journal of Consumer Research*, December 10, 1983, pp. 292–302.

examined by removing each item and recording, among other things, (1) the class of product by designated code number; (2) the number of items for that product; (3) the amount of product in the original container or the amount of the product (weight for solids, ounces for liquids, etc.); (4) price of the product appearing on the container; (5) amount of wasted product, if any; (6) brand name of the product; and (7) the product type (e.g., low-fat milk).

To illustrate, suppose a sorter picks up a plastic wrap with a white tag indicating that the wrapper was used for hamburger. The product class would be recorded as one item of beef, and the tag would also be used to obtain information about the weight of the package, the total cost of the product, and perhaps the purchase place of the product. The wrapper would be recorded as being made of plastic and paper, and it would be placed in a plastic bin.[15]

Unobtrusive methods of observation such as garbage analysis are desirable for several reasons. First, response errors are eliminated because respondents are unaware of the analysis. Second, the focus is on actual consumption as opposed to self-reported behavior. The evidence on the relationship between findings from garbage analysis and self-reported data indicate systematic biases. For example, it appears that respondents consistently overestimate the quantity of normatively valued items, such as milk, they consume, and they consistently underestimate the quantity of items with negative normative value, such as alcoholic beverages.[16]

On the negative side, problems with garbage analysis include

1. Distortions caused by recycling, compost piles, and so forth, which leaves no residue of the item consumed.

2. Limitations due to the restriction that items must be consumed in the home.

3. Distortions caused by a nonhousehold member bringing the item into the home.

4. Limitations due to the inability to determine the motivational and cognitive processes underlying the behavior.

Physiological Measurement

Methods that monitor a respondent's nonvoluntary responses to stimuli fall under the umbrella of physiological measurement. These methods involve mechanical devices, and they are typically obtrusive in nature. Two types of physiological measurement techniques that have been used, albeit limited, in studies of shopping behavior and reactions to advertising are briefly described below.

Pupilometer. A pupilometer attaches to a person's head and measures interest and attention by the amount of dilation in the pupil of the eye.

Galvanometer. A galvanometer measures excitement levels by using the electrical activity level in the person's skin.

---

[15]Cote, McCullough, and Reilly, "Effects of Unexpected Situations," p. 189.

[16]William L. Rathje, "Archeological Ethnography," in *Explorations in Ethnoarcheology*, ed. R. A. Gould (Albuquerque: University of New Mexico Press, 1978), pp. 49–76.

There are two difficulties with using physiological measures, and these relate to their obvious unnatural and obtrusive nature and the fact that such measurements lack a clear affective (i.e., like/dislike) component. For example, if a person's pupils dilate or if the electrical activity level in his or her skin increases, what can we conclude about the person's reaction—was it favorable or unfavorable?

Computerized/Electronic Measurement

Some variants of observational research involve computerized or electronic measurement of behaviors. The following describes several of the methods.

Scanners. Optical scanning via Universal Product Codes (UPC) is another form of mechanical observation measurement. Scanner services that permit extensive data on product category, brand, store type, price, quantity, and customer to be automatically recorded have been discussed in some detail in Chapter 4.

Eye Tracking. Eye movement research has been used in marketing research for many years. Technological advances in fiber optics, digital processing, and advanced electronics, however, have moved the field away from the old days of "eye cameras" and heavy equipment with bite bars and forehead restraints. Today, lightweight equipment is used, and, typically, a minicomputer paces the stimulus material for the respondent and records and displays eye movement automatically through a dual disk-drive system. Exhibit 5–10 provides details on the procedure used by Perception Research Services.

Eye-tracking measurement is used in advertising and package research. As indicated in Table 5–3, eye-tracking methods have considerable advantages over

EXHIBIT 5–10
—
Description of
Eye Tracking

The Procedure

The individual views a screen onto which 35mm slides (depicting store scenes, actual ads, etc.) are projected.

Each person is provided a remote control switch. The switch permits him or her to control viewing time.

The Perception Research Services, Inc. (PRS) eye tracker records each participant's visual experience. The tracker simultaneously pinpoints where the respondent is looking and superimposes that point directly onto the material being viewed. PRS is able to determine not only where the respondent looks, but how long he or she stays on a particular point.

Eye-tracking information is recorded directly onto computer tape for data processing. This allows for a continuous record of the visual response as it takes place. PRS has the capability of recording 60 eye movements per second. (It can also be placed on videotape for client viewing.)

For analytical purposes, a software program depicts the test item in terms of individual components. These components can be modified at any time for additional analysis. For shelf display work, each package on a shelf may become a component. For ad testing, headline, subhead, main illustration, subillustration, logo, product shot, and individual copy lines can be differentiated.

The movement of the eye is charted from the time the test item is first viewed until the time the viewing is terminated. Accordingly, there is a record of the viewing sequence, the time given to each item, copy readership, and most importantly, those areas that are quickly bypassed or totally overlooked. Eye tracking shows stopping power.

Source: Perception Research Services, Inc. Reprinted with permission.

T-Scope	Eye Tracking	
Sensitivity subject to selected exposure duration	No requirement to select exposure duration	TABLE 5–3
Discrete measurement	Continuous measurement	Advantages of Eye-Tracking Technology
Highly sensitive to lighting conditions	Stable across greater range of lighting conditions	
No ability to determine scan path	Ability to determine scan path	

Source: Lynn Lin and Y. S. Parkalleskog, "A State-of-the-Art Eye Movement Research Burke Diagnostic Package Test and Print Ad Test," paper presented at the ESOMAR Congress, Copenhagen, October 17–19, 1984.

early electronic measurement devices, such as the tachistoscope (T-scope), which varied the amount of time (e.g., $1/10$ of a second, $3/10$ of a second) a visual image was exposed to the subject, thereby attempting to simulate split-second duration of a consumer's attention in much the same way that a package might be part of a mass display.

Exhibit 5–11 depicts a classic example of how eye tracking has been used.

Response Latency.   Response latency measures the time interval between the asking of a question and the response to that question. The amount of deliberation spent answering a question is considered as an indication of the confidence or certainty of the answer.[17] The most common method of measuring response latency is to use the internal clock of a personal computer. The computer displays one question at a time and measures the lapse in time between the question being displayed and the respondent's response.

Response latencies are most useful when people are asked to choose between two options. For example, consider the following question:

Please check which brand of coffee you prefer.
Folgers _____   Yuban _____

From your answer, we can tell which brand of coffee you prefer, but we cannot tell by how much. Here, response latency would help to determine how much you preferred one of the brands over the other. The longer it takes you to respond, the more similar are the options. If immediately after being presented with this choice you checked Folgers, we would conclude that you strongly prefer Folgers to Yuban because you required almost no deliberation time. On the other hand, if after being presented with this choice, you spend a considerable amount of time deliberating, we would conclude that the two brands are similar and that you do not strongly prefer one brand over the other.

An advantage of response latency is that it is unobtrusive; that is, the respondent does not know that the measure is being recorded. In addition, it is relatively easy and inexpensive to implement, assuming of course that the necessary equipment (e.g., personal computer) is available.

---

[17]James MacLachlan, *Response Latency: New Measure of Advertising* (New York: Advertising Research Foundation, 1977).

EXHIBIT 5–11   Example of the Use of Eye-Tracking Technology

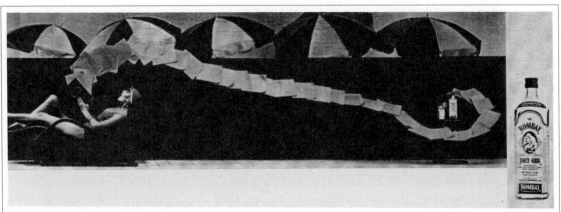

The original *Bombay* ad looked like this.

However, when pretested, the eye tracking showed that readership of the copy below the visual was virtually nonexistent, and the Bombay bottle on the far right was being ignored by 9 out of every 10 readers. As you might imagine, this translated to recall levels that could only be classified as disappointing.

When followed up with verbal questioning to uncover gin drinkers' attitudes toward the advertising and their perception of the product, we found the ad was confusing; it failed to convey an upscale image for Bombay and for the types of drinkers who were likely to buy Bombay. Most important, it required a copy link between the visual and the message because many readers failed to understand the relevance of the artwork.

Based on the pretest findings, the agency (TBWA) instituted a number of major, though subtle, revisions. You'll note that the size of the Bombay bottle on the far right has been increased. But, most important, the line "Nothing attracts like the imported taste of Bombay Gin," provides the explanation for the visual and the imported heritage of the product, which justifies premium pricing and positions Bombay as a quality gin.

NOTHING ATTRACTS LIKE THE IMPORTED TASTE OF BOMBAY GIN.

This revised execution was attention-getting, memorable, meaningful, and motivating. In fact, the unaided recall level for this ad was almost 100 percent higher than the level for the original execution.

Source: Perception Research Services, Inc. Reprinted with permission; photos courtesy of Carillon Importers.

SUMMARY

In this chapter we described what is meant by qualitative research. We saw that qualitative research generally possesses one or more of the following features: (1) small sample sizes, (2) unstructured question formats, (3) indirect measurement of respondents' feelings and beliefs, and (4) direct observation. Attention was then directed toward one of the most popular qualitative research techniques, namely, focus groups, and its companion, depth interviews. In the course of the discussion we described the major uses of focus groups and depth interviews and addressed various implementation issues. Next, the discussion turned to the primary techniques that involve the direct or indirect observation of behavior. In this section we discussed various human and mechanical ways of observing the relevant behavior under investigation. Finally, the last major section of this chapter discussed and illustrated a variety of projective techniques, all of which are based on the assumption that respondents cannot or will not communicate their feelings and beliefs directly, and, consequently, these techniques provide a format that allows respondents to project their own feelings and beliefs into the situation while they interpret the behavior of others.

KEY CONCEPTS

unstructured/structured interview

qualitative research

quantitative research

focus group interview

discussion guide

depth interviews

projective techniques

word association

sentence completion

unfinished scenario story completion

third person/role playing

cartoon completion test

observational methods

ethnography

physiological measurement

REVIEW QUESTIONS

1. Discuss the primary observational methods of interviewing. What are the advantages of using them, if any, compared with using quantitative research methods?

2. What are the factors that affect the number of focus groups that should be conducted?

3. Under what circumstances would you suggest that a depth interview be conducted rather than a focus group?

4. What role does the moderator play in focus group interviews? Can the moderator adversely affect the quality of the data?

5. Describe the distinguishing features of naturalistic inquiry studies.

6. Describe and illustrate the major types of projective interviewing techniques.

Survey-Interviewing Methods

— Describe the different types of survey-interviewing methods.

— Understand the distinctive nature of mail, telephone, personal in-home, and mall-intercept interviews.

— Describe how new and more sophisticated computer technology is being used in survey research.

— Discuss the problems and methods for handling nonresponse bias.

INTRODUCTION

In this chapter we continue our treatment of primary research and discuss the major types of survey-interviewing methods. We use the term *survey* to describe methods of gathering information from a number of individuals (the respondents, who collectively form the sample) in order to learn something about a larger target population from which the sample of respondents has been drawn. In contrast to the observational and qualitative methods of primary research discussed in Chapter 5, the survey-interviewing methods that are discussed in this chapter generally involve structured, paper-and-pencil measurement; a larger number of respondents; and inference (i.e., projections) to the larger target population.

Because faulty data collection procedures are probably the largest source of bias within the marketing research process, another related issue is addressed in this chapter, that is, problems due to low response rates. Low response rates, caused by factors such as not-at-homes and refusals, present the potential for nonresponse error, which is a particularly nagging problem in survey research. In the course of our discussion we explain the factors that contribute to low response rates and possible ways of handling this problem.

INFORMATION COLLECTED

The information collected in surveys will depend on the objectives of the research study. Concept tests, for instance, collect information on purchase intentions, likes/dislikes, and attribute ratings. This type of study attempts to

EXHIBIT 6–1

Types of Information
Collected in Surveys

Respondent Background Characteristics

- — Demographic variables.
- — Socioeconomic variables.
- — Ownership.
- — Media habits.

Personality Traits

- — Innovativeness.
- — Dogmatism.
- — Risk taking.
- — Inner-other directedness.

Attitude and Lifestyle Factors

- — Attitude measures.
- — Activities, interests, and opinions.

Product-Related Variables

- — Usage data.
- — Determinants of brand choice.
- — Situational factors.
- — Intentions.

---

strategies and provide direction for development of the product and product advertising. Tracking studies, on the other hand, collect information on measures such as awareness, trial, purchase, usage levels, and customer demographics because this type of study focuses specifically on the firm's product and customer markets and the competitive arena, in general. Exhibit 6–1 provides a brief description of the types of information collected in marketing research studies. Four broad categories of variables are listed: respondent background characteristics, personality traits, attitude and lifestyle factors, and product-related variables.

TYPES OF SURVEYS

Surveys can be classified in many different ways. We can classify them by the size and type of sample; for example, surveys can be conducted on a local, state, or national basis and may attempt to collect informative data from a few hundred or thousands of people. Surveys can also be classified on a temporal basis; for example, surveys can be distinguished according to whether a *cross-sectional* or *longitudinal* approach is adopted. **Cross-sectional surveys** collect data from a number of different respondents at a single point in time. The cross-sectional study typically examines the relationships among a set of relevant marketing-related variables across different cross sections of respondents. Market segmentation studies that attempt to identify subgroups of respondents who will respond to a given marketing-mix offering in a similar manner are examples. **Longitudinal surveys,** on the other hand, question the same or similar respondents at different points in

cross-sectional surveys
Collection of informative data from a number of different respondents at a single point in time.

longitudinal surveys
Questioning of the same or similar respondents at different points in time.

EXHIBIT 6–2
—
Survey Research
Techniques

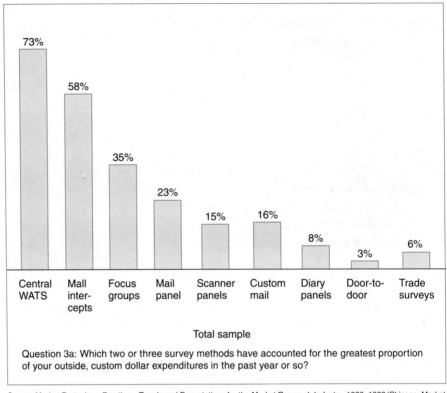

Total sample

Question 3a: Which two or three survey methods have accounted for the greatest proportion of your outside, custom dollar expenditures in the past year or so?

Source: Market Facts, Inc., *Practices, Trends and Expectations for the Market Research Industry, 1988–1989* (Chicago: Market Facts, Inc., October 1988), pp. 88–89.

time, examining the changes that occur with the passage of time. Tracking studies that provide information on changes in the marketplace and consumer diary panels that provide weekly information on purchases, usage, and media viewing for a group of respondents exemplify this type of survey. Alternatively, surveys also can be classified according to the interviewing method that is employed.

MAJOR DATA-COLLECTION METHODS

Researchers' choices of survey techniques can change over the years. A survey asking 140 corporate marketing research directors to name the two or three data-collection methods used most often in a past year indicates that the two most popular data-collection methods were central WATS (Wide Area Telephone Service, i.e., telephone surveys) and mall-intercept surveys.[1] Exhibit 6–2 shows the complete results. Compared with the results of a similar survey taken in 1987, the

---

[1]Market Facts, Inc., *Practice Trends and Expenditures for the Market Research Industry* (Chicago: Market Facts, Inc., April 1987).

1991 survey found an increase in the use of mail panels, direct ("cold") mail, focus groups, and central telephone (WATS) surveys; it found decreases in the use of purchase diaries and in-home interview surveys.

In this section we discuss direct, also called *cold*, mail surveys, mail panels, telephone surveys, personal in-home (or door-to-door) surveys, and mall-intercept interviewing. The newer technological approaches for interviewing will be deferred until the next section. Each of the alternative data collection methods will be compared with respect to the criteria described at the end of the chapter.

1. *Complexity and versatility.* Refers to the extent to which the format of the data collection must be simple and straightforward and to the extent to which the data-collection method can handle different question formats and scenarios, respectively.

2. *Quantity of data.* Refers to the amount of information that can be safely collected with the use of a particular type of data-collection technique.

3. *Sample control.* Refers to the ease or difficulty of ensuring that an element of the target population can be identified and further that he or she will be the one who responds to the data-collection instrument.

4. *Quality of data.* Refers to the accuracy of the data collected using a particular data-collection method.

5. *Response rate.* Refers to the percentage of the total number of respondents contacted who cooperate and complete the questionnaire.

6. *Speed.* Refers to the total time it takes to complete the study by using a particular data-collection method.

7. *Cost.* Refers to the total expenditure required to collect the necessary data by using a particular data-collection method.

8. *Uses.* Refers to the primary types of studies that rely on a particular data-collection method.

Mail Surveys

Mail surveys involve sending out a fairly structured questionnaire to a sample of respondents. Surveys are typically mailed directly to the respondent, and the completed questionnaire is returned by mail to the firm conducting the study. Alternatively, the survey can be dropped off to the respondent and arrangements can also be made for the completed questionnaire to be picked up.[2] Mail surveys can also be attached to products, as is standard practice with warranty cards, or distributed as inserts in magazines and newspapers.[3] Exhibit 6–3 (see page 142) presents an example of a survey using a warranty card.

mail surveys
Data-collection method that involves sending out a fairly structured questionnaire to a sample of respondents.

---

[2]See C. H. Lovelock, R. Stiff, D. Cullwick, and I. M. Kaufman, "An Evaluation of the Effectiveness of Drop-Off Questionnaire Delivery," *Journal of Marketing Research*, November 1976, pp. 358–64.

[3]J. K. Klompmaker, J. D. Lindley, and R. L. Page, "Using Free Papers for Customer Surveys," *Journal of Marketing*, July 1977, pp. 80–82.

EXHIBIT 6–3

Example of Warranty
Card Questionnaire

BLACK&DECKER ®

Product Registration Card

Thank you for purchasing this Black & Decker product. Please register your name and address right away to help us contact you in the unlikely event of a product recall. This information will also help us design new products and better understand our customers.

Return this card for a chance to <u>win</u> the Black & Decker small appliance of your choice!

A quarterly drawing will be held from the Product Registration Cards received during the preceding 3 months. We will send the winner a Black & Decker small appliance of their choice. In order to participate, simply complete and return this registration card at once. Offer void in Canada and other countries where restricted or prohibited by law. The odds of winning depend upon the number of participants.

❶ 1. ☐ Mr.   2. ☐ Mrs.   3. ☐ Ms.   4. ☐ Miss   83D01-01

First Name   **Initial**   **Last Name**

Street   **Apt. No.**

City   **State**   **ZIP**

❷ Home Telephone:
(Area code)

❸ Date of Purchase
Month   Day   Year

❹ Now that you have purchased this Black & Decker product, how has your opinion of Black & Decker changed?
1. Much more positive than before
2. Somewhat more positive than before
3. About the same as before
4. Somewhat more negative than before
5. Much more negative than before

❺ Do you or anyone else in your household own or plan to purchase any of the following in the next 6 months?

		Own	Plan to Buy
1.	Toaster Oven	1.	
2.	Food Processor	2.	
3.	Electric Can Opener	3.	
4.	Popcorn Popper	4.	
5.	Coffee Grinder	5.	
6.	Electric Juicer	6.	
7.	Slow Cooker	7.	
8.	Electric Food Steamer	8.	
9.	Electric Wok	9.	
10.	Microwave Oven	10.	
11.	Drip Coffeemaker	11.	
12.	Blender	12.	
13.	Appliance Mounted Under-The-Cabinet	13.	
14.	Mixer	14.	
15.	Food Chopper	15.	
16.	Sandwich Grill	16.	
17.	Crepe Maker	17.	
18.	Pasta Maker	18.	
19.	Espresso Maker	19.	
20.	Cordless Hand Held Vac	20.	
21.	Corded Hand Held Vac	21.	
22.	Auto-Off Iron	22.	
23.	Smoke Alarm	23.	
24.	Rechargeable Light	24.	

❻ Date of birth of person whose name appears above: 1 9
Month   Year

❼ <u>Excluding yourself</u>, what is the SEX and AGE (in years) of children and other adults living in your household?
1. No one else in household

Male	Female	Age		Male	Female	Age
1.	2.	years		1.	2.	years
1.	2.	years		1.	2.	years

❽ Marital status:
1. Married   3. Widowed
2. Divorced/Separated   4. Never Married (Single)

❾ Occupation:

	You	Spouse
Homemaker	1.	
Professional/Technical	2.	
Upper Management/Executive	3.	
Middle Management	4.	
Sales/Marketing	5.	
Clerical or Service Worker	6.	
Tradesman/Machine Oper./Laborer	7.	
Retired	8.	
Student	9.	
Self Employed/Business Owner	10.	

❿ Which group describes your annual family income?
1. Under $15,000   7. $40,000-$44,999
2. $15,000-$19,999   8. $45,000-$49,999
3. $20,000-$24,999   9. $50,000-$59,999
4. $25,000-$29,999   10. $60,000-$74,999
5. $30,000-$34,999   11. $75,000-$99,999
6. $35,000-$39,999   12. $100,000 & over

⓫ Education: (Please check those which apply) You   Spouse

	You	Spouse
Some High School or less	1.	
Completed High School	2.	
Vocational/Technical School	3.	
Some College	4.	
Completed College	5.	
Some Graduate School	6.	
Completed Graduate School	7.	

⓬ Which credit cards do you use regularly?
1. American Express, Diners Club
2. MasterCard, Visa, Discover
3. Department Store, Oil Company, etc.
4. Do not use credit cards.

⓭ For your primary residence, do you:
1. Own a House?
2. Own a Townhouse or Condominium?
3. Rent a House?
4. Rent an Apartment, Townhouse or Condominium?

Direct "cold" mail surveys involve mailing questionnaires to a group of individuals who have not agreed in advance to participate in the study.

Complexity and Versatility.   Because mail surveys must be self-administered, they must be simple and straightforward, and the questions must be presented in fixed order. Each question must be carefully constructed because no interviewer is present to clarify a question that the respondent doesn't understand; there is no opportunity for following up on incomplete or unclear responses or for additional probing. Finally, mail surveys are less versatile than personal interviews because they do not employ certain visual cues. For example, full-scale product prototypes cannot be used, even though it is possible to include drawings and photographs in a mailing.

Quantity of Data.   A key factor determining the quantity of data that can be collected via direct mail is the length of the questionnaire. Personal interviews can be longer than either mail or telephone interviews, and mail interviews can be longer than telephone interviews. Short questionnaires have not necessarily been shown to generate higher response rates than longer questionnaires.[4]

Sample Control.   Controlling who is in the sample with a cold mail survey can be difficult. Mail surveys require an explicit list of individuals or households that are eligible for inclusion in the sample. This list, called the **sampling frame,** must contain addresses, if not names and addresses, for the entire eligible population. In many instances, however, mailing lists are unavailable or, if available, are incomplete or dated. For example, Survey Sampling, Inc., estimates that in their national database of U.S. households, which consists of 74 million names and addresses, 12 to 15 percent of the names listed will have changed due to normal population mobility. In addition, 5 to 10 percent of their records nationwide are rural, with addresses consisting of only two lines and these sometimes are treated as undeliverable by local post offices.[5] Moreover, even if a complete and accurate mailing list is available, researchers have little control over who fills out the questionnaire and whether it will be returned. Catalogs of mailing lists are available, containing thousands of lists that can be purchased.[6] (See Chapter 8 for further discussion of sampling practices.)

On the positive side, mail surveys can reach geographically dispersed respondents and hard-to-reach areas (e.g., inner-city areas). In fact, the recent increase in use of mail surveys is probably due to the belief that hard-to-reach people will respond when they can do so at their own convenience.

direct "cold" mail surveys
Surveys in which questionnaires are sent to a "cold" group of individuals who have not previously agreed to participate in the study.

sampling frame
An explicit list of individuals or households that are eligible for inclusion in the sample.

---

[1]See L. Kanuk and C. Berenson, "Mail Survey and Response Rates: A Literature Review," *Journal of Marketing Research,* November 1975, pp. 440–53; Julie Yu and Harris Cooper, "Quantitative Review of Research Design Effects on Response Rates to Questionnaires," *Journal of Marketing Research,* February 1983, pp. 36–44.

[5]*Fact Sheets* (New York: Survey Sampling, Inc., 1988).

[6]For example, see 1993–94 *Directory of Mailing List Companies* (New York: Todd Publications, 1993).

Quality of Data   On the positive side, the absence of an interviewer eliminates interviewer bias caused by altered questions, appearance or speech, projection of cues to respondents, probing tactics, or cheating, that is, an interviewer's falsifying all or part of an interview. Also, because a mail survey does not involve any social interaction between an interviewer and a respondent, evidence suggests that for sensitive or embarrassing questions (for example, questions about drinking habits, sexual behavior, bank loans, etc.) mail surveys yield better-quality data than either personal or telephone interviews.[7] Finally because the instrument is self-administered, the respondent can work through the questions at his or her own pace.

On the negative side, however, the respondent cannot seek clarification without an interviewer, and the quality of data may be suspect due to inaccuracies caused by confusing questions. In the case of mail surveys the respondent is free to read through the entire questionnaire before answering the questions, and—as a result of a response to a question appearing near the end of the questionnaire—he or she can change a response made to an earlier question. Finally, because of the lack of control over who is included in the sample, respondents who return the completed questionnaires are often not representative of the total sample. For example, in a mail survey about a new product, respondents who return the questionnaire may be more likely to have had either an extremely favorable or a highly unfavorable reaction to the new product.

Response Rates.   Low response rates are among the most serious problems plaguing mail surveys. **Response rates** refer to the percentage of the total number of respondents sent questionnaires who complete and return the questionnaire:

response rates
The total number of respondents sent questionnaires who complete and return them, expressed as a percentage.

$$\text{Response rate} = \frac{\text{Number of completed questionnaires}}{\text{Number of eligible respondents}}$$

where the number of eligible respondents is equal to the number of questionnaires sent *minus* the number returned because of improper addresses, deaths, and so on. Because the response rate in mail surveys can be related to the respondent's interest in the survey topic, nonresponse bias can be a serious problem. For a mail survey sent to a cold list of randomly selected respondents, without any pre- or postmailing follow-up, typically no more than 10 to 20 percent of the questionnaires can be expected to be returned. If multiple premailings and postmailings are made, it is possible to generate response rates of 80 percent, possibly more. We will discuss methods for improving response rates in a later section of this chapter.

Speed.   It usually takes several weeks for completed questionnaires to be returned. The elapsed time for completing a mail survey will be even longer if follow-up mailings are required. Each follow-up mailing may require two or more weeks to determine whether an acceptable response rate has been achieved, so that a large

---

[7]B. Dunning and D. Calahan, "Mail versus Field Self-Administered Questionnaires: An Armed Forces Survey," *Public Opinion Quarterly*, Spring 1972, pp. 105–8.

mail survey may take several months to complete. Unfortunately, the marketing researcher has very little control over the time it takes for the completion and return of questionnaires.

Cost.   The relatively inexpensive cost of mail surveys is one of their most attractive features. For mail surveys, the data-collection cost, excluding analysis and report generation, can be as low s $2.50 per completed interview. However, if the response rates are low, the actual cost, including follow-up mailings, can be more expensive than other methods.

Uses.   Direct mail surveys are most often used in executive, industrial, or medical studies; readership studies are often conducted by using cold mailings. The selected respondents typically share a high interest in the survey topic, and the sample is small and geographically dispersed. On the other hand, unless up-to-date and complete mailing lists are available, the cold mail survey is rarely used in attitude and usage studies of consumer products and services because of the potential of low response rates.

Mail Panels

A mail panel consists of large and nationally representative samples of households that have agreed to periodically participate in mail questionnaires, product tests, and telephone surveys.[8] Thus, mail panels represent an important resource that offers marketing executives a pool of respondents who are ready to participate in research projects and ready to answer questions whenever they are asked to do so. Households that agree to participate in the mail panel are often compensated for their time and effort. Various forms of incentives are used.

   Mail panels are maintained by commercial marketing research suppliers. There are three major players in the mail panel market: National Family Opinion (NFO), Market Fact's Consumer Mail Panel (CMP), and Home Testing Institute (HTI).

Complexity and Versatility.   Like cold mail surveys, questionnaires sent to mail panel members need to be fairly simple and straightforward. Because the questionnaire is self-administered, the limitations associated with cold mail surveys also apply to mail panels. However, mail panel members tend to have greater expertise in filling out questionnaires, and this sometimes allows more complex skip patterns to be used.

Quantity of Data.   Compared with cold mail surveys, mail panels generally increase the quantity of data that can be collected. First, neither time nor effort is lost in qualifying or interviewing respondents, and the questionnaires are self-administered. Second, most panel members are available by phone for either more in-depth information or a more immediate response.

---

[8]This material follows the presentation found in *Why Consumer Mail Panels Is the Superior Option* (Chicago: Market Facts, Inc., 1986).

Sample Control. As Exhibit 6–4 reveals, recent changes in the demographic makeup of American households reflect a skew toward smaller families and more households with women employed outside the home. Mail panels afford much greater control over the characteristics of the sample. First, they can efficiently provide samples that have greater geographic dispersion than can alternative data-collection methods. Second, mail panels also offer samples that are matched to U.S. Census Bureau statistics on key demographic criteria. Basic demographics usually include geographical region, population density, household income, age of panel members, and household size. Third, specific user groups within a panel can be identified, and surveys can be targeted to households that have specific characteristics. Fourth, specific members of any panel household can be questioned. Finally, hard-to-reach and low-incidence groups can be surveyed. In order to provide this sort of control, mail panels are large; for example, the NFO panel has 400,000 households providing market researchers with cost-effective access to approximately 1 in every 226 American households.

On the negative side, however, are the issues of representativeness and response bias. The issue of representativeness involves the extent to which a panel can legitimately be considered representative of the overall population. Individuals who agree to serve on a panel are special because not everyone is willing to serve on a panel; in fact, only about 10 percent of those households approached agree to join. Moreover, cooperativeness may be unrelated to demographic variables, which means that it cannot be compensated for by matching the entire panel, or some portion of it, to census statistics.

EXHIBIT 6–4
—
Changing Times

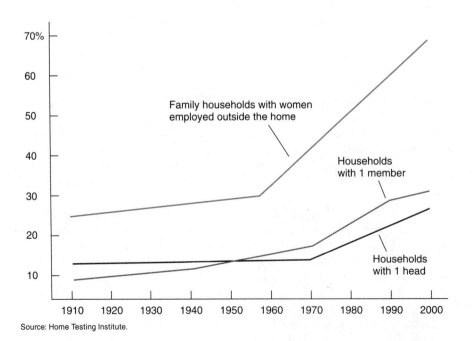

Source: Home Testing Institute.

Response bias involves the extent to which those panel members who respond to the mailing can be considered representative of the general population or, for that matter, of the entire panel of households. Again, interest in the survey topic and extreme reactions can motivate a respondent to complete and mail back a questionnaire. There is little control over which household member actually fills out the questionnaire, although, compared with cold mailings, mail panels make it easier to question specific members of any panel household. Finally, potential problems are caused by the natural tendency for panels to age (*maturation*) and by *conditioning/testing* effects that sensitize panel members over time to those products or services that have been the topic of the survey. Both maturation and conditioning effects can be reduced by "rolling out" panel members, that is, by systematically adding new panel members.

Quality of Data.   Mail panels can enhance the quality of the data collected. First, because respondents have more time to answer than with telephone or in-home personal interviewing, they can be thorough and thoughtful when they complete lengthy questionnaires. Second, aware of the confidentiality that mail panels provide, respondents can be more candid. Third, there is less risk of interviewer bias. Finally, consumer mail panels provide the prime tool for eliciting consumer answers in sensitive and/or personal areas where respondents would be reticent to answer interviewers.

Response Rates.   Because of assured respondent cooperation, response rates in mail panels are typically in the 70 to 80 percent range.

Speed.   As with cold mail surveys, it generally takes several weeks for complete questionnaires to come in. Because little follow-up action is usually required, the data-collection process is completed much faster than with cold mail surveys.

Cost.   Mail panels offer the lowest cost per respondent of any research medium. Access to a mail panel is often sold on a shared-cost basis. In a shared-cost mailing a limited number of firms have access to a proportion of the general panel sample for a specific dollar cost. As the name implies, each participating firm shares in the cost of the mailing. Restrictions are placed on the minimum number of mailings and the amount of information that can be obtained. For example, with the CMP service the minimum number of mailings is 1,000, with increments of 1,000, and the information is limited to a single two-sided card called a *Data Gage*. Exhibit 6–5 (see page 148) illustrates a Data Gage card. In a customized mailing, all aspects of the mailing have been tailored to the specific needs of a single firm. Essentially, for the right price, these mail panel services will allow almost any type of customized research project to be undertaken. In addition, mail panel firms also promote special subgroups of the total panel sample—for example, a baby panel or a student panel—and offer certain syndicated products such as beverage consumer mail panels. Because of economies of scale, monthly shared-cost computer card mailings can be as little as 30 cents per household. Mail panels are also cost-efficient because detailed demographic information on every household is already on file, and

EXHIBIT 6–5   Data Gage

ANSWER THIS SIDE FIRST   Job No. 1346

Please answer the following questions on this side and the other side of this card.

1. How frequently, if at all, do you purchase the following snack items? ("X" ONE FOR EACH ITEM)

	Once a Month or More	Every 2–3 Months	Less Often	Never
	1	2	3	4
Regular potato chips	[ ]	[ ]	[ ]	[ ] (9)
Flavored potato chips (Bar B-Q, Sour cream & onion, etc.)	[ ]	[ ]	[ ]	[ ]
Processed Potato Chips (Pringles, Munchos, etc.)	[ ]	[ ]	[ ]	[ ]
"Home style" Potato chips	[ ]	[ ]	[ ]	[ ]
	1	2	3	4
Cheese Puffs (Cheeto's etc.)	[ ]	[ ]	[ ]	[ ](13)
Corn chips (Frito's etc.)	[ ]	[ ]	[ ]	[ ]
Tortilla chips (Doritos, etc.)	[ ]	[ ]	[ ]	[ ]
Pretzels	[ ]	[ ]	[ ]	[ ]
Peanuts/other nuts	[ ]	[ ]	[ ]	[ ]
Flavored Crackers (Not Saltines	[ ]	[ ]	[ ]	[ ](18)
	1	2	3	4
Dips (Canned or refrigerated)	[ ]	[ ]	[ ]	[ ](19)
Dried fruit snacks (Fruit Roll-Ups, Fun Fruits, etc.)	[ ]	[ ]	[ ]	[ ]
Sweet baked goods (Hostess Snack Cakes, Twinkies, Dunkin Sticks, etc.)	[ ]	[ ]	[ ]	[ ]
Frozen potato products (French fries, Tator Tots, etc.)	[ ]	[ ]	[ ]	[ ]
Frozen dessert snacks (Pudding Pops, Eskimo Pies, Dole Fruit Bars, etc.)	[ ]	[ ]	[ ]	[ ](23)

ANSWER OTHER SIDE FIRST   Job No. 1346

2a. Within the past year, to which, if any, of the following charities have you contributed money? (RECORD UNDER 2a)
2b. To which of the following have you volunteered your time? (RECORD UNDER 2b)

	2a. Contributed Money	2b. Volunteered Your Time
American Cancer Society	[ ]1	[ ]1
American Heart Association	[ ]2	[ ]2
American Lung Association	[ ]3	[ ]3
Arthritis Foundation	[ ]4	[ ]4
Easter Seals	[ ]5	[ ]5
March of Dimes	[ ]6	[ ]6
Multiple Sclerosis (MS) Society	[ ]7	[ ]7
Muscular Dystrophy Assn. (MDA)	[ ]8	[ ]8
National Kidney Foundation	[ ]9	[ ]9
United Way	[ ]0	[ ]0
Other	[ ]-0	[ ]-0
None	[ ]-X	[ ]-X
	(24-25)	(26-27)

3. Do you own

	Yes	No
A programmable calculator?	[ ]1	[ ]2 (28)
A calculator with a tape print out?	[ ]1	[ ]2 (29)

4. Are you, or is someone in your household, a member of the American Automobile Association (AAA)?
   Yes   [ ]1   No   [ ]2   (30)

5. Does anyone in your household normally pack a lunch to school or work?
   School [ ]1   Work [ ]2   Neither [ ]3 (31)

6a. Which of the stores listed below have you heard of?

6b. Which, if any, have you visited within the past year?

	Heard of?		Visited in past year?		
Stores	Yes	No	Yes	No	
Pier 1 Imports	[ ]1	[ ]2	[ ]1	[ ]2	(32-33)
Color Tile	[ ]1	[ ]2	[ ]1	[ ]2	(34-35)
Eckerd Drugs	[ ]1	[ ]2	[ ]1	[ ]2	(36-37)
					(38-78 Open)
					79 [0][1] 80

Source: Market Facts, Inc., used with permission.

consequently no interviewing expenditures are necessary. The availability of demographic data permits identification of specific targets at a reasonable cost.

Uses.   Mail panels provide a vehicle for collecting meaningful data in virtually all areas of marketing research. Panels provide a very effective way to handle in-home product testing because specific user groups can be identified and targeted to receive the product, and, ultimately, they will use it in a normal home environment. Another important application is the ability to survey low-incidence groups in a cost-efficient manner by using the entire panel to identify users of a low-incidence product and then following up with a mail or telephone survey. This two-step procedure can greatly reduce the cost of surveying low-incidence groups. Also, the entire panel can be used to target special panels of households. For example, NFO provides "special panels" such as the Baby Panel—households with new babies and expectant mothers, the 50 Plus Panel—households with members 50 years of age or older, etc.

Mail panels also have been used very successfully and innovatively to gather national and/or regional information. For example, panel members have been used as a national consumer field force to audit and report on a variety of products and services. Among other things, panel members have been asked to visit department stores and request catalogs, to visit fast food restaurants and record prices, and to buy products and report satisfaction.

Telephone Surveys

Telephone surveys involve phoning a sample of respondents drawn from an eligible population and asking them a series of questions. The use and percentage of dollar budgets allocated to WATS telephone interviewing continues to increase, and it is still the most frequently used data-collection method.

telephone surveys
Surveys that involve phoning a sample of respondents drawn from an eligible population and asking them a series of questions.

Complexity and Versatility. Because an interviewer is involved with the questioning, telephone surveys can include complex questionnaires with features such as skip patterns, probes, refer-backs, and various termination points that are not possible in mail surveys. However, telephone surveys do not offer the degree of complexity found in personal interviews, nor are they as versatile. Complex or lengthy scales or unstructured questions are difficult to administer via telephone. Consider a question that asks a respondent to allocate 100 points among several brands according to his or her likelihood of purchase. Also, the respondent may tire very quickly if repeatedly exposed to similar scales on the telephone instead of in person. Finally, it is impossible to show a respondent anything during a telephone interview. Thus, it is impractical to conduct advertising copy testing or package tests, for example, via telephone. In certain instances this can be overcome by mailing the respondent a visual cue before conducting the telephone interview. Nevertheless, inability to use visual cues remains an inherent problem with telephone surveys.

Quantity of Data. Telephone interviews typically last about 15 to 30 minutes, although interviews of up to one hour have been successful.[9] Telephone interviews tend to be shorter than either mail surveys or personal interviews because (1) respondents can terminate the telephone conversation at their own discretion and (2) respondents may distrust telephone contacts. Of course, if respondents are

---

[9]S. Sudman, "Sample Surveys," *Annual Review of Sociology,* 1976, pp. 107–20.

extremely interested in the survey topic, they will probably remain on the telephone.

Sample Control.   Telephone surveys provide control over who is interviewed. Like mail surveys, telephone surveys can reach geographically dispersed respondents and hard-to-reach areas; they also are highly dependent on the sampling frame.

Nontelephone Households.   Although 94 percent of U.S. households have telephones, households that do not have telephones present an immediate problem, regardless of the sampling frame selected. Available data[10] indicate that nontelephone households tend to be

- Low income.
- Low education.
- Single person or very large household.
- Rural/nonfarm.
- Minority.
- Southern.
- Separated.

These differences between telephone and nontelephone households are not a major concern to commercial marketing research studies, however, because nontelephone households usually are low-consumption families and not the target market for many goods or services.

Unlisted Telephone Households.   In contrast to nontelephone households, unlisted telephone households represent a serious source of bias. Nationally, about 30 percent of all households have unlisted telephones, and the number is increasing by about 1.5 percentage points a year. There also are important demographic and attitudinal differences between listed and unlisted telephone households. For example, unlisted telephone households tend to be

- Urban, especially inner city.
- Younger.
- Single and single parent.
- Lower status occupations.
- Low or high income.
- Black.
- Renters.
- Pacific and Mid-Atlantic census regions.

And they tend to have different attitudes with respect to

- Political affiliation.
- Voting.

---

[10]Data and findings reported in this section have been taken from *Fact Sheets* (New York: Survey Sampling Inc., 1988).

TABLE 6–1   Metropolitan Areas with Highest Incidence of Unlisted Numbers

Metro Area	Total Households	Households with Telephones (%)	Estimated Telephone Households Unlisted (%)
Oakland	790,900	95.6	59.6
Los Angeles–Long Beach	3,025,800	93.4	59.5
Las Vegas	299,600	90.8	59.5
San Jose	525,700	97.0	59.3
Fresno	226,200	93.0	59.0
Sacramento	572,800	94.6	55.8
Riverside–San Bernardino	913,700	93.6	55.3
San Diego	911,800	95.0	54.8
Anaheim–Santa Ana	841,200	96.6	54.3
Oxnard–Ventura	221,200	95.8	53.2
San Francisco	645,600	95.6	52.6
Bakersfield	186,800	91.8	51.6
Jersey City	207,900	88.8	49.1
Detroit	1,621,000	96.1	38.4
Portland	491,800	94.6	37.5
Tacoma	217,900	93.8	37.5
Chicago	2,224,300	94.2	36.6
Miami–Hialeah	701,800	90.8	36.5
Tucson	266,200	91.2	35.7
Newark	651,400	94.2	34.9
San Antonio	458,800	92.2	34.5
Phoenix	826,000	91.8	34.0
Philadelphia	1,788,400	95.7	33.2
Honolulu	267,300	95.4	32.4
Albuquerque	189,800	92.2	32.3

Note: The unlisted rate is determined by comparing the estimated number of telephone households with the actual number of households found in telephone directories. Estimated telephone households are computed by taking projected household estimates at the county level calculated by Market Statistics for *Sales & Marketing Management* magazine and applying a figure from the U.S. Census that indicates the percent of households with a telephone.

Source: *Fact Sheets* (New York: Survey Sampling, Inc., 1991). © Copyright Survey Sampling, Inc., 1991. All rights reserved.

— Religious views.
— Media habits.

Table 6–1 presents the 1991 25 metropolitan areas that had the highest incidence of unlisted telephones among the top 100.

There are two types of sampling frames used in telephone surveys.[11]

---

[11]*Fact Sheets*, (New York: Survey Sampling, Inc., 1988). For more details see C. L. Rich, "Is Random Digit Dialing Really Necessary," *Journal of Marketing Research*, August 1977, pp. 300–301; A. B. Blankenship, "Listed versus Unlisted Numbers in Telephone Survey Samples," *Opinion Quarterly*, February 1977, pp. 39–42; G. J. Glasser and G. D. Metzger, "National Estimates of Nonlisted Telephone Households and Their Characteristics," *Journal of Marketing Research*, August 1975, pp. 359–61; and J. Honomichl, "Arbitron Updates Unlisted Phone Numbers," *Advertising Age*, January 15, 1979, p. 40.

TABLE 6–2
—
Directory-Based
Samples

National, manually drawn from directories
   Clerical nightmare.
   Duplication.

National, computer database of listed households
   Survey Sampling, Inc.
   No duplication.

Local, White Pages directory
   Good geographic area definition.

Local Reverse directory
   Better geographic area definition.
   Available for few markets.

directory-based sampling designs
Sample where telephone numbers are selected from the directory in some prescribed way.

Directory-Based Sampling Designs. With **directory-based sampling designs,** telephone numbers are selected from the directory in some prescribed way, and so the sample is restricted to households that have published telephone numbers. If the directory is not current (the average age of a directory is 18 months) then households that have moved into the geographical area covered by the directory cannot be included in the sample. The directory also may not adequately represent people who have moved or that have dissolved households. Furthermore, if the geographic area to be sampled is not concomitant with the area covered by the telephone directory, then much of the ease of drawing the sample will be negated because each selected telephone number must be identified as belonging to the eligible population by inspecting its address—a process that can prove cumbersome and can lead to inclusion errors. Table 6–2 contrasts several of the possible directory-based sampling frames that can be used.

random-digit directory sample designs
Samples of numbers drawn from the directory, usually by a systematic procedure. Selected numbers are modified to allow all unlisted numbers a chance for inclusion.

To overcome exclusion bias, **random-digit directory sample designs** have been used.[12] The first step in these random designs is to draw a sample of numbers from the directory, usually by using a systematic procedure such as picking every 10th telephone number. Next, the selected telephone numbers are modified to allow all unlisted numbers a chance for inclusion. Three popular approaches for correcting exclusion bias with directory frames are (1) *addition of a constant to the last digit,* (2) *randomization on the r last digits,* and (3) *inverse sampling with probabilities proportional to size.* The first approach, addition of a constant to the last digit, calls for an integer (between 0 and 9) to be added (arithmetically) to the telephone number selected from the directory. The second approach, randomization on the r last digits, replaces the r last digits ($r = 2$, 3, or 4) of the selected telephone number with an appropriate number of random digits. The third approach involves a two-stage procedure. First, the directory is used to select a sample of telephone numbers from a specific exchange. The last three digits of each number are then removed. Next, a block of three-digit random numbers, between 000 and 999, is selected and appended to the four digits remaining to form a

---

[12]For example, see Matthew Hauck and Michael Cox, "Locating a Sample by Random Digit Dialing," *Public Opinion Quarterly,* Summer 1974, pp. 253–60; and Seymour Sudman, "The Uses of Telephone Directories for Survey Sampling," *Journal of Marketing Research,* May 1973, pp. 204–7.

EXHIBIT 6–6
—
Description of
Directory Sampling
Designs

Addition of a Constant to the Last Digit
Selected telephone number: 456   6612
                              exchange   block
Add one to the last digit to form the selected number 456–6613.

Randomization on the *r* Last Digits
Selected telephone number: 456   8329
                              exchange   block
Replace last two digits of block with randomly selected numbers 4 and 5 to form the number 456–8345.

Two-Stage Procedure
Cluster one—selected exchange 265; selected telephone number
        265   9592
    exchange   block
Replace last three digits 592 with randomly selected digits 045 to form selected number 265–9045. Repeat process until desired sample of households (telephone numbers) from this cluster is obtained.

complete seven-digit telephone number. Exhibit 6–6 briefly illustrates each of these approaches. If the geographic area to be sampled is concomitant with the area covered by the telephone directory, random-digit directory sampling can prove effective. Out of the three methods, addition of a constant has been shown to produce high contact rates and representative samples.[13] Exhibit 6–7 (see page 154) examines some of the issues a researcher should consider when deciding on a random-digit or listed sample.

Nondirectory Sampling Designs.   The **nondirectory sampling design** approach does not make direct use of telephone directories. Instead, numbers are prescriptively added to working exchanges (also called prefixes). There are three kinds of nondirectory sampling designs: *simple two-stage, two-stage cluster,* and *stratified.*[14] A simple two-stage sample randomly selects a working exchange and appends a block of four-digit random numbers. A two-stage cluster design first clusters telephone numbers by exchange. Next, a sample of exchanges is selected either

nondirectory sampling designs
Telephone survey samples that do not make direct use of telephone directories. Instead, numbers are prescriptively added to working exchanges (also called prefixes).

---

[13]E. L. Landon, Jr., and S. K. Banks, "Relative Efficiency and Bias of Plus-One Telephone Sampling," *Journal of Marketing Research,* August 1977, pp. 294–99.

[14]For example, see A *National Probability Sample of Telephone Households Using Computerized Sampling Techniques* (Radnor, Pa.: Chilton Research Services, 1976); Research Services, "Telecentral Communication: An Innovation in Survey Research," presented to the Advertising Research Foundation, 11th Annual Conference, New York, October 5, 1965; Stanford L. Cooper, "Random Sampling by Telephone—An Improved Method," *Journal of Marketing Research,* November 1964, pp. 45–48; J. O. Eastlack, Jr., and Henry Assael, "Better Telephone Surveys through Centralized Interviewing," *Journal of Advertising Research,* March 1966, pp. 2–7; Gerald J. Glasser and Dale D. Metzger, "Random Digit Dialing as a Method of Telephone Sampling," *Journal of Marketing Research,* February 1972, pp. 59–64; Gerald J. Glasser and Dale D. Metzger, "National Estimates of Nonlisted Telephone Households and Their Characteristics," *Journal of Marketing Research,* August 1975, pp. 359–61; William R. Klecka and Alfred J. Tuchfarber, Jr., "Random Digit Dialing as an Efficient Method for Political Polling," *Georgia Political Science Association Journal,* Spring 1974, pp. 133–51; and E. Laird London, Jr., and Sharon K. Banks, *Boulder Shopping Survey: Shopping Habits and Attitudes of Boulder Residents* (Boulder, Colorado: Department of Community Development, March 1976).

EXHIBIT 6–7

—

Random-Digit versus
Listed Telephone
Sample

Let's examine some of the issues a researcher should consider when deciding between a random-digit or listed sample. The first step is to evaluate whom you would or would not be reaching by using either of the two methods. A random-digit method will allow all telephone households—whether listed in telephone directories or not—to be represented in your sample. Therefore, study results could be projected to the approximately 93 percent of all U.S. households with telephones.

A listed sample, on the other hand, will allow only households with their phone numbers listed in directories to be included. Nationally, this means you will miss the approximately 25 percent of telephone households with unlisted numbers, and in areas such as Los Angeles and Chicago, over 40 percent of telephone households will be missed.

These unlisted households tend to be different than their listed counterparts. People who choose to have unlisted phone numbers tend to have either very high incomes, better educational backgrounds, and white-collar jobs or very low incomes and less educational backgrounds. Further, the unlisted group includes some younger, more urban households that do not appear in directories because of their high level of mobility.

Given these characteristics, a researcher must consider the potential bias introduced (by not including unlisted households in the sampling frame) in relation to the purpose of the study at hand. You might ask yourself these two questions:

1. Do you think that listed and unlisted households would exhibit any differences in the respondents' attitudes and behavior concerning the product or service under study?

2. How will the study results be used? And, therefore, how representative and projectable do the results need to be?

For example, is the overall purpose of the research to size a potential or existing market; is it to profile users or nonusers; is it to determine advertising effectiveness; or is it to simply take a quick "snapshot" of consumers' likes and dislikes about a product or service?

After evaluating the issues mentioned above, most researchers would prefer a random-digit method. And in the majority of cases, the precision and projectability inherent to random-digit sampling will be worth any extra cost.

Unfortunately, random-digit sampling isn't always feasible. Take, for example, a study where it's crucial that consumers be interviewed within a very tightly defined geographic area (e.g., a set of census tracts or block groups). A sample constrained by such a specific definition is feasible only via a listed method that uses actual street addresses to code households to fine levels of geography.

Although you could start out with a random-digit sample for a larger geographic area and then screen for actual addresses as part of the interview, the interviewing costs (not to mention problems) may override the value of including unlisted households. The trade-off becomes one of projectability versus cost and feasibility.

Low incidence population groups present a similar problem. For example, say you're trying to reach households with a particular demographic characteristic at about a 6 percent level of incidence. There are few study budgets that can justify the high cost of employing a random-digit technique under such circumstances. A well-targeted listed sample, though, could significantly increase the incidence of finding rare market segments—making such a study financially feasible.

Source: Survey Sampling, Inc., 1988.

randomly or systematically. Then, within these selected exchanges, four digits are generated to yield the sample of telephone surveys. The stratified sampling design also adds random digits to exchanges. However, in stratified designs, working exchanges and working banks are first determined. Each exchange consists of 10 banks of 1,000 numbers each. For example, the 1,000 numbers between 8,000 and 8,999 are a bank. Information on working banks are kept by the telephone company; however, it may be difficult to obtain this information. Next, four-digit random numbers that fall within working banks are added to each working exchange to form the selected telephone number. The number of households taken from each exchange is based upon a prespecified allocation rule. Stratified designs typically are used in local or regional telephone surveys because it is not feasible to stratify by exchange at the national level—there are over 28,000 working exchanges.[15]

<u>Quality of Data.</u> Numerous studies have shown that telephone surveys produce data essentially comparable to that collected via mail surveys and personal interviews.[16] Telephone surveys do have several unique features, however. First, compared with mail surveys, telephone survey respondents show a greater tendency not to include information on income and personal finances.[17] Second, interaction between the respondent and the interviewer can create a tendency to give socially acceptable answers to sensitive or embarrassing questions.[18] In this regard, telephone surveys fall somewhere between mail surveys and personal interviews. Third, on the one hand, an interviewer reduces respondent confusion, permits probing, and allows respondents to clarify their responses; on the other hand, even though interviewers are not physically present during the interview, they may transmit cues that can bias respondents' answers. Interviewers can project a "warm" or "cold" image or, for that matter, convey their own attitudes through inflection and tone of voice, thereby either influencing the responses or suggesting the appropriate response.[19] Finally, on the positive side, telephone interviewing that is conducted at a central telephone facility allows the person who is supervising the survey to monitor a portion of each interviewer's work to ensure that the questionnaire is being administered properly and that no cheating is taking place.

<u>Response Rates.</u> The proportion of completed interviews in telephone surveys typically ranges from 50 to 60 percent.

$$\frac{\text{Response}}{\text{rate}} = \frac{\text{Number of complete interviews with those contacted}}{\text{Number of complete} + \text{Number of} + \text{Number of}}$$
$$\text{interviews} \quad\quad \text{refusals} \quad\quad \text{terminations}$$

Such high response rates are obtained by initiating multiple contacts with potential respondents. In the case of telephone surveys, call-backs are easily implemented at little cost. Many telephone surveys use a three-call-back procedure.

---

[15]Chilton Research Services, A *National Probability Sample*, p. 2.

[16]See, for example, C. S. Aneshensed, R. R. Frerichs, V. A. Clark, and P. A. Yokopenic, "Measuring Depression in the Community: A Comparison of Telephone and Personal Interviews," *Public Opinion Quarterly*, Spring 1982, pp. 110–21; and J. R. Hochstim, "A Critical Comparison of Three Strategies of Collecting Data from Households," *Journal of the American Statistical Association*, September 1967, pp. 876–89.

[17]T. F. Rogers, "Interviews by Telephone and In Person: Quality of Response and Field Performance," *Public Opinion Quarterly*, Spring 1976, pp. 51–65.

[18]T. T. Tyebjee, "Telephone Survey Methods: The State of the Art," *Journal of Marketing*, Summer 1979, pp. 68–78.

[19]E. Telser, "Data Exercises Bias in Phone vs. Personal Interview Debate, But If You Can't Do It Right, Don't Do It At All," *Marketing News*, September 10, 1976, p. 6.

EXHIBIT 6–8   A Survey Researcher's View of the United States

Unlisted rate	17.6%
Contact rate	59.4%
Cooperation rate	50.3%
Surveyed rate	24.4%

Unlisted rate	29.1%
Contact rate	57.1%
Cooperation rate	47.8%
Surveyed rate	26.7%

Unlisted rate	21.8%
Contact rate	56.0%
Cooperation rate	59.3%
Surveyed rate	25.8%

Unlisted rate	33.7%
Contact rate	55.1%
Cooperation rate	55.7%
Surveyed rate	31.3%

Unlisted rate	30.6%
Contact rate	57.8%
Cooperation rate	57.1%
Surveyed rate	24.2%

Unlisted rate	49.1%
Contact rate	53.1%
Cooperation rate	46.1%
Surveyed rate	29.4%

Unlisted rate	31.3%
Contact rate	53.5%
Cooperation rate	53.5%
Surveyed rate	20.9%

Unlisted rate	26.0%
Contact rate	59.7%
Cooperation rate	60.8%
Surveyed rate	27.0%

Unlisted rate	26.4%
Contact rate	57.4%
Cooperation rate	54.9%
Surveyed rate	25.9%

Total United States

Unlisted rate	31.1%
Contact rate	56.4%
Cooperation rate	53.2%
Surveyed rate	26.0%

Source: Survey Sampling, Inc., 1990.

The map shown in Exhibit 6–8 was constructed by Survey Sampling, Inc. The map consists of the nine census divisions and presents the highlights for these geographical areas: the unlisted rates (the number of homes with unlisted numbers), the contact rate (the proportion of calls resulting in contact with an English-speaking person), the cooperation rate (how likely people in these regions are willing to cooperate), and the survey frequency (how often surveys are conducted in that region). Note that the unlisted rate can range from as high as 49.1 percent for the Pacific region to 17.6 percent for the New England region.

Speed.   When a central telephone facility is used, always the case in WATS telephone surveys, enough interviewers can be assigned to a study to ensure that several hundred telephone interviews can be scheduled and completed each day. Large national studies can then be collected in a week or two.

Cost.   The data collection cost for a WATS telephone survey will depend on the incidence rate (the percentage of the total population)[20] and the length of the

---

[20]Incidence rates are discussed in Chapter 8. To give a specific example, suppose that the target population is all females between the ages of 18 and 35 who have used a hand lotion product during the past 30 days. The incidence rate is the percentage of the target population who satisfy these criteria.

| Interview Length (minutes) | Incidence | | TABLE 6–3 |
	80%	10%	
10	8.50	28.00	Cost Per Interview—
15	11.90	31.40	Central Location
20	15.30	34.80	Interviewing by
25	18.70	38.20	Phone

interview. Table 6–3 shows a sample of the suggested cost breakdowns for surveys expected to have an 80 percent and a 10 percent incidence.

Uses. Telephone surveys are used in studies that require national samples. In addition, when dealing with a small geographically dispersed group of respondents, telephone interviewing may be the only practical way of reaching them. It has replaced door-to-door personal interviews for many attitude and usage studies, particularly in *market tracking studies* that periodically assess customer awareness, attitudes, and usage behavior in a product category. Telephone surveys are also used in *product tests* to obtain opinions after respondents have used the test product. Finally, telephone surveys are used increasingly as an efficient way to conduct call-back interviews with respondents who were previously contacted through a mail survey or by a personal interview.

Personal In-Home Surveys

The **personal in-home survey** involves asking questions of a sample of respondents face-to-face in their homes. In the case of in-home personal surveys the responsibilities of the interviewer are to (1) locate the appropriate sample of respondents, (2) ask them a set of questions, and (3) record their responses. There has been a marked decrease in the use and percentage of dollar budgets allocated to in-home personal interviewing.

personal in-home survey *Survey that involves asking questions of a sample of respondents face-to-face in their homes.*

Complexity and Versatility. Personal surveys are by far the most flexible and versatile of the data-collection methods. They afford the greatest freedom in questionnaire length and format. Complex questionnaires having involved skip patterns, lengthy scales, projective techniques, probes, refer-backs, and various termination points can be easily used by an experienced interviewer. Because the interviewer and respondent interact, the interviewer can observe the respondent directly and, thus, can ensure that the instructions have been properly understood. In addition to asking and clarifying questions, an interviewer also can provide other valuable information. For example, in a *package-test* study, the interviewer can record whether the respondent opens the package as it was designed or whether the package design is faulty. Finally, being able to present the respondent with visual cues is one of the most attractive features of in-home personal surveys.

Quantity of Data. Because the effort required by the respondent is substantially less than in a mail survey and often less than in a telephone survey, the quantity of data that can be collected with an in-home personal survey exceeds that of either of the other data-collection methods. Open-ended questions are recorded by the interviewer and responses to lengthy scales can be made easier by presenting the respondent with a card that lists the various categories.

Sample Control. In principle, by applying probabilistic sampling designs, a very representative sample of the total population can be drawn, using homes as a basis for the sampling; specifically, with in-home personal surveys the researcher can control which households are interviewed, who within the household is interviewed, the degree to which other members of the household participate in the survey, and other aspects of the data-collection process. Unfortunately, although the potential exists for a high level of sample control, serious execution problems can break down this potential. First, since nearly half of all women are employed outside the home, it has become increasingly difficult to find respondents home during the day (see Exhibit 6–4). The interviewer must contact the household either on weekends or at night, and he or she will likely have to make several callbacks to respondents who are not at home or who are unavailable. Second, sample control with in-home personal surveys is seriously jeopardized by the increasing reluctance of interviewers to venture into inner-city neighborhoods. Furthermore, increasing crime rates have led many people to become cautious about letting strangers into their homes or even opening the door to strangers.

Quality of Data. Because the interviewer can directly observe the respondent, ensuring that instructions are properly understood, and can monitor exposure to the test stimuli, in-home personal interviews can yield more in-depth responses and more complete data than can telephone interviews.[21]

On the other hand, because of interaction between the interviewer and the respondent, the respondent may be reluctant to accurately answer potentially embarrassing questions and may give socially acceptable answers to sensitive questions.[22] The interviewer is a dominant force in personal surveys; therefore, potential for interviewer effects is greatest with this method of data collection. Interviewers can alter questions; change the sequence of questions asked; change the appearance of questions; and give intentional or unintentional cues by their tone of voice, vocabulary, and verbosity, as well as through probing. In effect, each respondent could receive a different survey instrument.[23] Some evidence suggests that, depending on the survey topic, the interviewer's age, gender, race, social class, authority, or opinions can affect the respondent's answers to the questions.[24]

---

[21]See, for example, E. Telser, "Data Exercises," p. 6; and T. F. Rogers, "Interviews by Telephone," pp. 51–65.

[22] J. Colombotos, "Personal vs. Telephone Interviews Effect Responses," *Public Health Report*, September 1969, pp. 773–820.

[23]See M. Collins, "Interviewer Variability," *Journal of the Market Research Society* 2, 1980, pp. 77–95.

[24]See P. B. Case, "How to Catch Interviewer Errors," *Journal of Advertising Research*, April 1971, pp. 39–41; J. Freeman and E. W. Butler, "Some Sources of Interviewer Variance in Surveys," *Public Opinion Quarterly*, Spring 1976, pp. 84–85; and B. Bailar, L. Bailey, and J. Stevens, "Measures of Interviewer Bias and Variance," *Journal of Marketing Research*, August 1977, pp. 337–43.

Finally, the interviewer can cheat; that is, he or she can intentionally falsify all or part of the interview. All of these potential effects can be minimized through proper control and design. The best advice is to hire only the best-trained and experienced interviewers. Since some degree of interviewer bias is likely to be present, methods have been developed to account for such effects by using subjective and statistical adjustments.[25] To safeguard against interviewer cheating, the standard practice today is to validate the interviewer's work by reinterviewing a sample of the respondents and asking several of the original questions again; this also will help to determine whether the interview actually took place and if it was conducted properly.

Response Rates. Response rates with personal interviewers are high and can exceed 80 percent.

$$\frac{\text{Response}}{\text{rate}} = \frac{\text{Number of complete interviews with those contacted}}{\text{Number of complete} + \text{Number of} + \text{Number of}}$$
$$\text{interviews} \qquad \text{refusals} \qquad \text{terminations}$$

Higher response rates can be obtained through increased numbers of call-backs. Most personal surveys vary the call-back schedule by time of day and day of week. Two factors, the larger proportion of women employed outside the home (necessitating call-backs) and high-crime areas, can seriously affect response rates.

Speed. If the total sample can be judiciously split among several markets, and if interviews can be conducted in each market simultaneously, it is possible to complete a large study relatively quickly. In general, personal surveys can be completed faster than mail surveys, but probably not as fast as telephone surveys.

Cost. Compared with mail and telephone surveys, personal surveys are relatively expensive. As the need for call-backs increases, the cost of a personal survey can skyrocket because the interviewer may have to make repeated visits to a distant urban neighborhood just to complete a single interview. For in-home personal surveys, the cost of data collection, excluding analysis and report generation per completed interview, can be as low as $5 to $10; however, the cost per completed interview can be in the $100s or even $1,000s, depending on the length of the interview and the incidence of the sample group under study.

Uses. Historically, in-home personal interviews were used frequently because of the low incidence of telephone ownership and the nonexistence of shopping malls; in addition, they were almost exclusively used when visual cues or exhibits needed to be shown and in complex attitude and opinion studies. Today, the trend is to use mall-intercept interviewing.

---

[25]For details see D. S. Tull and L. E. Richards, "What Can Be Done about Interview Bias," in *Research in Marketing*, 3rd ed., ed. J. Sheth (Greenwich, Conn.: JAI Press, 1980), pp. 143–62.

Mall-Intercept Interviewing

mall-intercept
personal survey
*Survey method using
a central-location test
facility at a shopping
mall; respondents are
intercepted while they
are shopping.*

A **mall-intercept personal survey** involves a central-location test facility at a shopping mall where respondents are intercepted while they are shopping. This type of data-collection method is extremely popular (see Exhibit 6–2). Underlying this interviewing method is the rationale that it's more efficient to have the respondent come to the interviewer than to have the interviewer go to the respondent. This method has been used for more than 20 years, dating back to the first enclosed shopping mall. Today, there are more than 325 permanent mall research facilities.[26]

Complexity and Versatility. Because of the presence of an interviewer and the ability to bring into the mall any materials deemed necessary, mall-intercept personal surveys have even more flexibility and versatility than in-home personal surveys. Greater flexibility and versatility in the use of visual cues and exhibits are possible—be they concepts, products, packages, or advertisements. In addition, marketing or technical people can easily observe or interact with the respondents.

Quantity of Data. In contrast to in-home personal interviews, interview time with mall intercepts generally is limited because respondents are usually hurried. For example, General Foods, a heavy user of mall-intercept surveys, typically keeps the interview time to 25 minutes or less.[27]

Sample Control. Usually the interviewer chooses which respondents will be intercepted, and the choice is limited to mall shoppers, creating two primary problems. First, frequent mall shoppers have a greater chance of being included in the sample; in fact, the problem is complicated further because interviewing is often limited to Thursday, Friday, and Saturday shoppers. Second, a potential respondent can intentionally avoid or initiate contact with the interviewer. Furthermore, the demographics of shoppers can vary drastically from mall to mall. On the positive side, however, easy access to respondents is a clear benefit of mall intercepts: The limitations of night work involved with in-home personal surveys don't apply. Weather is not a problem. And finally, it is easy to determine which family member is the respondent.

Quality of Data. The overall quality of data from mall intercepts appears to be equivalent to that of telephone interviewing in terms of the ability to provide complete and in-depth responses.[28] In addition, because of the opportunity to closely supervise the interviewing process, interviewer bias can be reduced. Finally,

---

[26]*Market Research Association Research Services Directory* (Chicago: Marketing Research Association, 1986).

[27]Al Ossip, "Mall Intercept Interviews," *Second Annual Advertising Research Foundation Research Quality Workshop* (New York: Advertising Research Foundation, 1984), p. 24.

[28]A. J. Bush and J. F. Haire, Jr., "An Assessment of the Mall Intercept as a Data Collection Method," *Journal of Marketing Research*, May 1985, pp. 158–67.

Interview Length (minutes)	Incidence	
	80%	10%
10	11.20	24.50
15	15.20	28.50
20	18.70	32.00
25	22.20	35.50

TABLE 6–4
—
Cost Per Interview—
Central-Location
Interviewing

limited evidence suggests that mall-intercept interviewing yields more accurate or less distorted responses in comparison to telephone interviews.[29]

On the negative side, however, the unnatural testing environment of the shopping mall can potentially produce biased responses from respondents, particularly in food testing and advertising test studies. Another factor detracting from the overall quality of data collected with mall intercepts is what can be called "mall burnout." The same people might be repeatedly interviewed. Finally, because sometimes only one-third of the people intercepted agree to participate, the potential for selection bias is quite serious.[30]

Response Rates. Response rates in intercept surveys usually are comparable to those obtained in in-home personal interviews. The percentage of people contacted who refuse to participate typically varies between 10 and 30 percent, which is slightly lower than in telephone surveys.[31]

Speed. By employing several central mall facilities, even moderately large studies (say, 500 respondents) can be completed in a few days. Next to telephone surveys, mall-intercept surveys are the fastest.

Cost. Mall intercepts generally cost less than in-home personal surveys. Prerecruiting respondents to a central location is relatively inexpensive, and only limited quantities of the visual cues or exhibits are needed because such materials can be used repeatedly. Table 6–4 provides cost information, which is broken down by incidence rate (80 percent and 10 percent) and length of interview.

Uses. Mall-intercept personal surveys are regularly used in concept tests, name tests, package tests, product tests, copy tests, and in some simulated test-market studies. In general, the type of visual cues and exhibits will dictate whether a mall-intercept personal survey should be used.

Table 6–5 (see page 162) provides a comparative summary account of the survey interviewing methods discussed so far.

---

[29]Ibid.
[30]Ossip, "Mall Intercept," p. 25.
[31]Bush and Haire, "An Assessment," p. 165.

TABLE 6–5   Summary Comparison of Major Data Collection

Criteria	Direct/Cold Mailing	Mail Panels	Telephone	Personal In-Home	Mall Intercept
Complexity and versatility	Not much	Not much	Substantial but complex or lengthy scales difficult to use	Highly flexible	Most flexible
Quantity of data	Substantial	Substantial	Short, lasting typically between 15 and 30 minutes	Greatest quantity	Limited to 25 minutes or less
Sample control	Little	Substantial, but representativeness may be a question	Good, but non-listed households can be a problem	In theory, provides greatest control	Can be problematic; sample representativeness may be questionable
Quality of data	Better for sensitive or embarrassing questions; however, no interviewer present to clarify what is being asked	Better for sensitive or embarrassing questions; however, no interviewer present to clarify what is being asked	Positive side, interview can clear up any ambiguities; negative side, may lead to socially accepted answers	In addition, there is the chance of cheating	In addition, unnatural testing environment can lead to bias
Response rates	In general, low; as low as 10%	70–80%	60–80%	Greater than 80%	As high as 80%
Speed	Several weeks; completion time will increase with follow-up mailings	Several weeks with no follow-up mailings, longer with follow-up mailings	Large studies can be completed in 3 to 4 weeks	Faster than mail but typically slower than telephone surveys	Large studies can be completed in a few days
Cost	Inexpensive; as low as $2.50 per completed interview	Lowest	Not as low as mail; depends on incidence rate and length of questionnaire	Can be relatively expensive, but considerable variability	Less expensive than in-home, but higher than telephone; again, length and incidence rate will determine cost
Uses	Executive, industrial, medical, and readership studies	All areas of marketing research; particularly useful in low-incidence categories	Particularly effective in studies that require national samples	Still prevalent in product testing and other studies that require visual cues or product prototypes	Concept tests, name tests, package tests, copy tests

NEWER TECHNOLOGICAL APPROACHES

The marketing research business is constantly responding to the explosion in computer technology. Sophisticated computer technology is being introduced and integrated into existing services to create more flexible, easier-to-use, and more accurate data-collection methods. Computer-assisted interviewing is fast becoming a dominant force in collecting data from respondents. The following sections discuss these newer technological approaches, according to the same criteria used to evaluate the major data-collection methods.

CATI Interviewing

A **computer-assisted telephone interviewing (CATI)** system involves a computerized survey instrument. The survey questionnaire is entered into the memory of a large mainframe computer, into a smaller microprocessor, or minicomputer, or even into a personal computer. The interviewer conducts the interview in front of a CRT terminal, which has a television-like screen and typewriter-like terminal keyboard. The interviewer reads the questions from the screen and records the respondent's answers directly into the computer memory banks by using the terminal keyboard or special touch- or light-sensitive screens. In addition, the CATI system can provide labor-saving functions such as automatic dialing.

> **computer-assisted telephone interviewing (CATI)**
> *Survey systems involving a computerized survey instrument. The survey questionnaire is entered into the memory of a large mainframe computer, into a small microprocessor, or even into a personal computer. The interviewer reads the questions from the CRT screen and records the respondent's answers directly into the computer memory banks by using the terminal keyboard or special touch- or light-sensitive screens.*

Complexity and Versatility. CATI systems allow "individualized" questionnaires to be used for each respondent; that is, the set of questions that each respondent receives depends on the respondent's answers to earlier questions. Complex skip patterns are done automatically; in addition, question wording, format, and sequence can be easily changed, and the order of response alternatives can be rotated at virtually no additional cost.

Quality of Data. Because the questionnaire is computerized, such problems as skipping over questions, misunderstanding instructions, ignoring skip patterns, or giving contradictory responses to two or more questions are solved. However, there is still the potential for interviewer bias, for example, interviewer cheating. A comparison of the CATI interviewing procedure with nonsignificant CATI interviews showed no significant differences between the two procedures[32] among interviewers or respondents.

Speed. Data analysis and report generation can be carried on as the data are being collected. Because the data are entered directly into computer memory, interim reports can be produced daily and preliminary data analysis (e.g., top-line reports) can be generated in a more timely fashion.

Costs The startup costs for CATI interviews tend to be higher than for studies conducted exclusively by human interviewers. However, the productivity of

---

[32]R. M. Groves and N. A. Mathiowefz, "Computer Assisted Telephone Interviewing: Effects on Interviewers and Respondents," *Public Opinion Quarterly* 48, 1984, pp. 356–69.

interviewers with CATI can be as much as 20 percent greater than traditional survey methods, which may offset the startup costs, especially for large studies.[33]

Self-Administered CRT Interviews

self-administered CRT interview
An interviewing method where the respondent sits at a computer terminal and answers the questionnaire by using a keyboard and a screen.

Another recent innovation in data-collection methods is the onsite, **self-administered CRT interview.** In principle, a CRT self-administered interviewing station can be set up anywhere there is electrical and telephone service. Typically, self-administered CRT interviews have been used to collect data at trade shows, professional conferences, product clinics, central interviewing locations, and shopping malls.[34] The computer configuration of the onsite location can vary. The site can be computerized by the use of personal computers, and each PC can support three or four CRTs. CRTs can be hardwired directly to a microcomputer or minicomputer, or the CRTs can be linked directly through telecommunications equipment to a centrally located mainframe computer.

Flexibility and Versatility.   Like CATI systems, onsite self-administered CRT interviews afford greater flexibility and versatility in handling individualized questionnaires; question wording, format, and sequence; response alternative ordering; and complex skip patterns. On the negative side, however, open-ended questions can be a problem. Open-ended questions require that the respondent type in answers—in this case phrases or sentences. Although respondents generally have no difficulty in entering numbers, some may have poor typing skills. This problem can be handled by minimizing the number of open-ended questions, assisting the respondent through the help of a host or hostess, having the respondent handwrite the open-ended answers, or having the open-ended responses tape-recorded.[35]

Sample Control.   Self-administered CRT interviews provide automatic control over who is sampled. Because the CRTs are linked and because predetermined sample quotas are stored in the memory system, each respondent can be checked to determine which quota group he or she belongs to and whether the interview should be administered. In addition, respondent randomization can be accomplished automatically.

Quality of Data.   Because the interview is self-administered, no interviewer is needed, and interviewer bias is not a problem. These interviews may induce respondents to answer sensitive or socially embarrassing questions because they may feel less threatened by a machine. A comparison of the responses to a need-for-approval scale indicated that subjects responding to an electronic survey gave less

---

[33]Michael J. Havice and Mark J. Banks, "Live and Automated Telephone Surveys: A Comparison of Human Interviewers and an Automated Technique," *Journal of the Market Research Society* 32, no. 2, 1991, pp. 91–102.

[34]For prototypical applications see B. Whalen, "On-Site Interviewing Yields Search Data Instantly," *Marketing News*, November 9, 1984, pp. 1, 17.

[35]J. E. Rafael, "Self-Administered CRT Interview: Benefits Far Outweigh the Problems," *Marketing News*, November 9, 1984, p. 16.

socially desirable responses than respondents using a paper and pencil method.[36] In addition, as with CATI systems, self-administered CRT interviews solve such problems as skipping over questions, misunderstanding instructions, ignoring skip patterns, or giving contradictory responses to two or more questions. The computer will not allow a respondent to make these kinds of errors.

Speed. As with CATI systems, data are entered into computer memory directly by the respondent. Data analysis can proceed quickly, and interim reports can be generated daily.

Costs. A reasonable estimate of data-collection costs for 300 to 600 respondents, excluding data analysis and report generation, ranges from $6 to $10 per interview for a syndicated study or $18 to $23 per interview for a customized, exclusive study.[37]

NONRESPONSE ERRORS

Failure to obtain information from respondents of the target population that were selected to be in the sample can result in nonresponse errors. The first issue in understanding nonresponse is to anticipate what can go wrong in a study. For example, Exhibit 6–9 (see page 166) presents several of the possible outcomes of attempting to make a telephone contact.

Not-at-Homes

Low response rates caused by not-at-homes can be a serious problem with in-home personal and telephone surveys; however, employing a series of call-backs can drastically reduce the percentage of not-at-homes.

The minimum number of call-backs in consumer surveys is typically three to four. The percentage of not-at-homes will vary according to such factors as (1) the nature of the respondent—individuals more likely to be at home include married people with small children, as opposed to single or divorced people; (2) the day and time of call—contact is more likely on the weekend than on a weekday, in the evening as opposed to in the afternoon; and (3) the interview situation—if all else is equal, advance appointments made by telephone or by mail increase contact. In general, not-at-homes tend to be[38]

- Residents in central cities.
- Urban.
- Higher income.
  Younger
- Live in the Northeast.

---

[36]Havice and Banks, "Live and Automated Telephone Surveys."
[37]Whalen, "On-Site Computer Interviewing," p. 17.
[38]*Fact Sheets*, Survey Sampling, Inc.

EXHIBIT 6–9   Telephone Contacts: Possible Outcomes

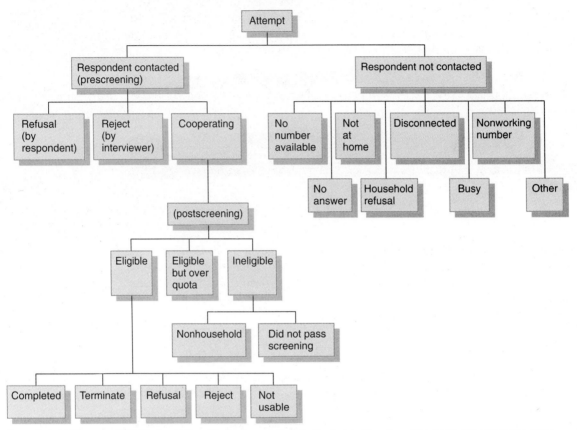

Source: Frederick Wiseman and Philip MacDonald, *Toward the Development of Industry Standards for Response and Nonresponse Rates* (Cambridge, Mass.: Marketing Science Institute, 1980), p. 29.

Available data clearly indicate that (1) people are generally not home as much as they used to be and (2) the best time to contact an individual is in the evening. For example, societal and lifestyle changes, working wives, fewer children, higher divorce rates, and the diminishing role of the family can explain why it is becoming increasingly more difficult to contact respondents.

The successful use of call-backs is based on two assumptions: (1) the number of nonresponses due to not-at-homes and the probability of response must be large enough to justify the effort—if the number of hard-core zero responses is large, then call-backs will be fruitless, and (2) call-backs should be different from those respondents who are already in the sample.

There should be a prescribed plan for and control over call-backs. A control sheet is commonly used in telephone surveys to record the outcome of each attempted contact. Typically, the first call yields the most responses, but the second

---

Households contacted on first attempts are different from those contacted in later attempts:

If you make only one attempt, your respondents will not be representative of the frame, that is, in terms of demographics and possible attitudes.

Not-at-homes are, generally, important consumer segments.

Unless absolutely sure topic is not correlated with prior demographic factors.

The general recommendation is to make three attempts.

Make more attempts if topic known to be correlated with "at homeness," for example.

Control timing of attempts.

EXHIBIT 6–10

How Many Attempts Should You Make?

and third calls have higher responses per call.[39] The first call frequently screens out businesses, disconnects, and refusals, and it provides information about the respondent that allows subsequent calls to be scheduled more efficiently. The ultimate decision concerning the number of call-backs involves weighing the benefits of reducing nonresponse bias by initiating further call-backs against their additional cost. As call-backs are initiated and completed, an evaluation of the difference between the call-back respondents and the respondents already in the sample should be conducted. If the differences are minor, or if a trend develops on the survey variable of interest, fewer call-backs may be warranted or no further call-backs may be warranted at all. Exhibit 6–10 gives some guidelines on the number of attempts to make.

Refusals

The second component contributing to low response rates is refusals. The unwillingness or inability of respondents to answer specific questions or to participate in the survey at all is a potential problem for in-home personal, mail, telephone, and mall-intercept personal surveys. Procedures for reducing refusals vary depending on the method of data collection.

The proportion of refusals depends upon a diverse set of factors. As we indicated, refusal rates in *personal and telephone surveys* can be high. Procedures for reducing refusals in these surveys have emphasized prior notification, motivating the respondent, and proper writing and administration of the questions.

1. **Prior notification** involves sending potential respondents an advance letter to notify them of the impending telephone or personal contact. Advance letters appear to positively affect response rates for samples of the general public.[40] The rationale behind this procedure is simple: Respondents often react with suspicion when reached by an unexpected telephone caller or

prior notification
Method of reducing non-response that involves sending potential respondents an advance letter to notify them of the impending telephone or personal contact.

---

[39]Leslie Kish, *Survey Sampling* (New York: John Wiley & Sons, 1965), p. 552.
[40]D. A. Dillman, J. G. Gallegos, and J. H. Frey, "Reduced Refusal Rates for Telephone Interviews," *Public Opinion Quarterly*, Fall 1976, pp. 66–78.

contacted by an interviewer either in their homes or at a shopping mall. This element of surprise and uncertainty contributes to refusals and diminishes the overall quality of the data collected. The advance letter tries to relieve potential anxiety regarding a survey while at the same time it tries to create a cooperative atmosphere. Regarding mall-intercept personal surveys, respondents can be prerecruited; that is, respondents can be screened ahead of time by telephone. If the respondent qualifies, he or she is asked to come to the central mall-testing location at a specific time to be interviewed. A prerecruiting strategy works best in situations in which the proportion of qualified respondents is low—for example, for low-incidence product categories or when the interview is lengthy. Prior notification cannot be used in all instances, however. For example, it is not possible with random-digit dialing.

foot-in-the-door technique
Method of reducing non-response involves first getting respondents to complete a relatively short, simple questionnaire and then, at some later time, asking them to complete a larger questionnaire on the same general topic.

2. *Motivating the respondent* involves procedures that can potentially increase respondents' interest or involvement and thereby gain their cooperation. One type of procedure, called the **foot-in-the-door technique,** involves first getting respondents to complete a relatively short, simple questionnaire and then, at some later time, asking them to complete a longer questionnaire on the same general topic. The rationale behind this procedure is based on **self-perception theory,** which proposes that individuals come to know their attitudes through interpreting the causes of their behavior.[41] To the extent that one's behavior is attributed to internal causes and not to circumstantial pressures, a positive attitude toward the behavior develops; these attitudes, or self-perceptions, exert a direct influence on subsequent behavior. Thus, the self-perception paradigm predicts that persons who actually comply with the small request will view themselves as persons who engage in such activities and, therefore, will be more likely to perform similar, more substantial activities. Although the evidence indicates that this procedure generally increases response rates, it may not be significant in view of the substantial added expense.[42]

self-perception theory
Theory proposing that individuals come to know their attitudes through interpreting the causes of their behavior. To the extent that one's behavior is attributed to internal causes and not to circumstantial pressures, a positive attitude toward the behavior develops, and these attitudes, or self-perceptions, exert a direct influence on subsequent behavior.

refusal conversion (persuasion)
Method of reducing nonresponse; skilled interviewers reduce the proportion of refusals by not accepting a refusal to a request for cooperation without making an additional plea.

3. *Proper writing and administration of the questions* relates to the skills and expertise of both the person putting together the questionnaire and the interviewer who administers it. Interviewers who have learned how far to probe and encroach on respondents' privacy and patience without outraging their stamina will reduce the proportion of refusals. Skilled interviewers can reduce the proportion of refusals by not accepting a no answer to a request for cooperation without making an additional plea. This procedure, called **refusal conversion** or **persuasion,** has been found to decrease refusal on the average by about 7 percent.[43]

---

[41]D. Bern, "Self-Perception Theory," in *Advances in Experimental Social Psychology,* ed. L. Berkowitz (New York: Academic Press, 1972), pp. 1–62.

[42]R. M. Graves and L. J. Magilavy, "Increasing Response Rates to Telephone Surveys: A Door in the Face for Foot-in-The-Door," *Public Opinion Quarterly,* Fall 1981, pp. 346–58.

[43]Ibid. p. 357.

Refusals to specific questions can be reduced by proper attention to question wording and format. Interviewing respondents by telephone or in person means that the questions asked are usually communicated orally. Oral communication means that many questions that are appropriate in mail surveys will not work if asked in the same form on the telephone or in person. Finally, question format and wording also affect respondents' willingness to answer socially threatening or embarrassing questions. We return to this issue and we give some general guidelines for properly writing and administering questionnaires in Chapter 12.

A relatively large number of procedures have been investigated as potential ways to improve refusals in *mail surveys.*

1. *Prior notification* to inform[44] or motivate respondents has successfully increased response rates. In addition, it can accelerate the rate of return. An advance letter or phone call generally informs respondents that they will be receiving a questionnaire shortly and requests their cooperation. The *foot-in-the-door* technique previously described also can be used, although evidence seems to indicate that this approach does not generate higher response rates than does standard prenotification.[45]

2. *Characteristics of the cover letter and questionnaire* that could be useful in reducing refusals have been extensively investigated. The cover letter is integral to the mail survey and may be the most logical and efficient vehicle for persuading individuals to respond. The cover letter is the first part of the mail-out package that respondents are likely to read. It introduces the survey and motivates the respondent to fill it out and return it as quickly as possible. Specific elements that should be included in the cover letter are discussed in Chapter 12.

3. *Follow-up action* involves contacting the respondent periodically after the initial mailing. **Follow-ups,** or reminders, are almost universally successful in reducing refusals and usually are less costly than prior notification procedures. Follow-up procedures involve a sequence of mailings. Exhibit 6–11 (see page 170) describes a typical sequence identified by the number of weeks that elapsed after the original mailing.[46]

follow-ups
Ways of contacting the respondent periodically after the initial contact.

Yammarino, Skinner, and Childers have recently conducted a meta-analysis of mail survey response behavior. Their findings indicated that repeated contacts in the form of preliminary notification and follow-ups, appeals, inclusion of a return

---

[44]See, for example, B. J. Walker and R. B. Burdick, "Advance Correspondence and Error in Mail Surveys," *Journal of Marketing Research*, August 1977, pp. 379–83.

[45]For experimental results on the foot-in-the-door technique, see C. T. Allen, C. D. Schewe, and G. Wijk, "More on Self-Perception Theory's Foot Technique in the Pre-Call Mail Survey Setting," *Journal of Marketing Research*, November 1980, pp. 498–502; and R. A. Hansen and L. M. Robinson, "Testing the Effectiveness of Alternative Foot-in-the-Door Manipulations," *Journal of Marketing Research*, August 1980, pp. 359–64.

[46]Dillman et al., "Reduce Refusal Rates," p. 183.

EXHIBIT 6–11

Sequence of Follow-Ups in Mail Survey

One week:	A postcard reminder sent to everyone. It serves as both a thank-you for those who have responded and as a friendly and courteous reminder for those who have not.
Three weeks:	A letter and replacement questionnaire sent only to nonrespondents. Nearly the same in appearance as the original mailing, it has a shorter cover letter that informs nonrespondents that their questionnaire has not been received and appeals for its return.
Seven weeks:	This final mailing is similar to the one that preceded it, except that it is sent by certified mail to emphasize its importance. Another replacement questionnaire is enclosed.

Source: D. A. Dillman, J. G. Gallegos, and J. H. Frey, "Reduce Refusal Rates for Telephone Interviews," *Public Opinion Quarterly*, 1976, pp. 68–78.

envelope, postage, and monetary incentives were effective in increasing response rates.[47]

Evidence on Response Rate Facilitators

Specific aspects of the questionnaire have been investigated for their potential to reduce refusals. Two of the obvious and possibly important aspects affecting response rates are questionnaire length and the absence or presence of an incentive. A recent comprehensive literature review of the techniques used to increase response rates made the following conclusions.[48]

1. Questionnaire length is nearly uncorrelated with response rates. The evidence revealed a negative but very weak relation between length and response rates.

2. Monetary incentives, whether prepaid or promised, increased response rates. Prepaid monetary incentives do, however, increase response rates over promised incentives. In addition, the amount of incentive paid has a strong positive relation to response rate. However, the use of large monetary incentives may well exceed the value of the additional information obtained by the increases in response rate.

3. Nonmonetary incentives, that is, offering premiums and rewards (for example, pens, pencils, or books), increased response rates over not offering any nonmonetary incentive, although this finding is based on only a few studies.

From this same study there is evidence on the effectiveness of several other potential response rate facilitators.[49] Specifically the following aspects of the questionnaire were found to increase response rates

Prior notification.

Personalization.

Follow-up letter.

---

[47]Francis J. Yammarino, Steven J. Skinner, and Terry L. Childers, "Understanding Mail Survey Response Behavior: A Meta-Analysis," *Public Opinion Quarterly*, 1991, pp. 613–39.

[48]Yu and Cooper, "Quantitative Review of Research Design Effects," pp. 39–41.

[49]Ibid.

Questionnaire response facilitators not effecting a positive impact on response rates include

Cover letter.

Anonymity.

Inclusion of a deadline date.

Return postage.

Appeals (neither social utility nor help-the-researcher).

Handling Nonresponse

Several different remedies for nonresponse error have been proposed. We discuss five approaches to dealing with it.[50]

Estimation of Effects. Whenever possible, the researcher should attempt an **estimation of the effects** of nonresponse. However, this process is complicated because direct validation rarely will be possible. One approach is to link non-response rates to nonresponse effects.

As a first step, nonresponse rates should always be reported. As we indicated, although high response rate is not in itself enough evidence to conclude that non-response bias is small, it does reduce the probability of nonresponse effects. In most instances, it seems reasonable to assume that a small nonresponse is unlikely to produce a large effect on the sample mean value of the variable of interest. To estimate the effects of nonresponse, nonresponse size must be linked to estimates of differences between respondents and nonrespondents. How? The key is to find out information about these differences. This information can be obtained from the sample itself, for example, from follow-ups on a subsample of the nonrespondents or from extrapolating any differences found through call-backs. Another frequent source of information on these differences is the knowledge base accumulated in past studies.

> **estimation of the effects**
> *Method of handling nonresponse error by linking nonresponse rates to nonresponse effects; to estimate the effects of nonresponse, nonresponse size is linked to estimates of differences between respondents and nonrespondents.*

Simple Weighting. **Simple weighting** procedures attempt to remove nonresponse bias by assigning weights to the data to help account for nonresponse. Suppose that in a national survey, response rates differed in each of four major geographical regions. Assume that the response rates were 80 percent in the East, 50 percent in the South, 75 percent in the North, and 60 percent in the West. For the East the weight would be 1.25 (100/80); for the South 2.00 (100/50); for the North 1.33 (100/75); and for the West 1.67 (100/60). Weighting subclasses inversely to their response rates can correct for differences between them; however, this weighting destroys the self-weighting nature of a sample design, and the complications of weighting can sometimes be expensive. We comment on this issue further in Chapter 13.

> **simple weighting**
> *Procedures that attempt to remove nonresponse bias by assigning weights to the data that in some sense account for nonresponse.*

---

[50]Parts of this treatment follow the discussion in Kish, *Survey Sampling*, pp. 557–60.

substitutions
*Method of handling non-
response; nonresponses
are replaced with other
substitute respondents
who are expected to
respond.*

Substitutions. **Substitutions** for nonresponse simply involve replacement—non-responses are simply replaced with other respondents—that is, substitutes that are expected to respond. This approach is based on dividing the overall sample into subclasses. The subclass should be internally homogenous for respondent background characteristics but should vary greatly in terms of response rates. If the subclasses are so constructed, then a substitute can be identified who is similar to a particular respondent and not to respondents already in the sample. The substitution approach is useless for reducing nonresponse bias when replacing a nonrespondent with a respondent who resembles other respondents in the same way.

Imputation. This approach attributes nonresponses to specific questions or an entire questionnaire on the basis of a set of characteristics available for both respondents and nonrespondents. **Imputation** is based on the notion that if there is high correlation between a set of characteristics and the response variable under study, a reasonably good prediction of the "missing" variable (nonresponse) may be obtained from capitalizing on this correlation. In many surveys imputation for nonrespondents is carried out by adjusting the weights of the respondents to account for nonresponse, similar to the simple weighting approach described above, or by a replacement procedure, which was initiated in the 1960 Census, in which a nonresponding household was replaced by the questionnaire responses of the previously listed responding household.[51]

imputation
*Approach that imputes
nonresponses to specific
questions or an entire
questionnaire on the
basis of a set of charac-
teristics available for
both respondents and
nonrespondents.*

Replacement. The **replacement** approach works as follows: Included in the survey are the addresses (or telephone numbers) of nonrespondents from an earlier survey that used similar sampling procedures. When a nonresponse is obtained in the current survey, the interviewer replaces the nonresponse address with an address of a nonrespondent in a previous survey. This approach was originally proposed for in-home (dwelling) personal surveys; through minor modification it can be applied in other survey settings. Obviously, the replacement approach works best in situations in which a firm conducts surveys routinely involving similar survey sampling procedures.

replacement
*Approach to reducing
nonresponse; included
in the survey are the
addresses (or telephone
numbers) of nonrespon-
dents from an earlier
survey that used similar
sampling procedures.
When a response is ob-
tained in the current
survey, the interviewer replaces the nonresponse
address with an address
for a nonresponse in a
previous study.*

For the replacement approach to be successful, three conditions must be in place: (1) the earlier survey nonresponse addresses must be numerous enough and have significantly high chance of response to justify the effort; (2) the relationship of the probability of response to the survey should be strong so that additional responses tend to yield correspondingly large reductions in nonresponse bias—in other words, nonresponse addresses in the earlier survey should be different from respondents already in the sample; and (3) nonresponses of the current survey must be similar in nature to nonresponse from the earlier survey from which the replacement addresses have been taken—ideally, the time between the two surveys should be brief, and both surveys should use similar kinds of respondents.

[51]A comprehensive review of alternative and weighting imputation procedures can be found in D. W. Chapman, "Survey of Nonresponse Imputation Procedures," *Proceedings of the Social Statistics Section, American Statistical Association*, Part I (Washington: American Statistical Association, 1976), pp. 245–51.

SUMMARY

In this chapter we have introduced issues involved in collecting primary research information; our emphasis has been on the major data-collection interviewing methods and the advantage and problems inherent in each. Selecting the appropriate method of data collection is not easy; no single interviewing method provides data more accurate than all the others. The choice among survey-interviewing methods depends on two issues: (1) the suitability of the data-collection method in light of the objectives of the research study and (2) the feasibility (that is, cost, speed, quality of data) of the method. Some of the newer computer-assisted data-collection techniques manage to solve serious problems of traditional methods, and use of these methods will probably increase.

KEY CONCEPTS

survey

cold mail surveys

mail panels

cross-sectional surveys

longitudinal surveys

mail surveys

direct "cold" mail surveys

sampling frame

response rates

telephone surveys

in-home personal interviews

directory-based sampling designs

directory-based telephone interviewing

random-digit directory sample designs

nondirectory-based telephone interviewing

nondirectory sampling designs

personal in-home surveys

mall-intercept personal survey

computer-assisted telephone interviewing (CATI)

self-administered CRT interview

CATI systems

self-administered CRT systems

estimation of effects

simple weighting

substitutions

imputation

replacement

REVIEW QUESTIONS

1. What factors would you consider when choosing among mail, telephone, personal, and mall-intercept interviews?

2. What specific research objectives would lead you to use the new computer approaches to interviewing?

3. Discuss and contrast directory and nondirectory telephone sampling methods.

4. Discuss the issues involved in dealing with non-response errors. What approaches are available for handling this potentially serious problem?

Experimental Research Methods

— Understand the distinction between laboratory and field environments.

— Introduce the concepts of experimentation and causality.

— Explain the necessary and sufficient conditions for inferring cause-and-effect relationships and what is meant by spurious correlation.

— Define the basic concepts of experimentation: *experimental design*, *treatments*, *experimental effects*, and *extraneous causal factors*.

— Discuss the various types of validity.

— Examine the factors that can jeopardize internal and external validity.

INTRODUCTION

Primary research is frequently conducted in an attempt to shed light on the *causal* relationships between the marketing-mix elements and various consumer responses. For example, do consumers view price as an indicator of quality? Does an aggressive couponing program lead to more sales? Questions like these involve *cause and effect* and, consequently, the concept of *experimentation*.

Like scientists, marketing executives and researchers are practicing experimenters; however, their laboratory is often the marketplace and their subjects human beings, which makes cause-and-effect relationships more difficult to assess.

Chapter 7 considers the role of experimentation in marketing research. We begin with a brief discussion of research environments. Next we examine causality and the conditions necessary for testing cause-and-effect relationships. We turn to a discussion of validity and the factors that can jeopardize internal and external validity. Our major emphasis is on the more frequently used experimental designs, those that marketing researchers employ regularly. Throughout the discussion, we describe the factors that can jeopardize the validity of our experiments.

RESEARCH ENVIRONMENTS

Research environments can be classified by the degree to which they provide a realistic or artificial setting. In a **realistic research environment,** the respondent is placed in a situation similar to that in which the behavior under study would naturally occur.

realistic research environment
Situation similar to the normal situation in which the behavior under study would naturally occur.

Laboratory Experimental Environments

The **laboratory experimental environment** allows the experimenter to have direct control over most, if not all, of the crucial factors that might affect the experimental outcome. Experiments take place in environments constructed solely for that purpose. The setting is rigorously specified and controlled. Laboratory experiments have been used in concept testing, taste testing, package testing, advertising effectiveness studies, and simulated pretest markets, though the degree of control exercised varies with the specific nature of the research project.

laboratory experimental environment
Research environment constructed solely for the experiment. The experimenter has direct control over most, if not all, of the crucial factors that might possibly affect the experimental outcome.

Field Experimental Environment

A **field experimental environment** is a natural setting—the environment in which the behavior under study would likely occur. Many marketing research studies are conducted in natural settings. Control is still a factor in field experiments. In fact, as the situation permits, the marketing experimenter should impose as much control as possible over those factors that could influence the experimental outcome.

field experimental environments
Natural settings; experiments undertaken in the environment in which the behavior under study would likely occur.

EXPERIMENTATION

An experiment entails some sort of test. The test should allow us to discern the effects of an independent variable on a dependent variable, controlling for extraneous factors that might influence the outcome. An **independent variable** is a variable that the researcher has some control over. It can be manipulated in that its value can be changed independently of other variables. The independent variable is generally assumed to be related in some way to the dependent variable under study. This is why independent variables are sometimes referred to as *explanatory variables*. The **dependent variable,** also referred to as the criterion variable, is the response measure or criterion that is under study. Its value is presumed to be determined at least in part by the independent variable that has been manipulated. To better understand experimentation we need to become familiar with the concept of causality and with several basic aspects of experiments.

independent variable
A factor in an experiment over which the experimenter has some control; if the experimenter manipulates its value, this is expected to have some effect on the dependent variable.

dependent variable
The response measure under study in an experiment whose value is determined by the independent variable.

Causality

By **causality** we mean that a change in one variable produces a change in another variable or, in other words, that one variable affects, influences, or determines some other variable. In many cases causality is difficult to prove because most effects have multiple causes. Hence, in attempting to establish causality, we must

causality
Relationship where a change in one variable produces a change in another variable. One variable affects, influences, or determines some other variable.

be particularly sensitive to competing explanations, to other extraneous variables that might have produced the observed cause-and-effect relationship. To infer causality requires at least three conditions: (1) concomitant variation, (2) time order of occurrence of variables, and (3) control over other possible causal factors.

Concomitant Variation. Without concomitant variation, causality cannot be proved or even inferred. **Concomitant variation** is the degree to which a variable X (for example, advertising expenditures) thought to be a cause covaries with a variable Y (for example, sales) thought to be an effect. Concomitant variation is another way of saying that two variables are associated. In Chapter 16 we present several different statistical measures used to compute the extent to which two variables are associated (i.e., covary). For now, we will refer to association in a general way.

Consider Exhibit 7–1, which shows three different patterns of covariation, or association, for two variables. In panel a the two variables, price and quantity, are **negatively associated**—high values of price are associated with low values of quantity demanded. In panel b the two variables, unit sales and advertising expenditures, are **positively associated**—high values of unit sales are associated with high values of advertising expenditures. And in panel c the two variables, automobile sales per month and inches of rainfall in 1993 per month, exhibit no association—high values of automobile sales are associated with both high and low values of rainfall per month. The tendency is to say that the positive or negative association shown in panel a or panel b is evidence of causation between price and quantity and between unit sales and advertising expenditures, whereas the lack of association shown in panel c is evidence of the lack of causation between automobile sales per month and inches of rainfall per month.

Unfortunately, association by itself does not demonstrate causation. If two variables are causally related they must by necessity share association or covary, but the converse is not true. In fact, two variables can be associated because of a third variable that has not been accounted for. Consider the data shown in Table 7–1. The table gives hypothetical data on the relationship between top box intent (percent definitely would buy) scores and respondent attitudes toward a new product concept. One commonly accepted idea is that attitude change leads to behavior change and, indeed, in panel a we see a strong positive association between liking the product concept and top box intent scores. Of the 362 respondents who indi-

concomitant variation
The degree to which a variable (X) *thought to be a cause covaries with a variable* (Y) *thought to be an effect.*

negative association
Relationship where high (low) values of one variable are associated with low (high) values of another variable.

positive association
Relationship where high (low) values of one variable are associated with high (low) values of another variable.

EXHIBIT 7–1
———
Patterns of
Association

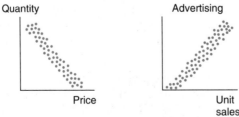
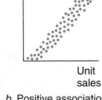
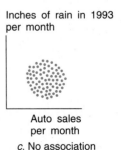

a. Negative association
b. Positive association
c. No association

cated that they liked the new product concept, 68 percent checked the top box on the purchase-intent scale; similarly, of the 638 respondents who indicated dislike, 82 percent also indicated that they would not likely purchase the product.

However, suppose that the marketing researcher suspects that the attitude-behavior relationship is actually influenced by another variable relating to whether the respondent has previously used items in this product category. The aggregate table is then split to form a prior-user panel b and a nonuser panel c. In the user group the chance of a respondent liking the new product idea is 80 percent (300/375); similarly, the likelihood of a respondent checking the top box on the purchase-intent scale is also 80 percent (240/300). On the other hand, in the non-user group, the chances are 10 percent in both cases: (62/625) and (6/62). Thus, if we control for prior respondent use, we can "explain" the apparent cause-and-effect relationship between a respondent's attitude and purchase intentions. In trying to demonstrate cause-and-effect relationships, it is necessary to investigate whether some other variable is the source of the association.

In cases in which a third variable is the actual cause of the observed association between two or more variables, we say that the original association was "spurious." **Spurious association** simply means an inappropriate causal interpretation of an observed association; it is not the association that is inappropriate, but rather the imputed cause-and-effect relationship.

spurious association
Inappropriate causal interpretation of an observed association.

Temporal Ordering of Variables. To say that a change in variable A produces a change in variable B requires that A occurs either before or simultaneously with B and not after it. For example, to say that price changes have a causal impact on quantity sold requires that a price change occur before measuring units sold. **Temporal ordering** of variables is necessary to ensure the proper link between the cause and the effect events. A problem arises when two variables can legitimately be both a cause and an effect of each other. For example, increasing advertising budgets can lead to increases in sales volume, yet increases in sales volume can lead

temporal ordering
The cause of an event should precede its occurrence in time.

TABLE 7–1
———
Spurious Association

Attitudes	Top Box Intent Score		
	No	Top Box	Total
a. Aggregate			
Like	116 (.18)	246 (.68)	362 (.36)
Dislike	522 (.82)	116 (.32)	638 (.64)
	638	362	1,000
b. User			
Like	60	240	300 (.80)
Dislike	15	60	75 (.20)
	75 (.20)	300 (.80)	375
c. Nonuser			
Like	56	6	62 (.10)
Dislike	507	56	563 (.90)
	563 (.90)	62 (.10)	625

to increases in advertising expenditures, especially in cases in which advertising budgets are a fixed percentage of sales. In any event, when demonstrating cause-and-effect relationships, be sure to justify the presumed causal time order among the respective variables.

Control over Other Possible Causal Factors. Even if we observe concomitant variation among two variables and can verify time order, causality is still questionable if the researcher has not searched for other factors that might have influenced the results. Cause-and-effect relationships must be inferred; therefore, to avoid misleading and perhaps erroneous inferences, other competing explanations for the observed effect must be investigated.

The Pepsi Challenge campaign began in 1975 in the Dallas, Texas, market, where Pepsi-Cola had an 8 percent share of market compared with Coca-Cola's 27 percent share.[1] PepsiCo, Inc., retained an independent research firm to conduct double-blind taste-tests, where cola drinkers tasted Coca-Cola and Pepsi-Cola without knowing which was which. The tests were aimed at finding out which cola consumers really preferred.

The results indicated that more than half the Coca-Cola drinkers tested actually preferred the taste of Pepsi. The research was translated into local television and print advertising and was called the Pepsi Challenge.

The Pepsi Challenge campaign was considered a success. In the Dallas area, for example, Pepsi-Cola's share of market increased 50 percent within a year after the Pepsi Challenge TV and local print campaign was launched. However, it is legitimate to ask whether there were other factors that might explain the apparent cause-and-effect relationship between Pepsi's increase in market share and the taste-test results as reported in the Pepsi Challenge campaign. Coca-Cola contended in a television commercial airing in the Dallas market that the blind taste-tests were misleading and inaccurate. Price-cutting promotional activities conducted simultaneously by both Coke and Pepsi might have seriously confounded the taste-testing results. Our point is that although these alternative explanations for Pepsi's increased market share are conjecture, they nevertheless must be considered and controlled for in order to unequivocably substantiate the reasons for Pepsi's success occurring concurrently with the airing of the challenge campaign.

Each of the three conditions we have described is necessary but not sufficient for inferring causality. To appropriately infer causality requires that *all* three conditions be in place. Let's examine the difficulty of satisfying each of these conditions. Because many different types of variables covary, especially over time, concomitant variation is generally very easy to satisfy. Advertising expenditures and sales volume covary, top box purchase-intent scores are associated with product-feature evaluations, and favorable test market results are related to the commercial success of a new product. The marketing researcher will find plenty of relationships, only the cause-and-effect inference is elusive.

---

[1]This material has been adapted from W. W. Talarzyk, *Cases for Analysis in Marketing* (Hinsdale, Ill.: Dryden Press, 1977).

In certain settings it is easy to say that X precedes Y, whereas in others it is almost impossible. Where the effect is measured after exposure to the cause agent, we can be sure of the time order of variables. Whenever the marketing researcher has control over exposing respondents to the cause agent (as in split-cable TV, advertising effectiveness studies, or a mall intercept), it is relatively easy to ensure that the cause variable precedes the presumed effect variable.

Because marketing related effects can be produced by multiple factors, many of which are difficult to control, the marketing researcher will typically find it difficult to present compelling evidence eliminating all other possible causal factors, unless the study is undertaken in rigorously specified, operationalized, and controlled settings.

Experimental versus Nonexperimental Designs

Experimental Designs.   In an **experimental design** the researcher has direct control over at least one independent variable, manipulates at least one independent variable, and controls which respondents will be exposed to the manipulated independent variable. The key elements involved in experimental design are

experimental design
Research concept where the researcher has direct control over at least one independent variable and manipulates at least one independent variable.

1. The treatment conditions that will be manipulated.
2. The respondents who will be exposed to the manipulation.
3. The respondents who will not be exposed to the manipulation.
4. The dependent variable that will be measured.
5. The procedure that will be used in testing.

A **treatment** refers to the independent variable that is manipulated. **Manipulation** means that the researcher has purposely set the levels of the independent variable to test for a specific cause-and-effect relationship. For example, to test the relationship between price and imputed quality the experimenter might expose respondents to four different price levels and record the quality ratings associated with each price level. In this case, price is the manipulated independent variable; the single treatment factor, price, has four treatment conditions, defined by the specific price levels used. Thus, the treatment conditions specify the manipulation under which the measurements on the dependent variable, in this case, quality ratings, are taken. Note that in this simple price-quality experiment, the researcher presumably has control over which treatment condition a respondent is exposed to; in other words, who sees what. Finally, as we will soon discuss, the way this price-quality experiment is implemented will determine the extent to which we can comfortably say that the price does or does not affect imputed quality, and it will affect the ability to generalize the results to the wider population at large.

treatment
Term for that independent variable that has been manipulated.

manipulation
Setting the levels of an independent variable to test a specific cause-and-effect relationship.

Nonexperimental Designs/Ex Post Facto Research.   In nonexperimental designs there is no manipulation of an independent variable nor does the researcher have control over which respondents are exposed to the independent variable. Nonexperimental designs are typically referred to as *ex post facto* (after the fact) because the outcome is first observed and then an attempt is made to find the causal factor that presumably has caused the effect. Consider, for example, the following scenario.

> A research manager for a regional bank was concerned with assessing customer images of their various branch locations. A mail survey was sent to a sample of the bank's customers. Among other things, the survey asked whether they were satisfied with the services provided by the branch location that they used. Each respondent rated his or her branch location on a number of attributes, for example, friendliness of bank personnel, convenience of location, parking facilities, and so forth. After receiving the questionnaires, the manager divided the sample into two groups; those who expressed satisfaction with the branch location and those who expressed dissatisfaction. An analysis of these two groups revealed that compared with customers who expressed satisfaction, dissatisfied customers rated their branch location as unsatisfactory with respect to friendliness of service. The researcher concluded that friendliness of service is the primary factor leading to customer satisfaction, and, consequently, it plays an important part in the decision about which bank to use.

In the study described above the treatment conditions, in this case, satisfaction/dissatisfaction with a branch location, were formed after the fact, and then the researcher looked for possible causal factors that could explain these two conditions. There was no manipulation nor did the researcher exercise any control over the respondent. One of the problems here is that the satisfied and dissatisfied groups have been self-selected; that is, respondents actually determined, by their answers to the satisfaction question, which group they would be placed in. It may well be that another factor accounts for the association between branch location satisfaction and rating of personnel friendliness; for example, the dissatisfied group may contain a greater percentage of customers who bank via an automatic teller machine (ATM). The point here is that the observed association may be spurious. Although nonexperimental designs/ex post facto research may be indicative of possible causal relationships, they must be supplemented with more controlled testing, tests that are more closely aligned with experimental designs, in order to make the researcher feel more comfortable with making cause-and-effect type statements.

Experimental Effects

experimental effect
Impact of the treatment conditions on the dependent variable. Each treatment condition's effect indicates the influence of that condition on the dependent variable.

The **experimental effect** denotes the impact of the treatment conditions on the dependent variable. We want to determine how each treatment condition influences the dependent variable; in other words, we want to determine the *effect* of each treatment condition.

To better understand the concept of an effect and how it might be computed, consider the following. Suppose that 20 respondents, who have agreed to participate in an experiment, are assigned to one of five treatment conditions, each reflecting a different advertising execution. In other words, there are four respondents per treatment condition, and each treatment group is exposed to one of the five advertisements. The objective of the study is to measure the effects of the different advertising executions on aided 24-hour day-after recall scores. Aided 24-hour day-after recall scores could be collected by telephoning the respondents one day (24 hours) after exposure to the advertisement and asking whether they recall any features or aspects of what they saw—for example, brand name, price, or package design.

Let y_{ij} denote the 24-hour day-after recall score for the ith respondent who saw the jth treatment condition. Assume, for simplicity, that the 24-hour day-after recall has been coded so that the highest recall score is 10 and the lowest recall score is 0. Table 7–2 shows hypothetical data for each of the 20 respondents. The five different treatment conditions have been assigned the numbers 1 through 5. Note that the table reveals a distinct ordering of the recall scores by treatment condition. Let $\bar{y}_{+j}$ denote the mean recall score in the jth treatment condition, where the "+" subscript indicates that we have summed over those respondents belonging to the jth treatment condition in computing the mean. From Table 7–2 we find that

$$\bar{y}_{+1} = (0 + 1 + 2 + 1)/4 \quad = 4/4 \; = 1$$
$$\bar{y}_{+2} = (3 + 2 + 1 + 2)/4 \quad = 8/4 \; = 2$$
$$\bar{y}_{+3} = (5 + 7 + 4 + 4)/4 \quad = 20/4 = 5$$
$$\bar{y}_{+4} = (9 + 10 + 7 + 10)/4 = 36/4 = 9$$
$$\bar{y}_{+5} = (7 + 8 + 5 + 8)/4 \quad = 28/4 = 7$$

Treatment conditions 4 and 5 produce much higher recall scores than treatment conditions 1 or 2. It seems that the variation in recall scores has something to do with which treatment condition a respondent saw. However, recall scores are not constant within a treatment condition; that is, not all respondents exposed to the same advertisement exhibit the same recall score. Each respondent would seem to have a unique reaction to the advertisement that is unshared by the other respondents who saw the same treatment condition. Based on this line of reasoning, each respondent's recall score can be viewed in terms of three components: an overall mean, which does not depend on which advertisement the respondent saw; an estimated effect that is due to the particular advertisement that the respondent did see; and an error effect that is unique to each respondent. Some interesting insights follow. For example, the deviation of any respondent's recall score from

Treatments									
Ad1		Ad2		Ad3		Ad4		Ad5	
Person	Recall	Person	Recall	Person	Recall	Person	Recall	Person	Recall
1	0	1	3	1	5	1	9	1	7
2	1	2	2	2	7	2	10	2	8
3	2	3	1	3	4	3	7	3	5
4	1	4	2	4	4	4	10	4	8
Total (y_{++})	4		8		20		36		28
Average ($\bar{y}_{+j}$)	1		2		5		9		7

TABLE 7–2
—
Hypothetical Data for an Advertising Experiment

the overall common mean is composed of two parts, namely, an estimated effect associated with the jth treatment condition and an estimated effect unique to the ith respondent.

The estimated effect of the jth treatment condition on a respondent's recall score can also be easily obtained by asking a simple question: Why should a respondent's score be higher or lower than the overall common mean? Well, one source of difference is due to the particular advertisement seen by the respondent. Thus, we can compare the treatment condition means with the overall common mean obtained from summing all of the recall scores and dividing by the number of respondents $[(0 + 1 + 2 + \cdots + 8 + 5 + 8)/20 = 96/20 = 4.8]$. We can say that the differences between the mean-treatment-condition recall scores and the overall-common-mean recall score represents explained or accounted for variation because we know that such differences exist since the treatment conditions have different effects on 24-hour day-after recall scores.

From the preceding discussion it also follows that the estimated error effect for the ith respondent in the jth treatment condition represents all of the effects on a respondent's recall score that are not due to or accounted for by the treatment condition seen by the respondent. In other words, we cannot explain why respondents who have seen the same advertisement have different recall scores. In this sense, we can say that such differences are unexplained and due to the unique reactions of each respondent. For example, in Table 7–2 we see that respondents' recall scores in treatment condition 5 range from a low of 5 to a high of 8. This variation must be due to an error component of the recall score, since for respondents who saw the same advertisement the overall mean effect and the treatment effect are constants. What are the sources of error variation? Unique respondent effects, chance fluctuations in a respondent's behavior, extraneous factors—in short, all other effects not due to the treatment condition. These then constitute error effects whose size the researcher attempts to minimize by using appropriate design and experimental controls.

Controlling Extraneous Causal Factors

Extraneous causal factors are variables that can affect the dependent variable and, therefore, must be controlled. Such factors are typically referred to as **confounds or confounding variables** because, unless controlled for, they are confounded with the treatment conditions. They make it impossible to say that differences in the dependent variable are due to the different treatment conditions alone. For example, in the advertising execution/recall experiment of Table 7–2, it would have been incorrect to attribute higher recall scores to treatments 4 and 5 if we had found that respondents in these treatment conditions had greater brand familiarity than respondents who had been assigned to the other treatment groups.

There are four basic strategies for controlling extraneous factors: randomization, physical control, design control, and statistical control. All attempt to remove the differential effect of extraneous causal variables across the various treatment conditions.

confounds or confounding variables
Extraneous causal factors (variables) that can possibly affect the dependent variable and, therefore, must be controlled.

By randomizing respondents to treatment conditions we would hope that the extraneous causal factors will be equally represented in each treatment condition. Respondents can be randomly assigned to treatment conditions by using what are called *random numbers.* Using random numbers to assign respondents to treatment groups results in each respondent having the same chance of being assigned to each treatment condition. Thus, we can view the **randomization** process as being equivalent to pulling a respondent's name out of a hat and then assigning the respondent to one of the treatment conditions. Random assignment helps ensure that the treatment groups do not differ before the treatment begins. We can check whether the randomization process worked by collecting measures on each possible causal factor and then examining the distribution of these extraneous variables across the treatment condition. The distribution of these extraneous variables should not be too different across the treatment conditions. In Chapter 16 we discuss different ways of statistically testing for group differences that can be used to perform a formal check on the randomization process.

Physical control means that we hold constant the value or level of the extraneous variable. For example, in our advertising execution/recall experiment the researcher could screen respondents for brand familiarity and sample only those with equivalent prior brand experience and usage behavior. Physical control often involves **matching** respondents. By *matching* we mean that respondents are matched on a set of background characteristics before being assigned to the treatment conditions. We discuss two different matching procedures later in this chapter.

Extraneous causal factors can also be controlled by using specific types of experimental designs. As we will see, several types of experimental designs are available; they differ according to the kinds of extraneous causal factors that they can control for. Later in the chapter we discuss several types of experimental designs.

Finally, extraneous causal factors can be statistically controlled, if the extraneous causal variable can be identified and measured. Statistical control of a causal variable employs **analysis of covariance (ANCOVA).** ANCOVA removes the effects of the confounding variable on the dependent variable by a statistical adjustment of the dependent variable's mean value within each treatment condition. We will discuss ANCOVA in the appendix of Chapter 15.

VALIDITY

There are two principal goals in conducting an experiment: (1) to draw valid conclusions about the effects of an independent variable and (2) to make valid generalizations to a larger population or setting of interest. We now discuss types of validity.[2]

randomization
Process by which respondents are randomly assigned to treatment conditions for the purpose of controlling extraneous factors in an experimental setting.

physical control
An attempt to hold constant the value or level of the extraneous variable.

matching
Involves matching respondents on one or several background characteristics or other factors before assigning them to treatment conditions.

analysis of covariance (ANCOVA)
A means of statistical control where the effects of the confounding variable on the dependent variable are removed by a statistical adjustment of the dependent variable's mean value within each treatment condition.

---

[2]This definition of validity and our ensuing discussion is based on the work of P. T. Campbell and S. T. Stanley, *Experimental and Quasi Experimental Design for Research* (Chicago: Rand McNally, 1963); and T. D. Cook and P. T. Campbell, *Experimentation: Design Analysis Issues for Field Settings* (Chicago: Rand McNally, 1979).

validity
Refers to the best approximation to truth or falsity of a proposition, including propositions concerning cause-and-effect relationships.

internal validity
Determination of whether the experimental manipulation actually produced the differences observed in the dependent variable.

external validity
Determination of whether the research findings of a study (cause-and-effect relationships) can be generalized to and across populations of persons, settings, and times.

In general, **validity** refers to the approximation to the truth or falsity of a proposition. In the context of experimentation, these propositions typically relate to statements concerning cause-and-effect relationships.

— **Internal validity** examines whether the experimental manipulation (the treatment conditions) actually produces the differences observed in the dependent variable. In other words, internal validity focuses on evidence demonstrating that the variation in the dependent variable was the result of exposure to the treatment conditions rather than to other extraneous causal factors. Obviously, control is a key requisite in demonstrating internal validity and, thus, laboratory experimental settings offer greater internal validity than do field experimental settings.

— **External validity** refers to whether the research findings of a study (cause-and-effect relationships) can be generalized to and across populations of persons, settings, and times.[3] In essence, external validity asks the question: To what extent do samples represent the population? Thus, because of their realism, field experimental settings offer greater external validity than do laboratory experimental settings.

FACTORS JEOPARDIZING VALIDITY

If not controlled for, extraneous factors pose threats that can jeopardize the internal and external validity of every experiment. To ensure that the experiment will not be confounded, the researcher must try to rule out all rival explanations that might produce differences in the dependent variable. Even though this task is formidable, the following discussion of threats to valid inference making provides an excellent starting point.[4] Exhibit 7–2 offers a brief description of errors that can confound the results of an experiment.

Threats to Internal Validity

As we discussed earlier, internal validity is concerned with whether the differences between treatment conditions are in fact due to the treatment conditions themselves, or whether rival hypotheses can explain the differences. We now turn to several common threats to internal validity.

history
Threat to internal validity; refers to those specific events that occur simultaneously with the experiment but that have not been controlled for.

History.   **History** refers to those specific events that occur simultaneously with the experiment but that have not been controlled for. Because these events occur at the same time as the experiment, they can affect the dependent variable and, thus, are confounded with the treatment conditions. For example, consider a "heavy-up" advertising program, in which a greater-than-average amount of advertising money is allocated to a mature brand (e.g., Bromo Seltzer) that is currently not being supported. The advertising program is launched in one or two test mar-

---

[3]Ibid, p. 38.
[4]Campbell and Stanley, *Experimental and Quasi Experimental Design*, pp. 5–6; Cook and Campbell, *Experimentation: Design Analysis Issues*, chapter 2.

EXHIBIT 7–2
———

Threats to Internal
and External Validity

Internal

— History—events occurring simultaneously with the experiment.
— Maturation—biological and/or psychological changes in respondents.
— Testing—after measurements taken on same subjects as before measures.
— Instrumentation—changes in calibration of the measurement instruments.
— Selection bias—improper assignment of respondents to treatment conditions.
— Mortality—differential loss of respondents from treatment groups.

External

— Reactive or interactive effects of testing—pre-exposure measurement sensitizes respondent to treatment.
— Interactive effects of selection bias—improper (nonrandom) assignment of subjects to groups results in different responses to treatment.
— Surrogate situations—experimental setting (test units, treatment, or other elements) differs from real world.

kets, and sales are monitored before and after the program launch. The difference between before-and-after sales levels is the assumed change due to the manipulated variable, that is, the increased advertising expenditures. However, other factors related to competitor's attempts to "jam" the test (e.g., trade promotions, couponing) that occur at the same time as the heavy-up advertising experiment could have produced (or nullified) the observed change in sales levels. In general, test markets are particularly vulnerable to historical factors because of the intentional jamming activities of competitors.[5] Or consider the effects of a feature news story about Bromo Seltzer aired nationally just after a pre- and post-advertising test is begun in several geographically dispersed markets. The news story could affect post-exposure levels. These effects are uncontrollable and are classified as history.

Maturation. **Maturation** refers to changes in the biology (growing older, more experienced) or psychology (changes in beliefs, perceptions) of the respondent that occur over time and can affect the dependent variable irrespective of the treatment conditions. During the experiment respondents may become tired, bored, or hungry—influencing the response to the treatment condition. In general, tracking and market studies that span several months or years are particularly vulnerable to maturation factors because there is no way to know how respondents might be changing over time. Also, maturation can be prevalent in experiments dealing with psychological responses, such as taste-testing studies.

maturation
Threat to internal validity; refers to changes in biology or psychology of the respondent that occur over time and can affect the dependent variable irrespective of the treatment conditions.

Testing. **Testing** refers to the consequences of taking before-and-after exposure measurements on respondents. It occurs when the first measurement, before exposure to the treatment condition, affects the second measurement, taken after

testing
Threat to internal validity; refers to the consequences of taking before-and-after exposure measurements on respondents.

—————
[5]N. Giges, "No Miracle in Small Miracle: Story Behind Failure," *Advertising Age*, August 16, 1982, p. 76.

exposure to the treatment condition. Thus, the post-exposure measurement on the dependent variable is not due to the experimental treatment conditions alone but is a direct result of the respondent's pre-exposure measurement. For example, consider an advertising test service in which respondents are prerecruited and asked to appear at a central testing location. These respondents are given a pretreatment exposure questionnaire covering, among other things, attitudes and intentions to buy a certain brand, which the respondent is aware of but has never tried. After viewing an advertisement for the test brand, they are again asked to fill out the questionnaire. Suppose that the experimenter finds no change when comparing pre- and post-exposure attitudes or intention-to-buy scores. The researcher might conclude that the advertising execution has had no effect. An alternative explanation is that respondents have sought to maintain consistency in their pre- and post-exposure measurement responses. Thus, what drove post-exposure measurement was not the experimental treatment condition but simply the respondent's pre-exposure responses. In general, testing effects occur because the respondent becomes expert at completing the measurement instrument, becomes annoyed at being asked to complete the same questionnaire twice, or becomes "frozen" in the sense of giving a consistent answer based on the initial questioning, and so on. If the respondent is unaware of being measured, testing effects are unlikely to surface.

instrumentation
Threat to internal validity; refers to changes in the calibration of the measurement instrument or in the observers or scorers themselves.

Instrumentation. **Instrumentation** refers to changes in the calibration of the measurement instrument or in the observers or scorers themselves. Instrumentation is most likely to occur when interviewers are used in a before-and-after exposure study. In such settings, interviewers may, with practice, acquire additional skills that make the second reading more precise. On the other hand, interviewers may become bored or tired, and by the time of the second measurement, their performance may have diminished and the recordings may have become less precise. Interviewer bias, discussed in Chapter 6, is an example of instrumentation.

selection bias
Threat to internal validity; refers to the improper assignments of respondents to treatment conditions.

Selection Bias. **Selection bias** refers to the improper assignment of respondents to treatment conditions. It occurs when selection assignment results in treatment groups that differ on the dependent variable before their exposure to the treatment condition. In general, selection bias can occur if respondents are allowed to self-select their own treatment condition or if treatment conditions are assigned to groups. Consider a pricing study in which two price conditions are assigned to various retail outlets. Because of store size differences the experiment can become confounded. The problem is one of nonequivalence of groups. That is, store size affects sales levels irrespective of which price condition was assigned to a store.

mortality
Threat to internal validity; refers to the differential loss (refusal to continue in the experiment) of respondents from the treatment condition groups.

Mortality. **Mortality** refers to the differential loss (that is, refusal to continue in the experiment) of respondents from the treatment condition groups. In general, experimental studies spanning a year or more, even several months, are particularly vulnerable to mortality effects. This is a serious problem in purchase diary panel studies. In addition, mortality effects can surface in experiments where one (or more) of the treatment conditions is relatively undesirable. For example, the recent trend toward irregular-sized, shorter umbrellas has made it difficult to product test normal-sized, new product versions because of their greater inconvenience. Over time, the treatment group with regular-sized umbrellas experiences some loss of respondents, and the respondents who do remain may be different from the other respondents participating in the experiment.

The threats to internal validity are not mutually exclusive. They can occur simultaneously and in certain instances can also interact with one another. For example, *selection-maturation-interaction* refers to the case where, perhaps because of self-selection, the treatment groups change with respect to the dependent variable at different rates over time.

Threats to External Validity

You will recall that external validity is concerned with generalizing research findings to and across populations of persons, settings, and times. Let's turn to several common threats to external validity.

Reactive or Interactive Effects of Testing. The **reactive or interactive testing effect** occurs when a pre-exposure measurement increases or decreases the respondent's sensitivity or responsiveness to the experimental treatment conditions and, thus, leads to unrepresentative results. In contrast to other testing effects with reactive or interactive testing effects, the pre-exposure measurement does not directly affect the post-exposure measurement; rather, the experimental treatment *condition* gains more notice and reactions than it would have if the pre-exposure measurement had not been taken. For example, consider an advertising study designed to assess attitude change for an improved product. The pretreatment exposure questionnaire could heighten respondents' interest, thus making them particularly sensitive to the advertising that they see. Reactive or interactive testing effects occur when the pre-exposure measurement and the treatment conditions interact to produce a joint effect on the dependent variable.

reactive or interactive effects of testing
Threat to external validity that occurs when a pre-exposure measurement increases or decreases the respondent's sensitivity or responsiveness to the experimental treatment conditions and thus leads to unrepresentative results.

Interactive Effects of Selection Bias. **Interactive effects of selection bias** is a situation that occurs when the improper selection of respondents interacts with experimental treatment conditions to produce misleading and unrepresentative results. Because of improper assignment of respondents to treatment conditions, some of the groups have a differential sensitivity or responsiveness to the experimental treatment conditions that cannot be generalized to the wider population.

interactive effects of selection bias
Threat to external validity; situation where the improper selection of respondents interacts with experimental treatment conditions to produce misleading and misrepresentative results.

Surrogate Situations. This threat to external validity occurs because of the use of experimental settings, test units, and/or treatment conditions that differ from those encountered in the actual setting that the researcher is interested in. **Surrogate situations** produce ungeneralizable results. Consider the case where we are interested in measuring subjects' reactions to various advertisements—for example, the five ads used in the 24-hour day-after recall experiment described earlier in this chapter. The subjects view the ads in a controlled environment, and their attention to the ad is more or less forced as a result of the experimental procedure.

surrogate situations
Use of experimental settings, test units, and/or treatment conditions that differ from those to be encountered in the actual setting that the researcher is interested in.

We must ask ourselves if the ads will capture the same attention and subsequent information processing when viewed in a naturalistic setting. Recall scores could be lower or higher for all five treatment conditions simply due to the way people process the ad when it is aired outside the controlled laboratory setting.

Demand Artifacts

demand artifacts
Those aspects of the experiment that cause respondents to perceive, interpret, and act upon what is believed to be the expected or desired behavior.

Demand artifacts are those aspects of the experiment that cause respondents to perceive, interpret, and act upon what is believed to be the expected or desired behavior.[6] Demand artifacts occur because human respondents do not respond passively to experimental situations. Suspicion about the purpose of the experiment, the respondent's prior experimental experience, and obtrusive pre- and postmeasurements are just a few of the possible extraneous factors that can produce demand bias if these artifacts either increase the possibility that the respondent knows the true purpose of the experiment or if the artifacts influence the respondent's perceptions of appropriate behavior.[7]

Demand artifacts may have affected the early experimental studies investigating the quality connotations of price.[8] Early price-quality studies typically presented respondents with brands differentiated only by some letter identification and the relative price (the brands were exactly the same) and found that respondents usually would choose the high-priced brand.[9] Respondents may have correctly guessed the purpose of the study and hypothesized that the experimenter expected them to choose higher priced brands.

Shimp, Hyatt, and Snyder reappraised the potential role of demand artifacts in consumer behavior experiments.[10] They contend that although demand artifacts are an ever-present threat to the internal validity of experimental results, it is difficult to know the extent to which a particular experiment is contaminated or biased by demand artifacts.

Demand artifacts pose serious threats to both internal and external validity. They can confound the internal validity of an experiment when they interact with the experimental treatment conditions to produce misleading results. They also affect generalization of the findings because it is very unlikely that the same set of demand characteristics operating in a laboratory setting will characterize a real-life situation.

---

[6]A. G. Sawyer, "Demand Artifacts in Laboratory Experiments in Consumer Research," *Journal of Consumer Research*, March 1975, pp. 20–30.

[7]See, for example, R. Rosenthal and R. L. Rosnow, *Artifacts in Behavioral Research* (New York: Academic Press, 1969); R. L. Rosnow and L. S. Aiken, "Mediation of Artifacts in Behavioral Research," *Journal of Experimental Social Psychology*, May 1973, pp. 181–201.

[8]Sawyer, "Demand Artifacts," p. 31.

[9]See J. D. McConnell, "The Price-Quality Relationship in an Experimental Setting," *Journal of Marketing Research*, August 5, 1968, pp. 300–303.

[10]T. A. Shimp, B. M. Hyatt, and D. J. Snyder, "A Critical Appraisal of Demand Artifacts in Consumer Research," *Journal of Consumer Research* 18, no. 3 (1991), pp. 273–83.

EXPERIMENTAL DESIGNS

Many different experimental designs are available—so many that it would be unrealistic to try to provide a complete and comprehensive treatment in one chapter. Our strategy is to introduce specific experimental designs that are frequently employed in marketing research studies and to provide examples of how they are used. These designs vary in the degree to which they control for extraneous factors that can jeopardize both internal and external validity. Before discussing specific experimental designs, let's look at the notation used to describe the various designs.

Notation

When discussing specific experimental designs, we use symbols that describe how each works.

- *RR* indicates that respondents have been randomly assigned to treatment conditions.
- *EG* refers to the experiment group, that is, one of the treatment conditions.
- *CG* refers to the control group—the group that is not exposed to the experimental treatment.
- *X* represents the exposure of a group of respondents to one of the experiment treatment conditions.
- *O* refers to the observation or measurement of the dependent variable for each respondent.

In delineating each design we array symbols horizontally and vertically. A horizontal string of symbols indicates movement through time and refers to a specific treatment group. A vertical string of symbols indicates events or activities that occur simultaneously. Subscripts delineate one treatment condition from another and denote order in the measurements.

To clarify how the symbolic scheme is used, let's use these symbols to describe five types of experimental designs.

1. *After-only design*—single group is studied only once.

$$EG: X\ O_1$$

2. *One-group before-after design*—single group is studied twice, once before exposure to the experimental treatment and once after the exposure.

$$EG: O_1\ X\ O_2$$

3. *After-only with control design*—two groups are studied; one group is exposed to the experimental treatment, one group is not, and subjects are randomly assigned to the groups.

$$EG: RR\ X\ O_1$$
$$CG: RR\ \ \ \ O_2$$

4. *Before-after with control-group design*—two groups are studied twice, before and after exposure to the experimental treatment, where respondents are assigned randomly to treatment conditions.

$$EG: RR\ O_1\ X\ O_2$$
$$CG: RR\ O_3\quad O_4$$

5. *Time-series design*—single group is studied over time, before and after exposure to the experimental treatment.

$$EG: O_1\ O_2\ O_3\ X\ O_4\ O_5\ O_6$$

Specific Experimental Designs

We now examine and illustrate some experimental designs that are frequently employed in marketing research. We emphasize the nonstatistical aspects of each design, how it is actually used in real-life marketing settings, and the extent to which it controls for extraneous factors. The testing of treatment effects for statistical significance will be treated in Chapter 15, which discusses *analysis of variance* (ANOVA) models.

after-only design
Experiment that exposes respondents to a single treatment condition followed by a post-exposure measurement.

After-Only Design.   This design exposes respondents to a single treatment condition and follows it with a post-exposure measurement. Exhibit 7–3 presents an abridged marketing research proposal that describes an after-only design involving an advertising recall study. The design calls for telephoning 200 respondents who claim to have watched a particular TV show the night before in any of 34 cities. Respondents are asked both unaided and aided recall questions. First, respondents are asked if they remember seeing a commercial for a product in the product category of interest (**unaided recall**). If they can recall the commercial, they are asked what specific copy execution points of the advertisement they remember. If the commercial they remember is not for the test brand, the respondent is asked whether he or she recalls the commercial for the brand being tested (**aided recall**). All results are compared with Burke category norm scores and are indexed for easier interpretation. The following example summarizes this design.

unaided recall
Respondents are asked if they remember seeing a commercial for a product in the product category of interest.

aided recall
Respondents are asked if they remember a commercial for the brand being tested.

EXAMPLE	EG:	X	O_1
	Respondents who claim to have watched a specific TV show the night before	Test-market advertisement	Unaided, aided recall of specific copy points

The presumption with after-only designs is that there is a causal relationship between exposure to the treatment condition, that is, the manipulation, and the post-exposure reading (measurement). In the context of the study described above, the presumption is that the ability to recall the commercial and the recol-

EXHIBIT 7–3

Marketing Research
Proposal: After-Only
Design

Brand:	Brand Z hair conditioner
Project:	Recall (R) study
Background & Objectives:	The brand group has developed a TV advertisement introducing Brand Z. The objective of this research is to evaluate this copy in a real-life setting.
Research Method:	A minimum of 200 respondents who claim to have watched a particular TV show the night before will be contacted by telephone in any of 34 cities.
Information to Be Obtained:	This study will provide information on the incidence of unaided and aided recall along with specific information on which copy execution points were remembered.
Action Standard:	In order to be judged successful, the percentage of unaided and aided recall scores must be significantly above category norms at the 80 percent confidence level.
Supplier:	Burke Marketing Research Service

lection of specific copy executions is due to the effectiveness, or lack thereof, of the commercial. However, although this inference may, on the surface, have some intuitive appeal, it is actually an assertion that may, in fact, not be accurate. The reason for this is that after-only designs generally afford no control over extraneous factors that could have contributed to the post-exposure readings that were observed. In other words, there may be many other factors, other than the commercial, that could have caused the unaided and aided recall and copy execution scores that were observed. For example, the program in which the test advertisement was aired could be carried by one of the cable TV companies, or the network that is showing the program may have more than one affiliate in the areas in which the study is being conducted. In either event the respondent may have watched the program but may not have been exposed to the new copy execution, but rather to the current advertisement.

Another general problem with after-only designs is the absence of any objective measure to evaluate the experimental effect. In the absence of a control group, a group that has not been exposed to the experimental treatment, it is often extremely difficult to interpret the post-exposure readings. For example, consider the unaided and aided recall scores presented in Table 7–3 (see page 192). Knowing that 27 percent of those who saw the program were able to recall, on an unaided basis, the test advertisement says very little. Is this high? Is it low? Well, it probably depends. Typically, when possible, norms can be used with after-only designs to provide some objective measure of performance. A norm reflects the collective wisdom or experiences of the firm in doing research in a particular product category. For example, we see from Table 7–3 that the norm reported for unaided recall is 30 percent. This might reflect the average of all advertising recall scores obtained over the last three years in this product category. Thus, this design does assess whether or not the test advertisement produces recall scores that are significantly above (or below) category norms. To be statistically significant at the 80 percent confidence level we need percentage differences between actual and norm percentage scores of about 6 to 7 percentage points (see Chapter 15).

	Recall	Index (relative to norm)
Unaided (% of time test ad is named)	27*	90
Norm	30	100
Aided (% of time test ad is named after prompting)	42*	111
Norm	38	100

*Not significantly different from the norm at the 80 percent confidence level.

Brand:	Branded women's hair shampoo
Project:	Advertising study
Background & Objectives:	The brand group has developed a new advertising campaign for branded women's hair shampoo. The objective of this research is to evaluate the effectiveness of a TV advertisement that portrays the brand's new image.
Research Method:	A minimum of 150 respondents will be recruited to central theater locations in four test cities. At the central testing location respondents are first given a personal interview. Next, they view a TV show in which the test advertisement is embedded twice. After viewing, they are again given a personal interview.
Information to Be Obtained:	This study will provide information on brand attitude, image, and purchase intent change scores as well as overall reaction to the test commercial and recall scores.
Action Standard:	All results are compared with category norms at the 80 percent confidence level.
Supplier:	McCollum-Spielman

Before-After Design. In this design, a measurement is taken from respondents before they receive the experimental treatment condition. After the treatment a post-exposure measurement is taken. The treatment effect (TE) is computed by taking $O_2 - O_1$. However, to safely conclude that X and X alone produced the observed $O_2 - O_1$ effect, we must verify that no other possible extraneous factors could have produced the observed result.

Exhibit 7–4 is an abridged marketing research proposal that describes a before-after design. The following example summarizes this design.

EXAMPLE

EG:	O_1	X	O_2
	Recruited respondents are given a questionnaire covering attitude, images, and intention measures	Test advertisement	Respondents are again given a questionnaire covering attitude, images, and intention measures as well as overall reaction to the test advertisement

	Norm		Test Advertisement	
	Percent Change Before-After	Index	Percent Change Before-After	Index Relative to Norm
Overall brand attitude				
Liked extremely	10	100	9	90
Brand image				
Strong agreement with:				
For today's woman	5	100	11	220
Gives hair body	7	100	12	171
Makes hair silky	7	100	13	186
Protection against dryness	8	100	5	63
For all kinds of hair	9	100	4	44
Purchase intention				
Extremely likely to buy	12	100	15	125

TABLE 7–4

Test Results

Table 7–4 presents hypothetical results. The test advertisement appears to have had substantial effects on before-after image and purchase-intent ratings. The principal extraneous factors that could have caused the observed before-after treatment effects appear to be testing, instrumentation, and interactive effects of testing. Moreover, the artificiality of the test environment (surrogate situation— TV program viewing in a theater) might also adversely affect the extra validity of the study.

Before-After with Control Design. This design adds a control group to the basic before-after design just discussed. Respondents are assigned randomly to one of the treatment conditions or to the control group. Random assignment is an important characteristic of this design, which entails the standard before-after exposure measurement in the experimental treatment groups and an analogous before-and-after measurement in the control group, which is never exposed to the experimental treatment. The treatment effect is computed by taking

$$TE = (O_2 - O_1) - (O_4 - O_3)$$

The difference $(O_2 - O_1) - (O_4 - O_3)$ reflects the effect obtained by using a before-after design. We are, in effect, adjusting the standard before-after treatment effect $(O_2 - O_1)$ by the effect that would have been obtained without the experimental treatment $(O_4 - O_3)$.

The experimental group was exposed to the manipulation (X). Hence, any difference in the before-after scores $(O_2 - O_1)$ is due to the manipulation (X) and extraneous error (E). The control group was not exposed to the manipulation; therefore, any difference in the before-after scores for the control group $(O_4 - O_3)$ can only be due to the extraneous error (E). Hence, taking the difference between the two groups controls for the extraneous error,

$$(O_2 - O_1) - (O_4 - O_3) = (X + E) - (E) = X$$

before-after with control design
Experiment that adds a control group to the basic before-after design; the control group is never exposed to the experimental treatment.

EXHIBIT 7–5

Marketing Research
Proposal: Before-
After with Control

Brand:	Brand A mouthwash
Project:	Dollar-off promotional study
Background & Objectives:	The marketing management team has proposed a dollar-off promotional study for Brand A, a brand that is not currently supported. The object of this research is to assess the likely impact that such a program will have.
Research Method:	The Buffalo, New York, area was selected as the test market. A total of 30 retail outlets participated in the study. Stores were randomly assigned to an experimental treatment group (dollar-off promotion) and to the control group (no promotion).
Information to Be Obtained:	This study will provide information on before-and-after share of market.
Action Standard:	To be judged successful the promotional campaign should produce at least a 1.0 percent change in share of market.
Supplier:	Market Facts, Inc.

Exhibit 7–5 presents an abridged marketing research proposal that describes this type of design involving a dollar-off promotional program for a brand currently unsupported by promotional dollars. The following example summarizes this design.

EXAMPLE

EG	RR	O_1	X	O_2
	15 outlets randomly assigned	Share of market, week ending 11/17	Dollar-off promotion, week of 11/18	Share of market, week ending 11/24
CG:	RR	O_3		O_4
	15 outlets randomly assigned	Share of market, week ending 11/17		Share of market, week ending 11/24

Hypothetical results in terms of market share for the experimental and control groups are

− Before week ending 11/17—5.3 (experimental); 5.4 (control).
− After week ending 11/24—6.8 (experimental); 5.6 (control).

Note that with only a before-after design, the estimated effect of the dollar-off promotional program would have been calculated to be 1.5 share points (6.8 − 5.3). However, it is necessary to adjust this effect by what would have been gained without the dollar-off promotional program. Hence, the true treatment effect is calculated to be

$$TE = (6.8 - 5.3) - (5.6 - 5.4)$$

or 1.3 share of market points, which exceeds the action standard requirement.

In general, before-after with control group designs control for all possible extraneous factors except mortality and the interactive effects of testing. History, maturation, and instrumentation should affect the treatment and control groups equally. Testing effects are also controlled for. Since both groups receive the pre-exposure measurement, any effect it has on the post-exposure measures should be the same regardless of treatment group. The effect of pre-exposure measurement can interact with the experimental treatment to affect the post-exposure measurement. In this application, however, interactive testing *effects* are unlikely because the dependent variable is share of market, measured unobtrusively via sales records.

After-Only with Control Design.   In this design a control group is added to the standard after-only design to remove extraneous sources of bias. Respondents are randomly assigned to the treatment and control groups. Typically, in real-life applications respondents are also matched on one or a set of background characteristics. Without a pretest there is no way to assess whether the treatment and control groups are equivalent. The treatment effect is computed by taking the difference, $O_1 - O_2$.

after-only with control design
Experiment where a control group is added to the standard after-only design to control for extraneous sources of bias.

Exhibit 7–6 (see page 196) is an abridged marketing research proposal that describes an after-only with control group design involving a two-cell monadic concept test. In a monadic test the respondent rates the item in question on a scale without reference to other comparison items. In the context of the study described in Exhibit 7–6 respondents rate one of the two checking account programs without any instructions about what specifically to compare it with. Each respondent is free to use whatever reference is most appropriate. However, it is reasonable to suspect that a respondent might use the current fee program when evaluating the new fee schedule; and when evaluating the current fee program the respondent might use a fee program consistent with his or her experiences with checking accounts. We discuss monadic scales in more detail in Chapter 10. The following summarizes this design.

				EXAMPLE
EG:	*RRM* Respondents are matched and randomly assigned	X 15 cents per check condition	O_1 Overall opinion and purchase-intent scores	
CG:	*RRM* Respondents are matched and randomly assigned	Fixed monthly fee of $5.50	O_2 Overall opinion and purchase-intent scores	

Note that we have introduced some new notation. The symbol *RRM* indicates that respondents have been matched and then randomly assigned to one of the

EXHIBIT 7–6

———

Marketing Research
Proposal: After-Only
with Control

Service:	Checking-account fee schedule
Project:	Two-cell monadic concept test
Background & Objectives:	The vice president of a regional commercial bank must decide whether to initiate a new checking-account fee schedule. The new alternative considered is a variable 15 cents per-check-used fee schedule. The current program is a fixed $5.50-per-month fee schedule.
Research Method:	A two-cell monadic after-only concept test was selected. The design calls for 200 bank customers per cell with matched random assignment. Respondents will be matched on checking-account balance and average number of checks used per month. Data collection will take place at four regional branches located in major shopping malls that are geographically dispersed within the state. Thus, there are 50 respondents in each of the two cells in each of the four data-collection cities. After being randomly assigned to one of the treatment groups, respondents are shown a concept board that describes one of the two checking-account fee schedules.
Information to Be Obtained:	The study will provide information on overall opinions, purchase intent scores, and account characteristics.
Action Standard:	To be judged superior, the following should hold: (1) the percentage of respondents checking top box opinion ("excellent") for one of the checking-account fee schedules should exceed the other by at least 10 percentage points; and (2) top box purchase-intent scores in the experimental group should exceed 55 percent. If criteria 1 and 2 are both realized, the decision will rest on criterion 2.
Supplier:	Market Facts, Inc.

TABLE 7–5

———

Opinion and
Purchase Intention
Results

Location	Treatment Composition	Excellent	Most Definitely Would Use
A	$0.15/check $5.50/month	38 62	8
B	$0.15/check $5.50/month	42 60	16
C	$0.15/check $5.50/month	40 64	14
D	$0.15/check $5.50/month	44 58	20
Overall	$0.15/check $5.50/month	41 61	17

two treatment groups. That is, one member of the matched pair is randomly assigned to one of the groups and the other member is assigned to the other group. As we indicated, in this application there is no control group per se, but rather the current fee-schedule program acts as the control group.

Table 7–5 presents hypothetical results as the percentage of respondents who checked top box opinion ("excellent"), and top box purchase-intent (most definitely would use). It is clear from the table that the fixed $5.50 monthly fee schedule had greater appeal than the alterative 15 cents per-check-used fee schedule and exceeds the action standards.

In general, after-only with control designs do not control for selection bias. However, respondent matching coupled with random assignment can control selection bias. Finally, since there is no pre-exposure measurement, this design also eliminates the possibility of interactive testing effects.

Nonequivalent Before-After with Control Quasi Design. This **nonequivalent before-after with control quasi design** is similar to the before-after with control design but does not use a random assignment rule; we will use the term *quasi* when referring to experimental designs where the researcher is unable to achieve complete control over the scheduling of the treatments or cannot randomly assign respondents to experimental treatment conditions. **Quasi-experimental designs** are frequently used in marketing research studies because cost and field considerations often prohibit direct control over randomization of respondents or the scheduling of treatments. However, in the absence of such controls, the chance of obtaining confounded results is greatly increased and the marketing researcher must recognize what specific factors have not been controlled for and, wherever possible, incorporate their effects into the interpretation of the research finding.[11]

The quasi before-after with control design can be symbolically represented as

$$EG: RM\ O_1\ X\ O_2$$
$$CG: RM\ O_3\ \ \ \ O_4$$

Once again we have a standard before-after exposure measurement in the experimental treatment group and an analogous before-and-after measurement in the control group, which is never actually exposed to the experimental treatment. In this case, however, respondents are not randomly assigned to treatment and control groups. Instead, respondents are first matched on one or a set of relevant background factors to produce two groups of matched pairs and then a decision is made as to which respondent group will receive which condition, either experimental treatment or control. Thus, treatments are randomly assigned to groups as opposed to randomly assigning each member of a matched pair to a treatment. The symbol *RM* is used to denote this kind of assignment procedure. Exhibit 7–7 (see page 198) illustrates the difference.

Exhibit 7–8 (see page 198) presents an abridged marketing research proposal that describes a quasi before-after with control design involving a *heavy-up* advertising program for a branded antacid product not currently supported, that is, the brand's advertising budget has been held relatively constant and has not been increased above maintenance-level expenditures. The following example summarizes this design.

---

[11]For a comprehensive discussion of quasi-experimental designs see Cook and Campbell, *Experimentation: Design Analysis Issues.*

nonequivalent before-after with control quasi design
Experimental design similar with the before-after with control design except not utilizing a random assignment rule. Respondents are first matched on one or a set of relevant background factors to produce two groups of matched pairs, and then one group receives the experimental treatment.

quasi-experimental design
Experimental designs in which the researcher is unable to achieve complete control over the scheduling of the treatments or cannot randomly assign respondents to experimental treatment conditions.

EXHIBIT 7–7

———

Random Matched
Pair Assignment
versus Quasi Design
Approach

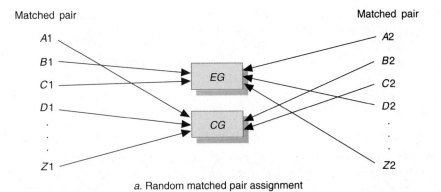

a. Random matched pair assignment

b. Quasi design approach

EXHIBIT 7–8

———

Marketing Research
Proposal: Quasi
Before-After with
Control

Brand:	Branded antacid (mature product)
Project:	Heavy-up advertising tracking study
Background & Objectives:	The brand group has decided to investigate the potential impact of a heavy-up advertising program for a mature branded antacid product that has not been supported with promotional programs. The objective of the study is to measure changes in brand awareness, usage, and perceptions resulting from the advertising program.
Research Method:	The decision was to create a spending program in a definable test-market area. The Buffalo area was selected as the test market with a matched control market consisting of the Albany, Schenectady, and Troy areas. Matched samples of 400 antacid users were contacted by telephone and measured with respect to brand awareness, usage, and perceptions before and three months after the advertising program began.
Information to Be Obtained:	The study will provide information on before-and-after brand awareness, usage, and perceptions.
Action Standard:	A necessary condition for management to recommend a national heavy-up advertising program for this brand is a test-market increase of at least 6.0 percent in the size of the group of people who have "ever" tried the test brand. Final decision rests on the perception and awareness results.
Supplier:	Market Facts, Inc.

EG	RM	O_1	X	O_2
	Matched sample of 400 users identified in the Buffalo, N.Y., test market	Measures of: brand awareness, brand usage (trial/most often used); perceptions of gentleness, efficacy	Translated heavy-up advertising program begins	3 months later— measures of: brand awareness, brand usage (trial/most often used); perceptions of gentleness, efficacy
CG:	RM	O_3		O_4
	Matched sample of 400 users identified in the Albany, Schenectady, and Troy, N.Y., control market	Measures of: brand awareness, brand usage (trial/most often used); perceptions of gentleness, efficacy		3 months later— measures of: brand awareness, brand usage (trial/most often used); perceptions of gentleness, efficacy

Table 7–6 (see page 200) presents hypothetical results in terms of before-and-after brand awareness, trial, and perceived gentleness and efficacy for the test and control markets. From the table we can calculate the treatment effects in the same way as with the standard before-after with control design. Hence, we calculate the effects to be

$$\text{Awareness: } TE = (66 - 65) \quad - (65 - 65) \quad = 1.0$$
$$\text{Trial: } TE \quad = (18.7 - 12.1) - (12.0 - 11.9) = 6.5$$
$$\text{Gentleness: } TE = (46 - 35) \quad - (37 - 36) \quad = 10.0$$
$$\text{Efficacy: } TE \quad = (56 - 55) \quad - (54 - 53) \quad = 0.0$$

It appears that although the heavy-up advertising program has not affected brand awareness, it has increased trial use by 6.5 percentage points, which exceeds the action standard requirement. Also, the advertising campaign appears to have increased the perception that this brand of antacid is gentle while preserving the perception of its effectiveness. Of course, the crucial question about this interpretation is whether it is correct to attribute these results to the heavy-up advertising program alone. Even though this application called for matched samples of respondents and matched test and control markets, a random assignment rule was not used; that is, members (respondents) of each matched pair were not randomly assigned to the experimental test and control groups; thus, we cannot be absolutely sure that the advertising program alone produced these results. The problem

TABLE 7–6

Results of the
Tracking Study

	Test Market Buffalo (%)	Control Market Albany/Schenectady/Troy (%)
Before		
Aware of product	65.0	65.0
Ever tried	12.1	11.9
Respondents indicating product is		
Gentle	35.0	36.0
Effective	55.0	53.0
After		
Aware of product	66.0	65.0
Ever tried	18.7	12.0
Respondents indicating product is		
Gentle	46.0	37.0
Effective	56.0	54.0

is that it is never possible to match respondents in test and control markets exactly.[12] There is always the chance that the experimental test and control groups are nonequivalent, that their pre-exposure measurement on the dependent variable(s) is significantly different. In general, the more similar the pre-exposure measurements, the more we can feel comfortable in asserting that the two groups are equivalent and the more effective is this design. In the present application, the two groups were matched and recruited similarly; thus, it is not surprising to note the similarity in the pre-exposure brand awareness, usage, and perception scores. Note, however, that this design does not generally control for interactive testing effects or interactive effects of selection bias, both of which can seriously confound the results.

two-factor after-only with control design *Experiment differing from the after-only with control group designs by having more than one independent variable.*

Two-Factor After-Only with Control Design. This design differs from the previously discussed after-only with control group designs in having more than a single treatment; that is, the researcher manipulates more than one independent variable. Additional treatment factors are incorporated into a design so that the researcher can control for the interaction of the various treatment factors. With more than a single treatment, the number of cells in the study equals the number of possible combinations of treatment factors. For instance, with three treatment factors, each having three levels, there are nine (3×3) possible combinations or cells. Recall that by treatment factor we mean an independent variable that the researcher has manipulated (for example, price); by treatment level we mean the particular conditions or values of the independent variable that are of interest (for example, in the case of price, $1.00, $1.25, and $1.50 per unit). In such designs respondents are typically randomly assigned to the various experimental cells, though a matching procedure could also be used. Symbolically, a two-factor

---

[12]Electronic test markets (e.g., BehaviorScan) make an attempt to overcome this problem.

after-only (with control) design with six cells (2 × 3), two levels of treatment 1, and three levels of treatment 2 can be represented as

$$
\begin{array}{cc}
X_{1a}X_{2a} & O_1 \\
X_{1a}X_{2b} & O_2 \\
X_{1a}X_{2c} & O_3 \\
EG: \quad RR\ X_{1b}X_{2a} & O_4 \\
X_{1b}X_{2b} & O_5 \\
X_{1b}X_{2c} & O_6 \\
\end{array}
$$

Because each level of treatment 1 (X_{1a}, X_{1b}) is crossed with each level of treatment 2 (X_{2a}, X_{2b}, and X_{2c}), the (statistical) generic name for this class of designs is **completely randomized factorial designs.** In general, factorial designs allow us to estimate the respective effects of each treatment condition alone—commonly referred to as *main effects*—as well as joint effects of the two (or more) treatments—commonly referred to as *interaction effects*. Two treatments are said to interact when a change in a level of one treatment produces a different change in the dependent variable at one level of another treatment than at other levels of this treatment. Note also that typically one level of each treatment represents the control condition, which provides a basis for comparing the individual effect estimates.

completely randomized factorial designs
Generic name for class of designs where each level of a particular treatment is crossed with each level of another treatment.

Exhibit 7–9 (see page 202) presents an abridged marketing research proposal that describes a two-factor, six-cell (3 × 2) after-only with control design involving a package and pricing test study for a mature woman's facial moisturizer. Exhibit 7–10 (see page 203) summarizes this design. Note that the control condition is the cream-colored package, priced at $6.29.

Table 7–7 (see page 203) shows hypothetical results in terms of visibility, brand imagery, and top box purchase-intent scores. The elements in the table give percentages for each cell in the design computed across the two cities. Also shown in the table are the total percentages computed for the package and price treatment factors separately—that is, the total percentages for a factor are computed by averaging the appropriate percentages over the levels of the other treatment factor; in part a of the table the total percentage of respondents who mentioned the test brand name when exposed to the cream-colored package was 25.5 percent ([25 + 26]/2), regardless of the retail price.

Although these total percentages can give us a rough feel for the effects of each treatment factor, they must be interpreted carefully because, if interaction effects are present, sole reliance on the main effect estimates can lead to erroneous conclusions. We will demonstrate how main effects and interaction effects are estimated in the appendix of Chapter 15. However, for now, let us examine Table 7–7 and Exhibit 7–11 and attempt to make some tentative conclusions. Exhibit 7–11 (see page 204) shows bivariate plots based on the data given in Table 7–7. In each figure, percentages are on the vertical axis, and package design occupies the horizontal axis. The two solid lines in each figure trace the movement in percentages for each price level. For example, if the solid lines cross, there is evidence to

Brand: Womans' facial moisturizer

Project: Package/pricing test study

Background & Objective: The beauty-aid brand group is considering replacing the current package design for a mature woman's facial moisturizer. In conjunction with a possible change in package, the brand group is also considering pursuing a premium pricing strategy. Two alternative packages (green and yellow) have been developed to possibly replace the current cream-colored package. The alternative pricing structure being considered is to retail a 6-ounce container for $6.79 as compared with the current price of $6.29. The objective of the study is to assess consumer reactions to the alternative package and price strategies in terms of visibility, consumer perceptions of product end benefits, and consumer purchase intentions.

Research Methods: Three alternative packages (cream, green, and yellow) and two alternative prices ($6.29 and proposed $6.79) will be evaluated monadically in central location shopping centers in Des Moines, Iowa, and Minneapolis, Minnesota. Each combination of package and price alternatives will be viewed among 300 female facial-moisturizer users aged 18 to 64. Age quotas will be established in each of six package-price cell combinations as follows:

Age	Percent
18–24	27
25–34	25
35–49	35
50–64	13

Fifty respondents will be randomly assigned to each of the six cells according to these age quotas. In order to determine consumers' reactions to each alternative package-price combination, respondents in each cell will be exposed to a slide containing the package and price variation and competitive leading brands. The test brand is shown in three positions within each cell to control position order bias. Each slide is shown for one second; the respondents are then asked to recall the brands they have seen. After this questioning the test brand is shown again for a prolonged period, and respondents are questioned about purchase likelihood and product imagery. An after-exposure reading is then taken.

Information to Be Obtained: Information on visibility (percent of respondents mentioning test-brand name after one-second exposure), package imagery (percent of respondents indicating that test brand makes their skin soft and young-looking), and purchase intentions.

Action Standard: A recommendation to replace the current package with either of the two new designs (green or yellow) will be made if the following conditions are met: (1) one of the new designs must be found to be more visible (at the 80 percent confidence level or higher) than the current design, and (2) the new design that generates greater visibility also must produce higher ratings (80 percent confidence level or higher) on the "keeps skin soft" and "keeps skin younger-looking" attributes.

A decision to change the price from $6.29 to $6.79 per 6-ounce container will be made if there are no significant differences (at the 80 percent confidence level or higher) between the respective top box purchase-intent scores.

Supplier: Burke Marketing Research.

EXHIBIT 7–10   Design for Two-Factor After-Only Experiment with Control

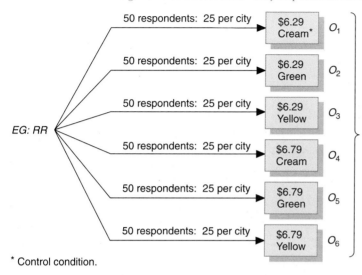

Measures of

Visibility: % of respondents mentioning test
brand name

Imagery: % of respondents indicating
"Makes my skin soft"
"Makes my skin look young"

Purchase intention: % of respondents
checking top box

300 nontest-brand female moisturizer
users who use at least one 6-oz. container
per year, aged 18–64 with the following
age quotas in each cell: 18–64, 27%;
25–34, 25%; 35–49, 35%; and 50–64, 12%

* Control condition.

TABLE 7–7

Results of the
Package/Price Study

a. Visibility

Package Design	$6.29	$6.79	Color Totals*
Cream	25	26	25.5
Green	38	39	38.5
Yellow	30	31	30.5
Price totals	31.0	32.0	

b. Imagery
"Makes My Skin Soft"

Package Design	$6.29	$6.79	Color Totals*
Cream	39	41	40.0
Green	33	58	45.5
Yellow	35	31	33.0
Price totals	35.7	43.3	

"Makes My Skin Look Young"

Package Design	$6.29	$6.79	Color Totals*
Cream	36	38	37.0
Green	35	63	49.0
Yellow	38	40	39.0
Price totals	36.3	47.0	

c. Purchase Intention

Package Design	$6.29	$6.79	Color Totals*
Cream	55	40	47.5
Green	58	62	60.0
Yellow	58	40	40.5
Price totals	56.3	48.3	

*Totals give row and column margin averages.

EXHIBIT 7–11   Plots of Interaction for Two-Factor After-Only with Control Design

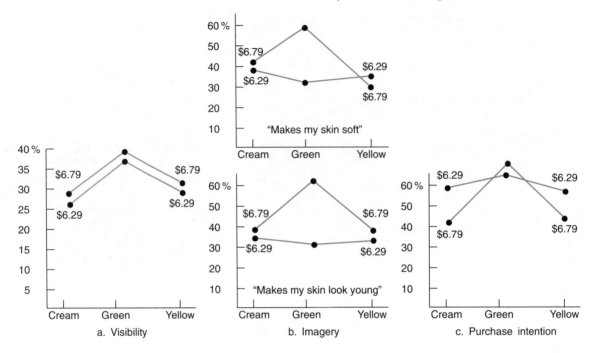

a. Visibility   b. Imagery   c. Purchase intention

suggest that the treatment factors interact. (Actually, any nonparallelism is a sign of interaction.) First, consider panel a, which reports on the percentage of respondents who mentioned the test brand name after a one-second exposure. Note that the solid lines are parallel and do not cross. In this case there appears to be a clear effect due to package color. Regardless of price, the green package produces greater visibility. In panels b and c the results are not so simple. For both imagery questions and purchase intentions there is some indication of an interaction between package and price. For the image questions there is not much difference between the various cell percentages with one important exception: Green at $6.79 does appreciably better than the others. Thus, there appears to be some synergistic effect produced by pairing these two treatment conditions. A similar result is obtained for top box purchase intentions. In general, and as expected, the lower price condition generates a greater percentage of top box purchase-intent scores than does the higher price condition with one important exception; green at $6.79 does slightly better than any of the other package and price variations. Barring problems of selection bias, which can always confound after-only with control designs, the results of the study will likely lead management to recommend a green package design and a retail price of $6.79.

Time-Series Quasi Design. The **time-series quasi design** involves periodic measurements on some group or individual, introduction of an experimental manipulation, and subsequent periodic measurements. As such, it represents a

time-series quasi design
Experiment that involves periodic measurements on some group or individual, introduction of an experimental manipulation, and subsequent periodic measurement.

EXHIBIT 7–12

Marketing Research
Proposal: Time-Series
Design

Brand:	Chewing gum
Project:	National tracking study
Background & *Objective:*	The chewing gum brand group has requested that a national tracking study be conducted next year. The objective of the study will be to track changes in awareness, consumer perceptions, and use resulting from any proprietary or competitive changes in the chewing gum market.
Research *Method:*	The study will be conducted over the next year in monthly waves beginning in February. Interviewing will be conducted by long distance from a central location. Strict probability methods will be used to select telephone numbers from all working exchanges and numbers in the continental United States. Respondents will be randomly selected within a household. Two hundred (200) past-30-day chewing gum users will be interviewed for 11 months, February through December, yielding a total sample of 2,220.
Information to *Be Obtained:*	The study will provide information on changes in brand awareness, consumer perceptions, and use patterns.
Supplier:	Leggett Lustig Firtle, Inc.

longitudinal study. We use the term *quasi* to describe this design because there is no randomization and because the timing of treatment presentation as well as which respondents are exposed to the treatment may not be directly under the control of the researcher. This design appears to be very similar to the before-after $(O_1 \ X \ O_2)$ design discussed at the beginning of this section. As we demonstrate in the example that follows, although this design bears a basic similarity to the before-after design, a time-series design provides more control over extraneous factors, because we take many pre-exposure and post-exposure measurements.

Exhibit 7–12 presents an abridged marketing research proposal requested by the Chewing Gum Brand Group for a national tracking study to be conducted next year.[13] Exhibit 7–13 (see page 206) summarizes this design.

To better understand the effects of the new competitive entry on the market, we have plotted the share of last purchase data for the established brand in Exhibit 7–14 (see page 206). In the figure, the X denotes the approximate market entry of the new diet chewing gum. From the figure it appears that in market A the new competitive product entry has had both a short-run and a long-run negative effect on share of last purchase for the established brand. In market B, the new competitive product entry has had only a temporary short-run negative effect on share of last purchase, as our share of market has bounced back to preentry levels by the end of the year. In markets C and D, the new competitive product entry has not had a real effect, for the changes that have occurred since its introduction are consistent with the prior preentry share of last purchase history. It is important to note that if we had examined only the change between June and July, as would be done if a one-group after-only design was used, the conclusion would have been that the new competitive product entry had a detrimental effect on our share of

---

[13] In commercial marketing research studies using this type of design, respondents would be scheduled so that there would be 200 different respondents in each month.

EXHIBIT 7–13   Time-Series Quasi Design

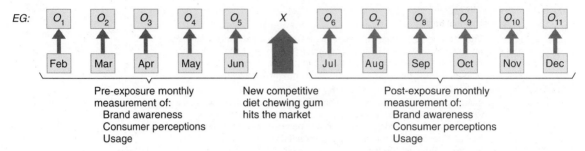

EXHIBIT 7–14   Share of Last Purchase for Established Brand

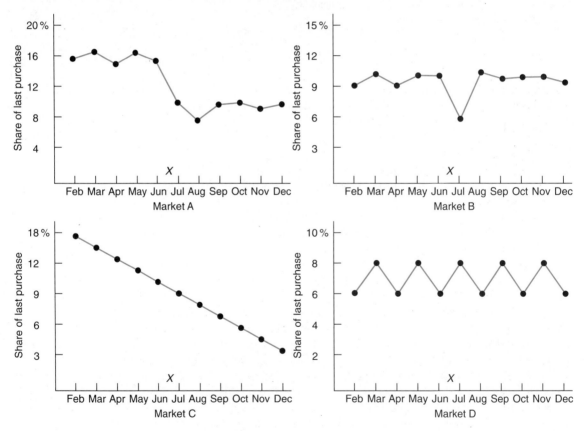

last purchase in all four markets; in addition, we would never have understood the nature of the effects in markets A and B.

Because of the multiple measurements, February through December, this design provides controls over several types of extraneous variables. A maturation effect, which could have produced the June through July change, is ruled out because this effect would show up in the other monthly measurements as well; that is, it would not affect the June through July months alone. Testing and instrumentation effects can also be ruled out for similar reasons; and if some care is taken, selection bias and mortality can be minimized. The possible uncontrollable sources of bias relate to history (for example, competitive activity) and interactive testing effects due to the repeated measurements taken on each respondent. In addition, selection bias, mortality, and interactive effects of selection bias are not controlled for; however, with some rare exceptions these potential errors can be minimized.

Selection of a Design

By way of summary, Table 7–8 provides information on the potential threats to validity in each of the designs discussed above. A "C" indicates that the design in question explicitly provides a control for this type of potential error; an "NC" indicates that no explicit control is provided. Most important, note that we have used the phrase *potential errors* in discussing threats to validity. This refers to the fact that potential errors are not actual errors and that although a design, in principle, does not control for a potential source of error, the marketing researcher may build in specific controls when designing the experiment for the study that will be implemented. (For this reason we have used a "+" under certain designs in Table 7–8.)

The challenge facing marketing researchers is that those experimental designs providing the tightest controls over internal validity may be the most artificial and, thus, may compromise our ability to generalize the research findings. However, the pragmatics of marketing research often necessitate that we project the sample results to the larger untested population. Hence, the issue of internal

TABLE 7–8   Experimental Design and Potential Errors

	Potential Error									
	History	Maturation	Testing	Instrumentation	Selection Bias	Mortality	Interactive Effects of Testing	Interactive Effects of Selection Bias	Surrogate Situation	Demand Artifacts
1. After-only	NC	NC	C	C	NC	NC	C	NC	NC	NC
2. Before-after	NC	NC	NC	NC	C	C	NC	NC	NC	NC
3. Before-after with control	C	C	C	C	C	NC	NC	NC	NC	NC
4. After-only with control (RRM)	C	C	C	C	C	NC	C	C	NC	NC
5. After-only with control (RM)	C	C	C	C	NC+	NC+	C	NC	NC	NC
6. Time series	NC	C	C	C	NC+	NC+	NC	NC+	NC	NC

Note: C indicates a method of controlling for the error is provided by the design; NC indicates no method of controlling is incorporated in the design; a + indicates that with some care these potential errors can be minimized.

versus external validity is an important one. This conflict has led many researchers to suggest that designs that are tight in internal validity be used in early stages of marketing research projects to identify treatment conditions known to have specific effects under controlled conditions. Then, depending on the costs and risks involved, these conditions can be subjected to further testing in more natural settings through the use of quasi-experimental designs.[14] Quasi-experimental designs, if properly developed, can provide the marketing researcher with a vehicle for extending experimentation into real market settings.

SUMMARY

In this chapter we have explained the distinction between laboratory and field experiments, especially in regard to their ability to provide control of those crucial factors that might affect the experimental outcome. Next, we discussed the necessary and sufficient conditions for inferring cause-and-effect relationships and what is meant by spurious correlation. Much of the chapter was devoted to the issue of validity and to discussing and illustrating basic concepts on experimentation. In the course of that discussion we introduced several different types of experimental designs and discussed their ability to provide control over potential sources of error that can threaten both internal and external validity.

KEY CONCEPTS

realistic research environment

laboratory experimental environment

field experimental environments

independent variable

dependent variable

causality

concomitant variation

negative association

positive association

spurious association

temporal ordering

experimental design

treatment

manipulation

experimental effect

confounds or confounding variables

randomization

physical control

matching

analysis of covariance (ANCOVA)

validity

internal validity

external validity

history

maturation

testing

instrumentation

selection bias

mortality

reactive or interactive effects of testing

interactive effects of selection bias

surrogate situations

demand artifacts

after-only design

unaided recall

aided recall

before-after design

before-after with control design

after-only with control design

nonequivalent before-after with control quasi design

quasi-experimental design

two-factor after-only with control design

completely randomized factorial designs

time-series quasi design

---

[14]See A. G. Sawyer, P. M. Worthing, and P. E. Sendak, "The Role of Laboratory Experiments to Test Marketing Strategies," *Journal of Marketing*, Summer 1979, pp. 60–67.

REVIEW QUESTIONS

1. Discuss the advantages and disadvantages of laboratory versus field experiments.

2. What are the requirements for a causal relationship between two variables?

3. Discuss the various methods for controlling extraneous sources of variation.

4. Discuss the differences between internal and external validity.

5. Compare the before-after with the before-after with control experimental designs with respect to controlling for threats to internal validity.

CASE STUDIES FOR
PART II

CASE 1:
Consumers' Attitudes and Perceptions Toward
Seafood when Eating Out: Preliminary Phase

The lack of acceptance by the consumer of squid, mackerel, pollock, whiting, hake, and other underutilized species impedes the fishing industry from developing and using these existing fisheries despite the abundance of the available product. The specific problems being encountered are in the marketplace. Although problems of quality and handling techniques also exist, solutions to these problems are to little or no avail unless consumers will accept the product.

All sectors of the fishing industry that are concerned with these species, from harvesting to processing to distribution, are affected by the problem of consumer nonacceptance. Even popular species are underused at certain times of the year. In this area of scarce resources, the result is to deny use of abundant resources to all sectors of the fishing industry. Such denial affects the costs of other processing and distribution resources and capabilities, contributes to greater cyclical fluctuations within the industry, denies greater employment opportunities, and inhibits commercial food-service establishments from providing lower cost seafood menu items, which would benefit the consumer and increase consumption of all species.

A major market for fish is the food-service industry. As viable as this industry is, however, it selects only certain seafood products and sells them with a minimum of marketing effort and much ignorance about the consumer who eats seafood away from home.

Marketing research has explored the attitudes, perceptions, and behavior of the food-market seafood buyer and resultant home-consumption patterns. The away-from-home seafood buyer, however, consumes twice as much seafood as the at-home eater and provides a vital link not only in total consumption, but also in the exploration of new uses and species. Yet he or she orders seafood or fish only about 7 percent of the time in all restaurants.

This research is directed at understanding the marketing process that is most effective for expanding consumption of both traditional and nontraditional fish in commercial food-service establishments. This knowledge is essential to the stabilization, maintenance, and growth of the fishing industry, and it is advanced by empirical identification of consumers' beliefs, attitudes, intentions, and behaviors toward seafood products and their promotion. Specifically, the broad objective of the full research project is threefold:

1. To provide an analysis of consumer beliefs, attitudes, intentions, and behavior toward product characteristics of fish eaten in commercial food-service establishments, especially underutilized species, both fresh and frozen.

2. To develop an effective foundation for generating marketing tactics and strategies for food-service operators in preparing, serving, merchandising, advertising, promoting, menu listing, naming, and pricing of fish products, especially underutilized species.

3. To provide an analysis of delineated market segments that will orient the food-service operator toward optimal marketing effectiveness for fish and fish products, especially underutilized species.

The research was confined to Massachusetts for funding and resource-limitation reasons. As such, it pays particular attention to fish species of the northeastern seaboard and to the attributes of Massachusetts consumers. Generalizations beyond Massachusetts should be made with caution, but it is believed that the findings have nationwide implications.

Part I of the Research

The purpose of this part of the research project was to provide a foundation and qualitative basis for the more extensive quantitative research that would follow. As the first phase of a comprehensive study, it examines

- General attitudes and perceptions toward seafood.
- Factors affecting those attitudes and perceptions.
- Attitudes, feelings, and beliefs that influence consumers' behavior patterns toward eating fish when dining out.

Specific objectives were to explore

- Tastes and preferences.
- Familiarity with the product.
- Knowledge of nutritional attributes.
- Previous consumption.
- Present consumption.
- Home versus away-from-home usage.
- Associations.
- Awareness, knowledge, familiarity, consumption, and attitudes toward nontraditional species.

Focus group research was undertaken to collect data. Four focus group interviews of 8 to 10 persons each were held in geographically different areas, including both inland and coastal markets. This enabled us to examine any differences that might exist between consumers who have immediate access to a wide variety of fresh fish and those who are farther removed from it.

Sample

Two focus groups, one male and one female, were held in the Boston and Springfield, Massachusetts, areas. Participants for the interviews were prescreened on several factors so that they would represent a cross section of the restaurant-eating public. These factors included age, income, education, marital status, frequency of eating in restaurants, type of restaurant visited, and frequency of selecting seafood when eating out.

Virtually all participants had attended high school and most had completed college. The groups were about evenly divided between married and single or divorced participants. Representative job descriptions included clerk, secretary, homemaker, bookkeeper, supervisor, draftsperson, teacher, and contractor. About 75 percent were Massachusetts natives.

All participants had eaten dinner at least twice in a table-service restaurant during the previous month. Approximately one-third claim they eat out at least eight times a month; some claim they eat out as often as five times a week.

All participants order finfish for their main course at least occasionally when dining out. Over half reported they eat fish frequently when at restaurants. Half of these say they always eat fish at restaurants.

Method

Each focus group session began with an introduction to what a focus group is and how one is conducted. The moderator emphasized that there were no right or wrong answers and strongly encouraged participants to express their own opinions. Discussion was free-flowing and generally exploratory, but it also was probing and directed toward certain topic areas. (The full moderator's guide for conducting the sessions is shown in Exhibit 1.)

Case Question

Critique and evaluate the approach taken in the focus group phase of this study.

Source: Material for this case was supplied by Dr. Robert C. Lewis, Department of Hotel Administration, University of Massachusetts.

CASE 2:
Coke Targets Youth Market with CD, Tape Promotion

ATLANTA—Opting for the sound of music rather than the dubious whiz-bang technology of last year, Coca-Cola Co. is planning a huge compact disc and cassette giveaway for its summer promotion.

The Atlanta-based soft-drink maker said it will place 5.6 million mini CDs and 100 million certificates for $1 cassettes inside multipacks of Coca-Cola Classic, Diet Coke, and Sprite beginning in May. The CDs and tapes will feature youth-oriented artists from Sony Music's Columbia and Epic labels.

The promotion is aimed squarely at the youth market, with the featured artists heavy on the dance and rock side.

"We feel strongly we have the right music at the right time," said Ted Host, senior vice president at Coca-Cola USA. "The music is top of the chart artists."

The new promotion follows last summer's "Magi-Cans," which offered cash prizes stuffed into ejector-equipped cans. That promotion, billed as one of Coke's largest, was killed early amid complaints of malfunctioning prize mechanisms and reports that the chlori-

EXHIBIT 1   Moderator's Guide

Introduction
A. Moderator.
B. Focus-group technique, taping, etc.
C. Participant introductions (name, where live, where born, how often eat out [non-fast food])

Background Information
A. Favorite restaurant/why?
B. What influences our choices of food?
1. Things in childhood—As a child did you try new foods?
2. Peer group.
3. Religion.
4. Geographical preferences (where).
5. Parental pressure.

Seafood Consumption
(Not shellfish such as crab, lobster, shrimp; talk about fish such as sole, halibut, cod.)
A. How frequently eat seafood when eat out?
1. What kinds?
2. Why? (benefits).
   a. Health.
   b. Taste.
   c. Price.
   d. Nutrition.
3. More or less than in the past?
4. Eating habits change as you get older.
5. Why not others?
B. Present consumption habits.
1. Home.
2. Away from home.
   a. Why at restaurant and not at home?
   b. Is restaurant an experience or just a place?
C. Favorite seafood
1. Why/what makes it a favorite?
   a. Fish itself.
   b. Sauce.
   c. Texture.
   d. Manner in which it is prepared.
2. Elements that appeal the most.
3. How important familiarity?
D. Describe a typical dining out experience—in terms of menu selection.
E. Influencers/preconceived ideas.
1. Waiter/waitress.
2. Menu.
3. People you are with.
4. Specials of the day.
5. Table tents on tables.
6. Any particular tastes or names that may have an influence.
F. Do you try new dishes?
1. Why?
2. Why not?

G. What catches your attention?
1. Description.
2. Name.
3. Price.
4. Others.
H. Expectations.
1. What will it taste like?
2. What kinds/names?
I. Types of restaurants.
1. More likely to trust a particular type of restaurant.
2. More likely to try something new in a restaurant you trust.
3. How does type of restaurant influence choice?

Menu Evaluation (hand-cut menus)
A. What catches your eye first?
1. Price.
2. Descriptions of fish.
3. Benefits seen in eating fish.
B. Probe for specifics of factors making favorite/underutilized species.
1. Would you eat this kind? (Try new terms).
2. Why?
3. Why not?
4. Would you try it?
5. How familiar are you with these species? (Some on menu, others like monkfish, dog fish.)
C. Fresh fish versus frozen.
1. Likes/dislikes.
2. Do you trust the menu?
3. Trust the waiter/waitress?
D. Methods of preparation.
1. Broiled.
2. Baked.
3. Fried.
4. Steamed.
5. Sautéed.
6. In chowders.

Marketing Influence/Strategy
A. Restaurant's role in educating the consumer.
1. Waiter/waitress.
2. Special promotions.
3. Descriptions.
B. Other media used to influence.
1. TV
2. Articles.
3. Commentaries.
4. News item.
5. Julia Child-type program.

nated water used to make the winning cans feel like the real thing would leak.

Host rejected the suggestion that the company was trying to play it safe with the music giveaway after the widespread publicity over the problems with MagiCan. While it was in progress, the 1990 promotion gave Coke sales increases, he said.

"We thought the MagiCan was extremely successful," Host said. "We just see this as another Coke promotion."

For most consumers, the MagiCan probably is long forgotten, said AMA Chairman Kenneth L. Bernhardt, head of the marketing department at Georgia State University, Atlanta.

"I think people have fairly short memories on promotions, unless you remind them enough of it," he said. If they [Coke] came out with something similar to last year's, people probably would remember.

Summer promotions are important to the industry, with hot weather and added leisure time making it a prime season for soft-drink consumption.

Under the new "Coca-Cola Pop Music" promotion, one in 19 multi-packs will contain one of four 3-inch CDs with at least four songs each. All other packages will contain a certificate that can be redeemed with $1 for a six-song cassette.

Case Question

Coke management was quite certain that the ultimate consumer, the soda drinking market, would react favorably to the promotion. However, Coke was less certain of the feelings of its other customers, the trade—that is, distributors, wholesalers, retailers, and so forth. Coke wanted to conduct focus group interviews with members of the trade.

What recommendation would you provide for this audience as compared with the typical consumer focus group? Prepare a moderator's guide for the focus group sessions.

Source: *Marketing News*, April 29, 1991, p. 5. Reprinted with permission.

CASE 3:
McDonald's Tests Catfish Sandwich

NASHVILLE, TENNESSEE—McDonald's Corp. is trying to hook customers in southern test markets, including one in Kentucky, on a new catfish sandwich.

The chain is serving its newest sandwich in Bowling Green, Ky.; Memphis, Chattanooga, and Jackson,

Tenn.; Huntsville, Ala.; Jonesboro, Ark.,; and Columbus, Tupelo, Greenville, and Greenwood, Miss., said Jane Basten, a marketing specialist for McDonald's in Nashville.

The sandwich consists of a 2.3-ounce catfish patty, lettuce, and tangy sauce served on a homestyle bun.

The company will evaluate the sandwich based on sales and supply availability after a six-week ad campaign ends in mid-April.

"The advertising will be similar to what we're doing right now with the grilled steak sandwich," Basten said. "We will promote it to the fullest and see what happens."

She said the catfish is being supplied by The Catfish Institute, an industry promotion association based in Belzoni, Miss.

Catfish Institute director Bill Allen said catfish farmers, processors, and marketers are "very excited about this prospect for our industry. This is super good news.

"But we don't want to get our hopes up too much and start thinking this is going to be our salvation, because we already have a viable industry."

Allen said that catfish firms that remember earlier tie-ups with major restaurant chains such as Church's Fried Chicken are cautiously optimistic about the McDonald's deal.

Case Question

The management team for new-product development was interested in assessing the relevancy of the chosen test markets to the three states designated for rollout if the test market was satisfactory. If successful, the product was designed to be introduced into Tennessee, Alabama, and Georgia.

What are your conclusions about the representativeness of the test cities to the designated rollout states? Present secondary data to support your conclusions.

Source: *Marketing News*, March 18, 1992, p. 10. Reprinted with permission.

CASE 4:
Researcher: Test Ads First to "Zap-Proof" Them

By Joe Agnew

Consumers' potential for zapping, skipping, and ignoring ads should be measured before the ads are placed on the air and in print, according to Lee Weinblatt, president of the Pretesting Co., Englewood, N.J.

Although exceptionally strong media campaigns might eventually reach the eyes and ears of audiences, he said, it is more efficient to design commercials and ads that gain and hold the audience's attention and deliver a message that is relevant and believable.

"Our data clearly show that it is exceptionally difficult to force communication on an audience," Weinblatt said. "Communication and pretesting efforts must reflect this fact."

In most studies conducted in forced-exposure situations, Weinblatt said, "executions strong on hard facts and product comparisons usually had the highest levels of communication and 'convinceability.'"

He said, however, that studies using "real-world" simulations have found that few of these executions were ever listened to or read.

"Besides entertainment, care must also be taken to leave behind a strong, relevant, and believable message to reach nonusers," Weinblatt said. "While a number of 30-second commercials which achieve both goals have been tested, this has not been found among many 15-second executions."

He said data strongly suggest that simply increasing broadcast budgets will not solve the problem of a commercial or ad that does not gain and hold the attention of people who don't use the products and services.

To measure the impact of zapping over a wide variety of product categories, Weinblatt said his company conducted five tests, each using the same controlled test design.

Each test consisted of at least 100 respondents who went through the Pretesting Company's two patented methodologies, the Simulated Network and PeopleReader.

For testing TV commercials, respondents were seated individually before a color TV, were given a remote control, and were told to choose from three different popular programs for the next half hour.

Respondents could view each show for as long as they wished, and they could switch back and forth among the three networks, Weinblatt said. Respondents selected the one show they liked best, and then they described that program's strengths and weaknesses.

The programs came from three videotape recorders synchronized with each other. At exactly the same time on all three networks, a commercial pod appeared consisting of five commercials: three 30-second and two 15-second spots.

Three of the five commercials were different on all three stations, while two of the commercials—a 15-second and a 30-second spot—appeared at the same moment on all three networks.

If respondents zapped a commercial, Weinblatt said, they would find different commercials on each of the other programs. However, if either two of the same test commercials were zapped, the exact commercial would be found on all three channels.

Toward the end of the half-hour program, there was another commercial pod and the same two test commercials were repeated, synchronized on all three channels.

Case Questions

1. Comment on the research design utilized by the Pretesting Co. to assess the amount of zapping.

2. A brand manager was trying to decide between two advertising campaigns for the introduction of a new brand. One advertising campaign used a humorous approach, while the other utilized a celebrity endorsement. Both campaigns communicated the same end benefit information and only varied by the executional technique. The brand manager was interested in the three criteria: Would the ads attract the attention of the viewers? Would the ads hold the viewers' attention long enough to communicate the prime end benefit of the brand? And would the ads' ability to attract and hold attention wear out (i.e., would they lose effectiveness over time)?

    Use the basic format of the Pretesting Company to design an experiment that will provide the information necessary to recommend to the brand manager which of the two advertising campaigns he or she should use for the introduction of the brand.

Source: *Marketing News*, February 29, 1988, p. 18. Reprinted with permission.

CASE 5:
Retailers Unhappy with Displays from Manufacturers

Supermarket executives are unhappy with manufacturer-provided displays, according to a recently released study by the Howard Marlboro Group (HMG), New York.

Of the 129 members of HMG's Retail Advisory Board who were surveyed, 60 percent indicated they were at most marginally satisfied with their current racks.

Reasons for dissatisfaction included such things as the racks were ineffective for inventory control, they used space poorly, and they did not aid consumers in

Courtesy of S. C. Johnson & Sons, Inc.

shopping, the study said. Retailers also noted many of the racks were unattractive and did not fit in with their store's decor.

Although supermarket executives were not enthused with most manufacturer-provided racks, they rated L'eggs displays the best, the study said. The retailers indicated the racks had a "consistent presentation and appearance," and that the company showed its support by regularly providing renewal parts for the displays, according to the survey.

HMG also questioned retailers on their use of interactive merchandising systems (IMS).

Forty-five percent of the retailers already use at least one IMS, and these displays are used in a variety of departments, the study said, including generic grocery, meat and seafood, spices, and electrical and hardware.

Seventy-seven percent of the retailers surveyed said IMS use will continue to increase, the report found, and 93 percent were interested in learning more about the systems.

Raid, the popular insecticide, has developed an Insect-A-Guide to help people learn about the pests they're trying to kill. The in-store display features various Raid products arranged under a color code to help consumers pick the right spray for the right bug. A flip chart gives information on the habits of insects and suggests ways to knock 'em dead. The unit, designed by the Howard Marlboro Group, New York, can be arranged in three configurations to accommodate various store sizes.

Case Question

Design an experiment to test the new display for Raid. Be sure your design will test for both customer and retailer satisfaction with the design.

Source: *Marketing News*, October 10, 1988, p. 21.

SAMPLING THEORY AND PRACTICES

After the researcher has decided how the data will be collected, the next concern is how to obtain a sample of respondents that is representative of the target population of interest. In Part III, attention is directed to sampling theory and practices. There is voluminous literature on the theory and practices of sampling; indeed, entire textbooks are devoted to this subject. Nevertheless, the next two chapters and accompanying appendixes will expose you to the major sampling techniques and how they are used in marketing research studies. Sampling techniques can be divided into *probability designs* and *nonprobability designs*. As you will come to understand, in a probability sampling design each element of the population has a known nonzero chance of being selected. In such cases sampling variation can be computed, and results can be projected to the entire population. In contrast, because in nonprobability sampling designs (for example, *convenient samples*) the chance of selecting any particular population element is not known, sampling variation cannot be computed, and results cannot, in a strict sense, be projected to the entire population. This is not to imply that probability sampling designs are "good" and that nonprobability sampling designs "bad." As you will see, both probability and nonprobability procedures have appropriate uses in marketing research.

The subject of sampling can be technically rigorous. The level of technical rigor that is required ultimately depends on the specific application. In certain instances only a few basics and some common sense are needed, whereas in other instances sampling decisions involve complex statistical concepts and the use of a host of computational formulas. Some of you will never be responsible for designing a sampling plan, nor will you have to evaluate the technical aspects of a sampling design, but because others may want to know a little about the technical aspects of sampling theory, we have presented two chapters on the theory and practice of sampling. In Chapter 8 we present a nonquantitative treatment of sampling fundamentals in which particular emphasis is placed on the decisions that must be made by a manager or research analyst. Chapter 9 is devoted to a more technical treatment of sampling and should be of interest to those who want to know more about determining how large a sample to draw and how to actually draw various kinds of probability samples.

Sampling Fundamentals

- Discuss the key elements involved in devising a sampling plan.
- Explain the importance of properly defining the target population of interest.
- Illustrate the distinctive features of probability and nonprobability samples.
- Describe the major types and pimary practical uses of both probability and non-probability samples.
- Discuss the primary approaches for determining sample size.
- Define the concepts of *sampling* versus *nonsampling* errors.
- Explain what factors contribute to *nonresponse* and *response* errors.
- Describe how response rates can be improved.
- Discuss the proposed remedies for nonresponse error.

INTRODUCTION

Put simply, **sampling** involves identifying a group of individuals or households who can be reached by mail, by telephone, or in person and who possess information relevant to solving the marketing problem at hand. A logical first question is: *Why sample at all?* The answer is simple and straightforward: Sampling is practical and economical. Recall that the objectives of survey research are to describe and explain selected characteristics of a prespecified group of individuals, households, institutions, or objects. However, complete enumeration of the group, called a **census**, is rarely undertaken because it is usually much too expensive in terms of time, money, and personnel. Even the most notable exception, the *U.S. Census of Population*, conducted each decade, generates an enormous amount of data about many subjects by surveying a small sample of the entire population. As we will see, there is simply no need to survey every individual to obtain an accurate representation of the group as a whole. With proper care and control, only a very small fraction of the entire population is needed to obtain an accurate representation of the group as a whole.

Although sampling may appear somewhat foreign, it actually is a common occurrence in our everyday events. For example, to determine what a marketing research course is like, a student may quickly thumb through the book to get a feel for the entire course. As another example, suppose you are cooking some pasta and want to determine if it is ready to serve. Most likely, you would first stir the pot and then select one or two pieces of the pasta and taste them. This is sampling. The pot of pasta represents the **target population.** A target population is that set of people, products, firms, markets, and so forth, that contains the information that is of interest to the researcher. The one or two pieces of pasta selected is the sample. A **sample** is a subset of the target population from which information is gathered to estimate something about the population.

The objective of sampling is to learn something about the population without taking a census. That is, based on the information derived from the sample we will make an inference about the entire population. In this case, we infer whether or not the pasta is ready by testing a sample from the pot.

Sampling issues are primarily concerned with (1) the membership of the population that should be included in the sample (i.e., what size sample do we need), (2) the selection of the items from the target population so that the sample is representative of the entire population, and (3) the computation of an estimate about the target population for some variable of interest which is based on what is observed in the sample.

Remember that sampling may not always be necessary. Instead of immediately running out and asking a group of individuals a series of questions, the marketing analyst should first exhaust all relevant sources of secondary data—reinventing the wheel is often costly and time-consuming, and it can be embarrassing.

With this caveat in mind, let us begin our treatment of the theory and practice of sampling. The discussion begins by describing the key elements that a market-ing manager or researcher must consider when devising a sampling plan. These elements, which together form the overall sampling design, provide the organiza-tion for the remainder of this chapter. Although many of you may never actually draw a sample or compute sample-based statistics in a real-life marketing research setting, at some point you may be responsible for overseeing the sampling design and play an important role in evaluating the overall plan. Consequently, you need to understand the basic issues of sample design.

SAMPLING DESIGN CONSIDERATIONS

Exhibit 8–1 provides a schematic overview of the sampling process. The first step requires the specification of the data that must be collected for the research proj-ect. In general, this will be determined by the background and objectives section of a marketing research proposal. Once the researcher and/or manager determines what information will be collected, the next step is to define the target population. Here the researcher and/or manager must specify the target population, determine the relevant sampling units, determine incidence rates, and select a sampling frame. The third step of the sampling process involves data-collection issues, that is, what method will be used to collect the data. Data-collection methods can affect other aspects of the sampling design. For example, incidence rates may change if the data collection is implemented with a mall intercept versus a tele-phone interview.

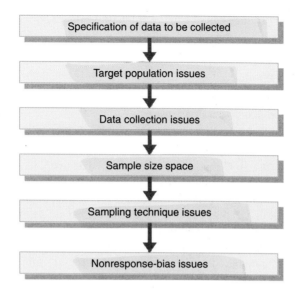

EXHIBIT 8–1
—
Overview of the
Sampling Process

The next step is to determine the required sample size. This is usually one of the first questions asked, "What size sample do we need?" As we will see there are many ways to determine the required sample size for a project. Some of the methods are based on statistical theory, whereas other methods are based on industry practices. The next step requires a selection of a sampling technique. The sample may be either a probability sample or a nonprobability sample, and there are a variety of specific sampling techniques for each of these major categories. The last step of the sampling process relates to issues concerning nonresponse bias. That is, what are the potential sources of error due to the fact that not all of the sample elements responded to the survey.

Each of these stages, following the specification of the data to be collected, are covered in this chapter. The diagram shown in Exhibit 8–1 presents the sampling process as hierarchical. This diagram is simply an overview that outlines the issues that must be addressed when constructing a sample design. These issues are interrelated, and a decision at one stage may require revising decisions at previous stages.

TARGET POPULATION AND FRAME ISSUES

A sample does not have to be representative of the general population, but it must be representative of the population of interest. The population of interest is called the target population. Precise definition of the target population is absolutely essential. If you define your target population improperly, the research will likely be ineffectual for solving your problem.

To be precise, a population must be defined in terms of *elements*, *units*, and *time*. The population for a new "tuna-in-a-jar" concept test, for example, was defined as females between the ages of 18 and 54 who purchased at least one

6.5-ounce can of tuna in the past 30 days and shopped in supermarkets during the period September 15–30.

Elements:	Females between the ages of 18 and 54 who purchased at least one 6.5-ounce can of tuna in the past 30 days and shopped in
Units:	Supermarkets
Time:	During the period September 15–30

Once the population of interest has been defined, it is commonly referred to as the *target population*. The elements that make up that population are called **sampling units.** In the new tuna-in-a-jar concept test study, supermarkets are designated as the sampling units. That is, although females between the ages of 18 and 54 who purchased a 6.5-ounce can of tuna in the past 30 days might be sampled directly, it is easier to select supermarkets, the place at which canned tuna is purchased, as the sampling unit and interview all females who qualify as elements of the population. In some situations the population element and sampling unit will be the same; in others they will be different.

Let's consider another illustration. Suppose the brand manager of a new safety door lock system is interested in determining the awareness of and attitudes toward the locking system. The target population is single women between the ages of 25 and 54 who rent apartments in high-rise apartment buildings in Dallas, Texas, as of January 1992.

sampling units
Elements making up the population.

Elements:	Single women between the ages of 25 and 54 who rent apartments in
Units:	High-rise apartment buildings in Dallas, Texas, as of
Time:	January 1992

It is the responsibility of the marketing research supplier to provide explicit instructions to the field service concerning the qualifications of the target population. This is accomplished by providing a list of *screening* questions that are used to qualify respondents. A set of screening questions for a burger image study is provided in Exhibit 8–2. To be eligible to be included in this study, an individual must be between the ages of 18 and 34 (see Question B) and must have eaten a hamburger at a fast food chain in the past month (see Question C).

Screening questions explicitly define who should be included in the sample and who should be excluded. Most marketing research surveys exclude certain individuals for a variety of reasons. For example, in the burger image study, the first question on the questionnaire asks whether the individual or any household member works in advertising, in marketing research, or for a fast food chain. Typically, this is the first question asked, and the interview is terminated at this point if the individual indicates that he or she or someone else in their household works in one of these industries, or in the product or service area dealt with in the survey. These individuals are excluded for so-called security reasons—they may be

EXHIBIT 8–2

Screening Questions

> APPROACH MALE OR FEMALE ADULTS WHO APPEAR TO BE BETWEEN 18 AND 34 YEARS OF AGE. CHECK INTERVIEWER INSTRUCTIONS FOR SEX QUOTAS.

Hello, I'm_____from_____, a marketing research firm. We are conducting a study in this area and would like to include your opinions.

> IF RESPONDENT'S ANSWER TO ANY QUESTION IS MARKED, "TERMINATE," CIRCLE THE NEXT AVAILABLE NUMBER IN THE TERMINATION BOX FOR THAT <u>ANSWER</u>. THEN, ERASE AND RE-USE SCREENER. <u>NEVER</u> ERASE CIRCLED TERMINATION BOX NUMBERS!

A. First, do you or does any member of your household work in any of the following: advertising, marketing research, or a fast food chain?

TERMINATE ◄ YES
CONTINUE ◄ NO

> <u>YES TO SENSITIVE INDUSTRY: TERMINATE.</u>
>
> 1 2 3 4 5 6 7 8 9 10 11 12   (12)

B. In the past 6 months, have you participated in any research interview that took more than 3 minutes to complete?

TERMINATE ◄ YES
CONTINUE ◄ NO

> <u>INTERVIEWED IN PAST 6 MONTHS: TERMINATE.</u>
>
> 1 2 3 4 5 6 7 8 9 10 11 12   (13)

We would like to speak to people of various ages today. Are you . . . (READ LIST)?

TERMINATE ◄ UNDER 18   (14)
CHECK QUOTAS AND CONTINUE WITH Q.C. ◄ 18–34... 25–34
TERMINATE ◄ 35 or over / Refused

> <u>UNDER/OVER/REFUSED AGE, OVER QUOTA: TERMINATE.</u>
>
> 1 2 3 4 5 6 7 8 9 10 11 12   (15)

C. In the past month have you eaten a hamburger at a fast food chain such as McDonald's, Hardee's, or Wendy's?

CONTINUE WITH Q.D. ◄ YES
TERMINATE ◄ NO

> <u>DID NOT EAT A HAMBURGER AT A FAST FOOD RESTAURANT: TERMINATE.</u>
>
> 1 2 3 4 5 6 7 8 9 10 11 12   (16)

D. Have you eaten a hamburger, cheeseburger, or other burger product at any of the following chains during the past three months?

	YES (17)	NO (18)	
McDonald's . . .	1	1	
Hardee's . . .	2	2	CHECK QUOTA
Wendy's . . .	3	3	
Burger King . . .	4	4	

competitors or work for competitors, and the researchers would not want to alert them to what the study is about.

Sampling Frames

Selecting a sample means that one selects some number of elements from the target population. The ability to select a sample of elements from a target population is based on the presumption that we are able to identify (locate) the target population of interest. A **sampling frame** is simply a list or set of directions (e.g., a geographic breakdown) that identifies the target population. A sampling frame can be a list of names and telephone numbers, as in a telephone survey; an area map of dwellings, as in an in-home personal survey; or a list of household addresses obtained from a local utility company, as in a mail survey. Exhibit 8–3 provides an example of the type of mailing lists available from Alvin B. Zeller, Inc. These lists can be ordered geographically; for example, by state, city, county, and so on. Additionally, telephone numbers are available for most lists. If no list or organized breakdown of the target population exists, then location sampling (as in mall-intercept surveys) or random-digit dialing (as in telephone surveys) is probably the only alternative. In some cases sample elements are found within sample units. For example, suppose we were interested in sampling the Head of Household for families living in apartments. The sample frame would consist of apartment complexes. The individual apartments within the complexes would be the sampling units. One of the biggest problems in probability sampling, and especially in simple random sampling, is obtaining an appropriate sampling frame.

Actually, lists or other geographical breakdowns are available from a variety of sources. Local community utility companies have a fairly complete list of households. Area telephone branches frequently cooperate and give out a list of working exchanges. Magazine subscriptions, organization membership rosters, credit card companies, and professional associations are well-known sources of lists. Many companies are in the business of selling lists. For example, the Donnelley Company maintains a list drawn from telephone directories and automobile registrations that contains around 88 percent of U.S. households. Some companies compile catalogs of lists. Even though costs do vary, a list can usually be obtained for between $50 and $120 per 1,000 names.

Although lists or other geographic breakdowns exist, the list rarely matches the target population exactly. For example, a list of residents of a given community usually does not include new arrivals or households living in dwellings built since the list was created. Lists are rarely current; in addition, lists frequently contain duplication—households with multiple telephone numbers or individuals whose names and addresses appear on two or more lists (combined to gain a better representation of the target population) have an increased chance of being selected. Thus a list can overrepresent or underrepresent a target population.

The list (sampling frame) that is used defines what can be called the **operational** or *working* **population**. If a sampling frame consists of all the sampling units in the target population *plus* additional units, then it suffers from

EXHIBIT 8–3   Mailing List Example

QUANTITY		PRICE	QUANTITY		PRICE
3,400	Moose Lodges	$40/M	675	Newspapers, Weekly, with	
3,400	Mortgage Banking Companies	$40/M		circulation of 10,000 or more	$75
11,350	Mortgage Banking Executives	$40/M	9,200	Night Clubs, Discos	$40/M
19,300	Mortgage Companies	$40/M	220,000	Non-Profit Tax Exempt Organizations	$40/M
21,900	Morticians	$40/M	8,600	Notaries, Public	$40/M
41,000	Motels	$40/M	8,275	Novelties (Advertising) Jobbers	$40/M
57,000	Motels & Hotels	$40/M	1,900	Novelty & Souvenir Shops	$40/M
545	Motel & Hotel Chains	$75	22,500	Nuclear Industry Executives	$40/M
3,900	Motion Picture Producers	$40/M	1,200	Nuclear Medicine Specialists	$75
12,100	Motion Picture Theaters	$40/M	1,900	Nuclear Physicists	$40/M
8,550	Motorcycle Dealers	$40/M	150	Nudist Clubs	$75
3,500,000	Motorcycle Owners	Inquire	13,750	Nurseries & Greenhouses	$40/M
12,000	Moving & Storage Companies	$40/M	53,000	Nursery Schools & Kindergartens	$40/M
9,600	Muffler Shops	$40/M	8,000	Nurses, Directors of	$55/M
38,200	Municipal Government Officials	$40/M	205,000	Nurses, Hospital	Inquire
5,770	Museums	$40/M	4,600	Nurses, Private Duty	$55/M
790	Museums, Art	$75	2,000,000	Nurses, Registered	Inquire
18,600	Museum Officials	$40/M	9,400	Nurses, Registries	$40/M
2,400	Music Department Chairmen, Colleges	$60/M	21,200	Nursing Homes	$40/M
22,000	Music Professors, College	$60/M	12,800	Nursing Homes, 50 beds or more	$40/M
15,000	Music Teachers, High School	$45/M	6,700	Nursing Homes, 100 beds or more	$40/M
3,950	Music Instruction, Private	$40/M	14,800	Nursing Homes, Private	$40/M
7,600	Musical Instrument Dealers	$40/M	1,300	Nursing Schools	$75
21,000	Music, Records, Tapes, Musical Instruments Dealers	$40/M	1,765	Nutritionists	$75
65,000	Musicians (Select Instrument)	$50/M			
425	Mutual Funds	$75		**O**	
1,750	Mutual Fund Executives	$75			
465	Mutual Savings Banks HQ	$75	23,350	Obstetricians & Gynecologists	$40/M
			30,000	Occupational Therapists	Inquire
	N		15,500	Oceanographers	$40/M
			3,400	Odd Fellows Lodges	$40/M
15,700	Nail Salons	$40/M	5,500	Office Building Management Companies	$40/M
18,000	National Advertisers	$40/M	31,300	Office & Building Cleaners	$40/M
69,000	National Advertisers Executives	$40/M	14,200	Office Equipment & Supplies Dealers	$40/M
340	National Parks	$75	9,300	Office Machine Dealers	$40/M
2,100	Naturalists	$40/M	1,200	Office Machine Manufacturers	$75
5,900	Naval Engineers	$40/M	10,050	Office (Commercial) Stationers	$40/M
235,000	Navy Officers, Retired & Reserved	Inquire	389	Office Parks	$75
3,950	Narcotics & Drug Abuse Centers	$40/M	2,000,000	Office Workers, Home Address	Inquire
40,630	Navigators (Air), Flight Engineers	$40/M	115,000	Offices, Government, All Levels	Inquire
10,900	Needlework & Yarn Shops	$40/M	19,000	Oil Burner & Furnace Dealers & Distributors	$40/M
16,350	Neon Sign Dealers	$40/M	17,400	Oil (Fuel) Dealers	$40/M
2,500	Neurologists	$40/M	52,000	Oil Industry Executives	$40/M
5,260	Neuroscientists	$40/M	15,500	Oil (Petroleum) Bulk Stations	$40/M
160	News Features Syndicates	$75	18,000	Oil (Petroleum) Wholesalers	$40/M
2,400	Newsdealers & Newsstands	$40/M	8,100	Oil (Petroleum) Producers & Refiners	$40/M
3,175	Newsdealers, Wholesalers & Distributors	$40/M	935	Oil Pipeline Companies	$75
11,200	Newsletter Publishers	$40/M	3,650	Oilwell Drilling Contractors	$40/M
22,130	Newspaper Executives	$40/M	6,200	Oilwell Drilling Companies	$40/M
3,500	Newspapers, College	$40/M	735	Opera Companies	$75
1,710	Newspapers, Daily	$75	300,000	Opinion Leaders	$40/M
520	Newspapers, Daily with circulation of 25,000 or more	$75	310,000	Opportunity Seekers (Male/Female)	$40/M
1,040	Newspapers, Daily with circulation of 10,000 or more	$75	12,200	Ophthalmologists	$40/M
			2,100	Optical Equipment & Supplies, Wholesale	$40/M
115	Newspapers, Daily, Canadian	$75	15,300	Opticians	$40/M
6,900	Newspapers, Weekly	$40/M	23,200	Optometrists	$40/M
			4,400	Oral Surgeons	$40/M

Source: Alvin B. Zeller, Inc., 37 East 28th Street, New York, N.Y., 10016.

underregistration
*Condition that occurs
when a sampling frame
contains fewer sampling
units than the target
population.*

gap
*Difference between the
operational population
and the target
population.*

overregistration. If, on the other hand, a sampling frame contains fewer sampling units than the target population, it suffers from **underregistration.** The difference between the operational population and the target population is commonly referred to as the sampling **gap.** It is probably safe to say that a gap exists in most surveys, including the majority of market-research studies. When you select a sampling frame, you should try to minimize the gap because the larger the gap, the greater the potential for misleading results.

Once the target population has been properly defined and an appropriate list or geographic breakdown selected, you must address the question of how many contacts (telephone calls, mailings, and the like) will be required.

Incidence Rates

One of the key components of estimating both the cost and timing of a research study is the incidence rate.[1] The incidence level determines how many contacts need to be screened for a given sample size or quota requirement.

In most commercial marketing research studies a criterion for inclusion in the survey is past use of the brand or product/category under study. Product/category use incidence is ordinarily known and supplied by the client (the firm commissioning the research). This defines the **gross incidence**—the percentage of the entire population who are product-category users. **Net incidence** is the factored-down gross incidence, which includes *all* target population qualifications. It is also called the *effective* or *overall* incidence. To illustrate, we consider a survey in which a qualified respondent must meet the following requirements:

gross incidence
*Product/category use inci-
dence for the entire
population.*

net incidence
*The factored-down gross
incidence that includes
all target population
qualifications.*

- 18–55 (no specific age breakouts).
- Used any over-the-counter (OTC) cold remedy in the past month.
- No known health restrictions, drug allergies.
- No one in household employed by advertising agency, marketing research company, or drug manufacturer.
- Has not participated in a marketing research study in the past three months.

The product/category use incidence was quoted at 60 percent. This was confirmed to be the gross incidence level—that of "past one-month OTC cold-remedy usage." The next step is to calculate the net incidence level. This involves taking the gross incidence of 60 percent and reducing it for all other qualifications. Note that the screening/data-collection method affects the qualification percentages. Let us assume an in-person mall-intercept screening method was used. Calculating the net incidence is a multiplication process. As shown below, the gross incidence is multiplied by the qualification percentages for all inclusion components.

---

[1]Much of this material has been adapted from G. Lee, "Incidence Is a Key Element," *Marketing News*, September 13, 1985, pp. 50–52.

Net incidence = Gross incidence $\times$ Qualification percentages
Qualification percentages = 92% age 18–55
$\qquad\qquad\qquad\qquad$ 88% no health restrictions/drug allergies
$\qquad\qquad\qquad\qquad$ 97% no household employment
$\qquad\qquad\qquad\qquad$ 96% no past research participation
Qualification percentage = 92% $\times$ 88% $\times$ 97% $\times$ 96%
$\qquad\qquad\qquad\qquad$ = 75.4%
Net incidence = 60% $\times$ 75.4% = 45.2%

The net incidence will determine the number of contacts required for a given sample size or quota. The relationship between incidence and the number of contacts needed is given by

$$\text{Total contacts} = \frac{\text{Total qualified (needed)}}{\text{Net incidence}}$$

Thus, for a quota of 100 qualified respondents and a net incidence level of 45 percent, the number of contacts required, assuming no refusals, will be

$$100 \div 45\% = 222$$

Using the gross incidence level of 60 percent we would need only 167 contacts. You can see that serious problems surface if the gross incidence is mistakenly used as the net. Moreover, the magnitude of the error in miscalculating the net incidence escalates as the overall sample size or quota increases.

Exhibit 8–4 (see page 228) presents an example of using both incidence and completion rates to determine the number of contacts. It is extremely important to identify all of the requirements needed for a respondent to be eligible. The reason for this is that every time an additional requirement is imposed, the incidence is changed, and when the incidence changes, both the cost and the timing of the project change. Exhibit 8–5 (see page 229) presents an example of how unforeseen requirements can affect the incidence rate and, subsequently, the timing and the cost of the study. Exhibit 8–6 (see page 229) presents points about ethical considerations that should be noted when using a mall-intercept procedure for selecting sample elements.

Select the Sampling Units

Once the appropriate sampling design has been selected and the required sample size determined, the next step is to use the sampling frame available to select (or draw) the required number of sampling units in the appropriate manner. How sampling units are selected will vary with the sampling design. Explicit instructions are needed as to how the sampling units should be selected. Operational procedures to be used in the selection of sampling units in the data-collection phase of a study are specified in the instructions to the field service. Exhibit 8–7 (see page 230) presents an example of an operational sampling plan.

DATA-COLLECTION ISSUES

An important decision in devising a sampling plan involves the choice of a method for collecting data. For survey research, you have a choice between telephone, mail, in-person, at-home, or mall-intercept interviews, among others. We

EXHIBIT 8–4

——

Incidence Rate and
Sample Size
Considerations

Calculation of sample size involves four factors:

1. The number of completed interviews desired, divided by:
2. The working phone (or "reachable") rate, divided by:
3. The incidence rate, divided by:
4. The completion rate.

Let's focus on the two most critical factors, incidence and completion rates. By using the word *incidence,* we refer to the percentage of contacts that will qualify for the interview. Put another way, What percentage of people who answer the phone (or reply to your mail questionnaire) will pass your screening questions?

For example, let's say that you're conducting a national study on cat food purchasing habits. Obviously, you need to talk to people who buy cat food. But what is the incidence of people who buy cat food? Studies show that cat food is purchased by about 30 percent of the country's households.

There are many sources for this type of data. However, past experience has shown that a client's own product and brand managers usually have the best information on incidence at their disposal.

Also, accurate incidence data is critical to determining the proper size of your sample because an incidence figure that is too high will probably leave you short of sample, once your study is in the field. So, even if any adult who answers the phone will qualify for your interview, we recommend you use an incidence rate of 90 percent to cover those instances where an adult answers the phone, but there is a language or other communication problem.

Now let's look at how we establish the completion rate. We define the completion rate as the percentage of people who, once they qualify for your study, will agree to cooperate by completing the interview. There are several important elements to consider when trying to reasonably estimate the completion rate:

The length of your interview.

The sensitivity of the topic.

The time of year.

The number of attempts to be made to reach a respondent.

The length of time that the study will be in the field.

Returning to our cat food study, we will try to determine a completion rate. We'll assume that we're planning a 10-minute interview, one that's not terribly sensitive.

The study will be conducted in August, and it will be conducted in the field for four days. During that time we'll make one initial attempt and up to three call-backs in our effort to reach a qualified respondent at each phone number we try.

Because the interview is relatively short and not sensitive, we would probably start by recommending a 50 percent completion rate. But conducting a study during August, when many families tend to be on vacation, may mean that it will be harder to reach people. So, it would be wise to drop the completion rate to 45 percent.

If we had a longer interview (15 minutes or more), we would subtract another 5 to 10 percent from the completion rate. The same is true for a sensitive topic (e.g., political issues, personal finance, hygiene). Finally, if we were to reduce the number of call-backs, we would also reduce the completion rate by 5 to 10 percent for each attempt that we eliminate.

Adding the final fact to the question, let's say we want to complete 300 interviews and that we'll be using Survey Sampling, Inc.'s random-digit super sample, which yields a working-phones rate of at least 55 percent. Now we are equipped with all the information we need in order to calculate our sample size. We start by dividing the number of completed interviews (300) by the working-phones rate (0.55), which equals 545. Next, we divide that answer by the incidence rate for cat food purchasers (0.30), which equals 1,817. Next, we divide that answer by the completion rate (0.45), which gives us a sample size of 4,038.

Finished? Not quite. Remember we said that we'd have our study in the field for only four days. Because such a short amount of time doesn't always allow for all the intended call-backs to be made, we strongly recommend that you increase your total sample size by 20 percent for any study that will be in the field less than one week. Thus, we end up with a final sample size of 4,845.

EXHIBIT 8–5

Unforeseen
Requirements

We are conducting a mall-intercept study among "buyers of Brand X coffee." In order to qualify, the respondent must be the female head of the household, must pass an occupational security screen, could not have been interviewed within the past three months, and must have bought Brand X coffee during the past three months. The anticipated incidence was estimated at 30 percent. This figure represents the "working" or effective study incidence for this study. That is, we would expect that 3 out of every 10 females screened (asked all of the screening questions or terminated via instruction to response category) will be eligible to be interviewed.

After several days in the field, the reports indicate that the project is proceeding at a slower rate than planned. The results are examined from the supervisors' reports of the screenings.

$$a = \ \ \text{20 not female head of household.}$$
$$b = \ \ \text{30 work in industry (do not pass security screen).}$$
$$c = \ \ \text{15 have been interviewed within past 3 months.}$$
$$d = \text{200 refused (screening information incomplete).}$$
$$e = \ \ \text{15 language barrier.}$$
$$f = \text{300 have not bought coffee during past 3 months.}$$
$$g = \text{500 bought coffee, but not Brand X, during past 3 months.}$$
$$h = \ \ \text{25 eligible, but refused to participate in study.}$$
$$i = \ \ \ \text{5 eligible, but terminated in middle of interview.}$$
$$j = \text{200 completed interviews.}$$

1,310 total $(a + b + c + d + e + f + g + h + i + j)$
1,095 total screened $(a + b + c + f + g + h + i + j)$
  230 total eligible $(h + i + j)$

Note that refusals or language barriers were not included because a screening was not completed (the formula states total screened, not total "attempts"). The 230 "eligible" (including those who did not complete an interview) is divided by the 1,095 "screened" to compute the incidence. In this instance, the actual incidence of 21 percent is considerably lower than the 30 percent planned for and provides an explanation, at least in part, as to why the study is taking longer to complete and why it will probably involve more effort than was anticipated.

Source: 1988, Survey Sampling, Inc., All Rights Reserved, One Post Road, Fairfield, CT 06430.

EXHIBIT 8–6

Ethical
Considerations

Frequently, when mall-intercept samples are used, the sampling plan uses a systematic procedure for selecting respondents. For example, one interviewer may be given the following assignment: Select every tenth person entering the mall through the south entrance on Monday between 9:00 A.M. and 11:00 A.M. and between 2:00 P.M. and 5:00 P.M. Interview 10 people in the morning session and 10 people in the afternoon session. It is unethical to collect all the interviews starting at 9:00 A.M. Certainly, it is more convenient for the interviewer, but this would endanger the representativeness of the sample. In addition, it is unethical to select only the people you want to interview. That is, when the sampling plan calls for the selection of every tenth person, the interviewers must stick to this plan and not simply interview the people they want to interview.

discussed various survey-interviewing methods in Chapter 5. In review, the choice of a data-collection method affects (1) the quality of data, (2) the quantity of data that can be collected, (3) the types of questions that can be asked, (4) the speed with which the data can be collected, (5) the incidence of nonresponse, and (6) the cost of the study. In addition, with respect to sampling design, the choice of a data-collection method directly influences (1) the number of contacts required, (2) the type of sample to be drawn, (3) how sample size is determined, and (4) the approach to handling nonresponse. As an example, consider

EXHIBIT 8–7
—
Operational
Sampling Plan

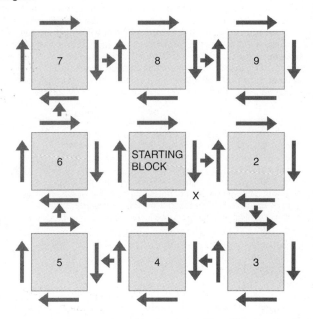

A. **Block diagram**

If for any reason this map does not adequately depict the area indicated by the intersections we have outlined above, please draw a map of the area, as it actually looks, on the back of this sheet. Once you have done so, follow the normal instructions for interviewing as detailed below.

B. **Where to start interviewing**
Starting at the corner indicated by the X, go around the entire block in a clockwise manner until you have reached your quota. If you have not reached your quota, follow the arrow to the next block; again start at the corner and follow the same procedure as before. Start interviewing at the _____ dwelling unit you come to.

C. **How to select subsequent households for interviewing**
When you encounter a dwelling where (1) no one is at home, (2) the respondent refuses to be interviewed, or (3) no qualified respondent is available, go to the very next dwelling unit. Follow this procedure until an interview is obtained. After each completed interview, skip _____ households and continue interviewing until you have completed your quota of _____ interviews.

Table 8–1, which compares the number of contacts required for in-home versus telephone interviewing.

SAMPLE SIZE DETERMINATION ISSUES

An important issue in survey research is how large a sample to draw. Large samples are generally more precise than small samples. In other words, if all else is the same, with large samples the researcher is generally more confident that the results are representative of the target population. However, large samples are also generally associated with higher costs. Marketing researchers use at least five

Qualifications	In-Person	Random Telephone	TABLE 8–1
18–55	92%	86%	Comparison of Net
Used any OTC cold remedy during the past month	60	60	Incidence—
No health restrictions/drug allergies	88	88	In-Person versus
No prior research participation	96	96	Telephone Screening
No employment by advertising agency, marketing research company, or drug manufacturer	97	97	
Net incidence	45	42	
Contacts required	222	238	

different methods of determining sample size. Sample size can be determined based on (1) blind guesses, (2) statistical precision, (3) Bayesian considerations, (4) cost limitations, and (5) industry standards.

Blind Guesses

Blind guessing, clearly the most unsatisfactory method of determining sample size, uses informed intuition as the basis for determining how many units to sample. This approach to determining sample size is completely arbitrary and does not consider the likely precision of the survey results or the cost of obtaining them.

blind guessing
Using informed intuition to determine how many units to sample.

Statistical Precision

Statistical precision relies on traditional statistical formulas for determining sample sizes. For example, consider the formula shown in Equation 8–1, which is used to determine the sample size for estimating the population mean.

$$n^* = \frac{(Z_{1-\alpha/2})^2 \, (\hat{\sigma})^2}{(P)^2} \qquad (8\text{--}1)$$

Note that the required sample size (n^*) depends on three criteria:

1. The desired confidence level ($Z_{1-\alpha/2}$).
2. The desired precision (P).
3. The variability, as measured by the estimated standard deviation ($\hat{\sigma}$) of the variable to be estimated.

To see how these three criteria affect the required sample size, consider the case in which a brand manager for a frozen foods corporation was interested in estimating the number of main dishes prepared by microwave in a typical month for dual-income families. The research design calls for a telephone interview, and the manager wants to know what size sample he or she should use.

First, the manager must determine how confident he or she wants to be. That is, does the manager want to be 90 percent confident in estimating the true population

Americans, More Optimistic About the Economy, Have Become Less Eager for Federal Remedies

WASHINGTON—When it comes to what the government should be doing to get the country out of the recession, most Americans seem ready to heed the advice of former Carter administration economist Charles Schultze: "Don't just do something—stand there."

A new nationwide *Wall Street Journal*/NBC News poll shows that, for the first time since the end of World War II, voters aren't clamoring for any of the traditional government tools to pull the country out of an economic downturn.

Moreover, there is a growing feeling that the worst of the recession is already over—an attitude fueled by the outcome of the Persian Gulf war. In the survey, nearly half of the voters—46 percent—expect the national economy to get better in the next year. In a poll just a month ago, only 25 percent thought so. That striking change in attitude could give a major boost to the economy by spurring consumer and business spending.

"The poll shows a sharp turnaround in people's attitude toward the economy," say pollsters Peter Hart, a Democrat, and Robert Teeter, a Republican, who conducted the survey for the *Journal* and NBC. "The first peace dividend is a psychological sense that we're going to come out of the economic doldrums. This isn't to say that everything is terrific, but that we've turned a corner" toward recovery.

To be sure, voters say the Bush administration, Congress, and the Federal Reserve aren't doing enough to combat the recession. But majorities say that tax cuts, interest-rate reductions, and increased government spending, the traditional solutions, won't do much good.

mean, 95 percent confident, etc. Once this has been established, the $Z_{1-\alpha/2}$ value is found by using a standard Z-table (see Table 2 of the Statistical Appendix). Assume that the manager determines that he or she wants to be 95 percent confident in estimating the true number of main dishes prepared by microwave in a typical month. In this case, from the Z-table, the value of $Z_{1-\alpha/2}$ is 1.96.

Second, the manager must determine how precise the estimate should be. Does he or she want to be able to estimate the true number of main dishes prepared by microwave in a typical month within a range of plus or minus two meals, four meals, or more? Assume that the manager states the estimate must be within plus or minus one meal; hence, $P = 1$.

The last piece of necessary information is an estimate of the variability of the variable being estimated. In this case, we need to estimate the standard deviation (or the variance) of the number of main dishes prepared by microwave during a typical month. This estimate can be based on prior studies, a small-scale pilot sample, or guessing. Let's assume that a pilot sample indicated that the estimated standard deviation was six meals.

We are now ready to determine the required sample size to estimate the number of main dishes prepared by microwave at a confidence level of 95 percent within plus or minus one meal. Using Equation 8–1, the required sample size is

Further, they clearly believe that the economy is getting better on its own. Nearly 7 out of 10 voters now believe that the recession will be a mild one; in December, only 45 percent thought it would be mild.

How Poll Was Conducted

The Wall Street Journal/NBC News poll was based on nationwide telephone interviews of 1,505 registered voters conducted Friday through Tuesday by the polling organizations of Peter Hart and Robert Teeter.

The sample was drawn from 315 randomly selected geographic points in the continental United States. Each region of the country was represented in proportion to its population. Households were selected by a method that gave all telephone numbers, listed and unlisted, an equal chance of being included. One registered voter, 18 years or older, was selected from each household by a procedure to provide the correct number of male and female respondents. The results of the survey were minimally weighted by gender, race, and income to ensure that the poll accurately reflects registered voters nationwide.

Chances are 19 of 20 that if all registered voters in the United States had been surveyed using the same questionnaire, the findings would differ from these poll results by no more than 2.6 percentage points in either direction. The margin of error for subgroups would be larger.

Source: Michel McQueen, *The Wall Street Journal*, March 22, 1991, p. A10.

$$n^* = \frac{(1.96)^2\,(6)^2}{(1)^2} = 138.3$$

Because sample size calculations are always rounded up, the required sample size would be 139. Note that the confidence level and the estimated standard deviation are in the numerator of the formula. Therefore, as the confidence level increases (e.g., moving from a 95 percent confidence to a 99 percent confidence) and/or the estimated standard deviation increases, the required sample size will also increase. Alternatively, since the desired precision is in the denominator of the formula, as the precision increases (i.e., the value of P decreases), the required sample size increases.

Appendix 8A provides a nomograph, which can be used to ascertain the required sample size when estimating a proportion for a given confidence and tolerance level. These devices are frequently utilized by political pollsters to ascertain the required sample size in order to estimate a proportion, typically voters, within plus or minus 3 percentage points. An explanation of what political pollsters mean when they say the results will differ by no more than plus or minus some percentage is provided in From the World of Research 8–1.

Bayesian Considerations

Bayesian decision analysis
Process that bases the decision on how large a sample to draw on both the expected value of the information obtained by the sample and the cost of taking the sample.

Bayesian decision analysis can also be used to determine sample size. The Bayesian approach, although not used much in practice, bases the decision regarding how large a sample to draw on both the expected value of the information obtained by the sample and the cost of taking the sample (see Appendix 2A). This approach involves computing a difference known as *expected net gain* from sampling for various sample sizes and choosing the sample size with the largest positive expected net gain.[2]

Cost Limitations

The cost limitations method, or "all-you-can-afford," determines sample size on the basis of the budget allocated to the project. This approach involves (1) subtracting from the available budget all nonsampling-related costs (for example, fixed cost of designing the survey, questionnaire preparation, data analysis, and report generation) and (2) dividing this amount by the estimated cost per sampling unit to arrive at the desired sample size. This approach is unsatisfactory because it emphasizes *cost* to the exclusion of all other factors, especially precision.

Industry Standards

industry standards
Those rules of thumb, developed from experience, that have become standard industry guidelines for determining how large a sample to draw.

Industry standards refer to those rules of thumb, developed from experience, that have become standard industry guidelines for determining how large a sample to draw. Conventional guidelines on sample size vary with the type of marketing research study as well as with the number of cells included in the study. The conventional approach to determining sample size is frequently used in nonprobability designs, especially in *quota samples*. In quota samples, for example, the minimum number of respondents per cell is usually no less than 50. Table 8–2 presents a summary of minimum sample sizes and typical sample sizes for various commercial marketing research studies. For example, 1,000 to 1,500 is usually considered to be a reasonable sample for a national (probability) market study. Also, 200 to 300 per cell is the convention for a typical concept or product test.

Although we have discussed the various methods of determining sample size separately, rarely will the marketing researcher rely on any one approach. The practicing marketing researcher has to consider statistical precision, financial constraints, and company policy (industry standards) when deciding on how many to include in the sample.

SAMPLING TECHNIQUE ISSUES

An important issue that must be resolved about sampling design concerns the method of drawing the sample. There are two broad categories: *probability samples* and *nonprobability samples*. Exhibit 8–8 presents a taxonomy of the specific sampling techniques that will be considered.

---

[2]Because the Bayesian approach is not frequently used in practice (primarily due to its complexity and perceived difficulty) we do not discuss it further. The interested reader can consult P. Schlaifer, *Analysis of Decisions Under Uncertainty* (New York: McGraw-Hill, 1969), for a comprehensive treatment.

Study	Minimum Size	Typical Size (range)
Market studies	500	1,000–1,500
Strategic studies	200	400–500
Test-market penetration studies	200	300–500
Concept/product tests	200	200–300/cell
Name tests	100*/name variant	200–300/cell
Package tests	100*/package variant	200–300/cell
TV commercial tests	150/commercial	200–300/commercial
Radio commercial tests	150/commercial	200–300/commercial
Print ad tests	150/advertisement	200–300/commercial
Test-market audits		
Projectable number of stores accounting for:		
Food	50% of ACV†	
Drugs	50% of ACV†	
Controlled		
Food	10 stores	10–12 stores
Drugs	10 stores	10–12 stores
Focus group	6/region	8–12/region

*If quota samples are used, the minimum cell size for analysis is 50 respondents.
†ACV—average all commodity volume.

Typical Sample Size Used in Different Types of Marketing Research Studies

EXHIBIT 8–8 Taxonomy of Sampling Designs

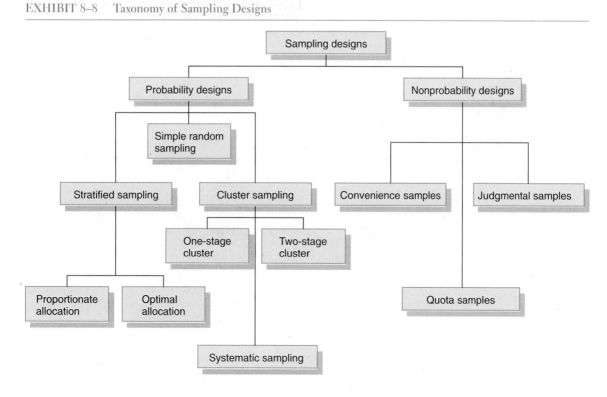

Probability Samples

All probability sampling procedures share two fundamental characteristics.[3]

1. Before the sampling takes place, it is always possible to specify every potential sample of a given size (samples of size two, of size three, and so on) that could be drawn from the population and the probability of selecting each sample.

2. Every sampling unit must have some nonzero chance of being selected.

Thus, in probability sampling designs, the population must be clearly defined, enabling the researcher to tell which sampling units belong to the population of interest and which sampling units do not. This means that a sampling frame (a list or other organized breakdown of the target population) must be available. There is no requirement that every potential sample have the same probability of selection, but the probability of selecting any particular sample of a given size can be specified.

The ability to determine this probability means that the precision of the estimated value of the characteristics under study can be computed. In other words, confidence intervals into which the true population value will fall with a given level of certainty can be computed. And, in essence, this allows the researcher to make inferences (projections) to the target population from which the sample was drawn. The primary probability sampling methods are simple random sampling, systematic sampling, stratified sampling, and cluster sampling.

Simple Random Sampling (SRS). The simplest method of drawing a probability sample is to do it randomly. This method is equivalent to a lottery system in which names are placed in an urn and drawn out randomly. **Simple random sampling** guarantees that every sample of a given size, as well as every individual in the target population, has an equal chance of being selected. To draw a simple random sample requires a list or other organized breakdown that specifically enumerates each individual, household, or other element in the target population. Numbers from 1 to N (the size of the target population) are assigned to each element in the list and a random number table (see Table 1 in the Statistical Appendix) is used to select n (the desired sample size). In other words, the elements with numbers corresponding to the random numbers are selected into the sample.

simple random sampling
Design guaranteeing that every sample of a given size as well as every individual in the target population has an equal chance of being selected.

Simple random samples have many desirable features. For example, they are easily understood and used, and they allow one to project sample results to the target population. Nevertheless, simple random samples are rarely used in practice. First, SRS may be infeasible—it requires that all elements in the target population be identified and labeled (numbered) prior to sampling. Prior identification is often impossible. Second, SRS can be expensive—it can result in especially large samples or in samples spread out over a large geographical area, making data collection time consuming and costly. This occurs because SRS gives each element

---

[3]R. J. Jaeger, *Sampling in Education and the Social Sciences* (New York: Longman, Inc., 1984), pp. 28–29.

in the target population an equal chance of being included in the sample. Consider the use of SRS in a study designed to compare various brand-user groups of a target population. Under SRS the expected representation of a brand-user group is its population proportion, or market share. If a brand has a small market share, we would need a relatively large simple random sample to adequately represent users of this brand. Finally, SRS does not guarantee that the sample drawn will be representative of the target population—it may not include specific subgroups of the population. Consequently, the sample ultimately drawn may contain too few or too many individuals from certain subgroups. A simple random sample of past-30-day facial cream moisturizer users, for example, could result in a sample in which specific brands of the category are overrepresented or underrepresented in relation to their actual market shares. In such a case, resulting brand profiles could be quite distorted. In other words, though random samples will represent a population well *on average*, a given random sample (and particularly a small one) may not represent the target population well at all. For this reason, some sample procedures attempt to guarantee that the correct proportion of subpopulation elements will find their way into the ultimate sample.

Systematic Sampling.   With **systematic sampling** the target sample is generated by picking an arbitrary starting point (in a list) and then picking every *n*th element in succession from a list. For example, if one wanted a target sample of 60 from a target population of 3,600 and assuming that the 21st element (or any number between 1 and 60) was selected as the arbitrary starting point, then elements 81, 141, 201, . . . , 3,561 would make up the remaining 59 elements of the target sample. Systematic sampling is very easy to use. Note also that although a list of all individual elements in the population is required, there is no need to generate a set of random numbers, and, therefore, the random numbers do not have to be matched with individual elements as in SRS. Since some lists contain millions of elements, considerable time can be saved by not having to scan the entire list and pull off, say, the names and addresses or phone numbers of the designated elements. Thus, it is not too surprising to note that many consumer phone and mail surveys use a systematic sampling procedure.

systematic sampling
Design whereby the target sample is generated by picking an arbitrary starting point (in a list) and then picking every nth element in succession from a list.

Stratified Sampling.   **Stratified sampling** involves partitioning the entire population of elements into subpopulations and then selecting elements separately from each subpopulation. Consequently, stratified sampling necessarily involves two types of variables: a **classification variable,** which is used to place each population element into a particular subpopulation, and a **sampling variable,** which represents the characteristic of the population that we wish to estimate.

Stratified sampling can be described by four steps:

1   Based on some classification variable, the entire population of sample units is divided into distinct subpopulations called *strata*.

2. Within each stratum a separate sample of elements is selected from all of the elements composing that stratum, usually by SRS.

stratified sampling
Design that involves partitioning the entire population of elements into subpopulations, called strata, and then selecting elements separately from each subpopulation.

classification variable
Variable used to place each population element into a particular subpopulation.

sampling variable
Variable that represents the characteristic of the population that we wish to estimate.

3. For each separate sample an estimate of the characteristics of interest is calculated and properly weighted; this is then added to obtain a combined estimate for the entire population.

4. The variances of the estimates also are computed separately for each stratum, and these are properly weighted and added to form a combined estimate for the entire population.

Stratified sampling is more complex than SRS and, because at least one classification variable must be observed for each sampling unit, potentially more costly. On the positive side, however, stratified sampling can be much more efficient than SRS. For a given sample size, the standard deviation of the estimated value can often be significantly reduced through the use of stratified sampling design—a smaller confidence interval is often obtained. This is frequently accomplished by stratifying to preclude the selection of undesirable samples that might be selected under some other sampling design. For example, suppose we wish to estimate the total number of interviews completed per day by all of the field service companies that have performed field operations for our company last year. Further, suppose we know that the majority of the field services are small and primarily perform mall-intercept surveys, while the few large field-service companies perform the vast majority of in-home personal interviews. Under these conditions, an SRS taken from the list of all field-service companies may not necessarily represent the population since it might contain too few or too many of the very large field-service companies.

A solution to this problem might be to stratify on the basis of the size of the field-service company; that is, we could stratify each sampling unit (field-service company), prior to sampling, into two groups (small, large), and then using SRS techniques we could select certain numbers of field-service companies from each of the two strata. A very simple illustration of this is shown in Exhibit 8–9.

The efficiency of stratified sampling is directly tied to the efficacy of the (classification) variable used to classify the sampling units into strata. We want the sampling units that are assigned to a particular stratum to be very similar to each other with respect to the characteristic being measured (within-strata homogeneity) but very different from the elements assigned to other strata (between-strata heterogeneity). In most applications the population is stratified on the basis of a

EXHIBIT 8–9
———
Stratified Sampling

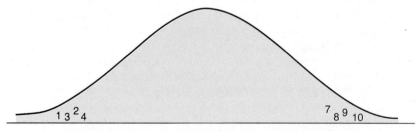

In this case the classification variable has divided the population into two halves. We choose a sample of one from each stratum. Thus, the procedure rules out undesirable samples like 1, 2; 2, 3; 9, 10; 8, 9; and so on.

variable that can be conveniently measured, for example, by geographical region, age, gender, and so on. Remember that a good classification variable for one study may be quite unsatisfactory for another.

An important decision in stratified sampling is the number of elements that will be sampled from each stratum. For example, suppose we decide on a sample size of 100 and are stratifying based on usage: light versus heavy. The questions are, How many light users do we sample, and how many heavy users do we sample under the constraint that the total sample size must equal 100. In practice, two procedures have been used extensively for allocating the total sample size among strata. One procedure, **proportional allocation,** guarantees that stratified random sampling will be at least as efficient as SRS. When proportional allocation is used the number of elements selected from a stratum is proportional to the size of the stratum with respect to the population. For example, if light users represented 35 percent of the population, then 35 percent of the sample (or 35 people) would be sampled from the light stratum, and the remaining 65 percent would be from the heavy stratum.

The second procedure, called **disproportional or optimal allocation** produces the most precise (reliable) estimates. Optimal allocation involves a double weighting scheme. The first weight reflects the size of the stratum, as in proportional allocation. The second weight reflects the variance or standard deviation of the variable that will be estimated in each stratum. From the previous example, if the light users had a greater standard deviation than heavy users, more than 35 percent of the sample would be taken from the light users. In general, more observations will be taken from stratum that have large standard deviations of the variable that will be estimated. Note that optimal allocation reduces to proportional allocation if the standard deviations are similar across strata.

Stratified random sampling is a popular sampling procedure because it combines the conceptual simplicity of SRS with potentially significant gains in precision. An increasing trend today is the use of stratified sampling designs in telephone interviewing (see Chapter 6). Exhibit 8–10 (see page 240) and Table 8–3 (see page 241) describe the telephone sampling procedure used by Survey Sampling, Inc., a research supplier specializing in survey sampling methods. This sampling procedure combines systematic and stratified sampling concepts to gain efficiency for nondirectory telephone interviewing.

Cluster Sampling. **Cluster sampling procedures** can be described broadly by the following features:

1. Based on some classification variable or natural grouping, the entire population of sampling units is divided into mutually exclusive and exhaustive subsets, called **clusters.**

2. Clusters are then selected based on a specified probability design such as SRS.

3. Elements are either probabilistically drawn from each selected cluster, or for each selected cluster all of the elements are included in the sample. Note

proportional allocation
Sampling design guaranteeing that stratified random sampling will be at least as efficient as SRS. The number of elements selected from a stratum is directly proportional to the size of the stratum.

disproportional or optimal allocation
Double weighting scheme where the number of sample elements taken from a given stratum is proportional to the relative size of the stratum and the standard deviation of the distribution of the characteristic under consideration among all elements in the stratum.

cluster sampling
Design whereby a sample of clusters is first selected and then a decision on which sampling units to include in the sample is made.

clusters
Groups or collections of sampling units.

Stratification to Counties

To equalize the probability of telephone household selection from anywhere in the area sampled, samples are first systematically stratified to all counties in proportion to each county's share of telephone households in the survey area. After a geographical area has been defined as a combination of counties, the sum of estimated telephone households is calculated and divided by the desired sample size to produce a sampling interval:

Total estimated telephone households ÷ Desired sample size = Interval
750,000 ÷ 6,000 = 125

A random number is drawn between 0 and the interval (125) to establish a starting point. Assuming the starting point is 86, then the 86th, 211th, 336th, 461st, . . . , records would be selected for the sample, each time stepping through the database by a factor of 125. This is a systematic random sample because the sample is selected in a systematic "nth" fashion from a random starting point. Any county whose population of estimated telephone households equals or exceeds the sampling interval is automatically included in the sample, while smaller counties are included with a probability proportionate to their size.

Using our example, where the sample size is 6,000, let us also assume that the geographical area selected covers three counties. The sampling interval allows the proportionate distribution of the sample over three counties as shown in Table 8–3.

Selection of Numbers within Counties

For each county included in the sample, one (or more) unique telephone number is selected by systematic sampling from among all working blocks of numbers in all telephone exchanges assigned to the county. A working block is defined as 100 contiguous numbers that contain three or more residential telephone listings:

the phone number 266/7558
exchange/block

In this example, for the exchange 266, the entire block comprises the number 7500–7599. Exchanges are assigned to a single county on the basis of where listed residents live. For those overlapping county lines, the exchanges are assigned to the county with the highest number of listed residents.

Selection among Exchanges

Once the sample has been allocated, a second sampling interval is calculated for each county by dividing the number of listed telephone households for the county by the portion of the sample allocated to that county. In our earlier example, it was determined that 28 percent of the sample (1,680 numbers) would be drawn from County A. Each exchange and working block within an exchange are weighted by their share of listed telephone households. If the total number of listed telephone households in the database for this county is 159,600, that number is divided by 1,680, which gives us an interval of 95.

Next, from a random start between 1 and 95, the exchanges and working blocks that fall within the interval are sampled on a systematic basis. Next, two more digits are randomly chosen from the range 00–99 and added to each of the selected blocks. The result is a complete number made up of the exchange, the block, and the two random digits (e.g., 266 + 75 + 59).

Source: Survey Sampling, Inc., used with permission.

that in contrast to SRS and stratified sampling, with cluster sampling, a sampling frame is needed only for those clusters selected into the sample.

There are many different types of cluster sampling designs. At the most general level, cluster sampling can involve either a single stage or multiple stages. By a stage we simply mean a step in the sampling process. For example, if stores that participate in a test-market study are the clusters and calendar weeks are sampling

	Total Households	Percent with Phone	Estimated Phone Households	Percent of Sample	
County A	223,404	94	210,000	28.0	TABLE 8–3
County B	393,258	89	350,000	46.7	——
County C	204,301	93	190,000	25.3	Proportionate
Total	820,963		750,000	100.0	Distribution Through Systematic Sampling

units, then there might be two steps involved in selecting the sample of calendar weeks on which to base the estimate of volume sold for the test brand under study. The first step might involve selecting a sample of stores, and the second step might involve selecting a sample of calendar weeks for each of the stores selected at the first step. The clusters used at the first stage of sampling are usually referred to as **primary sampling units (PSUs),** and the sampling units selected at the second stage of sampling are usually referred to as **secondary sampling units (SSUs).**

A **single-stage cluster sample** entails one step because once the sample of clusters is selected, every sampling unit within each of the selected clusters is included in the sample. If the clusters are chosen by SRS, and within each cluster all sampling units are selected, we refer to this design as **simple one-stage cluster sampling.**

Multiple-stage cluster sampling designs entail two or more steps. For example, in a telephone survey we might first take a sample of states. Second, we might take a sample of counties within each sample cluster (states). Third, we might take a sample of working telephone exchanges within each of the counties selected at the second stage. And finally, we might take a sample of telephone numbers within each working exchange selected at the third stage. Note that in multistage cluster sampling more than one sampling frame is likely to be used in drawing the sample. However, after each stage, the sampling frame for the next stage involves only those clusters chosen at the preceding stage. If the clusters at the first stage are selected by SRS and if at the second stage the sampling units are selected probabilistically by SRS from each sample cluster so that the same fraction of sampling units is drawn from each sample cluster, we refer to this design as **simple two-stage cluster sampling.** In cases in which the clusters are of unequal size, it is not always possible for the fraction of sampling units at the second stage to be exactly the same within each sample cluster. A frequently used type of two-stage design that does not entail SRS of clusters at the first stage is called sampling with **probability proportional to size (PPS) sampling.** Under PPS sampling, clusters are sampled at the first stage with probability proportional to the number of sampling units in the cluster.

The two primary advantages of cluster sampling are feasibility and economy. For these reasons, cluster sampling is frequently used in practice, especially in surveys covering large geographical areas. The practical feasibility of cluster sampling comes about because in many settings the only sampling frame readily available for the target population is one that lists clusters. Lists of geographical

primary sampling units (PSUs)
Clusters used at the first stage of sampling.

secondary sampling units (SSUs)
Sampling units selected at the second stage of sampling.

single-stage cluster sample
One-step design where, once the sample of clusters is selected, every sampling unit within each of the selected clusters is included in the sample.

simple one-stage cluster sampling
One-step design in which first-stage clusters are selected by SRS, and within each selected cluster all sampling units are chosen.

simple two-stage cluster sampling
Design in which the clusters at the first stage are selected by SRS; at the second stage the sampling units are selected probabilistically by SRS from each sample cluster so that with clusters of equal size the same fraction of sampling units is drawn from each sample cluster.

probability proportional
to size (PPS) sampling
*Design in which clusters
are sampled at the first
stage with probability
proportional to the num-
ber of sampling units in
the cluster.*

regions, blocks, telephone exchanges, and the like can usually be easily compiled, and the researcher can thus avoid compiling a list of all individual elements for the target population, a process almost never feasible in terms of time and resources for populations of any reasonable size.

Cluster sampling is generally the most cost-effective means of sampling. Cost efficiencies come about because of the relative ease with which sampling frames can be assembled and the reduced costs associated with traveling. For example, with in-home personal surveys, if a geographical area such as a census tract defines the clusters, then once the sample of census tract clusters is selected and households are selected from within the sample census tracts, the cost of traveling from household to household will usually be low. Cost economies arise from selecting a relatively small number of census-tract clusters and sampling many households from the sample census tracts, as opposed to taking an SRS of households (of a given size) spread across many census tracts—the traveling costs for visiting households that are in different census tracts are considerably higher than the traveling costs of visiting households in the same tract.

Although it is practical and economical, cluster sampling is not without disadvantages. First, and perhaps most serious, for a given sample size the estimates obtained from cluster sampling designs are frequently not as precise as those obtained from samples drawn with the use of other sampling designs. The reliability of cluster samples will be poor, depending on the extent to which sampling units within a cluster are homogeneous. The procedure with cluster sampling is to select many sampling units from very few clusters to capitalize on traveling cost savings. However, if the within-cluster sampling units are homogeneous, then selecting more than one of these sampling units provides very little additional information on the population characteristic under study. Thus, the ultimate sample selected from the small number of cluster PSUs can be unrepresentative of the entire target population, and highly unreliable estimates can be obtained. In cluster sampling, we want the within-cluster sampling units to be somewhat heterogeneous with respect to the sampling variable to ensure representativeness. However, in practice, clusters tend to be homogeneous. For example, households on the same block are frequently similar with respect to socioeconomic and demographic factors; patrons who regularly frequent the same store are often similar with respect to social class as well as other variables.

The aim in choosing a sampling design is to select the one that yields the most precise estimates at a specified cost or, conversely, the design having lowest cost that yields estimates with specific precision. If cost and feasibility were the sole concerns, then rarely would one choose any design other than cluster sampling. On the other hand, if reliability of estimates was the sole concern, then one would rarely choose cluster sampling. In choosing between cluster sampling and other designs, we must incorporate reliability, cost, *and* feasibility.

The second principal disadvantage associated with cluster sampling designs is their complexity. The most complex cluster sampling designs occur when each cluster in the population does not have the same number of sampling units. The complexity of cluster sampling manifests itself in several difficulties. The procedure for drawing the sample becomes more difficult, and estimation formulas become much more involved; in fact, standard statistical software packages usually cannot be used to estimate population parameters under cluster sampling, except in simple one-stage designs where formulas for estimates resemble the formulas used in SRS.

Use of Probability Samples.   In commercial marketing research studies, probability samples are drawn when the need is for highly accurate estimates of share of market or volume that can be statistically projected to the entire market. Heterogeneous markets favor the use of nationwide studies and probability samples. In nationwide studies a high degree of accuracy is generally worth the extra cost because of the information needed and the decisions to be made. For example, national market tracking studies provide information on category and brand-use incidence rates and demographic and psychographic user profiles. Among other things this information is used to measure the relative effectiveness of the organization's marketing program, to define target audiences, to identify marketing opportunities, and to provide direction for developing marketing strategies. Such decisions are vitally important to the organization and require accurate estimates that can be statistically projected to the entire market. Finally, as we indicated in Chapter 6, the clear trend is away from in-home personal surveys. It is not surprising that most studies that use probability samples are conducted via the telephone. These designs generally call for a two-stage procedure in which systematic and stratified sampling are combined with some form of random digit dialing (see Exhibit 8–10).

Nonprobability Samples

All **nonprobability sampling procedures** share a common characteristic. There is no way of determining exactly what the chance is of selecting any particular element into the sample. Consequently, estimates are not statistically projectable to the entire population. We don't mean that nonprobability samples are necessarily inaccurate and always inferior to probability samples. Rather, nonprobability samples can be good (representative) or bad (unrepresentative) depending on the approach and controls used in selecting who is included in the sample. Certain nonprobability designs produce what are called *purposive samples* because certain "important" segments of the target population are intentionally overrepresented in the sample. Some of the major nonprobability sampling approaches include convenience samples, judgmental samples, and quota samples.

nonprobability samples *Form of sampling where there is no way of determining exactly what the chance is of selecting any particular element or sampling unit into the sample.*

Convenience Samples.   If **convenience sampling** is used, there is very little or no control over who is included in the sample. If respondent participation is voluntary or if the interviewer selects sampling units, then convenience samples are produced. For example, 100 women might be intercepted in a shopping mall and interviewed with no quotas or qualifications for participation in the study. There is no way to access the representativeness of the sample. Mail surveys often produce convenience samples. Because of the self-selection and voluntary participation that accompany this data-collection method, the issue of nonresponse is extremely important. We will discuss nonresponse bias shortly.

convenience sampling *Studies in which respondent participation is voluntary or which leaves the selection of sampling units primarily up to the interviewer.*

judgmental sampling
Studies in which respondents are selected because it is expected that they are representative of the population of interest and/or meet the specific needs of the research study.

snowball design
Sample formed by having each respondent, after being interviewed, identify others who belong to the target population of interest.

quota sampling
Design that involves selecting specific numbers of respondents who possess certain characteristics known or presumed to affect the subject of the research study.

Judgmental Samples. **Judgmental sampling** involves selecting certain respondents for participation in the study. Respondents are selected because they are presumably representative of the population of interest and/or meet the specific needs of the research study. Judgmental samples are frequently used in commercial marketing research studies. For example, a concept product test may specify that only past-30-day facial-moisturizer category users should be interviewed. Test markets exemplify judgmental samples, that is, the specific community, neighborhood, or metropolitan area is presumed to be representative of the entire market. Scanner services also use what must be considered judgmental samples of cities. As we discuss in Chapter 21, a debate centers on whether the judgmentally selected sample of cities represents only those specific cities or the entire United States.

A special kind of judgmental sampling is the **snowball design,** frequently used when it is necessary to reach a small, specialized target population. Under a snowball design, after being interviewed, each respondent is asked to identify others who belong to the target population.

Quota Samples. **Quota sampling** involves selecting specific numbers of respondents who possess certain characteristics known or presumed to affect the subject of the research study. It is extremely common in commercial marketing research studies to set quotas on interviews based on age, gender, or income. Quota samples are designed to ensure that the proportion of the sample elements possessing a certain characteristic is approximately the same as the proportion with the characteristic in the population of interest. In other words, the sample is representative of the entire population. An interviewer at the testing location, who is responsible for conducting 20 interviews, might be instructed to intercept and interview nine female past-30-day category users, aged 18–34; six female past-30-day category users, aged 35–54; and five female past-30-day category users, 55 years or older. Table 8–4 presents some representative quota sample requirements based on category users and/or category volume for several product categories.

Whether quota samples actually produce representative samples is often a difficult question to answer.[4] If an important characteristic that affects the subject of the research study is overlooked, then the quota sample will not be representative. Because quota samples are frequently used in mall-intercept surveys, there is potential for overrepresenting the kinds of people who frequent high-traffic shopping malls (see Chapter 6). To improve the quality of mall-intercept quota samples we suggest the following guidelines.[5]

- Use several different shopping malls in different neighborhoods so that differences between them can be observed.
- To minimize biases caused by traffic and parking flows, stratify by mall-entrance location and take a separate sample from each entrance.

---

[4]See Leslie Kish, *Survey Sampling* (New York: John Wiley & Sons, 1965), pp. 562–66, for a discussion of the problems in quota sampling.

[5]The following guidelines were adapted from Seymour Sudman, "Improving the Quality of Shopping Center Sampling," *Journal of Marketing Research*, November 1980, pp. 423–31.

	Chewing Gum		Breath Sweetners		Antacid		Cough Drops	
	% of Users	% of Volume	% of Users	% of Volume	% of Users	% of Volume	% of Users	% of Volume
Male	45	45	45	45	45	NA	40	45
Female	55	55	55	55	55	NA	60	55
8–11	10	10	—	—	—	—	10	5
12–17	20	25	20	20	—	—	15	10
18–24	20	20	20	20	15	NA	25	25
25–34	20	20	20	20	25	NA	25	25
35–49	15	15	25	25	25	NA	15	20
50+	15	10	15	15	35	NA	10	15

TABLE 8–4

Representative Quota Sample Requirements

Razor Blades % of Volume			Hand/Body Lotions % of Volume			Mouthwash			
	Males	Females		Males	Females		% of Users		% of Users
18–34	45	60	18–34	60	30	Male	45	35–49	25
35–49	25	20	35–54	30	60	Female	55	50–64	25
50–65	30	20	55–65	10	10	16–24	20	65+	5
						25–34	25		

— To minimize biases caused by shopping patterns, stratify by time segments—such as weekdays, weekday evenings, and weekends—and interview during each segment.

Use of Nonprobability Samples. Nonprobability samples are frequently used in commercial marketing research studies. In many instances the cost of conducting a national probability sample is prohibitively expensive, given the information needed and the decisions to be made. In practical settings the objectives of the study dictate what method of sampling will be used. For example, in concept tests, product tests, package tests, name tests, focus groups, and copy tests, all using nonprobability samples, projectable totals are usually not needed; rather we need to know only the proportion of the sample checking top box purchase-intent scores or favorable brand attitudes. Moreover, since these studies typically focus on brands for which shopping mall customers represent a major share of the market, mall shoppers can provide an adequate population, and mall-intercept quota samples are often used.[6] Exhibit 8–11 (see page 246) presents a type of sampling method, target sampling, that is a blend of probability and nonprobability sampling.

---

[6]Ibid., p. 423.

CHOOSING BETWEEN PROBABILITY AND NONPROBABILITY DESIGNS

When faced with the decision of whether to use a probability sample or a nonprobability sample, the marketing researcher must choose between projectability and efficiency. Probability samples allow statistical projection of the results to a target population, but usually they are not very efficient with respect to cost per respondent. Alternatively, nonprobability samples are typically efficient with respect to cost per respondent, but they are not statistically projectable. When the research objectives do not require a statistical projection to some target population, a nonprobability sampling design can supply the desired accuracy for substantially less cost per respondent. Consider Exhibit 8–12, which describes several criteria for choosing between a probability sample and a targeted sample.

EXHIBIT 8–11
—
Target Samples

A target sample is a blend of judgment sampling and probability sampling. The purpose of target sampling is to increase the field efficiency of the survey. In essence, when we conduct a target sample we specifically limit sampling to certain households, geographical areas, ethnic groups, and so on. For example, if a politician is interested in college students' opinion on a certain issue, a national probability telephone sample would be less efficient than a sample that targets cities and towns containing universities.

Assume that you are interested in conducting a survey and the target population consists of black households. The percentage of black households identified by the 1980 census is 11.2 percent. In this case you may want to consider a targeted sample. Using 1980 census data, SSI has identified census tracts where the density of black households is 30 percent or higher. Those census tracts constitute the standard SSI sampling frame for targeted black samples, which are available for mail, door-to-door, and listed telephone studies.

At the 30 percent level, some 5,900 tracts qualify across the United States. They represent 13.7 percent of all 43,000 U.S. tracts. Distributed across 39 states, these 5,900 tracts comprise some 5 million black households, according to the 1980 census.

Source: 1988, Survey Sampling, Inc., All Rights Reserved, One Post Road, Fairfield, CT 06430.

EXHIBIT 8–12
—
Decision Between Probability versus Targeted Sample Designs

There are three areas to consider before deciding the appropriate use of a targeted sample. First, is it critical that the study results be projectable to the entire universe? If so, a targeted sample may be inappropriate. Instead, disproportionate probabilities could be used so that areas with a higher incidence would have a greater chance of being selected. Next, by weighting the survey results, the projections could be adjusted back to their appropriate level.

Second, is there an economic benefit in targeting for the desired characteristic? Can we identify clusters of that trait in the census geography? If so, we may be able to significantly increase our sample incidence and reduce our field screening costs.

Third, assuming that targeting our sample proves to be a worthwhile approach, how narrowly should we define the target population? Or, to put it another way, what level of density of the desired trait will allow a geographical area to qualify for inclusion in the sample?

Here we face a trade-off between efficiency and projectability. A very narrow definition will increase efficiency by increasing incidence. But, at the same time, it will exclude those geographical areas where the incidence of the trait is somewhat lower, thus reducing projectability.

Source: 1988, Survey Sampling, Inc., All Rights Reserved, One Post Road, Fairfield, CT 06430.

> It is unethical, and potentially extremely misleading, to treat a nonprobability sample as if it were a probability sample. For example, consider the case where people are asked to call a 900 telephone number to express their views on a particular subject. The temptation is to project what is found in the sample to a larger population. However, because the respondents were self-selected, this is not possible. It is the responsibility of the supplier to inform the user(s) of the sample information about any caveats there may be regarding the statistical precision of the sample.

EXHIBIT 8–13

———

Ethical
Considerations

Exhibit 8–13 presents some ethical considerations for probability versus nonprobability samples.

NONRESPONSE BIAS ISSUES

The quality of the data in a particular survey is a function of what can be called the **total survey error**.[7] Total survey error reflects the difference between the overall population's true mean value (of the characteristic of interest) and the mean observed value (of the characteristic of interest) obtained from the particular sample of respondents. A matter of some importance is what causes the information obtained from a sample of respondents to differ from that of the entire population. Total survey error is composed of two components: **random sampling error** and **nonsampling error**.

Total survey error = Random sampling error + Nonsampling error

Random sampling error occurs because the selected sample is an imperfect representation of the overall population. Random sampling error represents how accurately the chosen sample's true mean value reflects the population's true mean value. It can be controlled by employing appropriate statistical design considerations and by increasing the sample size.

Nonsampling error represents the degree to which the mean observed value (on the characteristic of interest) for the respondents of a particular sample disagrees with the mean true value for the particular sample of respondents (on the characteristic of interest). The size of the nonsampling error depends on two factors: **nonresponse error** and **response error**. Nonresponse error occurs because not all of the respondents included in the sample respond; in other words, with nonresponse, the mean true value (on the characteristic of interest) of those sample respondents who do respond may be different from the entire sample's true mean value (on the characteristic of interest). The other component of nonsampling error, response error, occurs when respondents give inaccurate answers.

total survey error
The difference between the overall population's true mean value (on the variable of interest) and the mean observed value (of the variable of interest) obtained from the particular sample of respondents.

random sampling error
Error caused because the selected sample is an imperfect representation of the overall population; therefore, the true mean value for the particular sample of respondents (on the variable of interest) differs from the true mean value for the overall population (on the variable of interest).

nonsampling error
Degree to which the mean observed value (on the variable of interest) for the respondents of a particular sample disagrees with the mean true value for the particular sample of respondents (on the variable of interest).

---

[7]The discussion of total survey error and its components follows the presentation in H. Assael and J. Keon, "Nonsampling vs Sampling Errors in Sampling Research," *Journal of Marketing*, Spring 1982, pp. 114–23.

Nonsampling errors are more complex and harder to control than are sampling errors. Some evidence also suggests that nonsampling errors are a much larger part of the total survey error than are sampling errors.

Response Errors

Response errors occur when respondents do not provide accurate answers. A respondent may give inaccurate responses intentionally or unintentionally because of interviewer effects and biases as well as other external or societal factors.

1. *Intentional factors.* Respondents may purposely misreport their answers because they want to "help" the researcher; therefore, they either agree or disagree with all statements. This is called **acquiescence bias,** and it is particularly prominent in new-product tests. When faced with a new-product concept, certain respondents will respond very positively to the concept, regardless of their true feelings.

2. *Unintentional factors.* Even though a respondent intends to respond accurately, response errors arise because of faulty recall, fatigue, question format, question content, or some other unintentional factor. (We discuss the proper way to construct and format questions in Chapter 12.)

    Response errors also arise when respondents are unfamiliar or have little experience with the topic of the survey. For example, asking low income respondents about what is most important in choosing a European vacation spot and their intentions about which vacation spots they will go to may result in intention scores that have little or no relationship to the respondent's actual behavior.

3. *Interviewer effects and biases.* Remember that interviewers can influence respondents' answers, misrecord respondent's answers, or even cheat by falsifying respondents' answers.

4. *Extended or societal factors.* Respondent errors can arise because the respondent is influenced either positively or negatively by the organization conducting the study. Also, the desire to give socially acceptable answers to sensitive or potentially embarrassing questions leads to response errors.

Nonresponse Errors

Very few studies achieve a 100 percent response rate. The problem of nonresponse error occurs because those who agree to participate in the study are different, in some way, from those who are unable or unwilling to participate. In general, the higher the response rate, the lower the probability of nonresponse effects. However, response rate can be a poor indicator of nonresponse error. First, response rates provide no information about whether the respondents are good representatives of the original target sample. Second, an increasing response does not necessarily reduce nonresponse error. For example, if those nonrespondents who are induced to respond, through call-backs or some other method, are no different from the respondents already in the sample, nonresponse bias may still be a problem.[8] Third, the notion of response rate is ambiguous since the number of eligible respondents used in the calculation of response rates frequently differs across studies; in some instances, for example, poor health or an inability to communicate in English are considered acceptable reasons for not counting a contact in the response rate calculation, whereas in other instances, they are not considered legitimate. Finally, another difficulty is that researchers often fail to report the way in which the response rate was calculated.[9]

Unfortunately, the extent of the differences between respondents and nonrespondents seldom can be directly determined. Indirect methods sometimes provide very limited checks for respondent and nonrespondent differences. For example, if the sample is drawn from available records (e.g., personnel files or warranty cards), whatever information is available from those sources can be used to check for respondent-nonrespondent differences.[10] If the sample is supposed to be representative of the general population, comparisons can be made against the U.S. Census.[11] Note, however, that indirect comparisons may be of little use and may even be misleading if the characteristics employed for comparison purposes are not closely related to the variable under study. For example, if age and occupation information are available from warranty card records, but these variables have no relationship to receptivity to a new direct mailing appeal, then to use them as a basis for comparing respondents and nonrespondents may be of little value.

By using personal and telephone surveys, the interviewer can make limited judgments about a person's background characteristics when a refusal occurs. For example, the interviewer may be able to make judgments about the nonrespondent's age, gender, marital status, family size, socioeconomic status, and so on. This is not the case with mail surveys; because there is no interviewer, nonrespondent characteristics cannot be determined. Mail surveys present the researcher with much more serious respondent-nonrespondent differences than do either personal or telephone surveys. The reason for this is the chance for response selectivity.[12] Recipients of mail questionnaires can examine the instrument thoroughly before deciding to respond. Interest in the particular survey topic is likely to be a primary factor in whether the questionnaire is completed and returned. As a result, respondents may not be representative of the original target sample.

---

[8]See L. Leslie, "Are High Response Rates Essential to Valid Surveys," *Social Science Research*, September 1971, pp. 332–34.

[9]See J. Williams-Jones, "Lack of Agreement on the Standardization of Response Terminology in the Survey Research Industry," in *Advances in Consumer Research VIII*, ed. K. B. Monroe (Association for Consumer Research, 1981), pp. 281–86.

[10]D. A. Dillman, *Mail and Telephone Surveys: The Total Design Method* (New York: John Wiley & Sons, 1978), p. 53.

[11]D. A. Dillman, J. A. Christenson, E. H. Carpenter, and R. M. Brooks, "Increasing Mail Questionnaire Response: A Four-State Comparison," *American Sociological Reviews*, 1974, pp. 744–56.

[12]Dillman, *Mail and Telephone Surveys*, p. 53.

SUMMARY

In this chapter we have presented a treatment of the fundamental concepts of sampling. We organized our discussion in terms of the five key decision issues that a marketing manager or researcher must consider when devising a sampling plan. Sampling decisions are complex; there is no single "right" way to make sampling decisions. As we emphasize, cost, reliability of the estimates, industry practices, and convenience all influence the choice of a sample design. Because of the interrelationships among the decision issues (e.g., the method of data collection is related to the method of drawing the sample), compromises will undoubtedly have to be made. Since most serious errors in sample design occur because of nonsampling errors, we suggest that the researcher be particularly sensitive to nonresponse bias and errors in logic.

KEY CONCEPTS

target population	probability samples	nonprobability samples	target samples
sampling frames	simple random samples	convenience samples	nonresponse bias
incidence rates	stratified samples	judgment samples	nonresponse errors
sample size determination	cluster samples	quota samples	response errors

REVIEW QUESTIONS

1. Identify the target population and a likely sampling frame for the following scenarios.
    a. A café in downtown New York City develops a new blend of coffee and would like to conduct a taste test with their patrons.
    b. A private Minneapolis country club debates offering a discount program to those wanting joint use of the golf course and the tennis courts.
    c. The United States Army conducts a national search for eligible recruits.
    d. A professional golfer begins a national campaign to sell his latest instructional video.
    e. The mayor of Atlanta wants to increase small business development in the city in order to increase productivity and decrease unemployment.
    f. A local fitness club would like to double its current membership by promoting greater awareness of its facilities as well as the long-term benefits to its consumers.
    g. Over 10,000 assembly-line employees are sponsoring a national push for better working conditions at all U.S. assembly plants.

2. A handful of the PAY-LO grocery stores in a southeastern city noticed diminishing store traffic during the previously busy 5 P.M. to 8 P.M. time period. The area manager found that other chain stores had not seen such a decrease in store traffic during the same time slot. Store management commissioned a survey to study changing shopping patterns. In order to encourage participation, the research department offered each participant $5.00 worth of groceries. The written survey took only five minutes, and most participants were able to complete the survey instrument while waiting in the checkout line.
    a. What type of sampling method was used?
    b. Outline the advantages and disadvantages of the method used.

3. A southwestern company that manufactured and distributed a newly patented sunglass lens decided it was time to expand. Potential test areas in four southeastern states were reviewed and analyzed in terms of demographics, purchase patterns, and so on. Finally, Miami, Florida, and Savannah, Georgia, were selected.

a. What type of sampling method was used?

b. Outline the advantages and disadvantages of the method used.

4. Weight-Loss Center of America wanted to assess its spring advertising campaign. The company's research department decided on the use of a number of focus groups. They selected 8 to 12 overweight individuals who were walking around a local mall.

a. What type of sampling method was used?

b. Outline the advantages and disadvantages of the method used.

5. For each of the situations described in question 1, discuss whether a probability or a nonprobability design is more appropriate and which particular design you would select.

SAMPLE SIZE CALCULATOR

HOW TO USE THE SAMPLE SIZE CALCULATOR

Scale A is graduated proportionally to the percent of favorable responses received (or expected) in a sampling survey. Values from 1 to 50 percent are graduated on the left side of this scale, and values from 50 to 99 percent are graduated on the right side of the scale.

Scale B is graduated proportionally to sample sizes ranging from 30 to 10,000.

Scale C is graduated proportionally to the sampling error (plus or minus) in the percent of favorable responses. Graduations on the left side of this scale are for 95 percent probability of being correct (i.e., 95 percent confidence), and graduations on the right side of the scale are for 99.7 percent confidence.

To use the chart, lay a straightedge to connect known values on any two of the scales. Read the unknown value where the straightedge intersects the third scale. You can use the chart to determine proper sample size from an expected favorable response rate and desired maximum error level; or you can use it to determine expected (or actual) error levels with an expected (or actual) favorable response rate and a given sample size.

Reprinted from the Marketing Problem Solver, authored by Kenneth Barasch, and originally published by Cochrane Chase & Company.

SAMPLE SIZE CALCULATOR

An easy method of obtaining approximate answers to a variety of sampling problems.

To use the chart, lay a straightedge to connect known values on any two of the scales. Read the unknown value where the straightedge intersects the third scale.

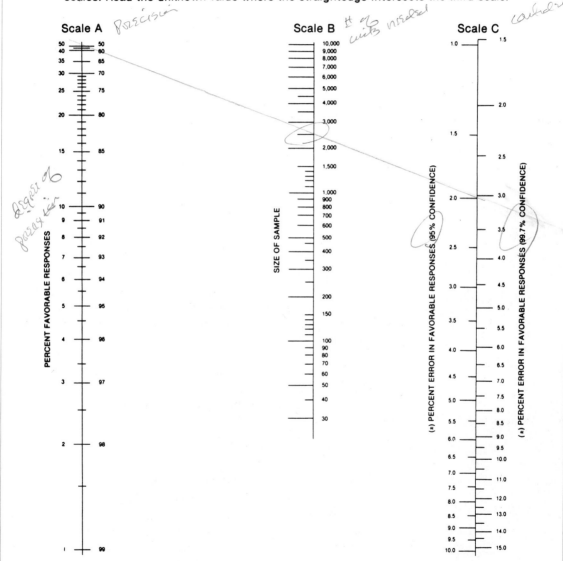

Kennedy Research, Inc., Waters Building, Grand Rapids, Michigan 49503 616/458-1461

Procedures for Drawing Probability Samples

— Discuss the mechanics of probability sampling designs.
— Explain how to draw simple random samples, systematic samples, stratified samples, and cluster samples.
— Illustrate how population characteristics are estimated under simple random sampling, systematic sampling, stratified sampling, and cluster sampling.
— Demonstrate how required sample sizes are calculated under various probability sampling designs.

INTRODUCTION

This chapter presents the mechanics of drawing probability samples. The material will be of interest to those of you who want (or need) to understand more about how the various probability sampling designs work in general, and specifically how probability samples are drawn. In our discussions of simple random sampling, systematic sampling, stratified sampling, and cluster sampling, we emphasize various issues that are likely to arise in practical application and, wherever possible, compare the benefits of each.

SIMPLE RANDOM SAMPLING PROCEDURES

As we indicated in Chapter 8, simple random sampling (SRS) is based on the simplest probabilistic model: A *simple random sample* (SRS) of n elements from a target population of N elements is one in which each of the M samples in the target population has the same chance of being selected, equal to $1/M$. In addition, the probability of selecting any individual element is equal to n/N, the ratio of target sample size to target population size.

Selecting the Sample

If a sampling frame is available, a simple random sample is drawn according to the following steps:

1. Assign a number from 1 to N to each element.
2. Using the random number table (Table 1 in the Statistical Appendix) and as many digits consistent with N, begin at some arbitrary point and proceed either up, down, or diagonally until *n* different numbers greater than zero but less than or equal to *n* have been selected. If you reach the bottom line of a particular page, proceed to the top line of the very next column on that same page. If you run out of columns on the current page then proceed to the next page of random numbers.
3. The numbers selected identify the elements that should be included in the sample.

EXAMPLE

Suppose that, as part of your duties as a junior analyst, you are responsible for overseeing field-service operations. Specifically, you are responsible for estimating the average number of interviews completed daily by all of the field services that have conducted mall-intercept surveys for your department in 1993. This information is to be used for 1994 budget-planning purposes. You are beginning to plan the 1993 sampling design. To decide on how many field services to include in the sample, you take a simple random sample of field interviews from an "average" field-service operation in order to obtain sample estimates of the mean and variance of the number of interviews completed per day. Table 9–1 lists the number of completed interviews per day for 15 field interviewers who are employed by the XYZ Field Service—a presumably average field-service operator.

The following procedure is used to draw a simple random sample of $n = 5$ field interviewers. Because $N = 15$, two-digit random numbers are used. Beginning at some arbitrary point in a random number table (Statistical Appendix, Table 1), at row 16, and the first two columns in the second block, for example, select the needed interviewers. Moving down the columns pick out five different numbers between 01 and 15. Numbers equal to 00 or greater than 15 are discarded as well as any duplication. From the random number digit table we find that the first two-digit number satisfying these conditions is 12, followed by 04, 01, 06, and 11. Note that the number 04 was encountered twice, but it was discarded the second time. Also note that when the bottom of the page is reached, you proceed to the first two columns in the third block of numbers, although you could have proceeded to any previously unused set of two columns in the table.

Estimating Population Characteristics

Estimates obtained under SRS are unbiased estimators of their corresponding population values. If, for simplicity, we assume infinite (or at least very large)

TABLE 9–1
———

Completed
Interviews per Day,
Mall-Intercept in
Cincinnati, Ohio,
XYZ Field Service

Interviewer	Completed Interviews/ Day (Y_i)
1*	4.5
2	3.5
3	6.5
4*	2.5
5	5.5
6*	3.5
7	3.5
8	2.5
9	4.5
10	5.5
11*	6.5
12*	6.5
13	5.5
14	4.5
15	2.5
	67.5

*Interviewers selected into the sample—see text discussion.

target populations, we can estimate the mean and variance of the characteristic being measured in the entire target population under SRS as follows:[1]

$$\bar{y} = \sum_{i=1}^{n} y_i / n \qquad (9\text{–}1)$$

———
[1]For computational purposes we recommend the following algebraically equivalent form for calculating the variance and standard deviation:

$$s_y^2 = \frac{\sum_{i=1}^{n} y_i^2 - \dfrac{\left(\sum_{i=1}^{n} y_i\right)^2}{n}}{n - 1}$$

and

$$s_y = \sqrt{\frac{\sum_{i=1}^{n} y_i^2 - \dfrac{\left(\sum_{i=1}^{n} y_i\right)^2}{n}}{n - 1}}$$

where $\sum_{i=1}^{n} y_i^2$ = Summation of the squares of each observation

$\left(\sum_{i=1}^{n} y_i\right)^2$ = Square of the total summation.

$$s_y^2 = \frac{\sum\limits_{i=1}^{n} (y_i - \bar{y})^2}{n - 1} \qquad (9\text{--}2)$$

where

n = Total sample size

y_i = Value of the characteristic being measured for the ith element in the target sample

$\bar{y}$ = Estimated mean value (unbiased estimator of population mean)

s_y^2 = Estimated sample variance (unbiased estimator of population variance)

In Chapter 8 we introduced the concept of reliability in discussing sample size determination. The reliability of an estimated *population parameter* (for example, a mean value or a proportion) refers to its reproducibility, that is, how reproducible the estimate of a population parameter is over different samples of a given size. Assuming no measurement error, the reliability of an estimate of a population parameter can be judged in terms of its **standard error.** For instance, the estimated standard error of the sample mean is given by

standard error (s_y) *Indication of the reliability of an estimate of a population parameter; it is computed by dividing the standard deviation of the sample estimate by the square root of the sample size.*

$$s_{\bar{y}} = \frac{s_y}{\sqrt{n}} \qquad (9\text{--}3)$$

The smaller the estimated standard error associated with the sample mean, the greater the reliability of the sample estimate.

The standard error of an estimate can be used to form confidence limits on *population estimates.* To construct confidence intervals, we must make certain assumptions about the sampling distribution of the sample estimates. For reasonably large sample sizes (say $n > 30$), the sampling distributions of sample estimates (such as means or proportions) are close to the normal distribution, and normal theory can be used to construct confidence intervals for the unknown population parameters being estimated. For example, an appropriate $100(1 - \alpha/2)$ percent confidence interval for the true population mean is

$$\bar{y} \pm (t_{1 - \alpha/2} s_y / \sqrt{n}) \qquad (9\text{--}4)$$

All of the terms appearing in Equation 9–4, except t, have been previously defined. The symbol t refers to students' t-distribution. We use the t-distribution instead of the standard normal z-distribution since in most cases the population variance will be unknown. Tabulated values for the standard normal z-distribution and the t-distribution are given in Tables 2 and 3, respectively, in the Statistical Appendix. The value of t is read from the table of students' t-distribution for $n - 1$ degrees of freedom.[2] If the sample size is greater than 30, the value of t is the same as the

---

[2] Recall from your basic statistics course that the term *degrees of freedom* refers to the total number of observations in the sample ($= n$) less the number of independent restrictions (parameters estimated).

value of z read from a standard normal table for the same level of significance; in other words, with large sample sizes, regardless of whether the variance is known or unknown, we may substitute the approximate z-value for t in Equation 9–4.

The preceding formulas strictly apply to situations in which the target population is infinitely large. When the target sample is large in relation to the target population, these formulas will overestimate the estimated variance (standard deviation) of a population parameter (mean or proportion). A correction factor is used whenever the target sample represents 10 to 20 percent or more of the target population. The **finite population correction factor (fpc)** is given by $\left(\dfrac{N-n}{N-1}\right)$. The fpc "corrected" variance formula is thus

$$s_{\bar{y}}^2 = \left(\frac{\sum\limits_{i=1}^{n}(y_i - \bar{y})^2}{n-1}\right)\left(\frac{N-n}{N-1}\right) \tag{9–5}$$

Essentially, the fpc depends upon the relation of n to N. If the population size N is very large and the sample size n is small, then the fpc will be close to 1; if, on the other hand, the sample size n is close to the population size N, then the fpc will be less than 1 and will decrease the numerical value of the estimated population variance. In most consumer goods studies the assumption of infinite target populations is probably reasonable because target populations typically include millions of individuals or households.

EXAMPLE

Having drawn the sample (see Table 9–1), you, the junior analyst, turn to estimating the mean and variance of the number of interviews completed per day. Noting the finite nature of the population and that $n/N > 20$ percent you decide to use the fpc corrected variance formula. Applying Equations 9–1 and 9–5 yields the following results

$$\bar{y} = \frac{4.5 + 2.5 + 3.5 + 6.5 + 6.5}{5} = 4.7 \text{ interviews/day}$$

$$s_{\bar{y}}^2 = \frac{(4.5 - 4.7)^2 + (2.5 - 4.7)^2 + (3.5 - 4.7)^2 + (6.5 - 4.7)^2 + (6.5 - 4.7)^2}{5 - 1}\left(\frac{15-5}{14}\right)$$

$$= (3.2)\left(\frac{10}{14}\right) = 2.29$$

Thus the estimated standard error of the mean number of interviews completed per day is

$$s_{\bar{y}} = s_y/\sqrt{n}$$
$$= \sqrt{2.29}/\sqrt{5} = 0.68$$

Finally you compute a 95 percent confidence interval around this estimate. Setting $\alpha = 0.05$, we find, from Table 3 in the Statistical Appendix, that $t_{1-\alpha/2;n-1} = 2.776$ and therefore

$$\bar{y} + t_{(1-\alpha/2;\, n-1)}s_{\bar{y}}$$
$$4.7 + 2.776(0.68) = 4.7 \pm 1.89$$
$$= \text{Between 2.81 and 6.59 interviews/day}$$

Sample Size Determination

It is frequently necessary to determine the size of the sample required to estimate a population parameter with a certain level of precision. Following the discussion provided in Chapter 8, the procedure for determining such a sample size is

1. Specify the acceptable **tolerance level** (p). This is the difference between the estimate and its unknown true population value. One approach to specifying the acceptable tolerance level is to take one-half of the desired confidence interval (range).

2. Determine the reliability coefficient ($z_{1-\alpha/2}$), which depends on the desired level of certainty ($1 - \alpha/2$).

3. Obtain an estimate of the standard deviation ($\hat{\sigma}_y$) of the characteristic to be measured in the target population. This can be based on prior studies, on a small-scale pilot study, on a subjective guess, or by taking one-sixth of the estimated range of the distribution of the characteristic (if normally distributed).

4. Apply the following formula to obtain the required sample size n^*

$$n^* = \frac{(z_{1-\alpha/2})^2 \, (\hat{\sigma}_y)^2}{(p)^2} \qquad (9\text{–}6)$$

tolerance level
The allowable difference permitted between the estimate and its known true population value.

To ensure an estimate is within a fixed percent of the anticipated mean value, the following procedure should be followed:

1. Specify the acceptable **relative tolerance level** (r), which is expressed as a fixed percent (for example, 5 percent or 10 percent).

2. Determine the reliability coefficient ($z_{1-\alpha/2}$).

3. Obtain an estimate of the **coefficient of variation** of the characteristic to be measured in the target population. The coefficient of variation (C_y) is a measure of relative dispersion given by σ/μ, where σ is the (true) standard deviation of the population mean and μ is the (true) population mean value. For the purpose of determining the required sample size, obtain an estimate of the anticipated mean value of the characteristic in the target population ($\bar{y}$) and the estimated standard deviation ($\hat{\sigma}_y$) of the characteristic in the target population and compute the estimated coefficient of variation

$$\hat{C}_y = \hat{\sigma}_y/\bar{y}$$

relative tolerance level (r)
The difference between the estimate and its unknown true population value, expressed as a percentage.

coefficient of variation (C_y)
A measure of relative dispersion given by dividing the population mean by its (true) standard deviation.

4. Apply the following formula to obtain the required sample size n^*

$$n^* = \frac{(z_{1-\alpha/2})^2 \, (\hat{C}_y)^2}{(r)^2} \qquad (9\text{–}7)$$

At this point, you, the junior analyst, have all of the information needed to determine the sample size required to achieve a desired level of precision. Because results of the survey

EXAMPLE

will be used for budgetary purposes, your estimate of the mean number of interviews completed per day needs to be virtually certain ($z_{1-\alpha/2} = 3$) to be within 10 percent of the true population value. Using the "anticipated" mean ($\bar{y} = 4.7$) and standard deviation ($\hat{\sigma}_y = \sqrt{2.29} = 1.51$) obtained in the preliminary study, you first compute an estimate of the coefficient of variation

$$\hat{C}_y = 1.51/4.7$$
$$= 0.32$$

Next, Equation 9–7 was applied:

$$n^* = \frac{(3)^2(0.32)^2}{(0.10)^2}$$
$$= 92.16 \rightarrow 93$$

Since fractional interviewers cannot be sampled, the 92 will not be quite enough precision. In this case, you decide to include 93 interviewers in the target sample.

STRATIFIED SAMPLING PROCEDURES

In many studies, the target population of interest can be divided into different segments (strata), where each segment has a distinctive character. Under *stratified random sampling,* the information about the strata is used in designing the overall sampling plan. As discussed in Chapter 8, the following steps describe the essence of stratified sampling:

1. Based on some classification variable, the entire population of sample units (or elements) is divided into distinct subpopulations called strata.
2. Within each stratum a separate random sample of elements is selected from all of the elements composing that stratum.
3. A separate mean (or proportion) is computed for each stratum and these separate estimates are properly weighted and added to obtain a combined estimate for the entire population.
4. The variances of the estimates are also computed separately for each stratum, and these are also properly weighted and added to form a combined estimate for the entire population.

The objective of stratification is to maximize the homogeneity of the sampling elements *within* strata. Thus a reasonable approach would be to use a classification variable that is highly associated with the sampling variable. Indeed, the stronger the relationship between the classification variable and the sampling variable, the greater will be the effect of stratification.

A decision about how many strata to form can be based on efficiency. In terms of efficiency, many strata should be used: Increasing the number of strata provides increased precision since the variance of the estimates is determined by the within-stratum variation;[3] in principle, more strata provide finer delineations of

---

[3]W. Cochran, *Sampling Techniques,* 3rd ed. (New York: John Wiley & Sons, 1977), p. 132.

the population, which, if all else is the same, should yield more homogeneous stratum elements. However, in practical applications the number of strata that should be formed depends on such considerations as (1) the classification variables available for stratification, (2) their degree of association with the sampling variable, (3) the cost of defining the strata, and (4) the cost of allocating the population elements among the strata. The general consensus is that most practical applications do not demand the use of many strata. The gains from stratification are proportional to the relative size of the stratum. If many strata are used, many of them will likely be small (containing few population elements) and contribute little to the gains from stratification. Typically, only a few strata yield most of the gains from a given classification variable.[4]

Selecting the Sample

The procedure for selecting a stratified random sample is as follows:

1. Decide on a classification variable and the number of strata to employ.
2. Obtain a list or other organized breakdown of all elements in the target population; and on the basis of the classification variable, assign each element to one of the H strata.
3. Number each element in each stratum from 1 to N_h.
4. Decide on the number of sample elements (n_h) to be selected from each stratum, where $\sum_{h=1}^{H} n_h = n$.
5. Using a random number table (see Table 1 in the Statistical Appendix), draw a simple random sample of size n_h from each stratum.

EXAMPLE

Table 9–2 presents results in terms of units sold for a controlled store promotion test conducted in five geographical regions. Data on shelf space measured in 5-inch length increments [the brand under study is packaged in a 5-inch (length) × 2-inch (width) × 3-inch (height) box] and whether the promotion included an exclusive newspaper feature are also given in the table. Consider the stores participating in the promotion test as the elements and volume (in units) sold as the characteristic being measured. Assume further that you, the junior analyst assigned to this study, decide to use geographical region as the classification variable. Note that in Table 9–2 the stores appear by region (the stratifying variable) and within a region each store is identified by a number between 1 and N_h.

You decide to take a sample of 12 stores from the 50 stores participating in the study with the following breakdown: three stores from stratum 1 (Buffalo), three stores from stratum 2 (Cincinnati), two stores from stratum 3 (Kansas City), two stores from stratum 4 (Minneapolis), and two stores from stratum 5 (Phoenix). Having determined how many stores to sample from each of the five strata, you then employ a random number table (Table 1, Statistical Appendix) and randomly select the appropriate number of elements from each stratum. The procedure for selecting the elements from the five strata parallels

---

[4]For additional details see L.Kish, *Survey Sampling* (New York: John Wiley & Sons, 1965), p. 102.

TABLE 9–2   Strata for 50 Stores—Controlled-Store Promotion Test

Store	Volume (units)	Shelf Space (inches)	Exclusive Feature	Store	Volume (units)	Shelf Space (inches)	Exclusive Feature
Buffalo store (Stratum 1)				*Kansas City store (Stratum 3)*			
1 $(y_{1,1})$	55	15	0	1 $(y_{1,3})$	109	30	1
2 $(y_{2,1})$	35	10	0	2 $(y_{2,3})$	57	15	0
3 $(y_{3,1})$	68	20	0	3 $(y_{3,3})$	71	15	1
4 $(y_{4,1})$	38	10	0	4 $(y_{4,3})$	49	10	0
5 $(y_{5,1})$	90	20	0	5 $(y_{5,3})$	75	15	0
6 $(y_{6,1})$	98	25	0	6 $(y_{6,3})$	39	10	0
7 $(y_{7,1})$	62	15	1	7 $(y_{7,3})$	81	20	1
8 $(y_{8,1})$	42	10	1				
9 $(y_{9,1})$	89	20	0				
10 $(y_{10,1})$	36	10	1	*Minneapolis store (Stratum 4)*			
11 $(y_{11,1})$	51	15	0	1 $(y_{1,4})$	43	10	1
12 $(y_{12,1})$	65	15	0	2 $(y_{2,4})$	83	20	0
				3 $(y_{3,4})$	131	35	1
Cincinnati store (Stratum 2)				4 $(y_{4,4})$	98	25	0
1 $(y_{1,2})$	30	10	0	5 $(y_{5,4})$	73	20	0
2 $(y_{2,2})$	85	20	0	6 $(y_{6,4})$	35	10	0
3 $(y_{3,2})$	66	15	1	7 $(y_{7,4})$	69	15	1
4 $(y_{4,2})$	40	10	0	8 $(y_{8,4})$	21	5	0
5 $(y_{5,2})$	100	25	0	9 $(y_{9,4})$	87	20	0
6 $(y_{6,2})$	67	15	1	10 $(y_{10,4})$	100	25	1
7 $(y_{7,2})$	72	20	1	11 $(y_{11,4})$	29	5	0
8 $(y_{8,2})$	84	25	0				
9 $(y_{9,2})$	51	10	1				
10 $(y_{10,2})$	19	5	0	*Phoenix store (Stratum 5)*			
11 $(y_{11,2})$	65	15	0	1 $(y_{1,5})$	63	15	0
12 $(y_{12,2})$	113	30	1	2 $(y_{2,5})$	60	15	0
13 $(y_{13,2})$	21	5	0	3 $(y_{3,5})$	121	30	1
14 $(y_{14,2})$	78	20	1	4 $(y_{4,5})$	140	35	1
15 $(y_{15,2})$	110	30	1	5 $(y_{5,5})$	100	25	1

that used in SRS. For each stratum we will begin with an independent random start and will select the elements whose within-stratum numerical label matches the random number that is between 1 and N_h. Table 9–3 presents the sample drawn following this procedure.

Estimating Population Characteristics

In defining the estimation of population characteristics for stratified random sampling we use the same type of notation that we used for simple random sampling.

TABLE 9–3

Sample Elements
from Table 9–2

Population Label	Sample Label	Volume Units	Shelf Space (inches)	Exclusive Feature
Buffalo store (Stratum 1)				
5 ($y_{5,1}$)	1 ($y_{1,1}$)	90	20	0
6 ($y_{6,1}$)	2 ($y_{2,1}$)	98	25	0
10 ($y_{10,1}$)	3 ($y_{3,1}$)	36	10	1
Cincinnati store (Stratum 2)				
1 ($y_{1,2}$)	1 ($y_{1,2}$)	30	10	0
6 ($y_{6,2}$)	2 ($y_{2,2}$)	67	15	1
11 ($y_{11,2}$)	3 ($y_{3,2}$)	65	15	0
Kansas City store (Stratum 3)				
3 ($y_{3,3}$)	1 ($y_{1,3}$)	71	15	1
7 ($y_{7,3}$)	2 ($y_{2,3}$)	81	20	1
Minneapolis store (Stratum 4)				
2 ($y_{2,4}$)	1 ($y_{1,4}$)	83	20	0
10 ($y_{10,4}$)	2 ($y_{2,4}$)	100	25	1
Phoenix store (Stratum 5)				
2 ($y_{2,5}$)	1 ($y_{1,5}$)	60	15	0
4 ($y_{4,5}$)	2 ($y_{2,5}$)	140	35	1

All the formulas that follow assume infinite populations and apply only to the estimation of a population mean using stratified random sampling.

Consider a population containing N elementary units grouped into H mutually exclusive and exhaustive strata. Let $N_1, N_2, \ldots, N_H$ denote the number of elements in each of the strata, that is, the size of the subpopulations. Since the total population (N) was divided into H strata, $N = \sum_{h=1}^{H} N_h$. The size of the sample chosen from each stratum is denoted as n_h, and $n = \sum_{h=1}^{H} n_h$ where n is the total sample size. In a later section we discuss how to determine the sample size in each stratum (n_h) given an overall sample size (n) under two types of allocation rules.

Under stratified random sampling, the mean and sampling error associated with a characteristic in the entire target population can be estimated as

$$\bar{y}_{(ST)} = \sum_{h=1}^{H} w_h \bar{y}_h \qquad (9\text{–}8)$$

and

$$s_{\bar{y}(ST)} = \sqrt{\sum_{h=1}^{H} w_h^2 s_{\bar{y}h}^2} \qquad (9\text{–}9A)$$

$$= \sqrt{\sum_{h=1}^{H} w_h^2 \frac{s_{yh}^2}{n_h}}$$

or

$$s_{\bar{y}(ST)} = \sqrt{\sum_{h=1}^{H} w_h^2 \left(\frac{s_{yh}^2}{n_h}\right) \left(\frac{N_h - n_h}{N_h - 1}\right)} \tag{9–9B}$$

if the sample represents 10 to 20 percent or more of the population. Note that in Equations 9–8 and 9–9

w_h = Weight attached to the hth stratum equal to N_h/N

$\bar{y}_h$ = Mean in the hth stratum

s_{yh}^2 = Variance in the hth stratum

The variance in the hth stratum is calculated from

$$s_{yh}^2 = \sum_{i=1}^{n_h} (y_{ih} - \bar{y}_h)^2/(n_h - 1) \tag{9–10}$$

Most important, from Equation 9–9 we see that the estimate of the standard error of the mean under stratified sampling depends *only* on the within-stratum variability.

EXAMPLE   Having drawn the sample (Table 9–3), you, the junior analyst, focus on estimating the mean number of units sold and the sampling error of the estimate.

The estimated mean volume in units sold per store in the entire target population can be estimated from Equation 9–8 as follows:

$$\begin{aligned}
\bar{y}_{(ST)} = {} & \left(\frac{12}{50}\right)\left(\frac{90 + 98 + 36}{3}\right) + \left(\frac{15}{50}\right)\left(\frac{30 + 67 + 65}{3}\right) + \left(\frac{7}{50}\right)\left(\frac{71 + 81}{2}\right) \\
& + \left(\frac{11}{50}\right)\left(\frac{83 + 100}{2}\right) + \left(\frac{5}{50}\right)\left(\frac{60 + 140}{2}\right) \\
= {} & 74.89 \text{ units per store}
\end{aligned}$$

Similarly, the estimated within-stratum variances are, according to Equation 9–10,

$$s_{y1}^2 = \frac{(90 - 74.67)^2 + (98 - 74.67)^2 + (36 - 74.67)^2}{2} = 1137.33$$

$$s_{y2}^2 = \frac{(30 - 54)^2 + (67 - 54)^2 + (65 - 54)^2}{2} = 433.00$$

$$s_{y3}^2 = \frac{(71 - 76)^2 + (81 - 76)^2}{1} = 50.00$$

$$s_{y4}^2 = \frac{(83 - 91.5)^2 + (100 - 91.5)^2}{1} = 144.50$$

$$s_{y5}^2 = \frac{(60 - 100)^2 + (140 - 100)^2}{1} = 3200.00$$

Now, to obtain the estimated standard error of the mean units sold per store in the target population, you apply the appropriate fpc correction factor

$$s_{\bar{y}(ST)} = \sqrt{\left[\left(\frac{12}{50}\right)^2\left(\frac{1137.33}{3}\right)\left(\frac{9}{11}\right)\right] + \left[\left(\frac{15}{50}\right)^2\left(\frac{433}{3}\right)\left(\frac{12}{14}\right)\right] + \ldots + \left[\left(\frac{5}{50}\right)^2\left(\frac{3200}{2}\right)\left(\frac{3}{4}\right)\right]}$$

$$= \sqrt{44.56} = 6.68$$

Thus, a 95 percent confidence interval for the true population mean number of units sold per store is

$$\bar{y}_{(ST)} \pm t_{(1-\alpha/2;n-1)}s_{\bar{y}(ST)}$$
$$74.89 \pm (2.201)(6.68) = 74.89 \pm 14.70$$
$$= \text{Between 60.19 and 89.59 units sold per store}$$

Sample Size Determination

We can determine the sample size required to estimate a population mean within a specified error limit at a specified level of confidence. As in SRS, estimates of the anticipated variance of the characteristic to be measured in the target population must be known; however, for stratified random sampling, estimates of the within-stratum variances must also be known for all strata.

Following standard notation, under stratified random sampling, the formula for determining the (approximate) number of elements needed to be $100(1 - \alpha/2)$ percent certain of obtaining an estimated mean that differs from the true population mean by no more than a fixed percent is, for reasonably large N, given by

$$n^* \approx \frac{N(z_{1-\alpha/2})^2(\hat{\sigma}^2_{wy}/\bar{y}^2)}{(z_{1-\alpha/2})^2(\hat{\sigma}^2_{wy}/\bar{y}^2) + Nr^2} \tag{9-11}$$

where with the exception of $\hat{\sigma}^2_{wy}$ all terms have been previously defined.[5] In Equation 9–11 $\hat{\sigma}^2_{wy}$ is the "anticipated" or estimated weighted average of the individual within-stratum variances

$$\hat{\sigma}^2_{wy} = \sum_{h=1}^{H} N_h \hat{\sigma}^2_{yh}/N \tag{9-12}$$

Suppose that for the last five years records of all in-store promotion studies have been maintained. Among the information routinely recorded are (1) product category of test brand, (2) volume (in units), (3) shelf-space allocation, (4) promotional activity, and (5) testing location. Table 9–4 gives information on the distribution of units sold in 250 stores located in the Buffalo (Stratum 1), Cincinnati (Stratum 2), Kansas City (Stratum 3),

---

[5]In a strict sense Equation 9–11 is applicable only when the sample will be allocated across the strata in relation to the relative size of each stratum. Allocation of the sample across the strata will be discussed shortly.

TABLE 9–4

Distribution of Units
Sold

Strata	Size	Mean Units Sold	Variance of Distribution of Mean Units Sold
Buffalo	45	55	182
Cincinnati	70	68	221
Kansas City	50	70	210
Minneapolis	60	74	232
Phoenix	25	101	175

Minneapolis (Stratum 4), and Phoenix (Stratum 5) test markets. You, the junior analyst, decide to use this information in planning a controlled store-promotion test that will be conducted in these areas. Believing in history, the anticipated mean number of units sold in the future promotion test will likely be

$$\frac{45(55) + 70(68) + 50(70) + 60(74) + 25(101)}{250} = 70.8$$

The weighting factors are, respectively

$$w_1 = (45/250) = 0.18$$
$$w_2 = (70/250) = 0.28$$
$$w_3 = (50/250) = 0.20$$
$$w_4 = (60/250) = 0.24$$
$$w_5 = (25/250) = 0.10$$

To calculate the estimated number of stores needed to be virtually certain of estimating the mean number of units sold to within 20 percent of the true mean under stratified random sampling, an anticipated value for $\hat{\sigma}_{wy}$ is needed. Using Table 9–4 and Equation 9–12, you compute the anticipated value of the weighted average of within-stratum variances to be

$$\hat{\sigma}_{wy}^2 = \frac{45(182) + 70(221) + 50(210) + 60(232) + 25(175)}{250}$$

$$= \frac{52455}{250} = 209.82$$

$$\hat{\sigma}_{wy} = 14.48$$

Thus, applying Equation 9–11,

$$n^* \approx \frac{250(3)^2 (14.48/70.8)^2}{(3)^2(14.48/70.8)^2 + 250(0.20)^2} = \frac{94.18}{10.37} = 9.08 \rightarrow 10$$

so that you make plans to sample 10 stores.

Allocating the Sample

An important decision in stratified sampling is the number of elementary units to be sampled from each stratum, under the constraint that a total of n elements will be sampled over all strata. In practice, two procedures are used for allocating the total sample size n among the H strata. One procedure, *proportional allocation*, guarantees that stratified random sampling will be at least as efficient as SRS. The other procedure, *optimal allocation* or *disproportional allocation*, minimizes the standard errors of the estimated population parameters for a fixed sample size n and a predetermined number of strata, though it is more difficult to apply than proportional allocation.

In this section we illustrate these two allocation procedures. We are confining our discussion to stratified random sampling, and so, regardless of the allocation procedure, once the number of elements n_h is determined, an SRS procedure is used to select elements from each stratum.

Proportional Allocation. In proportional allocation the number of elementary units selected from stratum h is directly proportional to the size of the population in that stratum. In other words, with proportional allocation the sampling fraction $f_h = n_h/N_h$ is constant for all strata, which implies that the overall sampling fraction $f = n/N$ is the fraction taken from each stratum. Under this allocation procedure, the size of the sample to be drawn from each stratum is easily calculated. The number of elements drawn from each stratum, n_h is given by

$$n_h = \left(\frac{N_h}{N}\right)n \tag{9-13}$$

Optimal Allocation. The goal in optimal allocation is to allocate a fixed sample size among the strata to minimize the variance of the characteristic to be measured in the target population. Assuming equal per-element sampling costs, it can be shown that the allocation of n sample units into each stratum, which will yield a minimum variance estimate of a population parameter, is given by

$$n_h = \left(N_h\hat{\sigma}_{yh} \middle/ \sum_{h=1}^{H} N_h\hat{\sigma}_{yh}\right)n \tag{9-14}$$

Optimal allocation essentially involves a double weighting scheme; the number of sample elements taken from a given stratum is proportional to (1) the relative size of the stratum and (2) the anticipated standard deviation ($\hat{\sigma}_{yh}$) of the distribution of the characteristic under consideration among all elements in the stratum. As we mentioned in Chapter 8, the rationale for this dual weighting procedure is simple. First, size is important because strata with larger numbers of elements are the most important in determining the population mean. Second, stratum variability is important because, if the distribution of the characteristic under consideration has a large standard deviation in a particular stratum, then a relatively large number of elements must be selected from that stratum to obtain a reliable estimate of a stratum parameter. A smaller number of elements must be selected from a stratum in which the distribution of the characteristic under consideration has small standard deviation.

EXAMPLE   Having decided to sample 10 stores, you, the junior analyst, next examine how the sample would be allocated among the strata under proportional and optimal allocation.

Under proportional allocation the sample would be allocated to the five strata as follows

$$n_1 = \frac{45}{250}(10) = 1.8 = 2$$

$$n_2 = \frac{70}{250}(10) = 2.8 = 3$$

$$n_3 = \frac{50}{250}(10) = 2.0 = 2$$

$$n_4 = \frac{60}{250}(10) = 2.4 = 2$$

$$n_5 = \frac{25}{250}(10) = 1.0 = 1$$

If an optimal allocation plan is used, some estimate of the anticipated standard deviation of the characteristic under study must be available. Using the information presented in Table 9–4 and Equation 9–14, the sample would be allocated among the strata as follows

$$n_1 = \left(\frac{45\sqrt{182}}{45\sqrt{182} + 70\sqrt{221} + 50\sqrt{210} + 60\sqrt{232} + 25\sqrt{175}}\right)10 = 1.7 = 2$$

$$n_2 = \left(\frac{70\sqrt{221}}{45\sqrt{182} + 70\sqrt{221} + 50\sqrt{210} + 60\sqrt{232} + 25\sqrt{175}}\right)10 = 2.9 = 3$$

$$n_3 = \left(\frac{50\sqrt{210}}{45\sqrt{182} + 70\sqrt{221} + 50\sqrt{210} + 60\sqrt{232} + 25\sqrt{175}}\right)10 = 2.0 = 2$$

$$n_4 = \left(\frac{60\sqrt{232}}{45\sqrt{182} + 70\sqrt{221} + 50\sqrt{210} + 60\sqrt{232} + 25\sqrt{175}}\right)10 = 2.5 = 2$$

$$n_5 = \left(\frac{25\sqrt{175}}{45\sqrt{182} + 70\sqrt{221} + 50\sqrt{210} + 60\sqrt{232} + 25\sqrt{175}}\right)10 = 0.9 = 1$$

Note that in this case, the optimal allocation agrees with the proportional allocation computed earlier. The reason for this is the within-stratum variances are not sufficiently disparate to induce the sample to be allocated across the strata in a manner different from that which is obtained by considering only the relative size of each stratum.

To apply optimal allocation, we need to know the standard deviation of the distribution of the variable under consideration. In practice, this will rarely be known. There are, however, two ways in which to proceed.

1. Based on prior research surveys that have investigated similar sampling variables and used similar classification variables, obtain—through averaging or some other method—estimates of $\hat{\sigma}_{yh}$, the standard deviation of the distribution of the sampling variable within each stratum. Next, use these esti-

mates to calculate the optimal allocation of elements to draw from each stratum.

2. Draw a small "subordinate" sample from each stratum. Denote the subordinate sample elements by $n_1^*, n_2^*, \ldots, n_H^*$ with values of the sampling variable given by $y_{i1}^*, y_{i2}^*, \ldots, y_{iH}^*$. Next, on the basis of the subordinate sample, calculate s_{yh}^* the estimated standard deviation of the sampling distribution of the sampling variable. Using s_{yh}^*, calculate the optimal allocation of elements to draw from each stratum. As a precautionary step, after drawing the sample on the basis of the *pseudo*-optimal allocation procedure, check the estimated standard deviations against those obtained in the subordinate sample. If consistent, proceed. If not, draw another subordinate sample, and continue following the same procedure as before.

CLUSTER SAMPLING PROCEDURES

The sampling methods discussed so far require sampling frames that list or provide an organized breakdown of all elements (or sampling units) in the target population. An alternative strategy is to construct sampling frames that contain groups or clusters of elements (or sampling units) without explicitly listing the individual elements. Sampling can be performed from such frames by taking a sample of clusters, obtaining a list or other breakdowns only for those clusters that have been selected in the sample, and then selecting a sample of the individual sampling units. These sample designs are known as *cluster samples*, and they are widely used in practice because of their feasibility and economy. In the next two sections we discuss and illustrate one-stage and two-stage cluster sampling designs.

ONE-STAGE CLUSTER SAMPLING PROCEDURES

In Chapter 8 we briefly mentioned an extremely easy-to-apply approach to drawing samples, namely, the method of systematic sampling. All systematic sampling designs have two characteristics in common: (1) The elements of a population are treated as an ordered sequence, and (2) the elements are selected according to some fixed interval from an ordered sampling frame. Put simply, systematic sampling consists of taking every kth sampling unit (or element) after a random start. Application of systematic sampling is quite easy because, typically, it involves selecting every kth line from listing sheets or every kth block from numbered maps. In systematic sampling of one in k elements, there are k possible samples, and, although each element has the same chance $(1/k)$ of being included in the sample, the particular sample selected depends on the random number used as the starting point. Thus, each of the k possible samples can be viewed as a "cluster" of n elements with each element being k units apart. In addition, because each sampling unit (or element) appears only once in each possible sample, each unit has a probability of selection also equal to $1/k$. For this reason, systematic sampling is actually a one-stage cluster sampling design (Chapter 8).

To draw a systematic sample, certain elements (or sampling units) in the target population must be identified; for example, one may want to select the elements labeled $j, j + k, j + 2k, j + 3k \ldots$. Note, however, that in contrast to SRS the size of the target population (N) need not be known prior to sampling, nor does a list or other organized breakdown of the elements in the target population need to be available beforehand; in other words, the list can be compiled during the sampling process. An example of such a list would be the situation in which you are sampling one of every five customers entering an entrance of a mall shopping center. The sampling can be done while the frame is being constructed.

We must emphasize two features of systematic sampling. First, the order of elements (or sampling units) in the list is relevant. For example, consider the case of a researcher who is looking at supermarket sales over 365 consecutive days and who decides to select every seventh day's sales into the sample. In this case, the sample of 52 days of sales ($365 \div 7$) could produce misleading results because, depending on where in the list of sales data the researcher started, the samples would reflect the sales for all Mondays, all Tuesdays, and so forth. The ordering of elements can affect the efficiency of the estimates obtained under this sampling design. Second, in contrast to SRS, in which *every one* of the (N) samples has the same chance of being selected, a systematic sample of one in k contains only k possible samples, and the particular sample selected depends on which random number was originally selected.

Selecting the Sample

Assuming that some list or other organized breakdown of the elements in the target population is available, a systematic sample can be drawn by the following procedure:

1. For each element in the target population, assign the numbers 1 to N. We will refer to the number assigned to an element as its *index*.
2. Suppose n elements will be sampled. Compute $k = N/n$ where k is called the **sampling interval**. If k is a fraction, choose that integer closest to the ratio N/n.
3. Using a random number table, select a number, r, in the range 1 to k.
4. Select as the first element for inclusion in the sample the element with the index r.
5. Continue to select elements according to the following scheme

$$r + k$$
$$r + 2k$$
$$\cdot$$
$$\cdot$$
$$\cdot$$
$$r + (n - 1)k$$

An example will help to clarify the procedure.

Let us return to the data on the number of completed interviews per day for the mall-intercept package test conducted in Cincinnati, Ohio, by the XYZ Field Service Company (see Table 9–1). However, suppose now that we wish to effect a systematic sample of size $n = 5$. The first step is to calculate the sampling interval

$$k = N/n = 15/5 = 3$$

Since k is an integer we need neither round up nor down. Next, using Table 1 in the Statistical Appendix, we need to select a random number, r, in the range 1 and 3. Assume that $r = 2$. Thus, the systematic sample would consist of elements

$$r = 2$$
$$r + k = 5$$
$$r + 2k = 8$$
$$r + 3k = 11$$
$$r + (5 - 1)k = 14$$

We indicated earlier that a list would not need to be available prior to sampling. The following example illustrates how to draw systematic samples when no list is available.

Suppose that detailed records on all of the field-service companies employed by the marketing research department over the last year are located in six file drawers, each having a depth of 32 inches. If a sample of 75 records is needed, a systematic sample could be drawn as follows:

1. Determine the total length of field records (that is, $32 \times 6 = 192$ inches).
2. Determine k, where in this case $k = 192/75 = 2.56$ inches, or the total length divided by the number of records.
3. Using a random number table select a number between 0 and k—that is, between 0.00 and 2.56. (Suppose that $r = 1.65$.)
4. Using some kind of measuring device, take the record that is $r = 1.65$ inches from the front of the first file drawer. Select next the record that is $k = 2.56$ inches from the first record selected. Continue this process, moving to other drawers when necessary, until the end of the last drawer is reached.

Estimating Population Characteristics

In general, estimation of population parameters and, in particular, the estimate of the variance of the characteristic under study in the target population can become quite complex. However, if the list from which the systematic sample is drawn represents a random ordering with respect to the variable being measured, then the estimates obtained under systematic sampling will be identical to those obtained under SRS; in other words, we can use the same formulas as in SRS.

Sample Size Determination

In general, the determination of sample size for systematic samples is quite difficult. However, if we assume that the list from which the systematic sample was drawn represents a random ordering regarding the variable being measured, then the methods for determining sample size developed for SRS can be used. If the assumption of random ordering is not defensible, little can be done. The problem is that the variance of estimates obtained under systematic sampling depends on the sampling interval. For example, a one-in-four systematic sample from a list of 100 observations will yield a sample of size 25; a one-in-five systematic sample will yield a sample of size 20. Intuition coupled with what we now know about sampling theory would lead us to expect that the variance of estimates from the larger sample should be smaller than the variance of estimates obtained in the smaller sample. However, depending on the ordering of elements in the list, the smaller sample may produce estimates that have smaller variances than those obtained in the larger sample. The point here is that, in practice, we will rarely know the nature of the list (that is, its ordering), and, therefore, care must be exercised.

TWO-STAGE CLUSTER SAMPLING PROCEDURES: PPS SAMPLING

As we indicated in Chapter 8, to the extent that the elements within clusters exhibit homogeneity with respect to the variables being measured, cluster sampling and especially simple one-stage cluster sampling will be relatively inefficient compared with other sampling designs. Because it is likely that there will be much redundancy among the elements within a cluster, it may be better to take a sample of the elements rather than to select all of them. In such cases, the sample would be drawn in two stages: In the first stage a sample of clusters from the population would be selected, and in the second stage a sample of the elements (or sampling units) within each sample cluster would be drawn.

There are several types of two-stage sampling designs. One type is called simple two-stage cluster sampling because it involves SRS at both the first and second stages in the sampling design. In other words, SRS sampling is used at the first stage to select a sample of clusters from the population and at the second stage to draw a sample of elements from each sample cluster. Under this design the fraction of elements selected at the second stage is the same for each sample cluster. This design is strictly appropriate only when each cluster contains the same number of sampling units. If the cluster sizes are different, it is impossible to take the same percentage of elements from each sample cluster.

Because it is extremely unlikely that clusters will contain exactly the same number of elements (or sampling units), we confine our discussion to a two-stage cluster sampling design that accommodates clusters of varying sizes. This design, called probability proportionate to size, or PPS sampling, results in the same number n of sampling units (or a multiple of n) being selected from each sample cluster.

In PPS sampling, clusters are sampled with probability proportional to the number of sampling units within the cluster. Thus large clusters are more likely to be included in the sample than small clusters. PPS sampling is self-weighting in that the probability of selecting a sampling unit in a cluster, given that the cluster has been selected at the first stage of sampling, varies inversely with the size of the sample cluster. PPS sampling results in selecting approximately equal numbers of sampling units from each sample cluster.

Selecting the Sample

Let M denote the total number of clusters available and m the number of clusters to be sampled. The following outlines the steps involved in drawing a PPS sample:

1. Generate cumulative measure of size, denoted by MOS. The measure of size for a particular cluster will be denoted by MOS_i, where $MOS_i = N_i$. Note that the cumulative MOS simply equals N, the total population.
2. Compute the sampling interval, s, where $s = MOS/m$.
3. Consulting a random number table or some other device, choose a random number between 1 and s; let r denote the first random number chosen.
4. Select clusters having the following numerical labels

$$r$$
$$r + s$$
$$r + 2s$$
$$r + 3s$$
$$\cdot$$
$$\cdot$$
$$\cdot$$
$$r + (m - 1)s$$

A cluster is selected if the selection number falls into its sequence of numbers; that is, the selection number is greater than the MOS of all previous clusters, but less than or equal to the MOS including the designated cluster.

5. Selection of sampling units within each sample cluster proceeds as follows: Select n_i sampling units from each sample cluster based on SRS or systematic sampling; the number of sampling units selected from a sample cluster is given by

$$n_i = f_2 \times N_i$$

where f_2, the second-stage sampling fraction, is equal to f/f_1. Noting that f, the overall sampling fraction, is equal to n/N, and f_1, the first-stage sampling fraction, is equal to N_i/s.

PPS results in an equal number of sampling units being selected from each sample cluster. In general, the number of sampling units selected from each sample cluster will be (approximately) equal to

$$n_i = \bar{n} = n/m$$

It can happen that a cluster's MOS can exceed the sampling interval. In such cases, the cluster will automatically be included in the sample; that is, this cluster will be selected with certainty. Because of the existence of clusters that will be included in the sample with certainty, we must modify the PPS sampling selection procedure to identify and remove such clusters.

To be more specific, after computing s, the sampling interval, we check whether $MOS_i > s$ for each cluster i in the population. If $MOS_i > s$, cluster i is removed from further consideration, and a new cumulative MOS is computed. Denoting the new sampling interval s^*, we again check whether any $MOS_i > s^*$. If a cluster's $MOS > s^*$, then that cluster is also removed, and a new MOS is once again computed. This process continues until no remaining cluster has an MOS greater than s^*, the relevant sampling interval. For the remaining clusters, the PPS sampling procedure then continues in the manner described above. However, note that from the remaining clusters we will select only $m^* = m - c$, where c denotes the number of clusters selected with certainty. For clusters selected with certainty, we would sample

$$n_c = (f \times N_1) + (f \times N_2) + \ldots + (f \times N_c)$$

so that we end up selecting

$$n^* = n - n_c$$

sampling units from the sample of clusters selected under PPS sampling.

EXAMPLE

Let's consider the 10 test-market cities given in Table 9–5 and suppose that you, the junior analyst responsible for this study, wish to take a PPS sample of $n = 25$ stores from $m = 5$ cities. The first step in the procedure is to form the cumulative MOS, which is generated by cumulating the number of stores in each city. From the data presented, MOS $= 500$.

Next you compute s where

$$s = \frac{500}{5} = 100$$

and note that MOS_7 (Buffalo) exceeds 100. Consequently, following the procedure described earlier, Buffalo is selected with certainty. The new MOS is then calculated. The cumulative MOS for the remaining nine cities (excluding Buffalo) is $395(500 - 105 = 395)$ and therefore

$$\begin{aligned} s^* &= MOS/(m - 1) \\ &= 395/4 \\ &= 98.75 \text{ or } 99 \end{aligned}$$

Noting that no city exceeds s^*, you now use Table 1 of the Statistical Appendix to generate a random number between 1 and 99. Assume the number 26 is selected. Thus

$$\begin{aligned} r &= 26 \\ r + s^* &= 26 + 99 = 125 \\ r + 2s^* &= 26 + 198 = 224 \\ r + 3s^* &= 26 + 297 = 323 \end{aligned}$$

The sample cities, from Table 9–5 are

Fargo, North Dakota

Pittsburgh, Pennsylvania

Cincinnati, Ohio

Minneapolis, Minnesota

with Buffalo being included (from step 1) to obtain the required five clusters.

City	Number of Stores (MOS)	Cumulative MOS	Cumulative MOS—Excluding Buffalo	Random Number	Random Number Chosen	
Erie, Pa.	20	20	20	001–020		TABLE 9–5
Fargo, N. Dak.	10	30	30	021–030	26	
Green Bay, Wis.	40	70	70	031–070		Procedure for PPS
Pittsburgh, Pa.	90	160	160	071–160	125	Sampling
Portland, Oreg.	20	180	180	161–180		
Cincinnati, Ohio	75	255	255	181–255	224	
Buffalo, N.Y.	105	360	—			
Lexington, Ky.	20	380	275	256–275		
Minneapolis, Minn.	70	450	345	276–345	323	
Nashville, Tenn.	50	500	395	346–395		
Total	500	500	395			

We will not discuss or illustrate how to estimate population characteristics under PPS sampling, nor will we consider sample size determination. The fact that cluster samples have unequal numbers of sampling units creates some problems when it comes to estimation and sample size determination that are beyond the scope of our discussion.[6]

In closing our discussion of PPS sampling we should note that two-stage cluster sampling designs are generally more cost-effective than SRS and, in many instances, can provide cost efficiencies over simple one-stage cluster sampling designs. In addition, as we mentioned in Chapter 8, PPS sampling procedures can be used to improve mall-intercept surveys.

---

[6]See, for example, Cochran, *Sampling Techniques*; P. S. Levy and S. Lemeshow, *Sampling for Health Professionals* (Belmont, Calif.: Lifetime Learning Publications, 1980), pp. 75–78, for a discussion illustrating this procedure.

SUMMARY

Sampling is often referred to as being more of an art than a science. This sentiment reflects the fact that a great deal of creative ingenuity is generally required in reaching the individual households that possess information relevant to solving the marketing problem at hand. As we indicated in Chapter 8, sampling decisions are often complex, and there is no single "right" way to make them. Deciding on the specific sampling design to use may often not be straightforward; sampling professionals may be needed. This chapter has explained the mechanics of probability sampling designs for those of you who want (or need) to understand how such designs work.

KEY CONCEPTS

selecting the sample	simple random sampling	stratified sampling procedures	cluster sampling procedures
estimating population characteristics	systematic sampling procedures	allocating sample units to strata	PPS sampling
sample size determination			

REVIEW QUESTIONS

1. The average tee shot for golfers on the PGA tour is 262 yards (μ). Suppose a random sample of $n = 20$ is selected from the total of 200 players. What are the chances (the probability) that the sample mean ($\overline{X}$) will fall within 5 yards of the population mean (μ), assuming that the normal approximation rule is in effect with $\overline{X}$ normally distributed and $\sigma = 10.2$?

2. The president of a large Florida resort area, called Mickey World, has decided to hire your services in order to estimate the number of non-Floridians entering Mickey World each day, within $\pm$ 500. The president figures that "about 15,000 ($\overline{X}$) non-Floridians enter the park daily, with a standard deviation ($\hat{\sigma}$) of 2,000." Will a sample of 125 be large enough to ensure 99 percent confidence?

3. Your marketing professor wants you to determine the sample size necessary to estimate the number of students that will make the Dean's List this year with 99 percent certainty, within ± 1 student. The average number receiving the honor from previous years in the overall student body (population) is 35. You know that $\sigma^2 = 9.82$.

   a. Compute the required sample size.

   b. Last year's records show a variance of 22.34. Recompute the necessary sample size. Discuss why the necessary sample size has increased or decreased.

   c. How would the sample size change if the only information your professor shared with you was that former students making the Dean's List ranged from 25 to 48?

4. A large computer company estimates the variance for the number of defective computers coming off the production line to be 10.0. A sample of 27 computers are needed from the population in order to be 90 percent sure that the average number of defects differs by no more than ± 1 unit from the true mean.

   a. If this computer company then decides it wants to be twice as precise, what is the new required sample size?

   b. How would your results differ if the computer company decided to increase the confidence interval from 95 percent to 99 percent?

5. A local newspaper decided to call 2,000 of its subscribers and inquire about satisfaction with delivery

(yes/no). The newspaper company wanted findings that would differ from the true results of the population by no more than ± 2.5 percentage points in either direction at the 99 percent level of confidence. Was the sample size selected large enough to meet the newspaper's requirements? If not, how large a sample was needed?

6. A state university athletic department has $85,000 to hire a research firm in order to contact as many alumni as possible at any collegiate game to determine if a new concept for "one price gets you a season ticket to all home sporting events" is in the best interest of their alumni. Past studies show that three in four attendees of any school event are alumni and are willing to be interviewed. You know that a 50 percent profit margin is required by the research firm. If the nonsampling costs total $44,500 and the sampling cost per unit is $17.75, how many alumni can the university expect to be included in the study?

CASE STUDIES FOR
PART III

CASE 1
A Head & Shoulders Study

A market researcher calls with the following specs:

> Three hundred interviews with females 18 years old or older who shampoo their hair at home. One hundred will be with Head & Shoulders users, the rest with users of any other shampoos. The effective telephone incidence for Head & Shoulders users is 20 percent; all-other-brand users is 75 percent. The interview length is 15 minutes.

In response to these specifications, the junior research analyst estimates that 767 contacts will be needed, 500 for the Head & Shoulders quota and 267 for all-other-users quota (100 ÷ 0.20 = 500; 200 ÷ 0.75 = 267). With 767 contacts required and assuming a 30 percent productive dialing ratio (finding a respondent home), the number of dialings needed was estimated at 2,557 (767 ÷ 0.30 = 2,557). The total hours required for interviewing was estimated as

2,557 dialings × 1.5 minutes =	3,835.5 minutes	
767 contacts × 3 minutes =	2,301	
300 completes × 15 minutes =	4,500	
10,636.5 minutes =	177.28 hours	

The junior research analyst also included time spent on qualified refusals and breakoffs, estimated at 10 percent. Thus, the estimate of total hours of interviewing was 195 hours. At $20 an hour, the bid submitted was $3,900.

Case Questions

1. Comment on the incidence-rate projections.
2. Develop a probabilistic sampling design for this study. What potential problems do you anticipate?

CASE 2
Changing Complexion of Restaurant Industry

In response to the dramatic changes that have taken place in the restaurant industry, the Restaurant Association of America recently commissioned a survey of restaurant owners. The study called for a national probabilistic sample; its objectives were to estimate the incidence of the following types of eating establishments:

1. Fast food.
2. Casual.
3. Dinner.
4. Fine dining.

Another objective was to collect various data on menu offerings and price structures. Subgroup analysis will be undertaken by restaurant type and geographical region. Assume that you have been retained to evaluate the procedures used. The necessary details follow.

Sampling Plan

Selection of firms to conduct the sampling. Various firms specializing in drawing probabilistic telephone samples were solicited and asked to supply a national probability sample of restaurant establishments; in addition, several county samples also were requested. These samples were judged for accuracy and completeness in relation to census and county data. A single firm was selected.

Selection of sampling frame. The chosen sample was based on a frame of all restaurant establishments located in the contiguous United States.

Sample selection procedures. The chosen design was that of a probability-replicated sample, comprising 70 randomly selected, stratified, and matched samples of 50 restaurants, each from a frame of all eligible restaurants in the United States and each having a known chance of selection.

The total database was filtered to create a population consisting only of telephone numbers falling into the *Yellow Pages* categories of restaurants. The filtering process resulted in a population of 302,247 restaurants. The file was then geographically sorted by area codes and exchange, and a systematic selection was made to produce the final sample. A sample of 10,000 restaurants was first sampled from this list and was verified; then 5,000 restaurants were selected into the final target sample.

Sample size considerations. The objective was to estimate the incidence (proportion) of each of the five categories of eating establishments with ±5 percent. After some discussion it was felt that a sample of 1,000 establishments would be sufficient.

Response rates. Great care was given to achieve high response rates by completing five call-backs. The total number of calls made exceeded 3,000, which represented about a 30 percent response rate.

Survey instrument (questionnaire construction and administration). The following procedures were undertaken:

1. Questionnaire was subjected to rigorous pretests, and the instrument was constructed according to acceptable standards.
2. Questionnaire was administered by executive interviewers, especially those trained in the food-service industry, to ensure objective and accurate responses.
3. Computer-driven CRT interviewing center was employed.
4. Twenty-five percent of the interviews were verified.

Case Question

Prepare in memo format an evaluation of the sampling design and procedures used.

CASE 3
Bigger TV Guide Tuned to Readers

By George Lazarus

Is bigger better for *TV Guide*?

So far, it's thumbs up for a larger format of the digest-sized weekly under test in three markets, Pittsburgh, Nashville, and Rochester, N.Y., for the last two months.

With positive newsstand response for the 7½-by-10-inch format, exactly twice the current digest size, *TV*

Guide boss Joseph Cece is encouraged enough to expand the test shortly to "a bigger market," likely in the western part of the country.

Cece, the Radnor, Pa.-based president-publisher of Rupert Murdoch-owned *TV Guide*, in Chicago this week to meet with the advertising community, declined to identify the fourth test market. Sources suggest it might be San Diego.

Beyond reporting that sales have increased in initial test areas—the bigger size is being distributed exclusively in Nashville and Rochester, with both the bigger and digest sizes available in Pittsburgh—Cece is understandably keeping open the publication's options.

A larger format for the digest-sized weekly, which made its debut in 1953, has been rumored for some time, more so since Murdoch's $3 billion buyout in 1989 of Triangle Communications, most of the money going for *TV Guide*. Murdoch since has said he overpaid for *TV Guide*, sources saying by as much as $400 million to $500 million.

Readers and advertisers, attracted by a more inviting layout, will prefer a larger format, but a bigger size will present additional production costs, including paper, of course.

Observers believe the 15.8 million-circulation *TV Guide* eventually will go to the larger format, best indications being by mid-1992. The format change is a much safer bet than *TV Guide* ever returning to the 20 million-circulation peak enjoyed in 1978.

Under Murdoch, Cece contends the weekly is much more profitable, $20 million to $30 million extra annually from a publication that already was a good bottom-line producer. Total profitability probably tops $100 million annually, but *TV Guide* won't divulge a figure.

Even in a weak-advertising environment that has affected all media, *TV Guide* has pockets big enough to splurge for the larger size, which will finally match the format of TV weekly publications of many newspapers.

Source: *Chicago Tribune*, May 17, 1991, p. 3–2. Reprinted with permission.

Case Question

Assume that the new 7½-by-10 inch format was introduced 16 months ago and now Mr. Cece is interested in conducting a telephone interview of 3,000 people nationally to assess their opinions of the new format.

Choose from among simple random sampling, stratified sampling, or cluster sampling, and design a sampling plan to interview 3,000 people.

CASE 4
Bar Code Technology Helps Track Florida Tourists

By W. Lynn Seldon, Jr.

When it comes to tourism, it's tough finding out exactly who's going where and why.

In an industry where marketing is so important, tracking tourists is a game many tourism officials must play. But there's never been an efficient and convenient way to track tourists until now.

Florida is at the forefront of tracking tourists with technology. The force behind this development is SouthEast Advantage (SEA) and its CEO and chairman, John L. Welday.

SEA took grocery store technology and brought it to tourism.

SEA is a discount travel club that recently devised a coupon book for Florida attractions that allows marketing officials to track tourists.

The company developed a proprietary Tourist Tracking Systems (STTS) bar code that identifies each merchant discount coupon, as well as the individual or company redeeming it, Welday said.

"It offers a detailed audit of all coupons redeemed and by whom, as well as mailing lists and disks," he said.

This system is arranged by selling or giving coupon books to incoming Florida tourists, distributed through direct mail to more than 1.4 million Florida-bound vacationers two or three months before they arrive.

They also are distributed through 32,000 travel agents, who issue more than 11 million Florida airline tickets each year, meeting planners, thousands of major corporations, and to TV viewers.

Alamo Rent A Car's promotion alone promises to distribute more than 132 million merchant's discount cheques.

The coupons provide consumers with a merchant's best discount. Participants include Universal Studios Florida, Rivership Grand Romance, Mardi Gras, the Miami MetroZoo, PGA Passport (200 PGA golf courses), and many more.

According to the Florida Division of Tourism, the average family spends more than $3,500 on its Florida vacation. Visitors who come by auto have an annual family income of about $25,000, while visitors who fly in top $60,000. Knowing where and how the money is spent obviously is important.

When travelers receive the coupon book, they give the issuer vital information about themselves and receive a set of bar code labels they must affix to each coupon they redeem.

Each tourist has his or her own bar code, and, when used, their names, addresses, and phone numbers are known and traced by STTS users. The coupons and the bar codes are nontransferable.

Official Airline Guides, publishers of many magazines for travel agents and frequent travelers, said of SEA's efforts: "An exciting breakthrough is taking place in Florida, which is sure to have a dramatic effect on the way the state is promoted."

This comes at a crucial time for state officials, when their tourism budget was just cut by more than $500,000 and visitor figures are down.

When coupons are redeemed, the bar codes and SEA do the rest. SEA already knows who "owns" each bar code. It uses the information to give merchants a monthly computer printout and diskette listing SEA discount users and distributors of the merchant's coupons. Merchants then can use the lists for marketing efforts.

The Florida Retail Federation is seeking to promote SEA's program to its more than 7,000 major and local retail members.

These simple bar codes can lead to user printouts, mailing labels, and statistical tracking. For a fee, SEA can provide tourist figures generated by the bar codes.

The net result of this program is the development of Florida's largest computer database of tourist profile information.

Sixty-eight percent of the state's visitors come back within about a year, according to the Florida Division of Tourism. The coupon books are good for 18 months, and return visitors can still use them on the next trip.

The benefits of tracking tourists this way, according to SEA, can help merchants do the following:

- Plan advertising by reviewing user printouts of tourist origins by area code, city, zip code, state, or country.
- Know which travel agents and tour operators have done the best job promoting the merchant's business.
- Track foreign visitors who have received coupons from airlines or foreign travel consultants.
- Discover which auto rental agencies recommend a merchant's business to their customers.

- Establish a relationship with major corporations that have used coupons for incentive travel.

- Align marketing promotions with cruise lines offering both land and sea packages.

- Support the local chamber of commerce's or tourist development council's worldwide marketing activities.

- Review referrals from hotel and motel corporations, franchises, and local establishments.

- Encourage return of associations, colleges, and universities for annual meetings and reunions.

- Expose and test performance of new products and services by issuing different coupons.

Source: *Marketing News*, November 12, 1990, pp. 8–9. Reprinted with permission.

Case Question

Comment on the sampling plan used by SouthEast Advantage to distribute its coupon books.

MEASUREMENT, SCALING, AND QUESTIONNAIRE DESIGN

We now turn our attention to the topics of measurement, scaling, and questionnaire design. Specifically, in Part IV we present four chapters that together provide a comprehensive treatment of the process of measurement, both in theory and in application.

Chapter 10 introduces basic concepts of measurement and presents details about different types of measurement scales. Chapter 11 is totally devoted to attitude scaling; here we apply several of the scaling techniques, discussed in Chapter 10, to the problem of measuring attitudes and discuss the concepts of reliability and validity. In Chapter 12 we turn to issues involved in questionnaire design and field execution; now that we know what measurement is and how its techniques work, we use them to form our questions. Finally, Chapter 13 discusses issues related to processing the data; in essence these procedures prepare the data for analysis, which is the subject of Part V.

Concepts of Measurement and Measurement Scales

- Introduce and define basic concepts of measurement and scaling.
- Distinguish among the various types of measurement scales.
- Describe and illustrate *comparative* types of measurement scales.
- Describe and illustrate *noncomparative* types of measurement scales.
- Discuss single-item versus multiple-item scales.

INTRODUCTION

It's easy to dance to. Give the song a 10. From the simple to the complex, assigning scores is how we find out who or what is the best in any given field. *Consumer Reports*, for instance, has made a reputation for accurately rating a wide variety of nondurable and durable products. Developing accurate and reliable rating systems is what measurement is all about. Simply put, *measurement* is the process by which scores or numbers are assigned to the attributes of people or objects.

The type of information being sought strongly influences how scores or numbers will be assigned. If you want precise information on cigarette consumption, for example, you might ask individuals to report how many packs of cigarettes they smoke in a day, or in an average week. On the other hand, if you want to collect information on perceptions of cigarette smoking, you might ask individuals to classify themselves as either heavy or light smokers. These two questions yield very different types of measurements. In the former case, responses are given in packs per day (or packs per week), whereas in the latter case, responses are classificatory, producing two categories of smokers.

Measurement involves the use of some sort of scale: feet, inches, centimeters, yards, dollars, and so on. There are many different types of measurement scaling techniques. Various scaling techniques have different properties, and you must understand the proper way to use them because the way in which a characteristic or trait is measured has important implications for the interpretation and analysis of the data collected.

This chapter illustrates a variety of frequently used measurement scales. We start by introducing basic concepts of measurement and scaling. Then we distinguish between two general types of measurement scales: *noncomparative* and *comparative*. We describe the particular ways many of the commonly used comparative and noncomparative scales are used. We complete our discussion by comparing single-item and multiple-item scales.

MEASUREMENT DEFINED

We have discussed methods of obtaining primary information and methods of choosing a sample; now we turn to more specific details on the theory and application of measurement techniques. Because the information collected will be analyzed, numbers must be assigned to the responses to the questions that are asked. As you will see, these numbers have important implications in terms of how the answers to questions can be interpreted and analyzed. Thus we need to understand the properties of the various scaling techniques and the proper way to use them.

measurement
Process of assigning numbers to objects to represent quantities of attributes.

Measurement involves "rules for assigning numbers to objects to represent quantities of attributes."[1] Stated somewhat differently, **measurement** relates to the procedure (the rules) used to assign numbers that reflect the amount of an attribute possessed by an object, a person, an institution, a state, or an event. Think of the everyday occurrence of rating a movie on a scale of 1 to 10. That is very simple measurement. Note that measurement does not pertain to objects themselves—we never measure an object or a person, per se—but rather the amount of an attribute or characteristic possessed by the object. To be more specific, we never measure the movie but rather its entertainment value or how likable it is; similarly, we never measure consumers—only their age, income, social status, perceptions of brand benefits, purchase intentions, or some other relevant characteristic.

The most important and critical aspect of measurement is specifying the rules for assigning numbers to the characteristics to be measured. Once a measurement rule has been selected, the characteristics of objects or persons take on meaning only in the context of the numbers assigned; therefore, if we don't know the rule being applied, we cannot completely or accurately understand the characteristic in question. Consider the characteristic of consumer *brand loyalty* and the following pattern of purchases for two hypothetical consumers during a given period.

> Consumer 1: A B C A B B
> Consumer 2: A C B C C C

If, for example, brand loyalty is measured by computing the proportion of total purchases devoted to the most frequently purchased brand, then the brand loyalty score for consumer 1 is 3/6 = 0.50 and for consumer 2 it is 4/6 = 0.67. On the other hand, if brand loyalty is measured by counting the number of different brands purchased, then both consumers would be given the same brand loyalty score. Conclusions about the brand loyalty of these two consumers depend on which measurement rule the researcher adopts.

A question that follows naturally from this illustration is: Which of the two measurement rules is more correct? This question is difficult to answer. Many

---

[1]J. C. Nunnally, *Psychometric Theory* (New York: McGraw-Hill, 1967), p. 2.

characteristics that we investigate in marketing research studies can be measured in a variety of ways. Particular attention must be given to the objectives of the study, the precise definition of the characteristic to be measured, and the correspondence between the measurement rule and the characteristic.

Concepts, Constructs, and Definitions

The term **concept(s)** refers to the name(s) given to characteristics that we wish to measure. The terms **construct** and *concept* are frequently used interchangeably. Concepts and constructs are abstractions that are formed for a specific research purpose. For example, in Chapter 11 we discuss the **attitude** construct in some detail. Attitude is a concept that most of us would say relates to a person's feelings about or predispositions toward an object. However, when used in a research setting, attitude becomes a construct that must be specifically defined and measured by the researcher.

concept/construct
Names given to characteristics that we wish to measure.

attitude
Concept that relates to a person's feelings about an object or thing.

Constitutive Definitions.
A **constitutive definition** delineates the major characteristics of a given construct. Constitutive definitions allow us to distinguish the concept in question from other similar but different concepts.

For certain concepts the definition found in a dictionary will serve as an appropriate constitutive definition, while for others the constitutive definition will need to be more precise and tailored to the specific research question under study. We cannot overemphasize that the constitutive definition must be consistent with the objectives of the study. If, for example, we are interested in consumer attitudes toward purchasing new Coke, then the attitude concept in question is not the object (new Coke) but instead a consumer's attitude toward *purchasing* new Coke on, say, the next purchase occasion.

constitutive definition
Specifications for the domain of the construct of interest so as to distinguish it from other similar but different constructs.

Measurement/Operational Definitions.
The proper specification of a concept also involves linking the constitutive definition to observable events. A **measurement/operational definition** translates the constitutive definition into steps that must be followed in order to assign numbers to the characteristics being measured. The numbers must be assigned in a way that will reflect the properties of the construct under study; in other words, the measurement definition provides a correspondence between the concept and the real world. As such, a measurement definition clearly defines which observable events (traits, characteristics, variables, etc.) will be measured and the procedure for assigning a value to the concept. It determines which question will be asked.

measurement/ operational definitions
Specifications as to how unobservable constructs are related to their observable counterparts; that is, the procedure that provides a correspondence between the concept and the real world.

Many of the constructs measured in typical marketing research studies are directly observable, but many are not. For example, the concepts of sales and market share have easily observable physical referents; that is, each of those concepts can be directly tied to observable events. In contrast, the concepts of attitude, product perceptions, or consumer satisfaction involve an individual's mental states and, consequently, must be measured indirectly. Whether a concept is directly or indirectly observable is not the critical issue. In either case, the researcher must define precisely what is meant by the construct under study.

EXAMPLE

Attitude

*Constitutive
Definition:*   A predisposition to react to a brand in a favorable or
unfavorable way.

*Operational
Definition:*   On your next purchase occasion, do you intend to purchase
Brand X?

0 _____ X _____ 100%
Definitely   Definitely
will not buy   will buy

0   X

| 1 in. |

1 in. = 25 percent chance of buying

To summarize, constitutive definitions specify the characteristics of a construct—what the construct is—while measurement definitions link the construct, as reflected by its constitutive definition, to the real world.

LEVEL OF MEASUREMENT

To the extent that we have identified the proper characteristics to measure (constitutive definition) and have applied the correct rules for assigning numbers to reflect the quantity of the characteristic possessed by an individual, household, or object (operational definition), we will have captured the construct that we wish to study. The end result of measurement is to assign to each individual, household, or object a number that reflects the amount of a characteristic possessed; in this way, individuals, households, or objects can be distinguished according to how much of the underlying construct they possess. However, depending on the characteristics being measured, the numbers assigned have different properties that determine the kinds of statements we can make about the amount of a characteristic possessed by one individual relative to another.

Measurement can be undertaken at different levels. The levels reflect the correspondence of the numbers assigned to the characteristic in question and the meaningfulness of performing mathematical operations on the numbers assigned. The numbers assigned to reflect the amount of a characteristic possessed by an individual, household, or object can be described in terms of the following properties:

- Order—the numbers assigned produce an ordering with respect to a characteristic.
- Distance—the differences between the numbers assigned produce an ordering with respect to a characteristic.

Scale	Basic Empirical Operations	Some Permissible Statistics
Nominal	Determination of equality	Number of cases Percentages Mode
Ordinal	Determination of greater or less	Mode Median Percentages
Interval	Determination of equality of intervals or differences	Arithmetic mean Standard deviation Product-moment correlation
Ratio	Determination of equality of ratios	Coefficient of variation

TABLE 10–1
—
Types of
Measurement Scales

Source: Adapted from S. S. Stevens, "On the Theory of Scales of Measurement," *Science* 7, June 1946.

– Origin—the number zero indicates the true absence of a characteristic (that is, a unique origin).

There are four basic types of **measurement levels** that can be distinguished by the underlying assumptions regarding the correspondence of numbers assigned and the meaningfulness of performing mathematical operations on the numbers— that is, on the basis of order, distance, and origin. Table 10–1 describes some of the most important features of each.

Nominal Measurement

Nominal-scaled data are described in terms of classes; that is, the numbers assigned allow us to place an object in one and only one of a set of mutually exclusive and collectively exhaustive classes with no implied ordering. **Nominal data** provide a system that "maps" a characteristic of an object to a number; in other words, a number is assigned that identifies a specific object or characteristic. For example, a person's telephone number and social security number are examples of nominally scaled data. The numbers assigned have no specific properties other than to identify the person assigned the number.

Nominal-scaled variables are frequently referred to as *qualitative* or *nonmetric*. For example, variables such as gender, religious denomination, and political affiliation are generally viewed as qualitative because the numbers assigned actually do not reflect the amount of the attribute possessed by an individual.[2] In fact, any reassignment of the numbers (such as reversing the numbers assigned) would have no effect on the numbering system because nothing is implied by the numbers in the first place. Because nominal data do not possess order, distance, or origin, only a limited number of statistics are permissible. To be more specific, with nominal-scaled data it is not meaningful to compute the mean because average gender or

measurement levels
Measurements that can be distinguished according to the underlying assumptions regarding the correspondence of numbers assigned to the properties of objects and the meaningfulness of performing mathematical operations on the numbers.

nominal data
Measurements in which the numbers assigned allow us to place an object in one and only one of a set of mutually exclusive and collectively exhaustive classes with no implied ordering.

---

[2]For this reason some have argued that nominally scaled variables do not actually represent measurement.

average political affiliation, for example, has little meaning. Nominal-scaled data can be counted—it is legitimate to say that 55 percent of the sample is female. The correct measure of central tendency is the *mode*, the value that appears most frequently.

Ordinal Measurement

Ordinal-scaled data are ranked data; consequently, all that we can say is that one object has more or less or the same amount of an attribute as some other object. Thus, with **ordinal data** the response alternatives define an ordered sequence so that the choice listed first is less (greater) than the second, the second less (greater) than the third, and so forth. In other words, ordinal data possess order; however, no distance property is implied since the numbers assigned do not reflect the magnitude of a characteristic possessed by an object. If, for example, a person's rank ordering of four brands according to overall performance is A(2), B(1), C(4), D(3), where the number in parentheses is the respective brand's rank order, we can say nothing about the difference in overall preference among the brands. In addition, even though the difference between the rank order numbers 1 and 2 equals the difference between the rank order numbers 2 and 3, we cannot say the difference in overall preference between the first- and second-ranked brands equals the difference in overall preference between the second- and third-ranked brands.

By using ordinal data any transformation is permissible as long as the basic ordering of the objects is maintained. Thus, we could have assigned the numbers 40 to brand C, 35 to brand D, 30 to brand A, and 10 to brand B. Note that this assignment preserves the relative preference rank ordering of the four brands. Because only order is implied, in the case of ordinal-scaled data the appropriate measures of central tendency are the *mode* and the *median*, the latter of which gives the value below which 50 percent of the observations lie.

Ordinal measurements frequently are used in commercial marketing research studies. Preference data typically are collected with ordinal measures, as the following example illustrates.

ordinal data
Measurements in which the response alternatives define an ordered sequence so that the choice listed first is less (greater) than the second, the second less (greater) than the third, and so forth. The numbers assigned do not reflect the magnitude of an attribute possessed by an object.

EXAMPLE

Read the list of packaged ice cream brands on the card I just gave you.

A. Breyers
B. Sealtest
C. Häagen-Dazs
D. Frusen Glädjé
E. Hood
F. Borden

Tell me which packaged ice cream brand you prefer most. Now excluding that brand, mention the brand of packaged ice cream that you next most prefer.
[*Continue until all brands have been considered.*]

(1) C	(3) F	(5) B
(2) D	(4) A	(6) E

Interval Measurement

Interval-scaled data allow us to say how much more one object has of an attribute than another; thus, if **interval data** are used we can tell how far apart two or more objects will be regarding the attribute, and therefore the difference between the numbers assigned can be compared. In other words, by using an interval scale the difference in the amount of an attribute between a measurement of 2 and a measurement of 3 is equal to the difference in the amount of the attribute between a measurement of 3 and one of 4; furthermore the difference between a measurement of 1 and one of 2 is one-half the difference between a measurement of 2 and one of 4. Thus, interval data possess order and distance properties. With interval-scaled data, the most frequently used measurement of central tendency is arithmetic *mean*, and the standard deviation is the most frequently used measure of dispersion. Virtually the entire range of statistical analysis can be applied to interval measurement scales (see Chapters 15 and 16).

This is not to say, however, that interval data allow comparison of the absolute magnitude of the measurements across objects. Stated differently, we cannot say that the object assigned the number 4 has twice the characteristics being measured as the object assigned the number 2 on an interval scale. The reason is that while interval data possess the characteristics of order and distance, they lack a natural or absolute origin (zero point). Because of the arbitrary nature of the zero point, any positive linear transformation (that is, $y = a + bx$, where x is the original scale value, y is the transformed scale value, a is any constant, and $b > 0$) will preserve the interval scale properties of the data. Thus, if interval data are used, neither ratios nor differences are unique; however, ratios of differences are. To see this, consider the following example.

interval data
Measurements that allow us to tell how far apart two or more objects are with respect to the attribute and consequently to compare the difference between the numbers assigned. Because the interval data lack a natural or absolute origin, the absolute magnitude of the numbers cannot be compared.

EXAMPLE

Person	Original Value (x)	Transformed Value (y = 5 + 3x)
A	5	20
B	10	35
C	15	50

The data consist of the interval-scaled values for three hypothetical individuals. The original values have been transformed according to the transformation $y = 5 + 3x$. We can see that it is incorrect to conclude that Person B has twice the characteristic being measured as Person A—for the transformed values, 35 is not twice 20. We can, however, conclude that the difference in the characteristic possessed by Person A and Person B is the same as the difference in the characteristic possessed by Person B and Person C; that is

Person B	–	Person A		Person C	–	Person B
10	–	5	= 5 =	15	–	10

And we see a corresponding equality of differences in the transformed values.

Person B	–	Person A		Person C	–	Person B
35	–	20	= 15 =	50	–	35

The ratio and differences between the values of the individuals are not unique, but the ratios of the differences are.

$$(10 - 5)/(15 - 10) = 1 = (35 - 20)/(50 - 35)$$

To summarize, the difference in the characteristic possessed by Person A and Person B is the same as the difference between Person B and Person C, using either set of values. Thus, for a given set of values, comparisons across people are permissible.

Interval measurements are frequently used in commercial marketing research studies, especially when a researcher collects attitudinal and overall brand rating information. For example, consider the following two prototypical question formats.

EXAMPLE

A. Please indicate your degree of agreement or disagreement with each of the following statements by selecting the appropriate response.

Breyers Ice Cream Is	Strongly Agree	Agree	Neither Agree nor Disagree	Disagree	Strongly Disagree
Wholesome	———	———	———	———	———
Healthy	———	———	———	———	———
Premium-priced	———	———	———	———	———
Unique	———	———	———	———	———
Good value	———	———	———	———	———

B. I would like you to rate the six brands of packaged ice cream on an overall basis. [*Hand respondent the card.*] Using the phrases on this card, please tell me how you would rate [*Brand checked following "x".*] overall? [*Record in appropriate place below.*] And how would you rate [*Insert next brand.*]? [*Record in appropriate place below. Continue for each checked brand.*]

	Excellent	Very Good	Good	Fair	Poor
( )Häagen-Dazs	5	4	3	2	1
(x)Breyers	5	4	3	2	1
(✓)Hood	5	4	3	2	1
(✓)Frusen Glädjé	5	4	3	2	1
(✓)Sealtest	5	4	3	2	1
(✓)Borden	5	4	3	2	1

It is unlikely that the interval between each of the scale categories in both of the questions shown above is exactly equal. In fact, the data resulting from either of these two scales are, strictly speaking, ordinal, but typically they are analyzed as if they were interval. If the interval between successive scale categories is grossly unequal, then applying statistical analysis that requires interval measurement can produce badly misleading results.

Ratio Measurement

ratio data
Measurements that have the same properties as interval scales but which also have a natural or absolute origin.

Ratio-scaled data have the same properties as interval-scaled data—with one important difference. **Ratio data** possess a natural or absolute origin. Thus, we can legitimately say that the object assigned the number 4 has twice the characteristic being measured as the object assigned the number 2 on a ratio scale. Ratio data are frequently associated with directly observable physical events or entities. Directly observable relevant marketing constructs that have ratio data properties include market share, sales, income, number of salespersons per territory, and so forth.

Because of the legitimate zero point, ratio data allow only for proportionate transformations. For example, the proportionate transformation of the form $y = bx$, where x is the original value, y is the transformed value, and $b > 0$, will preserve all of the relationships among the objects. Ratio data are the most powerful of the measurement types; they have the properties of the other types and more because they possess the characteristics of order, distance, and unique origin.

We need to make three points before proceeding. First, the measurement level categories (nominal, ordinal, interval, and ratio) we've discussed are not necessarily exhaustive. It is possible to have nominal data scales that convey partial information on order or ordinal data scales that convey partial information on distance.[3] Second, keep in mind that the measurement level adopted for the given characteristic being measured ultimately defines the construct's metric. For example, if the characteristics that purportedly reflect the construct in question are measured at the ordinal level, then the construct's metric will also be ordinal. Finally, the progression from nominal to ratio data implies an increasingly restrictive set of measurement rules. The arithmetic operations that are permissible for a higher scale of measurement should never be applied to a lower scale of measurement, as Exhibit 10–1 (see page 294) illustrates.

SCALE TYPES

The various types of measurement scales fall into two broad categories: *comparative* and *noncomparative scales.*

In **comparative scaling** the subject is asked to compare one set of stimulus objects directly against another. For example, a respondent might be asked to compare directly, on the basis of a set of salient attributes, his or her current brand against the other brands that are considered when making a purchase from this product category. Because the scaling is comparative, results must be interpreted in relative terms and have ordinal or rank-order properties; that is, the scores obtained indicate that one brand is preferred to another, but not by how much. An attractive feature of comparative scales is that relatively small differences among the objects being compared can be detected. Note, however, that since the respondent is instructed to directly compare objects, differences are effectively "forced" to surface. Finally, in general, comparative scales are easily understood by the respondent.

In **noncomparative scaling** the respondent is asked to evaluate each object on the scale provided independently of the other objects being investigated. Because each object is rated independently, noncomparative scaling is frequently referred

comparative scaling (nonmetric scaling) *Scaling process in which the subject is asked to compare a set of stimulus objects directly against one another.*

noncomparative scaling (monadic scaling) *Scaling method whereby the respondent is asked to evaluate each object on a scale independently of the other objects being investigated.*

---

[3]Between nominal and ordinal measurement lies the *partially ordered* measurement; between the ordinal and interval data is *ordered metric* data. It is beyond the scope of this text to discuss these measurement types in any detail. Further discussion can be found in C. H. Coombs, "Theory and Methods of Social Measurement," in *Research Methods in the Behavioral Sciences*, ed. L. Festinger and D. Katz (New York: Holt, Rinehart and Winston, 1953).

EXHIBIT 10–1
—
Be Careful What You
Do with Numbers

Consider the following scenario:

In a recent taste-test 100 respondents were asked to indicate their purchase intentions for two brands of soft drinks. The soft drinks were tasted blind. After tasting the first soft drink, respondents indicated their purchase intent on the following scale.

A. Definitely would buy.   _____
B. Probably would buy.   _____
C. Might or might not buy.   _____
D. Probably would not buy.   _____
E. Definitely would not buy.   _____

After recording their intentions, respondents were instructed to drink some water (to clear their taste buds) and then to taste the second soft drink. After tasting the second soft drink they were again asked to indicate their purchase intent (on the identical scale). The order of tasting the two brands was randomly assigned across the respondents.

The following summarizes the results.

	Brand X	Brand Z
A. Definitely would buy.	15	20
B. Probably would buy.	50	15
C. Might or might not buy.	20	50
D. Probably would not buy.	10	10
E. Definitely would not buy.	5	5
Total	100	100

These results were forwarded to the brand group responsible for this category. At a general meeting of the group some time later, the three brand managers who had worked on this study presented their conclusions. Brand Manager 1 concluded that, "based on the data our brand (Brand X) is 100 percent more preferred than the competition (Brand Z)." Brand Manager 2 concluded that, "based on the data our brand (Brand X) is 7.5 percent more preferred than the competition (Brand Z)." Brand Manager 3 concluded that, "based on the data our brand (Brand X) is 9.4 percent more preferred than the competition (Brand Z)."

The apparent inconsistency among the brand managers is a bit puzzling, especially since the same data and computational procedure were used by each manager. Each calculated an average score for each brand, took the difference, and then divided the difference (ignoring sign) by the competitive brand's score to obtain a percentage.

You might be wondering, What possibly could account for the different conclusions? Well, it seems that each brand numbering manager used a different numbering system in computing the mean scores. Brand Manager 1 decided to code Category A as $+2$, Category B as $+1$, Category C as 0, Category D as -1, and Category E as -2. This resulted in mean scores of 0.6 (Brand X) and 0.3 (Brand Z) and since the 0.6 score is 100 percent more than the 0.3 level obtained by the competition, this brand manager concluded that Brand X is 100 percent more preferred. In contrast to Brand Manager 1, the second brand manager assigned Category A as $+1$ and continued up to $+5$ for Category E. This yielded mean scores of 3.6 (Brand X) and 3.35 (Brand Z). Finally, Brand Manager 3 essentially used the same coding system as the second brand manager but assigned a $+5$ to Category A and a $+1$ to Category E. This resulted in mean scores of 2.4 (Brand X) and 2.65 (Brand Z).

Which brand manager is right? Well, as you might suspect, none of them. The reason is that, for this type of data, calculation of ratios is not appropriate.

to as **monadic scaling.** Monadic scales are the most widely used scaling technique in commercial marketing research studies.

COMPARATIVE SCALES

Comparative scales ensure that all respondents approach the rating task from the same known reference point.

	Package Design			
	A	B	C	D
Package design A	—	0.20	0.75	0.40
B	0.80	—	0.90	0.70
C	0.25	0.10	—	0.35
D	0.60	0.30	0.65	—

TABLE 10–2

Proportion of Times
Column Package
Design Chosen Over
Row Package Design

Paired Comparisons

The **paired comparison scale** presents the respondent with two objects at a time and asks the respondent to select one of the two according to some criterion. Paired comparisons yield ordinal-scaled data; for example, Brand A is preferred to Brand B: Brand A tastes better than Brand B, and so on. This type of scale is frequently used, especially when the objects are physical products. As the following example illustrates, paired comparison scales are extremely easy to administer, and the resulting data are generally easy to analyze and interpret.

paired comparison scale
*Scale that presents the
respondent with two ob-
jects at a time and asks
the respondent to select
one of the two according
to some criterion.*

EXAMPLE

To scale consumers' response to four alternative package designs for a new product, a mall-intercept study of 100 consumers was used. After qualifying the respondents, the interviewer presented each one with an 8-inch by 8-inch poster. The poster contained a color picture of two alternative package designs, and the respondent was asked to indicate which he or she preferred most. Because there were a total of four package designs, the respondent was presented with six posters, one at a time, in random order.

To tabulate the paired comparison data, a matrix was formed that indicated the percentage of people who chose each package design when paired with the other three designs. Table 10–2 presents this matrix with the four package designs labeled A, B, C, and D. The numbers in the matrix represent the proportion of people choosing the column entry over the row entry. For example, A was chosen 80 percent of the time when paired with B (consequently, B was chosen 20 percent of the time when paired with A); A was chosen 25 percent of the time when paired with C, and so forth.

Note that Package Design C was preferred to all other package designs, and Package Design B was not preferred to any of the other designs. A rank ordering of the designs with respect to preference would be $C > A > D > B$. To obtain this ranking, we form another matrix. In this matrix, shown in Table 10–3 (see page 296), if the column design was preferred (that is, a proportion > 0.5) to the row design, we place a 1 in that cell, whereas if the column design was not preferred (that is, a proportion < 0.5), we place a zero.[4] The rank-order value is calculated by simply summing the columns. (Proportions equal to 0.5 are randomly assigned a value of one or zero.)

[4]An alternative approach to handling paired comparison data used in commercial marketing research is to look at the proportion of times a given package design is chosen out of the total number of comparisons involving that package design.

	A	B	C	D
A	—	0	1	0
B	1	—	1	1
C	0	0	—	0
D	1	0	1	—
Sum	2	0	3	1

This example includes four brands and six comparisons. In general, with n brands there are $n(n - 1)/2$ comparisons along one criterion; therefore, with k criteria, there $k \times [n(n - 1)/2]$ comparisons in total. Obviously, with many brands or criteria, the number of comparisons can become unwieldy. In addition, because objects are compared two at a time, respondents' judgments may not obey the rule of transitivity; that is, if Brand A is preferred to Brand B, Brand B is preferred to Brand C, then, by the rule of transitivity, Brand A should be preferred to Brand C; however, if Brand C is preferred to Brand A, then an intransitivity exists. If a large number of intransitivities exist, then the paired comparison data will be uninterpretable.

Another important property of paired comparison scales is that the ordinal data can be converted to interval-scaled data, as the following example illustrates.

EXAMPLE

To convert the ordinal data resulting from the paired comparison procedure reported in Table 10–2, we use an approach that, in essence, converts the proportions to z-values (standard normal deviates—see Chapter 15).[5] For example, from Table 10–2 the proportion of people choosing A over B is 0.80. From the cumulative normal distribution shown in the Statistical Appendix, Table 2, we see that the z-value for 0.80 is approximately equal to 0.84. If the proportion is less than 0.5, we subtract the proportion from 1, and the resulting z-value carries a negative sign. For example, only 10 percent of the people chose B over C; consequently, this cell would contain a z-value of -1.28. Table 10–4 contains the z-values corresponding to the proportions reported in Table 10–2.

Let us determine the interval-scale value for Package Design A (column one). From Table 10–4 the value would be $[0.0 + 0.84 + (-0.67) + 0.25]/4 = 0.105$. As previously noted, the zero point of an interval scale is arbitrary. For ease of interpretation we can rescale the interval-scale values just obtained. This involves adding the absolute value of the smallest mean-scale value to original mean-scale values. For instance, in this example, Alternative B has the smallest mean-scale value (-0.66); thus we add 0.66 to all four mean-scale values. The resulting scale values (I^*) are shown in Table 10–4. Based on these scale values we would conclude that C is preferred to A, A is preferred to D, and D is preferred to B. The advantage of converting to interval data is that additional statistical operations can be undertaken.

---

[5] L. L. Thurstone, "A Law of Comparative Judgment," *Psychological Review* 34 (1927), pp. 273–86.

Brand	A	B	C	D
A	0.00	−0.84	0.67	−0.25
B	0.84	0.00	1.28	0.52
C	−0.67	−1.28	0.00	−0.39
D	0.25	−0.52	0.39	0.00
Total	0.42	−2.64	2.34	−0.12
Mean	0.105	−0.66	0.585	−0.03
r^*	0.765	0.00	1.245	0.63

TABLE 10–4

Z-Values Resulting from Table 10–2

Dollar Metric Comparisons

An extension of the paired comparison method is the **dollar metric scale** or **graded paired comparison** procedure.[6] The dollar metric scale extends the paired comparison method by asking respondents to indicate which brand is preferred and how much they are willing to pay to acquire their preferred brand. As the following example demonstrates, this scaling technique allows you to obtain an interval-scaled measure of preferences.

dollar metric scale (graded paired comparison) *Scale that extends the paired comparison method by asking respondents to indicate which brand is preferred and how much they are willing to pay to acquire their preferred brand.*

EXAMPLE

As we indicated above, the dollar metric scale is an extension of the paired comparison method. The respondents are presented with pairs of brands and, in the same manner as with paired comparisons, are asked to select the one they prefer most. However, with the dollar metric scale respondents also are asked how much more, in dollars, they would be willing to pay for the brand selected. For example, suppose a manufacturer of fruit juices wanted to scale preference for different types of containers (glass, plastic, can, or paper box). Table 10–5 (see page 298) presents the responses of one hypothetical person.

A preference scale can be created by summing the dollar (cents) amounts reported for the various comparisons. For each comparison when the alternative is preferred the additional amount willing to be paid carries a positive sign, whereas if it is not preferred, the sign is negative. From the data presented in Table 10–5 we can compute the following preferences.

Glass:	0.07 +	0.07 +	0.02 = 0.16
Plastic:	0.06 +	(−0.02) +	(−0.05) = −0.01
Can:	−0.07 +	0.03 +	0.05 = 0.01
Box:	−0.06 +	(−0.07) +	(−0.03) = −0.16

Thus glass is most preferred, followed by can, plastic, and finally box. Again, with transformation to interval data, additional statistical analyses can be performed.

---

[6]E. A. Pessemier, *Experimental Methods of Analyzing Demand for Branded Consumer Goods with Application to Problems in Marketing Strategy*, Bulletin 39 (Pullman: Washington State University, Bureau of Economic and Business Research, June 1963).

TABLE 10–5	With respect to fruit juice, which container do you prefer?		How much more in cents would you be willing to pay for the preferred container?
Dollar Metric Method	Glass ✓	Can ___	$0.07
	Box ___	Plastic ✓	0.06
	Glass ✓	Box ___	0.07
	Plastic ___	Glass ✓	0.02
	Can ✓	Box ___	0.03
	Plastic ___	Can ✓	0.05

Rank-Order Scales

rank-order scale
Scale in which respondents are presented with several objects simultaneously and requested to "order" or "rank" them.

Next to paired comparison scales, the most widely used comparative scaling technique is simple rank-order scaling. With a **rank-order scale,** respondents are presented with several objects simultaneously and requested to "order" or "rank" them. The following example illustrates how this type of scale works.

EXAMPLE

To illustrate the use of simple rank order, consider that we have 10 people ranking four brands with respect to preference. We show each subject a list of the four brands and ask them to place a 1 beside the brand they most prefer, a 2 beside their second choice, and so forth. Table 10–6 presents the ordering of the 10 subjects; for example, the first subject ranks B first, A second, C third, and D fourth, whereas the second subject ranks A first, B second, D third, C fourth, and so on. Note that B was ranked first by 60 percent (6/10) of the subjects, whereas D was never ranked first. Table 10–7 tabulates the raw data presented in Table 10–6. Here the numbers in the table represent the number of times each brand was ranked either first, second, third, or fourth; for example, Brand A was ranked first twice, while Brand B was ranked first six times, and so forth.

One way to scale the brands with respect to preference is to multiply the frequency of times a brand was ranked first, second, third, and fourth by the ranking. The resulting scale values represent an ordinal scaling with low numbers representing higher preferences. The ordinal scale values for the four brands follow:

$$\text{Brand A: } (2 \times 1) + (4 \times 2) + (2 \times 3) + (2 \times 4) = 24$$
$$\text{Brand B: } (6 \times 1) + (3 \times 2) + (1 \times 3) + (0 \times 4) = 15$$
$$\text{Brand C: } (2 \times 1) + (2 \times 2) + (3 \times 3) + (3 \times 4) = 27$$
$$\text{Brand D: } (0 \times 1) + (1 \times 2) + (4 \times 3) + (5 \times 4) = 34$$

The ranking is therefore B > A > C > D where ">" indicates preferred to.

conditional rank-order scale
Procedure whereby respondents consider each object in turn as a standard for comparison. Respondent assigns ranks to other objects according to this standard.

A variation of the conventional rank-order method, which is sometimes used in order to obtain similarity judgments, is the **conditional rank-order scale.** The conditional rank-order method takes each object, in turn, as a standard for comparison. Each respondent is asked to rank the remaining objects in order of, say, their similarity to this standard. Exhibit 10–2 (see page 300) contains the typical instructions provided to respondents and an example of how the conditional rank-

| Respondent | Brands | | | | TABLE 10–6 |
	A	B	C	D	
1	2	1	3	4	Rank-Order Data
2	1	2	4	3	
3	2	1	3	4	
4	4	2	1	3	
5	3	1	2	4	
6	2	1	3	4	
7	1	3	2	4	
8	4	2	1	3	
9	2	1	4	3	
10	3	1	4	2	

| Brand | Ranking | | | | TABLE 10–7 |
	1st	2nd	3rd	4th	
A	2	4	2	2	Tabulated Rank-Ordered Data
B	6	3	1	0	
C	2	2	3	3	
D	0	1	4	5	

order method would be used to judge the perceived similarities and dissimilarities for a set of carbonated soft drinks.

Constant Sum Scales

The **constant sum scale** is a popular technique that overcomes the problem of having respondents evaluate objects two at a time. Rather, respondents are instructed to allocate a number of points or chips—say, for example, 100—among alternatives according to some criterion (for example, preference or importance). Respondents are instructed to allocate the points or chips in such a way that if they like Brand A twice as much as Brand B, they should assign it twice as many points or chips.

The use of the constant sum scale can differ depending on the type of interview. For example, with a mall-intercept or personal interview, we may actually give a respondent 100 *chips* and have them allocate the chips among a set of alternatives with respect to some criterion, (for example, importance). This method has the advantage of allowing visual inspection of the actual height or number of chips allocated, and the respondent is free to move the chips around to represent his or her feelings. In a telephone interview we probably would ask the respondent to allocate 100 *points* among the alternatives. The respondent is still free to change his or her allocation; however, since chips are not actually being

constant sum scale Procedure whereby respondents are instructed to allocate a number of points or chips among alternatives according to some criterion—for example, preference or importance.

EXHIBIT 10–2
—
Conditional Rank-
Order Scale

We are going to ask you about how similar you think certain types of carbonated soft-drink brands are to each other. Considering each of the various types of carbonated soft-drink brands in turn please place a 1 beside the brand you think is most similar to the brand being considered, a 2 beside the brand next most similar to the brand being considered, and so on. For example, considering diet Pepsi, if you think that diet Coke is most similar to this brand, followed by Dr Pepper, 7UP, Diet 7UP, and finally Sprite, you would have given the following responses:

diet Pepsi

7UP	3
Dr Pepper	2
Sprite	5
Diet 7UP	4
diet Coke	1

[*Hand respondent card with the first brand.*]

7UP

Sprite	1
diet Coke	3
diet Pepsi	4
Diet 7UP	2
Dr Pepper	5

[*Hand respondent card with the second brand.*]

Sprite

diet Coke	3
diet Pepsi	4
Diet 7UP	2
Dr Pepper	5
7UP	1

[*Continue until all brands are considered.*]

Once the data-collection task is completed, a similarity data matrix can be constructed in which each row shows the similarity or dissimilarity with respect to the standard. That is, each row element corresponds to the rank order given to the brand appearing in that column when the brand appearing in the row was the standard for comparison. For example, for the respondent described above we might have found the following. (Note that the elements in row 1 correspond to this respondent's rank ordering when 7UP was the standard of comparison.)

	7UP	Sprite	diet Coke	diet Pepsi	Diet 7UP	Dr Pepper
7UP	—	1	3	4	2	5
Sprite	1	—	3	4	2	5
diet Coke	4	5	—	1	3	2
diet Pepsi	3	5	1	—	4	2
Diet 7UP	1	2	3	4	—	5
Dr Pepper	3	4	2	1	5	—

Note: In the example above, respondents indicated the perceived similarity among the brands. If preference information is desired, respondents can be asked to provide a conditional rank order of the brands with respect to each anchor brand.

distributed, inspection is more difficult. Exhibit 10–3 contains a typical application of the constant sum method.

To scale the characteristics, we simply count the points assigned to each characteristic by each person. Note that the scale, using 100 points, ranges from 0 to

EXHIBIT 10–3
—
Constant Sum Scale

Below are five characteristics that you might consider when purchasing an automobile. Please allocate 100 points among the characteristics so that the allocation represents the importance of each characteristic to you. The more points a characteristic receives, the more important the characteristic is. If the characteristic is not at all important, it is possible to assign zero points. If a characteristic is twice as important as some other characteristic, it should receive twice as many points.

Characteristics	Number of Points
1. Styling	50
2. Ride	10
3. Gas mileage	35
4. Warranty	5
5. Closeness to dealer	0
	100

$n \times 100$ for each object, where n equals the number of respondents (the sample size).

A problem with using a constant sum scale in mail surveys is that the respondent may allocate more or less of the points or chips available. Thus, if the respondent is instructed to allocate 100 points but instead allocates 112 points, the researcher must adjust the data in some way or delete this respondent's data.

Another problem relates to the cognitive effort that is required. For example, in the example presented in Exhibit 10–3 respondents may find it cognitively taxing to allocate points in a manner consistent with the way they value each characteristic.

Constant sum scales have been used in commercial concept-testing studies. Exhibit 10–4 (see page 302) provides an illustration of its use in collecting information on purchase behavior, and Exhibit 10–5 (see page 302) provides an illustration showing how the constant sum method can be used with a paired comparison scale. Note that the illustrative data shown in Exhibits 10–4 and 10–5 indicate a relatively strong preference for Alberto VO-5.

Line Marking/Continuous Rating Comparative Scale

A **line marking scale** is frequently used to obtain similarity judgments. In prototypical applications the respondent is presented with object pairs and asked to judge their similarity by marking a 5-inch line anchored by the phrases "Exactly the same" and "Completely different."

Exhibit 10–6 (see page 303) contains the typical instructions provided to respondents and an example of how the line marking scale would be used in understanding the perceived similarities and dissimilarities among a set of carbonated soft drinks.

Q-Sort Scales

A **Q-sort scale** uses a rank-order procedure in which objects are sorted into piles based on similarity with respect to some criterion. Respondents are given a set of

line marking scale
Procedure whereby the respondent is presented with object pairs and asked to judge their similarity by placing a mark on a continuous line.

Q-sort scales
Rank-order procedure in which objects are sorted into piles based on similarity with respect to some criterion.

Now I'd like you to think about the <u>last 10 times</u> you bought shampoo or asked someone to buy it for you. Please <u>divide 10 points to indicate</u> how many of each brand you bought (or requested) the last 10 times. Please give us your best estimates, even if you can't remember exactly what you bought. You may assign the points any way you wish, as long as the points add up to 10. [*Hand questionnaire with pencil to respondent.*] [*After respondent has finished, take back questionnaire. Total must add up to 10.*]

Agree II	(6)	
Alberto VO-5	(7)	5
Body on Tap	(8)	
Breck	(9)	3
Fabergé Organic	(10)	
Finesse	(11)	
Flex	(12)	
Halo	(13)	
Halsa	(14)	
Head and Shoulders	(15)	2
Ivory	(16)	
Jhirmack	(17)	
Johnson's Baby Shampoo	(18)	
L'Oreal	(19)	
Mink Difference	(20)	
Pert	(21)	
Sesame Street	(22)	
Silkience	(23)	
Suave	(24)	
Tame	(25)	
Timotei	(26)	
Vidal Sassoon	(27)	
Other brand(s): _____	(28)	

SPECIFY

Total must equal   10

Now, we would like you to divide 11 points, or "chips," between each pair of hand and body lotions listed below. You can divide the 11 chips any way you like, depending on how much more you like one product than the other. Some possible combinations are 11 & 0, 1 & 10, 9 & 2, 3 & 8, 7 & 4, or 5 & 6. The two numbers you assign to the products in each pair must add to 11. Always give the product you like more in each pair the larger of the two numbers. Now, please rate each pair of products going <u>across</u> the page. The number of chips you decide to give a product should be recorded in the <u>box</u> next to it.

Chips   Chips

A.   Agree   3 B. Alberto VO-5   8

B.   Alberto VO-5   10 C. Body on Tap   1

A.   Agree   7 C. Body on Tap   4

objects (e.g., brands, concepts, words, or phrases) and are instructed to sort them into piles according to some criterion. For example, a respondent might be given a set of brands and asked to sort them according to which are most similar to that person's ideal brand. The following example illustrates how a Q-sort scale works.

EXHIBIT 10–6

Line Marking Scale

[*Have the respondent read the instructions along with you.*]
You have previously indicated the set of carbonated soft drinks that you considered when making your last purchase. Now, I'm going to present you with pairs of carbonated soft drinks, and I would like you to indicate how similar the brands are to each other. We are going to make this easy for you by having you mark a line anchored by the phrases "exactly the same" and "completely different." For example, if you thought that Diet Pepsi is extremely similar to diet Coke, your response might have looked like this.

Diet Pepsi versus diet Coke
Exactly the   Completely
same ___ X _____ different

[*Hand respondent first pair.*]
7UP versus Coca-Cola Classic
Exactly the   Completely
same _____ X _____ different

[*Hand respondent second pair.*]
Sprite versus 7UP
Exactly the   Completely
same _____ X _____ different

Note: The judgments as measured from the left-hand end of the scale indicate dissimilarity, that is, the larger the number, the more dissimilar is the pair. Judgments can be coded from 0 to 127 (millimeters) or 0 to 100 (1/20 inch).

EXAMPLE

One of the major airlines was interested in determining the magazines that frequent flyers would most prefer to have available for reading while in flight. Management had a list of 75 magazines and wanted to scale the preferences of frequent flyers with respect to these.

To employ the Q-sort method, each magazine cover was photographed and reduced to a 3-inch by 5-inch picture. A cluster sample, clustering on major airports, of 100 frequent flyers was used to scale preferences.

Exhibit 10–7 (see page 304) presents the instructions and rating form used to scale the preferences.

Once the respondent has completed the Q-sort, each object is assigned a rank order. The data are ordinal in nature and can be analyzed with statistical procedures that are suitable for this type of data.

The number of items included in a Q-sort scale should be no less than 60 and no more than 140; 60 to 90 items appear to be a good range.[7] The instructions on how the items should be sorted determine the Q-distribution, although in general Q-distributions are an arbitrary matter. In the preceding example, respondents are specifically instructed to sort the magazines to produce a distribution that will probably be reasonably close to a normal distribution.

By way of summary, Table 10–8 (see page 305) presents a comparison of the various comparative scales just described.

___

[7] K. M. Kerlinger, *Foundations of Behavioral Research*, 3rd ed. (New York: Holt, Rinehart and Winston, 1973), pp. 583–92.

EXHIBIT 10–7

Q-Sort Procedure

The deck in front of you contains pictures of 75 magazines. Please choose the 9 magazines you most prefer of the 75. Once you have selected the 9 you most prefer, please list the magazine name on the form provided under the column "Prefer Most." Now, we would like you to select the 9 magazines you *least* prefer from the remaining 66 magazines. Please list these nine under the column "Prefer Least." Of the remaining 57 magazines, please select the 15 you most prefer and list these 15 under the column labeled "Like." Of the remaining 42 magazines, please choose the 15 you like the least and place these names under the column "Dislike." There should be 27 magazines remaining; please list the titles of these magazines under the column "Neutral."

Tabulation Sheet

Prefer Most	Like	Neutral	Dislike	Prefer Least
___	___	___	___	___
___	___	___	___	___
___	___	___	___	___
___	___	___	___	___
___	___	___	___	___
___	___	___	___	___
___	___	___	___	___
___	___	___	___	___
___	___	___	___	___
(9)	___	___	___	(9)
	___	___	___	
	___	___	___	
	___	___	___	
	___	___	___	
	___	___	___	
	(15)	___	(15)	
		___		
		___		
		___		
		.		
		.		
		.		
		___		
		(27)		

NONCOMPARATIVE SCALES

With noncomparative rating scales, the respondent is not instructed to compare the object being rated against either another object or some specified standard. Thus, in rating a specific brand, the respondent assigns the rating based on whatever standard is appropriate for that individual; no comparison baseline such as "your ideal brand" is provided. Of course, in assigning the rating, each respondent must use some standard; however, the researcher has not provided it.

TABLE 10–8

Comparative
Summary of
Comparative Scales

Scale Type	Measurement	Properties	Advantages/Disadvantages
Paired comparison	Ordinal	Order/distance with transformation	Easy to administer. Easy to analyze. May force differences to be obtained when none exist. Large number of comparisons may cause respondent fatigue.
Dollar metric	Interval	Order/distance	Information on intensity is obtained. Respondents may have difficulty in articulating preferences in terms of dollars and cents, especially when alternatives are similar. May force differences to be obtained when none exist.
Rank order	Ordinal	Order	Easy to administer. Can be used to handle large number of alternatives. Respondents may have difficulty in ranking a large number of alternatives. May force differences to be obtained when none exist.
Conditional rank order	Ordinal	Order	Easy to administer. Ranks are derived from some reference point. Respondents may have difficulty in ranking a large number of alternatives.
Constant sum	Interval	Order/distance	Information on intensity is obtained. Easy to administer. Can be cognitively taxing. Respondents may allocate more points or less points than the specified number.
Line marking	Interval	Order/distance	Information on intensity is obtained. Easy to administer. Requires template for coding. Large number of comparisons may cause respondent fatigue.
Q-sort	Ordinal	Order	Works well with large numbers of objects. Reduces cognitive effort when large number of objects are involved. Because sorting of objects is required, interviewer presence may be needed to ensure that the task is conducted properly.

Line Marking/Continuous Rating Scales

A **line marking/continuous rating scale** also can be used in a noncomparative format. Here the respondent is instructed to assign a rating by placing a mark at the appropriate position on a line, usually 5 inches long, that best describes the object under study. Note no explicit standard for comparison is given. Exhibit 10–8 (see page 306) demonstrates two versions of a continuous rating scale.

In one case (Type A), the respondent is assisted in localizing the rating by the use of numbers and descriptions along the continuum. However, in the other case

line marking/ continuous rating noncomparative scale *Procedure that instructs the respondent to assign a rating by placing a marker at the appropriate position on a line that best describes the object under study. There is no explicit standard for comparison.*

EXHIBIT 10–8

Continuous Rating
Scales

Please indicate your overall opinion of President Clinton by placing a mark (X) at the appropriate location on the line shown below.

Type A

0	10	20	30	40	50	60	70	80	90	100

Unfavorable   Neutral   Favorable

Type B

Unfavorable   Favorable

EXHIBIT 10–9

Itemized Rating
Scale

Please indicate your overall opinion of President Clinton by placing a mark (X) in one of the categories shown below.

Type A

Favorable   Unfavorable

___ :	___ :	___ :	___ :	___ :	___ :	___
Extremely	Quite	Slightly	Neither	Slightly	Quite	Extremely

Type B

Favorable   Unfavorable

___ :	___ :	___ :	___ :	___ :	___ :	___

Type C

Favorable   Unfavorable

___ :	___ :	___ :	___ :	___ :	___ :	___
7	6	5	4	3	2	1

Type D

Favorable   Unfavorable

7	6	5	4	3	2	1

(Type B), the respondent is free to check anywhere on the line. After the respondent has assigned a rating with Scale Type B, a score is determined usually by dividing the line into as many categories as desired and assigning the respondent a score based on the category into which his or her mark falls; it also can be determined by measuring the distance, in millimeters or inches, from the left- or right-hand end of the scale and coding the distance from 0 to 127 (millimeters) or 0 to 100 (1/20 inch). In either case, the resulting scores are typically analyzed as interval data.

Itemized Rating Scales

itemized rating scale
The respondent is provided with a scale having numbers and/or brief descriptions associated with each category and asked to select one of the limited number of categories, ordered in terms of scale position, that best describes the object under study.

In the case of an **itemized rating scale** the respondent is provided with a scale that has numbers and/or brief descriptions associated with each category and asked to select one of the limited number of categories, ordered in terms of scale position, that best describes the object under study. Several different types of itemized rating scales are demonstrated in Exhibit 10–9.

As demonstrated in the exhibit above, itemized rating scales can take on many different formats depending upon the number of categories, the nature and degree of verbal description, the number of favorable and unfavorable categories, the presence of a neutral position, and the forced or nonforced nature of the scale.

1. *The number of categories.* Theoretically, itemized rating scales can include any number of response categories. The basic issue concerns the respondent's ability to discriminate among categories. To be more specific, researchers who favor using a large number of scale categories argue that respondents are capable of making fine discriminations, whereas those who favor using only a limited, and usually small, number of scale categories argue that respondents are not capable of making fine discriminations and to force them to do so would produce ambiguous data at best. Is there an optimal number of categories to employ in all situations? Probably not. In most marketing research applications rating scales typically include between five and nine response categories; however, as we indicated, little can be said about an optimal number of response categories that can be generalized to all circumstances.[8]

2. *Nature and degree of verbal description in itemized rating scales.* Various types of verbal descriptions and numeric formats can be used. Verbal category descriptors help to ensure that each respondent is operating from the same base; however, note that the presence and nature of verbal category descriptors will affect the responses.[9] Pictures and other types of graphic illustrations can also be used, especially if the respondents are children. Two graphic itemized rating scales are shown in Exhibit 10–10 (see page 308).

3. *The number of favorable and unfavorable categories.* If an equal number of favorable and unfavorable scale categories are used, the scale is called **balanced**; otherwise, the scale is said to be **unbalanced**. An unbalanced itemized rating scale is shown below:

> **balanced scale**
> *Scale using an equal number of favorable and unfavorable categories.*
>
> **unbalanced scale**
> *Scale using an unequal number of favorable and unfavorable scale categories.*

Excellent	_____
Very good	_____
Good	_____
Fair	_____
Poor	_____

When should unbalanced rating scales be used? It seems reasonable that when the distribution of responses is likely to be skewed, either positive or

---

[8]For additional evidence, see E. P. Cox, II, "The Optimal Number of Response Alternatives for a Scale: A Review," *Journal of Marketing Research*, November 1980, pp. 407–22; A. M. Givon and Z. Shapira, "Response to Rating Scales: A Theoretical Model and Its Application to the Number of Categories Problem," *Journal of Marketing Research*, November 1984, pp. 410–19.

[9]A. R. Wildt and M. B. Mazis, "Determination of Scale Response: Label Versus Position," *Journal of Marketing Research*, May 1978, pp. 261–67; R. I. Haley and P. B. Case, "Testing Thirteen Attitude Scales for Agreement and Brand Discrimination," *Journal of Marketing*, Fall 1979, p. 31; and H. H. Friedman and J. R. Leefer, "Label Versus Position in Rating Scales," *Journal of the Academy of Marketing Science*, Spring 1981, pp. 88–92.

EXHIBIT 10–10

Graphic Itemized
Rating Scales

A. Please mark (X) on the face that best describes how you feel about the Bill Cosby Show.

B. Now I would like to know how you would expect these new cough drops to taste *just* based on what I read to you. Picture a thermometer scale that goes from 0 to 100, where 100 is the very best, and 0 is the very worst. As a cough drop for your own use, what number from 0 to 100 would best describe your expectation of the *overall taste qualities* of the cough drops I read about? (DO *NOT* READ LIST. RECORD ONE ANSWER.)

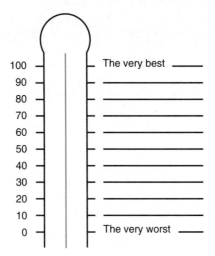

negative, an unbalanced scale that has more categories in the direction of the skewness should be used. For example, unbalanced scales are frequently used when asking socially threatening questions (see Chapter 12). Also, in studies of the heavy users of a product or service, an unbalanced scale may be justified because most of the respondents are likely to have favorable reactions to product features and imagery.

4. *Specification of a neutral position.* If a balanced rating scale is used, the researcher must decide whether to employ an *even* or *odd* number of scale items. With an odd number of scale items, the middle scale position is generally designated as a neutral point. The argument against neutral positions is that respondents really are not neutral and should be forced to indicate their feelings. On the other hand, proponents of scales with neutral positions argue that it is possible for the respondent to be neutral. If respondents can indeed be neutral regarding the object under study, then they

EXHIBIT 10–11
——
Purchase-Intent
Scales

If this new product were available at an outlet where you usually shop, how likely would it be that you would purchase it?

Five-Point Scale	Eleven-Point Scale
_____ Definitely would buy.	10—Certain (99 in 100).
_____ Probably would buy.	9—Almost sure (9 in 10).
_____ Might or might not buy.	8—Very probably (8 in 10).
_____ Probably would not buy.	7—Probably (7 in 10).
_____ Definitely would not buy.	6—Good possibility (6 in 10).
	5—Fairly good possibility (5 in 10).
	4—Fair possibility (4 in 10).
	3—Some possibility (3 in 10).
	2—Very slight possibility (2 in 10).
	1—Almost no chance (1 in 10).
	0—No chance (0 in 100).

should be able to express their neutrality. A balanced, odd-number itemized rating scale is presented below.

Strongly Agree	Agree	Neither Agree nor Disagree	Disagree	Strongly Disagree
_____	_____	_____	_____	_____

5. *The forced or unforced nature of a scale.* In a **forced itemized rating scale** the respondent indicates a response, even though he or she may have "no opinion" or "no knowledge" about the question. In such cases, the respondent may mark the midpoint of the scale; however, if enough respondents have no opinion or knowledge, marking the midpoint will distort measures of central tendency and variance. Thus, it is reasonable to suggest the use of a scale with a "no opinion" or "no knowledge" category.

forced itemized rating scale *Procedure in which a respondent indicates a response on a scale, even though he or she may have "no opinion" or "no knowledge" about the question.*

Itemized rating scales are frequently used to measure purchase intentions. Purchase intention scales represent an attempt to measure a respondent's interest in a brand or product. More specifically, they provide information to get at the key issue: How likely is a respondent to purchase a given brand, product, or concept? Two types of purchase-intent scales are frequently used: a 5-point itemized rating scale and an 11-point purchase probability scale. Exhibit 10–11 presents each type of scale.

The 5-point itemized rating scale is the more commonly used purchase-intent scale, at least in commercial marketing research. Interest typically focuses on top box purchase-intent scores. **Top box** refers to the percentage of respondents rating a brand, product, or concept in the most favorable category on the rating scale, that is, those checking the first choice (e.g., the "definitely would buy" category

top box *Percentage of respondents rating a brand, product, or concept in the most favorable category on the rating scale.*

TABLE 10–9

Comparative
Summary of
Noncomparative/
Monadic Scales

Scale Type	Measurement	Properties	Advantages/Disadvantages
Continuous rating	Interval	Order distance	Information on intensity is obtained; easy to administer, not very cognitively taxing. Differences among objects may not surface; requires template for coding.
Interval rating	Interval	Order distance	Information on intensity is obtained. Easy to administer, not very cognitively taxing; with use of verbal descriptors and different numbers of response item categories highly flexible. Differences among objects may not surface.

on the 5-point scale). Top box percentages are routinely used as a criterion of performance in marketing research, and the item achieving the highest top box score is deemed the strongest or most acceptable.

By way of summary Table 10–9 presents a comparison of the monadic scales just discussed and illustrated.

SINGLE-ITEM VERSUS MULTIPLE-ITEM SCALES

A multiple-item scale usually consists of a number of statements that the respondent must react to; for example, Indicate how favorable or unfavorable each statement is. An overall score is then determined by combining the reactions to each of the statements.

Multiple-item scales are frequently used in attitude measurement. Attitudes represent a person's likes and dislikes of an object or a situation, based on the person's beliefs; to some degree, attitudes determine how a person will *respond* to that object in the future.

> For our purposes we agree that: Attitude is a learned predisposition to respond in a consistently favorable or unfavorable manner with respect to a given object.[10]

This description specifies three fundamental characteristics about attitudes: They are learned, they affect behavior, and they are consistent with regard to an object.

Although attitudes can be measured with a single-item rating scale, multiple-item scales provide at least two principal advantages. First, because attitudes are complex, reflecting much of a person's learned beliefs and experiences, a single-item scale may provide only a crude measure of an individual's overall feelings about an attitude object. Attitudes are likely to be multifaceted; many different

---

[10]M. Fishbein and I. Ajzen, *Belief, Attitude, Intention and Behavior* (Reading, Mass.: Addison-Wesley, 1975), p. 6.

factors influence how a person feels about an object or issue. Single-item scales provide no information about the possible reasons for why the specific attitude has taken shape. Second, including multiple items in a scale and then combining the ratings on the various statements to form a combined score permits an assessment of two important measurement properties: validity and reliability. We discuss these and describe several multiple-item scales that are frequently used in marketing research in the next chapter.

SUMMARY

This chapter has explained measurement concepts and illustrated a variety of measurement scales. An understanding of complex measurement issues is essential in understanding the way to analyze the numeric scores that are assigned to respondents' answers. Two varieties of single-item measurement scales, noncomparative and comparative, were discussed and illustrated. The discussion concluded by focusing on the advantages of using multiple-item scales as opposed to single-item scales.

KEY CONCEPTS

comparative scaling (nonmetric scaling)

noncomparative scaling (monadic scaling)

paired comparison scale

dollar metric scale (graded paired comparison)

rank-order scale

conditional rank-order scale

constant sum scale

line marking scale

Q-sort scales

continuous rating scale (graphic rating scale)

itemized rating scale

balanced scale

unbalanced scale

forced itemized rating scale

purchase-intent scales

REVIEW QUESTIONS

1. From the following questions, name the type of scale (nominal, ordinal, interval, or ratio) being used. Justify your answers.
   a. Which of the three major networks do you watch most frequently?
      _____ NBC   _____ CBS   _____ ABC
   b. The temperature today will reach a high of?
      _____ 0°F–25°F   _____ 51°F–75°F
      _____ 26°F–50°F   _____ 76°F 100°F
   c. How much do you typically spend at the grocery?
      _____ Under $20.00   _____ $40.01–$60.00
      _____ $20.00–$40.00   _____ Over $60.00

   d. How would you rank the following items where 1 is most preferred and 5 is least preferred?
      _____ Milky Way   _____ Baby Ruth
      _____ Almond Joy   _____ Reeses
      _____ Snickers
   e. How many animals do you have? _____
   f. How close are you in pounds to your ideal weight?
      _____ Within 10 lbs   _____ Within 20 lbs.
      _____ Within 30 lbs.
   g. Your best SAT score falls in which of the following groups?

_____ Below 800   _____ 1101–1250

_____ 800–950   _____ 1251–1400

_____ 951–1100   _____ 1401 and above

2. Think about your university's cafeteria. Suppose that the university is interested in measuring the image it has with its student body. Develop a set of scale items to measure the perceived image of the cafeteria. Identify the type of scale being used and its properties.

3. Consider the set of instructions and measurement scale shown in Exhibit 1 below.

     a. What type of measurement scale is being used?

     b. Is this scale monadic or comparative? Explain.

4. The following question appeared on a survey for potential television buyers and received the response shown in the following table.

     a. What type of measure scale was used?

     b. What can you conclude from these data?

Five characteristics of television are listed below. Please allocate 100 points among the characteristics so that your allocation represents the importance of each characteristic to you when making a purchase decision.

Characteristics	Number of Points
1. Clear picture	40
2. Price	20
3. Warranty	15
4. Year of make	10
5. Name of brand	15

EXHIBIT 1

Q. Which brand(s) of medicine(s) for allergies listed below have you used in the past year? (CHECK AS MANY AS APPLY.) Now, for each brand of medicine for allergies that you indicated you have used in Q17, please rate that brand on a scale of "Excellent" to "Poor" for each characteristic listed below.

To do this, think about the brand and write the number on the line under the remedy and next to the characteristic that best expresses your opinion of its rating regarding that characteristic.

Please use the following scale:

Excellent = 1	Very Good = 2	Good = 3	Fair = 4	Poor = 5

Used past year (CHECK AS MANY AS APPLY)	Allerest [ ] 1	Chlortri-meton [ ] 2	Benadryl [ ] 3	Dimetapp [ ] 4	Drixoral [ ] 5	Sudafed [ ] 6	Dimetane [ ] 7	Contac [ ] 8 (66)
								67–78 OPEN

18. Characteristic Ratings

Treats more than one symptom at a time	___(13)	___(13)	___(13)	___(13)	___(13)	___(13)	___(13)	___(13)
Doesn't make you drowsy	___(14)	___(14)	___(14)	___(14)	___(14)	___(14)	___(14)	___(14)
Relieves nasal congestion/stuffiness	___(15)	___(15)	___(15)	___(15)	___(15)	___(15)	___(15)	___(15)
Is specifically for children under 12	___(16)	___(16)	___(16)	___(16)	___(16)	___(16)	___(16)	___(16)
Gives relief for four hours or less	___(17)	___(17)	___(17)	___(17)	___(17)	___(17)	___(17)	___(17)
Can use as frequently as needed	___(18)	___(18)	___(18)	___(18)	___(18)	___(18)	___(18)	___(18)
Helps you breathe easier	___(19)	___(19)	___(19)	___(19)	___(19)	___(19)	___(19)	___(19)
Is a product that was previously available only by doctor's prescription	___(20)	___(20)	___(20)	___(20)	___(20)	___(20)	___(20)	___(20)
Relives itchy skin	___(21)	___(21)	___(21)	___(21)	___(21)	___(21)	___(21)	___(21)
Provides fast relief	___(22)	___(22)	___(22)	___(22)	___(22)	___(22)	___(22)	___(22)
Relieves a headache	___(23)	___(23)	___(23)	___(23)	___(23)	___(23)	___(23)	___(23)
Contains just enough medication	___(24)	___(24)	___(24)	___(24)	___(24)	___(24)	___(24)	___(24)

Attitude Scaling and Concepts in Reliability and Validity

— Explain what is meant by an attitude.
— Describe and illustrate the more popular multiple-item scales used for measuring attitudes.
— Explain the classical true-score model of measurement.
— Discuss the theory and measurement of reliability.
— Discuss the theory and measurement of validity.
— Describe a procedure for developing sound constructs.

INTRODUCTION

In Chapter 10, we discussed and illustrated various types of measurement and a variety of different measurement scales. Now we continue our treatment of measurement and scaling, with particular emphasis placed on issues and problems that surface in measuring directly unobservable constructs and specifically the concept called *attitude*. You may wonder: Why the concern with attitudes? To put it simply, attitudes are presumed to be a precursor of behavior; that is, attitudes are thought to reflect a person's beliefs and in some sense to determine that person's ultimate behavior. Indeed, the vast majority of commercial marketing research studies contain questions to measure the respondent's attitude. One problem when dealing with *attitudes*, however, is that the term means different things to different researchers.

Although our attention is primarily placed on the measurement and scaling of an attitude, we also must understand what is meant by an attitude and its relationship to other constructs. Thus, the first step in understanding how attitudes can be measured is to provide a brief description of (1) what we mean by an attitude, (2) its constituent components, and (3) the conceptual framework that links attitudes to behavior. We next discuss specific scale types that have been used to measure attitude components. These range from simple single-item scales to multiple-item composite scales. The final sections of this chapter are devoted to an introduction to the concepts of reliability and validity. We conclude our discussion by describing an approach for developing sound constructs.

ATTITUDES

attitude
A learned predisposition to respond in a consistently favorable or unfavorable manner with respect to a given object.

What is an **attitude**? Each of you probably has a different definition. However, it is reasonable to suspect that in describing an attitude such terms as *feelings, emotions,* and *likes/dislikes* would be used. This is not too surprising because attitudes represent a person's *evaluation* of an object, based on the person's beliefs about that object; and, to some degree, attitudes determine how the person will *respond* to that object in the future.

Even though there have been many definitions of attitudes, most researchers would probably agree with the following description.

> Attitude is a learned predisposition to respond in a consistently favorable or unfavorable manner with respect to a given object.[1]

This description involves three fundamental characteristics: the notion that attitudes are learned, the notion that attitudes are a precursor to behavior, and the notion of stability—that behavior is consistently favorable or unfavorable toward the object.

ATTITUDE MEASUREMENT TECHNIQUES

Several types of scaling techniques have been employed to measure a person's overall evaluation of an object. We discuss and illustrate four popular scaling techniques: single-item formats, Likert scales, semantic differentials, and stapel scales. In contrast to the single-item format scale, Likert scales, semantic differential scales, and stapel scales all use a multiple-item format. As we demonstrate, these standard methods are based on responses to statements about beliefs or intentions and yield a single score that represents the person's location on an evaluative scale.

Single-Item Formats

single-item formats
Scaling technique that involves asking the respondent to make a judgment about the object in question.

Single-item format measures involve asking the respondent to make a judgment about the object in question. Typically, single-item measurement scales use a verbal, self-report, nonforced choice, monadic format, although formats do vary with respect to the labels used. Itemized rating scales (Chapter 10) are frequently employed. With such scales, the respondent places a check mark on the scale, which may be a continuous line or a line divided into categories.

EXAMPLE

Single-Response Format
My attitude toward shopping at Kmart is

| Extremely favorable | Quite | Slightly | Neither | Slightly | Quite | Extremely unfavorable |

---

[1]M. Fishbein and I. Ajzen, *Belief, Attitude, Intention and Behavior* (Reading, Mass.: Addison-Wesley, 1975), p. 6.

Multiple-Item Formats

If **multiple-item format** attitude-scaling methods are used, the respondent is asked to respond to a number of items that reflect statements of beliefs and/or feelings about the attitude object under investigation. A person's attitude score is obtained by combining the responses to each of the items.

multiple-item formats
Attitude scaling techniques that ask the respondent to respond to several (usually many) items that are statements of beliefs, feelings, and/ or intentions.

Semantic Differential Scale

Charles Osgood, George Suci, and Percy Tannenbaum are credited for the development of the semantic differential scale.[2] Their scale was originally used in psychological and personality research to measure the perceived meanings of words and concepts. They found that the perceived meaning of a variety of words and concepts could be decomposed in terms of three components: *potency, activity,* and *evaluation.* In marketing research studies, the semantic differential scale is frequently used to measure attitudes toward and imagery surrounding products and services. Generally, only the evaluative (e.g., good/bad) component is measured.

The **semantic differential scale** consists of a number of bipolar (opposite) adjective phrases or statements that could be used to describe the objects being evaluated. In the original scale development work of Osgood, Suci, and Tannenbaum, only single-word bipolar adjectives, not phrases, were used. However, common practice in marketing research applications is to use adjective phrases as well.

semantic differential scale
Scaling technique where a measure of the person's attitude is obtained by rating the object or behavior in question on a set of bipolar adjective scales.

The semantic differential scale in Exhibit 11–1 (see page 316) consists of bipolar adjective phrases and statements that pertain to Kmart. Each bipolar adjective rating scale consists of seven categories, with neither numerical labels nor category descriptions other than for the anchor categories. To remove any position bias, favorable and unfavorable adjective phrases are randomly distributed to the left-hand and right-hand anchor positions. The respondent is asked to check one of the seven categories that best describes his or her views about the object (Kmart) along the continuum impled by the bipolar adjective pair. An overall attitude score is computed by summing the responses on each adjective pair. Before computing the overall score, the response categories must be coded. Usually the categories are assigned values from 1 to 7, where a 1 is assigned to the unfavorable adjective phrase and a 7 is assigned to the favorable adjective phrase. Thus, before assigning codes and summing, the researcher must be careful to reverse the individual scale items where necessary so that each attitude continuum ranges from unfavorable to favorable, or vice versa.

Ratings on each of the bipolar adjective pairs are frequently used to provide a profile or image of the objects being investigated. This is accomplished by plotting the mean ratings on each bipolar adjective pair for each of the objects. Exhibit 11–2 (see page 317) presents illustrative pictorial profiles for Kmart and JC Penney. Note that to facilitate interpretation of the profiles, all of the favorable

---

[2]C. Osgood, G. Suci, and P. Tannenbaum, *The Measurement of Meaning* (Urbana: University of Illinois Press, 1957).

EXHIBIT 11–1   Semantic Differential Scale

We would like you to tell us what you think about Kmart. Below are a number of statements that could be used to describe Kmart. For each pair of adjective phrases, please check the category that best describes your feelings about Kmart.

Modern	_____ : _____ : _____ : _____ : _____ : _____ : _____	Old-fashioned
Low prices	_____ : _____ : _____ : _____ : _____ : _____ : _____	High prices
Unfriendly employees	_____ : _____ : _____ : _____ : _____ : _____ : _____	Friendly employees
Knowledgeable employees	_____ : _____ : _____ : _____ : _____ : _____ : _____	Unknowledgeable employees
Limited product assortment	_____ : _____ : _____ : _____ : _____ : _____ : _____	Wide product assortment
Sophisticated customers	_____ : _____ : _____ : _____ : _____ : _____ : _____	Unsophisticated customers
Quick service	_____ : _____ : _____ : _____ : _____ : _____ : _____	Slow service
Inviting atmosphere	_____ : _____ : _____ : _____ : _____ : _____ : _____	Cold atmosphere
Attractive interior	_____ : _____ : _____ : _____ : _____ : _____ : _____	Unattractive interior
Inconvenient store hours	_____ : _____ : _____ : _____ : _____ : _____ : _____	Convenient store hours

adjective phrases are positioned on the same side. From this "snake plot" it appears that, among other things, JC Penney has an edge over Kmart when it comes to attractiveness of interiors, friendly and knowledgeable employees, wide product assortment, sophisticated customers, and inviting atmosphere. Kmart has an edge over JC Penney when it comes to low prices, quick service, and convenient store hours. Overall it appears that JC Penney is more favorably perceived than Kmart since the profile of JC Penney is in general closer to the more favorable end (the left end) of the scales.

Stapel Scale

stapel scale
Procedure using a single criterion or key word and instructing the respondent to rate the object on a scale.

A modification of the semantic differential scale, the **stapel scale** uses a single criterion or key word and instructs the respondent to rate the object on a scale from, for example, "does not describe" to "describes completely." Typically, each scale item has 10 response categories with no neutral or indifference category. The scale is generally presented with numerical labels, but no verbal labels. Exhibit 11–3 presents an example using four of the adjective phrases used in the previously described semantic differential scale.

Ratings given in response to a stapel scale can be analyzed by using procedures similar to those used for analyzing responses to the semantic differential scale. An overall evaluative score can be computed for each respondent by summing the ratings given to each scale item. Similarly, snakelike profile plots can also be constructed from the mean rating on each scale item.

EXHIBIT 11–2   Semantic Differential Profiles for Kmart and JC Penney

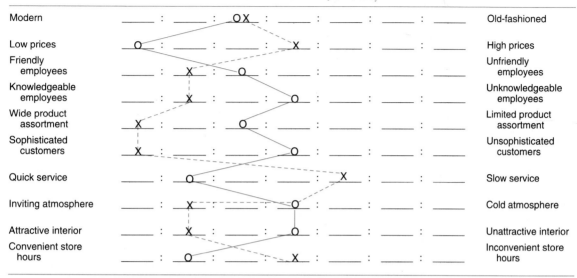

Modern				Old-fashioned
Low prices				High prices
Friendly employees				Unfriendly employees
Knowledgeable employees				Unknowledgeable employees
Wide product assortment				Limited product assortment
Sophisticated customers				Unsophisticated customers
Quick service				Slow service
Inviting atmosphere				Cold atmosphere
Attractive interior				Unattractive interior
Convenient store hours				Inconvenient store hours

Key: Kmart ————— ; JC Penney -----------

EXHIBIT 11–3

Stapel Scale

Please select a plus (+) number for words or phrases that you think describe Kmart accurately. The stronger you feel the word or phrase describes the store, the larger the plus number you should choose. Select a minus (−) number for words or phrases that you think do not describe Kmart accurately. The less you feel the word or phrase describes the store, the larger the minus number you should choose. You can therefore select any number from + 5 for words or phrases you think are very accurate, to − 5 for words or phrases you think are very inaccurate.

+ 5	+ 5	+ 5	+ 5
+ 4	+ 4	+ 4	+ 4
+ 3	+ 3	+ 3	+ 3
+ 2	+ 2	+ 2	+ 2
+ 1	+ 1	+ 1	+ 1
Low prices	Friendly employees	Cold atmosphere	Slow service
− 1	− 1	− 1	− 1
− 2	− 2	− 2	− 2
− 3	− 3	− 3	− 3
− 4	− 4	− 4	− 4
− 5	− 5	− 5	− 5

Compared with the semantic differential scale, the stapel scale is easy to construct since the researcher can avoid the difficult task of developing bipolar adjective phrases or statements. The stapel scale, however, has not enjoyed much popularity in commercial marketing research. There are perhaps two reasons for this. First, compared with the semantic differential scale, the instructions and format of the stapel scale appear to be more complex. Second, the descriptor adjectives can be phrased in a positive, neutral, or negative vein. There is some evidence suggesting that the use of different phrasings can have an affect on scale results and on a respondent's ability to respond.[3] The choice between using a semantic differential scale or a stapel scale will probably have to be decided on the basis of the particular research setting at hand since very little evidence has appeared favoring the superiority of one scale over the other. In fact, two studies have found no significant differences between these two scale types.[4]

Likert Scale

Likert scale

A measurement scale consisting of a number of evaluative statements.

The Likert scale bears the name of its originator, Renis Likert.[5] A **Likert scale** consists of a number of evaluative statements concerning an attitude object. The number of statements used will depend on the number of salient characteristics associated with the attitude object and, therefore, will vary from study to study. Usually, a Likert scale will have 20 to 30 statements. An even number of favorable and unfavorable statements should be used so that the scale is balanced. A balance of unfavorable and favorable statements reduces the likelihood of acquiescence bias (the tendency to agree or disagree with a set of questions), which is more likely if all of the statements are in the same direction.

Exhibit 11–4 presents an illustrative Likert scale that a store like Kmart could use to measure customer attitudes toward itself and a competitor like JC Penney. As shown in the exhibit, the response categories of a Likert scale usually will not have numerical labels, just verbal labels.

For analysis purposes, numerical codes are assigned to each response category in order to compute an overall evaluative score that reflects the respondent's attitude toward each attitude object, in this case, Kmart and JC Penney. The most typical way to code response categories is to assign the numbers 1 through 5, although in some cases other codes have been used, for example, $+2$, $+1$, 0, -1, -2. When assigning the numbers, care must be taken to ensure that response categories are coded in a consistent fashion. The "strongly agree" category for a favorable statement should receive a value of 5; similarly, the "strongly disagree" category for an unfavorable statement should also receive a value of 5. A respondent's overall evaluative score is computed by summing his or her numerical ratings on all of the statements making up the scale.

The success of using a Likert scale will in large measure be determined by the quality of the scale items used. The scale items selected should possess three qualities: (1) they should capture all relevant aspects of the attitude object, (2) they should be unambiguous, and (3) they should be sensitive enough to discriminate among respondents with respect to the attitude object under investigation. The

---

[3]Michael J. Etzel, Terrell G. Williams, John G. Rogers, and Douglas J. Lincoln, "The Comparability of Three Staple Forms in a Marketing Setting," in *Marketing Theory: Philosophy of Science Perspectives*, ed. R. F. Bush and S. D. Hunt (Chicago: American Marketing Association, 1982), pp. 303–6.

[4]See Del I. Hawkins, Gerald Albaum, and Roger Best, "Staple Scale or Semantic Differential in Marketing Research," *Journal of Marketing Research* 11 (August 1974), pp. 318–22; and Dennis Menezes and Norbert F. Elbert, "Alternative Semantic Scaling Formats for Measuring Store Image: An Evaluation," *Journal of Marketing Research* 16 (February 1979), pp. 80–87.

[5]Renis Likert, "A Technique for the Measurement of Attitudes," in *Attitude Measurement*, ed. Gene F. Summers (Chicago: Rand McNally, 1970), pp. 149–58.

EXHIBIT 11–4   Likert Scale

Please indicate by checking (X) the appropriate category the extent to which you agree with the following statements about Kmart.

	Strongly Disagree	Disagree	Neither Agree nor Disagree	Agree	Strongly Agree
1. The store has an inviting atmosphere.	_____	_____	_____	_____	_____
2. The clerks are knowledgeable.	_____	_____	_____	_____	_____
3. The store's checkout lines move slowly.	_____	_____	_____	_____	_____
4. The store offers a wide product assortment.	_____	_____	_____	_____	_____
5. The store has an unattractive interior.	_____	_____	_____	_____	_____
6. The clerks are unfriendly.	_____	_____	_____	_____	_____

recommended practice is to first generate a relatively large pool of statements and then prune the number of statements according to how well each statement discriminates between respondents holding favorable and unfavorable attitudes.

RELIABILITY AND CONSTRUCT VALIDITY

In a 1978 issue of *Marketing News*, Burleigh Gardner, president of Social Research, Inc., made the following comment.[6]

> Today the social scientists are enamored of numbers and counting. . . . Rarely do they stop and ask, "What lies behind the numbers?"
>
> When we talk about attitudes we are talking about constructs of the mind as they are expressed in response to our questions.
>
> But usually all we really know are the questions we ask and the answers we get.

These comments reflect the fact that attitudes are directly unobservable. As such, we must be particularly sensitive to the properties of the measurements used. In this section we discuss two standard measurement criteria—reliability and validity. *Reliability* indicates the precision of measurement scores, or how accurately such scores will be reproduced with repeated measurement. *Construct validity* refers to the extent to which differences in observed measurement scores reflect true differences in the characteristic being measured. Before we give further details about these two criteria, we introduce what is called the *true-score model* of measurement, which will provide a perspective on the issue of reliability and construct validity.

True-Score Model

The **true-score model** provides one framework for understanding what requirements our measures must satisfy.[7] Consider, for example, the attitude construct.

true-score model
A person's specific attitude toward buying and using the brand, denoted by X_T. The true score is composed of X_O, the observed score component, and X_E, the error score component.
$X_O = X_T + X_E$.

_____

[6] D. Gardner, *Marketing News*, May 5, 1970, p. 1.

[7] Note that the true-score model is not the only theory of measurement. For further details see F. M. Lord and M. R. Novick, *Statistical Theories of Mental Test Scores* (Reading, Mass.: Addison-Wesley, 1968).

We assume that a person holds a specific attitude toward buying and using a brand. This specific attitude is called his or her "true" attitude, and we denote this level by X_T. To capture the person's attitude, we use a particular measurement scale that produces an observed score, denoted by X_O. The measurement scale is usually composed of a number of scale items (questions), all presumed to be measuring the construct under study. These items represent a sample of items from the population of items that define the domain of the construct, for example, feelings, beliefs, and intentions.

Ideally, we would like the measurement scale to produce an observed score equal to the person's true attitude level, that is $X_O = X_T$. It rarely happens, however, that the observed score will equal the **true score**. The discrepancy between the two is usually referred to as the error score, given by the difference between the observed score and the true score

true score
Component part of a person's observed score that reflects the person's actual score on the construct of interest.

$$X_E = X_O - X_T \tag{11–1}$$

where X_E denotes the error score. By simple manipulation, we have the classic true-score model of measurement

$$X_O = X_T + X_E \tag{11–2}$$

which states that the observed scale score is composed of a true-score component and an **error component.** The true-score component represents the person's actual score on the construct of interest, whereas the error component is due to all those factors that cause the person's observed score to differ from the person's true score.

error component
Those factors that cause the person's observed scale score to differ from the person's true score.

The variation in a set of measurements obtained from a given measurement instrument arises from a variety of specific sources or factors. Exhibit 11–5 summarizes the possible sources of variation in measurement scores. Note that the true score is only one of nine possible sources of variation. All of the remaining sources constitute the error component in the classical true-score model.

EXHIBIT 11–5
———

Possible Sources of
Variation in
Measurement Scores

1. True differences in the characteristic being measured.
2. Characteristics of individuals that affect scores: for example, intelligence, extent of education, information processed.
3. Short-term personal factors: health, fatigue, motivation, emotional strain, among others.
4. Situational factors: for example, rapport established and distractions that arise.
5. Variations in administration of measuring instrument: interviewers, for example.
6. Sampling of items included in the instrument.
7. Lack of clarity of the measuring instrument: ambiguity, complexity, interpretation, for instance.
8. Instrument factors: lack of space to record response, appearance of instrument, and so on.
9. Analysis factors: for instance, scoring, tabulation, and statistical compilation.

RELIABILITY

Reliability in a measurement context is not really different from the layperson's definition.[8] Essentially, reliability denotes stability or consistency; that is, reliable measures are consistent—stable from one administration to the next. Consider Table 11–1, which shows three sets of scale scores for five individuals. The first column in the table displays each person's true score. (For discussion purposes we will assume that the respondent's actual value on the construct of interest is known, when in fact this will rarely, if ever, be the case.) The second and third columns show observed scale scores obtained under an unreliable test and a reliable test, respectively. Note that the rank orders of the first and third columns covary exactly; in other words, even though the observed scale scores obtained with this test are not identical to the true scores, they are in the exact rank order. And in this sense, this test is reliable. In contrast, the observed scale scores that appear in the second column do not covary with the true scores. And in this sense, this test is unreliable.

reliability
The extent to which measures are free from random error and yield consistent result.

Reliability Theory

The error score is an increase or decrease from the true score caused by measurement error. Measurement error is the primary source of unreliability. Unreliability comes about primarily because the items that make up the measurement scale do not measure the same construct. The error component in the classic true-score measurement model (see Equation 11–2) is itself composed of two components. That is

$$X_E = X_S + X_R \qquad (11\text{–}3)$$

where X_S denotes **systematic sources of error** representing stable characteristics such as *instrument factors*, which affect the observed scale score in the same way each time the test is administered, and X_R represents **random sources of error** such as *short-term personal factors*, which affect the observed scale score in different ways each time the test is administered.

systematic sources of error
Denoted by X_S, component made up of stable characteristics that affect the observed scale score in the same way each time the test is administered.

From Table 11–1 we saw that a test is reliable if it consistently rank orders individuals. Since systematic errors do not contribute to inconsistency, they affect the observed scale scores in the same way each time the test is administered and consequently do not adversely affect reliability. However, random error does, and therefore it lowers reliability. Based on this discussion, reliability can be simply defined as the extent to which measures are free from random error and yield consistent results. Stated somewhat more formally, a measure is reliable if independent but comparable measures of the same construct agree. Since reliability

random sources of error
Denoted by X_R, component made up of transient personal factors that affect the observed scale score in different ways each time the test is administered.

---

[8]Parts of this section are based on the work of J. P. Guilford, *Psychometric Methods* (New York: McGraw-Hill, 1954); K. N. Kerlinger, *Foundations of Behavioral Research*, 3rd ed. (New York: Holt, Rinehart and Winston, 1973); F. M. Lord and M. R. Novick, *Statistical Theories of Mental Test Scores* (Reading, Mass.: Addison-Wesley, 1968); J. C. Nunnally, *Psychometric Theory*, 2nd ed. (New York: McGraw-Hill, 1978); and J. P. Peter, "Reliability: A Review of Psychometric Basics and Recent Marketing Practices," *Journal of Marketing Research*, February 16, 1979, pp. 6–17.

(1) True Scores	Rank	(2) Scores from Unreliable Test	Rank	(3) Scores from Reliable Test	Rank
42	1	27	4	45	1
35	2	44	1	37	2
31	3	30	3	33	3
28	4	20	5	27	4
22	5	36	2	21	5

*Adapted from F. N. Kerlinger, *Foundations of Behavioral Research,* 3rd ed. (New York: Holt, Rinehart and Winston, 1973).

depends on how much random error is present in our measures, we can say that if $X_R = 0$, the measure is perfectly reliable.

Reliability Measurement

The general approach for assessing reliability is to determine the proportion of systematic variation in a measurement scale. To accomplish this, the various methods determine the association between scores obtained from two scales, where one of the scales is a similar replicated version of the other. If the association between the scores derived from the two scales is high, the scales are consistent in yielding the same results and are therefore reliable.

Several methods for calculating the reliability of a measurement scale involve the use of a correlation coefficient. As we discuss in Chapter 16 correlation coefficients measure the association between two variables. The values that a correlation coefficient can assume fall between $+1$ and -1. A value of $+1$ indicates perfect positive association; a value of -1 indicates perfect negative association. Computational formulas are given in Chapter 16.

test-retest reliability
Method for calculating reliability; respondents are administered identical sets of scale items at two different times under similar conditions. The reliability coefficient is computed by correlating the scores obtained from the two administrations.

reliability coefficient
Measure that indicates the amount of systematic variation, relative to the total observed scale variation.

Test-Retest Reliability.   In the **test-retest reliability** assessment method, respondents are administered identical sets of scale items at two different times under similar conditions. The suggested retest period is two weeks after the initial test. The **reliability coefficient** is computed by correlating the scores obtained from the two administrations.

There are several problems with the test-retest method. First, it is sensitive to the time interval between test occasions. All else the same, the longer the time interval between test occasions, the lower the reliability.[9] Second, a low reliability coefficient will be obtained if a change in the phenomenon under study has occurred between the first and second administrations; however, it may be difficult to distinguish this change from unreliability. Finally, the reliability coefficient as

———
[9]G. W. Bohrnstedt, "Reliability and Validity Assessment in Attitude Measurement," in *Attitude Measurement,* ed. G. F. Summers (Chicago: Rand McNally, 1970), p. 85.

computed in the test-retest method can be inflated because of the correlation of each scale item with itself. In computing the reliability coefficient, the correlation of each scale item with itself across the two administrations is not excluded. It is reasonable to expect that these correlations are likely to be much higher than correlations between different scale items across administrations; thus, the reliability coefficient can be high simply because of the high correlations that are present between the same scale item measured at different times, even though the correlation between different scale items is quite low.[10]

Internal Consistency Reliability.   One simple measure of **internal consistency reliability** is the **item-to-total correlation.** This is obtained by computing the correlation of each item with the total score, when by the total score we mean the score obtained from summing each person's responses to the entire set of items. According to the criterion of internal consistency, the relationship between attitude score and the probability of endorsing a given item should be linear. To be more specific, the more favorable a person's attitude, the more likely he or she should be to endorse favorable items and, conversely, the less likely he or she should be to endorse unfavorable items. From the assumed linear relationship between attitude score and probability of item endorsement, it follows that an individual item satisfies the criterion of internal consistency if the item score significantly correlates with the (overall) attitude score.

There are a number of other approaches to computing internal consistency reliability. If these approaches are used the item scores obtained from administering the scale are in some way split in half, and the resulting half scores are correlated. Large correlations between **split-halves** indicate high internal consistency. The simplest approach is to split the scale items in terms of odd- and even-numbered items or randomly. There is, however, one fundamental problem with using split-halves to assess internal consistency: Depending on how the scale items are split in half, different results will be obtained. This raises the important question of which one is the "real" reliability coefficient.

A popular approach to overcoming this limitation is to form all possible split-half partitions of a measurement scale and to compute the mean reliability coefficient. **Cronbach's alpha**[11] (α) is one of the most commonly accepted methods for assessing the internal consistency of a multi-item measurement scale.

Alternative Form Reliability.   In the **alternative form reliability** assessment approach, the same subjects are measured at two different times, usually two weeks apart, with two scales designed to be similar in content but not so similar that the scores on the scale administered first affect the scores on the scale administered after two weeks have elapsed. The reliability coefficient is obtained by correlating the scores from the two administrations of the alternative scale forms.

---

[10]For further discussion of this point see J. C. Nunnally, *Psychometric Methods.*
[11]L. J. Cronbach, "Coefficient Alpha and the Internal Structure of Tests," *Psychometrika,* September 16, 1951, pp. 297–334.

internal consistency reliability
Method of calculating reliability; the item scores obtained from administering the scale are in some way split in half and the resulting half scores are correlated. Large correlations between split-halves indicate high internal consistency.

item-to-total correlations
A measure of internal consistency in which each item is correlated with the total score obtained from summing the entire set of items used in computing the attitude score.

split-halves
Scale items split in terms of odd- and even-numbered items or randomly.

Cronbach's alpha
Mean reliability coefficient calculated from all possible split-half partitions of a measurement scale.

alternative form reliability
Method of calculating reliability; the same subjects are measured at two different times, usually two weeks apart, with two scales designed to be similar in content but not so similar that the scores on the scale administered first affect the scores on the scale administered after two weeks have elapsed.

Alternative forms implicitly assess the equivalence of the content of sets of scale items. And herein lies the problem. If this approach is used, we presume that substantially equivalent forms can be developed. Strictly speaking, alternative forms require that the alternative sets of scale items used have equivalent means, variances, and intercorrelations.[12] Even if these conditions are satisfied, it may be difficult to assess the equivalence of the alternative sets with respect to content. Low correlation between the alternative form scores could be due to low reliability or nonequivalence of content. This approach appears best suited to situations in which the construct under study is expected to vary over short time periods. In such cases, alternative form measures can allow the researcher to investigate these changes.

CONSTRUCT VALIDITY

Even if a measurement scale is reliable, it may or may not be construct valid. In other words, a measurement scale can consistently yield the same (or similar) scores, but the scores obtained need not reflect the construct that the researcher wishes to study. Reliability does not guarantee that a measurement scale will be construct valid because construct validity is most directly related to the question of what the measurement scale is in fact measuring. As such, reliability places an upper bound on validity. A measurement scale is said to possess **construct validity** to the extent that differences in the observed scale scores reflect true differences in the characteristic or construct being measured.

construct validity
The extent to which differences in the observed scale scores reflect true differences in the characteristic or construct being measured.

Construct Validity Theory

At the heart of construct validity is nonrandom error. Matters of construct invalidity arise when other factors (confounds—see Chapter 7) affect the characteristics being measured in addition to the one underlying construct and random error. The presence of nonrandom errors can result in scale items that represent something other than the intended construct, perhaps an extremely different construct altogether. For instance, if a researcher uses a particular set of scale items to represent brand loyalty but later discovers that the scale actually taps only repeat-purchase behavior irrespective of attitude, then the scale is an incomplete and possibly invalid indicator of loyalty.

Validity depends on the extent of nonrandom error present in the measurement process. Just as reliability is a matter of degree, so is validity. One can probably never attain a perfectly valid measurement scale, that is, one that represents the intended construct and no other. For example, high scorers on a brand loyalty scale may not only be persons who exhibit loyalty (both favorable attitude and purchase behavior) but also people who buy the same brand(s) because of their limited

---

[12]H. Gulliksen, *Theory of Mental Tests* (New York: John Wiley & Sons, 1950).

availability. This is another way of saying that validity critically depends on the extent of nonrandom error—that is, confounds—and, like reliability, is a matter of degree.

Types of Construct Validity and Measurement

The term *construct validity* has come to be used generically to provide a broad umbrella under which the other types of validity are subsumed. We now describe several types of construct validities that you should be aware of and briefly comment on how each is measured.[13] In the course of the discussion, we refer to the attitude construct in order to provide specific illustrations of what is meant by the various types of validity.

Content Validity.   In this case we are concerned with the representativeness of the content of a measurement scale. **Content validity** focuses on whether the scale items adequately cover the entire domain of the construct under study. Consider, for example, the attitude construct, which is presumably composed of three subdimensions relating to a person's likes/dislikes, beliefs, and behavioral intentions. To be content valid, an attitude score should contain scale items that tap all three subdimensions. The content validity of a measurement scale would be assessed by evaluating the closeness of the scale items to the characteristic or construct under study.

content validity
Indication of the representativeness of the content of a measurement scale; focuses on whether the scale items adequately cover the entire domain of the construct under study.

Convergent Validity.   This type of validity indicates that measurement scales designed to measure the same construct should be related. In attitude measurement, the scale items purportedly measuring the affective (like/dislike) subdimension of attitude should be related to the scale items purportedly measuring the cognitive (belief) subdimension because both measurement scales presumably reflect a person's attitude. **Convergent validity** generally is assessed by the extent to which two (or more) measurement scales designed to measure the same construct correlate.

convergent validity
Indication of the extent to which measurement scales designed to measure the same construct are related.

Discriminant Validity.   This type of validity examines the extent to which the measurement scale is novel and not simply a reflection of some other variable. Measurement scales can correlate too highly. To quote a seminal article on convergent and discriminant validity: "Tests can be invalidated by too high correlations with other tests from which they were intended to differ."[14] If two

---

[13]Our treatment of how to measure validity will be elementary. Details on validity measurement require a level of sophistication beyond the scope of this textbook. Readers who want further details can consult N. Schmitt, B. W. Coyle, and B. B. Saari, "A Review and Critique of Analyses of Multitrait-Multimethod Matrices," *Multivariate Behavioral Research*, 1977, pp. 447–78; and N. Schmitt and D. M. Stults, "Methodology Review: Analysis of Multitrait-Multimethod Matrices," *Applied Psychological Measurement* 10 (1986), pp. 1–22.

[14]Campbell and Fiske, 8.

presumably distinct measurement scales correlate very highly, then they may be measuring the same characteristic or construct rather than different characteristics or constructs. Suppose that when we measure attitude the correlation between the affective (like/dislike) measurement scale items and cognitive (belief) measurement scale items approaches unity; in this case the two measurement scales would be indistinguishable, and we would conclude that the two scales are not reflecting *separate* and *distinct* components of attitude but rather just a single component. **Discriminant validity** is assessed by examining the correlation between the measure of interest and other measures that purportedly measure a different, but related, characteristic or construct.

discriminant validity
Indication of extent to which the measurement scale is novel.

Criterion Validity.   This type of validity investigates whether the measurement scale behaves as expected in relation to other constructs. For example, in the context of the attitude construct, we might investigate whether persons with positive attitudes, as indicated by the measurement scale being used, also have a tendency to perform favorable behaviors with respect to the attitude object. **Criterion validity** generally is assessed by determining the extent to which the observed measurement scale scores can predict some criterion measure. For this reason, this type of validity is sometimes referred to as *predictive validity*.

criterion validity (predictive validity)
Indication of whether the measurement scale behaves as expected in relation to other constructs.

VALIDITY VERSUS RELIABILITY

A measurement scale can be reliable, yielding consistent and stable results over time and situations, yet not valid. In contrast, however, a measurement scale that is unreliable cannot be valid. Reliability, then, is a *necessary* but not *sufficient* condition for validity.

Exhibit 11–6 illustrates the concepts of reliability and validity in the context of a dartboard game involving three players. The first situation shows holes all over the target. This dart thrower is neither consistent nor very accurate. This illus-

EXHIBIT 11–6

Illustrations of
Possible Reliability
and Validity
Situations in
Measurement

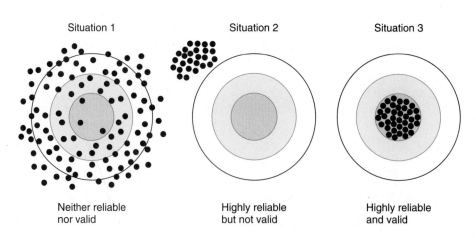

Situation 1 — Neither reliable nor valid

Situation 2 — Highly reliable but not valid

Situation 3 — Highly reliable and valid

trates a lack of reliability and validity. The second dart thrower is much more consistent. This illustrates reliability, but the holes in the target are far from the center, which means that he or she is off the mark. The final dart thrower is highly reliable and valid. This dart thrower has a steady eye that is on target.

DEVELOPING SOUND CONSTRUCTS[15]

Based on the discussion presented so far, we can outline a recommended procedure for developing sound constructs in terms of five essential steps.

1. *Specify constitutive definition.* This involves a clear and precise definition of the domain of the construct in question.

2. *Specify measurement/operational definition.* This involves specifying the items (questions) to be asked and the rule for assigning numbers to the characteristics of interest, that is, specifying the scale of measurement.

3. *Perform item analysis.* After the items have been placed in an appropriate format, data should be collected from members of the relevant target market of interest, and an *item analysis* should be performed. The items making up a scale should correlate highly with the total score for the overall measurement instrument; in this sense the scale can be said to be *internally consistent.* Items showing low correlation with the total score for the overall measurement instrument should be deleted. The exact procedure for conducting an item analysis will depend on the specific type of scale that is used.

4. *Perform reliability checks.* Once an item analysis has been performed, new data should be collected with the purified measurement instrument, and a reliability check should be performed. We have discussed various methods for measuring reliability.

5. *Perform validity checks.* After the reliability of the measurement instrument has been established, a validity analysis must be performed. Where appropriate, each type of validity should be examined.

Unfortunately, the procedure for developing sound constructs that is described above is rarely completely followed in commercial marketing research studies. The reason for this is simple; time and cost constraints often make it impossible to completely follow such an elaborate procedure. Nonetheless, we suggest that the steps described above serve as a framework for construct development that can be implemented in whole or in part, depending on the resources available.

---

[15]See Gil Churchill, "A Paradigm for Developing Better Measures of Marketing Constructs," *Journal of Marketing Research* 16 (February 1979), pp. 64–73; or W. J. Lundstrom and Lawrence M. Lamont, "The Development of a Scale to Measure Consumer Discontent," *Journal of Marketing Research* 8 (November 1976), pp. 373–81.

SUMMARY

In this chapter we have considered the measurement and scaling of attitude. Attitudes play a central role in our understanding and anticipation of consumer behavior and, thus, are important to many marketing research investigations. Our emphasis has been on issues and problems that surface when measuring attitude and its constituent components. Among other things, we described how attitude is linked to behavior, and we discussed and illustrated the major scaling techniques used to measure attitude. In addition, we have introduced the concepts of reliability and validity and described an approach for developing sound constructs.

KEY CONCEPTS

attitude	reliability	internal consistency	convergent validity
semantic differential scale	test-retest reliability	validity	discriminant validity
Likert scales	reliability coefficient	content validity	criterion validity
true-score model			

REVIEW QUESTIONS

1. Suppose that your university is interested in measuring students' attitudes toward the cafeteria. Develop a set of 10 scale items to measure attitudes toward the cafeteria, using each of the three multiple-item scale formats discussed in this chapter.

2. The table below shows responses to 10 Likert items and item-to-total correlations.

   a. What statements can you make about the reliability of the 10 items?
   b. Why are some of the item-to-total correlations negative?
   c. Should those items having negative item-to-total correlations be removed?
   d. Could the negative item-to-total correlations be changed? If so, how?

A. Likert Items	Strongly Agree	Agree	Neither Agree nor Disagree	Disagree	Strongly Disagree
1. The commercial was soothing.	5	4	3	2	1
2. The commercial was not entertaining.	5	4	3	2	1
3. The commercial was insulting.	5	4	3	2	1
4. The commercial was silly.	5	4	3	2	1
5. The commercial was too "hard-sell."	5	4	3	2	1
6. The characters in the commercial were realistic.	5	4	3	2	1
7. The commercial was not creative.	5	4	3	2	1
8. The commercial clearly demonstrated the product's advantages.	5	4	3	2	1
9. I will remember this commercial.	5	4	3	2	1
10. The commercial had meaning to me personally.	5	4	3	2	1

B. Responses to 10 Likert Items

Individual	Item										Sum of Ten Items
	1	2	3	4	5	6	7	8	9	10	
1	5	5	1	3	1	2	5	2	5	2	31
2	3	4	2	2	2	1	5	3	4	3	29
3	4	2	4	2	5	4	2	4	5	5	37
4	1	4	2	3	2	1	4	1	4	3	25
5	3	1	5	3	4	4	2	4	5	5	36
6	3	5	2	4	2	2	5	1	4	3	31
7	4	3	3	3	2	3	3	3	4	4	32
8	3	4	2	3	1	1	4	2	4	3	27
9	4	2	5	3	5	5	2	4	5	5	40
10	3	5	1	3	1	2	5	2	4	2	28

C. Item-to-Total Correlations

| | 0.58 | −0.75 | 0.84 | −0.14 | 0.87 | 0.96 | −0.77 | 0.82 | 0.79 | 0.81 | |

3. By applying the variance operator to the true-score measurement model (Equation 11–2), we obtain the following:

Var(Observed Score) = Var(True Score) + Var(Error)

a. What interpretation do you give to the quantity

$$\frac{\text{Var(True Score)}}{\text{Var(Observed Score)}}$$

b. What arguments can you provide to support the contention that the mean of the error scores is 0?

4. Comment on the following statements:

a. Systematic error contributes to unreliability.

b. Random error contributes to invalidity.

c. An item that is valid must be reliable.

Questionnaire Design
Including International Considerations

- Explain the importance of questionnaire design and field execution.
- Discuss the basic activities involved in designing questions.
- Briefly discuss design and field considerations when conducting international marketing research.

INTRODUCTION

A critical element in a survey research study is the construction of a properly designed questionnaire. A questionnaire is simply a data-collection instrument that sets out in a formal way the questions designed to elicit the desired information. The questionnaire continues the research process that began with identification of the management problem, specification of the information needed to solve this problem, selection of an appropriate method for collecting the necessary data, and identification of the target population of individuals who can provide the needed information. As we discussed in Chapter 6, a questionnaire can be administered with the aid of a computer, by means of the telephone, by a personal interviewer, or by mail, and although we associated questionnaires with survey research projects, they can be used in experimental designs as well (Chapter 7). Questionnaires can be used to collect information on a diverse set of topics. In Chapters 10 and 11 we introduced measurement scales that can be used when researchers collect information on product ratings, attitudes and opinions, purchase intentions, and behaviors. In this chapter we focus first on design issues, that is, how scales should be worded in light of the specific objectives of the study and the target group of respondents who will be questioned. Included in our coverage is a discussion of relevant questionnaire design issues that surface when researchers conduct marketing research studies in foreign markets. Although the marketing problem may appear well defined in terms of hypotheses, information needs, and the appropriate target population, effective operationalization of these components in the data-collection phase is needed to achieve valid and reliable results.

A questionnaire is a data-collection instrument. It formally sets out the way in which the research questions of interest should be asked. On first thought, it may seem that questionnaires should be simple to put together—all that is re-quired is to know what questions you wish to ask.

However, even simple questions require proper wording and organization if the researcher wants accurate information. The format, the content, or the organiza-tion of the questions can induce a respondent to give an accurate or an inaccurate response, as the examples in From the World of Research 12–1 (see pages 332–333) illustrate.

In this chapter we focus first on design issues such as how questions should be worded, given the specific objectives of the study, and the target group of respon-dents who will be questioned. We then turn our attention to how the question-naire should be organized and pretested. The general principle and procedures we recommend apply to mail, telephone, personal, and computer-assisted telephone interviews (CATI). Finally, recognizing the opportunities of the opening of mar-kets abroad, we discuss questionnaire design issues that should be considered in conducting marketing research studies in international markets.

QUESTIONNAIRE DESIGN

By the time the researcher arrives at the questionnaire design stage of a given study, the marketing problem has probably been expressed in a set of appropriate research questions. Now these questions must be translated into the language of the respondent and then arranged in a questionnaire in a valid, logical fashion that will produce meaningful results.[1] Hence, we can view questionnaire design in terms of four interrelated activities: (1) preliminary considerations, (2) asking questions, (3) constructing the questionnaire, and (4) pretesting the questionnaire.

Exhibit 12–1 (see page 334) provides a summary of these activities.

Preliminary Considerations

Before you even start to consider how questions should be asked, you must trans-late the marketing problem into a set of research questions that identify (1) ex-actly what information is required; (2) exactly who the appropriate target respondents are, and (3) what data-collection method will be used to survey these respondents. These questions were covered earlier in Chapters 2, 7, and 9. We repeat them here because there is no way to overstate their importance.

Asking Questions

All too often, formulation of the questionnaire is thought to be the easiest part of designing a survey. Yet question wording is a crucial element in maximizing the validity of survey data. Building good questions seems like a simple task. After all, we ask questions all the time. Often the responses we get, however, are based on

---

[1] An excellent source for a detailed treatment of questionnaire design and construction issues is D. A. Dillman, *Mail and Telephone Surveys: The Total Method* (New York: John Wiley & Sons, 1978).

From the World
of Research
—
12–1

Asking Questions

You may think that asking questions and designing a questionnaire are simple matters. Yet, faulty questionnaire design is a major contributor to nonsampling errors and specifically to response errors. Response errors occur because respondents do not give accurate answers to questions that have been asked, and many factors that lead a respondent to give inaccurate responses can be traced directly to improper questionnaire design and construction. As the examples below demonstrate, the format of a question, the content of a question, or the organization of the questions can induce a respondent to give an inaccurate response.

Format problem

What is your religious preference?

Jewish __Catholic __Protestant denomination __Other __Specify __None

The blank lines may be confusing. The respondent may wonder whether the blank lines should be used for the response category before it or the one after it.

Content problem

Do you believe that IBM personal computers are the most compatible and the best buy for the money?

how we word our questions. Seemingly small changes in wording can cause large differences in responses.

Consider a well-known example: Two priests, a Dominican and a Jesuit, are talking about whether it is a sin to smoke and pray at the same time. After failing to reach a conclusion, each goes off to consult his respective superior. The next week they meet again. The Dominican says, "Well, what did your superior say?" The Jesuit responds, "He said it was all right." "That's funny," the Dominican replies, "my superior said it was a sin." Jesuit: "What did you ask him?" Reply: "I asked him if it was all right to smoke while praying." "Oh," says the Jesuit, "I asked my superior if it was all right to pray while smoking."[2]

General Guidelines

When you construct a questionnaire a general rule is to always ask yourself, "Why am I asking this question?" You must be able to explain how each survey question is closely related to the research question that underlies management's problem.

Three general guidelines help in devising a good questionnaire:

1. Write specific questions only after you have thoroughly thought through your research questions. Write the research questions down.

---

[2]Adapted from Seymour Sudman and Norman M. Bradburn, *Asking Questions* (San Francisco: Jossey-Bass, 1983).

The question considers *two* aspects of IBM's product performance—compatibility and value. If a respondent feels that IBM personal computers are the most compatible *but* not necessarily the best buy for the money, how should the person respond?

Organization problem

Q1. Did you purchase a maintenance contract for your FAX machine?
Yes . . .
No . . .

Q2. Do you think that maintenance contracts are a good investment?
Yes . . .
No . . .

Q3. What is the anticipated cost of the maintenance contract?
Less than $50 per year
$50–$100 per year
$101–$200 per year
More than $200 per year

The confusion in the questions shown above relates to whether question Q3 should be answered by all respondents or only by those who have purchased a maintenance contract.

2. When you are working on the questionnaire, constantly refer to your research questions.

3. For each question you write, explain how the information obtained from responses will help in answering your research questions.

Satisfactory questions on generic issues may already exist. Before you attempt to create new questions, search for questions on the same topic that may have been asked by other researchers in other studies. Most questionnaires contain some questions that have been used before; in fact, even some new questions probably have been adapted from questions used in the past. The point is that the repetition of questions is not only permitted but it is also encouraged in survey research and in social science in general.[3] Repeating questions that have demonstrated acceptable levels of reliability and validity can allow you to (1) reduce the time needed for testing, (2) compare results across a number of studies, and (3) establish response reliabilities for the study at hand.

Basic Principles

A number of specific considerations should be kept in mind when asking questions; the following basic principles form what could be called the "art" of asking questions.

---

[3] Normally no permission from the originator of the question is required or expected, although you may want to communicate with the originator to find out whether there were difficulties with the question that were not reported in the publisher's source. For questionnaires that have been copyrighted, permission from the publisher is required.

EXHIBIT 12–1

Questionnaire
Design
Considerations

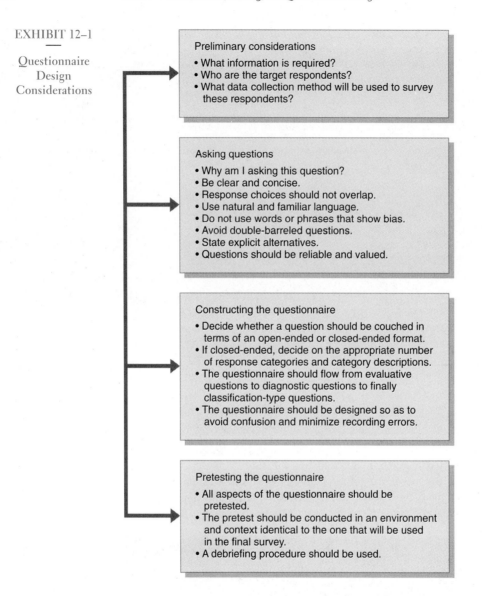

Preliminary considerations

• What information is required?
• Who are the target respondents?
• What data collection method will be used to survey
  these respondents?

Asking questions

• Why am I asking this question?
• Be clear and concise.
• Response choices should not overlap.
• Use natural and familiar language.
• Do not use words or phrases that show bias.
• Avoid double-barreled questions.
• State explicit alternatives.
• Questions should be reliable and valued.

Constructing the questionnaire

• Decide whether a question should be couched in
  terms of an open-ended or closed-ended format.
• If closed-ended, decide on the appropriate number
  of response categories and category descriptions.
• The questionnaire should flow from evaluative
  questions to diagnostic questions to finally
  classification-type questions.
• The questionnaire should be designed so as to
  avoid confusion and minimize recording errors.

Pretesting the questionnaire

• All aspects of the questionnaire should be
  pretested.
• The pretest should be conducted in an environment
  and context identical to the one that will be used
  in the final survey.
• A debriefing procedure should be used.

Principle 1: Be Clear and Precise. The question should be understandable to both researcher and respondent, and it should allow responses consistent with the desired level of measurement and response options that will afford actionable results. For example, consider the following two questions intended to identify volume of coffee consumption.

(A) How many cups of coffee do you drink in a typical work day?

———————

[*Write in number.*]

(B) How frequently do you drink coffee? [*Record choice below.*]

Extremely often	1
Very often	2
Not too often	3
Never	4

Note that question B is not precise. It neither specifies the consumption period, that is, daily, weekly, or monthly consumption, nor does it result in a precise measure of coffee consumption. Question B yields responses that have, at best, ordinal properties; in fact, one could argue that such a question would yield nominal data because it may not be possible to legitimately make comparisons across respondents—each response category may imply very different consumption frequencies to each respondent. In contrast, question A yields more precise information about the amount of coffee consumed and the time interval in which consumption takes place. Finally, the data collected from question A has ratio-scaled properties.

Principle 2: Response Choices Should Not Overlap. Along with the tenets of clarity and precision goes the idea of **mutual exclusivity.** What this means is that the response choices to a question should not overlap with one another. Consider the following question.

> Which of the following categories best describes your total household income before taxes in 1993? [*Circle one answer only.*]
>
> | | |
> |---|---|
> | Less than $10,000 | 1 |
> | $10,000–$15,000 | 2 |
> | $15,000–$25,000 | 3 |
> | $25,000 or higher | 4 |

mutual exclusivity
Condition in which the response choices to a question do not overlap with one another.

As you may have noticed, it is possible for individuals who live in households with incomes of exactly $15,000 or $25,000 to choose two response categories. Choices 2 and 3 should have been written as $10,000–$14,999 and $15,000–$24,999. Without this mutually exclusivity, it is difficult to say where the "true" response lies.

Principle 3: Use Natural and Familiar Language. Consider who makes up your sample when constructing your questions. Phrase questions in the colloquial language of your respondent group. Not only do different ethnic and social groups express their thoughts differently but so do people who live in different regions within the same country. Think about a sandwich prepared on a large loaf of bread: This is variously referred to as a "grinder," "hoagie," "hero," and "submarine" in different parts of the country. We don't mean to imply that the intent is to be chatty. Your language should always mean what you intend and should convey the intended meaning to the respondents in a clear and precise fashion.

The familiarity of language also has been shown to influence respondents' willingness to give accurate responses to threatening questions.[4] Threatening

---

[4]Ed Blair, Seymour Sudman, Norman M. Bradburn, and Carol Stocking, "How to Ask Questions about Drinking and Sex: Response Effects in Measuring Consumer Behavior," *Journal of Marketing Research*, August 1977, pp. 316–21.

questions ask respondents to report on illegal or contrary-to-norm behaviors or conditions not generally discussed in public without tension. Response effects to such questions can be quite severe and can result in (1) the overstatement of desirable behavior (for example, voting) and (2) the understatement of behaviors perceived as being socially unacceptable (for example, alcohol or drug abuse). One study showed that response effects due to threatening questions can be decreased by allowing the respondents to select their own words for describing the threatening behavior under study.[5] One of the threatening behaviors investigated was intoxication.

EXAMPLE

The standard question for intoxication read

> During the past year, how often did you become intoxicated while drinking any kind of alcoholic beverage?

Respondents were handed a card containing the following response categories:

- Never.
- Once a year or less.
- Every few months.
- Once a month.
- Every few weeks.
- Once a week.
- Several times a week.
- Daily.

The alternative procedure allowed respondents to first provide their own word for intoxication through the following question:

> Sometimes people drink a little too much beer, wine, or whiskey so that they act different from usual. What word do you think we should use to describe people when they get that way so that you will know what we mean and feel comfortable talking about it?

The intoxication question then read:

> Occasionally, people drink on an empty stomach or drink a little too much and become (respondent's word). In the past year, how often did you become (respondent's word) while drinking any kind of alcoholic beverage?

No response categories were offered for either item.

Other techniques have been used to improve response accuracy for threatening questions. For example, as we indicated in Chapter 10, *unbalanced scales* that include additional categories on the heavy end have been used in collecting data on alcohol consumption.

---

[5]Ibid., p. 318.

Principle 4: Do Not Use Words or Phrases that Show Bias. Biased or leading words or phrases are emotionally charged and suggest an automatic sentiment of approval or disapproval. **Loaded questions,** as they are called, suggest what the answer should be or indicate the researcher's position on the issue under study. In both instances, the respondent is not given a fair chance to express his or her own opinion, and a consistent measurement error is introduced that would not exist if neutral phrasings were used (see next example).

loaded questions
Questions that suggest what the answer should be or indicate the re-searcher's position on the issue under study.

Leading questions can take a variety of forms. Consider the following question.

What did you dislike about the product you just tried?

The respondent is not given a "way out" if he or she found nothing to dislike. A more suitable way to ask this question would be to first ask:

Did you dislike any aspects of the product you just tried?
_____ Yes _____ No

Certain words and phrases also can induce bias. For example:

Do you think Exxon did everything possible in its handling of the Alaskan oil spill situation?

This is a leading question because the use of the phrase *everything possible* can produce biased responses. The issue is whether Exxon acted *reasonably* in the aftermath of this accident.

Another type of bias can occur when a respondent is required to rate a series of objects (such as brands of toothpaste) on the same set of characteristics. **Order bias** can be particularly troublesome in concept and product testing. Research has shown that the ratings of objects may be related to the order in which they were presented for evaluation; in other words, brands receive different ratings depending on whether they were shown first, second, third, and so on.

order bias
Condition whereby brands receive different ratings depending on whether they were shown first, second, third, etc.

Shown below are the mean brand ratings of 60 respondents who evaluated three brands of analgesics (Bufferin, Excedrin, and Tylenol) where the order of rating was varied. For each of the six possible combinations each brand was evaluated monadically on a 7-point itemized scale.

Tylenol	1.0	Tylenol	1.5	Bufferin	3.0
Bufferin	6.0	Bufferin	5.5	Tylenol	1.0
Excedrin	3.0	Excedrin	3.0	Excedrin	6.0
Bufferin	3.5	Excedrin	2.5	Excedrin	3.5
Excedrin	3.0	Tylenol	1.5	Bufferin	3.5
Tylenol	3.5	Bufferin	6.5	Tylenol	3.0

It is clear from the preference ratings that the brand rated immediately following Tylenol received relatively higher scores. Thus the order in which the brands of analgesics were presented to the respondent may have affected the ratings given.

In order to control for this kind of order bias, both the order of object presentation and attribute presentation should be varied (rotated) across respondents. Rotating objects and/or attributes across respondents minimizes the chance that systematic order effects will be misinterpreted because any biases are now randomly (uniformly) distributed. Note that with self-administered interviews, the rotation of questions is extremely difficult to implement and often impractical.

Principle 5: Avoid Double-Barreled Questions. Questions in which two opinions are joined together are called **double barreled**. With these questions, the respondent must answer two questions at once even though his or her opinions about the two may diverge. Consider, for example, the following question:

> Do you believe that McDonald's has fast and courteous service?

Here, questions about two different attitude objects, speed and courteous service, are conjoined. A customer might agree with the claim of fast service but not with the claim that it is courteous.

Principle 6: State Explicit Alternatives. The presence or absence of an explicitly stated alternative can have dramatic effects on responses. Consider, for example, the following two forms of a question asked in a "Pasta-in-a-Jar" concept test.

> Version A: Would you buy pasta-in-a-jar if it were available in a store where you normally shop?
>
> Version B: If pasta-in-a-jar and the canned pasta product that you are currently using were both available in the store where you normally shop, would you
>
> *a.* buy only the canned pasta product?
> *b.* buy only the pasta-in-a-jar product?
> *c.* buy both products?

The stated alternatives provide a context for interpreting the reaction to this new concept for Version B. For example, if with Version A, 42 percent of the respondents indicated that they would buy the new pasta-in-a-jar product, we would expect when specific alternatives were added (Version B) the number of respondents indicating that they would buy only the new pasta-in-a-jar product would drop.

Principle 7: Questions Should Meet Criteria of Validity and Reliability. The issues of whether or not we are truly measuring what we are attempting to measure and whether or not we can replicate these responses at a later point in time should certainly be considered in question building (see Chapter 11). You should not assume that the same questioning approach will work similarly well for all product/service categories and all interviewing methods.

The validity and reliability of data can be severely compromised if respondents cannot accurately answer the questions. Two aspects of questions might make it impossible for a respondent to answer:

1. *Relevance.* It is possible to ask respondents questions on topics about which they are uninformed; in other words, the question is not relevant because the respondent has never been exposed to the answer; that is, the respondent lacks experience. An all-too-common example is to ask a respondent's opinion, in general or on specific performance characteristics, about a product, brand, store, or service that he or she has never heard of or has never consumed. Furthermore, respondents typically do not indicate their lack of knowledge—thereby compromising validity. The problem of relevance can be minimized by (1) selecting the proper target populations and (2) allowing the respondent to indicate his or her lack of knowledge by direct questioning or by including a "don't know" category on the scaling instrument.

2. *Memory.* In many instances a respondent is asked a question about something that has occurred in the past, and he or she may have forgotten the answer. Forgetting can cause three types of response effects: omission, telescoping, and creation.[6] **Omission** occurs when a respondent cannot recall that an event has occurred; **telescoping** occurs when a respondent compresses time or remembers an event as occurring more recently than it actually occurred (for example, in the case of a respondent indicating visits to a particular store twice in the last week although one of the visits occurred 10 days ago); **creation** occurs when a respondent recalls an event that did not actually occur.

   It is reasonable to expect that **unaided questions,** ones that do not provide any clues to the answer, can result in an understatement of specific events. On the other hand, **aided questions,** ones that provide clues that potentially help the respondent recall more accurately, can increase telescoping and creation. Response effects due to memory factors can be diminished by (1) asking respondents questions only about *important* events that occurred within the last few days[7] and (2) informing respondents that the aided-recall questions may contain some bogus items.[8]

omission
Interviewing condition that occurs when a respondent cannot recall that an event has occurred.

telescoping
Condition that occurs when a respondent either compresses time or remembers an event as occurring more recently than it actually occurred.

creation
Situation whereby a respondent recalls an event that did not actually occur.

unaided questions
Questions that do not provide any clues to the answer.

aided questions
Questions that provide clues that will potentially help the respondent recall more accurately.

CONSTRUCTING THE QUESTIONNAIRE

Now that we've discussed principles of good question design, we will present some suggestions for arranging the questions in a form that provides meaningful results in a cost- and time-efficient manner. Several important issues should be considered when constructing a questionnaire.

---

[6] Seymour Sudman and Norman M. Bradburn, "Effects of Time and Memory Factors on Response in Surveys," *Journal of the American Statistical Association,* December 1973, pp. 805–15.

[7] Yoram Wind and David Lerner, "On the Measurement of Purchase Data: Surveys Versus Purchase Diary," *Journal of Marketing Research,* May 1970, pp. 254–55.

[8] Daniel Starch, *Measuring Advertising Readership and Results* (New York: McGraw-Hill, 1966), p. 20.

Response Formats

Two general types of response formats can be used when researchers construct a questionnaire: *open-ended* and *itemized* (closed-ended).

open-ended questions
Questions that allow the respondent to choose any response deemed appropriate, within the limits implied by the question.

Open-Ended Questions. With an **open-ended question** format the respondent is free to choose any response deemed appropriate, within the limits implied by the question. The next example shows a question series that allows the respondent to choose his or her own words when describing the commercial.

EXAMPLE

What did the commercial say?

_____

_____

_____

What did the commercial show?

_____

_____

_____

What did you like about the commercial you just saw?

_____

_____

_____

Not all studies include open-ended questions. However, when they are included, their primary purpose is to obtain the respondent's own verbalization of, comprehension of, and reaction to stimuli. The stimuli may cover a broad range (such as ads, commercials, packages, products, concepts). Therefore, it is impossible to set rules for every possible situation in which open-ended questions might be used or to set rules for the processing of the open-ended questions. However, there are several good reasons for asking open-ended questions:

1. Open-ended questions may be used to check and/or corroborate the results of the quantitative or closed-ended questions. Along these same lines, open-ended questions also may be used to find a wider range of response and reaction than is included in the quantitative or structured questions.

2. Open-ended questions may be used to obtain direct comparisons and more specific areas of preference and rejection when two or more stimuli (e.g., products or concepts) are involved in a test.

3. Open-ended questions may be used to determine whether a particular communication vehicle (e.g., commercial or concept) conveys its intended objectives.

4. Open-ended questions may be used to determine respondents' affective reactions or feelings as a result of exposure to a stimulus (e.g., commercial, concept, package, product, or ad).

There are several drawbacks to using open-ended questions. First, they are not very well suited for self-administered questionnaires simply because most respondents will not write elaborate answers. Second, answers to open-ended questions may be a more direct result of the respondent's ability to articulate than a measure of the respondent's knowledge or interest in the issue being investigated. Third, interviewer bias can be a serious problem with the use of open-ended questions (see Chapter 6). Finally, open-ended questions must be coded or categorized for analysis purposes, and this is often a tedious task laden with ambiguities (see Chapter 13). An alternative is called **precoding.** Here the respondent is presented with an open-ended question such as

precoding
Procedure of assigning a code number to every possible response to an open-ended question.

What brand of shampoo did you last purchase?

After the respondent has indicated the brand last purchased, the interviewer checks off that brand on a list that contains the most popular brands in the product category. As such, this type of open-ended question is treated from the viewpoint of the interviewer as an itemized question or closed-ended question.

Precoded   EXAMPLE

Q. What brands of toothpaste have you ever heard of? [*Do not read list. Record below.*] Any others?

Aim	1
Aqua-Fresh	2
Colgate	3
Crest	4
Gleem	5
Pepsodent	6
Topol	7
Others (please specify) _____	
_____	
_____	

Uncoded

Q. What brands of toothpaste have you ever heard of? [*Record responses verbatim on lines provided below.*]

_____   _____

_____   _____

_____   _____

Itemized (Closed-Ended) Questions. With an itemized-question format the respondent is provided with numbers and/or predetermined descriptions and is asked to select the one that best describes his or her feelings. **Itemized questions** can take on many different formats. Recall that in Chapter 10 we discussed in some detail several issues related to itemized-question formats: namely, (1) the number of response alternatives (such as multiple-choice or dichotomous), (2) the nature and degree of verbal description, (3) the number of favorable and

itemized (closed-ended) questions
Format in which the respondent is provided with numbers and/or predetermined descriptions and is asked to select the one that best describes his or her feelings.

unfavorable categories, (4) the presence of a neutral position, and (5) the forced or nonforced nature of the scale. The next example presents several illustrations of an itemized-question format. It shows structured response alternatives to a purchase-intent question.

EXAMPLE

Balanced with neutral position
Definitely would buy
Probably would buy
Might or might not buy
Probably would not buy
Definitely would not buy

Balanced without neutral position
Definitely would buy
Probably would buy
Probably would not buy
Definitely would not buy

Balanced, nonforced
Definitely would buy
Probably would buy
Don't know/no answer
Probably would not buy
Definitely would not buy

Balanced, graphic rating
(Place an "X" in the position on the line that indicates your likelihood of buying Product X.)

Would _____ Would
not buy   Might or   buy
                            might not buy

Dichotomous
Would buy
Would not buy

Unbalanced
Definitely would buy
Probably would buy
Might or might not buy
Would not buy

The obvious advantages of itemized-question formats relate to their ease of use in the field, their ability to reduce interviewer bias (and specifically bias due to differences in how articulate respondents are), and, finally, the relatively simple approach required with respect to coding and tabulation. To be effective, however, itemized-question formats require a substantial amount of effort, particularly with respect to pretesting. The use of itemized-question formats presumes that the predetermined set of response categories adequately reflects all of the possible and

EXHIBIT 12–2

Questionnaire
Organization

— **Evaluative**
Purchase intent
— **Diagnostic**
Reasons for expressed level of purchase intent.
Uniqueness (of idea).
Believability (of idea).
Importance of main benefit.
Expected frequency of usage.
Ratings on a series of product benefits.
— **Classification**
Age.
Marital status.
Family size.
Education.
Occupation.
Income.

relevant responses at the appropriate level of precision and that it will not produce distortions in the data.

Logical Flow

To respondents, questionnaires should appear as logical, carefully-thought-out examinations. In everyday life, we generally are asked about what we have done and then about the details surrounding a given occurrence before we go on to talk about another unrelated situation. This is also the typical flow in marketing research surveys: there is a progression from evaluative to diagnostic questioning or vice versa and then on to classification questions. Exhibit 12–2 provides a sequence of question topics appearing in a product concept test that might be asked of a group of respondents after the interviewer has read a description of a new product idea to them. When designing the flow of the questionnaire, there are several specific issues to consider.[9]

Introducing the Questionnaire.   Many respondents will have some initial suspicions or fears concerning why they are being interviewed. The introduction must make clear the purpose of the study. It need not be long and complicated, however. Instead, the first several questions should indicate the nature and purpose of the study.

In personal interviews, for example, respondents should identify themselves and the organization(s) they represent, and they should immediately give a one- or two-sentence description of the purpose of the study. On the other hand, in mail surveys the nature and purpose of the study is given in the cover letter that accompanies the questionnaire. The major points that should be covered are listed in Exhibit 12–3.[10] Note that these points should be covered in one page or less.

---

[9]Parts of the following discussion were adapted from Sudman and Bradburn, *Asking Questions*, pp. 208–28.

[10]A careful discussion of these points can be found in Dillman, *Mail and Telephone Surveys*.

EXHIBIT 12–3
—
Major Points in a
Questionnaire
Introduction

> What the study is about and its social usefulness (if applicable).
>
> Why the respondent is important.
>
> Promise of confidentiality.
>
> Explanation of the identification number appearing on the questionnaire.
>
> Reward for participation.
>
> What to do if questions arise.
>
> Thank you.

funnel sequence
The procedure of asking the most general (or unrestricted) question about the topic under study first, followed by successively more restricted questions.

Funnel and Inverted-Funnel Sequences. Typically a **funnel sequence** is followed when the respondent is assumed to have some ideas about a topic. *Funnel sequence* refers to the procedure of asking the most general (or unrestrictive) question about the topic under study first, followed by successively more restrictive questions. This approach minimizes the chance that early questions will condition or bias responses to questions that come later. The funnel sequence technique is also useful when the interviewer needs to ascertain something about the respondent's frame of reference. A funnel sequence used to determine first what a respondent thinks about a new product concept in general and then his or her reactions to specific end-benefit claims is shown in the next example. If the ordering of the questioning is reversed, responses dealing with *aroma* might be emphasized when responding to the second question simply because the respondent has been sensitized to this particular end benefit.

EXAMPLE

1. What is your overall reaction to the new product concept?
2. Did you find anything hard to believe about the new product concept?
3. Did you find the claims made about aroma hard to believe?

inverted-funnel sequence
Sequence inverted in the sense that the questioning begins with specific questions and concludes with the respondent answering the general question.

In other instances, an **inverted-funnel sequence** can be useful. This technique inverts the funnel sequence in the sense that questioning begins with specific questions and concludes with general ones. Such an approach compels respondents to consider certain specific points in reaching their evaluations. This approach is useful when the interviewer wishes to ensure that all respondents base their evaluations on similar specific factors. The inverted-funnel sequence approach appears most useful for low-salience topics, that is, topics about which respondents are without strong feelings or about which they have not formulated a point of view.

Note that the funnel sequence approach is useful only in personal and telephone interviews. In mail and other self-administered questionnaires the respondent can circumvent the funnel design by looking over the entire questionnaire before starting to answer it. The inverted-funnel sequence approach can be used in all types of interviews since no bias is introduced if the respondent examines all of the questions before beginning.

Changing Topics. Questionnaires frequently include questions that deal with more than one topic. In such instances all the questions that deal with one topic should be listed together before a new topic begins. Transition phrases should be included between topics to direct attention to the next topic (e.g., We are now going to ask you about. . . .)

Q4. Have you heard of brand X?   EXAMPLE

Yes [*Ask a.*]
No [*Skip to Q8.*]
Not sure [*Skip to Q8.*]

If Yes,
a. Have you used brand X in the last 30 days?
Yes [*Skip to Q7.*]
No [*Ask b.*]
b. Have you used brand X in the last 6 months?
Yes [*Skip to Q6.*]
No [*Ask Q5.*]

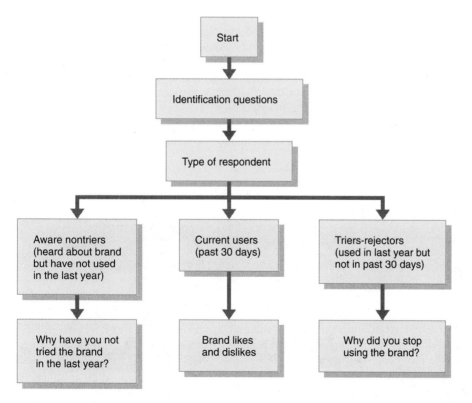

In this instance, answers to awareness and usage questions are used to ensure that all segments of the sample fall into one and only one question sequence.

Filter Questions. A question that is asked to determine which branching question, if any, should be asked is referred to as a **filter question**. Such questions are included to ensure that all possible contingencies are covered and to reduce the chance of interviewer or respondent error; they are also used to encourage complete responses.

Skip patterns in a questionnaire can become quite complicated for an interviewer or respondent. In many instances the appropriate skip pattern is based on several questions. A simple procedure the researcher can use to account for all contingencies is to make a flowchart of the logical possibilities and then to prepare the filter question and instructions according to the flowchart.

The example on the previous page provides an illustrative flowchart along with the corresponding filter questions. We see that a *yes* answer to question 4 qualifies the respondent as being aware of brand X. Questions 4a and 4b establish three distinct respondent groups and determine which questions will be asked next. For instance, respondents answering *no* to question 4a and *no* to question 4b constitute *aware nontriers* and are next asked about why they have not tried the brand in the last year.

Placement of filter questions is important, and two guidelines may be helpful. First, if only a single filter is used, it should be placed just before, or as close as possible to, its corresponding branching question. The interviewer wants to avoid having to flip back and forth in the questionnaire. Second, if multiple filter questions are required, they should all be asked before proceeding to more detailed questions. If all of the filter questions are not asked before the more detailed questions, respondents may discover that they can avoid answering detailed questions by giving certain answers to the filter questions.

Exhibit 12–4 provides a checklist of the major points that should be considered when planning the flow of the questionnaire.

Layout Considerations[11]

Use of Booklets. There are at least three reasons to recommend the use of a booklet format in questionnaires: (1) Booklets prevent pages from being lost or misplaced, (2) booklets allow the interviewer or respondent to move from one page to another more easily, and (3) booklets look professional and are easy to follow when used in self-administered interviews.

Appearance of Self-Administered Questionnaires. Just the appearance of mail and other self-administered questionnaires can have a dramatic effect on the respondents' cooperation. As a general rule, a questionnaire should look as easy to read (and answer) as possible to the respondent and should have a professional appearance. The date, title of the study, and name of the organization conducting the study should appear on the first page of the questionnaire.

---

[11]Parts of the following discussion are adapted from Sudman and Bradburn, *Asking Questions*, pp. 208–28.

---

1. Start with easy, salient, nonthreatening, but necessary questions. Put the more difficult or threatening questions near the end of the questionnaire. Never start a mail questionnaire with an open-ended question that requires a great deal of writing.

2. Since some demographic questions are threatening, put these questions at the end of the interview. If at all possible, avoid asking demographic questions first.

3. For personal interviews use funneling procedures to minimize order effects. Start with the general questions and move to specific questions. For low-salience topics, however, it may be necessary to ask questions about specific dimensions of the topic before asking for a summary view.

4. If questions deal with more than one topic, complete all questions on a single topic before moving to a new topic.

5. When switching topics, use a transitional phrase to make it easier for respondents to switch their trains of thought.

6. To ensure that all contingencies are covered, make a flowchart for filter questions. Filter questions should not require extensive page flipping by the interviewer or respondent or require remembering answers to earlier questions.

7. If multiple filter questions will be asked, try to ask all of them before asking the more detailed questions. Otherwise, respondents may learn how to avoid answering detailed questions.

Source: S. Sudman and N. M. Bradburn, *Asking Questions* (San Francisco: Jossey-Bass, 1983), pp. 207–8.

EXHIBIT 12–4
—
Checklist of Major
Points to Consider
When Planning the
Flow of the
Questionnaire

Use of Blank Space and Typeface. A tendency to guard against in questionnaire design is crowding questions together to try to make the questionnaire look shorter. Crowded questions with little blank space between them can, in fact, give the impression of a complicated questionnaire. And the respondent's perception of the difficulty involved is extremely relevant to cooperation rates, especially in self-administered questionnaires. Less-crowded questions with ample blank space look easier and generally result in higher cooperation rates and fewer response errors by interviewers or respondents. Along these same lines, the type should be sufficiently large and clear so as to cause no strain in reading; avoid photoreducing questionnaires whenever possible.

Color Coding. Although color does not influence response rates to questionnaires, or make them easier for interviewers to use, color coding can help in some respects. Printing a questionnaire designed for a certain group of respondents on one color of paper and a questionnaire designed for another respondent group on a different colored paper is useful. For example, one color could be used for respondents who have used a particular product in a test involving a number of products and a different color could be used for respondents who have not used the product.

Question Numbering. There are at least two good reasons for numbering questions in a questionnaire. First, numbering questions may help alert the interviewer or the respondent that a question has been skipped inadvertently. Second, numbering questions helps in developing interviewer instructions, especially with regard to appropriate skip patterns.

Fitting Questions on a Page.　Splitting questions, or response categories, between one page and the next is not recommended. Interviewers or respondents may assume that a question has ended at the end of a page, and this will result in misleading answers based on incomplete questions. You should also generally avoid splitting a series of related questions.

Interviewer Instructions.　Directions for individual questions should be placed as near as possible to the questions and usually just before or just after the question, depending on the nature of the directions. If the instructions deal with how the respondent should answer or how the question should be administered, they should be placed before the question. If, on the other hand, the instructions relate to how the answers should be recorded or how the interviewer should probe, they should be placed after the question. Distinctive type (e.g., capitals or italics) is commonly used to distinguish instructions from questions. The objective is to avoid having interviewers mistakenly read directions to respondents as part of the question.

Response Category Format.　The example below presents unacceptable formats of commonly asked demographic questions. Beginning questionnaire designers often make mistakes like these. In the example note that the page looks crowded and confusing. It is quite possible that respondents may be confused about whether the blank lines should be used with the response categories before or after them. This confusion can lead to response errors. Note also that there is no space provided for responses to question Q29.

EXAMPLE

Q22. Your sex: _____ Male _____ Female

Q23. Your present marital status: _____ Never married _____ Married _____ Separated _____ Widowed

Q24. Number of children you have in each age group: _____ Under five years _____ 5–13 _____ 14–18 _____ 19–25 and over

Q25. Your present age: _____

Q26. Do you own (or are you buying) your own home? _____ No _____ Yes

Q27. Did you serve in the armed forces? _____ No _____ Yes (Year entered _____ Year discharged _____)

Q28. Are you presently: _____ Employed _____ Unemployed _____ Retired _____ Full-time homemaker

Q29. Please describe the usual occupation of the principal wage earner in your household, including title, kind of work, and kind of company or business. (If retired, describe the usual occupation before retirement.)

Q30. What was your approximate net family income, from all sources, before taxes, in 1992?

Less than $3,000_____	10,000 to 12,999_____	20,000 to 24,999_____
3,000 to 4,999_____	13,000 to 15,999_____	25,000 to 30,000_____
5,000 to 6,999_____	16,000 to 19,999_____	Over $30,000_____
7,000 to 9,999_____		

Another tendency of beginning questionnaire designers is to place category or column headings in a sideways format to conserve space, as the next example illustrates. Sideways formatting requires constant shifting of the page or head-twisting to read the category headings. A better presentation is to design a questionnaire with ample space for conveniently placed category headings.

EXAMPLE

Much has been said about the quality of life offered by various sizes of cities. We would like to know how you feel. First, please show which city size is best for each of the characteristics by putting an "X" in the appropriate column by each item. Second, please look back over the list and show which three of these characteristics would be most important to you if you were selecting a new community in which to live by ranking them from 1 (most important) to 3 (third most important).

	City below 10,000 People	City of 10,000 to 49,999 People	City of 50,000 to 149,999 People	City of 150,000 People or Over
Equality of opportunities for all residents, regardless of race				
Place in which to raise children				
Community spirit and pride				
General mental health of residents				
Adequacy of medical care				
Protection of individual freedom and privacy				
Friendliness of people to each other				
Adequacy of police protection				
General satisfaction of residents				
Respect for law and order				
Lowest costs for public services (like water, sewer, and police)				
Recreational and entertainment opportunities				

Source: From D. A. Dillman, *Mail and Telephone Surveys: The Total Method* (New York: John Wiley & Sons, 1978), p. 139.

The generally accepted standard is to use vertical answer formats for individual questions, which means that the interviewer or respondent will be reading down a single column.

Another formatting strategy is to use *grids*, which are appropriate when there are a number of simultaneous questions that use the same set of response categories (e.g., What brands of toothpaste have you ever heard of? Which brand or brands of toothpaste have you used in the past 30 days? Which *one* brand do you use most often?). A grid format requires instructing the interviewer or respondent to record the response in the appropriate column. (See the following example.)

EXAMPLE

Fragrances

5a. [*Hand respondent card* A.] Listed on this card are several brands of fragrances. Would you please tell me which of these brands you have personally used in the past three months? [*Circle all mentioned below in column 5a.*]

5b. Which brands, if any, have you personally used in the past month? [*Circle all mentioned below in column 5b.*]

5c. Now, which one of these brands would you say you personally use most often? [*Circle one below in column 5c.*]

	(5a) Past 3 Months	(5b) Past Month	(5c) Most Often
Arpège	1 (20)	1 (23)	1 (26)
Aviance	2	2	2
Avon (all)	3	3	3
Babe	4	4	4
Cachet	5	5	5
Chanel No. 5	6	6	6
Chantilly	7	7	7
Charlie	8	8	8
Emeraude	9	9	9
Estée	1 (21)	1 (24)	1 (27)
Farouche	2	2	2
Intimate	3	3	3
Jean Naté	4	4	4
Je Reviens	5	5	5
Jontue	6	6	6
Joy	7	7	7
L'Air du Temps	8	8	8
Masumi	9	9	9
My Sin	1 (22)	1 (25)	1 (28)
Norell	2	2	2
Nuance	3	3	3
Rive Gauche	4	4	4
Shalimar	5	5	5
Tabu	6	6	6
Tigress	7	7	7
White Shoulders	8	8	8
Wind Song	9	9	9
Youth Dew	0	0	0
Other (specify)			
_____	X	X	X
_____			
None			Y

[*Take back card A.*]

Skip Instructions. Skip instructions are communicated to interviewers or respondents by two methods: verbal instructions and arrows that point to the next question. Both methods are acceptable.

Several guidelines should be followed with regard to skip instructions. First, the instruction should be placed immediately after the answer that generates the skip, not after the question. This format ensures that the interviewer or respondent will not forget or ignore the instructions. Second, skip instructions do not belong at the beginning of a subsequent question when there have been questions in between. For example, the instructions

> [If the respondent answered yes to Q10, ask Q15.
> Otherwise skip to Q12.]

placed at the beginning of question 15 would require the interviewer to turn back to locate the respondent's answer to question 10. In this case the skip instructions should be placed after the response to the filter question (that is, question 10), and the appropriate response categories should be placed before the follow-up question. Backward flow should be avoided.

Precoding. It is important when constructing the questionnaire to consider how the data ultimately will be processed and analyzed. If processing and analysis decisions are reserved until after the interviewing is complete, uncorrectable problems are likely to surface. Experienced researchers generally do as much precoding preparation as possible. Precoding of closed-ended questions and precolumning of the entire questionnaire is completed before using the questionnaire in the field. As we discuss in some detail in Chapter 13, precoding involves assigning a numerical value to every possible response to a closed-ended question. Precolumning involves assigning each question and response category contained in the questionnaire to a specific location in the data file, which allows the information to be "read-in" properly by the computer.

Exhibit 12–5 (see page 352) provides a checklist of the major points that should be considered when designing the questionnaire layout.

Pretesting the Questionnaire

Pretests are indispensable to the development of good questionnaires. In fact, the effectiveness of the itemized-question format is largely attributable to pretesting, which is necessary to determine the appropriate set of response categories. A thorough pretest exposes the potential for both respondent and interviewer error. There are at least five considerations involved in pretesting.[12]

1. *What items should be pretested?* All aspects of the questionnaire, including layout, question sequence, word meaning, question difficulty, branching instructions, and so on, should be part of the pretest.

---

[12]Our pretesting discussion is based on Shelby D. Hunt, Richard D. Sparkman, Jr., and James Wilcox, "The Pretest in Survey Research: Issues and Preliminary Findings," *Journal of Marketing Research*, May 1982, pp. 269–73.

EXHIBIT 12–5

Checklist of Major
Points to Consider
When Designing the
Format of the
Questionnaire

1. Use booklet format for ease in reading and turning pages and to prevent lost pages.

2. A mail or self-administered questionnaire should look easy to answer and should be professionally designed and printed. The date, the title of the study, and the name of the organization conducting the study should appear on the first page of the questionnaire.

3. Do not crowd questions. Be sure that sufficient space is left for open-ended questions since the answer will not be longer than the space provided.

4. Use sufficiently large and clear type so that there is no strain in reading.

5. Colored covers or sections of the questionnaire may be helpful to interviewers when multiple forms or complex skipping patterns are used.

6. Each question should be numbered, and subparts of a question should be lettered to prevent questions from being omitted in error and to facilitate the use of skip instructions. Indent subparts of questions.

7. Do not split a question between two pages because interviewers or respondents may think that the question is completed at the end of a page.

8. Provide directions and probes for specific questions at appropriate places in the questionnaire; identify these directions with distinctive type, such as capitals or italics.

9. Use vertical answer formats for individual questions.

10. Place skip instructions immediately after the answer to the filter question.

11. Precode all closed-ended questions to facilitate data processing and to ensure that all the data are in proper form for analysis.

12. Precolumn the questionnaire.

Source: S. Sudman and N. M. Bradburn, *Asking Questions* (San Francisco: Jossey-Bass, 1983), pp. 290–310.

2. *How should the pretest be conducted?* To whatever extent possible, the pretest should involve administering the questionnaire in an environment and context identical to the one to be used in the final survey. Essential features of a pretest are **debriefing** and/or **protocol analysis**. Debriefing, which takes place after a respondent has completed the questionnaire, involves asking respondents to explain their answers, to state the meaning of each question, and to describe any problems they had completing the questionnaire. Protocol analysis calls for the respondent to "think aloud" while completing the questionnaire.

debriefing
Procedure of asking respondents to explain their answers, to state the meaning of each question, and to describe any problems they had with answering or completing the questionnaire.

protocol analysis
Procedure in which the respondent "thinks aloud" while completing the questionnaire.

3. *Who should conduct the pretest?* In the case of telephone and personal pretest interviews, a number of parties should participate. First, the project director and/or person responsible for developing the questionnaire should complete several pretest interviews. The majority of the pretest interviews should be conducted by regular staff interviewers. It is a good idea to assign both experienced and relatively new interviewers to do the pretest interviews.

4. *Who should be the respondents in the pretest?* Respondents involved in the pretest should resemble the target population as much as possible in terms of familiarity with the topic, attitudes and behaviors associated with the topic, general background characteristics, and so on. This is absolutely critical to administering a pretest.

5. *How large a sample is required for the pretest?* To a large degree, sample size depends on the variation of the target population. The more heterogenous the target population, the larger the pretest sample required. Complex questionnaires also warrant a large pretest sample.

Pretesting questionnaires should be taken seriously: "No amount of intellectual exercise can substitute for testing an instrument designed to communicate with ordinary people."[13]

INTERNATIONAL CONSIDERATIONS

The success of a survey, whether international or domestic, rests on the ability of the researcher to ask the right questions in a manner that increases the likelihood that the respondent will provide the desired information. Beyond this challenge, there are additional considerations that are specific to conducting research in foreign markets. Many factors add to the complexity and diversity of conducting market research in international markets. These include the following:[14]

1. *Understanding the culture.* The first point to recognize is that consumers worldwide are a varied lot. For example, Table 12–1 (see page 354) presents an index of per capita spending in Europe by product and country. Note that there are substantial differences in all of the per capita spending indices. The second point to recognize is that a thorough understanding of the culture is necessary if the researcher is to obtain satisfactory response rates. Aside from the problems associated with high rates of illiteracy, in some cultures a woman will not consent to an interview by a stranger, let alone a man. In other cultures men will be reluctant to discuss topics such as personal hygiene or preferences in clothing because they feel this would be beneath their dignity—and they most definitely will not address these issues in the presence of a female interviewer. In addition, it is difficult, if not impossible, for respondents to answer questions concerning goods and services that have never been available or are not commonly used in the community, or whose use is not well understood.

2. *Lack of secondary data.* The usually voluminous amounts of secondary data available in U.S. markets are, in most cases, simply not available in every international market, especially in developing countries. Even when data are available, they may be of variable quality. For example, population censuses in some countries are frequently based on estimates made by nonprofessionals (e.g., village elders), and data on income and sales from tax returns can be grossly inaccurate in countries where such information is routinely undeclared or underreported. Table 12–2 (see page 355) presents census data from the last conducted censuses for European countries.

---

[13]C. H. Backstom and G. D. Hursch, *Survey Research* (Evanston, Ill.: Northwestern University Press, 1963).

[14]For further discussion, see S. P. Douglas and S. Craig, *International Marketing Research* (Englewood Cliffs, N.J.: Prentice Hall, 1983), chapter 1.

TABLE 12–1   European Differences: An Index of Per Capita Spending

	Luxembourg	Denmark	West Germany*	France	Great Britain	Belgium	Italy	Netherlands	Spain	Ireland	Greece	Portugal
Total spending	116.4	114.6	111.8	109.8	105.8	105.7	104.2	101.5	74.4	59.9	59.7	52.1
Food	105.3	92.7	91.3	114.9	83.8	102.4	121.4	89.2	94.2	85.0	105.0	79.6
Drinks	111.5	126.0	155.9	115.6	79.8	74.6	75.2	105.7	66.2	200.8	61.4	64.2
Tobacco	258.8	124.4	98.2	101.8	100.0	125.8	103.8	112.5	89.9	96.0	154.1	0.6
Apparel and footwear	89.8	89.7	128.4	93.7	109.7	86.3	118.6	101.4	54.2	55.0	59.5	49.4
Housing	87.4	126.7	79.7	94.0	117.5	83.8	112.2	80.0	131.2	51.6	38.2	78.0
Heat and light	222.7	141.3	139.3	101.5	119.6	142.0	78.4	133.6	44.2	68.4	40.0	32.9
Furniture	180.2	110.6	171.8	120.7	72.4	100.7	87.9	112.1	50.7	30.9	23.6	35.0
Household textiles	82.7	119.7	128.8	111.5	73.7	93.5	98.3	71.8	100.1	60.5	105.5	63.3
Home appliances	168.2	101.7	128.5	100.3	132.7	117.3	93.9	81.4	54.0	39.1	48.9	28.7
Other household	98.6	79.7	108.9	117.7	74.5	174.1	118.9	101.5	73.2	50.1	76.1	62.8
Health and medical	88.4	83.3	130.8	146.8	93.4	128.4	83.7	114.7	45.6	53.2	36.4	31.7
Transportation, vehicles	244.1	133.6	150.4	100.4	113.1	132.4	96.6	99.6	39.3	37.5	17.6	17.2
Transportation, maintenance	190.0	109.3	130.3	123.9	97.6	99.1	84.3	62.3	88.8	50.2	30.7	63.5
Public transportation	25.9	104.9	75.4	88.9	139.2	46.0	105.4	68.8	93.7	41.8	264.6	34.8
Communications	246.3	155.6	124.7	114.5	81.1	52.6	100.8	185.0	45.0	35.8	178.6	15.1
Entertainment, education, and legal	87.9	152.3	116.7	99.5	112.0	107.5	112.8	114.8	51.5	74.6	42.9	56.3
Restaurants and hotels	83.7	52.4	68.1	100.7	138.4	89.8	105.1	63.7	139.7	8.7	76.8	31.5
Other	155.8	187.3	93.8	109.2	123.0	107.5	115.8	127.5	56.7	45.8	27.2	30.2

Note: 100 equals the average for Europe. Low indices, in some cases, reflect sales to foreign nationals.

*Prior to reunification.

Source: *Donnés Sociales 1990*, Institut National de la Statistique et des Études Économiques, Paris, France.

	Population (millions)	Last Census	Lowest Level of Geodemographic Data Available
EEC Nations:			
West Germany	62.168	May 25, 1987	Teil (3,000 to 7,000 people)
Italy	57.664	October 25, 1981	Sezione di Censimento (an average of 125 families)
United Kingdom	57.366	April 5, 1981	Ward (8,000 to 10,000 people)
France	56.358	March 4, 1982	Chef lieu (up to 20,000 people)
Spain	39.269	March 1, 1981	Municipality (an average of 4,000 people)
Netherlands*	14.936	February 28, 1971	Postal code (an average of 15 households)
Portugal	10.354	March 16, 1981	Seccao/quarteiras (an average of 151 people)
Greece	10.028	April 5, 1981	Commune (an average of 1,500 people)
Belgium	9.909	March 1, 1981	Quarterier (an average of 508 people)
Denmark†	5.131	November 9, 1970	Commune (an average of 300 people)
Ireland	3.500	April 13, 1986	Ward (3,000 to 15,000 people)
Luxembourg	0.384	March 31, 1981	Commune (an average of 3,254 people)
Eastern Europe:			
Poland	37.777	December 7, 1978	n.a.
Yugoslavia	23.842	March 31, 1981	n.a.
Romania	23.273	January 5, 1977	n.a.
East Germany	16.307	December 31, 1981	n.a.
Czechoslovakia	15.683	November 1, 1980	n.a.
Hungary	10.569	January 1, 1980	n.a.
Bulgaria	8.934	December 4, 1985	n.a.

TABLE 12–2

European Scorecard: Census Data

*Last census supplemented by sample surveys and computerized population register.

†A computerized population register provides more up-to-date figures for 1976 and 1981.

Source: Midyear 1990 population projections and date of last census prepared by the Center for International Research; U.S. Bureau of the Census; CACI Limited in London; and embassy information offices.

3. *Cost of collecting primary data.* A researcher faced with collecting market-research information in international markets soon discovers that the costs of data collection can be considerably higher without a network of established marketing firms. Many foreign countries lack companies that are experienced in collecting information, which means that a sponsoring firm will have to invest in the development of sampling frames and other materials and in the training of interviewers and other necessary personnel.

Methodological Considerations

A number of methodological considerations influence the construction of questionnaires to be used in international research studies. These methodological problems essentially arise from two basic factors: (1) the complex cultural differences in the meaning of products and activities and (2) the paucity of standardized data-collection instruments to measure marketing-related variables.

functional equivalence
Refers to the extent to which the same product in two or more countries is used for the same function.

Functional Equivalence. The extent to which the same product is used for the same—or a similar—function in two or more countries is known as **functional equivalence.** However, possessions tend to be used for different functions in different societies. In India, for example, the accumulation of jewelry represents less an interest in the display of social status than in security and accumulation of wealth. Refrigerators, used to store food in some countries, are used primarily for chilling water and soft drinks in other countries.[15] When General Mills entered the United Kingdom's breakfast-cereal market, a box featured a freckled, red-haired, crew-cut kid saying, "Gee kids, it's great." What General Mills failed to recognize was that the British family is not as child oriented and permissive as the American family it was accustomed to, and that English parent-child relationships tend to be more authoritarian; consequently, the package had no appeal to the British housewife.[16]

A similar blunder was made by Binoca when it launched a talcum powder ad in newspapers in India. The ad showed an attractive, although apparently naked, woman dousing herself with talcum powder. The caption covering strategic portions of her body read: "Don't go wild—just enough is all you need of Binoca talc." The highly conservative Indian public found the advertisement distasteful and developed strong negative associations with the brand name.[17] To ask proper questions requires that researchers understand the functional equivalence, or lack thereof, of the activities being investigated.

conceptual equivalence
Refers to the extent to which the same concept has the same meaning in two or more countries.

Conceptual Equivalence. The extent to which the same concept (e.g., "family") has the same meaning in two or more countries is referred to as **conceptual equivalence.** However, concepts can have totally different meanings in different cultural environments. This requires the careful choice of the words used to convey the meaning of what the researcher is attempting to explore. The word *family*, for example, means something different in the United States, where it typically refers to only parents and children, than it does in many other cultures, where it may extend to grandparents, aunts, uncles, and other relatives.

Ethnic Influences. Researchers need to understand how the cultural values of a society will affect the approach to the research issue of interest. It may be possible

---

[15]Y. A. Choudhry, "Pitfalls of International Marketing Research: Are You Speaking French Like a Spanish Cow?" *ABER* 17, no. 4 (Winter 1986), pp. 18–28.

[16]David A. Ricks, Y. C. Fu, and S. Arpan, *International Business Blunders* (Columbus, Ohio: Grid, 1974).

[17]Ibid.

to research problems in one culture but not in another because of cultural taboos and different levels of abstraction. For example, researching attitudes and behaviors concerning personal hygiene products may simply not be possible in certain cultures where the norms clearly proscribe public discussion of such issues.

Instrument Equivalence. It may not be possible to use the same measuring instrument in every culture. For this reason the researcher may choose to use what are called *emic instruments. Emic* refers to analysis in terms of a situation's internal or functional elements. An **emic instrument** is one that is constructed specifically for investigating an attitude in a specific culture. Closed-ended questions, for example, may work well in one culture, but because of cultural differences may be inappropriate in others; certain categories of response may have to be omitted, or additional categories may have to be added. Open-ended questions also may pose some problems, especially in markets where the level of literacy is low and where interviewer bias is prominent. Other types of interviewing methods, such as focus groups and consumer panels, may face problems because of strong social-acquiescence tendencies that are the cultural norm in some countries.

emic instrument
An instrument constructed for investigating a construct in a specific culture.

In some instances the researcher may attempt to construct **etic instruments,** which are transcultural in application, relating to the behavioral analysis of attitudes considered in isolation. This would permit direct comparison of the same variable across cultures. Attempts at developing etic instruments have employed nonverbal instruments such as picture completion, TAT instruments, and semantic differentials.[18]

etic instrument
An instrument that can be used in different cultures to provide direct comparisons of the same variable across nations.

Instrument Translation. It may seem obvious to suggest that a survey developed in one country be carefully translated into the language of the country where it is going to be administered and assessed; however, mistakes can happen even in the case of literal equivalence. Classic examples of this are the translation into Flemish of General Motor's "Body by Fisher" slogan that became "Corpse by Fisher," and a U.S. airline's advertisement of its Boeing 747 "rendezvous lounge" that translated into Portuguese as the "prostitution chamber."[19]

Several translation methods have been used in international research projects:[20]

1. *Direct translation.* The survey undergoes a single translation from one language into another by a bilingual translator. This method, however, exposes the instrument to all the problems discussed above.

2. *Back translation.* A variation of direct translation, this method requires that the translated survey be translated back into the original language by another bilingual translator. This lets the researcher correct any meaning problems between the original and retranslated instruments. Note that back translation requires that equivalent terms for words or phrases exist in the other language, which may not always be the case.

---

[18]Choudhry, "Pitfalls of International Marketing Research," p. 23.
[19]See Ricks et al., *International Business Blunders.*
[20]Ibid., pp. 23–26.

3. *Decentering.* A hybrid of back translation, this method involves a successive iteration process: translation and retranslation of an instrument, each time by a different translator. The back-translated versions in the original language are compared sequentially. If discrepancies occur, the original is modified, and the process is repeated until both show the same or similar wordings. Generally, each iteration should show more convergence.

There are several ways to evaluate the quality of translations:

1. Have a monolinguist evaluate the translated questionnaire for clarity and comprehensiveness.
2. Determine the extent of change in the meaning between two versions examined by bilingual evaluators.
3. Assess the respondent's ability to answer the translated questions correctly.
4. Pretest both the original and the translated questionnaire with a bilingual individual.

Sampling and Fielding the Survey. In many countries telephone directories, census tract and block data, and detailed socioeconomic characteristics of the target population will not be available or are outdated. This adversely affects the ability to draw nonprobability as well as probability samples and to conduct personal interviews of any variety. For example, lacking age distributions for the target population, it is difficult for a marketing researcher to set representative age quotas. Moreover, in certain cultures, convenience samples are doomed to failure. In Saudi Arabia, for instance, because of the practice of purdah, the seclusion of women, shopping-mall interviews produce all-male samples.[21]

Inadequate mailing lists and rudimentary postal and telephone services can make marketing research in some countries extremely difficult. In many countries only a small percentage of the population has telephones, and an alarmingly large percentage of the telephone lines (over 50 percent) may be out of service at any one time.[22] Mail surveys suffer from similar problems. Delivery delays of weeks are common, and, in certain countries, expected response rates are lowered considerably because the questionnaire can be mailed back only at a post office.

The obstacles in conducting international marketing research studies are indeed formidable. Understanding the cultural environment in which the research is taking place is a necessary condition for success. The researcher must also avoid the tendency to blindly apply conventional research techniques and practices. Designing and implementing international research projects can be done effectively. It just takes effort and a sensitivity to asking the questions in a manner that increases the likelihood that respondents will provide the desired information.

---

[21]D. C. Pring, "American Firms Rely on Multinational Research Suppliers to Solve Marketing Problems Overseas," *Marketing News*, May 15, 1981, section 2, p. 2.

[22]"Cairo's Telephone System Improves," *World Business Weekly*, February 16, 1981, p. 19.

SUMMARY

In this chapter we have considered issues in questionnaire design and construction. The four major activities involved in questionnaire design are: (1) preliminary considerations, (2) asking questions, (3) constructing the questionnaire, and (4) pretesting the questionnaire. Our discussion emphasized general guidelines and offered basic principles involved in asking questions. The material on questionnaire construction focused on response formats, logical flow, and layout considerations. In our questionnaire pretest discussion we emphasized five decisions that the researcher must make. The remainder of the chapter considered the special case of conducting research in international markets, including methodological differences and concerns.

KEY CONCEPTS

mutual exclusivity	creation	filter questions	ethnic influences
loaded questions	open-ended questions	skip patterns	instrument equivalence
order bias	closed-ended questions	skip instructions	instrument translation
double-barreled questions	questionnaire flow	pretesting	direct translation
omission	funnel sequence	functional equivalence	back translation
telescoping	inverted-funnel sequence	conceptual equivalence	decentering

REVIEW QUESTIONS

1. Analyze the following questions and make any corrections needed.

   a. How much do you make?_____

   b. Which sporting event do you attend most frequently?

      _____ Baseball   _____ Hockey

      _____ Football   _____ Tennis

      _____ Basketball _____ Golf

   c. Do you agree with the president's intentions to lower taxes?

      _____ Strongly agree

      _____ Agree

      _____ Neither agree nor disagree

      _____ Disagree

   d. Name the last 3 movies you rented.

      _____

      _____

      _____

   e. How many hours of television do you watch in a typical week?

      _____ 0–10 hrs.   _____ 21–30 hrs.

      _____ 11–20 hrs.   _____ 30 or more hours.

   f. Don't you think MADD has saved many lives?

      _____ Yes   _____ No

   g. Check your favorite magazine.

      _____ *Time*   _____ *People*

      _____ *Newsweek*   _____ *Business Week*

      _____ *Money*   _____ *Life*

2. Select from the following list of open-ended questions those that would be better posed as closed-ended questions. Of those selected, rewrite them to make them closed-ended.

   − Exactly how much money does that job offer?

   − What are your favorite lines of clothing?

   − From which high school did you graduate?

   − How satisfied are you with your hair stylist?

   − Most of the office work gets done on which day of the week?

– Approximately how many jelly beans do you think there are in the jar?

3. Make up your own example to illustrate each of the following:
   a. Loaded question
   b. Double-barreled question
   c. An overlapping question
4. Distinguish among omission, telescoping, and crea-tion. Discuss how aided and unaided questions influence each of these response effects.

5. Develop an appropriate introduction for a questionnaire dealing with students' attitudes toward the university cafeteria.

6. Evaluate the following questionnaire before the owners of a new bar and grill pass it out. How could you improve it?

   1. What sex are you?
      _____ Male   _____ Female

   2. Are you part of the 67% who recently replied they were dissatisfied with the bars/restaurants in town?
      _____ Yes   _____ No

   3. What kind of music do you like to hear?
      _____ Rock   _____ Pop   _____ Jazz_____ Traditional country
      _____ Top 40   _____ Other

   4. Place an X on the line.

      The atmosphere is
      Good _____ Bad
      The managers are
      Good _____ Bad
      The service is
      Good _____ Bad

   5. About how much do you spend on a night out?
      _____ $0–$20.00   _____ $40.00–$60.00   _____ $20.00–$40.00
      _____ Above $60.00

   6. On a scale of 1 to 10, how would you rate your meal? _____

   7. Will you be coming back to see us soon?
      _____ Yes   _____ No

Data Processing and Tabulation

— Describe activities and elements in fielding a study.

— Describe the procedures for checking and editing questionnaires.

— Explain coding practices for closed-ended and open-ended questions.

— Describe the processes involved in transcribing raw data onto magnetic tape or disk or directly onto the computer.

INTRODUCTION

This chapter describes the activities necessary in administering a survey and in preparing the raw data for data analysis. The research activities to be described affect both the accuracy and the generalizability of the conclusions drawn from these data. The procedures and practices described serve two general purposes:

1. They establish, as far as possible, uniformity in fieldwork and in the processing of data.
2. They establish guidelines for the various steps in the processing of data.

FIELDING THE QUESTIONNAIRE

Fielding the questionnaire refers to the process of administering the data-collection instrument. We discuss how the data-collection (fieldwork) process actually works and describe procedures that are used to ensure that the information collected is, to the extent possible, free of errors caused by sloppy fieldwork.

Who Conducts Fieldwork?

You may recall from Chapter 1 our specification of three key players in the commercial marketing research business: corporations (manufacturers, the service industry, and the like), advertising agencies, and research suppliers. Corporations and ad agencies typically contract for a particular study, which the research supplier helps to design, execute, and analyze. The "execution" aspect includes data gathering.

At a research supplier, the data-collection function is the responsibility of the field department, a group normally headed by a director or vice president of field operations. Generally, the department is staffed by a number of field supervisors (who are responsible for day-to-day planning and control of specific studies), samplers (who purchase or establish samples firsthand), and people who provide clerical support for routing surveys to the interviewing sites and for checking the questionnaires in after data collection has been completed.

Depending on the supplier's size and staffing ability, data may be collected by personnel either within or outside the organization. It is fairly typical for medium-sized and large research firms to have their own WATS telephone-interviewing capabilities. Some companies such as Market Facts and MARC also have the capability to conduct full-scale, mall-intercept studies with their own personnel. In-house fieldwork operations give suppliers a competitive advantage because of cost efficiency and better quality control.

Suppliers that do not have their own means of data collection subcontract fieldwork to one or more of the thousands of independently owned and operated interviewing services. Many of these interviewing services are relatively small companies that conduct central-location personal interviews (mall intercept) and/or operate telephone interviewing facilities in one or more markets. An ever-decreasing number, however, conduct personal in-home (door-to-door) interviews.

Steps in Fielding a Study

The fielding of a study actually begins in the proposal stage of the research process (described in Chapter 2). At the time the supplier prepares its proposal, the project director and field director will discuss the research problem and a possible research method, including specification of the target audience, sampling, and interviewing methods. When all the study specifications have been determined, the field director prepares cost and timing estimates for conducting data collection. Activities in fielding a study follow this sequence:

1. Estimating costs.
2. "Alerting" the study.
3. Preparing field instructions.
4. Briefing.
5. Data collection.
6. Evaluation of fieldwork quality.

Estimating Costs. Estimating costs and time for conducting fieldwork is more an art than a science—no hard-and-fast rules exist. A sense of what it takes to collect the required number of interviews using a specific research approach comes from years of experience. Although there is no truly accurate estimation formula, there are a number of parameters you can consider in selecting specific sampling/interviewing methods.

In general, regardless of the method chosen, two factors determine the cost of the fieldwork: (1) incidence of qualified respondents and (2) questionnaire length.

Most studies require that respondents meet certain criteria in order to be interviewed. For example, a cola taste test may require a sample of people who have had at least two glasses of a carbonated cola beverage during the past week. Such individuals may account only for 35 percent of the population; that is, if you talk to 100 people, only 35 people will qualify (an incidence of 35 percent). As a general rule, the lower the incidence, the more people who must be screened for qualification, and the more the screening hours required.

The other key variable is questionnaire length. Interviewing hours are directly related to the amount of time it takes to administer a questionnaire to a qualified respondent. When questionnaire length goes beyond 15 to 20 minutes, other costs besides time can be incurred. With leisure time becoming more valuable, people tend to be less willing to participate in longer interviews. This results in lower cooperation rates for longer questionnaires; in this case, more screening may be needed and incentives may need to be used to increase response rates (see Chapter 7).

The effects of incidence and questionnaire length are compounded by administrative costs. An interviewing supplier, whether inside or outside the company, employs supervisors and other staff who are responsible for training personnel and supervising the interviews. These supervisory costs are usually covered by adding a percentage (about 50 to 60 percent) to the cost of interviewing.

Different costs are incurred depending on the type of interviewing method used. Exhibit 13–1 (see page 364) details one procedure for estimating the field costs for a telephone interview. Factors such as the time of day of the interview, sample administration and control, and the need for trained interviewers can affect the cost of data collection for whatever type of survey method used.

"Alerting" the Study. With a "ballpark" cost estimate and expected study specifications at hand, the field director begins to subcontract the data collection to one or more field services, whether they be internal or external to the research supplier. This process sounds easier than it is. After the cost estimate is constructed internally, the budgeted amount must be negotiated with the various services, usually through an oral agreement arranged by telephone. It is a real challenge for the field director to bring the study in under budget, given the variation of data-collection costs from market to market.

Once an agreement has been reached on the key parameters of the study in terms of sampling technique, questionnaire length, incidence, cost, and timing, an individual in the field department, usually called a *field supervisor*, prepares field instructions.

Preparing Field Instructions. The supplier formalizes the oral contract for services in its field instructions to the party (parties) conducting the fieldwork. Without mentioning the agreed-upon cost per interview, the instructions generally specify what are considered acceptable interviewing techniques, what can be expected from the field service operator or designated representative, and how

EXHIBIT 13–1
———
Fielding a Telephone
Study

Assumptions
A. Required sample size: $n = 300$
B. 225 = Number of telephone numbers an interviewer can dial per 8-hour shift assuming 6 1/2 productive hours
C. 65% = Category incidence rate
D. 60% = Cooperation rate
E. 15 minutes = Questionnaire length
F. 3 minutes = Interviewer checking time
G. $215 = Cost per workday

Calculating Interviews per Workday
1. Contacts per day = $B \times C \times D$
    $= 225 \times 0.65 \times 0.60$
    $= 87.75$
2. Contacts per hour = Contacts per day/6.5
    $= 87.75/6.5$
    $= 13.5$
3. Time in minutes to reach qualified contact
    $= 60/\text{Contacts per hour}$
    $= 60/13.5$
    $= 4.44$
4. Time to interview = $\begin{matrix} \text{Time in minutes} \\ \text{to reach qualified} \\ \text{respondent} \end{matrix} + \begin{matrix} \text{Interview} \\ \text{time} \end{matrix} + \begin{matrix} \text{Interview} \\ \text{checking} \\ \text{time} \end{matrix}$
    $= 4.44 + 15 + 3$
    $= 22.44$
5. Interviews completed per hour = 60/Time to complete interview
    $= 60/22.44$
    $= 2.67$
6. Interviews completed per workday = $6.5 \times$ Interviews completed per hour
    $= 6.5 \times 2.67$
    $= 17.36$

Calculating Field Costs
To determine field costs
1. Take completed interviews per workday (called *completes*):
    17.36
2. Divide required sample size by completes, which equals number of workdays needed to complete interviews:
    $300/17.36 = 17.28$
3. Field costs are equal to cost per workday to complete interviews including overhead and margin:
    $17.28 \times 215 = 3,715.2$
Hence, the field costs for the telephone survey are $3,715.20.

---

interviewers are to conduct the specific interview at hand. Instructions are commonly divided into three parts: general, supervisor, and interviewer.

1. *General instructions.* The general instructions to interviewers reiterate what is acceptable in both a technical and an ethical sense. They may include directions on how to screen respondents by asking questions as they are stated, rather than in a manner that increases the chance of finding a qualified respondent, and how to ask open-ended questions using the proper "probing" method.

2. *Instructions to the interviewing supervisor.* The instructions to the interviewing supervisor provide the field operators with guidance in the planning, organization, and control of the fieldwork for which they are responsible. They itemize all materials shipped for interviewers to use, such as questionnaires, display mate-

rials, report forms, and product. A second section of the instructions describes the organization and control of the sample; for example, it answers such questions as

- Who is a qualified respondent?
- How should quota groups be filled?
- How is incidence of the groups recorded, and how and when should the key figures be reported to the supplier?
- When and where should the sample be selected?

A third section of the supervisor's instructions describes the interviewing procedure itself, as it will be conveyed to the interviewers at a briefing session. Finally, the agreed-upon work schedule is laid out, and billing instructions are provided.

3. *Interview instructions.* The interviewers' instructions are key to valid and reliable data generation. They specify detailed sample selection and questionnaire administration procedures on a question-by-question basis. Interviewer instructions provide direction so that fieldwork is conducted in a consistent manner by all who are involved. (See From the World of Research 13–1 on pages 366–67.)

Briefing.   Having received the necessary materials and instructions from the supplier, the field operator holds a meeting of all interviewers taking part in the study. At the briefing session, which can be two to three hours long, the field service supervisor establishes what is expected of each interviewer working on the study. The field instructions are reviewed, and each interviewer gets a chance to administer the questionnaire before actually meeting with respondents. The briefing is typically held on the day that interviewing begins to keep the instructions clear in the interviewers' minds.

Data Collection.   Obviously, key to the quality of a study are the data. If quality data are not collected and provided in a timely manner, the marketing research effort is a waste of money.

The time needed for data collection can vary from a number of days to a number of months, depending on the incidence and/or the difficulty in finding the group under study, the length of interview, the sample size, and the number of interviewers working on the study. Typical studies take less than two weeks to complete.

The quality of fieldwork is enhanced by good communication between the supplier's field department and its subcontractors, the field services. This process begins with the initial telephone contact, continues with good written instructions by the supplier and daily progress reporting by the service, and concludes with the suppliers' feedback in the form of an independent validation report, as we describe below.

Evaluation of Fieldwork Quality.   At the completion of the data-collection phase, the interviewer's work is scrutinized in at least two ways. *check-in* and *validation*. The completed work from a particular field service is usually collected by one of the supplier's field supervisors; this is called the *check-in process*.

*From the World
of Research*
—
13–1

Interviewer Instructions—Be Precise!

Instructions to the interviewers should leave nothing to the imagination—they must be precise and unambiguous. A screener questionnaire for a carbonated soft drink study illustrates the degree of specificity that is required.

**Carbonated Soft Drinks
(Screening Questionnaire)**

Time Interview Begins: _____   ☐ 1/5-1 ☐
Time Interview Ends: _____
Total Time: _____   ☐ 1/6 ☐   ☐ 1/7 ☐ _____
Hello, I'm _____ from **Dimensions III**, a national market research company. We're conducting a study in your area, and I would like to ask you a few questions.

1. Are any members of your family or any of your close friends employed in any of the following occupations? [*Read list.*]

	Yes	No
Soft drink manufacturer or distributor	[ ]	[ ]
Selling soft drinks, vegetables, or fruit (wholesale or retail)	[ ]	[ ]
Advertising, sales promotion, public relations, or marketing research	[ ]	[ ]
Any form of radio or TV advertising	[ ]	[ ]
Editing or publishing	[ ]	[ ]

   [*If "Yes" to any of the above occupations, terminate and record in "Col. 1" on Call Record Sheet. Erase and reuse Questionnaire.*]
   [*Otherwise, continue with Q2.*]

2. Have you participated in any market research studies in the past three months?
   Yes [ ] [*Terminate and record in "Col. 2" on Call Record Sheet. Erase and reuse Questionnaire.*]
   No [ ] [*Ask Q3.*]

3. Which, if any, of the following products have *you, yourself* consumed at home in the past month?

		Yes	No
Instant coffee	☐ 1/9 ☐	[ ]-1	[ ]-2
Frozen orange juice	☐ 1/10 ☐	[ ]-1	[ ]-2
Carbonated soft drink	☐ 1/11 ☐	[ ]-1	[ ]-2

   [*Terminate and record in "Col. 3" on Call Record Sheet. Erase and reuse Questionnaire.*]

Questionnaires are counted to make sure that the necessary quotas (or cells) have been completed properly. For example, a quota for age might be 18–34 = 60%, 35–50 = 30%, and 51 + = 10%. Questionnaires usually are checked further in specific areas relating to complicated screening questions, skip patterns, open-ended question probing, and so on. Further details on check-in procedures are discussed in the following sections.

The second important quality check on fieldwork is making sure that the interview has actually taken place—the validation process. Some percentage, usually between 10 and 20 percent, of all respondents reported to have been interviewed

4. As you know, there are several brands of carbonated soft drinks. During the past three months, what specific brands of carbonated soft drinks have *you, yourself,* consumed at home [*Do not read list.*]

1/12 [ ]-1 Dr Pepper
      [ ]-2 Coke
      [ ]-3 Classic Coca-Cola
      [ ]-4 7UP
      [ ]-5 Sprite
      [ ]-6 Slice
      [ ]-7 Pepsi
      [ ]-8 Cherry Coca-Cola
      [ ]-9 RC Cola
      [ ]-0 Mountain Dew
      [ ]-x Other Brand _____
      [ ]-y Diet Brand _____

[INTERVIEWER'S INSTRUCTIONS:

1. *If respondent mentioned any of the soft drink brands in Q4, (boxes 1-x) continue to <u>blue</u> questionnaire and count toward nondiet soft drink quota.*

2. *If respondent <u>did not mention</u> any soft drink brand in Q4 but mentioned some diet carbonated soft drink brand (box y) continue to <u>yellow</u> questionnaire and count toward diet soft drink quota.*

3. *If any of the quotas above have been filled, terminate and record in appropriate over quota "Col. 4" on Call Record Sheet.*]

Among other things, note that the interviewer is *explicitly* instructed when to

1. Terminate the interview (see question 1).
2. Ask the next question (see question 2).
3. Read the set of appropriate answers (see question 1).
4. Not read the set of appropriate answers (see question 4).

The instructions given to the interviewers also clarify what to do after the screening questions have been asked. For example, the respondent receives a blue or yellow questionnaire, depending on his/her answer to question 4. Finally, the screener questionnaire has been precoded—examine, for example, questions 3 and 4.

are called again and asked a few questions to verify that the interview did take place. These questions may involve qualifying criteria (e.g., specific product usage) and/or questions generally related to the study (e.g., "Do you remember trying two cola soft drinks?"). When respondents cannot answer these questions satisfactorily, their interviews are often declared invalid and not processed. If more than one invalid questionnaire is traced to a given interviewer, it is often the practice to perform a 100 percent validation of that interviewer. If the interviewer was cheating, then all of his/her interviews would be discarded and the interviewer would not be paid.

STEPS IN PROCESSING THE DATA

Several functions must be performed in preparing the data for analysis. The major steps in processing the data are

1. Check-in.
2. Editing.
3. Coding.
4. Transferring the data.
5. Table specifications.

Check-In

check-in procedure
Initial step in data processing; involves a check of all question-naires for completeness and interviewing quality and a count of usable questionnaires by re-quired quota and/or use groups as per study design.

The **check-in procedure** involves checking a job in from the field. Activities in-volved in the check-in procedure are

1. A check of all questionnaires for completeness and interviewing quality.
2. A count of usable questionnaires by required quota and/or cell groups.

Checking for Acceptable Questionnaires. A questionnaire received from the field must be inspected to determine whether it is acceptable for use in the study. Several problems relating to completeness and interviewing quality can cause re-jection of a questionnaire:

1. Portions of the questionnaire, or key questions, are unanswered.
2. There is evidence that the respondent did not understand the instructions for filling out the questionnaire and/or did not take the task seriously. In the former instance, it may be obvious that skip directions were not followed properly; in the latter instance, answers to the questions may show very little variance, say, all 1s or all 7s on a seven-point rating scale.
3. The returned questionnaire is physically incomplete, with one or more pages missing.
4. The questionnaire has been filled out by someone who should have been screened out of the sample, that is, a respondent who does not qualify for the target population.
5. The questionnaire has been completed properly but returned after a pre-established cutoff date.

Check-in personnel should keep notes on the quality of the fieldwork through-out the process, as well as during subsequent processing functions, for feedback to local supervisors.

Counting the Questionnaires. A count of usable questionnaires by required quota and/or cell groups must be maintained to detect any problems in adhering to the sampling requirements and acceptable attention levels specified in the study design. Shortages must be identified and any corrective action determined while the study is still in the field. The local supervisor should forward returned questionnaires on schedule to the research firm so that check-in, editing, and code building can start as soon as possible, as opposed to holding questionnaires until all fieldwork is completed.

Editing

Editing involves reviewing the questionnaires for maximum accuracy and precision. Editing instructions are written to include as complete a check as possible to evaluate the consistency and accuracy of responses. When two answers are inconsistent—for example, the respondent indicates no familiarity with the test brand but also indicates that the brand was purchased on the last shopping trip—it may be possible to determine which, if either, of the two responses is correct. When this is not possible, both answers should be discarded. With respect to accuracy, the person responsible for editing concentrates on signs of interviewer bias or cheating; for example, common patterns of responses across different questionnaires for the same interviewer can signal potential problems. Finally, in addition to accuracy and consistency, the person who conducts the editing function is also concerned with response legibility, response clarity, and response completeness.

> **editing process**
> *Review of the questionnaires for maximum accuracy and precision.*

In all cases, the editor follows the editing instructions in resolving any ambiguities and may consult with the interviewer or recorder.

Coding Procedures

Put simply, **coding** involves assigning a numerical value (code) or alphanumeric symbol to represent (1) a specific response to a specific question and (2) the column position that the designated code or symbol will occupy on a data record. The coding process entails several different activities. For certain types of question formats (such as closed-ended questions), the coding specifications are designated before fieldwork begins (**precoding**). Coding specifications for open-ended questions are much more likely to be designated after the questionnaires have been returned from the field (**postcoding**), although in certain instances a coding scheme for such questions can be developed before completion of the fieldwork.

> **coding**
> *Assignment of a numerical value (code) or alphanumerical symbol to represent a specific response to a specific question along with the column position that the designated code or symbol will occupy on a data record.*

Coding language includes two special uses of terminology: case and record. **Case** refers to the unit of analysis for the study; in other words, a case is that thing, object, person, or whatever was interviewed or used to supply the answers to the survey questions. A respondent is the most common unit of analysis in commercial marketing research studies, so each respondent would constitute a case. The total number of cases equals the sample size.

> **precoding**
> *Coding specifications designated prior to fieldwork.*

Record refers to a string of coded data in machine-readable format. For historical reasons, it has become customary to view a record as consisting of 80 field positions where each field position contains the coded responses for a specific question. The early way of transferring raw data from questionnaire to computer was via a computer card with 80 vertical columns. Data were literally holes punched onto a card by a keypunch machine.

> **postcoding**
> *Coding specifications designated after the questionnaires have been returned from the field.*

Today data are entered into a computer memory via online CRT workstations. Tab houses normally use personal computers and programming that simulates a keypunch machine, with data first entered onto a floppy disk and then, in most cases, uploaded onto a mainframe computer. If the data take up more than 80

> **case**
> *The unit of analysis for the study.*

> **record**
> *A string of coded data in a machine-readable format.*

field positions (columns), another record is utilized; if the data exhaust the next 80 field positions (columns), yet another record is utilized, and so on until all of the data have been recorded. Thus, a case can consist of one or many records, depending on the number of questions asked; together the number of cases and the number of records per case define the data set.

Issues of data processing and analysis are best addressed during questionnaire construction. If processing and analysis of the data are considered only after the interviewing is complete, uncorrectable problems are likely to surface. Experienced researchers generally do as much preparation as possible for data processing before the questionnaire is printed. Advance preparation undoubtedly saves substantial amounts of time and money and can eliminate questions that may not provide the needed information.

Coding Closed-Ended Questions. Precoding and precolumning of the entire questionnaire are the two principal activities in preparing the data for processing. Precoding involves assigning a code number to every response to a closed-ended question; open-ended questions generally are not precodable. The precoding activity involves designating a coding scheme prior to undertaking fieldwork, and the actual codes as well as the field positions are printed on the questionnaire. The next example, which concerns breakfast foods and beverages (see next page), and Exhibit 13–2 show how this is done.

From Exhibit 13–2 we see that there are two records per case. The first respondent (case number 001) answered yes to consuming frozen waffles (a 1 in column 8 of record 1), frozen orange juice (a 1 in column 10 of record 1), and cold cereal (a 1 in column 11 of record 1), but answered no to consuming instant coffee (a 2 in column 9). Also, in a typical month five 13-oz. boxes of natural cereal were consumed (a 5 in column 21 of record 2).

Responses of "don't know" and/or "not applicable" are also precoded with an assigned number such as 9 for a single-digit response, 99 for a two-digit response, and so on. If a response of 9 or 99 could be considered a legitimate response, then either more columns could be used or alphanumeric codes such as x or y could be

EXHIBIT 13–2

———

Data Entry

Case #					Record #.		Frozen waffles	Instant coffee	Frozen orange juice	Cold cereal										Consumption					
1	2	3	4	5	6	7	8	9	10	11	12	13	14	15	16	17	18	19	20	21	22	23	...	79	80
0	0	1			1		1	2	1	1															
0	0	1			2															5					
0	0	2			1		2	2	1	1															
0	0	2			2														1	0					
0	0	3			1		1	1	1	1															
0	0	3			2															3					

used. For example, if an interviewee responded "I don't know" to the question of how many 13-oz. boxes of cereal are consumed in a typical month, then the response would be 99 in columns 20 and 21 of record 2.

Consider the following questionnaire concerning breakfast foods and beverages: EXAMPLE

	Yes	No
Frozen waffles	1/8[ ]-1	[ ]-2
Instant coffee	1/9[ ]-1	[ ]-2
Frozen orange juice	1/10[ ]-1	[ ]-2
Cold cereal	1/11[ ]-1	[ ]-2

The number to the left of the slash (/) denotes the record number (or card number); the number to the left of the box ([ ]) designates the field position that the response will appear in; the number to the right of the box([ ]) gives the appropriate code; the box ([ ]) itself is used by the interviewer to record the elicited response. The same approach is used to code responses that do not fall into categories; for example, a respondent's consumption of natural and/or cold cereal brands might be requested and coded as follows:

How many 13-oz. boxes of natural and/or cold cereal does your family consume in a typical month? _____ 2/20–21

Here the number 2 to the left of the slash (/) indicates that this response will appear on the second record for each respondent; the numbers 20–21 to the right of the slash (/) indicate that the response to this question should be entered into the 20th and 21st field positions (or columns). Note two points: first, by reserving two spaces for the response, the largest response that can be recorded is 99; second, if the response is 9 or less only the 21st field position (or column) will be used. In other words, the entered response is right justified. Exhibit 13-2 illustrates how the first three respondents' answers to these two questions would be entered into the computer.

We see that the first three field positions (or columns) are dedicated to a case identification number, which indicates the respondent; field position (or column) number 6 indicates the record number; field positions (columns) 8 to 11 are reserved for responses to question 5 where a 1 indicates that the product has been consumed in the past month and a 2 indicates that it has not; field positions (or columns) 20 and 21 on record 2 are reserved for the number of boxes of cold cereal consumed in a typical month.

Coding Open-Ended Questions. Open-ended questions are included in questionnaires to obtain a description of the respondent's reaction in the respondent's own words. The resulting variety of responses, however, makes coding open-ended responses difficult, and explicit instructions are necessary to ensure consistency among coders.

The coding of open-ended questions usually involves

1. Taking a sample from all respondents, or from each cell in the case of quotas.

2. Writing down all responses from this sample, trying to group responses in terms of general overall categories (e.g., taste, texture, efficacy).

3. Creating codes from these responses (e.g., Taste = 1, Texture = 2, Efficacy = 3).

4. Writing down all responses that do not fit neatly into the established codes. If enough respondents mention one of these responses, establish a new code.

Most codes require what are called *nets*, that is, basic category headings. Using category headings allows one to group different ways of expressing the same basic idea under a common heading. Examples are

Efficacy
  Relieves headache pain.

  Fast relief.

  Long-lasting relief.

  Extra strength relief.

Aroma
  Smells like an imported cigar.

  Smells like an expensive cigar.

  Smells good.

Category headings serve at least two purposes. First, they help to organize responses that relate to one idea. Second, and perhaps more important, category headings are used to determine how many *respondents* made comments related to the category as opposed to how many *responses* were made. For this purpose, it is necessary to net responses relating to the category. For example, if efficacy were an objective of an ad, you would want to know how many people expressed some reaction related to efficacy. We might have the following:

Efficacy	(86)
Relieves headache pain	50
Fast relief	35
Long-lasting relief	12
Extra strength relief	26

There are, in fact, 123 separate references to efficacy (50 + 35 + 12 + 26). These 123 responses were made by 86 respondents (note the 86 in parentheses for the category heading); hence, some respondents made more than one response relating to efficacy.

Transferring the Data

The next phase in data processing involves the physical transfer of the data from the questionnaires onto a magnetic tape or disk or directly into the computer via

CRT entry. CATI and computer-assisted systems do not require the transfer of data because data are directly put into computer memory at the time of collection. As we indicated earlier, tab houses typically use a PC-based program, which simulates a keypunch machine, to produce a binary-coded or ASCII file on diskette. The diskette (i.e., file) is then uploaded to a mainframe computer. Two other methods are available for transferring the data. The first uses machine-readable **mark-sensed questionnaires,** which require answers to be recorded with a special pencil in an area coded specifically for that answer. The second is **optical scanning,** which involves direct machine reading of the numerical values or alphanumeric codes and transcription onto magnetic tape or disk.

Verification. Data entry is relatively fast and inexpensive—an experienced operator can complete about 100 records per hour at a cost of 20 to 25 cents per record. Experienced operators do not make many errors. However, verification procedures are used to ensure that data from the original questionnaire have been transcribed accurately. Special verification programs are used for this purpose. These will increase the time and cost of data entry.

The automatic data entry in CATI or computer-assisted systems requires a different approach to verification. First, the system should allow a mistake to be corrected before it becomes part of the data file. Second, with CATI, it is often desirable to let the interviewer or respondent verify or contradict the response. If the answer is verified, the next question is repeated; if the answer is contradicted, the question is asked again.

Cleaning. Data must be **cleaned** prior to the final tabulation, which entails a check of all internal inconsistencies, all possible codes, and all impossible punch codes.

Frequency distribution. Typically, the initial step is to tabulate responses on a question-by-question basis. At the cleaning stage, these frequencies are sometimes called *marginals* because they give the number and percentage of respondents who chose each alternative. Consider, for example, the set of marginals shown in Exhibit 13–3 (see page 375), and, in particular, the 16th row, which gives information on the frequency distribution for 400 respondents who were asked the following question:

Last year what was your total taxable income?

Under $5,000	1/16	[ ]-1
$5,000–$9,999		[ ]-2
$10,000–$14,999		[ ]-3
$15,000–$19,999		[ ]-4
$20,000–$24,999		[ ]-5

mark-sensed questionnaire
Format that requires answers to be recorded with a special pencil in an area coded specifically for that answer and that can be read by a machine.

optical scanning
Direct machine reading of numerical values or alphanumeric codes and transcription onto magnetic tape, or disk.

cleaning
A check of all internal consistencies, all possible codes, and all impossible punches.

$25,000–$34,999	[ ]-6
$35,000–$49,999	[ ]-7
$50,000 and over	[ ]-8
No answer	[ ]-9

The total column in Exhibit 13–3 gives the number of respondents who participated in the study (400). The next column is labeled N/A, which stands for not applicable; that is, not all respondents may have been asked all of the questions, given the skip patterns that apply (in this case, all responses were applicable). The T/R column gives the total respondent base for each question. Note that Total minus N/A = T/R (400 − 0 = 400). The remaining columns give first the counts and then the percentages for each possible response. Note that the base for the percentages is the total column.

After the rough marginals are examined and cleaned, a final (cleaned) set of frequency distributions is usually prepared. The result in this case would look like the frequency distribution in Table 13–1, which presents the income question data.

The first column (or stub) in Table 13–1 is the category label describing the levels of the variable. The next column identifies the number assigned to each level in the precoding process. The third column gives the number of respondents checking a particular category; for example, 25 people in the sample reported income less than $5,000. The next column reports the percent of the total sample represented by each category; for example, 60 people reported income in the category $10,000 to $14,999, which represents 15 percent of the 400 people. The adjusted percentage column provides the percentages responding to each level after adjusting for the people that did not answer the question. In this example, 40 people did not answer the question; therefore the denominator for the adjusted percentage column is 360 rather than 400. The last column presents the adjusted cumulative frequencies; for example, 34.7 percent of the sample reported income of $14,999 or less (125/360 = 0.347).

TABLE 13–1

———

Frequency Distribution for Income Categories

Category Label	Code	Number	Percentage	Adjusted Percentage	Adjusted Cumulative Percentage
Under $5,000	1	25	6.3	6.9	6.9
$5,000–$9,999	2	40	10.0	11.1	18.0
$10,000–$14,999	3	60	15.0	16.7	34.7
$15,000–$19,999	4	70	17.5	19.4	54.1
$20,000–$24,999	5	90	22.5	25.0	79.1
$25,000–$34,999	6	40	10.0	11.1	90.2
$35,000–$49,999	7	25	6.3	6.9	97.1
$50,000 and over	8	10	2.5	2.8	99.9
No answer	9	40	10.0	—	
Total		400	100.0		

EXHIBIT 13–3 Marginals for Income Categories

Project Number and Name

Column		Total	N/A	T/R	1	2	3	4	5	6	7	8	9	0	X	Y	Project Number and Name
1	count	400	—	400	—	—	—	—	—	—	—	—	—	400	—	—	A01
	%	100.0	—	100.0	—	—	—	—	—	—	—	—	—	100.0	—	—	
2	count	400	—	400	100	100	99	1	—	—	—	—	—	100	—	—	A02
	%	100.0	—	100.0	25.0	25.0	24.8	.3	—	—	—	—	—	25.0	—	—	
3	count	400	—	400	40	40	40	39	41	40	41	40	39	40	—	—	A03
	%	100.0	—	100.0	10.0	10.0	10.0	9.8	10.3	10.0	10.3	10.0	9.8	10.0	—	—	
4	count	400	—	400	39	40	40	41	40	40	40	40	40	40	—	—	A04
	%	100.0	—	100.0	9.8	10.0	10.0	10.3	10.0	10.0	10.0	10.0	10.0	10.0	—	—	
5	count	400	400	—	—	—	—	—	—	—	—	—	—	—	—	—	A05
	%	100.0	100.0	—	—	—	—	—	—	—	—	—	—	—	—	—	
6	count	400	400	—	—	—	—	—	—	—	—	—	—	—	—	—	A06
	%	100.0	100.0	—	—	—	—	—	—	—	—	—	—	—	—	—	
7	count	400	—	400	154	172	59	14	1	—	—	—	—	—	—	—	A07
	%	100.0	—	100.0	38.5	43.0	14.8	3.5	.3	—	—	—	—	—	—	—	
8	count	400	—	400	94	216	65	22	3	—	—	—	—	—	—	—	A08
	%	100.0	—	100.0	23.5	54.0	16.3	5.5	.8	—	—	—	—	—	—	—	
9	count	400	—	400	51	176	136	36	1	—	—	—	—	—	—	—	A09
	%	100.0	—	100.0	12.8	44.0	34.0	9.0	.3	—	—	—	—	—	—	—	
10	count	400	198	202	13	52	58	77	2	—	—	—	—	—	—	—	A10
	%	100.0	49.5	50.5	3.3	13.0	14.5	19.3	.5	—	—	—	—	—	—	—	
11	count	400	200	200	2	19	13	154	12	—	—	—	—	—	—	—	A11
	%	100.0	50.0	50.0	.5	4.8	3.3	38.5	3.0	—	—	—	—	—	—	—	
12	count	400	202	198	6	47	52	87	6	—	—	—	—	—	—	—	A12
	%	100.0	50.5	49.5	1.5	11.8	13.0	21.8	1.5	—	—	—	—	—	—	—	
13	count	400	200	200	4	11	8	165	12	—	—	—	—	—	—	—	A13
	%	100.0	50.0	50.0	1.0	2.8	2.0	41.3	3.0	—	—	—	—	—	—	—	
14	count	400	400	—	—	—	—	—	—	—	—	—	—	—	—	—	A14
	%	100.0	100.0	—	—	—	—	—	—	—	—	—	—	—	—	—	
15	count	400	400	—	—	—	—	—	—	—	—	—	—	—	—	—	A15
	%	100.0	100.0	—	—	—	—	—	—	—	—	—	—	—	—	—	
16	count	400	—	400	25	40	60	70	90	40	25	10	40	—	—	—	A16
	%	100.0	—	100.0	6.3	10.0	15.0	17.5	22.5	10.0	6.3	2.5	10.0	—	—	—	
Column		Total	N/A	T/R	1	2	3	4	5	6	7	8	9	0	X	Y	

Note: Percentages may not add to 100 percent due to rounding.

Missing responses. The final step in the cleaning process is consideration of missing responses. After isolating the questions for which missing responses have occurred, perhaps through frequency distributions or by obtaining a column-by-column count of the responses to each question, it is necessary to decide how to treat questions that some respondents did not answer. All of the popular statistical packages allow the user to designate which codes refer to missing values; for example, all missing values could be assigned the value 999. There are several possible strategies:

1. Preserving missing or blank responses is an acceptable practice for certain types of analyses. For example, blanks can be accommodated in the case of simple tabulations simply by adjusting percentages and cumulative percentages for the percentage of missing responses, as in the final two columns of Table 13–1. For other types of analyses (such as regression analysis described in Chapter 17), blanks can be problematic.

   a. **Casewide deletion** calls for discarding any case (respondent) with missing values for any variable. The obvious problem is that much of the available sample can disappear in this way.

   b. **Pairwise deletion** preserves all the available nonmissing data for each calculation. For example, a respondent might have not answered the income question while providing complete answers to all other questions. This respondent's data would be included in all calculations except those involving the income variable. This approach works well for large samples where there are relatively few missing responses and where there is no reason to believe that missing responses follow a systematic pattern across certain questions.

2. Assigning value to the missing data is also an acceptable strategy.

   a. The **mean response** approach involves replacing a missing response with a constant—typically, the mean response to the question. Taking this approach lets the mean of the variable remain unchanged, and usually has very little effect on other statistics.

   b. Under the **imputed response** approach, a respondent's answers to other questions are used to impute or deduce an appropriate response to the missing question. For example, if you have information on the educational level attained, you might fill in missing income data either by estimating the relationship between income and education for all respondents who have answered both questions or by substituting the mean income level of all respondents having the same educational level as the respondents who did not provide income data. This approach can be risky because it can introduce considerable research bias into the results.

Table Specifications

A table consists of a number of columns, called *banners*, and a number of rows, called *stubs*. The banners represent the various subgroups in the analysis. Results

---

casewise deletion
Strategy for missing responses where any case (respondent) is removed if any of his or her responses are identified as missing.

pairwise deletion
Strategy for missing responses that involves using all of the available nonmissing data for each calculation.

mean response
Approach to missing responses that involves replacing a missing response with a constant—the mean, median, or mode response to the question depending on the measurement scale used.

imputed response
Approach to missing responses where the respondent's answers to other questions asked are used to impute or deduce an appropriate response to the missing question.

EXHIBIT 13–4 Table Specifications

		Stub						Banner			
Table Number	Table Title	Base	Question Number	Column Position	Description	(Code)	Banner Point	Question Number	Column Position	Description	(Code)
1	Overall rating of Carbonated Soft Drink— Coca Cola Classic	All	13	1/32	Excellent	(5)	A	14	1/15	Male	(1)
					Very good	(4)	B	14	1/15	Female	(2)
					Good	(3)	C	25	2/40, 41	Low income	(1–3)
					Fair	(2)	D	25	2/40, 41	Moderate income	(4–7)
					Poor	(1)	E	25	2/40, 41	High income	(8–10)

banner points
Form the columns of cross tabulations and represent subgroups of respondents.

for various subgroups of respondents are of special interest to the marketing research manager, so a cross tabulation singles them out for closer examination. Each particular subgroup (for example, light user, heavy user, male, female) is called a **banner point**. Typically, commercially available cross-tabulation programs allow up to 20 banner points per table, allowing simultaneous examination of a large number of subgroup interrelationships. The table **stub points** represent those questions in the questionnaire that the research analyst wishes to focus on. It is not uncommon to designate every question in an instrument as a stub, with the possible exception of the general variety of screener items used to qualify the respondent.

stub points
Make up the rows of a cross tabulation and usually delineate the response formats.

The research analyst generally provides tabulating specifications to the tab house, whose responsibility it is to form these tables. A typical tabulating specification form for a question rating Coca Cola Classic is shown in Exhibit 13–4. The specification form involves defining the following:

1. Table title.
2. Stub—The relevant base upon which the table will be formed (total respondents, brand X users, etc.), question number, column position(s), and the description, and code for the stub.
3. Banner specifications—Question number, column position, description, and code for each banner point.

SUMMARY

This chapter has discussed data-collection activities, with particular emphasis on fielding the questionnaire and data preparation. We began our discussion by explaining fieldwork procedures and practices. In the course of that discussion, we described procedures for checking in questionnaires and the process of editing. We then turned our attention to those functions that are necessary to transform the information collected into a form that allows the data to be analyzed. Among other issues, we discussed and illustrated coding procedures for closed-ended and open-ended questions. Finally, the chapter concluded by discussing how tables are specified.

KEY CONCEPTS

estimating costs	check-in	transferring data	banner
"alerting" the study	editing	table specifications	stub
field instructions	coding		

REVIEW QUESTIONS

1. What are some potential problems that might arise when coding open-ended questions?
2. After a job comes in from the field, list several reasons for rejecting a respondent's answers.

3. You are president of a company that analyzes and tabulates incoming data from mail surveys. One survey is causing you some trouble because a few of the questions deal with whether the respondent uses

drugs on occasion. What could you do to ensure that a high percentage of respondents answer these sensitive questions truthfully? If you end up having received many surveys with these questions left unanswered, what might you recommend to your client company?

4. Discuss the different methods for handling missing data.

5. From the cross tabulation shown on the next page, develop a frequency distribution (see Table 13–1) for (a) the total sample, (b) 1-line and 2-to-6-line businesses, and (c) the three regions.

6. You will have noticed that, for example, in the case of the "business customer" banner points shown in the cross tabulation of question 5, the frequency counts (826) do not add to the total number of respondents (836). Why?

Cross Tabulation of Likelihood to Purchase Repeat-Dialing Service

Q8B. LIKELIHOOD TO PURCHASE REPEAT DIALING FOR YOUR BUSINESS AT COST OF $4.00 EACH MONTH

	TOTAL	REGION			BUSINESS CUSTOMER			NUMBER OF TELEPHONE LINES					
		METRO	STATE	OHIO	LESS THAN 3 YRS	3–10 YRS	MORE THAN 10 YRS	1	2–6	PC 1+	MODEM 1+	FAX 1+	ANS MACH 1+
TOTAL RESPONDENTS	836	214	343	279	146	241	439	527	253	117	104	131	335
NO ANSWER	70	16	36	18	10	12	46	47	14	6	5	9	22
TOTAL ANSWERING	766	198	307	261	136	229	393	480	239	111	99	122	313
REPEAT DIALING													
VERY LIKELY TO BUY													
5	69	13	25	31	6	27	34	34	29	15	18	18	30
	9.0	6.6	8.1	11.9	4.4	11.8	8.7	7.1	12.1	13.5	18.2	14.8	9.6
4	88	18	35	35	21	29	38	49	35	19	13	19	38
	11.5	9.1	11.4	13.4	15.4	12.7	9.7	10.2	14.6	17.1	13.1	15.6	12.1
3	148	41	52	55	36	39	73	90	46	20	18	25	83
	19.3	20.7	16.9	21.1	26.5	17.0	18.6	18.8	19.2	18.0	18.2	20.5	26.5
2	74	25	27	22	9	33	32	45	28	14	11	8	26
	9.7	12.6	8.8	8.4	6.6	14.4	8.1	9.4	11.7	12.6	11.1	6.6	8.3
NOT VERY LIKELY TO BUY 1	387	101	168	118	64	101	216	262	101	43	39	52	136
	50.5	51.0	54.7	45.2	47.1	44.1	55.0	54.6	42.3	38.7	39.4	42.6	43.5
MEAN BASE	766	198	307	261	136	229	393	480	239	111	99	122	313
MEAN	2.19	2.08	2.09	2.38	2.24	2.34	2.09	2.06	2.43	2.54	2.60	2.53	2.36
STD DEV	1.39	1.29	1.38	1.46	1.31	1.44	1.38	1.33	1.46	1.48	1.55	1.52	1.39
STD ERR	.050	.092	.079	.090	.112	.095	.069	.061	.094	.141	.156	.138	.078

CASE STUDIES FOR PART IV

CASE 1
Olds Goal: Young and Stylish—GM to Sharpen Divisional Images

By Phil Frame

The foundering Oldsmobile Division will get the biggest makeover, moving to younger and more style-conscious buyers, as General Motors' new regime tries to focus the image of its car marketing divisions.

Marketing divisions would sacrifice models that blur their images and compete too closely with other GM vehicles, according to strategies for the mid-to-late 1990s under consideration by GM's North American Operations planners. While all product decisions are not final, conversations with many sources at the new North American Operations reveal general agreement on the focus each division will seek.

The plans under consideration include dropping Oldsmobile Cutlass Ciera and Bravada; Buick Roadmaster; Pontiac LeMans and the four-door Pontiac Grand Prix; and the 1997-model year remake of the Chevrolet Caprice, said sources at GM's new North American Operations.

Other product changes being considered:

- Replacing the Cadillac Allante with a domestic car.
- Dropping the Oldsmobile Ninety Eight.
- Dropping the Buick Skylark.

Spurred by angry investors and outside board members impatient with GM's $6.5 billion in losses over the past two years, planners are considering previously unthinkable options, NAO sources said. The sources also say the Buick Regal may be in jeopardy, but a division executive, who asked not to be named, strongly denied any plans to kill the model.

"It's totally untrue," the official said. "I don't know where that got started." He also said there is no plan now to eliminate the Skylark or Roadmaster.

"There's a danger in cutting too much—you can lose market share and volume forever," he said. "I'm not saying we won't have additions and deletions, though."

Among the five passenger-car marketing divisions plus Saturn Corp., Oldsmobile would have to shift the most dramatically from its current position on the GM perceptual map (see Exhibit 1, top right).

Oldsmobile. Outsiders commonly suggest eliminating the Oldsmobile division entirely. But GM executives steadfastly argue that they shouldn't discard a dedicated dealer body of 3,000 and decades of built-up brand equity.

Currently regarded internally as more conservative and nearly as pricey as Buick, Oldsmobile will get an image makeover by the late 1990s. It will embody the idea of cutting-edge expression for upscale customers between 30 and 45 years old.

Hard evidence of the change began two weeks ago when the division axed the slow-selling Custom Cruiser wagon and Toronado. Sources at NAO say the Bravada sport-utility could be dropped after the 1993 model year.

But Oldsmobile spokesman Guz Buenz said the Bravada is "very much a part of our product program going forward."

Another possible casualty is the Oldsmobile Ninety Eight, which may be dropped after the 1994 model year because it competes too closely with the Buick Park Avenue and is too conservative for Oldsmobile's intended new image, sources said.

Oldsmobile would continue selling the popular Achieva compact and mid-sized Eighty Eight.

The Toronado name is to be revived in the 1994 model year as a larger mid-sized four-door built on the all-new G-car platform. The 1996 model year would see a snazzy new Cutlass Supreme, based on the Anthem concept car displayed at several auto shows this year.

EXHIBIT 1

GM Car Markets

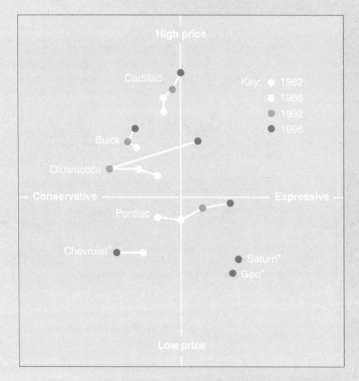

Source: GM and divisional sources.

Oldsmobile will sell a version of the next-generation U-body minivan due in the 1996 model year. Oldsmobile currently sells the Silhouette minivan.

The conservative Cutlass Ciera may again be on the chopping block. Although the Ciera/Buick Century program was approved last December for the 1995 model year, the new Ciera may be cut if NAO planners decide it's too conservative for Oldsmobile or too much like the Century, built on the same platform, sources said.

Any plans to drop the Cutlass Ciera would be met with stiff opposition from Oldsmobile and its dealers. It was Oldsmobile's top seller in 1991 and remains so this year. The dilemma illustrates the difficulty in moving Oldsmobile so far away from its current position on the perception scale.

The transformation of Oldsmobile has been in the works since the late 1980s, but it has not yet happened. Since 1986, Oldsmobile believes it has become even more conservative. It will have to change faster because of a GM board mandate to accelerate plant closings,

revamp North American operations, and quickly return to profitability.

GM's other marketing divisions will make smaller moves to refine their images and further differentiate themselves from external competitors and internal allies.

Buick. Buick will remain a division for conservative, wealthy, older people. Models such as the Regal, Skylark, and Roadmaster are in danger, sources said.

Planners may consider dropping the Skylark after the 1996 model year, NAO sources said. The model was redesigned for the 1992 model year, but the car is selling horribly. Skylark sales are down 61 percent from the previous model year and 41 percent for the calendar year, compared with the first quarter of 1991. The car is built on the N-car platform with the Pontiac Grand Am and Oldsmobile Achieva.

Buick wants the wildly styled and high-priced compact so it can draw younger buyers into the fold. But

NAO sources said GM can't afford that in a division that aims to cater to mature customers.

The B-body Roadmaster may die after the 1996 model year. Dwindling demand for large rear-wheel-drive cars has virtually killed off the B-body Chevrolet Caprice and did kill the Oldsmobile Custom Cruiser wagon. Although the Roadmaster is meeting its sales objectives, its life is tied to the Caprice, which is supposed to be the volume car on that platform.

Discussions about killing the Regal focus on whether it makes sense for Buick to have two mid-sized cars, NAO sources said. The sources said that if Buick keeps the Regal, it may be retained only as a coupe, while the Century would be sold only as a sedan.

When they are redesigned, the Century and Regal would be built off a single platform, instead of separate ones as they are now.

The Park Avenue would continue as Buick's flagship. A larger LeSabre, built off the G-platform beginning in 1996, could help fill the void if Roadmaster dies. The LeSabre now is built on the H-platform, which will be consolidated with the G-cars. The new G-platform debuts in the 1994 model year with the Buick Riviera and Oldsmobile Toronado.

Chevrolet. Chevrolet is likely to lose the Caprice, which planners believe has become too expensive (base price nearly $18,000 including destination charge) for the division's value-conscious customers. But Chevrolet and GM don't want to abandon the police-taxi-utility fleet market that takes 50,000 Caprices per year, so they may continue building the current version.

The 1997 Caprice replacement has been cancelled or shelved indefinitely, sources said.

A Chevrolet source said the company will wait until 1995 or 1996 to decide whether to continue the current car and will save money in the interim because it isn't committing money for research, development, and tooling.

Chevrolet spokesman Dave Hudgens declined comment on the division's future product plans.

Hudgens said earlier reports that the Caprice was killed caused concern at police agencies across the country because the car is the most popular pursuit vehicle.

"One police department went so far as to inquire about ordering more 1992s," Hudgens said.

The 1994-model W-body Lumina replacement, which will be larger than the current W-car, is expected to appeal to some Caprice buyers. A new all-aluminum small-block V-8 engine under development would be an option.

In the 1994 model year, Chevrolet also will debut a youthful, two-door, personal-luxury version of the Lumina called the Monte Carlo. It was not clear how such a vehicle would be reconciled with the value-conscious, conservative image other cars in the division are expected to carry.

The other Chevrolets are likely to remain, but the Cavalier and Corsica/Beretta will be combined onto one platform, and the Corvette and Camaro could share a platform in the future.

Chevrolet sources believe Geo has its own position in the market, nearly identical to Saturn's. It is not expected to change until perhaps 1997 when the Geo Prizm leaves the fold. Although Prizm is redesigned for 1993, it will leave at the expiration of GM's joint venture with Toyota Motor Corp. The joint venture—New United Motor Manufacturing Inc.—builds the Prizm and the Toyota Corolla.

Pontiac. Pontiac's image will be more expressive and sporty.

It probably will lose the Korean-built LeMans, which will be sold through the 1993 model year and then probably be dropped, a Pontiac source said. The TransSport minivan may survive the platform trims, although some NAO sources suggest Pontiac will not get a version of the 1996 replacement vehicle. The four-door Grand Prix probably will be dropped, NAO sources say.

Cadillac. Cadillac models will become slightly more upscale and more highly styled, sporty, and sleeker— along the lines of the 1992 Seville and Eldorado. Only the Allante may depart, but not until a replacement, which will be similar to the Aurora concept car shown in 1989, is ready in the 1995 or 1996 model year.

Saturn. Saturn will remain unchanged for now. Eventually, Saturn would like a mid-sized platform to compete against larger Japanese competitors such as the Honda Accord and Toyota Camry.

While Saturn officials have acknowledged the existence of such plans, they say they won't get the corporate go-ahead until they earn it by making a success of the compact car.

Suppose that GM is now interested in developing an "image" map for the subcompact market. The procedure agreed upon for collecting subcompact brand images resulted in the survey shown in Exhibit 2. At most, four ratings would be collected from each respondent. To be eligible for inclusion in the study, a respondent had to (1) have purchased a subcompact automobile within the last three years, (2) have been under 45 years of age, and (3) belong to a household, no member of which, including the respondent, was employed within the last three years by either an advertising, public relations, manufacturer/dealer of automobiles, or marketing research firm. The ratings would be taken on the respondent's *ideal* subcompact automobile, the subcompact that the respondent *currently owned,* and the two subcompacts that the respondent *considered* when making his or her last purchase of a subcompact. In other words, a respondent would be asked to rate, at most, four subcompact automobiles.

Each automobile would be rated on a set of 20 attributes. The attributes derived from focus-group interviews are listed below:

Sensible	Independent
Comfortable	Practical
Dependable	Down-to-earth
Luxurious	Youthful
Sporty	Contemporary
Family-oriented	Mature
High performance	Classic
Exciting	Affordable
Adventurous	Efficient
Fashionable	Economical

The automobile manufacturer was also interested in understanding the trade-offs subcompact car purchases make with respect to attributes such as

Economy.

High performance.

Ease in driving.

Dependability.

Standard demographic data also would be collected.

Source: *Automotive News,* May 11, 1992, pp. 1, 42. Used with permission.

Case Questions

1. Refer to Exhibit 2, the questionnaire developed by the marketing research group. Based on what you know about designing a questionnaire, discuss the following issues:

   — Is the questionnaire going to provide the necessary data?

   — Are there any problems with how the questions are asked?

   — Are there any problems with how the questions are constructed?

2. How can the questionnaire be improved? Develop a "better" questionnaire.

3. Prepare a set of interviewer instructions for your questionnaire.

EXHIBIT 2
—
Survey of
Subcompact Owners

Screener

Respondent's full name: _____

Address: _____

City: _____ State: _____ Zip code: _____

Telephone number: (_____) _____

Interviewed by: _____ Date: _____

Hello, I'm _____ from _____

We're conducting a study of automobile purchases, and I'd like to ask [*name from listing*] a few questions about his/her selection of [*car make and model and year*].

1. Are you or any member of your household employed by . . .?

An advertising or public relations firm	A
A manufacturer or dealer of automobiles, or	B
A marketing research company	C

EXHIBIT 2

(*continued*)

[*If "yes" to any, terminate and circle next highest number: 01 02 03 04 05 06 07 08 09 10 11 12 13 14 15. Reuse screener.*]

2. Which of the following groups includes your age?

18–24	1
25–34	2
35–45	3
46 or above	4

[*If 4, terminate and circle next highest number: 01 02 03 04 05 06 07 08 09 10 11 12 13 14 15. Reuse screener.*]

3. Are you . . .? [*Read list.*]

Married	1
Single	2
Divorced	3
Separated	4
Widowed	5
[*Do not read.*] Refused	y

4. What was the last grade of school you completed? [*Do not read list.*]

No formal schooling	1
Completed grammar school	2
Some high school	3
Graduated high school	4
Some college	5
Graduated college	6
[*Do not read.*] Refused	y

5. Is your annual household income before taxes . . .? [*Read list.*]

Under $15,000	1
Between $15,000 and $24,999	2
Between $25,000 and $34,999	3
Between $35,000 and $49,999	4
$50,000 or more	5
[*Do not read.*] Refused	6

6. Could you tell me the make, model, and year of your last car?

_____   _____   _____

7. Was your previous car new or used when you purchased it?

New
Used

8. Do you still own your previous car?

Yes
No

9. Including yourself, how many persons are there in your household?

One	1
Two	2
Three	3
Four	4
Five	5
Six or more	6

10. How many are over the age of 17?
Number over 17_____

11. Are there any other cars currently owned by members of your household?

Yes
No

EXHIBIT 2

——

(concluded)

Survey starts here

Scale or ranking question

12. Could you tell me their makes, models, and years?

————————   ————————   ————————
————————   ————————   ————————

13. [*If respondent still owns previous car or if other cars are owned by household members, ask:*] Would you consider your [*name of car from listing*] your main or second car?

Main
Second

14. From the following list of options, would you tell me which ones you purchased? [*For each "no," ask:*] Did you consider purchasing the option?

Air conditioning	Yes	Considered
Automatic transmission	Yes	Considered
Special radio or cassette	Yes	Considered
Sunroof	Yes	Considered
Special wheels	Yes	Considered
Turbocharger	Yes	Considered
Power steering	Yes	Considered
Dual mirrors	Yes	Considered
Tinted glass	Yes	Considered

15. Could you tell me which of the following features were major factors and which were minor factors in your choice of your [*car name from listing*]?

Economy

Easy to drive

High performance

Dependability

16. Which of the following words describe your ideal car? [*On "A" forms, start at top of list; on "B" forms, start at bottom of list*]

Sensible   ————
Comfortable   ————
Dependable   ————
Luxurious   ————
Exciting   ————
Adventurous   ————
Fashionable   ————
Independent   ————
Contemporary   ————
Generous   ————
Mature   ————
Classic   ————
Affordable   ————
Sporty   ————
Family-oriented   ————
Careful   ————
Performance   ————
Necessity   ————
Practical   ————
Down-to-earth   ————
Youthful   ————
Efficient   ————

CASE 2
BBQ Product Crosses Over the Lines of Varied Tastes

Rich Products Corp. is hoping its frozen barbecue will appeal to the wide tastes in its narrow market, but it realizes consumers will need a nudge in that direction.

Enter Ruby Raylene Dodge, waitress down at the Pork-O-Rama and major figure in the company's marketing campaign for its new product, Rich's Southern Barbeque.

Because barbecue is a regional delicacy—it varies in taste from county to county throughout the Southeast—Rich Products, Buffalo, New York, had to develop a tangy product to appeal to varied tastes and had to persuade consumers they'd like it, according to Joe Tindall, the company's product development manager of new products.

To cross over regional and local differences in the six-city market in the Southeast, Long, Haymes & Carr Advertising (LH&C), Winston-Salem, North Carolina, has launched a series of 30-second TV ads called "Please Don't Tell 'Em Ruby Sent You."

"The fictitious Ruby is supposed to give the product authenticity without trying to compete with barbecue restaurants or stands," said Don Van Erden, vice president/management supervisor, LH&C.

"Our research told us that no one has more rapport and credibility with the barbecue-eating public than the real-life barbecue waitress," Van Erden said. "In Ruby, we have a vivid persona who's believable because she's based on real barbecue waitresses we've observed."

Rich Products hopes Ruby will reach all consumers with her friendly Southern accent and down-home sincerity.

"I'm a loyal employee of the Pork-O-Rama, but my real true love is Rich's Frozen Barbecue," Ruby says in one spot. In another she's wearing a disguise. "I can't just go to my grocer's freezer for Rich's Barbeque," she says. "I've got a career at the Pork-O-Rama to consider."

She praises the product in all the spots, but fearful of losing her job, warns viewers, "Just please don't tell 'em Ruby sent you."

The microwavable barbecue entrees were test marketed last year in Nashville, Tennessee, Little Rock, Arkansas, and the Alabama cities of Birmingham, Huntsville, Montgomery, and Tuscaloosa. "That's the market now, but expansion into other areas is planned," Tindall said.

Source: *Marketing News*, September 12, 1988, p. 24.

Case Questions

1. What measurement and scaling issues should be considered when developing a study to measure consumers' attitudes toward barbecue in general and specifically Rich's Barbeque?
2. Assume Rich's wanted to test people's preference for their barbecue versus the other leading brands (of which there are five). What would you recommend to measure these preferences?

CASE 3
Consumer Attitudes and Perceptions Toward Seafood when Eating Out: Measurement Development

In Part II, Case Study 1, we introduced the preliminary phase of a study focusing on consumers' attitudes and perceptions toward seafood—in particular, nontraditional species—when eating out. The following describes the results from the focus-group interviews.

Eating Fish in Restaurants

Fish was seldom consumed at home. Participants objected to the residual odor after its preparation.

Those who do prepare fish at home emphasize the ease with which it can be prepared.

- "I like to eat foods I don't eat at home—my daughter is allergic to fish, so we don't eat it at home."
- "I like to eat fish when it's been cooked by someone else."
- "We never cook fish at home, but we love seafood, so we go out."
- "I don't like the smell of fish at home—when I go out that's my chance to have fish."
- "No one else in the house eats fish, so I get it when I go out."
- "I eat it more away from home because of the odor."
- "Fish out is a treat."
- "It's always a treat to have fish at home."

- "I don't think I've ever left home thinking about having a super fish meal. The only time I've done that is when I'm on vacation, down on the Cape or something."
- "Preparation of good fresh fish is quickly done at home—under the broiler—it's easy—so I order more difficult things when I go out."

Several participants established a link between trust in the knowledge of the restaurant staff and their willingness to try new dishes.

- "The better the restaurant—the more trust I have in the waiter and the more willing I am to try."
- "I'd have more trust in a more expensive restaurant—they pay their help better to be more informed."
- "If you've eaten in a restaurant before, you know how they cook."

Trust in the freshness of fish also was an issue.

- "I'll eat fish only in a restaurant that specializes—otherwise I feel it's not fresh—probably frozen."
- "I wouldn't ask them—they don't know."
- "If you're at the shore and you don't order seafood, you're foolish."

Some respondents were purists who preferred their fish broiled with butter and lemon, whereas others either had a favorite sauce or were willing to try new methods of preparation.

- "I don't like anything fried."
- "I like fish in a casserole."
- "Broiled or baked is always dry."
- "No bread crumbs—I like to see the fish."
- "It depends on the texture—is it flaky and moist or like rubber?"
- "If they're going to charge a big price I would hope they would do something to it."
- "I choose the fish first, then the method of preparation."

Some participants had tried a range of sauces and enjoyed them, while others had not.

Pro

- "Dill sauces."
- "Newburgh."

- "Ginger sauce."
- "Nothing too overpowering."
- "I had a good white cheese sauce—it was excellent."

Con

- "Never had any."
- "Don't like sauces—just butter."
- "Sauce could kill a good piece of fish—I like just lemon."
- "When I'm eating fish for health and weight, I stick to vegetables—no bread, no potatoes. I'd be defeating the purpose with a sauce."

Barriers to Fish Consumption

Some participants did not prepare fish at home because of the work involved in cleaning and deboning fish.

- "I don't like really strong fish."
- "I don't like the odor or a fishy taste."
- "I don't like bones—that's why I usually get scrod."
- "I don't like bones—I don't like to be surprised."
- "The skin is usually chewy and slimy."
- "I fish a lot—to get rid of bones it depends on the size of the fish and how you fillet it."

The discussion of odor led to some mention of freshness in several groups.

- "Fresh fish doesn't smell."
- "I get fish on the Cape—it has no odor."
- "Fresh-caught fish has no smell."
- "Supermarket fish smells when you cook it."
- "When you buy fish, you can see how fresh it is."
- "Oh, you can taste the difference."
- "In most big restaurants, it's easy to get fresh fish."
- "If I'm in another part of the country, I won't order fish."

Reactions to Specific Fish

None of the fish named as favorites could be considered nontraditional. Scrod and swordfish were named most often.

- "I like scrod—there's an occasional bone, but it's not too bad."

- "I'd go for swordfish, if you want a meatier fish."
- "I go deep-sea fishing—I like flounder."
- "I like scrod—it's tender and moist."
- "Swordfish is my favorite—it's meatier, solid, chewy."
- "Swordfish has more flavor—almost sweet."
- "Salmon for one—I love the color—I was brought up on it."
- "Scrod—it's light, not oily, juicy."
- "I like scrod—the taste isn't fishy, it's flaky."
- "I like white fish that are sweet."
- "Fillet of sole, sometimes scrod."
- "I like swordfish or salmon, for the taste and texture."
- "Haddock—flavorful but mild."
- "Haddock—out of habit."
- "Haddock—a nice piece of fish, not too gamy."
- "I like salmon with hollandaise sauce."

Attitudes Toward Nontraditional Fish

Of those people who were reluctant to try fish, the monetary risk was occasionally mentioned as a reason.

- "I don't want to pay $8 or $9 for something I might not like."
- "If you're going to spend $10 or $15, why try something you don't know you're going to like, when there are so many good things on the menu?"

For an overwhelming majority of participants, the name of the fish caused considerable reaction. Some reactions to specific fish are listed below.

Shark

- "I think it sounds unappetizing—*Jaws*–it bothers me to be deceived."
- "I suppose I would try it if I was in one of those moods to try something new."

Tilefish

- "Makes me think of Spanish or Italian tiles."

Monkfish

- "Doesn't sound tempting."

Skate

- "I think they ought to change the name—it sounds sharp."

In each of the groups there were participants who were eager to try new types of seafood or new methods of preparation and others who liked to play it safe.

- "I'll try something new if the ingredients look good."
- "I wouldn't order something I'd never had—a lot of fish is too strong."
- "I might taste someone else's."
- "If there is something in it that I know I like— otherwise, I wouldn't risk it."
- "I tried shark—it was really tasty—my dad came back from San Francisco and he was raving about it."

Participants were asked what they thought of specific seafoods named by the moderator. In some cases they reacted to the fish based on having tasted it, while in other cases they reacted to the name or its reputation. Some specific reactions are listed below.

Cod

- "Cod is a wormy fish."

Flounder

- "Flounder is a bottom feeder."

Pollock

- "I liked it; I've cooked it—it has a stronger flavor than scrod—it's a cheaper fish."

Whitefish

- "The only way I've had it was smoked—smoked was greasy."
- "It sounds like it's related to scrod or haddock."
- "Yes, sounds like scrod."

Mackerel

- "That's ok; it's a fish, not a predator."
- "You see them all the time in the grocery store."

Less well-known seafoods were greeted with a degree of suspicion. It may be inferred that the most common consumers' attitude is that if a species is underutilized, there must be a reason.

Shark

- "Most people have probably eaten shark and didn't realize it—it sometimes passes for swordfish or scallops."

- "Don't tell me its shark—I don't want to know."
- "I couldn't try shark—I don't know why—I just couldn't."

Butterfish

- "None would get my interest."
- "Maybe it's like sole or scrod."
- "It would be something I would ask about."
- "I would have to know what it tasted like."
- "I would try it if it were boneless, white."

Monkfish

- "They're the ugliest things in the world."

Skate

- "That doesn't sound good."
- "You know those perfectly round scallops, those are mostly skate, sometimes shark."
- "They look like rays."
- "If you saw one after you'd caught one, you'd probably never eat it."

Eel

- "I liked it."
- "No—I've caught one—they're slimy things."
- "No way I'd try it."
- "I've tried it—I didn't like the texture."
- "Definitely not—that's like a snake."
- "It tastes like salmon."
- "It's oily."
- "I've had it in a tomato and onion sauce—it's really not bad."

Squid

- "Definitely no."
- "I had it—didn't like it—nothing to do with the taste—it's the way they look."

- "My wife's family had it every Christmas—I've made it through all these years without trying it."
- "I think of those things as reptiles."
- "I would be more willing to try some of these exotic names if I was on vacation in a place where that might be the main food."

Source: Materials for this case were supplied by Dr. Robert C. Lewis of the Department of Hotel and Restaurant Administration, University of Massachusetts.

Case Questions

1. How can the results of the focus-group session help you to develop a questionnaire dealing with consumers' attitudes and perceptions toward nontraditional fish when eating out?

2. Prepare an outline of the questionnaire you would use to measure consumers' attitudes and perceptions toward nontraditional fish when eating out.

3. Based upon the information provided above and your answer to question 2, develop a set of measurement scales to measure consumers' attitudes and perceptions toward nontraditional fish when eating out.

CASE 4
National Wine Tracking Study

The following case exercise is used as an interviewing tool at a New York–based supplier for junior research project directors. Included are:

1. A questionnaire (Exhibit 1).
2. A grid page (Exhibit 2).

The assignment is to prepare a set of data-processing cleaning instructions for the grid page.

EXHIBIT 1
—
Questionnaire

National Wine Tracking Study
—Main Questionnaire—
[*Interviewer: Do Not Read List for Q's 1–6.*]

1. I'd like to ask you some questions about wine. Please tell me all the brands of wine you can think of. (Probe:) What others? [*Record all mentions on white grid page under Q.1, "Unaided aware."*]

2. What brands of wine do you recall having seen or heard advertised on TV, radio, or in magazines recently? (Probe:) What others? [*Record all mentions on white grid page under Q.2, "Unaided Advertising."*]

3. What brand of wine did you buy last? [*Record all mentions on white grid page under Q.3, "Bought last."*]
    [*If no brand is mentioned anywhere in Q's 1, 2, or 3, skip to Q.7. Otherwise, continue.*]

4. And what brand did you buy the time before that? [*Record all mentions on white grid page under Q.4, "Bought time before last."*]

5. What brand are you most likely to buy next? [*Record all mentions on white grid page under Q.5, "Will buy next."*]

6. What brand would you consider buying next? [*Record all mentions on white grid page under Q.6, "Would consider buying."*]

7. Have you ever heard of (*brand*)? [*Record "yes" answers on white grid page under Q.7, "Aided aware."*]
    [*Ask Q.8 for each (*) brand mentioned in Q.1 or Q.7 but not Q.2.*]

8. Do you recall having recently seen or heard advertising for (*brand*)? [*Record "yes" answers on white grid page under Q.8, "Aided ad aware."*]
    [*Ask Q.9 for each (*) brand mentioned in Q's 1, 2, or 7 but not Q's 3–4.*]

9. Have you ever bought (*brand*)? [*Record "yes" answers on white grid page under Q.9, "Ever bought."*]
    [*Ask Q.10a for each (*) brand mentioned in Q's 3, 4, or 9.*]

10a. Have you bought (*brand*) in the past *two months*? [*Record "yes" answers on white grid page under Q.10a, "Bought past two months."*]
    [*Ask Q.10b for each (*) brand mentioned in Q.10a.*]

10b. How many bottles of (*brand*) did you buy in the past two months? [*Record number legibly on white grid page under Q.10b, "# of bottles."*]

EXHIBIT 2   Sample Grid Page

CARD 4
continued DO NOT READ LIST

	Q. 1 Un-aided aware (18)	Q. 2 Un-aided advtg (24)	Q. 3 Bought last (30)	Q. 4 Bought time before last (36)	Q. 5 Will buy next (42)	Q. 6 Would consider buying (48)	Q. 7 Aided aware (54)	Q. 8 Aided ad aware (59)	Q. 9 Ever bought (64)	Q. 10a Bought past two months (69)	Start card 5 Q. 10b # of bot.
3-*Almaden	1	1	1	1	1	1	1	1	1	1	6-
Almaden Light	2	2	2	2	2	2					
Almaden Golden	3	3	3	3	3	3					8-
*B&G	4	4	4	4	4	4	4	4	4	4	10-
4-*Black Tower	5	5	5	5	5	5	5	5	5	5	12-
5-*Blue Nun	6	6	6	6	6	6	6	6	6	6	14-
*Bolla Or Soave Bolla	7	7	7	7	7	7	7	7	7	7	
Brolio	8	8	8	8	8	8	8				16-
*Carlo Rossi	9	9	9	9	9	9	9	9	9	9	18-
*Cella	0	0	0	0	0	0	0	0	0	0	
	(19)	(25)	(31)	(37)	(43)	(49)	(55)	(60)	(65)	(70)	
The Christian Brothers	1	1	1	1	1	1	1	1	1	1	
2-*Folonari	2	2	2	2	2	2	2	2	2	2	20-
Fontana Candida	3	3	3	3	3	3					
Franzia	4	4	4	4	4	4					
6-*Gallo	5	5	5	5	5	5	5	5	5	5	22-
*Giacobazzi	6	6	6	6	6	6	6	6	6	6	24-
Gold Seal Catawba	7	7	7	7	7	7					
Great Western	8	8	8	8	8	8					
7-*Inglenook	9	9	9	9	9	9	9	9	9	9	26-
Italian Swiss Colony/ Colony	0	0	0	0	0	0	0	0	0	0	
	(20)	(26)	(32)	(38)	(44)	(50)	(56)	(61)	(66)	(71)	
Krug	1	1	1	1	1	1	1	1	1	1	

8—*Lancers	2	2	2	2	2	2	2	2	2	2	____28-
Los Hermanos	3	3	3	3	3	3					
9—*Mateus	4	4	4	4	4	4	4	4	4	4	____30-
*Mondavi	5	5	5	5	5	5	5	5	5	5	____32-
*Monterey Vineyards	6	6	6	6	6	6	6	6	6	6	____34-
*Mouton Cadet (Moo-tawn ka-day)	7	7	7	7	7	7	7	7	7	7	____36-
Nectarose	8	8	8	8	8	8					
1—*Partager (Par-ta-jhay)	9	9	9	9	9	9	9	9	9	9	____38-
10—*Paul Masson (Ma-sahn)	0	0	0	0	0	0	0	0	0	0	____40-
	(21)	(27)	(33)	(39)	(45)	(51)	(57)	(62)	(67)	(72)	
*Masson Light	1	1	1	1	1	1	1	1	1	1	____42-
*Polo Brindisi	2	2	2	2	2	2	2	2	2	2	____44-
*Prego	3	3	3	3	3	3	3	3	3	3	____46-
11—*Riunite (Ree-u-nee-tee)	4	4	4	4	4	4	4	4	4	4	____48-
Ruffino	5	5	5	5	5	5					
*Sebastiani	6	6	6	6	6	6	6	6	6	6	____50-
*Sterling	7	7	7	7	7	7	7	7	7	7	____52-
12—*Taylor California Cellars (Calif. Cellars)	8	8	8	8	8	8	8	8	8	8	____54-
*Taylor California Cellars Light	9	9	9	9	9	9	9	9	9	9	____56-
*Taylor Lake Country	0	0	0	0	0	0	0	0	0	0	____58-
Taylor (Ask: ''could	(22)	(28)	(34)	(40)	(46)	(52)	(58)	(63)	(68)	(73)	
you be more specific'')	1	1	1	1	1	1					
*Valbon	2	2	2	2	2	2	2	2	2	2	____60-
*Vivante	3	3	3	3	3	3	3	3	3	3	____62-
Yago	4	4	4	4	4	4					
Other (specify)										80-4	80-5
____________	0	0	0	0	0	0					
____________	0	0	0	0	0	0					
____________	0	0	0	0	0	0					
None	x	x	x	x	x	x					
Don't Know	y	y	y	y	y	y					
	23-	29-	35-	41-	47-	53-					

DATA PROCESSING AND ANALYSIS

Having decided what information is needed to solve the marketing problem at hand—how to acquire the necessary data, who should be in the sample, what questions to ask, how to construct the questionnaire, and how to field the questionnaire and prepare the raw data—collection forms for analysis–we now turn to analysis and interpretation. Specifically, in Chapter 14 various methods for summarizing data are presented. These procedures are extremely useful for acquiring an understanding of the nature of a set of data. Chapter 15 discusses procedures for testing hypotheses concerning means and proportions. These procedures allow us to make inferences from the data collected (i.e., the sample) to the target population of interest. Finally, in Chapter 16 we take up the important topic of correlation and regression analysis. These procedures allow us to investigate the relationships among a set of variables while keeping a view toward explaining the phenomena under study.

An appendix that discusses several of the more popular multivariate data analysis procedures is also provided. Multivariate analysis deals with the *simultaneous* relationships among three or more variables, as opposed to the analysis of a single variable, or the analysis of pairwise relationship between two variables. Multivariate data analysis techniques have become more widely accepted and used in almost all fields of inquiry, due in large measure to the advent of high-speed, large–storage capacity computers and easy-to-use software packages for implementing multivariate analyses. Although it is beyond the scope of this text to discuss multivariate data analysis methods in great detail, the appendix material should nevertheless provide an adequate introduction to this class of procedures. In addition Chapter 17, Part VI, applies several of these procedures in the context of product positioning, market segmentation, and market structure analysis.

Data Analysis
Exploring Basic Relationships

- Discuss and illustrate data summary methods, including measures of central tendency and measures of variability.
- Discuss and illustrate how cross tabulations are used.
- Demonstrate how to graphically represent data and explain the pitfalls to avoid so that actual relationships are not distorted.

INTRODUCTION

You know the saying: A picture is worth a thousand words. In the context of data analysis, the *words* are the many responses that have been collected, and the *picture* refers to procedures that succinctly capture the relationships of interest in the data. As we have seen, *quadrant analysis* is one particular way of graphically representing data to provide insights into the composition of current users and brands. We will discuss quadrant analysis again after becoming familiar with some other approaches for summarizing data.

This chapter focuses on methods used for inspecting data before testing the formal research hypotheses related to the specific study objectives. These methods help us understand the nature of the data collected and, consequently, give a preliminary glimpse of what relationships to expect. We begin by discussing various descriptive statistics, many of them familiar from your basic statistics courses. We then return to cross tabulations, which we introduced in Chapter 13. We conclude with a discussion of graphic methods for displaying data.

DATA SUMMARY METHODS: DESCRIPTIVE STATISTICS

It would be extremely tedious to examine each response to every question appearing in a particular questionnaire. A researcher can use a variety of statistics to summarize data. Descriptive statistics use a single number to summarize data. If a researcher wanted to know, for example, the most likely response to a question, he or she could compute a measure of *central tendency* such as the *mean* for interval or ratio data. If, in addition, the researcher wanted to know how responses are dispersed around the mean, a measure of *variability* such as the *variance* could be computed.

Central tendency and dispersion represent two *informational components* of data. Measures of central tendency such as the mean tell you information about *elevation*—how high or how low the scores on a question tend to be. Measures of variability such as the variance tell you information about *dispersion*—how spread out are the responses to a question.

Measures of central tendency and variability are routinely reported when tabulating a study. Let's look at Table 14–1, for instance. The cross tabulation comes from a concept-product test for a new telecommunications redialing service. There are 13 banner points (including TOTAL) representing different subgroups of respondents. The table presents responses, labeled 1 through 5, to a likelihood-of-purchase question. Note that the total number of respondents answering this question is 766. The 70 "no" answers appearing in the total column relate only to question Q8B. If you examine the business customer banner points and add these frequencies counts, the base is 826, which is 10 respondents less than the total respondent count appearing in the total column. This means that 10 respondents did not provide information that would allow a classification into one of the three business customer types. Mean levels, the *standard deviation* (STD DEV), and the *standard error* (STD ERR) are reported at the bottom of the table.

Measures of Central Tendency: The Mean

The **mean** is by far the most frequently used measure of central tendency. In standard notation we let X_i denote the values that a variable can assume, n the sample size (i.e., the number of respondents), and $\overline{X}$ the mean. Then

$$\overline{X} = \sum_{i=1}^{n} X_i/n \qquad (14\text{--}1)$$

where Σ is the summation operator, with the subscript letter indicating the observations over which to sum.

To compute the mean, you add all the values given by respondents to that question and divide by the sample size. In other words, the mean is simply the average value of a variable. As we indicated earlier, the mean provides information on elevation—how high or how low the scores are for a particular question. Examining Table 14–1, for instance, shows that the mean likelihood-to-purchase score for the new redialing concept is 2.19 across the entire sample, which is rather low compared with the highest value of 5. Note that the mean level for this question can be obtained by the following operation:

$$\overline{X} = \frac{69(5) + 88(4) + 148(3) + 74(2) + 387(1)}{766}$$

or equivalently by

$$\overline{X} = 5(0.09) + 4(0.115) + 3(0.193) + 2(0.097) + 1(0.505)$$

TABLE 14-1   Cross Tabulation of Likelihood to Purchase Repeat-Dialing Service

Q8B. LIKELIHOOD TO PURCHASE REPEAT DIALING FOR YOUR BUSINESS AT COST OF $4.00 EACH MONTH

	TOTAL	REGION			BUSINESS CUSTOMER			NUMBER OF TELEPHONE LINES		PC	MODEM	FAX	ANS MACH
		METRO	STATE	OHIO	LESS THAN 3 YRS	3-10 YRS	MORE THAN 10 YRS	1	2-6	1+	1+	1+	1+
TOTAL RESPONDENTS	836	214	343	279	146	241	439	527	253	117	104	131	335
NO ANSWER	70	16	36	18	10	12	46	47	14	6	5	9	22
TOTAL ANSWERING REPEAT DIALING	766	198	307	261	136	229	393	480	239	111	99	122	313
VERY LIKELY TO BUY 5	69	13	25	31	6	27	34	34	29	15	18	18	30
	9.0	6.6	8.1	11.9	4.4	11.8	8.7	7.1	12.1	13.5	18.2	14.8	9.6
4	88	18	35	35	21	29	38	49	35	19	13	19	38
	11.5	9.1	11.4	13.4	15.4	12.7	9.7	10.2	14.6	17.1	13.1	15.6	12.1
3	148	41	52	55	36	39	73	90	46	20	18	25	83
	19.3	20.7	16.9	21.1	26.5	17.0	18.6	18.8	19.2	18.0	18.2	20.5	26.5
2	74	25	27	22	9	33	32	45	28	14	11	8	26
	9.7	12.6	8.8	8.4	6.6	14.4	8.1	9.4	11.7	12.6	11.1	6.6	8.3
1	387	101	168	118	64	101	216	262	101	43	39	52	136
NOT VERY LIKELY TO BUY	50.5	51.0	54.7	45.2	47.1	44.1	55.0	54.6	42.3	38.7	39.4	42.6	43.5
MEAN BASE	766	198	307	261	136	229	393	480	239	111	99	122	313
MEAN	2.19	2.08	2.09	2.38	2.24	2.34	2.09	2.06	2.43	2.54	2.60	2.53	2.36
STD DEV	1.39	1.29	1.38	1.46	1.31	1.44	1.38	1.33	1.46	1.48	1.55	1.52	1.39
STD ERR	.050	.092	.079	.090	.112	.095	.069	.061	.094	.141	.156	.138	.078

399

The first operation involves multiplying each response value by the number of respondents who gave that value and then, after summing, dividing by the total number of respondents. The second operation multiplies each response value by the percentage of respondents giving that response (for example, $0.09 = 69/766$), and then sums these products.

Examination of mean levels also provides for a quick assessment of differences across subgroups as well. In Table 14–1, for example, respondents are classified with respect to region, whether they are a business customer, number of telephone lines, and ownership of four types of telecommunications equipment. Note that mean purchase likelihood scores range from a low of 2.06 for respondents having only one telephone line to a high of 2.60 for respondents owning one or more modems. In general, the mean purchase likelihood scores for respondents owning telecommunication equipment is higher than the mean levels found in other subgroups, and, therefore, it appears that this type of respondent is, all else the same, more favorably disposed to the new redialing product concept.

mode
The most frequently occurring value; used as a measure of central tendency for data assuming a limited number of values.

There are other measures of central tendency that are applicable in the case of nominal or ordinal data. The **mode,** for instance, gives the most frequently occurring value. If you were to graph a distribution by counting up the number of times each unique response is given, the highest peak would be the mode. In Table 14–1 the mode is the fifth response category listed (the category labeled 1). The mode is best suited for categorical variables, or in cases where the responses to a variable have been categorized.

median
The value that is halfway between the highest and lowest values.

Another measure of central tendency is the **median.** The median is the value that is halfway between the highest and the lowest values. To determine the median you must first order the data either from high to low or from low to high and then record the number that is in the middle. When the sample has an even number of respondents, the median is calculated by adding the two numbers in the middle, and then dividing by two. For example, if you have a sample of 100, you add the responses for the 50th and the 51st observations in the arrayed data and divide by two.

Measures of Variability: The Variance

Measures of variability reflect the amount of dispersion or "spread" in the data. It is possible for two sets of data to differ in both central tendency and dispersion; another two sets of data may have the same central tendency but differ greatly in terms of dispersion. As we have indicated, the most commonly used measure of variability is the variance or standard deviation, although as demonstrated in Chapter 10, the range is also used as an approximation to the variance. The **range** is the difference between the largest and smallest observations in a data set. The range measures the total spread in any data set. It is simple and easily calculated but does not take into account how the data are distributed between the largest and smallest values.

range
The difference between the largest and smallest observations in a data set.

Recall that we discussed the variance and standard deviation in relation to sampling variability in Chapter 9. The **standard deviation** of a variable, X, denoted as s_x, is obtained by taking the square root of the variance:[1]

standard deviation
*Used as a measure of
variability when the data
have interval or ratio
scale properties—it is the
square root of the
variance.*

$$s_x = \sqrt{\frac{\sum_{i=1}^{n} (X_i - \overline{X})^2}{n-1}}$$

or   (14–2)

$$s_x = \sqrt{\frac{\sum_{i=1}^{n} X_i^2 - \frac{(\sum_{i=1}^{n} X_i)^2}{n}}{n-1}}$$ (14–3)

where

n = Total sample size
X_i = Value of the ith observation
$\overline{X}$ = Mean of the variable of interest

Note that the variance and standard deviation are calculated by taking the sum of squared deviations of X_i around its mean value $\overline{X}$. The more the individuals who participate in a study tend to give the same response to a particular question, the smaller will be the variance and standard deviation. When the standard deviation is small, you can conclude that the individuals are homogeneous (of like kind), and, consequently, the mean gives a good indication of the response of any particular individual. In contrast, if the variance or standard deviation is large, then individuals are heterogeneous and the mean may not be a very good indicator of the response of any particular individual.

Table 14–1 reports standard deviations for the entire sample as well as for each subgroup. Standard errors are also reported. Recall that we discussed standard errors in the context of sampling (Chapters 9 and 10) and used them in constructing confidence intervals. To compute the standard error of the mean, you divide the standard deviation by the square root of the sample size:

$$s_{\overline{x}} = \frac{s_x}{\sqrt{n}}$$

Note that the standard deviations for the subgroups are not very different, ranging from a low of 1.29 to a high of 1.55. The standard errors show more disparity, which is accounted for by the differences in the base sizes of the various

---

[1]From the definition of σ^2 and properties of the expected value, it can be shown that $E(s_x^2) = \frac{n-1}{n}\sigma^2$. Hence, s_x^2 is a biased estimator of σ^2 if we divide by n, but an unbiased estimator when we divide by $n-1$. For a complete discussion of this relationship, see P. G. Hoel, *Introduction to Mathematical Statistics*, 3rd ed. (New York: John Wiley & Sons, 1962), p. 229.

subgroups. We can use this information to construct 95 percent confidence intervals for the purchase likelihood of each subgroup by multiplying the standard error by 2 (actually 1.96, but let's use 2 for simplicity). It is interesting to note that none of the confidence intervals cover response category 3, a purchase likelihood value that might indicate some indifference to the new redialing product concept. Take the modem 1 + subgroup, for example. The lower bound of the confidence interval is 2.60 − 2(0.156) = 2.288, and the upper bound is 2.60 + 2(0.156) = 2.912.

Another illustration will help explain the information conveyed by mean and variance. Table 14–2 presents means and variances for five adjective statements used in an automobile name study. Two hundred respondents were asked to rate three existing automobiles (the Celica, the Fiero, and the Pulsar) on five characteristics along a seven-point scale, where 1 indicates "does not describe at all" and 7 indicates "describes completely." The means and variances reported in the table were computed by summing across individuals and automobiles. That is, because each individual rated three automobiles, there are in effect 600 observations (200 × 3). What can you conclude from this information? From the mean levels it appears that individuals on the average rated the three automobiles as being consistent with the adjectives "powerful" and "sporty."

The variances provide some interesting insights as well. Note that the variance of the ratings on "powerful" is relatively small, whereas the variance of the ratings

TABLE 14–2		
—		
Automobile Names Rated on Five Characteristics		

Adjective	Mean	Variance
For men	4.61	2.13
Sporty	5.93	4.31
Dependable	4.27	5.92
Powerful	6.11	1.78
High quality	4.09	2.47

Individual	Celica	Fiero	Pulsar
Small Variance: Parity			
1	5	5	5
2	4	4	4
3	5	5	5
4	4	4	4
Large Variance: Automobile Differences			
1	4	6	1
2	3	7	1
3	4	6	1
4	3	7	1
Large Variance: Individual Differences			
1	1	1	1
2	7	7	7
3	1	1	1
4	7	7	7

on "dependable" is relatively large. What can account for a large or a small vari- ance? In the context of this rating exercise, a small variance will be obtained if individuals are homogeneous in their perceptions—if most individuals rate each of the three automobiles similarly on "powerful." In the extreme case, if all indi- viduals gave the same rating to each automobile on an adjective statement, the variance would be zero, indicating that these automobiles are on *parity* with re- spect to this adjective statement. Two situations can account for a relatively large variance for an adjective statement: Either individual respondents differ in terms of their automobile perceptions (the automobiles are perceived differently), or the automobiles may have similar mean ratings but individuals are different (each in- dividual rates each of the three automobiles similarly on an adjective statement, but across individuals the ratings are different). The bottom portion of Table 14–2 illustrates these results.

DATA TABULATION PROCEDURES

Descriptive statistics of central tendency and variability, although informative, are frequently not sufficient to let a researcher fully understand the relationships among a set of variables. For this reason we often turn to tabulation procedures, which can provide additional insights into the data, before we consider what spe- cific statistical analyses to perform.

Our discussion uses data collected from 100 respondents who participated in a banking study dealing with the use of and attitudes toward automatic teller ma- chines (ATMs). A partial list of these questions is shown in Exhibit 14–1 (see page 404).

Frequency Distributions

Frequency distributions are useful for summarizing responses to specific ques- tions as well as for data cleaning (discussed in Chapter 13). Table 14–3 (see page 404) presents the frequency distributions for two variables: having an ATM card and age. From the table you can see that 61 percent of the sample have an ATM card. With respect to age, 22 percent of the sample were between the ages of 18 and 34; 33 percent were between the ages of 35 and 54; and 45 percent were 55 years of age or older.

frequency distributions
Statistical procedures useful for summarizing responses to specific questions.

Cross Tabulation

Given the distribution of the two variables in Table 14–3, you might want to con- clude that older people are more likely to have an ATM card because the majority of the respondents were over the age of 54 (45 percent) and most of the people in the sample have an ATM card (61 percent). This conclusion is, however, specula- tive because neither of the two frequency distributions provide information on the joint distribution of the two variables—for example, the percentage of the sample who have an ATM card *and* who are over the age of 54. To examine the joint distribution of two variables, we use a procedure called *cross tabulation*, which we introduced in Chapter 13.

EXHIBIT 14–1
—
Some Bank Survey
Questions Used in
ATM Study

1. Do you have a checking account with the bank?
   Yes   [ ]
   No   [ ]   [*If no, terminate and record.*]
2. Which type of checking accounts do you have?
   Senior   Yes   [ ]-1   No   [ ]-0   (1/1)
   Now   Yes   [ ]-1   No   [ ]-0   (1/2)
   State   Yes   [ ]-1   No   [ ]-0   (1/3)
3. Do you have an automatic teller card with your account? ·
   Yes   [ ]-1   (1/4)
   No   [ ]-0   [*If no, go to question 5.*]
4. Do you use the ATM for (read list)
   Deposits   Yes   [ ]-1   No   [ ]-0   (1/5)
   Withdrawals   Yes   [ ]-1   No   [ ]-0   (1/6)
   Transfers   Yes   [ ]-1   No   [ ]-0   (1/7)
   [*Show card demonstrating bank by phone service.*]
5. If the bank offered this service would you
   Definitely use   [ ]-1   (1/8)
   Probably use   [ ]-2
   Might or might not use   [ ]-3
   Probably not use   [ ]-4
   Definitely not use   [ ]-5
6. Gender [*Record, don't ask.*]
   Female   [ ]-1   (1/9)
   Male   [ ]-2
7. Age group
   18–34   [ ]-1   (1/10)
   35–54   [ ]-2
   55 +   [ ]-3
8. Household income
   Less than $15,000   [ ]-1   (1/11)
   $15,000 to $29,999   [ ]-2
   $30,000 to $49,999   [ ]-3
   $50,000 or more   [ ]-4

TABLE 14–3   Frequency Distributions

ATM

Value Label		Value	Frequency	Percent	Valid Percent	Cum Percent
NO		0	39	39.0	39.0	39.0
YES		1	61	61.0	61.0	100.0
		Total	100	100.0	100.0	
Valid cases	100	Missing cases	0			

AGE

Value Label		Value	Frequency	Percent	Valid Percent	Cum Percent
18–34		1	22	22.0	22.0	22.0
35–54		2	33	33.0	33.0	55.0
55 +		3	45	45.0	45.0	100.0
		Total	100	100.0	100.0	
Valid cases	100	Missing cases	0			

Source: N. H. Nie, C. H. Hull, J. G. Jenkins, K. Steinbrenner, and D. H. Beent, *SPSS: Statistical Package for the Social Sciences* (New York: McGraw-Hill, 1975).

A **cross tabulation,** which we introduced earlier in Table 14–1, is an extension of the frequency distribution and is a common method of describing two or more variables at a time. A table cross classifying the levels of one variable with the levels of some other variable provides the bivariate (two variables at one time) frequency distribution. These tables are also often referred to as *contingency tables.*

Table 14–4 presents the cross-tabulation table for ATM card ownership and age. The row and column totals (usually referred to as *marginals*) provide the same information as the frequency distribution where each is treated separately. The individual cells of the cross-tabulated table, though, provide additional information.

Note that there are four numbers in each cell of the cross-tabulated table. For ease of discussion, number the six cells or boxes of Table 14–4 from one to six beginning at the first row and continuing from left to right. Thus, cell 1 refers to individuals who do not have an ATM card and who are 18 to 34 years old, whereas cell 5 refers to individuals who have an ATM card and who are 35 to 54 years old. To understand the meaning of the four numbers appearing in each cell, look at the description of cell 1 in Exhibit 14–2 (see page 406). Only 5.1 percent (row percentage) of those respondents who do not have an ATM card are aged 18 to 34. Alternatively, if you look at the column percentage, you see that 9.1 percent of the people aged 18 to 34 do not have an ATM card. The conclusions drawn from cross tabulating these two questions are distinctly different from the speculative conclusions we had reached by examining each variable separately. This is not always necessarily the case. Sometimes the conclusions drawn from examining separate frequency distributions are consistent with the conclusions obtained by cross

TABLE 14–4
—
Cross Tabulation of
ATM and Age

	Count Row Pct		Age		
	Col Pct Total Pct	18–34 1	35–54 2	55+ 3	Row Total
ATM					
No	0	2 5.1 9.1 2.0	10 25.6 30.3 10.0	27 69.2 60.0 27.0	39 39.0
Yes	1	20 32.8 90.9 20.0	23 37.7 69.7 23.0	18 29.5 40.0 18.0	61 61.0
	Column Total	22 22.0	33 33.0	45 45.0	100 100.0
Number of Missing Observations:		0			

Source: The example was implemented with use of SPSS.

EXHIBIT 14–2
—
Annotated Cell (1,1)
of Cross Tabulation
in Table 14–4

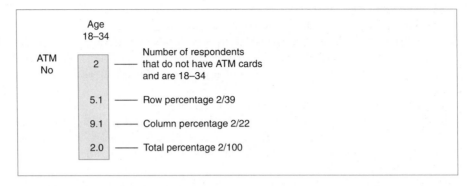

classifying two variables. This happens when the two variables in question are statistically independent, as we discuss further in Chapter 16.

Although cross tabulations provide an efficient way to summarize data, keep in mind that they provide information only on bivariate (two variables at a time) relationships—no information is provided on relationships among three or more variables taken simultaneously. Also, while cross tabulations can provide useful information in a condensed form, they are not an efficient way to search for results. For example, if you have 50 variables, there would be 1,225 possible two-way cross tabulations to examine—clearly an unwieldy number. Thus, cross tabulations are a useful tool in the initial examination of the nature of the data relationships, but they are not particularly well suited for searching for relationships among many variables.

The format of a cross tabulation will depend on the software used. As indicated previously, in commercial marketing research the rows of the table are identified as stub points and the columns of the table are called banner points. *Banner points* represent subgroups of respondents who are of special interest for some reason and, consequently, are singled out for closer examination. They might correspond to males and females, or different age groups, for example (see Table 14–5). The *stub points* represent the specific questions and the corresponding responses. In a readership study, for instance, the stub points might correspond to an individual's readership of news-related stories (as in Table 14–5). You might want to think of the banner points as explanatory variables and the stubs as either dependent or response variables. The elements of commercially prepared cross tabulations give the column frequency and column percentage for each stub point. For example, Table 14–5 reveals that 18 females, representing 32.1 percent of all females surveyed, indicated that they skimmed or glanced at news-related stories.

GRAPHIC REPRESENTATION OF DATA

Graphs are a valuable means of summarizing and displaying data. Constructed in certain ways, however, they can be misleading. Improper graphing procedures can

TABLE 14–5   Banner

Your readership of news-related stories

| | Total | Sex | | Age | | |
		Male	Female	Under 35	35+44	45 & Over
	132	67	56	68	27	35
	100.0	100.0	100.0	100.0	100.0	100.0
No answer	5	3	–	1	3	1
	3.8	4.5	–	1.5	11.1	2.9
Read most	32	15	15	21	2	9
	24.2	22.4	26.8	30.9	7.4	25.7
Read part	53	28	23	26	14	12
	40.2	41.8	41.1	38.2	51.9	34.3
Skimmed or glanced at	40	21	18	20	8	11
	30.3	31.3	32.1	29.4	29.6	31.4
Read none, skipped	2	–	–	–	–	2
	1.5	–	–	–	–	5.7

Source: The example shown was developed using ACROSS, Strawberry Software, Inc.

produce conclusions that are suspect.[2] Depending on their construction, graphs can hide differences or create them.

For example, consider Exhibit 14–3 (see page 408), which shows the number of public and private elementary schools for selected years between 1929 and 1970. According to the graph, we would conclude that the number of public schools has dropped substantially but that the number of private schools has remained about the same for the period of study. Now certainly we would expect that the number of private schools is only a small percentage of the total number of elementary schools. By plotting the number of private schools in thousands of schools from 0 to 400, any fluctuations in the number of schools are hidden by the scale. Exhibit 14–4 (see page 408), which also plots the number of private schools in thousands, but from 0 to 15, presents quite a different picture from that portrayed in Exhibit 14–3. The magnitude of a graph's scale is determined by the person who creates the graph. All observers should take care not to let the magnitude of a scale hide fluctuations when they exist or create fluctuations when they don't exist.

Consider next Exhibit 14–5 (see page 409), which presents circulation data for two New York City daily newspapers. It appears that by early 1981 the *Post* had caught up to the *Daily News* in circulation. Yet note the change in the scale at 800,000. Between 500,000 and 800,000 the scale intervals are 100,000, but now, at 800,000, the interval jumps to 700,000. This change of scale makes the difference in circulation appear smaller than it actually is. While it is true that the graph includes the circulation numbers, 1,191,000 for the *Daily News* and 732,000 for

---

[2]H. Wainer, "How to Display Data Badly," *The American Statistician*, May 1984, pp. 137–47.

EXHIBIT 14–3

—

Poorly Designed Bar
Graph of Number of
Public and Private
Elementary Schools,
1929–1970

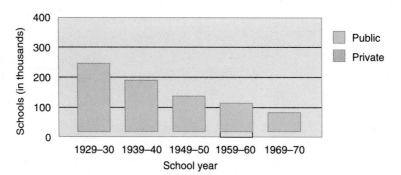

Note: The variation in the number of private schools is obscured by scale.

Source: From Howard Wainer, "How to Display Data Badly," *The American Statistician*, May 1984, p. 139.

EXHIBIT 14–4

—

Line Graph Showing
Increase in Number
of Private
Elementary Schools,
1930–1970

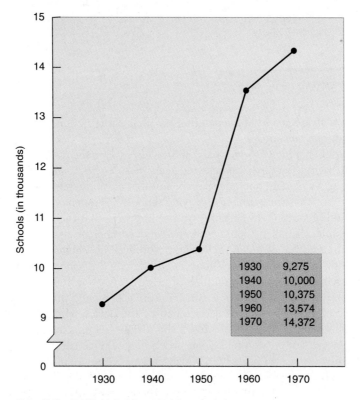

1930	9,275
1940	10,000
1950	10,375
1960	13,574
1970	14,372

Note: Unlike Exhibit 14–3, this graph shows a large increase.

Source: From Howard Wainer, "How to Display Data Badly," *The American Statistician*, May 1984, p. 140.

the *Post*, the crucial question is do readers of the graph rely on the numbers or the lines to make an interpretation?

Some of the more commonly used data graphics are bar charts and pie charts. Numerous graphic packages are available for both large mainframe computers and

EXHIBIT 14–5

Line Graph with
Change of Scale

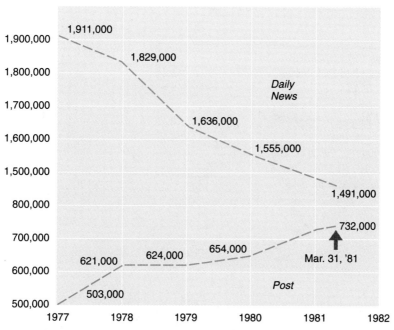

Source: From Howard Wainer, "How to Display Data Badly," *The American Statistician,* May 1984, p. 141.

IBM (and IBM clones) and Macintosh personal computers. The graphs illustrated here were constructed using CHARTMASTER℠ and SYSDAT℠. Spreadsheet programs such as LOTUS 1-2-3® and EXCEL 3.0 can also generate bar charts and pie charts.

Bar Charts

To illustrate the use of bar charts, let us consider an advertising study for a new suntan lotion. In this study, each respondent was assigned to one of three execution groups and, depending on the group to which the respondent was assigned, asked to evaluate one of three ads. After exposure to the particular advertising execution, each respondent rated the advertisement on six semantic differential items. Table 14–6 (see page 410) shows the mean ratings. If the researcher wants to compare the advertisement rating evaluations on each semantic differential item for each of the advertising execution groups, constructing bar charts is one possibility.

A stacked bar chart, which stacks the three executions in columns for each semantic differential scale, is shown in part *a* of Exhibit 14–6 (see page 410). A clustered bar chart, which graphs execution groups side by side for each semantic differential scale, is shown in part *b* of Exhibit 14–6. For both bar charts, the vertical axis gives the mean values and the six evaluative scales are spread along the horizontal axis. Consequently, the higher the bar, the greater the mean value for that characteristic of the advertisement.

From the clustered bar chart shown in part *b* of Exhibit 14–6, we can see that (1) execution group 1 is rated higher on each attribute than either of the other

TABLE 14–6

Mean Ratings on
Evaluative
Dimensions

	Group		
	1	2	3
High quality/low quality	4.32	4.00	2.68
Informative/uninformative	5.24	4.80	1.88
Good/bad	4.96	4.16	2.64
Persuasive/nonpersuasive	4.80	3.68	2.32
Artful/artless	3.76	3.04	2.92
Refined/vulgar	4.40	4.28	3.80

Group 1 = "Fun in the Sun"
Group 2 = "Serious Tanning"
Group 3 = "At the Lake"

EXHIBIT 14–6   Bar Charts

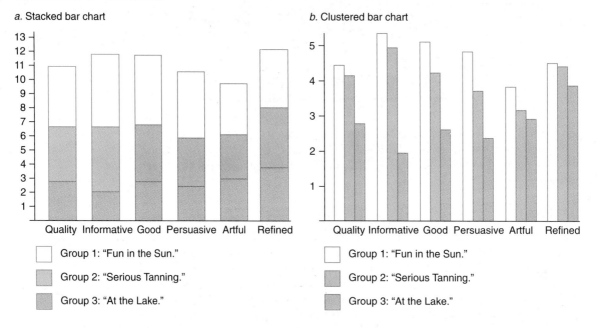

a. Stacked bar chart

b. Clustered bar chart

Group 1: "Fun in the Sun."
Group 2: "Serious Tanning."
Group 3: "At the Lake."

two executions and (2) execution group 1 received its highest rating on "informative/uninformative" and its lowest rating on "artful/artless." The same conclusions can be drawn from the stacked bar chart; however, in this form, across-group conclusions are sometimes more difficult to draw.

Pie Charts

Pie charts are an alternative method for presenting frequency distributions. The larger the slice of the pie, the greater the frequency. The pie chart in Exhibit 14–7 graphically depicts the overall attitude ratings of each advertising execution

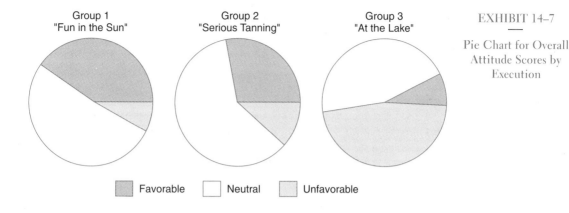

EXHIBIT 14–7
___

Pie Chart for Overall
Attitude Scores by
Execution

(group) for the new suntan lotion product. For translation into pie chart form, variables were interpreted such that a response of 6 or 7 represents a favorable attitude (top box score); a response of 3, 4, or 5 represents a neutral attitude; and a response of 1 or 2 represents an unfavorable attitude.

Quadrant Analysis

Quadrant analysis is a graphic technique that is typically used in commercial marketing research studies to analyze importance and attribute ratings. Many marketing research studies ask the respondent to indicate the importance that specific attributes play in his or her choice of one brand among various alternatives. The respondent is often asked to rate specified brands on their ability to deliver satisfactory amounts of the desired end benefits. Quadrant analysis produces a grid that shows which attributes are important and those attributes that a brand (or service) delivers. This type of analysis lets the researcher determine whether the attributes that a particular brand delivers are the attributes that respondents evaluate as being important.

An example can demonstrate how quadrant analysis works. In a study of the cold and cough remedy market category, respondents were asked to react to a list of characteristics that could be used to describe cold and cough remedy products and specifically to indicate how important each characteristic would be for the "ideal" cold and cough remedy product. Respondents were also asked to rate each brand that they had tried during the past 30 days on the same set of characteristics. Quadrant analysis was conducted on the top two box scores for both the importance (i.e., "extremely important" and "very important") and brand ratings (i.e., "describes completely" and "describes somewhat"). Table 14–7 (see page 412) presents the results of the first stage of the quadrant analysis for one of the brands, labeled simply brand L.

The second column of the table (labeled Y) gives the percentage of the sample who indicated that the characteristic in question is either extremely important or very important (i.e., top two boxes). The first column of the table (labeled X) gives the percentage of the sample who indicated that the characteristic in question is

TABLE 14–7
——
Quadrant Analysis

Y coordinate is percent top two box of importance.
X coordinate is percent of Y top two box and brand top two box.

Attribute	Brand L	
	X	Y
1. Relieve body aches	11.2	77.9
2. Be gentle to the stomach	40.5	88.3
3. Provide relief that lasts six hours or longer	20.7	79.8
4. Provide fast relief	45.2	96.4
5. Provide extra strength relief	22.4	65.7
6. Be in a liquid form	46.7	56.9
7. Relieve watery, itchy eyes	8.1	51.9
8. Treat more than one symptom at a time	17.6	76.2
9. Be a good value for the money	32.9	81.2
10. Be a product for one specific symptom	11.9	23.1
11. Help you fall asleep	20.0	60.0
12. Be good for nighttime use	38.3	77.1
13. Be non-habit forming	51.0	92.4
14. Be convenient to use away from home	32.6	80.7
15. Relieve head cold symptoms	19.3	86.2
16. Help you to breathe easier	23.1	96.4
17. Loosen upper chest congestion	36.4	92.6
18. Relieve a cough	65.5	94.0
19. Relieve a headache	6.4	81.0
20. Prevent a cold from developing	6.9	76.9
21. Be appropriate for the whole family	31.0	49.8
22. Relieve sinus congestion	12.4	78.8
23. Relieve sneezing	8.8	75.7
24. Relieve a runny nose	14.8	90.5
25. Relieve nasal congestion/stuffiness	17.1	91.2
26. Have no side effects	37.1	96.2
27. Be in a tablet form	1.0	15.2
28. Be safe to use	52.1	97.9
29. Be a good tasting chewable tablet	2.9	51.9
30. Doesn't make you drowsy	22.9	64.8

either extremely important or very important and who *also* agreed strongly or agreed somewhat (top two boxes for brand ratings) that brand L could be described by the respective characteristic. For example, the table indicates that 96.4 percent of the respondents felt that it is extremely important or very important that the "ideal" cold and cough remedy "provide fast relief" (characteristic 4); of those who rate this characteristic as top two box, 45.2 percent rated brand L as delivering this characteristic.

Exhibit 14–8 shows the quadrant map for this study. Characteristics are positioned in one of the four quadrants based on how their importance and delivery

EXHIBIT 14–8
—
Quadrant Map

The brand is brand L cold and cough remedy.
Median importance is 73.50 percent. Median delivery is 18.50 percent.

	Quadrant 2 High Importance Low Delivery		Quadrant 1 High importance High Delivery
1.	Relieve body aches	2.	Be gentle to the stomach
8.	Treat more than one symptom at a time	3.	Provide relief that lasts six hours or longer
19.	Relieve a headache	4.	Provide fast relief
20.	Prevent a cold from developing	9.	Be a good value for the money
22.	Relieve sinus congestion	12.	Be good for nighttime use
23.	Relieve sneezing	13.	Be non-habit forming
24.	Relieve a runny nose	14.	Be convenient to use away from home
25.	Relieve nasal congestion/stuffiness	15.	Relieve head cold symptoms
		16.	Help you to breathe easier
		17.	Loosen upper chest congestion
		18.	Relieve a cough
		26.	Have no side effects
		28.	Be safe to use

	Quadrant 3 Low Importance Low Delivery		Quadrant 4 Low Importance High Delivery
7.	Relieve watery, itchy eyes	5.	Provide extra strength relief
10.	Be a product for one specific symptom	6.	Be in a liquid form
27.	Be in a tablet form	11.	Help you fall asleep
29.	Be a good tasting chewable tablet	21.	Be appropriate for the whole family
		30.	Doesn't make you drowsy

scores, shown in Table 14–7, compare with the median importance and delivery scores that are reported on the top of the page. Consider, for example, the characteristic "relieve body aches" (characteristic 1). Note that it is positioned in Quadrant 2 because its top two box importance score of 77.9 percent exceeds the median score of 73.5 percent, while its delivery score of 11.2 percent is below the median delivery score of 18.5 percent.

SUMMARY

In this chapter we have considered procedures for examining data before testing formal research hypotheses related to the specific objectives of the study at hand. These procedures allow researchers to better understand the nature of the data collected and give some initial insights into the relationships between and among the various variables. The procedures illustrated include the basic descriptive statistics of central tendency (mean, median, and mode) and measures of variability (variance, standard deviation, and range). We then discussed cross tabulations and provided more complete illustrations of their uses. Finally, we considered graphic methods for displaying data that can be particularly effective in summarizing basic relationships.

KEY CONCEPTS

mean	variance	frequency distribution	pie charts
mode	range	cross tabulation	quadrant analysis
median	standard deviation	bar charts	

REVIEW QUESTIONS

1. Tables 1 and 2 (see the following pages) were obtained in a concept study for a new wine cooler. Based on the means and standard deviations (and standard errors) shown in Table 1, what conclusions can you draw concerning the purchase intentions of the various subgroups (i.e., banner points)?

2. Interpret the cross tabulation shown in Table 2.

3. Using the information given in Table 1, illustrate each of the graphic procedures discussed in this chapter.

TABLE 1

Q.14A APPEAL OF PHRASE AS IT RELATES TO COUGAR: J—NOT SWEET LIKE WINE COOLERS, NOT FILLING LIKE BEER, AND MORE REFRESHING THAN WINE OR MIXED DRINKS

	GRND TOTAL	GENDER MALE	GENDER FE-MALE	AGE 21-24	AGE 25-34	AGE 35-49	ALCOHOL 3-5/WK	ALCOHOL 6-10/WK	ALCOHOL 11+/WK	ALCOHOL 6+/WK	MALE 3-5/WK	MALE 6+/WK	FEMALE 3-5/WK	FEMALE 6+/WK	COMMIT. BEER	COMMIT. WINE OR WINE CLR	COMMIT. HARD ALC	CONCEPT VERY MUCH	CONCEPT SOME-WHAT	PROD. LIKE EXT/VERY	PROD. LIKE MOD	PROD. DIS-LIKE
TOTAL RESPONDENTS	300	150	150	101	123	76	131	91	78	169	42	108	89	61	158	108	101	130	170	127	86	11
TOTAL ANSWERING	300	150	150	101	123	76	131	91	78	169	42	108	89	61	158	108	101	130	170	127	86	11
SUBTOTAL..: TOP TWO BOX	242 80.7%	119 79.3%	123 82.0%	84 83.3%	102 82.9%	56 73.7%	108 82.4%	68 74.7%	66 84.6%	134 79.3%	31 73.8%	88 81.5%	77 86.5%	46 75.4%	126 79.7%	87 80.6%	89 88.1%	109 83.8%	133 78.2%	107 84.3%	65 75.6%	6 54.4%
EXTREMELY APPEALING (5)	151 50.3%	68 45.3%	83 55.3%	48 47.5%	66 53.7%	37 48.7%	71 54.2%	39 42.9%	41 52.6%	80 47.3%	20 47.6%	48 44.4%	51 57.3%	32 52.5%	81 51.3%	61 56.5%	59 58.4%	76 58.5%	75 44.1%	78 61.4%	31 36.0%	5 45.5%
APPEALING (4)	91 30.3%	51 34.0%	40 26.7%	36 35.6%	36 29.3%	19 25.0%	37 28.2%	29 31.9%	25 32.1%	54 32.0%	11 26.2%	40 37.0%	26 29.2%	14 23.0%	45 28.5%	26 24.1%	30 29.7%	33 25.4%	58 34.1%	29 22.8%	34 39.5%	1 9.1%
(3)	36 12.0%	21 14.0%	15 10.0%	9 8.9%	12 9.8%	15 19.7%	13 9.9%	15 16.5%	8 10.3%	23 13.6%	7 16.7%	14 13.0%	6 6.7%	9 14.8%	22 13.9%	12 11.1%	6 4.9%	16 12.3%	20 11.8%	11 8.7%	13 15.1%	4 36.4%
(2)	13 4.3%	7 4.7%	6 4.0%	4 4.0%	6 4.9%	3 3.9%	7 5.3%	4 4.4%	2 2.6%	6 3.6%	3 7.1%	4 3.7%	4 4.5%	2 3.3%	6 3.8%	6 5.6%	3 3.0%	5 3.8%	8 4.7%	5 3.9%	6 7.0%	1 9.1%
NOT AT ALL APPEALING (1)	9 3.0%	3 2.0%	6 4.0%	4 4.0%	3 2.4%	2 2.6%	3 2.3%	4 4.4%	2 2.6%	6 3.6%	1 2.4%	2 1.9%	2 2.2%	4 6.6%	4 2.5%	3 2.8%	3 3.0%	0 -%	9 5.3%	4 3.1%	2 2.3%	0 -%
MEAN BASE	300	150	150	101	123	76	131	91	78	169	42	108	89	61	158	108	101	130	170	127	86	11
MEAN	4.21	4.16	4.25	4.19	4.27	4.13	4.27	4.04	4.29	4.16	4.10	4.19	4.35	4.11	4.22	4.26	4.38	4.38	4.07	4.35	4.00	3.91
STD. DEV.	1.01	.97	1.06	1.03	.99	1.04	1.00	1.08	.94	1.03	1.08	.93	.95	1.18	.99	1.04	.95	.85	1.11	1.01	1.01	1.14
STD. ERR.	.059	.079	.086	.102	.089	.119	.087	.114	.107	.079	.166	.089	.101	.152	.079	.101	.094	.074	.085	.090	.108	.343

TABLE 2

Q.5 BEVERAGES CONSUMED AT LEAST OCCASIONALLY

VERSION A: POSITIVE PURCHASE INTENT

	GRND TOTAL	GENDER		AGE			ALCOHOL CONSUMPTION				CONSUMPTION BY GENDER				COMMITMENT			CONCEPT LIKEABIL.		PRODUCT TEST (EITHER)		
											MALE		FEMALE			WINE OR				LIKE		
		MALE	FE-MALE	21-24	25-34	35-49	3-5/WK	6-10/WK	11+/WK	6+/WK	3-5/WK	6+/WK	3-5/WK	6+/WK	BEER	WINE CLR	HARD ALC	VERY MUCH	SOME-WHAT	LIKE EXT/VERY	LIKE MOD	DIS-LIKE
TOTAL RESPONDENTS	300	150	150	101	123	76	131	91	78	169	42	108	89	61	158	108	101	130	170	127	86	11
TOTAL ANSWERING	300	150	150	101	123	76	131	91	78	169	42	108	89	61	158	108	101	130	170	127	86	11
SOFT DRINKS	281 93.7%	138 92.0%	143 95.3%	92 91.1%	118 95.9%	71 93.4%	122 93.1%	87 95.6%	72 92.3%	159 94.1%	39 92.9%	99 91.7%	83 93.3%	60 98.4%	144 91.1%	106 98.1%	97 96.0%	126 96.9%	155 91.2%	120 94.5%	78 90.7%	10 90.9%
JUICE	267 89.0%	132 88.0%	135 90.0%	86 85.1%	110 89.4%	71 93.4%	116 88.5%	81 89.0%	70 89.7%	151 89.3%	37 88.1%	95 88.0%	79 88.8%	56 91.8%	138 87.3%	100 92.6%	88 87.1%	117 90.0%	150 88.2%	111 87.4%	73 84.9%	11 100.%
BEER	261 87.0%	143 95.3%	118 78.7%	88 87.1%	112 91.1%	61 80.3%	103 78.6%	83 91.2%	75 96.2%	158 93.5%	40 95.2%	103 95.4%	63 70.8%	55 90.2%	158 100.%	90 83.3%	87 86.1%	112 86.2%	149 87.8%	110 86.6%	74 86.0%	11 100.%
WINE	201 67.0%	88 58.7%	113 75.3%	67 66.3%	81 65.9%	53 69.7%	102 77.9%	59 64.8%	40 51.3%	99 58.6%	31 73.8%	57 52.8%	71 79.8%	42 68.9%	98 62.0%	91 84.3%	75 74.3%	95 73.1%	106 62.4%	91 71.7%	50 58.1%	8 72.7%
ANY OTHER KIND OF BEVERAGE THAT INCLUDES ALCOHOL	236 78.7%	109 72.7%	127 84.7%	78 77.2%	99 80.5%	59 77.6%	109 83.2%	71 78.0%	56 71.8%	127 75.1%	29 69.0%	80 74.1%	80 89.9%	47 77.0%	124 78.5%	94 87.0%	95 94.1%	112 86.2%	124 72.9%	102 80.3%	65 75.6%	7 63.6%

416

Data Analysis
Hypothesis Testing

— Describe the procedure for testing hypotheses.
— Use hypothesis tests to test specific ideas concerning means and proportions obtained from independent samples and related samples.
— Explore the difference between statistical significance and practical importance.

INTRODUCTION

In Chapter 14 we discussed and illustrated various data analysis and graphing techniques that can provide a preliminary glimpse of the data. These techniques can provide suitable information for many of the marketing manager's needs. However, in some cases, the manager may want to test whether the collected data support some prespecified notion. In this chapter we present methods for testing whether or not the data support specific notions. These methods are called hypothesis tests. First, we present a general discussion of hypothesis testing. Then we move on to present many of the most commonly used hypothesis tests. The chapter closes with a discussion of statistical significance and its relationship to managerial and practical relevance.

HYPOTHESIS TESTING PROCEDURES

We begin our discussion of data analysis by describing procedures for testing hypotheses. A **hypothesis** is an assumption or guess that the researcher or manager makes about some characteristic of the sample population.[1] Throughout this book and especially in Chapter 7, we have provided examples of marketing research proposals, which typically contain an action standard. For example, consider the advertising study described in Exhibit 7–2. The action standard states that in order to be judged successful, the percentage of unaided and aided recall must be statistically significant from the norm.

Rarely will the sample data yield a value equal to the action standard. Hence, the manager is faced with the question: Is the percentage of recall

---

[1]Charles R. Hicks, *Fundamental Concepts in the Design of Experiments*, 3rd ed. (New York: Holt, Rinehart and Winston, 1982).

hypothesis
An assumption or guess the researcher or manager has about some characteristic of the population being sampled.

obtained from the sample different enough from the norm to conclude that we have better (worse) than average copy? Hypothesis testing is directed at answering such questions.

Let's consider another example. A sales manager might assume that on average all sales orders are received by retailers four days after the salesperson has called in the order. To empirically test this hypothesis, the sales manager takes a random sample of invoices and records the number of days between the retailer's placing the order and the retailer's receiving the shipment. Suppose that the data indicate that it takes 4.7 days on average for a retailer to receive the shipment. Now, what should the sales manager conclude about the stated hypothesis? That is: Is the hypothesis correct or incorrect? Clearly, the sample value of order-fulfillment time (4.7 days) is different from the hypothesized value (4.0 days). However, the question that hypothesis testing addresses is: Are the two values different enough for us to conclude that our hypothesis is incorrect? Or stated somewhat differently, is the value 4.7 close enough to 4.0 to lead us to believe that the mean time it takes to receive a shipment in the population is actually 4.0 days?

statistical hypothesis test
Test that determines the probability of observing a sample mean of $\bar{x}$ if indeed the population mean (or hypothesized mean) is μ.

In hypothesis testing we determine whether the hypothesis concerning a population characteristic is tenable. Using our example, the sales manager's hypothesis is that the population average (μ) of order fulfillment time is 4.0 days. A **statistical hypothesis test** determines the probability of observing a sample mean of 4.7 days if indeed the population mean (or hypothesized mean) is 4.0 days. In other words, if the hypothesis is true ($\mu = 4.0$), how likely is it that we should observe a sample with a mean value of 4.7 days?

Essentially, there are two explanations for observing a difference between the hypothesized value and the sample value: (1) The hypothesis is true, and the difference we observe is simply due to sampling error; or (2) the hypothesis is false, and the true mean is some other value. As we will see, hypothesis testing consists of using sample data to determine which explanation is more probable.

Steps in Hypothesis Testing

Hypothesis testing involves a series of steps. First, we must specify our hypothesis. Second, we must choose an appropriate statistical method for testing the hypothesis. And third, we must construct a decision rule that indicates whether or not we should reject the hypothesis.

null hypothesis
The hypothesis that is tested.

Step 1: Stating the Hypothesis. Hypotheses are stated using two forms: (1) a **null hypothesis** (*HO:*) and (2) an **alternative hypothesis** (*HA:*). The null hypothesis is the hypothesis that is tested. For example, in the sales manager's problem, the null hypothesis is:

$$HO: \mu = 4.0 \text{ days}$$

alternative hypothesis
A competing hypothesis to the null.

The alternative hypothesis (*HA:*) is simply a competing hypothesis to the null. An alternative hypothesis can be either directional or nondirectional. For example, we could specify the alternative hypothesis as

$$HA: \mu \neq 4.0 \text{ days}$$

Here we are specifying no direction to the competing hypothesis; if we decide *HO* is not true, μ can be greater than or less than the hypothesized value of 4 days. Conversely, we could specify a direction to the alternative hypothesis. For example, if the sales manager actually believed that the population average of fulfillment time is less than or equal to 4.0 days, then the null and alternative hypotheses would be

$$HO: \mu \leq 4.0 \text{ days}$$
$$HA: \mu > 4.0 \text{ days}$$

When the alternative hypothesis is directional, we have a **one-tail hypothesis test,** whereas when the alternative hypothesis is nondirectional we have a **two-tail hypothesis test.** We will return to the issue of one-tail versus two-tail hypothesis tests shortly.

Note that whether we specify a nondirectional or directional alternative hypothesis, the null and alternative hypotheses are in competition concerning a particular assumption about the population. Consequently, both cannot be true. This is the essence of hypothesis testing. We use sample evidence to determine which of the two hypotheses is more probable.

one-tail hypothesis test
Test used when the alternative hypothesis is directional—the entire region of rejection is in one tail of the distribution.

two-tail hypothesis test
Test used when the alternative hypothesis is nondirectional—the region of rejection is in both tails of the distribution.

EXAMPLE

Typically, the null and alternative hypotheses are formulated based on the action standard of a marketing research proposal. For example, consider the action standard for an advertising copy test that used a before-after experimental design. The action standard reads: "All results are compared with category norms at the 80 percent confidence level." Typically, ads are expected to exceed category norms to be considered for further development or continued use. Hence, either the brand manager's or his or her agency's hypothesis is that the ad being tested will exceed category norms. Since the expectation is that the test ad will exceed the standard, a one-tail hypothesis test is used. This is the relationship we want to test, but it cannot be tested directly. The hypothesis is tested by comparing it with a null hypothesis. "The null hypothesis is a statistical proposition which states essentially that there is no relation between the variables (of the problem). The null hypothesis says you are wrong, there is *no* relation, disprove me if you can."[2] Letting π be the percent change for purchase intent for the test ad and π^* be the norm, the null hypothesis is

$$HO: \pi \leq \pi^*$$

and the alternative hypothesis is

$$HA: \pi > \pi^*$$

You will note that the format of the null hypothesis says you are wrong, the test ad is not greater than the norm. Hence, for the manager to conclude that the test ad is greater than the norm he or she must statistically disprove the null hypothesis. This is the essence of hypothesis testing.

In some cases the action standard does not specify a direction. That is, there are no a priori expectations concerning the variable(s) that will be tested. For example, in package

[2]Fred N. Kerlinger, *Foundations of Behavioral Research* (New York: Holt, Rinehart & Winston, 1964), p. 174.

testing, a critical variable is the visibility score for a particular test package. Now suppose that a brand manager was testing two alternative package forms for a new brand. The action standard may read: "The package receiving the greatest visibility score will be considered for further development." In this case, a two-tail hypothesis test would be used. In this case the null hypothesis would be: "There is no difference in visibility for the packages, disprove me if you can." Letting μ_1 be the average visibility score for one package and μ_2 be the average visibility score for the other package, the null hypothesis is

$$HO: \mu_1 = \mu_2$$

and the alternative hypothesis is

$$HA: \mu_1 \neq \mu_2$$

Step 2: Choosing a Test Statistic.   Each hypothesis test has an accompanying test statistic (TS). For example, if we want to test the null hypothesis, $HO: \mu = 4.0$ days, we would use either a Z-test or a t-test. As you might recall from your basic statistics course, the t-distribution is recommended for situations in which the sample size (n) is less than 30. In contrast, the Z-distribution is used when the sample size exceeds 30. Although this rule generally applies, it would be helpful for you to understand the reasons and assumptions underlying its use.

To do so we need to make use of the sampling distribution. When the sample size is large, the shape of the sampling distribution is normal. In such cases, the mean of the sampling distribution is equal to the mean of the population with variance, given by $\sigma_{\bar{x}}^2 = \sigma^2/n$. When constructing confidence intervals we substituted s^2 for σ^2, where s^2 is the unbiased estimate of σ^2. Now the estimated variance of the mean, $s_{\bar{x}}^2 = s^2/n$, will most likely not equal $\sigma_{\bar{x}}^2 = \sigma^2/n$; however, when the sample size is large this is not a major concern because the sample-based estimate s^2 becomes more precise in the sense of being close to the population value σ^2.

When testing the hypotheses about μ, or alternatively, in making inferences about μ, we utilize standardized scores, or Z-values,[3] given by

$$Z = \frac{\bar{x} - E(\bar{x})}{\sigma_{\bar{x}}} \tag{15–1}$$

However, to utilize the standard scores or Z-values we need to know the population standard error, $\sigma_{\bar{x}}$, or equivalently the population variance σ^2, since $\sigma_{\bar{x}} = \sqrt{\sigma^2/n}$, but such information is rarely, if ever, known. A way to circumvent this problem is to substitute s^2 for σ^2; however, if we do this the explicit assumption is that the sample size is large enough to provide a value of s^2 that is close to the true value of σ^2. Thus, the Z-test statistic shown in Equation 15–1 is the appropriate test statistic to use when either the population variance σ^2 is known, or the sample is

---

[3]William L. Hays, *Statistics for the Social Sciences*, 2nd ed. (New York: Holt, Rinehart & Winston, 1973), p. 392.

large enough for us to believe that s^2 is a precise estimate of σ^2, and, therefore, $s_{\bar{x}}$ can be substituted for $\sigma_{\bar{x}}$ in Equation 15–1. In cases in which the available sample is not sufficiently large to let us believe that s^2 is reasonably close to σ^2, the appropriate test statistic is not the standardized score given in Equation 15–1. Instead, the appropriate test statistic is given by

$$ t = \frac{\bar{x} - E(\bar{x})}{\hat{\sigma}_{\bar{x}}} \qquad (15\text{--}2) $$

which is called the *t*-test statistic. Even though the *t*-test statistic bears a close resemblance to the Z-test statistic, there is a difference. Specifically, in comparing Equations 15–1 and 15–2 we can see the denominators are not the same. The denominator of the Z-test statistic, Equation 15–1, is a constant, whereas the denominator of the *t*-test statistic, Equation 15–2, is a random variable, which is reflected by the "^" over $\sigma_{\bar{x}}$. In other words, when using the *t*-test statistic we need to *estimate* $\sigma_{\bar{x}}$, the standard error of the mean, and $\bar{x}$, the mean, itself. However, in a strict sense, we can use the *t*-test statistic only if the distribution of x_i is normal. If the population distribution of x_i is not normal, the estimates of the mean and the variance of the mean are not statistically independent. In cases in which the normality of x_i is not satisfied, it is extremely difficult to specify the exact distribution of the *t*-test statistic.[4]

Step 3: Constructing a Decision Rule. Sample data are used to obtain a calculated value of the test statistic. For example, if the sample mean (4.7 days) was based on a sample of 25, we would use the *t*-test statistic. Now, if the standard deviation for this sample of 25 was, say 1.1, the calculated *t*-value (t_c) would be

$$ \begin{aligned} t_c &= \frac{\bar{x} - \mu}{s/\sqrt{n}} \qquad (15\text{--}3) \\ &= \frac{4.7 - 4.0}{1.1/\sqrt{25}} \\ &= 3.18 \end{aligned} $$

where we have used the fact that $\hat{\sigma}_{\bar{x}} = s/\sqrt{n}$. We must now decide whether the value of the test statistic is large enough to warrant rejection of the hypothesis. To do so we establish a **region of rejection**. Basically, this region of rejection is a cut point, often referred to as a critical value. Consider Exhibit 15–1 (see page 422), which illustrates the rejection region for a two-tail test. If the calculated value of the test statistic falls in the shaded area, we reject the null hypothesis.

To better understand the rationale underlying the use of the region of rejection in hypothesis testing let us once again consider the *t*-distribution, although the same results hold for the Z-distribution. The formula for the *t*-distribution shown in Equation 15–2 is

$$ t = \frac{\bar{x} - E(\bar{x})}{\hat{0}_{\bar{x}}} \qquad (15\text{--}4) $$

region of rejection
A cut point often referred to as a critical value; if the value of the test statistic falls to the right or the left of this critical value, we reject the null hypothesis.

---

[4]Ibid.

EXHIBIT 15–1

Two-Tail Region of
Rejection

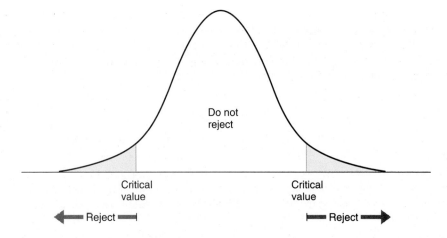

or, equivalently

$$t = \frac{\bar{x} - \mu}{s/\sqrt{n}} \qquad (15\text{–}5)$$

Hence, if we want the sampling distribution of t when the null hypothesis is true (when the mean is μ), then we would derive the frequency distribution for the values calculated from Equation 15–2 for all samples of size n.

Exhibit 15–2, part *a* presents the distribution when the sample size (n) equals 5. We can interpret the distribution as follows: If the null hypothesis is true, it is highly probable you will get a calculated value of t in the range -1 to 1. However, it is unlikely you will get a calculated value less than -2 or greater than 2 if the null hypothesis is true. Because this is a density function, we can determine the probability of observing a specific value of t, given that the null hypothesis is true. This value is our critical value. The shaded areas in Exhibit 15–2, part *b* represent 0.025 percent of the distribution. Hence, if our calculated test statistic was less than -2.776 or greater than 2.776 we would reject our null hypothesis and be confident of making the right decision in 95 out of 100 cases based on the sample data. Hypothesis tests are based on sample data; consequently, we never reject or fail to reject a hypothesis with certainty. The decision to reject or not reject the null is always subject to error.

Inspecting Table 3 of the Statistical Appendix gives us the tabled critical t-values. Note that for a specified level of α, the region of rejection changes for different degrees of freedom, denoted by df, where $df = n - 1$. Unlike the Z-distribution, the t-distribution is actually a family of distributions. The sampling distribution of the t-test statistic depends on the estimate of $\hat{\sigma}_{\bar{x}}$, which changes as the sample size is varied. Consequently, to determine the region of rejection for a t-test statistic we need to specify both the confidence level $(1 - \alpha/2)$ and the degrees of freedom (df).

The significance level for a statistical test is specified as $1 - \alpha$, or $1 - \alpha/2$, the difference being whether we want to conduct a one-tail $(1 - \alpha)$ hypothesis test

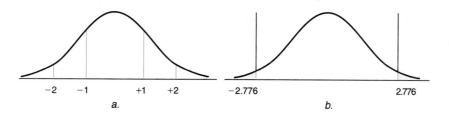

EXHIBIT 15–2

Critical Regions for
t-Distribution for
n = 5

or a two-tail $(1 - \alpha/2)$ hypothesis test. For example, if the sales manager wanted to test the hypothesis that delivery time was less than or equal to the hypothesized value of 4.0, then he or she would use a one-tail test. That is, the entire region of rejection would be in the left-hand tail of the distribution. Consequently, when specifying the tabled value of a test statistic, we use two subscripts: The first refers to the confidence level of the hypothesis test, and the second refers to the degrees of freedom. When we wish to use a one-tail test, the first subscript is denoted as $1 - \alpha$, whereas if we wish to use a two-tail test, the first subscript will be denoted as $(1 - \alpha/2)$. For example, $t_{(1 - \alpha;\, df = n - 1)}$ refers to a one-tail t-test that has $n - 1$ degrees of freedom (df), whereas $t_{(1 - \alpha/2;\, df = n - 1)}$ refers to a two-tail t-test that has $n - 1$ degrees of freedom (df).

Basically, the decision rules are to reject the null hypothesis if the calculated value of the test statistic falls in the region of rejection and to fail to reject the null hypothesis if the calculated value of the test statistic does not fall in the region of rejection. Letting TS_c be the calculated value of the test statistic and TS_t be the tabulated value of the test statistic for some specified α level, we reject HO: if

$$TS_c > TS_t \text{ or } -TS_c < -TS_t$$

Thus, the decision rule is simply to reject the null hypothesis if the value of TS_c lies in the region of rejection, as established by the critical values of TS_t.

Returning to the example we used to explain the steps in hypothesis testing, suppose we wanted to test the hypothesis that the population mean was 4.0 days. The sample of $n = 25$ elements from the population has a sample mean of 4.7 and a standard deviation of 1.1. The null and alternative hypotheses are

$$HO: \mu = 4.0$$
$$HA: \mu \neq 4.0$$

To test this hypothesis, we use the t-test statistic

$$t = \frac{\bar{x} - \mu}{s/\sqrt{n}} \qquad (15\text{–}6)$$

where in this case $\bar{x}$ is the sample mean (4.7) and μ is the assumed population parameter (mean) equal to 4.0. Now the calculated t-value is

$$t_c = \frac{4.7 - 4.0}{1.1/\sqrt{25}} = 3.18$$

EXHIBIT 15–3
——
Region of Rejection
for *t*-Test Statistic
for α = 0.05 and
df = 24

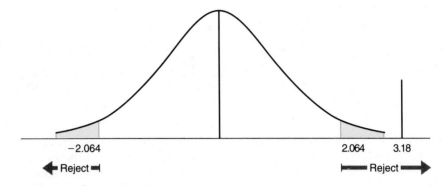

Given that the null hypothesis is true, the shaded areas of Exhibit 15–3 indicate that for *df* = 24(25 − 1), 95 percent of the *t*-values calculated will lie between the region −2.064 and +2.064, and these critical values constitute the region of rejection. Hence, with a calculated value of 3.18 we would reject the null hypothesis because the test statistic does fall within the region of rejection. The distribution in Exhibit 15–3 gives the *t*-values we would expect if the true mean of the population was the hypothesized value 4.0. Hence, what we are rejecting is the likelihood of observing a mean value of 4.7 (with a standard deviation of 1.1 based on a sample size of 25) coming from a population distribution in which the population mean is actually 4.0.

Type I error
Situation occurring when the null hypothesis is in fact true but is nevertheless rejected on the basis of the sample data.

alpha (α) level
The likelihood of committing Type I error.

Type II or beta (β) error
Situation occurring when we fail to reject the null hypothesis (HO:) when in fact the alternative (HA:) is true.

power of the test
(1 − β)
The probability of making a correct decision of rejecting the null hypothesis (HO:) when in fact it is false.

Error Types

Hypothesis testing is subject to two types of error, customarily referred to as Type I and Type II error. Suppose we specify a null hypothesis and, based on the sample data, we reject it. We may have reached a wrong conclusion simply because the observed difference between the sampled value and the hypothesized population value is due to sampling error. That is, the sample data actually come from a population whose mean is equal to the (null) hypothesized value but—because of sampling fluctuation—this particular value of $\bar{x}$ differs from μ. **Type I error** occurs when the null hypothesis is in fact true but is nevertheless rejected on the basis of the sample data. The researcher sets the tolerance of committing Type I error. The likelihood of committing Type I error is called the **alpha (α) level**. Hence $1 − α$ is the probability of making a correct decision, if we fail to reject the null hypothesis (*HO:*) when in fact it is true.

On the other hand, we could fail to reject the null hypothesis (*HO:*) when in fact the alternative (*HA:*) is true. This is referred to as **Type II or beta (β) error**. The value $1 − \beta$, which is called the **power of the test**, reflects the probability of making a correct decision of rejecting the null hypothesis (*HO:*) when in fact it is false. Consequently, α and β represent probabilities of error concerning whether or not we reject the null hypothesis, given that the null hypothesis is actually true or false. That is

Decision Based on Sample	Actual Value for Population	
	HO: True	*HO:* False
Reject *HO:*	Type I error (α)	1 − β
Fail to reject *HO:*	1 − α	Type II error (β)

TABLE 15–1

Errors in Hypothesis Testing

$$\alpha = \text{PR (reject } HO\text{:) when } HO\text{: true}$$
$$\beta = \text{Pr (not reject } HO\text{:) when } HO\text{: not true}$$
$$1 - \beta = \text{Power} = \text{Pr (reject } HO\text{:) when } HO\text{: not true}$$

The probabilities of making a correct decision are $(1 - \alpha)$ and $(1 - \beta)$. The probabilities of making an incorrect decision are α (Type I) and β (Type II). These probabilities are shown in Table 15–1. As we mentioned previously, the level of α is at the discretion of the researcher. However, the determination of β is more complicated. (For further information, the interested reader is referred to J. Freund's book on statistics.[5])

For an alternative explanation of the trade-offs between α error and β error, consider this analogy to jurisprudence:

> In a murder trial, the jury is being asked to decide between *HO:*, the hypothesis that the accused is innocent, and the alternative *HA:*, that he is guilty. A Type I error is committed if an innocent man is condemned, while a Type II error occurs if a guilty man is set free. The judge's admonition to the jury that "guilt must be proved beyond a reasonable doubt" means that α should be kept very small.
>
> There have been many legal reforms (for example, limiting the power of the police to obtain a confession) that have been designed to reduce α, the probability that an innocent man will be condemned. But these same reforms have increased β, the probability that a guilty man will evade punishment.
>
> There is no way of pushing α down to zero (ensuring absolutely against convicting an innocent man) without raising β to 1 (letting every defendant go free).[6]

The only way to simultaneously decrease both α and β would be, in our legal analogy, to collect more evidence. In research, we can collect more evidence by increasing our sample size.

HYPOTHESIS TESTS

In this chapter we present several of the most widely used hypothesis tests. We describe tests for proportions and means for hypotheses that relate to one, or more than one, independent sample(s). Examples are also provided for tests of means

---

[5]John E. Freund, *Statistics as a First Course*, 2nd ed. (Englewood Cliffs, N.J.: Prentice Hall, 1976), pp. 240–41.

[6]Thomas H. Wonnacott and Ronald J. Wonnacott, *Introductory Statistics for Business and Economics*, 2nd ed. (New York: John Wiley & Sons, 1977), pp. 259–60.

and proportions when the samples are not independent. Exhibit 15–4 presents a typology of statistical tests based on the number of groups, the level of measurement, and whether or not the samples are independent.[7]

To motivate the discussion of hypothesis testing, we use data collected from a product test. Exhibit 15–5 (see page 428) presents the project proposal.

Although each of the hypothesis tests invokes different test statistics, all involve the following ingredients.

1. *HO*: Specify the null hypothesis.
2. *HA*: Specify the alternative hypothesis.
3. *TS_c*: Choose the appropriate test statistic and calculate its value.
4. *TS_t*: Determine the value of the tabulated test statistic.
5. *DR*: Establish a decision rule for the rejection of the null hypothesis.

Before discussing and illustrating specific hypothesis-testing procedures, we need to explain the distinction between independent and related samples and the concept of degrees of freedom (*df*).

Independent versus Related Samples

In some cases the researcher might want to test the hypothesis that a parameter in one population is equal to the parameter in another population. The appropriate test statistic depends on whether the samples are independent or related. By **independent samples** we mean that the measurement of the variable of interest in one sample in no way affects the measurement of that variable in the other sample. It does not mean that we have two different surveys, although we could. By **related samples** we mean that the measurement of the variable of interest in one sample can influence the measurement of the variable in some other sample.

For example, in a mail survey we might collect information relating to frequency of eating fast food for lunch, and in addition we could collect information on the gender of the respondent. Now suppose we want to test the hypothesis of no difference in the incidence of fast-food consumption (at lunch time) between men and woman. In this case, a test statistic that assumes independent samples is appropriate since in no way would a man's response affect or alter the way a woman responds, and vice versa.

Alternatively, suppose we want to determine the effect of a cents-off promotion to retailers on the amount of shelf space given to the product. To determine this effect, we draw a random sample of retailers and measure shelf space for a four-week period. At the end of the four weeks we introduce the promotion and measure shelf space for the next four-week period. Note that these samples are not independent. The measurement of shelf space during the second four-week period

independent samples
The measurement of the variable of interest in one sample in no way affects the measurement of the variable in the other sample.

related samples
The measurement of the variable of interest in one sample can affect the measurement of the variable in some other sample.

---

[7]The statistical tests in Exhibit 15–4 highlighted by an asterisk (*) are nonparametric statistical tests and are not formally discussed. The interested reader is referred to Sidney Siegel, *Nonparametric Statistics for the Behavioral Sciences* (McGraw-Hill, 1956), for a discussion of each technique.

EXHIBIT 15–4   Typology Statistical Tests

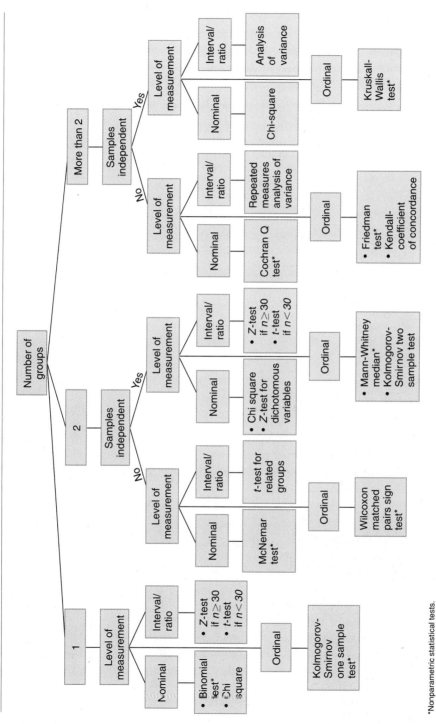

*Nonparametric statistical tests.

Source: Discussed in Sidney Siegel, *Nonparametric Statistics for the Behavioral Sciences* (McGraw-Hill, 1956).

EXHIBIT 15–5
—
Marketing Research
Proposal

Brand:	Burst chewing gum
Project:	Central-location product test
Background & Objectives:	R&D has developed a new chewing gum that is vitamin fortified. Previous concept testing has indicated strong support for the product from category users. The objective of this research is to assess consumers' attitude ratings of the product and intent to purchase. The chewing gum brand group has requested that research be conducted to determine if this product should be considered for a simulated/pretest market study.
Method:	Central-location interviews will be conducted in four geographically dispersed markets with 300 adult past-30-day users of chewing gum. Age and gender quotas will be

	Gender			*Age*
Male	50 percent		18–34	33.3 percent
Female	50 percent		35–54	33.3 percent
			55 +	33.3 percent

Respondents will be given three packages of the product to take home and try during the coming week.

Information to Be Obtained:	• Attribute ratings. • Likes/dislikes. • Overall rating. • Purchase intent.
Action Standard:	The product must equal or exceed past company product tests at the 95% confidence level for chewing gum with respect to average attribute ratings and top box intent scores to be considered for a pretest market.

can be, and most likely is, affected by the actions of the retailers during the first four-week period. This influence on the variable of interest must be taken into consideration when performing the test; in other words, to test the hypothesis of no difference between pre- and post-tests on shelf space, we would have to use a test statistic appropriate for related samples.

DEGREES OF FREEDOM

As we shall see, certain statistical tests require the specification of the degrees of freedom in order to select the tabled value of the test statistic. The concept of degrees of freedom is mathematical in nature. In essence, however, the concept determines the number of observations in a statistical problem that are not restricted, or alternatively that are free to vary. In this discussion, we approach the concept heuristically rather than mathematically. Suppose we measured a sample of 100 people on two variables, usage (high versus low) and intent to purchase (high versus low). Additionally, let's say that 60 percent of the people were low users (hence, 40 percent were high users) and 30 percent indicated a high intent to purchase (hence, 70 percent indicated a low intent to purchase). Now, let's say that 10 people were low users and intended to purchase. That is, the count for cell (2,1) is 10. If we cross tabulate these two variables, the table will look like

Usage

Intent	Low	High	
Low			70
High	10		30
	60	40	100

You will note that once the value for this cell is given, all of the other cells are determined; that is, they are not free to vary. For example, it must be that in this case there is one degree of freedom. In general there are $(r - 1)(c - 1)$, where r = number of rows and c = number of columns, degrees of freedom for a cross-tabulated table.

As another example, assume that we have a sample of five people and the mean, of some variable, for the sample is 10. There are only four elements of the sample that are free to vary: Once the value for any four of the five individuals is known then the last value is also known since the mean value must be 10. That is, if the four values are 8, 12, 9, and 13, the last value must be 8 in order to make the mean 10. Hence, the sample has $n - 1$ degrees of freedom. In other words, we could speak of the sample as if it consisted of one less observation.[8] In general, the greater the degrees of freedom, the more independent pieces of information the sample contains.

TESTS OF PROPORTIONS

One-Sample Test

To test the hypothesis that a proportion is equal to some prespecified value we use a **one-sample proportion test**. The appropriate test statistic is:[9]

$$Z_c = \frac{p - \pi^*}{\sqrt{\dfrac{\pi^*(1 - \pi^*)}{n}}}$$

(15–7)

one-sample proportion test
Test of the hypothesis that a proportion is equal to some prespecified value.

where

p = Sample proportion
π^* = Prespecified population proportion
n = Sample size

---

[8]Ya-Lun Chou, *Statistical Analysis with Business and Economic Applications* (New York: Holt, Rinehart & Winston, 1969), p. 374.

[9]We provide the Z-test; however, we could substitute the sample estimate of the population variance and use a *t*-test.

The steps for a two-tailed test of this hypothesis are

$$HO: \pi = \pi^*$$
$$HA: \pi \neq \pi^*$$
$$TS_c: Z_c = (p - \pi^*)/\sqrt{\pi^*(1 - \pi^*)/n}$$
$$TS_t: Z_{t(1 - \alpha/2)}$$
$$DR: \text{Reject } HO: \text{ if } TS_c > TS_t \text{ or } -TS_c < -TS_t$$

EXAMPLE

The action standard in the research project proposal presented in Exhibit 15–5 specifies that the brand's top box intent score must exceed the normed top box intent score that was achieved by previous products tested in this category in order to proceed to the next stage in the research process, which will involve implementing a pretest market. The company's norm for top box intent scores for this category is 19.5 percent and let us assume that 74 respondents checked the top box on purchase intent; thus the sample proportion (p) is 0.247(74/300). Since the action standard states that the test scores must exceed the norm, a one-sample test of proportions will be used.

Following the standard procedure we have

$$HO: \pi^* \leq 0.195$$
$$HA: \pi^* > 0.195$$
$$TS_c: Z_c = (p - \pi^*)/\sqrt{\pi^*(1 - \pi^*)/n}$$
$$TS_t: Z_t = Z_{t(1 - \alpha)}$$
$$DR: \text{Reject } HO: \text{ if } TS_c > TS_t$$

The calculated test statistic (Z_c) is

$$Z_c = \frac{0.247 - 0.195}{\sqrt{0.195(0.805)/300}}$$
$$= 2.27$$

Letting $\alpha = 0.05$ we note, from Table 2 of the Statistical Appendix, that $Z_t = 1.65$.

Because the calculated Z-value (TS_c) exceeds the tabled Z-value, we reject the null hypothesis. Therefore, the new brand would proceed to the next research stage and a pretest market study would be implemented.

Two-Independent Sample Test

two-independent sample test
Test whether the observed proportion (mean) in one sample is equal to the observed proportion (mean) in another sample.

In certain cases we want to test whether the observed proportion in one sample is equal to the observed proportion in another sample (the **two-independent sample test**). The appropriate test statistic is

$$Z_c = \frac{p_1 - p_2}{s_{\bar{p}_1 - \bar{p}_2}} \tag{15–8}$$

The numerator in Equation 15–8 is simply the difference between the proportions for the two samples. The denominator in Equation 15–8 is the standard error of the difference in the two sample proportions and is calculated as

$$s_{\bar{p}_1 - \bar{p}_2} = \sqrt{\left[p^*(1 - p^*) \right]\left[\frac{1}{n_1} + \frac{1}{n_2} \right]} \qquad (15\text{–}9)$$

where

$$p^* = \frac{n_1 p_1 + n_2 p_2}{n_1 + n_2}$$

p_1 = Proportion in sample one

p_2 = Proportion in sample two

n_1 = Size of sample one

n_2 = Size of sample two

The steps for a two-tailed test of this hypothesis are:

HO: $\pi_1 = \pi_2$

HA: $\pi_1 \neq \pi_2$

TS_c: $Z_c = (p_1 - p_2)/s_{\bar{p}_1 - \bar{p}_2}$

TS_t: $Z_{t(1 - \alpha/2)}$

DR: Reject HO: if $TS_c > TS_t$ or $-TS_c < -TS_t$

EXAMPLE

The research method section of the research project proposal shown in Exhibit 15–5 indicated that the sample of 300 respondents should be equally divided between men and women. Now, assume that management wanted to test whether there was any difference in top box intent scores between men and women. To test this hypothesis a two-sample proportion test for independent samples would be used. Following our standard procedure we have

HO: $\pi_1 = \pi_2$

HA: $\pi_1 \neq \pi_2$

TS_c: $Z_c = (p_1 - p_2)/s_{\bar{p}_1 - \bar{p}_2}$

TS_t: $Z_t = Z_{t(1 - \alpha/2)}$

DR: Reject HO: if $TS_c > TS_t$ or if $-TS_c < -TS_t$

In order to calculate the test statistic we must first determine the proportion of both men and women who are checking the top box; that is, we need to calculate p^*. Suppose that the data indicate that 42 men checked the top box, whereas 32 women checked the top box. Letting men be denoted by the subscript m and women by the subscript f we have

$$n_m = 150 \qquad n_f = 150$$
$$p_m = 0.28 \qquad p_f = 0.21$$

Therefore $p^* = \dfrac{(0.28)(150) + (0.21)(150)}{300} = 0.247$

Consequently, the calculated test statistic (Z_c) is

$$Z_c = \frac{0.28 - 0.21}{\left[(0.247)(0.753)\left(\frac{1}{150} + \frac{1}{150} \right) \right]^{\frac{1}{2}}}$$

$$= 1.41$$

Letting $\alpha = 0.05$, we find from Table 2 of the Statistical Appendix, that $Z_t = \pm 1.96$. Because Z_c is not greater than Z_t, we fail to reject the null hypothesis. That is, we would conclude that there is no statistical difference between top box intent scores for men and women.

More than Two Independent Samples

When we have more than two groups and are interested in testing a hypothesis of equality of proportions for some variable of interest among the groups, we must use a test statistic other than the Z- or *t*-test statistic. The test statistic most frequently used in this situation is the Pearson chi-square statistic. In essence, the **chi-square test statistic** measures the *goodness of fit* between the numbers observed in the sample and the numbers we should have seen in the sample if the null hypothesis is true. For this application the chi-square test statistic (χ^2) is calculated as

> chi-square test statistic *Measure of the goodness of fit between the numbers observed in the sample and the numbers we should have seen in the sample, given the null hypothesis is true.*

$$\chi_c^2 = \sum_{i=1}^{K} \frac{(O_i - E_i)^2}{E_i} \qquad (15\text{–}10)$$

where

O_i = Observed value in the *i*th sample
E_i = Expected value in the *i*th sample, given that the null
hypothesis is true
K = Number of sample groups being tested

Like the *t*-distribution, the chi-square distribution is a family of distributions. Consequently, to determine the region of rejection we must specify the degrees of freedom (df) in addition to a significance level $(1 - \alpha)$. With this application of the chi-square test statistic, the number of degrees of freedom is equal to the number of groups (independent samples) minus one. Thus, the degrees of freedom are[10]

$$df = K - 1 \qquad (15\text{–}11)$$

---

[10]The chi-square test statistic is widely used for testing for independence of variables constituting a contingency table having *I* rows and *J* columns. Here the degrees of freedom are equal to $(I - 1)(J - 1)$. This application of the Pearson chi-square statistic is demonstrated in Chapter 16.

The research method section of the research project proposal shown in Exhibit 15–5 also indicated that the sample of 300 respondents should be equally divided between the three age categories: 18–34, 35–54, and 55+ years of age. Now, assume that management wanted to test whether differences in top box intent scores exist across the three age categories. To statistically test the hypothesis of equal top box intent scores among the three age categories, a $K = 3$ independent sample proportion test would be used.

Following the standard procedure the test is

$$HO: \pi_1 = \pi_2 = \pi_3$$
$$HA: \text{Not all } \pi_i \text{ are equal}$$
$$TS_c: \chi_c^2 = \sum_{i=1}^{K} (O_i - E_i)^2/E_i$$
$$TS_t: \chi_t^2 \; (1-\alpha; \; df = K-1)$$
$$DR: \text{Reject } HO: \text{if } TS_c > TS_t$$

Results indicate that of the 300 respondents, 24.7 percent of the respondents, or 74 people, checked the top box for the intent question. If the null hypothesis were true (i.e., there was no difference among the age categories) then we would expect equal distribution of the 74 people across the three age categories; hence, $E_1 = E_2 = E_3 = 74/3 = 24.7$. Suppose that the number of respondents checking the top box for the three age categories is 5, 21, and 48, respectively. Hence, the chi-square test statistic is

$$\chi_c^2 = (5 - 24.7)^2/24.7 + (21 - 24.7)^2/24.7 + (48 - 24.7)^2/24.7$$
$$= 38.25$$

The tabulated value of the chi-square test statistic with $\alpha = 0.05$ and $df = 3 - 1 = 2$ is, from Table 5 of the Statistical Appendix, 5.99. Because the TS_c is greater than the TS_t, the null hypothesis is rejected. Hence, there are statistically significant differences in top box intent scores among the three age categories.

One heuristic for examining the differences among the categories is to assess the differences between the observed and expected values for each level of the variable tested. The rationale for this heuristic lies in the calculation of the chi-square statistic itself. Because the denominator for the test statistic (TS_c) is the same for all levels of the variable, those categories having the largest absolute discrepancy between the observed and expected values contribute most to the rejection of the null hypothesis of no differences. The differences between the expected and observed values for the three age categories are -19.7, -3.7, and 23.3, respectively. Hence, the first and third categories contribute most to the calculated value of the test statistic.

TESTS OF MEANS

One-Sample Test

Here we want to test if a sample mean is equal to, greater than, or less than some hypothesized mean value of a particular population. The test statistic, assuming a sample size of $n \geq 30$, is

$$Z = \frac{\bar{x} - \mu^*}{s/\sqrt{n}} \tag{15-12}$$

The steps for a two-tailed test of this hypothesis are:

$$HO: \mu = \mu^*$$
$$HA: \mu \neq \mu^*$$
$$TS_c: Z_c = \frac{\bar{x} - \mu^*}{s/\sqrt{n}}$$
$$TS_t: Z_{t(1 - \alpha/2)}$$
$$DR: \text{Reject } HO: \text{ if } TS_c > TS_t \text{ or } -TS_c < -TS_t$$

EXAMPLE

In addition to top box intent scores the respondents in the product test (Exhibit 15–5) also rated the new chewing gum on five 7-point attribute scales. An overall rating score for the product was obtained by summing the scores for each of the five attribute ratings. Because there were five 7-point scales, the scores could range from 5 to 35, and an average rating for the product on each scale would produce a score of (5×4), or 20.

Now, assume that management wanted to determine if the product scored above or below average for the composite score derived from the five attribute rating scales. To test this hypothesis a one-sample test of mean differences would be used.

Following the standard procedure, the hypothesis test is

$$HO: \mu^* = 20.0$$
$$HA: \mu^* \neq 20.0$$
$$TS_c: Z_c = (\bar{x} - \mu^*)/(s/\sqrt{n})$$
$$TS_t: Z_{t(1 - \alpha/2)}$$
$$DR: \text{Reject } HO: \text{ if } TS_c > TS_t \text{ or if } -TS_c < -TS_t$$

Assume that the average product rating from the sample was 24.55 with a standard deviation of 4.86 based on the responses from 288 people. That is, 12 of the people had a missing response on at least one of the attribute ratings; therefore, they were dropped for purposes of testing this hypothesis. With a hypothesized mean (μ^*) of 20.0, the calculated test statistic is

$$Z_c = (24.55 - 20.0)/(4.86/\sqrt{288})$$
$$= 15.89$$

Consequently, with $\alpha = 0.05$, the tabulated value of the test statistic for a two-tail hypothesis test is, from Table 1 of the Statistical Appendix, 1.96. Given the values of TS_c and TS_t we reject the null hypothesis and conclude that the product received above average attribute ratings.

Two-Independent Sample Test

Suppose that we want to test whether the observed means from two independent samples differ enough to conclude that the populations are statistically different with respect to their means. The most commonly used approach to test this hypothesis is the *t*-test. Note, however, that with large samples in each group or known variance we could use the Z-test statistic. The calculations are the same. The only difference is whether we utilize a Z- or *t*-distribution to establish the critical value.

The steps for a two-tailed test of this hypothesis are:

$HO: \mu_1 = \mu_2$

$HA: \mu_1 \neq \mu_2$

$TS_c: t_c = \bar{x}_1 - \bar{x}_2 / s_{\bar{x}_1 - \bar{x}_2}$

$TS_t: t_{t(1 - \alpha/2; df = n_1 + n_2 - 2)}$

DR: Reject $HO:$ if $TS_c > TS_t$ or $-TS_c < -TS_t$

Because we are using a t-test statistic we must assume that the two populations are normally distributed and that the samples are independent. The denominator of the t-test $(s_{\bar{x}_1 - \bar{x}_2})$ is the standard error of the difference in the means. It is calculated as

$$s_{\bar{x}_1 - \bar{x}_2} = \sqrt{s_p^2 \left(\frac{1}{n_1} + \frac{1}{n_2} \right)} \tag{15-13}$$

where s_p^2 is the pooled variance given by

$$s_p^2 = \frac{\sum\limits_{i=1}^{n_1} (x_{1i} - \bar{x}_1)^2 + \sum\limits_{i=1}^{n_2} (x_{2i} - \bar{x}_2)^2}{n_1 + n_2 - 2} \tag{15-14}$$

The calculation of the pooled variance can be simplified if we know the variance of each mean. Specifically, if we know the variance of $\bar{x}_i$, we can easily calculate $\sum (x_i - \bar{x})^2$ by the following relationships. Since

$$s^2 = \sum\limits_{i=1}^{n} (x_i - \bar{x})^2 / (n - 1) \tag{15-15}$$

we have, by simple manipulation,

$$\sum\limits_{i=1}^{n} (x_i - \bar{x})^2 = (n - 1)s^2 \tag{15-16}$$

The pooled variance t-test statistic discussed above requires the assumption of **homoscedasticity.** *Homoscedasticity* simply means that in the population the variance of the variable being tested is the same in all samples. Hence, in the case of two samples we are hypothesizing

$$HO: \sigma_1^2 = \sigma_2^2$$

homoscedasticity
In the population the variance of the variable being tested is the same in all samples.

To test this hypothesis we use an F-test. The F-distribution, like the t- and χ^2 distributions, is a family of distributions. Consequently, we must specify the degrees of freedom to determine the region of rejection. To determine the tabulated value of the F-distribution, in addition to the confidence level $(1 - \alpha)$, we need two measures of the degrees of freedom for the test, that is, the numerator and the denominator degrees of freedom. The test shown here is the ratio of the variance from one group divided by the variance of another group. Letting i reference one group and j the other, the TS_c is $F = s_i^2 / s_j^2$ with degrees of freedom for the numerator equal to $n_i - 1$ and the degrees of freedom for the denominator equal to $n_j - 1$. Note that the larger of the two variances is always placed in the numerator. The appropriate hypothesis test is

$$HO: \sigma_i^2 = \sigma_j^2$$
$$HA: \sigma_i^2 \neq \sigma_j^2$$
$$TS_c: F_c = \sigma_i^2 / \sigma_j^2$$
$$TS_t: F_{t(1 - \alpha; \, df = n_1 - 1, \, n_2 - 1)}$$
$$DR: \text{Reject } HO: \text{ if } TS_c > TS_t$$

If we do not reject this hypothesis, we simply use the pooled variance t-test statistic. However, if we do reject the hypothesis, we can use a separate variance t-test. The standard error of the difference $s_{\bar{x}_1 - \bar{x}_2}$ for a separate variance t-test is

$$s_{\bar{x}_1 - \bar{x}_2} = \sqrt{\frac{s_1^2}{n_1} + \frac{s_2^2}{n_2}} \tag{15–17}$$

Hence, we must first test for homogeneity of variance to decide which formulation of the t-test to use. We should note that if homogeneity of variance is rejected and separate variance estimates are used, the degrees of freedom associated with the test statistic can be approximated by $n_1 + n_2 - 2$.

EXAMPLE

Assume that management wanted to determine whether there was a difference in the attribute ratings between men and women. To test this hypothesis a two-sample independent test of means would be used. Letting, as before, men be denoted by the subscript m and women by the subscript f, sample results reveal the following:

$$n_m = 149 \qquad n_f = 139$$
$$\bar{x}_m = 24.21 \qquad \bar{x}_f = 24.92$$
$$s_m = 4.90 \qquad s_f = 4.79$$

Before we can test this hypothesis, we need to determine if the variances in the two samples are statistically equal. To test this hypothesis the procedure is

$$HO: \sigma_m^2 = \sigma_f^2$$
$$HA: \sigma_m^2 \neq \sigma_f^2$$
$$TS_c: F_c = s_m^2 / s_f^2$$
$$TS_t: F_t = F_{t(1 - \alpha; \, df = n_1 - 1, \, n_2 - 1)}$$
$$DR: \text{Reject } HO: \text{ if } TS_c > TS_t$$

The standard deviations for the males and females subsamples are 4.90 and 4.79, respectively. With these values our calculated F is

$$F_c = (4.90)^2 / (4.79)^2$$
$$= 1.05$$

The degrees of freedom for this test are $149 - 1 = 148$ for the numerator and $139 - 1 = 138$ for the denominator. Letting $\alpha = 0.05$, our tabulated value for F_t from Table 5 of the Statistical Appendix is 1.0. Therefore, we reject the null hypothesis and use the separate variance formulation for testing differences between means.

The hypothesis test using our standard procedure is

$$HO: \mu_1 = \mu_2$$
$$HA: \mu_1 \neq \mu_2$$
$$TS_c: t_c = \bar{x}_1 - \bar{x}_2 \Big/ \left[\frac{s_1^2}{n_1} + \frac{s_2^2}{n_2} \right]^{\frac{1}{2}}$$
$$TS_t: t_t = t_{t\,(1 - \alpha/2;\, df = n_1 + n_2 - 2)}$$
$$DR: \text{Reject } HO: \text{ if } TS_c > TS_t \text{ or if } -TS_c < -TS_t$$

Thus we find

$$t_c = \frac{24.21 - 24.92}{\left[\frac{(4.9)^2}{149} + \frac{(4.79)^2}{139} \right]^{\frac{1}{2}}}$$
$$= -1.24$$

The tabulated value of t with $\alpha = 0.05$ and $149 + 139 - 2 = 286$ degrees of freedom is ± 1.96. Consequently, we fail to reject the null hypothesis and conclude that there is no statistically significant difference between men and women in their attribute ratings of the product.

___

More than Two Independent Samples

When we want to test hypotheses of no differences among means for more than two independent samples we use a statistical technique called **analysis of variance (ANOVA)**. The null hypothesis to be tested is

$$HO: \mu_1 = \mu_2 = \mu_3 = \ldots = \mu_K$$

That is, the means for the K samples are not statistically different. Analysis of variance is applicable whenever we have interval measurement on K independent groups. Most applications of ANOVA are in the analysis of data resulting from experimental designs. As an example consider a study in which the objective is to measure the effects of five different advertising executions on aided 24-hour day-after recall scores. The data for the study are presented in Table 15–2 (see page 438). We will develop the basic one-way ANOVA design; Appendices 15A and 15B present extensions.

Let y_{ij} denote the 24-hour day-after recall score for the ith respondent who saw the jth treatment condition; $\bar{y}_{+j}$ denotes the mean recall score for the jth group and $\bar{y}_{++}$ denotes the overall mean. Hence, the quantity $(y_{ij} - \bar{y}_{++})$ gives the deviation of the ith respondent in the jth treatment from the overall or grand mean. Now it can be shown that if we square this quantity and sum the squared deviations, the following formula holds

$$\sum_i \sum_j (y_{ij} - \bar{y}_{++})^2 = \sum_j n_j (\bar{y}_{+j} - \bar{y}_{++})^2 + \sum_i \sum_j (y_{ij} - y_{+j})^2 \qquad (15\text{–}18)$$

| TSS | = | BSS | + | WSS |

analysis of variance (ANOVA)
A way to test hypotheses of no differences among means for more than two independent samples. ANOVA is applicable whenever we have interval measurement on K independent groups.

TABLE 15–2

Day-After Recall
Scores

	Ad 1	Ad 2	Ad 3	Ad 4	Ad 5
	0	3	5	9	7
	1	2	7	10	8
	2	1	4	10	8
	1	2	4	7	5
Total	4	8	20	36	28
$\bar{y}_{+i}$	1	2	5	9	7
$\bar{y}_{++}$	96/20 = 4.8				

The term on the left side of the equation is called the *total sum of squares* (TSS). The first term on the right side of the equation is called the *between sum of squares* (BSS), and the second term on the right is called the *within* or *error sum of squares* (WSS). We will discuss the between and the within sum squares soon, but first let us demonstrate how to calculate these quantities. The calculations are presented in Table 15–3.

Formula 15–18 is referred to as "the fundamental equation of analysis of variance."[11] The total sum of squared deviations from the overall mean is decomposed into the sum of squared deviations between treatment means and the overall mean, and the sum of squared deviations within a treatment. You will recall that in Chapter 7 we discussed experimental effects. Following the notation introduced above, a model of individual recall scores can be written as

$$y_{ij} = \bar{y}_{++} + T_j + e_{ij} \tag{15–19}$$

where

$$\bar{y}_{++} = \text{Overall mean}$$
$$T_j = \text{Effect of the } j\text{th exposure}$$
$$e_{ij} = \text{An error term}$$

Note the similarity between this formula and the fundamental equation of analysis of variance. In ANOVA, T_j is the effect of the jth treatment. We might ask why any one group has recall scores that are greater than (less than) the overall average. Note that if no group is very different from the overall average, then

$$\mu_1 = \mu_2 = \mu_3 = \mu_4 = \mu_5$$

which is exactly the hypothesis that is being subjected to testing. The within group or error sum of squares represents the variation in respondents' recall scores for people who have seen the same ad. Given that these people were randomly assigned to the treatment groups, any difference in their scores must be due to a unique reaction to the ad and is, therefore, called unexplained variation; that is, we cannot explain the variation due to exposure to a particular ad (within treat-

---

[11]Charles R. Hicks, *Fundamental Concepts in the Design of Experiments*, 2nd ed. (New York: Holt, Rinehart & Winston, 1964), p. 28.

TABLE 15–3
—
Calculations for
Total Sum of Squares
and Within Sum of
Squares for Data
Shown in Table 15–2

y_{ij}			
i	j	TSS	WSS
1	1	$(0 - 4.8)^2 = 23.04$	$(0 - 1)^2 = 1$
2	1	$(1 - 4.8)^2 = 14.44$	$(1 - 1)^2 = 0$
3	1	$(2 - 4.8)^2 = 7.84$	$(2 - 1)^2 = 1$
4	1	$(1 - 4.8)^2 = 14.44$	$(1 - 1)^2 = 0$
1	2	$(3 - 4.8)^2 = 3.24$	$(3 - 2)^2 = 1$
2	2	$(2 - 4.8)^2 = 7.84$	$(2 - 2)^2 = 0$
3	2	$(1 - 4.8)^2 = 14.44$	$(1 - 2)^2 = 1$
4	2	$(2 - 4.8)^2 = 7.84$	$(2 - 2)^2 = 0$
1	3	$(5 - 4.8)^2 = 0.04$	$(5 - 5)^2 = 0$
2	3	$(7 - 4.8)^2 = 4.84$	$(7 - 5)^2 = 4$
3	3	$(4 - 4.8)^2 = 0.64$	$(4 - 5)^2 = 1$
4	3	$(4 - 4.8)^2 = 0.64$	$(4 - 5)^2 = 1$
1	4	$(9 - 4.8)^2 = 17.64$	$(9 - 9)^2 = 0$
2	4	$(10 - 4.8)^2 = 27.04$	$(10 - 9)^2 = 1$
3	4	$(10 - 4.8)^2 = 27.04$	$(10 - 9)^2 = 1$
4	4	$(7 - 4.8)^2 = 4.84$	$(7 - 9)^2 = 4$
1	5	$(7 - 4.8)^2 = 4.84$	$(7 - 7)^2 = 0$
2	5	$(8 - 4.8)^2 = 10.24$	$(8 - 7)^2 = 1$
3	5	$(8 - 4.8)^2 = 10.24$	$(8 - 7)^2 = 1$
4	5	$(5 - 4.8)^2 = 0.04$	$(5 - 7)^2 = 4$

$$\sum_i \sum_j (y_{ij} - \bar{y}_{++})^2 = 201.2 \qquad \sum_i \sum_j (y_{ij} - \bar{y}_{+j})^2 = 22$$

BSS
$$n_i \sum_j (\bar{y}_{+j} - \bar{y}_{++})^2 = 4[(1 - 4.8)^2 + (2 - 4.8)^2 + (5 - 4.8)^2$$
$$+ (9 - 4.8)^2 + (7 - 4.8)^2] = 179.2$$

Note that we can also get the BSS by subtraction
Total variation = Between variation + Within variation
201.2 = Between + 22
Between = 201.2 − 22
= 179.2

ment). However, the between-group variation represents differences in recall scores for groups that were exposed to different treatments. Hence, we say we can explain the difference in group scores as a function of exposure to a particular treatment. As shown in Formula 15–18, the **total variation** is equal to the sum of **between-group variation** plus **within-group variation**; consequently, the larger the between sum of squares, the smaller the within sum of squares.

To test the hypothesis of no difference in group means

$$HO:\ \mu_1 = \mu_2 = \mu_3 = \mu_4 = \mu_5$$

we examine the ratio of between to within sum of squares.

Table 15–4 (see page 440) presents the typical analysis of variance table. To test the hypothesis of equality of group means we use an F-test with $K - 1$ degrees of

total variation
Sum of between variation plus within variation.

between-group variation
Between-group differences in scores for groups that were exposed to different treatments—represents "explained" variation.

TABLE 15–4	Source	Sum of Squares	Degrees of Freedom	Mean Sum of Squares	F
Analysis of Variance Table	Between *(BSS)*	$\sum_j n_j(\bar{y}_{+j} - \bar{y}_{++})^2$	$K - 1$	$BSS/(K - 1)$	$BSS/(K - 1)$
	Within *(WSS)*	$\sum_i \sum_j (y_{ij} - \bar{y}_{+j})^2$	$n - K$	$WSS/(n - K)$	$WSS/(n - K)$
	Total *(TSS)*	$\sum_i \sum_j (y_{ij} - \bar{y}_{++})^2$	$n - 1$		

TABLE 15–5	Source	Sum of Squares	Degrees of Freedom	MSS	F_c
ANOVA Table for Attribute Ratings by Age	Between	317.54	2	158.77	7.035
	Within	6431.68	285	22.57	
	Total	6749.22	287		

within-group variation
Within-group sum of squares; reflects differences in scores for respondents in the same group—represents "unexplained" variation.

freedom in the numerator and $n - K$ degrees of freedom in the denominator, where K is the number of treatment means tested. Note that in order for the F-test to be strictly valid, the variances must be the same in each sample (i.e., the assumption of homoscedasticity is required).

EXAMPLE

Management wanted to determine if there was any difference in the composite attribute ratings among the three levels of age. To test this hypothesis we need to use analysis of variance.

Following our standard procedure

HO: $\mu_1 = \mu_2 = \mu_3$
HA: Not all μ_k are equal
TS_c: $F_c = [BSS/(K - 1)]/[WSS/(n - K)]$
TS_t: $F_t = F_{t(1 - \alpha;\, df = K - 1,\, n - K)}$
DR: Reject HO: if $F_c > F_t$

The ANOVA table is presented in Table 15–5. With $\alpha = 0.05$ and 2 degrees of freedom in the numerator and 285 degrees of freedom in the denominator, the tabulated value of the test statistic, from Table 5 of the Statistical Appendix, is 3.0. Consequently, we reject the hypothesis of no difference in attribute ratings among the levels of age categories. The means for the three levels of age are 25.53, 23.09, and 25.04, respectively, from low to high. To determine which of these means are statistically different, we must use *a posteriori* comparisons or contrasts. Such comparisons are explained in the next section. However, before proceeding we must emphasize that, at this point, no conclusions about the differences in means among the three age groups can be made, except that we can safely conclude they are not equal.

A Posteriori Comparisons. In the two-group case the alternative hypothesis (HA:) simply states, for a two-tail test, that the groups are not equal. Hence, if our hypothesis test indicates that we should reject the null, we know that μ_1 is statistically different from μ_2. However, when we have more than two groups, the alternative hypothesis states that not all of the group means are equal. Some, but not necessarily all, of the means are statistically different. That is, returning to our example of day-after recall scores, we could find that some of the treatment ads are different, whereas some are not. Therefore, having concluded, by rejecting the null, that there is a statistically significant difference in the treatment ads, interest then centers on determining which of the means are different. To answer this question we select a method of **a posteriori comparisons.**

If we reject the null hypothesis

$$HO:\ \mu_1\ =\ \mu_2\ =\ \mu_3\ =\ \ldots\ =\ \mu_K$$

interest then centers on determining which of the means are statistically different. It would seem intuitive to calculate a *t-* or Z-test statistic since we now want to compare two means. However, the problem with this approach is that the α level is affected by the number of tests we perform since the tests are not independent. To test each pair of means, with $K = 5$, we would have to perform $[5(4)/2] = 10$ separate *t-* or Z-tests. The corresponding tabled values of *t* or Z would not reflect the appropriate α level. That is, we may think we have set $\alpha = 0.05$; however, the actual level of α is greater than $\alpha = 0.05$ and increases with the number of comparisons we make. For this reason we utilize a posteriori comparisons. These techniques specifically account for the number of comparisons made and hold α constant at the level specified by the researcher. There are a variety of a posteriori comparison methods. One popular method is the Newman-Keuls comparison procedure.[12]

a posteriori comparisons *Techniques used to determine which of the means are statistically different once the null hypothesis is rejected.*

Related Sample Tests

Previously, we stated that when we have more than one sample the assumption is that the samples are independent. That is, the measurement in one sample does not in any way affect measurement in the other sample. Whenever we measure the same set of individuals at two points in time, this assumption of independent samples is violated. For example, consider the approach taken in one type of advertising testing. Typically, the same set of individuals are measured both before and after viewing a test commercial for a brand with respect to attitude and top box intent scores. If we want to test for differences in, say, mean attitude scores or for differences in top box scores, we have to use hypothesis testing procedures that account for having dependent samples.

Means. To examine if there are any differences in mean scores for the before and after tests, we first must calculate a difference score (d_i) for each individual. This is accomplished by subtracting the after score from the before score for each person. Hence, we now have a new variable (d_i) for each person that represents their

---

[12]See Hicks, *Fundamental Concepts*, for further details on a posteriori comparisons.

change in attitude. If there was no change in attitude we would expect this new variable to have a mean of zero. The TS_c for this hypothesis test is

$$TS_c = \frac{\Sigma d_i/n}{s_d/\sqrt{n}}$$

where

d_i = Difference in scores, or in this case attitude change
s_d = Standard deviation of the differences
n = Sample size

Consequently, letting Δ represent attitude change, we can test the null hypothesis of no change in attitude scores with the following procedure:

HO: $\Delta = 0$
HA: $\Delta \neq 0$
TS_c: $t_c = (\Sigma d_i/n)/(s_d/\sqrt{n})$
TS_t: $t_t = t_{t(1 - \alpha/2;\ df = n - 1)}$
DR: Reject HO: if $TS_c > TS_t$

EXAMPLE

To determine how much attitude toward a brand changes as a result of exposure to a particular commercial, subjects were pretested to measure existing attitudes. Next, they were exposed to an ad, and their post-exposure attitude scores were obtained. The experimental results are shown in Table 15–6.

Now assume we ignore the fact that the samples are related. We would test the hypothesis of no attitude change as

HO: $\mu_{A1} = \mu_{A2}$
HA: $\mu_{A1} \neq \mu_{A2}$

$$TS_c: t_c = \frac{\bar{x}_{A1} - \bar{x}_{A2}}{\sqrt{s_p^2\left(\frac{1}{n_1} + \frac{1}{n_2}\right)}}$$

TS_t: $t_t = t_{(1 - \alpha;\ df = n_1 + n_2 - 2)}$
DR: Reject HO: if $TS_c > TS_t$ or $-TS_c < -TS_t$

The test statistic is

$$t_c = \frac{50.5 - 54.5}{8.55}$$
$$= -0.468$$

Since $t_{(0.95;18)} = 1.729$ we fail to reject our null hypothesis and conclude that the ad had no impact on attitude change. However, note from the attitude change column shown in Table 15–6 that in all cases except one (subject 7), post-exposure attitude was higher or more favorable than pre-exposure attitude. When we take into account that the samples are related, the hypothesis does not change, but the test statistic does. The t-test statistic for a related sample is

$$TS_c = \frac{\Sigma d_i/n}{s_d/\sqrt{n}}$$

Subject	Pre-exposure Attitudes (A_1)	Post-exposure Attitudes (A_2)	Attitude Change (d_i)
1	50	53	3
2	25	27	2
3	30	38	8
4	50	55	5
5	60	61	1
6	80	85	5
7	45	45	0
8	30	31	1
9	65	72	7
10	70	78	8

TABLE 15–6

Before-After
Experimental Results

where

d_i = Difference in the scores, or in this case the attitude change

s_d = Standard deviation of the differences

n = Sample size

From the data in Table 15–6 the test statistic is

$$TS_c = \frac{4.0}{3.02/\sqrt{10}}$$
$$= 4.19$$

The region of rejection is given by $t_{(1 - \alpha/2; \, df = n - 1)}$ which, with $n = 10$ and the α level at 0.05, is equal to 2.26. Hence, we now reject our null hypothesis and conclude that the ad does have a statistically significant impact on attitudes.

Proportions. To demonstrate the procedure for testing differences in proportions from related samples consider Table 15–7a (see page 444), which presents top box intent scores for a sample of 100 people before and after exposure to a commercial for a test brand. Before exposure 25 percent (25/100) of the respondents checked the top box of the intent scale, and after exposure to the test commercial 30 percent (30/100) checked the top box. Letting p_b represent the proportion of top box intent scores before exposure and p_a represent the proportion after exposure, the difference in proportions (Δ_p) is $p_a - p_b$. The standard error of this difference can be estimated, using the notation from Table 15–7b (see page 444)[13] as

$$\left[\frac{b + c - \{(b - c)^2/n\}}{n(n - 1)} \right]^{\frac{1}{2}}$$

---

[13]W. J. Dixon and F. J. Massey, *Introduction to Statistical Analysis* (New York: McGraw-Hill), p. 250.

TABLE 15–7
—

Before and After
Measurement of Top
Box Intent Scores

	a.	Before		Total		b.	Before		Total
		Yes	No				Yes	No	
	Yes	23	7	30		Yes	a	b	
After	No	2	68	70	After	No	c	d	
	Total	25	75	100		Total			

With a large sample (i.e., $n \geq 30$), a Z-test can be used to test for a significant difference in the before and after proportions.

Since the test commercial was expected to significantly increase the top box intent scores, a one-tail hypothesis test will be used. Following the standard procedure the hypothesis test for the differences in related proportions is

HO: $\pi_a \leq \pi_b$

HA: $\pi_a > \pi_b$

TS_c: $Z_c = p_a - p_b/[b + c - \{(b - c)^2/n\}/n(n - 1)]^{\frac{1}{2}}$

TS_t: $Z_t = Z_{(1 - \alpha)}$

DR: Reject HO: if $Z_c > Z_t$

For the example the TS_c is

$$TS_c = \frac{0.30 - 0.25}{\left[\dfrac{7 + 2 - \{(7 - 2)^2/100\}}{100(99)} \right]^{\frac{1}{2}}} = 1.68$$

The tabled value of the test statistic for a one-tail test with $\alpha = 0.05$ is 1.645. Hence, we reject the null hypothesis, no difference in top box intent scores before and after exposure to the test commercial.

Transition Tables. In Chapter 4 we discussed the use of diary purchase panels and scanners for recording the purchase of brands by households over time. These data are typically used to construct transition tables, which allow for an assessment of brand loyalty and brand switching. Table 15–8 presents a hypothetical transition table for four brands (A, B, C, and D) for two months (June and July).

The totals (or marginals) represent brand share for the respective months. For example, brand A had a share of 10 percent in June and a share of 15 percent in July. The main diagonal of the table represents the number of people who purchased the brand in June and who purchased the brand in July. For example, 80 people purchased brand A in June and July. These cells on the main diagonal provide a measure of repeat purchase behavior. Because there were 100 people that purchased brand A in June and 80 people that purchased brand A in both June and July, repeat purchase for A is (80/100) 80 percent. Likewise, the repeat purchase likelihoods for B, C, and D are 80 percent, 78 percent, and 78 percent, respectively. The off-diagonal cells represent brand switching. From the table we can see that 10 of the 100 people that purchased brand A in June switched to brand B in July.

TABLE 15–8

Transition Table for
Four Brands

		June Brand				
July		A	B	C	D	Total
Brand	A	80	25	20	25	150
	B	10	240	0	0	250
	C	0	20	310	20	350
	D	10	15	70	155	250
	Total	100	300	400	200	1000

Now, assume that management wanted to test the hypothesis that the level of brand switching was equal for all four brands. Because the data represent purchases for the same households over time, the samples for June and July are not independent. The appropriate test statistic for testing the hypothesis of equal brand switching is[14]

$$TS_c = \sum_{i < j} (n_{ij} - n_{ji})^2/n_{ij} + n_{ji}$$

where

i = Rows of the transition table
j = Columns of the table

This test statistic has an approximate chi-square distribution with

$$df = [K(K - 1)/2] \text{ where } K = \text{Number of brands}$$

Letting ϕ_i represent the percentage of switching for brand i, the test for equality of brand switching is:

$HO: \phi_1 = \phi_2 = \phi_3 = \phi_4$
$HA:$ Not all ϕ_i are equal
$TS_c: \chi_c^2 = \sum_{i<j} (n_{ij} - n_{ji})^2/(n_{ij} + n_{ji})$

$TS_t: \chi_t^2 {}_{(1 - \alpha; df = K(K - 1)/2)}$
$DR:$ Reject $HO:$ if $TS_c > TS_t$

Returning to our example of the four brands the TS_c is

$$TS_c = [(25 - 10)^2/35] + [(20 - 0)^2/20] + (25 - 10)^2/35] +$$
$$[(0 - 20)^2/20] + [0 - 15)^2/15] + [(20 - 70)^2/90]$$
$$= 95.63$$

Letting $\alpha = 0.05$ and with $[4(4 - 1)/2] = 6$ degrees of freedom, the tabled value of the chi-square is 12.59. Since $TS_c > TS_t$ we reject the null hypothesis of equal brand switching.

---

[14]Ibid.

STATISTICAL SIGNIFICANCE

A statistically significant finding means that our notions (hypotheses) about a population are likely given the sample evidence. We must remember that when we are conducting hypothesis tests we are dealing with samples and not populations. Whenever we sample we have the possibility of sampling error. Hence, the difference between what we hypothesize and what we observe may be due to sampling error or to our notions being incorrect. A statistically significant finding means that the difference is not, at some specified level of error (α), due to sampling error. Hence, the level of statistical significance should be related to sample size, and it is.

However, the relevance of the research finding to managerial decision making is a totally separate issue. "Statistical significance is a statement about the likelihood of the observed result, nothing else. It does not guarantee that something important, or even meaningful, has been found."[15]

For example, assume you were faced with the decision of choosing between two vacation spots for spring break, and an important factor in your decision is the average price for a hotel room. If we told you, because we know the actual average price, that the average price for one spot was $50.00 and the average price for another was $50.50, would this help you make your decision? That is, how relevant is the difference? Depending on the sample size, the difference may be statistically significant.

Consider the situation where an advertising manager is copy testing a print ad for day-after recall. The norm for brand recognition for this type of ad is 30 percent; that is, 30 percent of the people that were questioned report having seen the brand advertised. Results of a survey indicate that 37 percent of the people questioned report having seen this particular ad. To test the hypothesis of no difference between the sample results and the norm, we would use a one-sample proportion test. The calculated Z-values for different sample sizes are:

Sample Size	Z-Calculated
30	0.84
50	1.08
100	1.53
200	2.16
500	3.42

From our previous discussions we know that at $\alpha = 0.05$, the tabled value (Z_t) is 1.96. Hence, if we had a sample size of 30, 50, or 100 we would not reject the null hypothesis, whereas if we had a sample size of 200 or more, we would reject the null. The reason is that with the smaller sample sizes, the difference we observe (0.30 versus 0.37) could very likely be due to sampling error. However, with sample sizes in excess of 200 we have confidence that the difference is not due to

---

[15]Hays, *Statistics for the Social Sciences*, p. 384.

sampling error. Another way to look at this issue is to construct a 95 percent confidence interval for samples of size 100 and 500.

Sample Size	Confidence Interval
100	$0.28 \leq \pi \leq 0.46$
500	$0.33 \leq \pi \leq 0.41$

Note that with the sample of 500 we would expect to obtain a recall score for this ad not less than 33 percent in 95 of 100 trial samples; hence, we can safely conclude that it scores better than the norm. However, with a sample size of 100 it is inconclusive that the population recall score for this ad would be different from the norm since in 95 out of the 100 trial samples we would expect to find recall scores between 28 percent and 46 percent.

Before concluding this chapter we warn the reader of a problem concerning statistical significance when a number of statistical tests are conducted on the same variable from the same sample. For example, consider the case where a researcher is interested in testing for differences between groups on top-box intention scores and the groups are (1) gender at two levels, (2) income at two levels, and (3) age at two levels. In this case, the researcher might perform three 2-group tests of differences in proportions. A problem arises in choosing the critical value. If we set α at 0.05 and choose a critical value from Table 2, 3, 4, or 5 in the Statistical Appendix, this critical value does not reflect that we are conducting more than one statistical test. Consequently, the significance level will be less than the desired 95 percent level or, stated another way, the probability of a Type I error will turn out to be greater than 5 percent. The researcher faced with this situation should use tabled values that account for multiple tests.[16]

SUMMARY

Hypothesis testing procedures permit specific claims about a population of interest to be tested on the basis of data collected from a sample of customers. Essentially, statistical hypothesis testing allows the manager to assess the probability that the claims made about the population are true.

This chapter considered hypothesis testing procedures for proportions and mean scores under a variety of situations. We began by discussing those factors that influence the choice of a hypothesis testing procedure.

Next, attention was directed to hypothesis testing for proportions for one sample, two samples, and more than two samples. We discussed the appropriate testing procedure for independent and related samples when more than one sample is available. Hypothesis tests concerning mean scores were also treated. Again the discussion considered one-sample, two-sample, and more-than-two-sample hypothesis tests for independent and related samples.

---

[16]The interested reader should begin by consulting Mitchell Dayton and William D. Schafer, "Extended Tables of *t* and Chi-Square for Bonferoni Tests with Unequal Error Allocation," *Journal of the American Statistical Association* 68 (March 1973), pp. 78–83.

KEY CONCEPTS

hypothesis

statistical hypothesis test

null hypothesis

alternative hypothesis

one-tail hypothesis test

two-tail hypothesis test

region of rejection

Type I error

alpha (α) level

Type II or beta (β) error

power of the test
($1 - \beta$)

independent samples

related samples

one-sample proportion test

two-independent sample test

chi-square test statistic

homoscedasticity

analysis of variance (ANOVA)

total variation

between-group variation

within-group variation

a posteriori comparisons

statistically significant finding

REVIEW QUESTIONS

1. Discuss the difference between conducting an independent sample hypothesis test and a related sample test.

2. The brand group for a manufacturer of washing machines believed that at most 30 percent of the households owning a washing machine used liquid detergent. If the proportion was greater than the hypothesized value, management would consider adding a line of products specifically designed for the use of liquid detergent. A survey of 500 households indicated that 165 used liquid detergent. What do you conclude?

3. In a coupon test the action standard called for a difference between a test coupon and a control coupon at the 90 percent confidence level. That is, to be considered for use the test coupon must outscore the control coupon at the 90 percent confidence level. To this end, samples of 500 test coupons and 500 control coupons were randomly delivered. The results indicated that 7 percent of the control coupons and 10 percent of the test coupons were redeemed. What do you conclude and why?

4. Your college of business was interested in starting a program to prepare students for the GMAT exam. The program consisted of a three-week course designed to familiarize students with the content areas of the exam. To evaluate the program, the college randomly selected 10 students from among the 210 students in the senior class that had already taken the exam. These students participated in the three-week preparatory class. The average GMAT score for all 210 students was 570. The scores before and after the course are given in the table below.

   a. What do you conclude about the course? Be sure to substantiate your conclusions.

   b. Comment on the general procedure employed by the college.

Student	Before	After
1	550	555
2	580	590
3	560	555
4	570	575
5	565	580
6	585	590
7	560	570
8	570	565
9	575	585
10	585	595

ANALYSIS OF VARIANCE WITH MORE THAN ONE TREATMENT CONDITION

In Chapter 15 analysis of variance is used to test different treatment conditions for differences in mean scores for a criterion variable. The criterion variable (y_{ij}), the response for the ith person in the jth treatment, is modeled as

$$y_{ij} = \bar{y}_{++} + T_j + e_{ij} \qquad (15A\text{--}1)$$

where

$$\bar{y}_{++} = \text{Overall mean}$$
$$T_j = \text{Effect of the } j\text{th treatment condition}$$
$$e_{ij} = \text{Error term}$$

The total sums of squares (*TSS*) or $\Sigma\Sigma\,(y_{ij} - \bar{y}_{++})^2$, the difference between a person's score on the criterion variable and the overall mean, consists of two

parts: (1) between sums of squares $\left[\sum_{j=1}^{J} n_j\,(y_{+j} - \bar{y}_{++})^2 \right]$ and (2) within sums

of squares $\left[\sum_{i=1}^{n} \sum_{j=1}^{J} (y_{ij} - \bar{y}_{+j})^2 \right]$.

The between sums of squares (*BSS*) represent that part of the total sums of squares due to the treatment conditions (i.e., explained variation), whereas the within sums of squares (*WSS*) represent that part of the total sums of squares not due to the treatments (i.e., unexplained variation).

To test the null hypothesis of equality of treatment means, an *F*-test calculated as

$$F_c = \frac{BSS\,/\,df}{WSS\,/\,df} \qquad (15A\text{--}2)$$

is used. Hence, the more variation due to differences in treatment means (*BSS*), the more likely it is that the null hypothesis will be rejected.

In some cases the experimental design has more than one treatment condition. Consider the example of the completely randomized factorial design introduced in Chapter 7. Subjects are exposed to a color-of-package treatment condition and a brand-price treatment condition. Letting C_i be the effect of the ith color and P_j be the effect of the jth price, the model becomes

$$y_{ijk} = \bar{y}_{+++} + C_i + P_j + CP_{ij} + e_{ijk} \qquad (15A\text{--}3)$$

Note that to be consistent with standard notation we now subscript individuals by k. The total variation for the score on the criterion variable for the

kth person in the ith, jth treatment from the overall mean $(\bar{y}_{+++})$ can be decomposed into the variation due to the ith treatment condition, the variation due to the jth treatment condition, the interaction between the ith and jth treatment conditions, and the error or unexplained variation e_{ijk}. That is

$$\sum_i^I \sum_j^J \sum_k^K (y_{ijk} - \bar{y}_{+++})^2$$

$$= nJ\sum_i (\bar{y}_{i++} - \bar{y}_{+++})^2 + nI\sum_j (\bar{y}_{+j+} - \bar{y}_{+++})^2 \qquad (15A\text{--}4)$$

$$+ n\sum_i \sum_j (\bar{y}_{ij+} - \bar{y}_{i++} - \bar{y}_{+j+} + \bar{y}_{+++})^2$$

$$+ \sum_i \sum_j \sum_k (y_{ijk} - \bar{y}_{ij+})^2$$

where

$$\sum_i \sum_j \sum_k (y_{ijk} - \bar{y}_{+++})^2 = \text{Total sum of squares } (TSS)$$

$$nJ\sum_i (\bar{y}_{i++} - \bar{y}_{+++})^2 = \text{Sum of squares due to the } I \text{ color-of-package treatment conditions } (SSC)$$

$$nI\sum_j (\bar{y}_{+j+} - \bar{y}_{+++})^2 = \text{Sum of squares due to the } J \text{ brand-price treatment conditions } (SSP)$$

$$n\sum_i \sum_j (\bar{y}_{ij+} - \bar{y}_{i++} - \bar{y}_{+j+} + \bar{y}_{+++})^2 = \text{Sum of squares due to the interaction of color-of-package and brand-price treatment conditions } (SSCP)$$

$$\sum_i \sum_j \sum_k (y_{ijk} - \bar{y}_{ij+})^2 = \text{Error sum of squares } (SSE)$$

Now, SSC and SSP are the main effects of color and price, which are interpreted in the same manner as the main effect of the commercial on recall scores shown in Chapter 15. However, now we have an effect due to the interaction of color and price (SSCP). Before proceeding to an example demonstrating the calculation of these effects and subsequent hypothesis tests, let's first take a look at the interaction effect.

Exhibit 15A–1 presents the plots of the treatment means shown in Table 15A–1. Remember that in Chapter 6 we said an interaction was present when the factor level lines were not parallel. Consider panel *a* of Exhibit 15A–1. In this case we have three factor level lines. You will note that at either price level, yellow is always the most visible, cream the least visible, and green almost equidistant between the two. Hence, given statistical significance for the color factor, yellow is the most significant regardless of price. Now, consider panel *b* of Exhibit 15A–1. At the price level of $6.29 all colors generate about the same purchase-intent scores; however, at the $6.79 price level, purchase-intent scores for yellow and cream decrease considerably, whereas purchase-intent scores for green actually increase. The factor level lines are not parallel, which indicates interaction. It can be said that a significant interaction renders main effects tenuous. To understand the meaning of this statement assume that the main effect of color on purchase-intent scores is significant. Simply looking at the means for the main effect of color (see

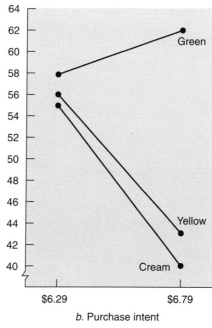

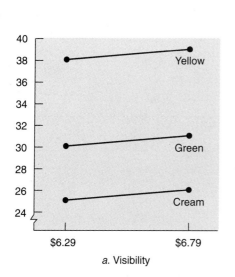

a. Visibility

b. Purchase intent

	Visibility				Purchase Intent		
Package Color	Price		Color Treatment Mean	Package Color	Price		Color Treatment Mean
	$6.29	$6.79			$6.29	$6.79	
Cream	25	26	25.5	Cream	55	40	47.5
Green	38	39	38.5	Green	58	62	60
Yellow	30	31	30.5	Yellow	56	43	49.5
Price Treatment Mean	31	32	31.5	Price Treatment Mean	56.3	48.3	52.3

TABLE 15A–1

Treatment Means

Table 15A–1) we would conclude that green produces the best purchase-intent scores. However, note that this is true for the $6.79 brand-price level, but it may not be true for the $6.29 brand-price level; that is, at this level the treatment means may not be statistically different. Hence, the choice of color depends on the level of price, and this is what is meant by a significant interaction; the effects of one factor depend on the level of another factor.

In the one-way analysis of variance presented in Chapter 15, we tested the null hypothesis of equality of treatment means for the levels of the treatment condition. When we have a two-factor design we test a hypothesis for the equality of treatment means for each of the factors and their interaction. Letting C_i be the effect for color, P_j be the effect for price, and CP_{ij} be the interaction effect, the hypotheses that will be tested are

TABLE 15A–2   Analysis of Variance Table—Two-Factor Design

Source	SS	df	MS	F_c
Factor C (SSC)	$nJ\sum_i (\bar{y}_{i++} - \bar{y}_{+++})^2$	$I - 1$	$SSC/(I - 1)$	$\dfrac{SSC/(I - 1)}{ESS/IJ(n - 1)}$
Factor P (SSP)	$nI\sum_i (\bar{y}_{+j+} - \bar{y}_{+++})^2$	$J - 1$	$SSP/(J - 1)$	$\dfrac{SSP/(J - 1)}{ESS/IJ(n - 1)}$
Interaction (SSCP)	$n\sum_i\sum_j (\bar{y}_{ij+} - \bar{y}_{i++} - \bar{y}_{+j+}$ $+ \bar{y}_{+++})^2$	$(I - 1)(J - 1)$	$\dfrac{SSCP}{(I - 1)(J - 1)}$	$\dfrac{SSCP/(I - 1)(J - 1)}{ESS/IJ(n - 1)}$
Error (ESS)	$\sum_i\sum_j\sum_k (y_{ijk} - \bar{y}_{ij+})^2$	$IJ(n - 1)$	$\dfrac{ESS}{IJ(n - 1)}$	
Total	$\sum_i\sum_j\sum_k (y_{ijk} - \bar{y}_{+++})^2$	$nIJ - 1$		

1. Main effect of color
   HO: $C_1 = C_2 = \ldots = C_I$
   HA: Not all C_i are equal
2. Main effect of price
   HO: $P_1 = P_2 = \ldots = P_J$
   HA: Not all P_j are equal
3. Interaction of color and price
   HO: $CP_{11} = CP_{12} = \ldots = CP_{IJ} = 0$
   HA: Not all $CP_{ij} = 0$

We again use an F-test to statistically test these hypotheses. The formula for the appropriate F-test for each hypothesis is shown in Table 15A–2.

We first test for the effects of color and price on visibility scores. The ANOVA table, including calculations of the sum of squares, is presented in Table 15A–3. Note that the sum of squares for the interaction term (SSCP) is zero, which reflects the parallelism of the treatment level lines shown in Exhibit 15A–1.

The calculated F-value for the color treatment conditions is 12.87

$$F_c = \frac{8600/2}{98223/294}$$

which allows rejection of the null hypothesis of the $\alpha = 0.05$ level. The calculated F-value for the price treatment conditions is 0.22

$$F_c = \frac{75/1}{98223/294}$$

consequently, the null hypothesis is not rejected, and we would conclude that with respect to visibility only the color of package had a statistically significant effect.

Let's now turn to the purchase-intent scores. Table 15A–4 presents the analysis of variance table, including the calculations of the sum of squares.

With a calculated F-value of 6.48 ($F_c = \dfrac{5450/2}{123626/294}$), the null hypothesis of no interaction is rejected at the $\alpha = 0.05$ level (critical value of $F_{t(1 - 0.05; 2,294)}$ is

Source	SS	df	MS
Color (SSC)	8,600	2	4300.00
Price (SSP)	75	1	75.00
Color × Price (SSCP)	0	2	0.00
Error (ESS)	98,223	294	334.09
Total (TSS)	106,898	299	

$$TSS = 106{,}898$$

$$SSC = nJ\sum_i (\bar{y}_{i++} - \bar{y}_{+++})^2 = (50)(2)[(25.5 - 31.5)^2$$
$$+ (38.5 - 31.5)^2$$
$$+ (30.5 - 31.5)^2]$$
$$= 100(36 + 49 + 1)$$
$$= 8.600$$

$$SSP = nI\sum_j (\bar{y}_{+j+} - \bar{y}_{+++})^2 = (50)(3)[(31 - 31.5)^2$$
$$+ (32 - 31.5)^2]$$
$$= 150(0.25 + 0.25)$$
$$= 75$$

$$SSCP = n\sum_i\sum_j (\bar{y}_{ij+} - \bar{y}_{i++} - \bar{y}_{+j+} + \bar{y}_{+++})^2 = 50\,[(25 - 31 - 25.5 + 31.5)^2$$
$$+ (38 - 31 - 38.5 + 31.5)^2$$
$$+ (30 - 31 - 30.5 + 31.5)^2$$
$$+ (26 - 32 - 25.5 + 31.5)^2$$
$$+ (39 - 32 - 38.5 + 31.5)^2$$
$$+ (31 - 32 - 30.5 + 31.5)^2]$$
$$= 50\,(0 + 0 + 0 + 0 + 0 + 0)$$
$$= 0$$

$$ESS = \text{(by subtraction)} = 106{,}898 - 8{,}600 - 75 - 0 = 98{,}223$$

Source	SS	df	MS
Color (SSC)	9,017	2	4,508.50
Price (SSP)	4,800	1	4,800.00
Color × Price (SSCP)	5,450	2	2,725.00
Error (ESS)	123,626	294	420.50
Total (TSS)	142,893	299	

$$TSS = 142{,}893$$
$$SCC = (50)(2)[(47.5 - 52.3)^2 + (60 - 52.3)^2 + (49.5 - 52.3)^2]$$
$$= 9{,}017$$
$$SSP = (50)(3)[(56.3 - 52.3)^2 + (48.3 - 52.3)^2]$$
$$= 4{,}800$$
$$SSCP = (50)[(55 - 56.3 - 47.5 + 52.3)^2 + (58 - 56.3 - 60 + 52.3)^2 + (56 - 56.3 - 49.5 + 52.3)^2$$
$$+ (40 - 48.3 - 47.5 + 52.3)^2 + (62 - 48.3 - 50 + 52.3)^2 + (43 - 48.3 - 49.5 + 52.3)^2]$$
$$= 5{,}450$$
$$ESS = \text{(by subtraction)} = 142{,}893 - 9{,}017 - 4{,}800 - 5{,}450 = 123{,}626$$

approximately 3.00 from Table 4 of the Statistical Appendix) In addition, the null hypotheses are rejected at $\alpha = 0.05$ for both of the main effects. Ignoring the significant interaction we conclude that the price of $6.29 and the color green produce the greatest purchase-intent scores. However, you will note from Exhibit

15A–1 that if we choose the price level of $6.29, there is not much difference in purchase-intent scores for the three colors. If there is a significant interaction we must assess differences in treatment conditions at each level of the other treatment condition. These tests are called tests of simple main effects, and the interested reader is referred to Winer.[1] Basically, what is involved is testing for differences among the color-package treatment conditions at the $6.29 brand-price level and then at the $6.79 brand-price level, or alternatively testing for differences in the brand-price treatment levels at each of the three color-package treatment conditions. Remember that significant interactions render main effects tenuous. Hence, whenever we have more than one treatment condition and a significant interaction term, care must be exercised when you interpret main effects.

---

[1] B. J. Winer, *Statistical Principles in Experimental Design* (New York: McGraw-Hill, 1971).

ANALYSIS OF COVARIANCE

In Chapter 6 we discussed concepts and issues related to experimental designs. In the course of the discussion we indicated that one method of controlling for extraneous sources of variation due to factors other than the variable that has been manipulated is via *statistical control*. In essence, statistical control involves purging the effect of the extraneous causal factor from the criterion measure. *Analysis of covariance* (ANCOVA) helps the researcher to increase the precision of an experiment by removing possible sources of variance in the criterion variable that are attributable to factors not controlled for by him or her. As we will see, these influences are removed statistically, and by so doing the error variance can be decreased, resulting in more sensitive (that is, precise) experiments.

THE ANCOVA MODEL

You will recall from Chapters 7 and 15 we introduced the following model

$$y_{ij} = \bar{y}_{++} + T_j + e_{ij} \tag{15B–1}$$

where $\bar{y}_{++}$ denotes the overall mean response and T_j ($j = 1, 2, \ldots, K$) denotes the differential effect of the Kth treatment condition on the criterion measure. As before e_{ij} denotes the error term.

Suppose now that in addition to the manipulated variable the researcher suspects that another extraneous factor has influenced the observed measures on the criterion variable. We refer to this other extraneous factor as the *covariate*. In ANCOVA the traditional ANOVA model is augmented in such a way as to account for the variation in the criterion variable that is due to the covariate. Specifically, we introduce another term, denoted as x_{ij}, representing the covariate and express the model shown in Equation 15B–1 as

$$y_{ij} = \bar{y}_{++} + T_j + c(x_{ij}\,\bar{x}_{++}) + e_{ij} \tag{15B–2}$$

The variable x_{ij} denotes the value of the covariate for the ith individual in the jth treatment condition; c denotes the coefficient representing the average effect of a unit change in the covariate on the criterion variable; and $\bar{x}_{++}$ is the overall mean of the covariate. [In Chapter 16 this effect (c) is known as a *regression coefficient*.] Verbally, the algebraic model shown in Equation 15B–2 can be expressed as

$$\begin{pmatrix} \text{Observed value} \\ \text{of dependent} \\ \text{variable} \end{pmatrix} = (\text{Constant}) + \begin{pmatrix} \text{Effect of} \\ \text{treatment} \\ \text{condition} \end{pmatrix} + \begin{pmatrix} \text{Effect} \\ \text{of} \\ \text{covariate} \end{pmatrix} + \begin{pmatrix} \text{Error} \\ \text{term} \end{pmatrix}$$

To better understand how ANCOVA works we can compare the error term with that obtained under the basic ANOVA model. We can view $c(x_{ij} - \bar{x}_{++})$ as representing that part of y_{ij} that is accounted for by changes in the covariate (x), while e_{ij} is the *residual* error that still remains. Letting e^*_{ij} denote the error term under ANCOVA and e_{ij} denote the error term under ANOVA we can write

$$e_{ij} = e^*_{ij} + c(x_{ij} - \bar{x}_{++})$$

If we assume that the e_{ij} and $c(x_{ij} - \bar{x}_{++})$ are independent, we have

$$\text{Var}(e_{ij}) = \text{Var}(e^*_{ij}) + \text{Var}(\text{due to } x)$$

Thus, the variance of the error term after covariance adjustment is no more than the variance of the error term under the standard ANOVA model, ignoring the variance due to the covariate (x).

SUM OF SQUARES AND TESTING

From Equation 15B–2 it is apparent that the criterion variable may be adjusted for the covariate as follows

$$y_{ij(\text{adj})} = y_{ij} - c(x_{ij} - \bar{x}_{++}) \tag{15B–3}$$

where $y_{ij(\text{adj})}$ denotes the value of the criterion variable adjusted for the covariate. In covariance analysis we are still concerned with testing the hypothesis that the treatment condition means are equal. Thus, based on the preceding discussion and Equation 15B–3, it would appear that we could accomplish this by conducting an analysis of variance on the adjusted scores $y_{ij(\text{adj})}$. However, unless the coefficient c is known, which rarely is the case, this is not the recommended approach. The problem is that c in most cases must be estimated from the sample by using data from all of the treatment conditions. Because the adjusted treatment condition means are not independent of each other, the F-test for testing the equality of treatment condition means is not strictly valid. Therefore, another approach must be followed.

The first step is to develop the necessary sum of squares. Let

TSS(·) = Total sum of squares for factor (·)
BSS(·) = Between sum of squares for factor (·)
WSS(·) = Within sum of squares for factor (·)

Table 15B–1 shows the necessary formulas for computing the unadjusted sum of squares and cross products. (By *cross products* we mean the yx effect.)

To perform the ANCOVA test we need to adjust these sums of squares. In essence, the adjustment removes the effect of the covariate from the total, between, and within sum of squares for the criterion variable y. These are shown below.

$$TSS(y_{\text{adj}}) = TSS(y) - \left(\frac{TSS(yx)^2}{TSS(x)}\right)$$

$$WSS(y_{\text{adj}}) = WSS(y) - \left(\frac{WSS(yx)^2}{WSS(x)}\right)$$

$$BSS(y_{\text{adj}}) = TSS(y_{\text{adj}}) - WSS(y_{\text{adj}})$$

The hypothesis testing procedure follows the standard format.

HO: $\mu_1 = \mu_2 = \ldots = \mu_K$

HA: not all μ_K are equal

$$TS_c\colon F_c = \frac{BSS(y_{\text{adj}})/(K - 1)}{WSS(y_{\text{adj}})/(n - K - 1)}$$

$TS_t\colon F_{t(1 - \alpha;\ df = K - 1,\ n - K - 1)}$

DR: Reject HO: if $F_c > F_{t(1 - \alpha;\ df = K - 1,\ n - K - 1)}$

Note that the degrees of freedom associated with the adjusted within sum of squares are $(n - K - 1)$. One additional degree of freedom is lost because of the estimation of the within-treatment effect $WSS(yx)^2/WSS(x)$.

Table 15B–2 (see page 458) shows data on pre- and post-exposure attitude scores for 12 respondents who participated in a three-cell *before-after* advertising execution test. Table 15B–3 (see page 458) shows summary computational details

---

Total:

$$TSS(y) = \sum_{j=1}^{K}\sum_{i=1}^{nj} (y_{ij} - \bar{y}_{++})^2 = \sum_{j=1}^{K}\sum_{i=1}^{nj} y_{ij}^2 - \left(\sum_{j=1}^{K}\sum_{i=1}^{nj} y_{ij}\right)^2 \Big/ n$$

$$TSS(x) = \sum_{j=1}^{K}\sum_{i=1}^{nj} (x_{ij} - \bar{x}_{++})^2 = \sum_{j=1}^{K}\sum_{i=1}^{nj} x_{ij}^2 - \left(\sum_{j=1}^{K}\sum_{i=1}^{nj} x_{ij}\right)^2 \Big/ n$$

$$TSS(yx) = \sum_{j=1}^{K}\sum_{i=1}^{nj} (y_{ij} - \bar{y}_{++})(x_{ij} - \bar{x}_{++})$$

$$= \sum_{j=1}^{K}\sum_{i=1}^{nj} y_{ij}x_{ij} - \left(\sum_{j=1}^{K}\sum_{i=1}^{nj} y_{ij}\sum_{j=1}^{K}\sum_{i=1}^{nj} x_{ij}\right)\Big/ n$$

Between:

$$BSS(y) = \sum_{j=1}^{K} n_j(\bar{y}_{+j} - \bar{y}_{++})^2$$

$$BSS(x) = \sum_{j=1}^{K} n_j(\bar{x}_{+j} - \bar{x}_{++})^2$$

$$BSS(yx) = \sum_{j=1}^{K} n_j(\bar{y}_{+j} - \bar{y}_{++})(\bar{x}_{+j} - \bar{x}_{++})$$

Within:

$$WSS(y) = \sum_{j=1}^{K}\sum_{i=1}^{nj} (y_{ij} - \bar{y}_{+j})^2$$

$$WSS(x) = \sum_{j=1}^{K}\sum_{i=1}^{nj} (x_{ij} - \bar{x}_{+j})^2$$

$$WSS(yx) = \sum_{j=1}^{K}\sum_{i=1}^{nj} (y_{ij} - \bar{y}_{+j})(x_{ij} - \bar{x}_{+j}) = \sum_{j=1}^{K}\sum_{i=1}^{nj} y_{ij}x_{ij} - \frac{n}{K}\left(\sum_{j=1}^{K} y_{+j}\bar{x}_{+j}\right)$$

TABLE 15B–1
—
Formulas for Computing Unadjusted Sum of Squares and Cross Products

TABLE 15B–2
—
Pre- and Post-
Exposure Attitude
Scores for Three-Cell
Before-After
Advertising
Execution Test

Respondent	Pre-Exposure Attitude Score (y)	Post-Exposure Attitude Score Covariate (x)
1	6	6
2	7	6
3	8	8
4	5	5
Cell 1	$\bar{y}_{+1} = 6.5$	$\bar{x}_{+1} = 6.25$
5	7	5
6	5	3
7	4	2
8	6	4
Cell 2	$\bar{y}_{+2} = 5.5$	$\bar{x}_{+2} = 3.5$
9	8	10
10	7	9
11	6	8
12	9	11
Cell 3	$\bar{y}_{+3} = 7.5$	$\bar{x}_{+3} = 9.5$
	$\bar{y}_{++} = 6.5$	$\bar{x}_{++} = 6.42$

TABLE 15B–3
—
Summary
Computations and
ANOVA Table

Source	SS	df	MSS	F_c
Between	$BSS = 8$	$K - 1 = 2$	$\dfrac{BSS}{(K-1)} = 4$	$\dfrac{4}{1.67} = 2.4$
Within	$WSS = 15$	$n - K = 9$	$\dfrac{WSS}{(n-K)} = 1.67$	
Total	$TSS = 23$	$n - 1 = 11$		

$$BSS = \sum_{j=1}^{K} n_j(\bar{y}_{+j} - \bar{y}_{++})^2 = [4(6.5 - 6.5)^2 + 4(5.5 - 6.5)^2 + 4(7.5 - 6.5)^2]$$
$$= 8$$

$$WSS = \sum_{j=1}^{K}\sum_{i=1}^{nj} (y_{ij} - \bar{y}_{+j})^2 = (6 - 6.5)^2 + (7 - 6.5)^2 + \ldots + (6 - 7.5)^2$$
$$+ (9 - 7.5)^2$$
$$= 15$$

$$TSS = \sum_{j=1}^{K}\sum_{i=1}^{nj} (y_{ij} - \bar{y}_{++})^2 = (6 - 6.5)^2 + (7 - 6.5)^2 + \ldots + (6 - 6.5)^2$$
$$+ (9 - 6.5)^2$$
$$= 23$$

and the resulting ANOVA table, ignoring the covariate, which in this case is the pre-exposure attitude score. From the table we would conclude that the three cells are not different; that is, the three advertising executions come from the same population, and therefore, their post-exposure mean attitude scores are the same.

TABLE 15B–4 Summary Calculations and ANCOVA Table

Source	SS	df	MSS	F_c
Between	$BSS = 5.17$	$K - 1 = 2$	$\dfrac{BSS}{(K-1)} = 2.59$	$\dfrac{2.59}{0.096} = 26.98$
Within	$WSS = 0.77$	$n - K - 1 = 8$	$\dfrac{WSS}{(n-K-2)} = 0.096$	
Total	$TSS = 5.94$	$n - 2 = 10$		

Preliminary Calculations	Cell 1	Cell 2	Cell 3	Total
n_j	4	4	4	12
Σy	26	22	30	78
Σx	25	14	38	77
Σy^2	174	126	230	530
Σyx	167	82	290	539
Σx^2	161	54	366	581

$$TSS(y) = \sum_{j=1i=1}^{K}\sum^{nj} (y_{ij} - \bar{y}_{++})^2 = \sum_{j=1i=1}^{K}\sum^{nj} y_{ij}^2 - \left(\sum_{j=1i=1}^{K}\sum^{nj} y_{ij}\right)^2 \Big/ n$$
$$= 530 - (78)^2/12 = 23$$

$$TSS(x) = \sum_{j=1i=1}^{K}\sum^{nj} (x_{ij} - \bar{x}_{++})^2 = \sum_{j=1i=1}^{K}\sum^{nj} x_{ij}^2 - \left(\sum_{j=1i=1}^{K}\sum^{nj} x_{ij}\right)^2 \Big/ n$$
$$= 581 - (77)^2/12 = 86.92$$

$$TSS(yx) = \sum_{j=1i=1}^{K}\sum^{nj} y_{ij}x_{ij} - \left(\sum_{j=1i=1}^{K}\sum^{nj} y_{ij} \sum_{j=1i=1}^{K}\sum^{nj} x_{ij}\right)\Big/ n$$
$$= 539 - (78)(77)/12 = 38.5$$

$$WSS(x) = \sum_{j=1i=1}^{K}\sum^{nj} (x_{ij} - \bar{x}_{+j})^2 = (6 - 6.25)^2 + (6 - 6.25)^2 + \cdots + (8 - 9.5)^2 + (11 - 9.5)^2$$
$$= 14.77$$

$$WSS(yx) = \sum_{j=1i=1}^{K}\sum^{nj} (y_{ij} - \bar{y}_{+j})(x_{ij} - \bar{x}_{+j}) = \sum_{j=1i=1}^{K}\sum^{nj} y_{ij}x_{ij} - \frac{n}{K}\left(\sum_{j=1}^{K} \bar{y}_{+j}\bar{x}_{+j}\right)$$
$$= 539 - 4[(6.5)(6.25) + (5.5)(3.5) + (7.5)(9.5)]$$
$$= 539 - 524.5 = 14.5$$

$$TSS(y_{adj}) = TSS(y) - \frac{TSS(yx)^2}{TSS(x)}$$
$$= 23 - \frac{(38.5)^2}{86.92} = 5.94$$

$$WSS(y_{adj}) = WSS(y) - \frac{WSS(yx)^2}{TSS(x)}$$
$$= 15 - \frac{(14.5)^2}{14.77} = 0.77$$

$$BSS(y_{adj}) = TSS(y_{adj}) - WSS(y_{adj})$$
$$= 5.17$$

The ANCOVA test is carried out in Table 15B–4. Note that the adjustment treatment condition mean sum of squares is 5.17, and the adjusted within-treatment condition mean sum of squares is 0.77. The associated F ratio of 26.98, with 2 and 8 degrees of freedom, is highly significant at the 0.05 level. Thus, in contrast to the ANOVA results, we conclude that the three advertising executions differ once the influence of the covariate is removed.

CONCLUSION

In the preceding example covariance adjustment led to an increase in precision; after adjustment the treatment conditions were found to be significant. However, it is possible for covariance analysis to lead to a decrease in precision. If the covariate is highly related to the manipulated variable (treatment conditions) and *not* highly related to the criterion variable, then covariance adjustment can remove a large part of the treatment effect, thereby reducing precision. In such cases partialing out the covariate is not appropriate.

Measures of Association and Regression Analysis

— Present the notion of covariation between two random variables.

— Demonstrate the calculation of correlation coefficients for variables measured on interval, ordinal, or nominal scales.

— Use simple regression analysis to predict values of one variable, given a value for another variable.

— Describe multiple regression analysis.

— Explain the effects of multicollinearity on the estimation of regression coefficients.

— Provide statistical tests for regression coefficients.

— Describe the assumptions underlying regression analysis.

INTRODUCTION

Chapter 15 focused on data analysis methods and tests of hypotheses that considered only one variable at a time. Although these methods did allow for group differences to be tested, the hypotheses were formulated in terms of a single variable.

Understanding the relationships that exist between sets of variables is extremely important in marketing research as well. In this chapter we discuss measures of correlation and regression analysis. Measures of correlation quantify the extent to which two variables are associated. Regression analysis is a model that attempts to understand the dependence on one variable, called the **dependent** or **criterion variable** (for example, CEO compensation), on one or more other variables, called the **explanatory** or **independent variables** (for example, performance). The point is to predict the mean or average value of the former on the basis of the known values of the latter.[1]

The chapter begins with a discussion of correlation and covariance, concepts that we introduced previously in Chapters 8 and 14. Next, the discussion turns to calculating correlation coefficients for different measurement scales, including nominal, ordinal, and interval. Because the two variables being

---

1D. Gujarati, *Basic Econometrics* (New York: McGraw-Hill, 1978), p. 12.

correlated may have different measurement properties, we then demonstrate how correlation coefficients can be computed for variables having mixed scales. The remainder of the chapter is devoted to the regression model. First, simple regression, which considers the relationship between a dependent variable and a single explanatory variable, is discussed. Then we turn to multiple regression, which considers the relationship between two or more explanatory variables, and discuss several important conditions underlying the proper use of this procedure.

ASSOCIATION BETWEEN VARIABLES

Before we investigate specific measures of correlation we need to understand what is meant by **covariation**. If two variables covary, there is a systematic relationship between the level of one variable and the level of some other variable.

Columns 2 and 3 of Table 16–1 present hypothetical data on size of sales force and market coverage. Inspection of the data provides support for association between the two variables. Note that those firms with a large sales force also tend to have high market coverage, whereas firms with a small sales force tend to have low market coverage. Exhibit 16–1, part *a* displays the bivariate plot of these two variables. These plots are typically called **scatter diagrams** and are useful for visually inspecting the association, if any, between two variables. The numbers in parentheses refer to the firms listed in Table 16–1.

The type of association shown in Exhibit 16–1, part *a* is called **direct or positive association** because as the value of one variable increases (decreases) there is a tendency for the value of the other variable to increase (decrease). It is also

TABLE 16–1
—

Hypothetical Data
Used for Measuring
Covariation

(1) Firm	(2) Sales Force	(3) Market Coverage (%)	(4) Out-of-Stock Items	(5) Average Dollar Sale	(6) Turnover Ratio
1	100	10	30	30	30
2	200	30	17	40	35
3	400	30	15	35	25
4	300	50	19	25	30
5	500	50	13	45	15
6	500	60	10	35	15
7	600	70	11	40	20
8	100	20	22	50	40
9	800	80	10	35	25
10	700	50	9	30	15
11	1000	80	3	35	40
12	700	60	12	45	20
13	800	70	2	45	30
14	900	90	2	40	30
15	1000	90	5	50	45

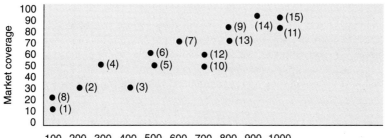

a. Sales force and market coverage

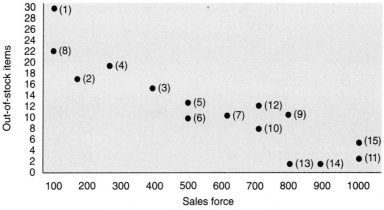

b. Sales force and out-of-stock data

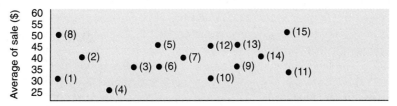

c. Sales force and average dollar amount of sale

Note: Number in parentheses refers to the firm number in Table 16–1.

EXHIBIT 16–1
—
Scatter Diagram for
Data in Table 16–1

possible to observe an **inverse or negative association** between two variables. The term *negative association* is used whenever the value of one variable increases (decreases) and the value of the other variable decreases (increases). Note that the terms *positive* and *negative* are not subject to value judgments; that is, positive relationships are not "good" and negative relationships are not "bad."

direct or positive
association
*Relationship where, as
the value of one variable
increases (decreases),
there is a tendency for
the value of the other
variable to increase
(decrease).*

EXAMPLE

Columns 2 and 4 of Table 16–1 present data for the size of the sales force and out-of-stock items for the same 15 firms. The scatter diagram for these data is displayed in Exhibit 16–1, part *b*. In contrast to the relationship shown in part *a* of this figure, there is an inverse relationship between size of sales force and out-of-stock items; that is, companies that have small sales forces were more likely to be out of stock.

inverse or negative association
Relationship where, as the value of one variable increases (decreases), the value of the other variable decreases (increases).

Our two examples demonstrate the case where an association, positive or negative, exists between two variables. However, there are circumstances when two variables may not be associated. By **no association** we mean that there is no systematic relationship between the level of one variable and the level of another variable. In other words, the variation in one variable is independent of the variation in the other variable.

EXAMPLE

Consider columns 2 and 5 of Table 16–1, which give information on the size of sales force for the 15 firms and the corresponding average dollar amount of a sale. The scatter diagram for the data is shown in Exhibit 16–1, part *c*. Note that smaller firms have *both* large and small average dollar sales and the same is true for larger firms—larger firms also have *both* large and small average dollar sales. Hence, there is no systematic relationship between size of sales force and the level of the other variable (average dollar sale).

no association
A situation in which there is no systematic relationship between the level of one variable and the level of another variable.

It is important to emphasize, however, that association does not imply causality. That is, you cannot conclude from the scatter diagram shown in Exhibit 16–1*b* that sales price level determines (i.e., *causes*) the level of out-of-stock. As we discussed in Chapter 8, there are a number of conditions that must be in place, for example, controlling extraneous factors, before causality can be proven. In this example, it may be that firms with large sales forces have inventory and distributional problems caused by operating at near-full capacity.

Although we must be careful in making statements about causality, correlation analysis does allow us to make inferences about the relationship between two variables. Consider the two cross tabulations shown in Table 16–2. The table cross classifies the responses of 100 individuals according to their gender and purchase behavior. Consider first the cross tabulation shown in panel *a*. Suppose you are asked to guess the probability that a female would purchase. Looking at panel *a*, your best guess is 0.50, because half of the females purchased (25/50) and half (25/50) did not. Knowledge of a person's gender does not help you very much in predicting purchase behavior. And, as we will see shortly, the correlation coefficient for these two variables is zero—gender and purchase behavior have no association.

Now consider panel *b* of Table 16–2. Here, the marginals are the same—50 percent of the sample purchased, while 50 percent did not, and the sample is evenly divided between males and females. Faced with the same question as before, you would now conclude that the probability of a female purchasing is 1.0—

a.

Purchase Gender	Yes	No	Total
Male	25	25	50
Female	25	25	50
Total	50	50	100

b.

Purchase Gender	Yes	No	Total
Male	0	50	50
Female	50	0	50
Total	50	50	100

TABLE 16–2

Cross Tabulation of
Purchase and Gender

all of the 50 females surveyed initiated a purchase. In this case, there is a very strong association between gender and purchase behavior. In fact, the correlation coefficient for panel *b* is 1.0, indicating that gender and purchase behavior are perfectly correlated.

To summarize, measures of correlation are symmetrical in nature. The correlation between variable *x* and variable *y* is the same as that between variable *y* and variable *x*. Two variables can be *positively correlated, negatively correlated,* or *uncorrelated*. Parts *c, d,* and *g* in Exhibit 16–2 (see page 466) depict these three conditions. In Exhibit 16–2*c* the two variables are positively correlated, $r > 0$. Note that there is an upward trend to the data—when *x* is large, *y* is also large. Exhibit 16–2*d* depicts negative correlation, $r < 0$. Note that there is an inverse relationship between the two variables—when *x* is large, *y* is small whereas when *x* is small, *y* is large. Exhibit 16–2*g* depicts the situation when two variables are uncorrelated, $r = 0$. Note that there is no systematic relationship between the two variables—when the values of *x* are large, some *y* values are large and some are small, and when the values of *x* are small some values of *y* are small and some are large.

The correlation between two variables lies between the limits of -1 and $+1$. If the correlation between two variables is equal to $+1$, we say that the two variables exhibit *perfect positive correlation* (see Exhibit 16–2*a*). If the correlation between two variables is equal to 1, we say that the two variables exhibit *perfect negative correlation* (see Exhibit 16–2*b*). As shown in these two figures, perfect positive or negative correlation means that there is an exact linear relationship between the two variables. Correlation measures the *linear association* between

EXHIBIT 16–2

Correlational
Patterns

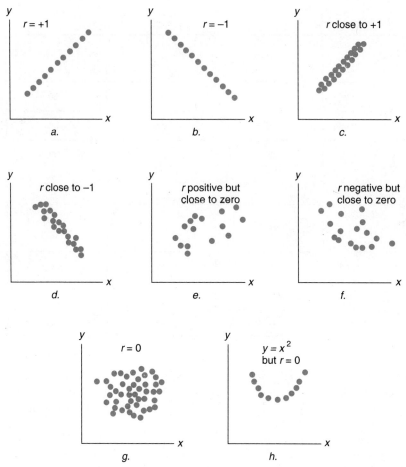

Source: Adapted from Henri Theil, *Introduction to Econometrics* (Englewood Cliffs, N.J.: Prentice Hall, 1978), p. 86.

two variables. Thus, as depicted in Exhibit 16–2h, $r = 0$ even though $y = x^2$ (where x assumes both positive and negative values).

MEASURES OF CORRELATION

Ultimately, the method or procedure used to measure the degree of association between two variables depends on the type of measurement scale used.

Interval- or Ratio-Scaled Variables

Pearson product moment correlation
Measure of the linear association between two interval- or ratio-scaled variables.

The most commonly used measure of correlation was developed by Carl Pearson in the early 1900s and is referred to as the **Pearson product moment correlation,** or simply as the product moment correlation between two variables. Denoting the variables as x_i and y_i and their corresponding linear correlation as r_{xy}, the formula for computing the sample-based product moment correlation is

$$r_{xy} = \frac{\sum_{i=1}^{n}[(x_i - \bar{x})(y_i - \bar{y})]/(n-1)}{\sqrt{\frac{\sum_{i=1}^{n}(x_i - \bar{x})^2}{n-1}} \sqrt{\frac{\sum_{i=1}^{n}(y_i - \bar{y})^2}{n-1}}} \qquad (16\text{--}1)$$

The denominator of Equation 16–1 may look familiar; it is simply the product of the standard deviation of x_i and y_i. The numerator of Equation 16–1 gives the covariance between x_i and y_i. Covariance measures the degree to which two variables covary, that is, the extent to which the variables display some degree of positive or negative association.

Computation shows that the covariance between sales force (y_i) and market coverage (x_i) is 99,800. However, does a covariance of 99,800 represent strong or weak association between the two variables? From Equation 16–1 we can see that the larger the values of y_i and x_i, the larger will be the covariance because we are summing the product of $(x_i - \bar{x})(y_i - \bar{y})$. In other words, the covariance between two variables is affected by the units of measurement. To illustrate this notion you can multiply the sales force size for each firm shown in Table 16–1 by 10. Hence, instead of 100 salespersons, firm 1 now has 1,000 salespersons, firm 2 now has 2,000 salespersons instead of 200 salespersons, and so forth. The covariance between the two variables is now 998,000; however, the basic relationship between the two variables has not changed. That is, the scatter diagram would be identical to Exhibit 16–1, and only the scale of the vertical axis would be changed. It is for this reason that we divide the covariance between y_i and x_i by the product of their standard deviations as shown in Equation 16–1. Unlike the covariance between x_i and y_i, the correlation (r_{xy}) is, as we indicated earlier, bounded by the range -1 to $+1$, where -1 represents perfect negative correlation, $+1$ represents perfect positive correlation, and zero represents no correlation. In the case of perfect positive or perfect negative correlation, all of the points in a scatter diagram would fall on a straight line. As the points deviate from a straight line, the correlation decreases.

In Chapter 13 the standardization transformation was discussed. If you let x_i' be the standardized value associated with x_i and y_i' be the standardized value associated with y_i, where with

$$x_i' = (x_i - \bar{x})/s_x$$

and

$$y_i' = (y_i - \bar{y})/s_y$$

we know that $\bar{x}' = \bar{y}' = 0$ and $s_{x'} = s_{y'} = 1$.

Hence, the correlation ($r_{x'y'}$) between the standardized variables (x' and y') is

$$r_{x'y'} = \frac{\sum_{i=1}^{n} (x_i' - 0)(y_i' - 0)/(n-1)}{\sqrt{1}\,\sqrt{1}}$$

$$= \sum_{i=1}^{n} (x_i' y_i')/(n-1) \qquad (16\text{--}2)$$

Thus, we see that the covariance between two standardized variables is the correlation between the variables.

EXAMPLE

To illustrate the calculation of the product moment correlation, we can return to the data shown in Table 16–1. Applying Equation 16–1, we find

$$r_{xy} = \frac{99{,}800/14}{(305.19)(25.0)} = 0.93$$

The correlation r_{xy} is the sample-based correlation between x_i and y_i. It is an estimate of the population correlation (ρ_{xy}) between the two variables. If we want to statistically test the hypothesis of no correlation in the population between x_i and y_i (that is, HO: $\rho_{xy} = 0$), the procedure is[2]

HO: $\rho_{xy} = 0$

HA: $\rho_{xy} \neq 0$

TS_c: $t_c = \dfrac{r_{xy}\sqrt{n-2}}{\sqrt{1-r_{xy}^2}}$

TS_t: $t_{t(1-\alpha/2;\ df\ =\ n\ -\ 2)}$

DR: Reject HO: if $TS_c > TS_t$ or $-TS_c < -TS_t$

With $r_{xy} = 0.93$ we find

$$t_c = \frac{0.93\sqrt{13}}{\sqrt{0.14}}$$

$$= 8.96$$

From Table 3 in the Statistical Appendix the region of rejection at $\alpha = 0.05$ and $df = n - 2 = 13$ is 2.160. Since the test statistic calculated (TS_c) exceeds the tabulated test statistic (TS_t), $TS_c > TS_t$, we reject the null hypothesis, concluding that sales force and market coverage are significantly correlated.

As stated previously, the product moment correlation measures the linear association between two interval-scaled or ratio-scaled variables. If two variables exhibit nonlinear association, the product moment correlation will likely be close to zero; however, this does not mean that the variables are not associated. Consider, for example, the data in columns 2 and 6 of Table 16–1. Plotting these data shows

---

[2]John Neter, William Wasserman, and Michael J. Kuter, *Applied Linear Statistical Methods*, 2nd ed. (Homewood, Ill.: Richard D. Irwin, 1985), pp. 501–3.

a U-shaped pattern. In other words, both large and small firms have high turnover ratios of salespeople, and midsize firms have lower turnover ratios. Hence, as the size of a firm increases, the turnover ratio decreases until some point and then reverses itself and increases as the size of a firm increases. The (linear) product moment correlation is close to zero (0.033), indicating little association between the variables. However, there is a fairly strong association between the variables, but it is not linear in character.

Ordinal Scales

As we discussed in Chapter 10, the mean is not the appropriate measure of central tendency when the data have ordinal-scale properties; consequently, we cannot use the product moment correlation. With variables having ordinal or rank-order properties, the appropriate measure of correlation is **Spearman's rank-order correlation coefficient**, which we will denote simply as ρ_s (and r_s for the sample-based estimate).

The sample-based Spearman's rank-order correlation coefficient can be calculated from the following formula:[3]

$$r_s = 1 - 6 \sum_{i=1}^{n} \frac{d_i^2}{n(n^2 - 1)} \tag{16–3}$$

Spearman's rank-order correlation coefficient *Measure of linear association between variables that have ordinal-scale properties.*

where d_i represents the difference in ranking for the ith object, n is the number of objects ranked, and the number 6 appearing in the numerator is a constant needed to ensure that the sample-based estimate of the correlation coefficient is an unbiased estimate of its population counterpart. How Equation 16–3 is applied will become clear through the following example.

EXAMPLE

To illustrate the calculation of the rank-order correlation coefficient, consider the following example. An advertising agency was interested in the relationship between the copy-testing procedures of two copy-testing suppliers. Each of the copy-testing services evaluated copy on a number of dimensions (e.g., attention, recall, and persuasion) and produced a rank ordering of the copy that purportedly reflected the advertisement's overall effectiveness. The advertising agency needed to select one of the copy-testing services; however, a major concern centered on the consistency of the rank orderings produced by each of the copy-testing services and the internal rank ordering of ads within the advertising agency itself. To investigate this issue, the agency asked each supplier to copy-test 10 ads and to rank order them with respect to overall performance. These rankings would be used to determine which, if any, of the suppliers' ranking was most associated with the agency's own ranking of the 10 ads.

Table 16–3 (see page 470) contains the rankings for the agency and the two suppliers. To determine the correlation between the advertising agency's rank ordering and those of each testing service, the difference in rank orderings (d_i) and the squared differences (d_i^2)

---

[3]Robert L. Winkler and William L. Hays, *Statistical Probability: Inference and Decision*, 2nd ed. (New York: Holt, Rinehart and Winston, 1975), pp. 867–70.

must first be calculated. (The d_i's are shown in Table 16–3.) Applying Equation 16–3, the correlation between the rank orderings of the advertising agency and supplier 1 is

$$r_s = 1 - (6)(14)/10(10^2 - 1) = 0.915$$

and the correlation between the advertising agency and supplier 2 is

$$r_s = 1 - (6)(62)/10(10^2 - 1) = 0.624$$

We can also perform a test of whether the rank-order correlation coefficient is statistically different from zero. The hypothesis and test statistic are described below:

$$HO: \rho_s = 0$$
$$HA: \rho_s \neq 0$$
$$TS_c: t_c = \frac{r_s \sqrt{n - 2}}{\sqrt{1 - r_s^2}}$$
$$TS_t: t_{t(1 - \alpha/2; \, df \, = \, n \, - \, 2)}$$
$$DR: \text{Reject } HO: \text{ if } TS_c > TS_t \text{ or } -TS_c < -TS_t$$

From previous results, the test statistics can be computed as follows:

$$t_c = 0.92\sqrt{8}/\sqrt{1 - 0.915^2} = 6.45 \text{ (supplier 1)}$$
$$t_c = 0.62\sqrt{8}/\sqrt{1 - 0.624^2} = 2.24 \text{ (supplier 2)}$$

Hence, for $t_{t(0.05; \, 8)} = 2.306$ (see Table 3, in the Statistical Appendix) we reject the null hypothesis of no association between the advertising agency's rankings and those of supplier 1, in the population, but cannot reject the null hypothesis of no association between the rankings of the advertising agency and those of supplier 2 in the population. Consequently, the advertising agency would select supplier 1 to perform their copy testing because the correlation between this supplier's rankings of ads and the advertising agency's own ranking was statistically significant and larger in magnitude than that associated with supplier 2.

TABLE 16–3

Ranking of Ads

Advertisement	Agency Ranking	Supplier 1 Ranking	d_i	Supplier 2 Ranking	d_i
A	1	2	−1	3	−2
B	8	9	−1	5	3
C	5	6	−1	6	−1
D	2	1	1	1	1
E	4	3	1	8	−4
F	7	7	0	9	−2
G	10	10	0	7	3
H	9	8	1	10	−1
I	3	5	−2	4	−1
J	6	4	2	2	4

Nominal Scales

When data adhere to a nominal scale the method of analysis typically consists of determining the number or proportion of observations for each level of the variable. When we have two variables that adhere to a nominal scale and we want to determine the degree of association between them, we first cross classify the variables to form a contingency table of dimensions $I \times J$, where I is the number of levels of one variable (typically, the variable constituting the rows) and J is the number of levels of the other variable (typically, the variable constituting the columns).

The most widely used measures of association for nominal data are those based on the **chi-square statistic**.

Measures Based on the Chi-Square Statistic. Table 16–4 presents the frequency distributions for ownership of automatic teller machine (ATM) cards and age collected in a regional banking study. Inspection of the frequency distributions tells us that 61 percent of the sample own an ATM card and that 45 percent of the sample is aged 55 +. Hence, intuitively, we might conclude that mostly older people own ATM cards. However, from the cross classification we can see that only 40 percent (18/45) of the older people own an ATM card. Because 61 percent of the sample own an ATM card and 45 percent of the sample are aged 55 +, it is reasonable to expect that 27.5 percent (0.61 × 0.45) of those age 55 + own an ATM card.

This intuition is actually well grounded in probability theory. Probability theory tells us that the joint probability is equal to the product of the marginal

chi-square statistic
A measure for the difference between what we observe from the sample and what we should have observed in the sample if the two variables were not associated.

Automatic Teller Machines (ATMs)			Age		
Code	Number	Percent	Code	Number	Percent
No	39	39.0	18–34	22	22.0
Yes	61	61.0	35–54	33	33.0
			55 +	45	45.0

		Age			
		18–34	35–54	55 +	Total
	No	2	10	27	39
		(5.1)	(25.6)	(69.2)	39.0
ATM		(9.1)	(30.3)	(60.0)	
		(2.0)	(10.0)	(27.0)	
	Yes	20	23	18	61
		(32.8)	(37.7)	(29.5)	61.0
		(90.9)	(69.7)	(40.0)	
		(20.0)	(23.0)	(18.0)	
	Total	22	33	45	100
		22.0	33.0	45.0	

TABLE 16–4

Frequency Distributions and Cross Tabulation of ATM and Age

probabilities when the variables are independent. Therefore, if age and ATM card ownership are independent, we would expect 27.5 percent, or 27.5 of the sample of 100, both to be age 55+ and to own ATM cards. The differences, or discrepancies, between what we would expect the cell counts to be, given that the variables are independent, and the cell counts we observe from the cross classification of the sample are used to calculate the chi-square statistic. The chi-square statistic is defined as

$$\chi^2 = \sum_{k=1}^{K} (O_k - E_k)^2 / E_k \qquad (16\text{--}4)$$

where

O_k = Observed count in the kth cell of the table

E_k = Expected count in the kth cell of the table

K = Number of cells in the table

Note that if the expected counts are equal to the observed counts, the chi-square statistic will be zero. As the expected counts differ from the observed counts, the chi-square statistic increases in magnitude. The actual value of the chi-square statistic is used to first test the hypothesis that the variables are independent; upon rejecting this hypothesis, the value of the chi-square statistic is used to determine the level of association between the two variables. Before demonstrating the use of the chi-square statistic for assessing the correlation between two cross-classified variables, we need to introduce notation that is commonly used for representing cross-classification, or contingency, tables.

Consider the case in which we have two nominal variables: gender (female, male) and coffee preference (drip, instant). The cross classification of these two variables produces a 2×2 contingency table that has four cells, shown in Table 16–5. Here the n_{ij} represent the observed counts. For example, letting $i = j = 1$ we have cell n_{11}, which is the number of observations in the sample that are female and prefer drip coffee, whereas letting $i = 1$ and $j = 2$ we have n_{12}, which is the number of observations in the sample that are female and prefer instant coffee. The same interpretations hold for n_{21} and n_{22}. Note that the totals for rows and columns use a "+" as a subscript. When the "+" is used for the j subscript (n_{i+}), it means that we are summing over j or the columns for the ith row. Hence, if we let $i = 1$ for n_{i+} we get n_{1+} or the total for the first row. Therefore, n_{i+} represents the totals for the rows and n_{+j} represents the totals for the columns. The total sample size (n) is expressed as n_{++}.

Dividing the observed counts (n_{ij}) by the total sample size (n_{++}) provides a corresponding probability table.[4] This table is shown in Table 16–5, part *b*. The numbers in the cells of the table are called joint probabilities. Hence p_{22} is the joint probability of a sample element being male and preferring instant coffee. The numbers representing row or column totals are called marginal probabilities.

---

[4]Stephen E. Fineberg, *The Analysis of Cross-Classified Categorical Data* (Boston: MIT Press, 1977), p. 11.

a.

Gender	Preference		
	Drip	Instant	
Female	n_{11}	n_{12}	n_{1+}
Male	n_{21}	n_{22}	n_{2+}
	n_{+1}	n_{+2}	n_{++}

b.

Gender	Preference		
	Drip	Instant	
Female	p_{11}	p_{12}	p_{1+}
Male	p_{21}	p_{22}	p_{2+}
	p_{+1}	p_{+2}	1

TABLE 16–5

2 × 2 Contingency Table for Coffee Preference

Consequently, p_{+1} is the probability of preferring drip coffee. Probability theory tells us that when two variables are independent, their joint probability is equal to the product of their marginal probabilities. Hence, the expected joint probabilities for the four cells, given the null hypothesis of no association, are calculated as

$$\text{Cell } (1,1) = p_{1+} \times p_{+1}$$
$$\text{Cell } (1,2) = p_{1+} \times p_{+2}$$
$$\text{Cell } (2,1) = p_{2+} \times p_{+1}$$
$$\text{Cell } (2,2) = p_{2+} \times p_{+2}$$

The expected values for each cell can be calculated by substituting the row or column totals for the row or column probabilities and by dividing by the sample size (n_{++}). For example, the expected count for Cell (1,1) would be:

$$\text{Expected count Cell } (1,1) = (n_{1+}n_{+1})/n_{++}$$

The chi-square statistic provides us with a measure for the difference between what we observe from the sample (O_k) and what we should have observed in the sample (E_k) if the two variables were not associated, that is, assuming the null hypothesis is true, in other words, that the two variables are not associated.

So far we have considered only the case of a 2 × 2 table. Frequently, either the rows, columns, or both have more than two levels. The calculations for the expected counts are the same for any size $(I \times J)$ contingency table. The expected count for any cell is equal to the product of the corresponding row and column marginals divided by the total sample size. For example, if we had a 4 × 5 contingency table and wanted to calculate the expected count for Cell (2,3) given the null hypothesis of independence, we would divide the product of the marginal totals for the second row and third column by the total sample size:

$$(n_{2+}n_{+3})/n_{++}$$

Once we have calculated the chi-square statistic (χ^2) we can use this value to calculate the correlation between the two variables. A variety of correlation coefficients have been proposed to measure the degree of association between two nominal variables based on the value of χ^2. However, some of the coefficients are only applicable for 2 × 2 tables, and some of the coefficients have an upper limit of less than one. Here we provide **Cramer's contingency coefficient (V)**, which is appropriate for any size contingency table and in the case of perfect correlation $V = 1$, whereas $V = 0$ if the variables are independent.

Cramer's contingency coefficient (V)
Measure of the degree of association between nominal variables, which is appropriate for any size contingency table.

Cramer's contingency coefficient (V) is calculated as:[5]

$$V = \sqrt{\frac{\chi^2/n}{q-1}} \qquad (16\text{--}5)$$

where

χ^2 = Chi-square statistic
n = Sample size
q = Smaller of I or J

In addition we can use the chi-square statistic to statistically test the null hypothesis of no association. Following the standard procedure, letting ρ_n be the correlation between two nominally scaled variables, the hypothesis test is

$HO: \rho_n = 0$
$HA: \rho_n \neq 0$
$TS_c: \chi_c^2 = \sum_{k=1}^{K} (O_k - E_k)^2/E_k$
$TS_t: \chi_{t(1-\alpha;\ df = (I-1)(J-1))}^2$
$DR:$ Reject $HO:$ if $TS_c > TS_t$

You will note that the degrees of freedom associated with the test statistic are

$$df = (I - 1)(J - 1) \qquad (16\text{--}6)$$

EXAMPLE

Table 16–6a provides the observed counts for the cross classification of age and ATM card ownership. The expected counts for the null hypothesis of no association also are provided in part b of the table.

The chi-square statistic (Equation 16–4) based on the discrepancy between the observed and expected counts is

$$\chi^2 = (2 - 8.58)^2/8.58 + (10 - 12.87)^2/12.87 +$$
$$(27 - 17.55)^2/17.55 + (20 - 13.42)^2/13.42 +$$
$$(23 - 20.13)^2/20.13 + (18 - 27.45)^2/27.45$$
$$= 17.66$$

We first use the value of χ^2 to test the null hypothesis of no association. With $I = 2$, and $J = 3$, we have $(2 - 1)(3 - 1)$ or 2 degrees of freedom. The tabulated test statistic $\chi_{t(1-\alpha;\ df)}^2$ for $\alpha = 0.05$ and 2 degrees of freedom is, from Table 4 of the Statistical Appendix, 5.99. Since the $TS_c > TS_t$, we reject the null hypothesis of no association.

The next step is to determine the level of association between the two variables. The level of association, using Cramer's V is,

$$V = \sqrt{[(17.66/100)/(2 - 1)]}$$
$$= 0.42$$

---

[5]Albert M. Liebetrau, *Measures of Association* (Beverly Hills, Calif.: Sage Publications, 1983), p. 14.

a. Observed counts (O_k)					b. Expected counts (E_k)					TABLE 16–6
	Age					Age				
Own ATM card	18–34	35–54	55 +		Own ATM card	18–34	35–54	55 +		Cross Classification
No	2	10	27	39	No	8.58	12.87	17.55	39	of Age and ATM
Yes	20	23	18	61	Yes	13.42	20.13	27.45	61	Card Ownership
	22	33	45	100		22	33	45	100	

$E_{11} = (n_{+1} \times n_{1+})/n_{++} = (22 \times 39)/100 = 8.58$
$E_{12} = (n_{+2} \times n_{1+})/n_{++} = (33 \times 39)/100 = 12.87$
$E_{13} = (n_{+3} \times n_{1+})/n_{++} = (45 \times 39)/100 = 17.55$
$E_{21} = (n_{+1} \times n_{2+})/n_{++} = (22 \times 61)/100 = 13.42$
$E_{22} = (n_{+2} \times n_{2+})/n_{++} = (33 \times 61)/100 = 20.13$
$E_{23} = (n_{+3} \times n_{2+})/n_{++} = (45 \times 61)/100 = 27.45$

Mixed Scales

It is not uncommon for the marketing research analyst to be faced with the task of determining the correlation between two variables that have different scale properties. We consider two specific situations.

Dichotomous and Interval-Scale Variables. A frequently encountered data analysis situation occurs when one variable has interval-scale properties and the other variable is dichotomous.[6] In such cases the dichotomous variable is coded such that its levels assume the values zero or one; for example, in the case of gender, males = 1 and females = 0. (Note that it makes no difference if the assigned codes are males = 0 and females = 1.) The correlation coefficient used to measure the association between a dichotomous variable and an interval-scaled variable is called the **point-biserial correlation coefficient,** which we will denote as simply r_{PB}. There are specific formulas for the calculation of the point-biserial correlation coefficient; however, the same estimate of r_{PB} can be obtained with the more familiar product moment correlation coefficient.

point-biserial correlation coefficient *Coefficient that measures the association between a dichotomous variable and an interval-scaled variable.*

EXAMPLE

A regional telephone company wanted to estimate the average family expenditure on long-distance calls. The research supplier thought that a stratified sampling design should be used; however the researchers were uncertain what specific factor to stratify the population on. Management suggested two variables: home ownership (own versus rent) and whether or not the family had lived out of state for at least six months during the past five years (yes or no). In Chapters 8 and 9 we mentioned that efficiencies gained through stratified sampling are a function of the correlation between the response variable (the variable

---

[6]When the dichotomous variable is actually a continuous variable that has been dichotomized, the appropriate correlation coefficient is the biserial correlation coefficient. See Warren S. Martin, "Effects of Scaling on the Correlation Coefficient: Additional Considerations," *Journal of Marketing Research*, May 1978, pp. 304–8, for a presentation of the results of a mathematical simulation comparing the use of Pearson's product moment correlation where the biserial-correlation coefficient is the appropriate measure.

whose mean value we wish to estimate) and the stratifying variable (the classification variable). To assess the correlation between these two potential stratifying variables and monthly expenditure on long-distance calls, the research supplier conducted a pilot survey of 15 local families. The data from the pilot sample are presented in Table 16–7.

The two stratification variables are dichotomous; therefore, the point-biserial correlation coefficient (r_{PB}) is the appropriate measure of association. There is a fairly strong association between living out of state for at least six months during the past five years and long-distance expenditures ($r_{PB} = 0.66$); however, there is less association between home ownership and long-distance expenditure ($r_{PB} = 0.04$). Thus, management would probably stratify based on whether a family lived out of state for at least six months during the past five years.

The algebraic sign of the point-biserial correlation coefficient is arbitrary because the researcher determines which level of dichotomous variable is coded 0 and which level is coded 1. If you switch the 0 and 1 codes for the respective categories of the dichotomous variable, the algebraic sign attached to r_{PB} coefficient will change, but its magnitude will not.

To statistically test the significance of a point-biserial correlation coefficient we use the same procedure as for the Pearson product moment correlation coefficient; hence, the test statistic is

$$t_c = \frac{r_{PB} \sqrt{n - 2}}{\sqrt{1 - r_{PB}^2}} \tag{16–7}$$

with $n - 2$ degrees of freedom.

TABLE 16–7
——
Pilot Survey Data

Element	Long-Distance Phone Bill	Home Ownership	Move
1	2.50	Own (0)	No (1)
2	25.75	Own (0)	Yes (0)
3	38.50	Rent (1)	Yes (0)
4	5.00	Rent (1)	No (1)
5	15.50	Own (0)	Yes (0)
6	9.20	Own (0)	No (1)
7	4.00	Own (0)	No (1)
8	45.00	Own (0)	Yes (0)
9	10.90	Rent (1)	No (1)
10	5.40	Rent (1)	No (1)
11	12.75	Rent (1)	No (1)
12	18.65	Own (0)	Yes (0)
13	23.40	Rent (1)	No (1)
14	18.50	Own (0)	No (1)
15	14.50	Own (0)	Yes (0)

Applying Equation 16–7 for each of the two stratification variables introduced in the previous example yields the following results

$$t_c = \frac{0.04\sqrt{13}}{\sqrt{1 - 0.04^2}} = 0.14 \text{ (home ownership)}$$

and

$$t_c = \frac{0.66\sqrt{13}}{\sqrt{1 - 0.66^2}} = 3.17 \text{ (out of state)}$$

The region of rejection with $\alpha = 0.05$ and $df = n - 2 = 13$ is, from Table 3 in the Statistical Appendix, 2.160. Therefore, only the correlation between long-distance expenditure and living out of state for at least six months during the past five years is statistically significant.

In Chapter 15 we used a t-test statistic of the form

$$t_c = \frac{\bar{x}_1 - \bar{x}_2}{\sqrt{s_p^2 \left(1/n_1 + 1/n_2\right)}}$$

in order to test for the statistical difference between two samples on some interval-scaled variable. The preceding examples of point-biserial correlation may appear similar to this test; in other words, we might simply ask if there is a statistically significant difference in average monthly long-distance expenditures between those families that have lived out of state for at least six months during the past five years and those families that have not. Although the t-test statistic can be used to evaluate this hypothesis, the test statistic does not provide information on the level of association between these variables. We can, however, convert the t-value calculated from the t-test statistic to a point-biserial correlation coefficient.[7] The appropriate conversion formula is

$$r_{PB} = \sqrt{\frac{t_c^2}{t_c^2 + df}} \tag{16–8}$$

Designate families that have lived out of state as group 1 members and all other families as group 2 members. Thus from Table 16–7 we have

$n_1 = 6$	$n_2 = 9$
$\bar{x}_1 = 26.32$	$\bar{x}_2 = 10.18$
$s_{x1} = 12.75$	$s_{x2} = 7.06$

[7] J. Welkowitz, R. B. Bower, and J. Cohen, *Introductory Statistics for the Social Sciences* (New York: Academic Press, 1976), p. 187.

Using the pooled variance Equation 15–13 and the *t*-test statistic, we find that

$$t = \frac{26.32 - 10.18}{\sqrt{93.20(1/6 + 1/9)}} = 3.17$$

The point-biserial correlation coefficient is, from Equation 16–8,

$$r_{PB} = \sqrt{\frac{3.17^2}{3.17^2 + 13}} = 0.66$$

which agrees with the previous result.

Categorical and Interval-Scale Variables.   In many situations, the marketing research analyst may be interested in the relationship between a categorical variable that has more than two levels and an interval-scaled variable. In this case, there is no specific formula for calculating the correlation between such variables. One approach is to transform the interval-scaled variable into a smaller number of categories, cross classify the transformed variable with the categorical variable, and then use a measure of correlation appropriate for contingency tables (such as Cramer's V). The number of categories formed for the continuous variable usually depends on sample-size considerations. Of course, with large sample sizes the continuous variable can be broken down into a large number of categories or classes. However, if we designate a large number of classes for the continuous variable, the

TABLE 16–8

Cross Classification
of Ice Cream
Consumption by
User Category

a. Observed counts

Users	Consumption			
	Light (1)	Average (2)	Heavy (3)	
Aware/not used (1)	150	125	25	300
Unaware (2)	40	20	5	65
Users (3)	10	5	20	35
	200	150	50	400

b. Expected counts

Users	Consumption		
	Light	Average	Heavy
Aware/not used	150.00[a]	112.50[b]	37.50[c]
Unaware	32.50[d]	24.38[e]	8.13[f]
Users	17.50[g]	13.13[h]	4.38[i]

[a] E_{11} = (300 × 200)/400 = 150
[b] E_{12} = (300 × 150)/400 = 112.5
[c] E_{13} = (300 × 50)/400 = 37.5
[d] E_{21} = (65 × 200)/400 = 32.5
[e] E_{22} = (65 × 150)/400 = 24.38
[f] E_{23} = (65 × 50)/400 = 8.13
[g] E_{31} = (35 × 200)/400 = 17.5
[h] E_{32} = (35 × 150)/400 = 13.13
[i] E_{33} = (35 × 50)/400 = 4.38

resulting contingency table may be very sparse; that is, each cell of the table will have only a small number of observations, and many cells may even have no observed counts. It is difficult to handle contingency tables in which many of the cells have few or no observations. A generally accepted practice is to have five responses per cell. This suggestion (five observations per cell) is, however, only a guideline; it is not a hard-and-fast rule.

A manufacturer of a super-premium brand of ice cream was interested in the association between total monthly consumption of ice cream and three categories of super-premium brand users: (1) aware of brand and not used in last 30 days, (2) unaware of brand, and (3) users. A mall-intercept interview method was used to collect the data from a sample of 400 consumers who reported having consumed ice cream in the last 30 days. Monthly consumption of ice cream, for analysis purposes, was categorized into three levels: (1) light, (2) average, and (3) heavy. Table 16–8, part *a*, presents the cross classification of the two variables. The expected counts given the null hypothesis of no association are provided in part *b* of the table.

EXAMPLE

To calculate Cramer's V (Equation 16–5) we first must calculate the chi-square statistic. The value of the chi-square from Equation 16–4 is

$$\chi^2 = (150 - 150)^2/150 + (125 - 112.5)^2/112.5 + (25 - 37.5)^2/37.5$$
$$+ (40 - 32.5)^2/32.5 + (20 - 24.38)^2/24.38 + (5 - 8.13)^2/8.13$$
$$+ (10 - 17.5)^2/17.5 + (5 - 13.13)^2/13.13 + (20 - 4.38)^2/4.38$$
$$= 73.23$$

From Table 4 in the Statistical Appendix the tabled value of the critical chi-square at $\alpha = 0.05$ with $(3 - 1)(3 - 1) = 4$ degrees of freedom is 9.49. Hence we reject the null hypothesis of no association and calculate the level of association using Cramer's V as

$$V = \sqrt{\frac{73.23/400}{3 - 1}}$$
$$= 0.30$$

Collapsing Variable Categories

When a continuous variable is artificially categorized or a categorical variable is collapsed to a smaller number of categories, the basic structure of the data has been changed and, consequently, the original association can be affected. However, there are no rules that allow us to know exactly the nature of the effect. The analyst must be aware that collapsing variables may mask or create structural relationships that did not originally exist. The following example illustrates this point.

If we dichotomize the two variables in Table 16–8 by collapsing the third level into the second level, the resulting contingency table is shown in Table 16–9 (see page 480). The calculated chi-square statistic for these data is zero, as opposed to 73.23. Hence, in contrast to our previous conclusion, we now conclude that the variables are independent.

EXAMPLE

	Consumption		
Users	1	2	
1	150	150	300
2	50	50	100
	200	200	400

TABLE 16–9
—
Cross Classification
of Collapsed
Variables

REGRESSION ANALYSIS

regression analysis
Procedure that deter-mines how much of the variation in the depen-dent variable can be ex-plained by the independent variable.

Correlation analysis investigates the extent to which two variables are associ-ated. When correlating two variables, the variables are treated symmetrically—there is no attempt to specify the relationship between the variables. In contrast, in **regression analysis** one of the variables is designated as the *dependent variable*, while the other variable is designated as the *explanatory variable*, and the aim is to predict the mean or average value of the dependent variable on the basis of the known values of the explanatory variable. Regression analysis attempts to answer two important questions:

1. What is the change in the dependent variable for a unit change in an ex-planatory variable?
2. Given a specific value of an explanatory variable, what is the most likely value of the dependent variable?

As an illustration consider Exhibit 16–3, which presents a scatter diagram for two variables: the number of people entering the showroom, hereafter referred to as *ups*, and the dollar amount of advertising expenditures for an automobile deal-ership. The Pearson product moment correlation between the two variables is 0.857, indicating that these two variables show a systematic relationship. Although this information is useful, a manager might also want to know

1. For each $100 in advertising expenditure, how many more people will visit the dealership?
2. If advertising expenditures were, say, $5,500 next year, how many people will visit the dealership?

These questions are important to the manager because they quantify the magni-tude of the relationship between advertising expenditures and the number of peo-ple visiting the dealership. If there is a large responsiveness to a dollar spent on advertising, then the manager may feel more comfortable in recommending that advertising budgets be increased.

simple regression model
Model that considers the case of a single indepen-dent variable.

The terms *simple regression analysis* and *multiple regression analysis* are used to describe the kind of regression model being fit. When only a single explanatory variable is being considered, we refer to this procedure as **simple regression analysis.** When two or more explanatory variables are being considered, we call

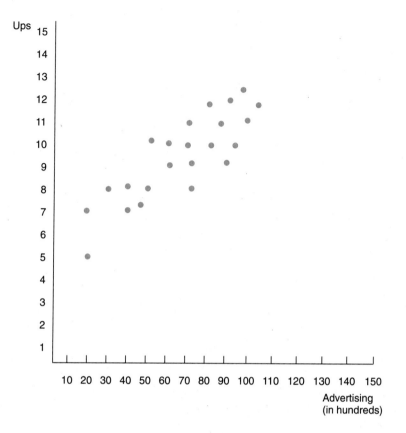

EXHIBIT 16–3
—
Scatter Diagram for
Number of Ups and
Advertising Level

this procedure **multiple regression analysis.** In this section, we introduce the simple regression model. In the section that immediately follows, we discuss multiple regression analysis.

multiple regression model
Model that considers the general case of more than one independent variable.

THE SIMPLE TWO-VARIABLE REGRESSION MODEL

Simple regression analysis considers the relationship between a dependent variable and a single explanatory variable. Following convention, the dependent variable will be denoted as y and the explanatory variable as x. The purpose of regression analysis is to develop an equation that can be used to predict the value of y on the basis of the known value of x. Looking at the scatter diagram shown in Exhibit 16–3, the problem can be solved by fitting a straight line through the data points. In general, the equation for a straight line is

$$y = a + bx$$

In the context of the regression model, the estimated **regression line** is written as

$$\hat{y}_i = \beta_0 + \beta_1 x_i \qquad (16–9)$$

regression line
A line fitted to the data that in some sense best captures the functional relationship.

where the subscript i denotes the observation number, $\hat{y}_i$ is the estimated value of y, β_0 is the intercept (that is, the value of y when $x = 0$), and β_1 is the slope coefficient that gives the rate of change in y for a unit change in x.

There are, however, many different straight lines that can be fit to the data shown in Exhibit 16–3 by varying the values of β_0 and β_1. For any specific values of β_0 and β_1, we have an estimated value $\hat{y}_i$. The difference between the actual and estimated y-values is called the *residual*, which we will denote as e_i:

$$e_i = y_i - \hat{y}_i \tag{16–10}$$
$$= y_i - \beta_0 - \beta_1 x_i \tag{16–11}$$

Among other things, the residuals reflect the fact that rarely will all of the variation in y be explained by x—there are other factors, perhaps unknown to the researcher, that possibly influence the dependent variable.

It is reasonable to want the differences between the actual and estimated y-values to be small. In the extreme case, if all of the residuals are zero, then each estimated value of y is exactly equal to its corresponding actual value. To this end, the regression model adopts the following criterion: Choose values for β_0 and β_1 in such a way that the sum of the squared residuals

$$\sum e_i^2 = \sum (y_i - \hat{y}_i)^2$$

is as small as possible. This criterion is known as the *least-squares criterion*.

Estimation of the Regression Coefficients

The simple two-variable regression model is

$$y_i = \beta_0 + \beta_1 x_i + e_i \tag{16–12}$$

where β_0 and β_1 are determined such that $\sum e_i^2$ is minimized. Having found sample-based estimates for the regression coefficients, we can write the estimated regression function as

$$y_i = \hat{\beta}_0 + \hat{\beta}_1 x_i + e_i \tag{16–13}$$
$$= \hat{y}_i + e_i \tag{16–14}$$

where the "hat" indicates an estimate.

We still are faced with the problem of which $\hat{\beta}$ values to choose. Applying the least-squares criterion, the following estimates are obtained:

$$\hat{\beta}_1 = \frac{\displaystyle\sum_{i=1}^{n} (x_i - \bar{x})(y_i - \bar{y})}{\displaystyle\sum_{i=1}^{n} (x_i - \bar{x})^2} \tag{16–15}$$

$$\hat{\beta}_0 = \bar{y} - \hat{\beta}_1 \bar{x} \tag{16–16}$$

The $\hat{\beta}$ estimates obtained produce a regression line such that the sum of squared residuals is minimized. There are no other estimates that provide "better" estimates of y or, alternatively, smaller residuals. These questions have a long history and are derived from what are referred to as the **normal equations.** The estimates are commonly referred to as the **ordinary least-squares (OLS)** estimates of β_0 and β_1.

*normal equations/
ordinary least-squares
Formulas that produce a
regression line such that
Σe_i^2 is minimized.*

Table 16–10 presents manual computations for estimating β_0 and β_1 for the data shown in Exhibit 16–3. Applying the estimation formula we find

EXAMPLE

$$\hat{\beta}_1 = \frac{74.3}{107.7}$$
$$= 0.689$$
$$\hat{\beta}_0 = \frac{129 - 0.689(83.0)}{15}$$
$$= 4.79$$

The estimated regression line therefore is

$$\hat{y}_i = 4.79 + 0.689x_i$$

From the estimated regression line we find that every \$100 in advertising generates about 0.689 visits, so that every \$200 spent on advertising would result in approximately one additional person visiting the dealership. We can also use the estimated regression line to ascertain the number of people expected to visit the dealership for any level of advertising. For instance, if the advertising expenditure is set at \$500, the estimated number of people visiting the dealership is $4.79 + 0.689(5)$, or roughly eight people.

TABLE 16–10   Manual Computations for Estimating β_0 and β_1

Advertising Expenditure (\$hundreds) x_i	$(x_i - \bar{x})$	$(x_i - \bar{x})^2$	$[(x_i - \bar{x})(y_i - \bar{y})]$	$(y_i - \bar{y})^2$	$(y_i - \bar{y})$	Ups y_i
1.00	−4.53	20.52	20.84	21.16	−4.60	4.00
2.00	−3.53	12.46	5.65	2.56	−1.60	7.00
2.00	−3.53	12.46	12.71	12.96	−3.60	5.00
10.00	4.47	19.98	10.73	5.76	2.40	11.00
9.00	3.47	12.04	1.39	0.16	0.40	9.00
6.00	0.47	0.22	0.66	1.96	1.40	10.00
7.00	1.47	2.16	3.53	5.76	2.40	11.00
6.00	0.47	0.22	0.19	0.16	0.40	9.00
6.00	0.47	0.22	−0.28	0.36	−0.60	8.00
4.00	−1.53	2.34	2.45	2.56	−1.60	7.00
3.00	−2.53	6.40	1.52	0.36	−0.60	8.00
5.00	−0.53	0.28	0.32	0.36	−0.60	8.00
5.00	0.53	0.28	−0.74	1.96	1.40	10.00
8.00	2.47	6.10	3.46	1.06	1.40	10.00
9.00	3.47	12.04	11.80	11.56	3.40	12.00
		107.72	74.30	69.60		

Evaluating the Regression

It seems reasonable to want to find out how well the estimated regression line fits the data. As we indicated earlier, it is presumptuous to think that all of the actual y-values will lie on the estimated regression line—rarely will a perfect fit be obtained. More likely there will be some positive e_i-values and some negative e_i-values. What we hope for is that these residuals around the estimated regression line are as small as possible.

How well the estimated regression line fits the data is determined by how much variation in y is explained by x. The total variation of the actual y-values about their sample mean, which may be called the total *sum of squares (TSS)*, is

$$TSS = \sum_{i=1}^{n} (y_i - \bar{y})^2$$

The total sum of squares can be partitioned into two components. The first represents the variation of the estimated y-values about their mean, which may be called the *sum of squares due to regression* [i.e., due to the explanatory variable(s)], or *explained by the regression*, or simply the *explained sum of squares* (ESS), and is given by

$$ESS = \sum_{i=1}^{n} (\hat{y}_i - \bar{y})^2$$

$$= \hat{\beta}_1^2 (x_i - \bar{x})^2$$

The second component of variation represents the residual or *unexplained* variation of the y-values about the regression line, or simply the *residual sum of squares* (RSS), and is given by

$$RSS = \sum_{i=1}^{n} e_i^2 = \sum_{i=1}^{n} (y_i - \hat{y}_i)^2$$

Thus,

$$TSS = ESS + RSS$$

These various sums of squares are graphed in Exhibit 16–4.

The ratio of explained to total variation is called the **coefficient of determination (R^2).**

coefficient of determination (R^2)
The ratio of explained to total variation.

$$R^2 = \frac{\text{Explained variation}}{\text{Total variation}} \tag{16–17}$$

$$= \frac{\sum_{i=1}^{n} (\hat{y}_i - \bar{y})^2}{\sum_{i=1}^{n} (y_i - \bar{y})^2} \tag{16–18}$$

$$= \frac{\hat{\beta}_1^2 \sum_{i=1}^{n} (x_i - \bar{x})^2}{\sum_{i=1}^{n} (y_i - \bar{y})^2} \tag{16–19}$$

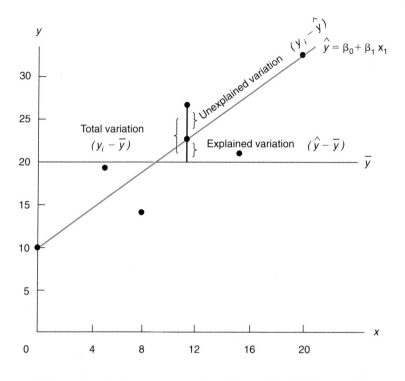

EXHIBIT 16–4

TSS, ESS, and *RSS*

The coefficient of determination is a measure of goodness of fit. It does not, however, indicate the percentage of correct predictions or the likelihood of correctly predicting the value of y given a specific value of x. The coefficient of determination simply tells us how much of the variation in the dependent variable is explained by the independent variable. The range of R^2 is 0 to 1. The closer R^2 is to 1, the stronger the linear relationship between the two variables.

We can use the manual computations appearing in Table 16–10 to calculate R^2 for the data on advertising expenditures and ups. From these summary computations we have

$$R^2 = \frac{(0.689)^2(107.70)}{69.60} = 0.735$$

Thus advertising expenditures explain 73.5 percent of the variation of people visiting the dealership.

EXAMPLE

Simple two-variable regression can be performed with the use of statistical software packages. Table 16–11 (see page 486) presents sample output from SPSSX. The sample output from regression analysis software packages provides a number of statistical tests and summary diagnostics. Notice first that the output presents the explained sum of squares (*ESS*) and the residual sum of squares (*RSS*). SPSSX labels these two sums of squares components *regression* and *residual*, respectively. Associated with any sum of squares are its degrees of freedom. For simple regres-

```
                          **** MULTIPLE REGRESSION ****
Listwise Deletion of Missing Data
Equation Number 1      Dependent Variable..      UP
Block Number  1.    Method: Enter      AD
Variable(s)  Entered on Step Number
1..    AD
Multiple R               .85689
R Square                 .73426
Adjusted R Square        .71382
Standard Error          1.19279
Analysis of Variance
                    DF        Sum of Squares      Mean Square
Regression           1         51.10433           51.10433
Residual            13         18.49567            1.42274
F = 35.91956         Signif F = .0000
                **** VARIABLES IN THE EQUATION ****
Variable        B         SE B        Beta         T        Sig T
              .688738    .114918     .856888      5.993     .0000
AD
(Constant)   4.788985    .706536                  6.778     .0000
```

sion, ESS has 1 *df*, RRS has $n - 2$ *df*, and TSS has $n - 1$ *df*. The various sums of squares are displayed in what is referred to as the *analysis of variance table*. Recall we discussed ANOVA in Chapter 15. The *mean square* column is obtained by taking each sum of squares component and dividing by its *df*.

Testing the significance of a regression model amounts to testing whether there is a stastistically significant relationship between y and x. If the explanatory variable x has no linear influence on the dependent variable y, then $\beta_1 = 0$. Thus, the appropriate null hypothesis for testing the significance of a regression model is

$$HO: \beta_1 = 0$$

The alternative hypothesis is generally stated as two-sided:

$$HA: \beta_1 \neq 0$$

although a one-sided test is appropriate when information on the expected algebraic sign of β_1 is available.

This test can be performed in one of two alternative but complementary ways. One approach is to form the *F*-ratio defined by

$$F = \frac{ESS/df}{RSS/df} \qquad (16\text{–}20)$$
$$= \frac{ESS/1}{RSS/(n-2)}$$

The alternative approach is to perform a *t*-test on the β_1 coefficient itself. The null hypothesis and alternative hypothesis are the same as before. The appropriate test statistic is

$$t = \frac{\hat{\beta}_1}{\hat{\sigma}_{\beta_1}} \qquad (16\text{–}21)$$

where $\hat{\sigma}_{\beta_1}$ is the estimated standard of β_1. Assuming that the disturbances, e_i, are normally distributed and HO: $\beta_1 = 0$, the t-statistic follows the student's t-distribution with $n - 2$ df. As shown in Table 16–11, computer programs for regression analysis provide standard errors, the values of t and F, and also the corresponding p-levels for the null hypothesis.

From the summary information provided in Table 16–11, we see that there is a statistically significant relationship between advertising expenditures and the number of people visiting the dealership. The F-value of 35.92 is significant at the $p < 0.0001$ level. The p-level is given by Signif F = .0000. The explanatory variable, denoted by AD in the output, is also statistically significant. The t-value is 5.993, which is significant at the $p < 0.0001$ level.

EXAMPLE

For the two-variable regression model there is really no need to perform both of these tests. When multiple regression is considered, however, these tests provide different information. Because computer programs for regression analysis do not distinguish between two and more than two explanatory variables, both tests are always routinely provided.

MULTIPLE REGRESSION

Multiple regression predicts the value of the dependent variable on the basis of the known values of two or more explanatory variables. Assuming that p explanatory variables, $x_1, x_2, \ldots, x_p$, are used, the estimated regression function is written as

$$y_i = \hat{\beta}_0 + \hat{\beta}_1 x_{1i} + \hat{\beta}_2 x_{2i} + \ldots + \hat{\beta}_p x_{pi} + e_i \qquad (16\text{--}22)$$

where the "hat" again indicates an estimate.

Frequently the explanatory variables are measured in different units. One explanatory variable may, for example, be measured in dollars, while another is measured in hours. When the explanatory variables are measured in different units, it is usually difficult to compare regression coefficients because the magnitude of each β is affected by the scale used in measuring each x. Stated somewhat differently, the regression coefficients are not independent of the change of scale—measuring an explanatory variable in terms of cents rather than dollars will change the magnitude of the resulting β. To remove the effects of scale, the standardized regression coefficients, often called *beta coefficients*, are computed. The beta coefficient associated with the kth explanatory variable, denoted by $\hat{\beta}_k^{\circ}$, is

$$\hat{\beta}_k^{\circ} = \hat{\beta}_k(s_{x_k}/s_y) \qquad (16\text{--}23)$$

where s_{x_k} and s_y are the standard deviations of x_k and y in the sample. The beta coefficients can also be obtained by standardizing x and y prior to estimating the regression function. Beta coefficients are bounded by -1 to $+1$; hence the larger the magnitude (in an absolute sense) of a beta coefficient, the more important is that explanatory variable.

TABLE 16–12
———

Sample Output for
SPSSX Multiple
Regression Analysis

```
                              **** MULTIPLE REGRESSION ****
Listwise Deletion of Missing Data
Equation Number  1       Dependent Variable..    ATTP
Block Number  1.      Method: Enter     LK1     LK2
Variable(s) Entered on Step Number
1..    LK2
2..    LK1
Multiple R                 .59250
R Square                   .35106
Adjusted R Square          .34669
Standard Error            2.73917
Analysis of Variance
                         DF       Sum of Squares   Mean Squares
Regression                2        1205.51489      602.75744
Residual                297        2228.40511        7.50305
F =     80.33502       Signif F = .0000
Variables in the Equation
Variable       B              SE B          Beta        T         Sig T
LK2              .881134     .152062       .289143     5.795      .0000
LK1             1.383171     .162099       .425782     8.533      .0000
(Constant)      7.942291    1.007959                   7.880      .0000
End Block Number  1     All requested variables entered.
```

When more than one explanatory variable is used, computations become quite tedious. For this reason, computer software is almost always used when estimating the β values and measures of goodness of fit. To illustrate, Table 16–12 presents SPSSX output from a concept-test study. The study focused on a new cold-remedy concept. Three hundred respondents indicated the likelihood that they would purchase the new concept if it were available. Respondents also rated the new concept with respect to their perceptions of the ability of the new concept to relieve cold-related symptoms without producing any undesirable side effects. The purpose of the regression analysis is to investigate the extent to which the product attribute perceptual ratings on relief and gentleness can explain a respondent's likelihood of purchase.

EXAMPLE

In the table, the dependent variable, likelihood of purchase, is denoted as *ATTP*, and the two explanatory variables, relief and gentleness, are denoted by *LK1* and *LK2*, respectively. Note first that there is a statistically significant relationship between likelihood of purchase and ratings on relief and gentleness. The *F*-value of 80.34 is statistically significant at the $p < 0.0001$ level. In terms of explained variation, the two perceptual attribute ratings explain a little over 35 percent of the variation in likelihood of purchase. You may not think this amount of explained variation is very high, but remember the hypothesis test is one of *no* relationship between the dependent variable and the two attribute rating explanatory variables. Both explanatory variables are statistically significant at the $p < 0.0001$ level. The beta values shown in Table 16–12 indicate that *LK1* is more important than *LK2* in influencing purchase likelihood.

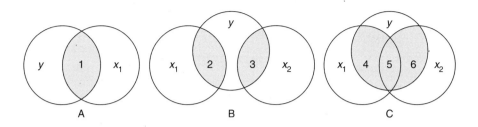

Effects of Multicollinearity

The term *multicollinearity* was apparently first coined by Ragnar Frisch.[8] Originally it was used to describe the existence of a "perfect," or exact, linear relationship among some or all explanatory variables of a regression model. If one or more exact linear relationships exist among a set of explanatory variables, then at least one of the explanatory variables can be written as a linear combination of the remaining explanatory variables. For example

$$x_i = ax_2 + bx_3 + \ldots + wx_p$$

where $a, b, \ldots, w$ are weights. Today, the term **multicollinearity** is more broadly used to include the case of perfect linear dependence as well as the case where the x variables are intercorrelated but not perfectly.

No multicollinearity is an assumption underlying the proper use of multiple regression analysis. No multicollinearity means none of the explanatory variables can be written as a linear combination of the remaining explanatory variables. What this means can be seen from the Venn diagram, or the *Ballentine*, shown in Exhibit 16–5.[9] (The name *Ballentine* is derived from the well-known Ballentine beer emblem with its circles.) In this figure, the circle y represents the variation in the dependent variable y and the circles x_1 and x_2 represent the variation in the explanatory variables x_1 and x_2, respectively. In panel *a*, there is a single explanatory variable, and area 1 represents the variation in y that is explained by x_1. With a single explanatory variable we do not need the assumption of no multicollinearity. In panel *b*, area 2 represents the variation in y that is explained by x_1, and area 3 represents the variation in y that is explained by x_2. In panel *c*, areas 4 and 5 show the variation in y explained by x_1, and areas 5 and 6 show the variation in y explained by x_2. Because area 5 is common to both x_1 and x_2, there is no way to assess which part of area 5 is due to x_1 and which part of area 5 is due to x_2. In other words, there is no way to apportion the common area to the explanatory variables. The common variation in area 5 represents the situation of multicollinearity. The assumption of no multicollinearity requires that x_1 and x_2 do not overlap.

The logic behind the assumption of no multicollinearity is intuitive. Suppose that y is the amount invested in the stock market and x_1 and x_2 are wealth and

multicollinearity
Correlation among independent variables. Multicollinearity causes problems in interpreting the individual regression coefficients because the values are affected by the amount of association between the independent variables themselves.

[8]Ragnar Frisch, *Statistical Confluence Analysis by Means of Complete Regression Systems* (Oslo University: Institute of Economics Publication no. 5, 1934).

[9]See Peter Kennedy, "Ballentine: A Graphical Aid for Econometrics," *Australian Economics Papers* 20 (1981), pp. 414–16.

TABLE 16–13

Regression of Sales
Volume (y) on
Shelf Space (x₁)
and Coupons
Distributed (x₂)

	Sales Volume y_i	Shelf Space x_{1i}	Coupons Distributed x_{2i}
1	50	13.0	12
2	57	13.0	14
3	65	14.0	18
4	72	15.0	15
5	77	14.5	13
6	84	15.0	16
7	88	16.0	20
8	90	17.0	18
9	93	17.5	22
10	97	18.5	19

TABLE 16–14

Estimated Regression
Coefficients

	Unstandardized		Standardized	
	β_1	β_2	β_1	β_2
Simple regression	8.00	3.75	0.94	0.76
Multiple regression	7.52	0.35	0.88	0.07

income of the consumer, respectively. In postulating that the amount invested in the stock market is linearly related to wealth and income, the presumption is that wealth and income have some *independent* influence on investment. In the extreme case, if wealth and income are perfectly correlated, then we have, in effect, only a single explanatory variable, not two, and there is no way to assess the *separate* effects of wealth and income on investment. In essence this is the problem of multicollinearity. When explanatory variables are correlated, the β estimates can be highly misleading and there is no way to assess the individual influence of each x on y.

To reinforce the concepts we have been discussing in this chapter, consider Table 16–13, which presents the data relating sales volume y to shelf space x_1 and in-store coupons distributed x_2 for 10 brands of hand soap. Table 16–14 presents β estimates derived by regressing y on each explanatory variable separately (simple regressions) and regressing y on x_1 and x_2 simultaneously (multiple regression). The table also reports the beta coefficients as well. Note that the estimate of the influence of x_2 on y varies rather dramatically depending on whether x_1 is included in the regression function. In the multiple regression it appears that the influence of coupon activity has little to do with sales volume—both the unstandardized and standardized coefficients are relatively small. In the simple regression, however, the influence is relatively strong, and, in fact, the product moment correlation between coupon activity and sales volume is equal to 0.76. This apparent inconsistency is due to the fact that coupon activity and shelf space are themselves highly correlated—there is more coupon activity for those brands that have larger amounts of shelf space.

Model Assumptions

There are other assumptions concerning the proper use of regression analysis. These assumptions concern the distribution of the residuals $e_i = (y_i - \hat{y}_i)$. One assumption is that at each of the various x-values the y's have the same variance. Technically, this assumption is referred to as the assumption of *homoscedasticity*, or *equal* (homo) *spread* (scedasticity), or *equal variance*. Another assumption, one that is needed in order to test the overall significance of the regression model as well as individual β coefficients, is that the residuals are normally and independently distributed.

Often plots of residuals and other types of residual analysis can provide useful information on whether these assumptions are in place. Residual plots, which are usually available in standard software packages (such as SPSSX), are used to determine whether the residuals exhibit any systematic pattern. If the residual plots show a systematic pattern, then the homoscedastic assumption and the normality assumption may be suspect.[10]

SUMMARY

Assessing the level of association (correlation) between two variables is a common practice in marketing research. In this chapter we have seen that the method used for calculating the correlation between two variables depends on the measurement properties of the variables. Correlation coefficients for nominal, ordinal, and interval variables were discussed and illustrated. We also considered the case of two variables having different units of measurement. This chapter also considered simple two-variable and multiple regression analysis. Regression analysis is a model for predicting the values of a dependent variable on the basis of the known values of one or more explanatory variables. Various aspects of regression analysis were discussed including the problem of multicollinearity and the assumptions underlying the proper use of the regression model.

KEY CONCEPTS

dependent or criterion variable

explanatory or independent variable

covariation

scatter diagram

direct or positive association

inverse or negative association

no association

Pearson product moment correlation

Spearman's rank-order correlation coefficient

chi square statistic

Cramer's contingency coefficient (V)

point-biserial correlation coefficient

regression analysis

simple regression model

multiple regression model

regression line

normal equations/ ordinary least-squares

coefficient of determination

multicollinearity

---

[10]Excellent discussions of residual analysis can be found in N. Draper and H. Smith, *Applied Regression Analysis* (New York: John Wiley & Sons, 1966).

REVIEW QUESTIONS

1. The following table shows data on sales, advertising expenditures, and the number of salespersons for 10 regional divisions of a large national distributor of hardware.

Sales ($000)	Advertising ($000)	Number of Salespersons
120	20	8
200	50	13
235	47	14
174	37	11
187	41	12
196	33	13
149	27	10
169	31	11
172	35	11
153	40	9

 a. Compute an appropriate correlation coefficient for each pair of variables.
 b. Interpret each correlation coefficient and determine which pairs of variables exhibit statistically significant association.

2. The following table shows data on the sales rankings and rankings of salesperson expertise for the 10 regional divisions shown in question 1. In the table, "1" denotes the highest ranking.

Sales Ranking	Salesperson Expertise Ranking	Sales Ranking	Salesperson Expertise Ranking
1	2	8	10
9	7	3	4
10	9	4	3
6	6	5	8
7	5	2	1

 a. Compute the correlation between sales and salesperson expertise.
 b. Interpret this relationship and determine whether it is statistically significant.

3. Each of 14 respondents were rated according to their exercise habits. Each respondent was classified as either above average (1), average (0), or below average (-1). The following table shows these data along with the gender of the respondents (coded 1 for males and 0 for females).

Gender	Exercise	Gender	Exercise
1	1	0	0
1	0	0	0
1	-1	0	1
1	0	0	-1
1	0	0	-1
1	1	0	0
1	0	0	-1

 a. What correlation coefficient is appropriate for these data?
 b. Compute the correlation between gender and exercise behavior.
 c. Interpret this correlation and determine whether it is statistically significant.

4. For the data shown in question 1, regress sales on advertising expenditures.
 a. How do you interpret the intercept and slope of the regression line?
 b. Plot the regression line of the estimate of advertising expenditures and sales.
 c. What percent of the variation in sales is explained by advertising expenditures?
 d. Is the regression model statistically significant?
 e. Compute the residual for the first regional division.
 f. What is the predicted sales volume for the first regional division?

5. For the data shown in question 1, regress sales on advertising expenditures and number of salespersons.
 a. Does the inclusion of the number of salespersons in the estimated regression model explain more of the variation in sales?
 b. Is the model significant?
 c. Interpret the regression model.
 d. Which explanatory variable is more important in explaining sales?

APPENDIXES: MULTIVARIATE ANALYSIS PROCEDURES

Multivariate analysis can be simply defined as the application of methods that *simultaneously* deal with reasonably large numbers of variables. In other words, multivariate techniques differ from univariate and bivariate analysis in that they direct attention away from the analysis of mean and variance of a single variable, or from the pairwise relationship between two variables, to the analysis of the relationship among three or more variables.

In this appendix we discuss several of the more popular multivariate techniques used in marketing research; in particular, these techniques are frequently used in various types of *market studies*. In Chapter 17, we discuss and illustrate how these techniques can prove useful in the context of market positioning, market segmentation, and market structure analysis.

MULTIDIMENSIONAL SCALING

In this appendix we present some technical details on multidimensional scaling (MDS).[1] The discussion is organized in terms of (1) derived distances, (2) nonmetric MDS, and (3) computer software.

DERIVED DISTANCES

The fundamental premise of MDS is that the derived distances in the space should match the original proximities (similarities). MDS programs find the positions in space or the coordinates for each of the objects such that the distances between them will correspond as closely as possible to the proximity values. The success of this process is judged by how well the derived distances in this space match the original proximities.

MDS attempts to determine a set of coordinates called the initial or starting configuration. Distances in the derived space are calculated from these coordinates and evaluated relative to the original proximity values. If the error is large (i.e., if the differences between the derived distances and the proximities are large), then the program moves the coordinates and recomputes the distances in the derived space. This process is repeated until the distances in the derived space adequately fit the data on the basis of some goodness-of-fit criterion (called *stress*).

NONMETRIC MDS

Nonmetric MDS assumes that the level of measurement is at the nominal or, at best, ordinal scale. It is quite common for the proximity values to have ordinal properties. In this case, the computation criterion is to relate the rank order of distances to the rank order of the proximity measures. Thus, in contrast to metric MDS, nonmetric MDS procedures yield solutions such that the distances in the derived space are merely in the same rank order as the original data.

An important secondary purpose in this type of analysis is to "metricize" the nonmetric data. Nonmetric MDS programs apply monotone transformations to the original data in order to permit arithmetic operations to be

---

[1]Much of this material has been adapted from W. R. Dillon and M. Goldstein, *Multivariate Analysis: Methods and Applications* (New York: John Wiley & Sons, 1984), chapter 4.

performed on the rank orders of the proximities. A monotone transformation maintains only the rank orders of the proximities. (The logarithm and exponential functions, for example, produce monotone transformations.) Monotone transformations of the data that are as much like the distances as possible are called *disparities*. As you will shortly see, these disparities, along with the derived distances, are used to judge the adequacy of the reduced space representation.

One popular approach to MDS with ordinal data is Kruskal's *least-squares monotonic transformation.*[2] This approach yields disparities that are a monotonic transformation of the data and that match the distances, in a least-squares sense, as closely as possible. To better understand how the process works consider Table 16A–1 (see page 496). Part a of the table shows the lower half of a hypothetical symmetric matrix of ordinal data on six stimuli.

First note that immediately below part a of Table 16A–1, the data have been arranged into a vector of numbers sorted in ascending order. Part b shows the matrix of derived distance, and they too have been arranged in vector form—not in ascending order, but rather in data order. For example, since the second element in the data vector corresponds to matrix position (2, 1) with a value of 2, the second element in the distance vector is 1.0; similarly, the last element in the data vector corresponds to matrix position (5,4) with a value of 15, and the last element in the distance vector has the value 8.4. It is now easy to see that if the elements in the distance vector were in the proper order in relation to the data vector, they too would be in ascending order—however, they are not. The procedure is to replace every sequence of two numbers that is out of order with the mean of the two numbers. Part c of the table shows how this works. Here NG (no good) indicates two numbers out of ascending order. For example, the distances 2.4 and 2.0 are out of order, and therefore we replace each with their mean value of 2.2. Next, this new value is compared with the number immediately following it, and an addition check is again undertaken. The next number is 3.2, and no replacement is needed (numbers in the proper order are indicated by OK). The process continues in a similar fashion. It may happen that the mean of two distances is not in the proper order; in such cases the mean of three (or more) distances is then formed. When the correct ordering of all the numbers in the distance vector is achieved, they are taken out of the vector and put back in matrix form. These numbers are now called the disparities. When there are ties in the data the process is altered slightly.

In practice, the process starts with an initial configuration of points (stimulus coordinates), perhaps determined randomly, in a specified dimensionality (number of dimensions). This configuration is moved iteratively to minimize some stress measure, subject to maintaining the monotonicity of the disparities with the original proximities. The process terminates when the value of the stress measure at a given iteration fails to improve by a specified amount from its value at the

---

[2] J. B. Kruskal, "Multidimensional Scaling by Optimizing Goodness of Fit to a Nonmetric Hypothesis," *Psychometrika* 29 (1964), pp. 1–27; and J. B. Kruskal, "Nonmetric Multidimensional Scaling: A Numerical Method," *Psychometrika* 29 (1964), pp. 28–42.

TABLE 16A–1
—
Kruskal's Least-Squares Monotone Transformation

a.   Raw data
```
0
2 0
5 1 0
  3  7  8  0
  9  6  4 15  0
14 12 13 11 10 0
```
Sorted into ascending order:
```
1 2 3 4 5 6 7 8 9 10 11 12 13 14 15
```
b.   Distances
```
0.0
1.0 0.0
3.2 0.8 0.0
2.4 3.8 4.0 0.0
4.2 2.6 2.0 8.4 0.0
9.2 6.0 7.2 5.4 5.6 0.0
```
Arranged in data order:
```
0.8 1.0 2.4 2.0 3.2 2.6 3.8 4.0 4.2 5.6 5.4 6.0 7.2 9.2 8.4
```
c.   Least-squares monotonic transformation
```
        OK  OK  NG       NG        OK
    0.8 1.0 2.4 2.0 3.2 2.6 3.8 4.0
            OK   2.2 OK
            OK   2.9 OK
        OK  OK  NG        OK  OK
        4.2 5.6 5.4 6.0 7.2 9.2 8.4
            OK 5.5   OK       OK 8.8
```
d.   Disparities
```
0.8 1.0 2.2 2.2 2.9 2.9 3.8 4.0 4.2 5.5 5.5 6.0 7.2 8.8 8.8
```
Optimally scaled:
```
0.0
1.0 0.0
2.9 0.8 0.0
2.2 3.8 4.0 0.0
4.2 2.9 2.2 8.8 0.0
8.8 6.0 7.2 5.5 5.5 0.0
```

Source: W. R. Dillon and M. Goldstein, *Multivariate Analysis: Methods and Applications* (New York: John Wiley & Sons, 1984), p. 128.

previous iteration. Exhibit 16A–1 summarizes the general procedure in flow chart form.

COMPUTER SOFTWARE

There are two requisites for an MDS analysis: a set of numbers, called proximities, which express all (or most) combinations of pairs of similarities within a group of objects; and a computer-based algorithm to implement the analysis. In the last decade or so there has been a rapid increase in the number of computer programs for MDS. Six of the major MDS computer programs are MINISSA, POLYCON, KYST, INDSCAL/SINDSCAL, ALSCAL, and MULTISCALE. Note that ALSCAL can be accessed through SAS (Supplemental Library User's Guide, 1980) and

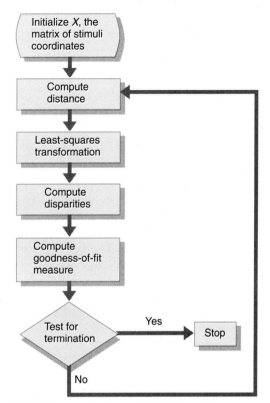

EXHIBIT 16A–1

The Nonmetric MDS
Procedure

Source: W. R. Dillon and M. Goldstein, *Multivariate Analysis: Methods and Applications* (New York: John Wiley & Sons, 1984), p. 130.

SPSSX. In addition, there is available MDS(X), which is an integrated series of MDS algorithms with common command language.

The various MDS programs differ in a number of fundamental ways. It is beyond our scope to discuss the mechanics of each computer program.[3]

References

1. Dillon, W. R., and M. Goldstein. *Multivariate Analysis: Methods and Applications*. New York: John Wiley & Sons, 1984, chapter 4.

2. Green, P. E., and F. J. Carmane. *Multidimensional Scaling and Related Techniques in Marketing Analysis*. Boston: Allyn & Bacon, 1970.

3. Green, P. E., and V. Rao. *Applied Multidimensional Scaling: A Comparison of Approaches and Algorithms*. New York: Holt, Rinehart & Winston, 1972.

---

[3]For a thorough discussion, consult S. S. Schiffman, M. L. Reynolds, and F. W. Young, *Introduction to Multidimensional Scaling* (New York: Academic Press, 1981).

FACTOR ANALYSIS TECHNIQUES

PRINCIPAL COMPONENTS ANALYSIS

Assume that n subjects have responded to a questionnaire containing p items. A basic purpose of *principal components analysis (PCA)* is to account for the total variation among these n subjects in p-dimensional space by forming a new set of orthogonal and uncorrelated *composite* variates. As we shall see, each member of the new set of variates is a linear combination of the original set of measurements. The linear combinations will be generated in such a manner that *each successive composite variate will account for a smaller portion of total variation*. Hence the first composite (that is, *principal component*) will have the largest variance, the second will have a variance smaller than the first but larger than the third, and so on. In general, the number of new composite variables that will be needed to account adequately for the total variation is less than p.

Model Development

Suppose that for a particular subject the observed responses for the p items on the questionnaire are represented by $x' = [x_1, x_2 \ldots, x_p]$. For all subjects let the population variance-covariance matrix of x by given by

$$\Sigma = \begin{bmatrix} \sigma_{11} & \sigma_{12} & \cdots & \sigma_{1p} \\ \sigma_{21} & \sigma_{22} & \cdots & \sigma_{2p} \\ \cdot & \cdot & & \cdot \\ \cdot & \cdot & & \cdot \\ \cdot & \cdot & & \cdot \\ \sigma_{p1} & \sigma_{p2} & \cdots & \sigma_{pp} \end{bmatrix}$$

The elements along the main diagonal of Σ are, respectively, the true population variances of each of the p original variables. The elements off the main diagonal are the true population covariances (i.e., the manner in which pairs of original variables relate to each other—positively, negatively, or not at all).

To find the first principal component $y_{(1)}$, we seek a vector of coefficients $a' = [a_1, a_2, \ldots, a_p]$ such that the variance of $a'x$ is a maximum over the class of all linear combinations of x subject to the constraint $a'a = 1$. The reason for

for requiring that the coefficients be normalized (i.e., $\mathbf{a'a} = 1$) is that otherwise the variance of $\mathbf{a'x}$ would increase by making the coordinates of $\mathbf{a}$ arbitrarily large. It can be shown that the set of coefficients $\mathbf{a}$ defining the first principal component is that which corresponds to the largest eigenvalue λ_1 of $\mathbf{\Sigma}$. An eigenvalue is merely the *variance of a particular principal component*. Thus, the largest eigenvalue is the variance of the first principal component $y_{(1)}$. Moreover, the set of coefficients defining this first principal component is called the eigenvector $\mathbf{a}_{(1)}$. The first principal component is given by $y_{(1)} = \mathbf{a'}_{(1)}\mathbf{x}$.

The second principal component is obtained by finding a second normalized vector (set of coefficients) $\mathbf{a}_{(2)}$, orthogonal to $\mathbf{a}_{(1)}$, such that $y_{(2)} = \mathbf{a'}_{(2)}\mathbf{x}$ has the second largest variance (i.e., eigenvalue) among all the vectors satisfying the constraints $\mathbf{a'}_{(2)}\mathbf{a}_{(2)} = 1$, $\mathbf{a'}_{(1)}\mathbf{a}_{(2)} = 0$. The process continues until all p sets of coefficients (eigenvectors) are generated in such a manner that each is normalized and orthogonal to the sets of coefficients generated for the other principal components.

The coefficients defining a given principal component have an interesting interpretation. Within the jth component the contribution of variable x_i is given by a_{ij}, where $y_{(j)} = a_{1j}x_1 + a_{2j}x_2 + \ldots + a_{pj}x_p$. The magnitude and sign of a_{ij} gives the strength and direction of the relationship between x_i and $y_{(j)}$. It can be shown that the covariance of x_i with the component y_{ij} is $\sqrt{\lambda_j}a_{ij}$, where λ_j is the eigenvalue whose associated set of coefficients of *component weights* a_{ij} can be converted into *component loadings* by dividing $\sqrt{\lambda_j}a_{ij}$ by the standard deviation of x_i. Component loadings represent the correlation between each variable x_i and the component $y_{(j)}$. Note that if all the variables defining x are first standardized, then $\mathbf{\Sigma}$ is a correlation matrix, and since all the variances will then be equal to 1, the scaled weights, $\sqrt{\lambda_j}a_{ij}/s_{x_i} = \sqrt{\lambda_j}a_{ij}$, represent the correlation between x_i *and* $y_{(j)}$.

How Many Components to Retain

One of our primary objectives in a PCA is dimensionality reduction; hence, if we use all or most of the possible new variates we are, in a sense, defeating our purpose. There is a rich class of statistical inference that can be helpful in determining how many components to generate. Most of the available statistical tests are applicable only for large samples and deal with a determination of whether the generated eigenvalues (i.e., component variances) appear significantly different from zero. Moreover, many users of these tests do not find them particularly helpful, and hence more ad hoc procedures are commonplace.

When the variance-covariance matrix is the basic input, components are usually generated until some prespecified amount of total variation is accounted for. This, of course, is a very subjective and arbitrary stopping rule. It is, however, the most frequently used rule. In the case of correlation input the "root greater than 1" criterion is frequently employed.[4] This criterion retains only those components whose eigenvalues are greater than 1. The rationale for this rule is that any

[4]H. F. Kaiser, "The Varimax Criterion for Analytic Rotation in Factor Analysis," *Psychometrika* 21 (1958), pp. 187–200.

component should account for more variance than any single variable in the standardized test score space. Both procedures are sensible and are recommended. There are also a number of graphic procedures that can be helpful in determining how many components to retain.

References

1. Dillon, W. R., and M. Goldstein. *Multivariate Analysis: Methods and Applications.* New York: John Wiley & Sons, 1984.
2. Gnanadesikan, R. *Methods for Statistical Data Analysis of Multivariate Observations.* New York: John Wiley & Sons, 1977.
3. Morrison, D. F. *Multivariate Statistical Methods*, 3rd ed. New York: McGraw-Hill, 1976.

FACTOR ANALYSIS[5]

Factor analysis is another linear reduction technique. However, factor analysis has more inherent structure since it assumes a specified model that implies a reduced form of the input matrix; that is, the factor analytic model presumes the existence of a smaller set of factors that can produce exactly the correlation in the larger set of variables.

Model Development

The basic model in factor analysis is usually expressed by

$$\mathbf{x} = \mathbf{\Lambda} \mathbf{f} + \mathbf{E} \tag{16B–1}$$

where

$\mathbf{x}$ = p-dimensional vector of observed responses
$\mathbf{\Lambda}$ = p × q matrix of unknown constants called factor loadings
$\mathbf{f}$ = q-dimensional vector of unobservable variables called common factors
$\mathbf{E}$ = p-dimensional vector of unobservable variables called unique factors.

We assume that the variance-covariance matrix of $\mathbf{E}$ is a diagonal matrix, $\mathbf{\Phi}$, with entries ϕ_i^2 and that all covariances between $\mathbf{E}$ and $\mathbf{f}$ are zero. The basic model along with the associated assumptions imply that $\mathbf{\Sigma}_{xx}$, the variance-covariance matrix of $\mathbf{x}$, is expressible as

$$\mathbf{\Sigma}_{xx} = \mathbf{\Lambda}\mathbf{\Sigma}_{ff}\mathbf{\Lambda}' + \mathbf{\Phi} \tag{16B–2}$$

Standardizing the vector of common factors and assuming that they are pairwise uncorrelated, one is led to

$$\mathbf{\Sigma}_{xx} = \mathbf{\Lambda}\mathbf{\Lambda}' + \mathbf{\Phi} \tag{16B–3}$$

---

[5]Much of this material has been adapted from W. R. Dillon and M. Goldstein, *Multivariate Analysis: Methods and Applications* (New York: John Wiley & Sons, 1984), chapter 3.

To get a better feel for the basic model, let us examine Equation 16B–1 in somewhat more detail. Writing Equation 16B–1 in terms of its elements we have

$$
\begin{bmatrix} x_1 \\ x_2 \\ \cdot \\ \cdot \\ \cdot \\ x_p \end{bmatrix} = \begin{bmatrix} \Lambda_{11} & \Lambda_{12} & \cdot \cdot \cdot & \Lambda_{1q} \\ \Lambda_{21} & \Lambda_{22} & \cdot \cdot \cdot & \Lambda_{2q} \\ \cdot & \cdot & & \cdot \\ \cdot & \cdot & & \cdot \\ \cdot & \cdot & & \cdot \\ \Lambda_{p1} & \Lambda_{p2} & \cdot \cdot \cdot & \Lambda_{pq} \end{bmatrix} \begin{bmatrix} f_1 \\ f_2 \\ \cdot \\ \cdot \\ \cdot \\ f_q \end{bmatrix} + \begin{bmatrix} E_1 \\ E_2 \\ \cdot \\ \cdot \\ \cdot \\ E_p \end{bmatrix}
$$

or

$$
x_i = \sum_{i=1}^{q} \lambda_{ij} \mathbf{f}_j + \mathbf{E}_i \tag{16B–4}
$$

This representation shows directly that, for the case of uncorrelated and standardized common factors, the common factor loading λ_{ij} expresses the correlation between the jth factor and the variable x_i. If we do not assume, however, that the common factors are pairwise uncorrelated, then the same interpretation does not prevail.

A further implication of the basic model as shown in Equation 16B–1 is that for the case of uncorrelated and standardized common factors, the correlation r_{ij} between any two variables x_i and x_j is expressible in terms of factor loadings by

$$
r_{ij} = \sum_{k=1}^{q} \lambda_{ik} \lambda_{jk} \tag{16B–5}
$$

Note that from Equation 16B–3

$$
\text{Var}(x_i) = \sigma_{ii} = \sum_{j=1}^{q} \lambda^2_{ij} + \phi^2_i \tag{16B–6}
$$

and hence we can think of λ^2_{ij} as the contribution of the common factor f_i to the variance of x_i. The contribution of all the factors to the variance of x_i (i.e., $\sum_{j=1}^{q} \lambda^2_{ij}$) is called the *commonality* of x_i; ϕ^2_i is the uniqueness of x_i and measures the extent to which the common factors fail to account for the variance of x_i. The total contribution of f_j to the variances of all the variables is

$$
v_j = \sum_{i=1}^{p} \lambda^2_{ij} \tag{16B–7}
$$

and hence the total contribution of all the common factors to the total variance of all the variables is the total commonality

$$
v = \sum_{j=1}^{q} v_j \tag{16B–8}
$$

To summarize,

$$\text{Total variance} = \sum_{i=1}^{p} \sigma_{ii}$$

$$= \sum_{i=1}^{p}\sum_{j=1}^{q} \lambda_{ij}^2 + \sum_{j=1}^{p} \phi_i^2 \qquad (16B\text{–}9)$$

$$= v + \phi^2$$

$$= \text{Total commonality} + \text{Total uniqueness}$$

Rotation of Factor Solution

When we introduced the notion of factoring the variance-covariance matrix $\mathbf{\Sigma}_{xx}$ (or the correlation matrix), we did not indicate that alternative solutions were possible and may be equally as valid. In fact, if the matrix $\mathbf{\Lambda}$ of factor loadings is postmultiplied by any orthogonal matrix $\mathbf{A}$, then $\mathbf{\Sigma}_{xx}$ will be reproducible through $\mathbf{\Lambda A}$ as well as through $\mathbf{\Lambda}$. The matrix of factor loadings $\mathbf{\Lambda}$ represents a particular interpretation of the data; that is, the variance-covariance or correlation matrix in terms of a set of factors. The rotated matrix of factor loadings $\mathbf{\Lambda}$ represents an alternative interpretation of the data that, in a mathematical sense, is equally as valid. The rotational process of factor analysis allows the researcher a degree of flexibility by presenting a multiplicity of views of the same data set in order to aid in interpretation.

Many procedures used to rotate the matrix of factor loadings do so in a manner to achieve simple structure. The major characteristics of simple structure are the following:

1. Any column of the factor loading matrix should have mostly small values, as close to zero as possible.

2. Any given row of the matrix of factor loadings should have nonzero entries in only a few columns.

3. Any two columns of the matrix of factor loadings should exhibit a different pattern of high and low loadings.

The idea of simple structure is not limited to orthogonal rotations but is equally reasonable for oblique rotations; that is, rotations that lead to nonorthogonal solutions.

Most computer software packages for factor analysis contain various rotational procedures. Factor loadings are automatically rotated to achieve certain criteria. Although options are given for oblique rotations, orthogonal rotations are without question the most frequently employed. Kaiser's Varimax method for factor rotation is probably the most popular of the computer-generated procedures.[6] The Varimax method rotates factors so that the variance of the squared factor loadings

---

[6]H. F. Kaiser, "The Varimax Criterion for Analytic Rotation in Factor Analysis," *Psychometrika* 23 (1958), pp. 187–200; and H. F. Kaiser, "Computer Programs for Varimax Rotation in Factor Analysis," *Educational and Psychological Measurement* 19 (1959), pp. 413–20.

for a given factor is made large. Most of the popular computer packages use Varimax rotation either with raw factor loadings or with normalized loadings, that is, by first dividing each variable loading by the square root of its commonality. By scaling, all variables are given equal weight in the rotation. However, some authors have argued against such scaling, especially when commonalities are very small.

Because of the computational complexities inherent in generating a matrix of factor loadings, today factor analyses are done almost exclusively by computer. Perhaps the most frequently employed methods are the principal factor solution and the maximum likelihood solution. Discussion of how each procedure operates is beyond our scope. For an in-depth presentation, we recommend the reader to Harman;[7] however, at least for the beginner, a step-by-step discussion of the nuances of each algorithm is not necessary in order to access an available computer package.

HOW DO PRINCIPAL COMPONENTS AND FACTOR ANALYSIS DIFFER?

There continues to be considerable confusion in many quarters about the differences between principal components and factor analysis. Recall that in PCA we find linear combinations of the original variables such that the jth component generated has the jth largest variance. Even though a few components may account for a large portion of the total variance, all p components are needed to recover the correlations exactly. In contrast, the common factor model posits the existence of a number of factors smaller than the number of original variables that will reproduce the correlations exactly but that may not account for as much variance as does the same number of principal components. Finally, it is important to note that while in PCA the factors are linear combinations of the observable variables, in common factor analysis the factors are linear combinations of only the common parts of the variables. Hence, it is understandable that principal components is viewed as variance oriented, whereas in common factor analysis the specific variance is expressed separately and, as such, it is correlation or covariance oriented.

References

1. Cattell, R. B. *Factor Analysis.* New York: Harper & Brothers, 1952.
2. Dillon, W. R., and M. Goldstein. *Multivariate Analysis: Methods and Applications.* New York: John Wiley & Sons, 1984.
3. Rummel, R. J. *Applied Factor Analysis.* Evanston, Ill.: Northwestern University Press, 1971.

---

[7]H. H. Harman, *Modern Factor Analysis* (Chicago: University of Chicago Press, 1967).

DISCRIMINANT ANALYSIS[8]

In discriminant analysis we have collected measurements on individuals who belong to one of several groups. The goal is to find linear composites (i.e., linear combinations) of the predictor variables that can distinguish the various groups. This is accomplished by finding axes that maximize the ratio of between-group to within-group variability of projections onto the axes. In general, with K groups and p predictor variables there are, in total, $\min(p, K - 1)$ possible discriminant axes (that is, linear composites). In most applications, since the number of predictor variables far exceeds the number of groups under study, at most $K - 1$ discriminant axes will be considered.

Determining the number of statistically significant discriminant functions is particularly important. The number of discriminant functions that provide statistically significant among-group variation essentially defines the dimensionality of the discriminant space. Thus, multiple discriminant analysis (MDA) can be viewed as a data reduction technique since it can, by uncovering a small number of discriminant functions (new axes), provide a condensed version of the factors that contribute to the among-group differences.

To better understand how MDA works, consider Exhibit 16C–1, which shows the scatterplot for the two predictor variables x_1 and x_2, and three groups. Note also that two new axes, denoted by y_1 and y_2, have been plotted in the space. Imagine now that we want to find the mean projection of each group on each axis by projecting the observations (i.e., points) first onto y_1 and then onto y_2. Essentially, this is what MDA does, in that its objective is to find those axes (in this case y_1 and y_2) with the property that the ratio of between-group to within-group variability is as large as possible. With more than two groups, however, there is an additional constraint. The discriminant functions are generated so that the scores on each new discriminant axis are uncorrelated with the scores on any previously obtained discriminant axis. In other words, y_1 is the single new axis that maximizes the ratio of between-group to within-group variability; y_2 is the second new discriminant axis that maximizes the ratio of residual between-group to within-group variability (after accounting for the between-group to within-group variability that is associated with y_1), subject to its point projections being uncorrelated with the projections on y_1. In addition, as we will see, the discriminant functions are extracted so that the accounted-for variation appears in decreasing order of magnitude.

---

[8]Much of the following discussion is extracted from W. R. Dillon and M. Goldstein, *Multivariate Analysis: Methods and Applications* (New York: John Wiley & Sons, 1984), chapter 11.

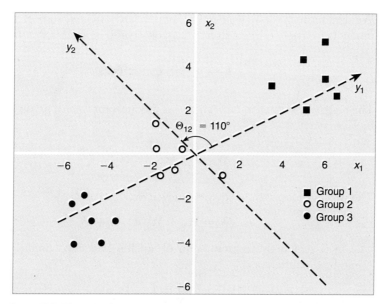

EXHIBIT 16C–1

Scatterplot of
Hypothetical Data
on Two Variables for
Three Groups

Source: W. R. Dillon and M. Goldstein, *Multivariate Analysis: Methods and Applications* (New York: John Wiley & Sons, 1984), p. 396.

OBJECTIVES OF MULTIPLE DISCRIMINANT ANALYSIS

The following summarizes five of the objectives that are typically found in MDA applications.

1. To find linear composites of the predictor variables having the property that the ratio of between-group to within-group variability is as large as possible, subject to the constraint that each uncovered linear composite must be uncorrelated with previously extracted composites. The linear composites are computed so that the accounted-for variation appears in decreasing order of magnitude.

2. To determine whether the group centroids are statistically different and the number of statistically significant discriminant axes (i.e., the dimensionality of the discriminant space).

3. To successfully assign new observations to one of the several groups, based on the observation's predictor-variable profile and resultant scores on the linear composites.

4. To determine which of the predictor variables contributes most to discriminating among the groups.

5. To identify the dimensions that underlie the discriminant space.

THE APPROACH

Assume that samples of n_i observations are available from the ith group, $i = 1, 2,$ ..., K, with each observation consisting of p measurements $x' = (x_1, x_2, \ldots, x_p)$.

We denote by T the matrix of the total mean corrected sum of squares of cross products for the scores on all $n = \Sigma_i n_i$ observations. That is,

$$T = \sum_{i=1}^{k} \sum_{j=1}^{n_i} (x_{ij} - \bar{x})(x_{ij} - \bar{x})' \qquad (16C-1)$$

The matrix of sum of squares and cross products for the ith group will be denoted by W_i:

$$W_i = \sum_{j=1}^{n_i} (x_{ij} - \bar{x})(x_{ij} - \bar{x}_i)' \qquad (16C-2)$$

The within-group sum of squares is given by

$$W = W_1 + W_2 + \ldots + W_k \qquad (16C-3)$$

The matrix of between-group sum of squares and cross products can thus be found by the difference

$$B = T - W \qquad (16C-4)$$

Define the linear compound $Y = a'x$. With respect to the linear composite y, the between-group sum of squares is given by $a'Ba$. Similarly, the within-group sum of squares is $a'Wa$. Thus,

$$\lambda = \frac{a'Ba}{a'Wa} \qquad (16C-5)$$

is the ratio of the between-group to within-group sum of squares for the K groups on the first linear compound. We wish to maximize λ with respect to a. Therefore, we take the partial derivative with respect to a and set it equal to zero. After some simplification we have

$$(B - \lambda W)a = 0 \qquad (16C-6)$$

Although Equation 16C–6 can be solved directly, it is more convenient to pre-multiply by W^{-1} and work with

$$(W^{-1}B - \lambda I)a = 0 \qquad (16C-7)$$

In this form it can be shown that the maximum value of λ is the largest eigenvalue of the matrix $W^{-1}B$, and a is the corresponding eigenvector, whose elements are the discriminant weights associated with the first linear composite.

In general there will be $r = \min(K - 1, p)$ linear composites. We will denote by λ_j the jth eigenvalue of $W^{-1}B$, where $j = 1, 2, \ldots, r$. The relative magnitudes of the respective eigenvalues, λ_j, give the descriptive index of the importance of each of the discriminant axes. For example, by expressing each eigenvalue as a percentage of the "total variance" accounted for, that is,

$$\frac{\lambda_j}{\Sigma_j \lambda_j} \qquad (16C-8)$$

we can determine which discriminant axes capture the major sources of variation separating the groups.

Associated with each linear composite is a set of discriminant weights (eigenvectors). We will denote by $\mathbf{a}_j$ the set of discriminant weights associated with the jth linear composite (eigenvalue). For interpretation it has become customary to transform the discriminant weights into what are called discriminant loadings. Discriminant weights can be adversely affected by predictor variables that are correlated. Thus, a better way of interpreting the relationship between the predictor variables and a discriminant function is to compute the simple correlation of the variable and the computed discriminant scores for that function. In other words, discriminant loadings are correlations, where the correlation is taken across the observed values of a given variable and the projection of points on a particular discriminant axis.

STATISTICAL TESTS

To assist in determining how many linear composites (i.e., axes) to retain, we can use Bartlett's statistic V and its χ^2 approximation to the significance of the eigenvalue of $\mathbf{W}^{-1}\mathbf{B}$. If $\mathbf{x}$ is multivariate normal within each group with equal variance-covariance matrices, the significance of the r discriminant functions can be assessed by computing a logarithmic function of Λ:

$$V = -[(n - 1) - \tfrac{1}{2}(p + K)]\ln \Lambda \qquad (16C\text{–}9)$$

where Λ is a Wilks' lambda variable. It can be shown that

$$\Lambda = \prod_{j=1}^{r} (1 + \lambda_j)^{-1} \qquad (16C\text{–}10)$$

Thus, since $-\ln a = \ln(1/a)$, we can write Bartlett's statistic as

$$V = [(n - 1) - \tfrac{1}{2}(p + K)] \sum_{j=1}^{r} \ln(1 + \lambda_j) \qquad (16C\text{–}11)$$

The statistic V is approximately distributed as a χ^2 random variable under the null hypothesis that the number of linear composites equals r with $p(K - 1)$ df. Thus, if the value of V is greater than a critical point from a χ^2 distribution with $p(K - 1)$ df, then we conclude that the discriminant solution is statistically significant. Because the discriminant functions are uncorrelated, the additive components of V are each approximately χ^2 variates. Thus, the significance of, say, the jth eigenvalue λ_j can be assessed by computing

$$V_j = [(n - 1) - \tfrac{1}{2}(p + K)]\ln(1 + \hat{\lambda}) \qquad (16C\text{–}12)$$

This statistic under *HO:* is approximately a χ^2 variate with $(p + K - 2j)$ df. Successive tests can be formed by cumulatively subtracting $V_1, V_2, \ldots, V_j$, from V.

References

1. Crask, M. R., and W. D. Perreault. "Validation of Discriminant Analysis in Marketing Research." *Journal of Marketing Research*, February 1977, pp. 60–64.

2. Dillon, W. R. "The Performance of the Linear Discriminant Function in Nonoptimal Situations and the Estimation of Classification Error Rates: A Review of Recent Findings." *Journal of Marketing Research*, February 1982, pp. 44–46.

3. Morrison, Donald G. "On the Interpretation of Discriminant Analysis." *Journal of Marketing Research*, May 1969, pp. 156–63.

CLUSTER ANALYSIS[9]

In many application settings there is reason to believe that the set of objects under study can be clustered into subgroups that differ in meaningful ways. The most commonly used term for the class of procedures that seeks to separate the component data into groups is *cluster analysis*. The cluster analysis procedure typically begins by taking, say, p measurements on each of the n objects. The $n \times p$ matrix of raw data is then transformed into an $n \times n$ matrix of similarity or, alternatively, distance measures where the similarities or distances are computed between pairs of objects across the p variables. Next a clustering algorithm is selected, which defines the rules concerning how to cluster the objects into subgroups on the basis of the interobject similarities. As we indicated, the goal in many cluster applications is to arrive at clusters of objects that display small within-cluster variation relative to the between-cluster variation. As a final step, the uncovered clusters are contrasted (that is, profiled) in terms of their mean values on the p variables or other characteristics of interest.

CLUSTERING CRITERIA

As we indicated, the researcher wanting to perform a cluster analysis is faced with what appears to be an endless list of clustering algorithms to choose among. For the most part, clustering algorithms depend on high-speed computer technology for computational efficiency and strive to meet some criterion that essentially maximizes the between-cluster variation relative to the within-cluster variation.

The between-cluster variation can be judged by assessing the distance between cluster centers in comparison with the distance of a cluster member to a cluster center. To understand how this criterion can be used to form clusters, imagine starting with a given number of cluster centers chosen arbitrarily, or on judgment, and assigning objects to the nearest cluster center. Next the mean or center of gravity of the resulting clusters are computed, and then objects are juggled back and forth between the clusters, each time recomputing the centers of gravity and the resultant between- and within-cluster variation until the ratio is sufficiently large.

---

[9]Much of this material is taken from W. R. Dillon and M. Goldstein, *Multivariate Analysis: Methods and Applications* (New York: John Wiley & Sons, 1984), chapter 5.

SIMILARITY MEASURES

Fundamental to the use of any clustering technique is the computation of a measure of similarity of distance between the respective objects. These measures can be separated into two broad classes based on the quality of the data available. With data having metric properties, a distance-type measure can be used, whereas with data having nominal components, a matching-type measure is appropriate.

Distance-Type Measures

Assume data have been collected on n objects or individuals. Let x_{ik}, $i = 1, 2, \ldots, n$, $k = 1, 2, \ldots, p$, be the measurement collected on the ith object or individual for the kth variable. Many measures of distance are special cases of the Minkowski metric defined by

$$d_{ij} = \left\{ \sum_{k=1}^{p} | x_{ik} - x_{jk} |^{r} \right\}^{1/r} \tag{16D–1}$$

where d_{ij} denotes the distance between the two objects i and j. If we set $r = 2$, then we have the Euclidean distance between objects i and j:

$$d_{ij} = \left\{ \sum_{k=1}^{p} (x_{ik} - x_{jk})^{2} \right\}^{1/2} \tag{16D–2}$$

If $r = 1$, then we have

$$d_{ij} = \left\{ \sum_{k=1}^{p} | x_{ik} - x_{jk} | \right\} \tag{16D–3}$$

which is referred to as the absolute or city-block metric. The use of the city-block metric results in two objects having the same distance regardless of whether they are two units apart, say, on each of two variables, or one unit apart on one variable and three units apart on the other—assuming, of course, scale units of equal value.

Euclidean distance is not scale invariant. Therefore, the use of raw data should be considered skeptically when computing distances between objects, since distance can be badly distorted by a simple change of scale.

Matching-Type Measures

Matching-type measures, perhaps better known as association coefficients, are appropriate when the data are nominally scaled. These types of similarity measures generally take on values in the range 0 to 1 and are based on the reasoning that two individuals should be viewed as being similar to the extent that they share common attributes.

CLUSTERING TECHNIQUES: HIERARCHICAL AND PARTITIONING METHODS

A rather large number of clustering algorithms have been proposed. There are two popular kinds of clustering techniques. The first group, called *hierarchical* techniques, clusters the clusters themselves at various levels. The second group, called *partitioning* techniques, forms clusters by optimizing some specific clustering criterion.

Hierarchical Techniques

Hierarchical techniques perform successive fusions or divisions of the data. One of the primary features distinguishing hierarchical techniques from other clustering algorithms is that the allocation of an object to a cluster is irrevocable; that is, once an object joins a cluster it is never removed and fused with other objects belonging to some other cluster. *Agglomerative* methods proceed by forming a series of fusions of the *n* objects into groups. *Divisive* methods partition the set of *n* objects into finer and finer subdivisions. Thus agglomerative methods eventually result in all objects falling in one cluster, whereas divisive techniques will finally split the data so that each object forms its own cluster. In either case, the obvious issue is where to stop. The output from both agglomerative and divisive methods is typically summarized by the use of a dendogram, which is a two-dimensional treelike diagram illustrating the fusions or partitions that have been effected at each successive level.

Agglomerative Methods.   These methods all proceed in a similar fashion: Each object starts out in its own cluster; at the next level the two closest objects (clusters) are fused; at the third level a new object joins the cluster containing the two objects, or another two-object cluster is formed, with the decision resting on some assignment criterion. The process continues in a similar fashion until eventually a single cluster containing all *n* objects is formed.

Agglomerative methods differ to the extent that alternative definitions of distance or similarity are used in the assignment rule. Two of the more popular agglomerative techniques are described below.

1. *Single linkage, or the nearest neighbor method.* Single linkage methods use a minimum-distance rule that starts out by first finding those two objects having the shortest distance. They constitute the first cluster. At the next stage one of two things can happen: Either a third object will join the already formed cluster of two, or the two closest unclustered objects are joined to form a second cluster. The decision rests on whether the distance from one of the unclustered objects to the first cluster is shorter than the distance between the two closest unclustered objects. The process continues until all objects belong to a single cluster. For this method, then, the distance between clusters is defined as the distance between their nearest neighbors.

2. *Complete linkage, or the furthest neighbor method.* This method is exactly opposite to the approach taken in single linkage, in the sense that distance is now defined as the distance between the most distant pair of individuals.

Divisive Methods. Hierarchical divisive methods start by splitting the total pool of objects into two groups. An immediate problem is how to effect the first split. With n objects there is a possibility of $2^{n-1} - 1$ different ways to form subsets of size 2. Hence, even with the recent advances in computer storage capacity, the number of subsets considered will have to be restricted in most realistic applications. Once the initial split is made, objects are moved from one cluster to another, or finer subdivisions of the already formed clusters are made. What distinguishes the various divisive methods is (1) how the initial split is effected and (2) how already formed clusters are subdivided.

Partitioning Techniques

Unlike hierarchical clustering techniques, methods that effect a partition of the data do not require that the allocation of an object to a cluster be irrevocable. That is, objects may be reallocated if their initial assignments were indeed inaccurate. These techniques partition the data based on optimizing some formal and predefined criterion. The use of partitioning techniques usually assumes that the number of final clusters is known and specified in advance, although some methods do allow the number to vary during the course of the analysis. A popular partitioning method is the K-MEANS clustering procedure.

References

1. Ball, G. H. *Classification Analysis.* Stanford Research Institute, SRI, Project 5533, 1971.

2. Cormack, R. M. "A Review of Classification." *Journal of the Royal Statistical Society Series* A (General), 134, pt. 3, 1971, pp. 321–53.

3. Hartigan, J. A. *Clustering Algorithms.* New York: John Wiley & Sons, 1975.

4. Johnson, S. C. "Hierarchical Clustering Schemes." *Psychometrika* 32 (1967), pp. 241–54.

CASE STUDIES FOR PART V

CASE 1
Kentucky Fried Chicken

The following provides details on a Kentucky Fried Chicken (KFC) concept study. Based on the information provided and any statistical tests you feel are appropriate, prepare a statement of findings.

Purpose

The objective of the research is to assess two alternative concept positionings for Kentucky Fried Chicken ("Chicken Superiority" and "Good for You") through a battery of evaluative scaled measurements that address (1) appeal and (2) relevance.

Method and Scope

Two hundred respondents were recruited via central-location shopping mall intercept. Qualified respondents were screened to meet the following requirements:

- Age 18–49
- Household income *under* $35,000
- At least four visits to a fast-food restaurant in the past month.
- Past six month KFC visitor.
- Not negative to future KFC visit.

Sample quotas were set to provide for a respondent sample that conformed to the following conditions:

- One-half male; one-half female.
- One-half with a child aged 6–18 at home; one-half without a child aged 6–18 at home.

Detailed Findings

Findings are listed in Tables 1 through 8.

Base: Total respondents	"Chicken Superiority" 200 %	"Good for You" 200 %
Excellent/very good	45	65
Excellent	20	40
Very good	25	25
Good	15	15
Fair	25	10
Poor	15	10

TABLE 1

Overall Rating of Kentucky Fried Chicken

TABLE 2
—
Summary of Mean
Score Agreement
Levels (7-Point
Scales)

Base: Total respondents	"Chicken Superiority" 200 $\bar{x}$	"Good for You" 200 $\bar{x}$
Appeal		
The way they described Kentucky Fried Chicken was appealing to me personally	3.80 (1.21)*	5.87 (0.98)
I really like the way she talked about Kentucky Fried Chicken	3.77 (1.12)	4.74 (1.01)
Listening to what she said could really make me hungry for Kentucky Fried Chicken	3.45 (1.01)	5.41 (0.95)

*Numbers in parentheses give variances.

TABLE 3
—
Summary of Mean
Score Agreement
Levels

Base: Total respondents	"Chicken Superiority" 200 $\bar{x}$	"Good for You" 200 $\bar{x}$
Relevance		
The Kentucky Fried Chicken experience described here is something I'd like to have more often	3.45 (1.45)*	3.52 (1.21)
She was talking about some things that matter to me when it comes to fast food	3.63 (1.23)	5.87 (1.01)
She described what I really like about eating Kentucky Fried Chicken	3.60 (1.5)	4.89 (1.01)

*Numbers in parentheses give variances.

Base: Total respondents	"Chicken Superiority" 200 %	"Good for You" 200 %
Appeal		
The way they describe Kentucky Fried Chicken was appealing to me personally	12	36
I really liked the way she talked about Kentucky Fried Chicken	14	36
Listening to what she said could really make me hungry for Kentucky Fried Chicken	15	40
Relevance		
The Kentucky Fried Chicken experience described here is something I'd like to have more often	8	15
She was talking about some things that matter to me when it comes to fast food	14	38
She described what I really like about eating Kentucky Fried Chicken	13	18

TABLE 4
—
Summary of Top Box Agreement Levels (Strongly Agree)

Base: Total respondents	"Chicken Superiority" 200	"Good for You" 200
Appeal		
The way they described Kentucky Fried Chicken was appealing to me personally	−0.154	0.654
I really liked the way she talked about Kentucky Fried Chicken	0.200	0.589
Listening to what she said could really make me hungry for Kentucky Fried Chicken	0.107	0.761
Relevance		
The Kentucky Fried Chicken experience described here is something I'd like to have more often	−0.140	0.641
She was talking about some things that matter to me when it comes to fast food	−0.200	0.742
She described what I really like about eating Kentucky Fried Chicken	0.109	0.451

TABLE 5
—
Simple Correlation of Attributes to Overall Rating of KFC

TABLE 6		"Chicken Superiority"	
Multiple Regression (Overall Rating Regressed on Specific Attribute Ratings)		Regression Coefficient	Standard Error
Eating Kentucky Fried Chicken is a more enjoyable experience than eating most other fast foods (x_1)		2.89	0.50
It made me look forward to the next time I get Kentucky Fried Chicken (x_2)		0.56	0.42
The way they described Kentucky Fried Chicken was appealing to me personally (x_3)		−1.85	1.01
I really liked the way she talked about Kentucky Fried Chicken (x_4)		−1.01	1.25
This reminds me of a lot of other Kentucky Fried Chicken commercials I've seen in the past (x_5)		−0.025	0.32

$R^2 = 0.262$; $RSS = 16543.21$; $ESS = 46542.3$

Correlation matrix

	y	x_1	x_2	x_3	x_4	x_5
y	1.0					
x_1	0.67	1.0				
x_2	0.23	0.45	1.0			
x_3	−0.36	−0.42	−0.67	1.0		
x_4	−0.31	−0.38	−0.42	0.50	1.0	
x_5	−0.15	−0.09	−0.16	0.25	0.10	1.0

TABLE 7		"Good for You"	
Multiple Regression (Overall Rating Regressed on Specific Attribute Ratings)		Regression Coefficient	Standard Error
Eating Kentucky Fried Chicken is a more enjoyable experience than eating most other fast foods (x_1)		2.25	0.87
It made me look forward to the next time I get Kentucky Fried Chicken (x_2)		1.32	0.35
The way they described Kentucky Fried Chicken was appealing to me personally (x_3)		0.87	0.25
I really liked the way she talked about Kentucky Fried Chicken (x_4)		1.01	0.87
This reminds me of a lot of other Kentucky Fried Chicken commercials I've seen in the past (x_5)		−1.25	0.65

$R^2 = 0.433$; $RSS = 19911.394$; $ESS = 26063.432$

Correlation matrix

	y	x_1	x_2	x_3	x_4	x_5
y	1.0					
x_1	0.59	1.0				
x_2	0.58	0.65	1.0			
x_3	0.46	0.23	0.32	1.0		
x_4	0.40	0.21	0.29	0.89	1.0	
x_5	−0.09	0.05	0.01	−0.14	−0.25	1.0

Base: Total respondents	"Chicken Superiority" 200 %	"Good for You" 200 %	TABLE 8 — Demographics
Age			
18–24	31	26	
25–29	24	26	
30–34	17	19	
35–39	15	14	
40–49	13	15	
Household size			
One	9	12	
Two	19	24	
Three	34	22	
Four	20	21	
Five or more	18	21	
Income			
Under $15,000	21	25	
$15,000 to under $25,000	38	35	
$25,000 to under $35,000	41	40	
Race			
White	72	66	
Black	25	26	
Other nonwhite	3	8	
Markets			
Atlanta	15	15	
Chicago	14	14	
Detroit	13	13	
Houston	23	22	
Los Angeles	21	22	
Seattle	14	14	

CASE 2
An Evaluation of One Print Advertisement for Velvet Liqueur

The following case exercise is used as an interviewing tool by Perception Research, Inc., Englewood, New Jersey. The instructions and materials that follow appear as they would if you were interviewing at Perception Research, Inc. Following, for a short print ad study, are

1. A background and objectives statement.

2. Discussions of methodology.

3. Tables of results.

Your assignment is to discuss detailed findings in writing, as if the next step were to give it to the typist. You may include a short summary and conclusions, if you wish.

Our purpose is simply to aid in the evaluation of your ability to organize your thoughts, to draw insights from the data, and to express yourself in writing.

You may type a rough copy or handwrite as you normally might do. Please take as much time as you need to produce what you feel is a representative sample of your work.

Background and Objectives

White Palace Partners, Inc., is currently considering a new advertising execution for a proposed new liqueur product called Velvet.

They have requested that PRS evaluate the new execution to determine if it appears to be a viable introductory vehicle for this new product. The *key* objectives of the new execution were

- An unaided recall score of at least 30 percent.
- A purchase-intent top box level of at least 15 percent.
- A "someone-like-me" level of at least +25 percent (see user image).

Sample Composition

A total of 75 interviews were conducted among purchasers (past year) and drinkers (past month) of a proprietary liqueur. One-half of the participants were men and one-half of them were women. In addition, one-half were of legal drinking age to 34 and one-half were aged 35–49.

Test Date and Locations

Interviewing was conducted at the PRS test facilities in New Jersey, Florida, California, and Minnesota.

Research Procedures

Participants were screened at each shopping mall location. They were not, however, prealerted as to the category under consideration.

Qualified respondents were seated in an interviewing booth that contained a slide projector. Participants were informed that they would be viewing a series of advertisements taken from a magazine. They were allowed to spend as much or as little time as they wished viewing each ad.

Unaided and aided recall was then obtained.

Participants were then reexposed to the test ad and asked to examine it in detail. A brief verbal interview was then conducted. Questioning focused on

- Future purchase intent and reasons.
- Product and user image.

Detailed Tables

Tabulated information from the questionnaire is listed in Tables 1 through 6.

TABLE 1
—
Unaided Recall

		Total
Base:		(75)
		%
Amaretto di Saronno		69
Kahlua		69
Volkswagen Jetta		65
American Express		63
Hilton Hotel		60
CocoRibe		59
Pentax		52
General Electric		47
Citizen Watches		40
Kool Lights		40
Velvet		33
Grand Marnier		31
Test Average*		54

Q. Thinking of the ads you just saw, which ones can you remember? Do you recall any other products or companies? Tell me the names of the products and companies you just saw advertised.

*Excluding Velvet.

	Base:	Total
		(75) %
Kahlua		97
American Express		95
Kool Lights		93
Amaretto di Saronno		91
Citizen Watches		91
Hilton Hotel		91
CocoRibe		87
Volkswagen Jetta		85
Pentax		84
General Electric		75
Grand Marnier		69
Velvet		61
Test Average*		87

Q. Here is a list of brand names. Some of these brands appeared in the ads you just saw, while others did not. Please tell me those which you definitely remember having seen, even though you may have mentioned them before.

*Excluding Velvet.

TABLE 2
—
Total Ad Recall
(Unaided or Aided)

	Base:	Total
		(75) %
Definitely would buy (5)	7	34
Probably would buy (4)	27	
Might or might not buy (3)	33	
Probably would not buy (2)	24	33
Definitely would not buy (1)	9	
Mean rating	3.0	

Q. Assuming Velvet were available at your liquor store, how likely would you be to buy a bottle based on what this ad shows and tells you about the brand? Please tell me the statement on the card that comes closest to describing how you feel about buying Velvet?

TABLE 3
—
Purchase Intent

TABLE 4

—

Reasons for Purchase
Intent

Base:	Total (75) %		Base:	Total (75) %
Favorable	51		*Other favorable*	20
Product attributes	37		Curious/try new products	12
Taste/flavor	33		Would buy for company/guests	4
Almond and orange flavor	20		For special occasions	4
Like almond	7		*Unfavorable*	28
Would taste good	4		Taste/flavor	23
Would taste similar to Amaretto	3		Dislike almond	11
Other product attributes	13		Wouldn't like orange and almond flavor	8
Like cordials/liqueurs	7		Would be too sweet	5
Italian/imported from Italy	5		Dislike coconut	3
Like the color of the liqueur	3		Visual	5
Visual	16		Bottle	3
Bottle	13		Other visual	3
Like the shape of the bottle	4		Dark color ad	3
Attractive bottle	4		Other unfavorable	4
Cut glass bottle	3		*Neutral/conditional*	39
Unusual shape bottle	3		Satisfied with current liqueur	11
Other visual	8		Not familiar with it	9
Almonds in the ad	7		Wouldn't buy a bottle until I've tasted it	9
Like the glass	3		Depends on price	9
			Don't drink much liqueur	5

Q. Why do you say that?

	Total
Base:	(75)
	%
Product Image	
High quality (versus low quality)	+69
Good after dinner (versus not)	+65
Good for serving to guests (versus not)	+52
Good straight or on-the-rocks (versus not)	+47
An Italian liqueur (versus not)	+44
Has a light orange taste (versus strong)	+43
Would make a good gift (versus would not)	+43
Good tasting (versus not)	+33
Has a light almond taste (versus strong)	+23
Different from other liqueurs (versus similar)	+21
More expensive than other liqueurs (versus less)	+ 5
User Image	
For selective drinkers (versus drink almost anything)	+68
For people who really know liqueurs (versus don't)	+35
For women (versus not for women)	+27
For men (versus not for men)	+24
For someone like me (versus not)	+ 1

Q. On this card are pairs of phrases that could be used to describe a product such as Velvet or the types of people who might buy a product such as this. For each pair of phrases, please indicate how this ad makes you feel about Velvet by placing an "X" in the space that best reflects your feelings.

*Percent selecting the two boxes closest to the description appearing first, minus the percent selecting two boxes closest to the description shown in parentheses, utilizing a five-point semantic differential scale.

TABLE 5

Product and User Image Net Differences*

TABLE 6   Summary for Key Dimensions

| | Base: | Previously Tested Velvet Ads | | | | | | New Product Liqueur Norm |
		Velvet	A	B	C	D	E	
		(75) %	(150) %	(151) %	(149) %	(150) %	(151) %	%
Unaided recall		33	15	17	26	28	27	32
Total recall		61	47	50	42	52	38	53
Likes and dislikes								
Any likes		NA	71	75	79	80	75	79
Any dislikes		NA	37	44	48	51	51	49
Net difference		NA	+34	+31	+31	+29	+24	+30
Purchase intent								
Definitely would buy		7 ⎤	1 ⎤	9 ⎤	6 ⎤	5 ⎤	5 ⎤	8 ⎤
Probably would buy		27 ⎦34	22 ⎦23	22 ⎦31	29 ⎦35	21 ⎦26	24 ⎦29	30 ⎦38
Product image—net differences*								
High quality		+69	+57	+72	+54	+55	+57	+51
Good after dinner		+65	+75	+76	+70	+70	+74	NA
Good for serving to guests		+52	+67	+60	+62	+62	+72	+68
Good straight or on the rocks		+47	+71	+72	+71	+66	+69	+65
An Italian liqueur		+44	+49	+89	+68	+81	+68	NA
Has a light orange taste		+43	+39	+23	+32	+39	+39	NA
Would make a good gift		+43	+39	+46	+40	+45	+42	NA
Good tasting		+33	+46	+39	+46	+42	+45	+55
Has a light almond taste		+23	+48	+47	NA	NA	NA	NA
Different from other liqueurs		+21	−3	−8	−7	−5	−13	+18
More expensive than others		+5	+17	+17	+9	+27	+19	+17
User imagery—net differences*								
For selective people		+68	+54	+43	+53	+54	+47	+40
For people who really know liqueur		+35	+48	+47	+50	+51	+54	+41
For women		+27	+46	+58	+57	+65	+64	+65
For men		+24	+27	+19	+29	+34	+35	+15
For someone like me		+1	+25	+34	+29	+28	+27	+29

*Top two boxes minus bottom two boxes, based on a 5-point scale.

CASE 3
Consumer Attitudes and Perceptions Toward Seafood when Eating Out: Positioning Phase

In earlier case studies, we introduced details on a study designed to collect information about consumers' attitudes and perceptions toward nontraditional fish consumption when eating out (in particular, see Part II, Case 4). Following is the executive summary for the focus-group phase of this study.

Executive Summary

Overall participants in these focus groups have a favorable attitude toward fish. They are eating more fish today than they ever have in the past, and they expect that consumption to increase. These consumers are more willing and more likely to try fish when eating out than they are at home. In fact, on many occasions they seem to relate eating out with eating fish.

On the other hand, despite the high propensity to eat fish in restaurants, there is significant resistance to trying the nontraditional species that were suggested to the participants in this study. Some participants are familiar with less traditional fish, if only by name, but none speak highly or very favorably about any of them. In some cases perceptions are negative; in many cases they are inaccurate.

In general, it might be said that there is an outright "suspicion" of nontraditional species, that is, that they project an unpleasurable experience. Those who are not familiar with the species mentioned seem to base their perceptions solely on the name. Other influential negative factors are the image of fish as an animal, its eating habits, its appearance, and its social behavior. Those who hold these perceptions are not influenced by those who do not, or by those who have had good experiences with nontraditional species.

Participants agree that they eat fish because they like the way it tastes. Health factors are also mentioned as reasons for consuming fish, particularly by the men. That fish is light and easily digested is mentioned more by the women. Fish is considered a good alternative to red meats, but generally it is not served at home. Many participants say they eat fish in restaurants because it is a change from what is prepared at home. This also depends on the amount of trust they put in the reputation of the restaurant and/or chef.

Factors that can either inhibit or promote the selection of fish include the method of preparation, previous experience, and cost. Although fish is not considered to be inexpensive, it is generally seen as a good food value. Yet some group participants said price prevents them from trying an unfamiliar fish. The risk of disliking the fish is too great relative to the cost in both dollars and the dining experience. A few participants feel that low-priced fish are of poor quality. Others complain about fish being "smelly," "bony," "oily," "slimy," or "too strong."

The consumption of fish in restaurants does not appear to have a direct correspondence with childhood, geographic, ethnic, or religious exposure or experience.

Several ideas for promoting nontraditional fish were suggested. Both men and women agreed that a description of the fish, its type, taste, and method of preparation enhances the likelihood of their trying it if it is unfamiliar.

Other frequently mentioned suggestions were to serve these fish as appetizers or "specials," or to include them in a combination plate. Free samples give people an opportunity to try an unfamiliar fish without the risk. Media suggestions include food preparation programs or morning talk shows with respected authorities like Julia Child.

Also mentioned was the implementation of an industrywide program, one comparable to the American Dairy Association, to promote fish in general. This was considered a good strategy to make consumers more aware of fish as an alternative to other foods.

Other means suggested to promote unfamiliar fish included:

- Make clear that the fish is fresh and prepared to order (but do not overdo, which causes suspicion).
- Offer in a "specialty" restaurant setting, especially a seafood restaurant.
- Price attractively—lower than steaks, for example, but not radically lower than other well-known fish.
- Have recommendations come from the restaurant—that is, from the chef, not from waiters or waitresses.

In addition, focus-group participants were also asked to provide similarity/dissimilarity ratings for eight traditional species of fish:

Fillet of sole	Blue fish	Halibut
Scrod	Salmon	Swordfish
Haddock	Cod	

In the next phase of this research study, interest centered on consumers' attitudes and perceptions of nontraditional fish. Specifically, the objectives were to explore

- Current eating-out habits of consumers in non-fast-food restaurants.
- Attitudes, beliefs, and intentions of consumers concerning the ordering of fish when eating out.
- Consumers' perceptions of nontraditional fish.
- Consumers' willingness to try nontraditional fish.
- Perception of nontraditional fish species' attributes held by consumers. Familiarity of and satisfaction with selected nontraditional fish.
- Different promotional techniques that might increase consumers' willingness to try nontraditional fish when dining out.
- The relationship among "ideal," perceived, and actual attributes of specific nontraditional fish.
- Characteristics of consumers who would be more willing to try nontraditional fish.

TABLE 1
—
Willingness to Try
Nontraditional Fish
[Scale (1) not very
willing to (5) very
willing]

Species	Willingness to Try (Mean Responses)	Not Willing (1 & 2)	Uncertain (3)	Very Willing (4 & 5)
Butterfish	3.39	27%	22%	51%
Hake	2.96	39	21	40
Mackerel	3.22	35	16	49
Monkfish	2.91	42	18	40
Squid	2.49	57	12	31
Pollock	3.52	24	21	55
Whiting	3.27	28	25	47
Skate	2.52	51	22	27
Eel	2.07	67	12	21
Cusk	2.81	43	21	36
Tilefish	2.41	51	26	23

Each of the 11 nontraditional fish species

Butterfish	Squid	Eel
Hake	Pollock	Cusk
Mackerel	Whiting	Tilefish
Monkfish	Skate	

were evaluated on 11 attributes and a "willingness to try" measure, as shown below:

Criteria	Range of Variation	
	(1)	(5)
Willingness to try	Not very	Very
Body	Soft	Firm
Flavor	Mild	Strong
Fat content	Low	High
Oily	Not oily	Very oily
Flaky	Not flaky	Very flaky
Color	White	Dark
Boniness	Not bony	Very bony
Odor	Mild	Strong
Moisture	Dry	Moist
Fleshiness	Lean	Meaty
Fishiness	Not fishy	Very fishy

Table 1 provides mean and percentage rating on "willingness to try" for each nontraditional fish species. Exhibit 1 presents the profile for the ideal fish, and Exhibits 2–12 (pages 525–27) present perceptual maps for three user groups ("not willing to try," "uncertain," "very willing to try") for each type of nontraditional fish.

Case Questions

Based on the results provided in Table 1 and in the perceptual maps, answer the following questions:

1. What are consumers' general attitudes and perceptions of consuming fish when eating out?

2. Recommend a strategy for increasing the consumption of nontraditional fish when eating out.

CASE 4
Banking Segmentation Study

The YMA advertising agency recently received a request by one of the leading banks in a medium-sized metropolitan area to present its approach to handling the bank's advertising program. The account executive assigned to the account was very interested in obtaining the bank as a client. To formulate the advertising strategy, the account executive decided to commission a research study to assess what consumers thought were the most salient characteristics of banks. The research objective was to obtain information for the design of advertising messages to specified segments.

The research would be conducted in two phases. Phase one would be a series of focus groups that would identify the salient attributes, and phase two would survey the importance that consumers placed on the salient attributes.

EXHIBIT 1   Profile of the Ideal Fish

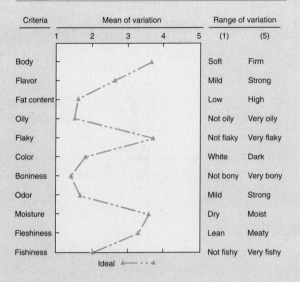

EXHIBIT 2   Discriminant Analysis of Butterfish

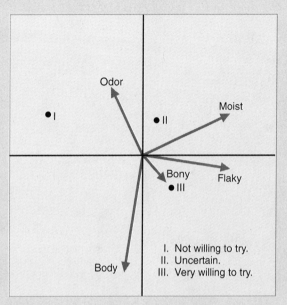

EXHIBIT 3   Discriminant Analysis of Cusk

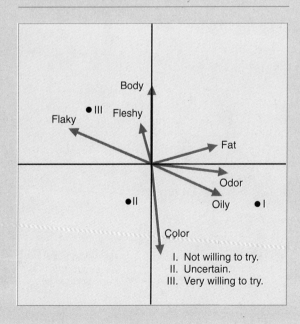

EXHIBIT 4   Discriminant Analysis of Eel

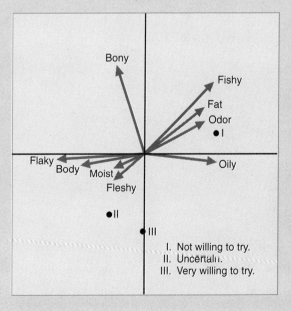

EXHIBIT 5   Discriminant Analysis of Hake

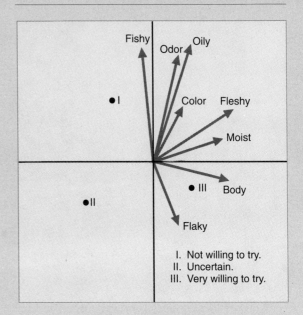

Odor
Moist
Fishy
●I
Flaky
●II
III
Flavor

I. Not willing to try.
II. Uncertain.
III. Very willing to try.

EXHIBIT 6   Discriminant Analysis of Mackerel

Fishy
Odor
Oily
Color
Fleshy
●I
Moist
III Body
●II
Flaky

I. Not willing to try.
II. Uncertain.
III. Very willing to try.

EXHIBIT 7   Discriminant Analysis of Monkfish

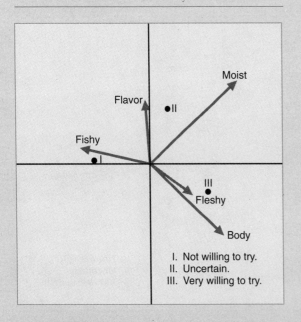

Moist
Flavor
●II
Fishy
●I
III
Fleshy
Body

I. Not willing to try.
II. Uncertain.
III. Very willing to try.

EXHIBIT 8   Discriminant Analysis of Pollock

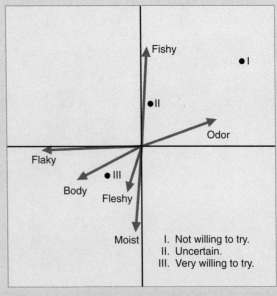

Fishy
●I
●II
Odor
Flaky
III
Body
Fleshy
Moist

I. Not willing to try.
II. Uncertain.
III. Very willing to try.

EXHIBIT 9 Discriminant Analysis of Skate

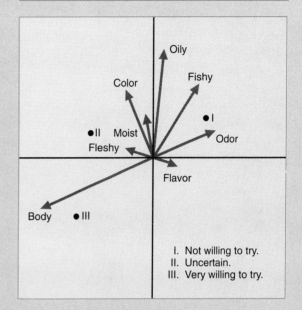

EXHIBIT 10 Discriminant Analysis of Squid

EXHIBIT 11 Discriminant Analysis of Tilefish

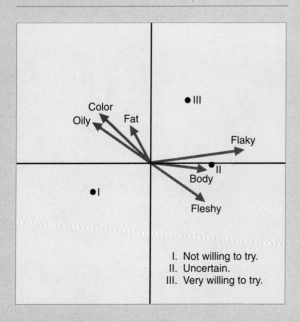

EXHIBIT 12 Discriminant Analysis of Whiting

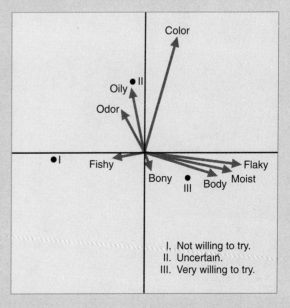

The series of focus groups identified 19 characteristics of banks that are important to consumers when choosing a bank or when switching their business to a new bank. The identified attributes are listed below:

1. Variety of services.
2. Reputation for quality service.
3. Convenient locations.
4. Convenient hours.
5. Quick service.
6. Friendly atmosphere.
7. Ease of parking.
8. Senior-citizen privileges.
9. Drive-thru tellers.
10. Banking by phone.
11. No minimum balance required.
12. No service charge for checking accounts.
13. Overdraft protection for checking accounts.
14. Level of interest rates for savings accounts.
15. Level of interest rates on loans.
16. Credit cards available.
17. Automatic teller machines (ATMs).
18. No fee for ATM usage.
19. Financial stability.

A mall-intercept study conducted by a local research supplier provided data for phase two. Quotas were specified for sex (50 percent female and 50 percent male) and age (60 percent less than age 35 and 40 percent age 35 or older). Eligible respondents were surveyed to determine (1) the importance of each of the attributes, (2) the usage patterns, and (3) the demographics. The appendix that follows (see pp. 528–29) contains the coding sheet utilized to punch the data.

Case Question

You have been assigned the task of tabbing the data, that is, generating tables for analysis. Prepare the relevant table specifications so that the tab house can generate the tables that you think would be required.

APPENDIX FOR CASE 4

Part One: Importance Ratings

	Not at All Important					Very Important		
Variety of services	0	1	2	3	4	5	6	(1)
Reputation for quality service	0	1	2	3	4	5	6	(2)
Convenient locations	0	1	2	3	4	5	6	(3)
Convenient hours	0	1	2	3	4	5	6	(4)
Quick service	0	1	2	3	4	5	6	(5)
Friendly atmosphere	0	1	2	3	4	5	6	(6)
Ease of parking	0	1	2	3	4	5	6	(7)
Senior citizens privileges	0	1	2	3	4	5	6	(8)
Drive-thru tellers	0	1	2	3	4	5	6	(9)
Banking by phone	0	1	2	3	4	5	6	(10)
No minimum balance required	0	1	2	3	4	5	6	(11)
No service charges for checking	0	1	2	3	4	5	6	(12)
Overdraft protection	0	1	2	3	4	5	6	(13)
Checks returned with statement	0	1	2	3	4	5	6	(14)
Level of interest rates for savings	0	1	2	3	4	5	6	(15)
Level of interest rates for loans	0	1	2	3	4	5	6	(16)
Credit cards	0	1	2	3	4	5	6	(17)
Automatic teller machines (ATMs)	0	1	2	3	4	5	6	(18)
No fee for ATM usage	0	1	2	3	4	5	6	(19)
Financial stability	0	1	2	3	4	5	6	(20)

Part Two: Usage:

Frequency of use for banking transactions:

In-bank tellers	_____ times per month	(22–23)
Drive-thru tellers	_____ times per month	(24–25)
ATM	_____ times per month	(26–27)

In an average month, approximately how many checks do you write?   (28)

[ ]   1–10   [ ]   11–20   [ ]   21–40   [ ]   41 +
(1)   (2)   (3)   (4)

In an average month, number of deposits/withdrawals: (29–30)

Deposits	(29)		*Withdrawals*	(30)
_____	(1)	0–3	_____	(1)
_____	(2)	4–10	_____	(2)
_____	(3)	11 +	_____	(3)

Part Three: Demographics

Are you: (1)   [ ]   Married   (3)   [ ]   Divorced/separated   (31)
           (2)   [ ]   Single, never married   (4)   [ ]   Widowed

Are you: (1)   [ ]   Male   (2)   [ ]   Female   (32)

Into which of the following age categories do you fall?   (33)

(1)   [ ]   19–24   (4)   [ ]   45–54
(2)   [ ]   25–34   (5)   [ ]   55–64
(3)   [ ]   35–44   (6)   [ ]   65 +

Do you rent or own your home?   (34)

(1)   [ ]   Rent   (2)   [ ]   Own

Please mark the income category that best matches your total annual household income.

(35)

(1)   [ ]   Under $15,000   (4)   [ ] $45,000–$59,999
(2)   [ ] $15,000–$29,999   (5)   [ ] $60,000–$74,999
(3)   [ ] $30,000–$44,999   (6)   [ ]   over $75,000

Which category below best describes the level of education you have
completed?   (36)

(1)   [ ]   Some high school   (5)   [ ]   Graduate work/degree
(2)   [ ]   High school graduate   (6)   [ ]   Technical school graduate
(3)   [ ]   Some college   (7)   [ ]   Community college graduate
(4)   [ ]   College degree

EXHIBIT 1
—
Framework for
Part VI

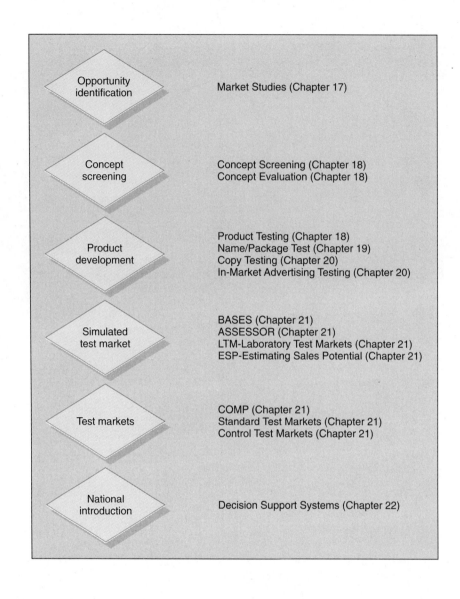

Opportunity identification — Market Studies (Chapter 17)

Concept screening — Concept Screening (Chapter 18) / Concept Evaluation (Chapter 18)

Product development — Product Testing (Chapter 18) / Name/Package Test (Chapter 19) / Copy Testing (Chapter 20) / In-Market Advertising Testing (Chapter 20)

Simulated test market — BASES (Chapter 21) / ASSESSOR (Chapter 21) / LTM-Laboratory Test Markets (Chapter 21) / ESP-Estimating Sales Potential (Chapter 21)

Test markets — COMP (Chapter 21) / Standard Test Markets (Chapter 21) / Control Test Markets (Chapter 21)

National introduction — Decision Support Systems (Chapter 22)

APPLICATIONS

In Part VI we introduce, discuss, and illustrate basic concepts and implementation of different types of market-research studies. Once again we use prototypical marketing research proposals as a framework for discussing the various applications considered in the remaining chapters.

Exhibit 1 outlines the specific areas considered. Note that our attention focuses primarily on the prelaunch stage of the research cycle. The reasons are simple: (1) the prelaunch stage is a particularly active one in terms of both the variety and volume of marketing research conducted, and (2) the prelaunch stage is crucial in determining the ultimate market acceptance of a new product. The reality of the marketplace is that most new products fail. Today, the evidence still suggests that two out of three new product entries eventually fail. More importantly, it appears that the reason for market failure is marketing related and can be avoided by effective marketing research testing in the prelaunch stage. Specifically, in the 75 consumer product failures studied by *Advertising Age* several years ago, most failures were marketing related, involving "value consumer difference" (36 percent), "poor product positioning" (32 percent), and "no point of difference" (20 percent).

Strategic Market Studies
Positioning, Segmentation, and Structuring

— Explain what is meant by a product/service market.

— Define the philosophy and objectives behind strategic market studies.

— Describe the role of strategic market studies.

— Discuss and illustrate three basic strategic market studies—*positioning studies, market segmentation studies*, and *market structure studies*.

— Acquire an understanding of the various methods used in the three basic types of strategic market studies.

INTRODUCTION

An essential ingredient in designing successful marketing strategies is a thorough understanding of the structure of markets and the patterns of competition that exist within the markets. It is difficult to conceive of a situation in which decisions concerning the marketing-mix elements (i.e., product design, price, advertising, and distribution) would be made without first acquiring an understanding of the competitive arena. The first step in this process is to define what is meant by a product/service market.

A **product/service market** consists of (1) a set of products/services that can be substituted for each other in those use situations where similar benefits are sought and (2) the customers for whom such uses are relevant.[1] In other words, product/service markets reflect the fact that individuals seek the benefits that products/services provide and that their decisions about the available alternatives are based on prior experience or the specific consumption situation that applies.

Acquiring an understanding of a product/service market may not be as simple as you might expect. First, the idea that product categories are unique and easily distinguishable is a gross simplification. In many instances, product/service market boundaries are amorphous, marked by arbitrary distinctions. For example, consider the snack food product category. In defining this

---

[1]G. S. Day, A. D. Shocker, and R. K. Srivastava, "Customer-Oriented Approaches to Identifying Product-Markets," *Journal of Marketing*, Fall 1979, p. 10.

product/service market
The set of products/services that can be substituted for each other within those use situations where similar benefits are sought and the customers for whom such usages are relevant.

product/service market should we include only "junk food" snacks, such as potato chips, pretzels, peanuts, and candy bars, or also fruits, or possibly even yogurt? Unfortunately, in this case, substitutability is a matter of degree and, ultimately, personal preference. Second, because the idea of a unique product/service market is an oversimplification, several different distinctions can be made.[2]

1. *Different product types* that serve the same generic need (e.g., pencils and pens), and, therefore, may be perceived as substitutes in the long run, but differ with respect to the specific need that is satisfied.

2. *Different product variants* that are available within the same overall type (such as low-fat and regular cottage cheese) and serve on certain occasions as substitutes.

3. *Different brands* produced within the same product variant (for example, Coca-Cola and Pepsi-Cola), differentiated on the basis of package, design, color, taste, shape, and so forth, and therefore serve as direct substitutes.

Third, because of the breadth and complexity of consumer need and the availability of a large number of alternatives to satisfy it, there is not a single product/service market, but rather there are several submarkets and strategic segments composed of customers who have common uses or applications for the product.

In this chapter we discuss marketing research studies that are designed to provide information about the composition and structure of a product/service market.

STRATEGIC STUDIES

strategic market studies
Studies that focus on in-depth analysis of a specific product/service market; they fall under the umbrella of custom research and are tailored to address specific marketing issues and/or problems.

Strategic market studies are conducted to provide marketing managers with information that is useful for them in understanding and coping with their current and future competitive environments. Because of the growing intensity of competition in most businesses, predicting the reactions of competitors to a firm's own marketing plans is a most pressing problem for many firms to face. Among the crucial managerial questions concerning competition are

— What is driving competition in my industry or in industries I am thinking of entering?

— What actions are competitors likely to take, and what is the best way to respond?

— How will my industry evolve (over time)?

— How can the firm be best positioned in order to compete with other firms during the long run?[3]

Typically, such types of studies fall under the umbrella of custom research and are tailored to address specific marketing issues and/or problems. We dis-

---

[2]T. Lunn makes these distinctions in "Segmenting and Constructing Markets," in *Consumer Market Research Handbook*, ed. R. M. Worcester (New York: McGraw-Hill, 1972). A similar discussion can be found in Day, Shocker, and Srivastava, "Product-Markets," pp. 10–11.

[3]M. E. Porter, *Competitive Strategy* (New York: Free Press, 1980).

cuss and illustrate three types of strategic market studies: **positioning studies, segmentation studies,** and **structure studies.** Positioning studies are an attempt to portray the interrelationships among a set of brands in terms of consumers' perceptions and preferences. Segmentation studies are an attempt to identify subgroups of consumers who will respond to a given marketing-mix configuration in a similar manner. Structure studies are an attempt to define the competitive relationships within a product/service market. In essence, all three are used to help marketing managers to understand and cope with their competitive environment.

POSITIONING STUDIES

Product-positioning studies provide "pictures" or maps of the competitive structure or other relationships among a predetermined set of products or brands. Such maps are based upon judgments by a sample of respondents who are familiar with the product category under study and who, presumably, represent how "the market" perceives the predetermined set of products or brands. **Product maps** provide management with a consumer perspective on competition in the marketplace. When used early in the marketing planning process, product maps can influence the alternative courses of action that are considered in later stages of the product's life and research cycles. In addition to providing a structure of competitive relationships, product maps have also been used to (1) develop and evaluate strategic plans, (2) track market changes, (3) investigate the relationship between the firm's actions and their market consequences, and (4) position or reposition a brand to appeal to specific consumers.

Philosophy and Objectives

It has been argued that firms compete to the extent that their "products are sufficiently similar so as to be close substitutes in the eyes of the buyer."[4] Through product maps we can graph the notion of close substitutes. Perceptual or preference data are analyzed to produce a representation in spatial form of the perceived relationships among a set of brands. In the product map, the closer the distance between any two brands (or product/services) the closer the brands are perceived as being in terms of relevant attributes or preferences.

Product maps consist of two essential elements:

1. A set of axes that reflect the dimensions on which the brands are judged. Typically, these dimensions represent product features or attributes that are judged as important to the consumer.

2. A set of coordinates (scores) that can be used to position each brand in the perceptual product space; in essence, the score gives a brand's position on the evaluative dimensions represented by the axes.

A perceptual product map is based on a plot of these coordinate scores in two or three, or possibly more, dimensions. The position of a brand on the map shows its

---

[4]A. Koutsouiannis, *Modern Microeconomics*, 2nd ed. (London: Macmillan, 1979), p. 8.

positioning studies
Attempts to portray the interrelationships among a set of brands in terms of consumers' perceptions and preferences for these brands.

segmentation studies
Attempts to identify subgroups of consumers who will respond to a given marketing-mix configuration in a similar manner.

structure studies
Attempts to define the competitive relationships within a product/service market.

product maps
Space that represents the perceived relationships among a set of brands; the spatial distance between any two brands represents the degree to which they are perceived as being similar in terms of relevant attributes or preferences.

EXHIBIT 17–1

Illustrative Product
Map for Soft-Drink
Market

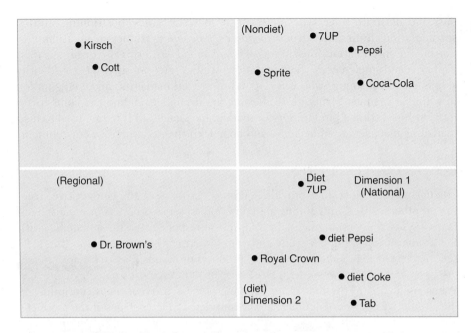

similarity to each other brand and the extent to which it possesses the characteristic or set of characteristics that define the dimensions of the space. Thus, the weight given to a dimension plays a crucial role in determining the derived distance between products in the dimensional space. A sample perceptual product map for the soft-drink product market is shown in Exhibit 17–1. The map indicates that consumers evaluate soft drinks on the basis of whether they are diet or regular brands and whether they are nationally or regionally distributed. (How the dimensions are uncovered will be discussed later.) According to the product map, diet Coke and Tab are perceived as very similar in terms of their underlying dimensions and therefore should be judged as more competitive than say diet Coke and Sprite.

Types of Product Maps

Product maps, regardless of their type, are generated from judgmental data that reflect the way consumers perceive similarities and preferences among competing brands. Although many different types of judgmental data have been used to construct product spaces, the most common forms of product maps incorporate preference or perceptual data. The choice of data affects not only the mode of collection but also the method used to produce the map.

Perceptual product maps are based upon consumers' perceived similarities and dissimilarities among a set of competing brands. The axes that define the resulting perceptual space represent the attributes that are most relevant to the consumer. For example, a perceptual product space for soft drinks may tell the brand manager that "diet versus regular" and "regional versus national" describe the evaluation process used by consumers. In addition to identifying the relevant

perceptual product maps
Maps based upon consumers' perceived similarities and differences among a set of competing brands.

dimensions, perceptual product spaces indicate how consumers view the brands of soft drinks along each dimension. Thus, perceptual product spaces represent psychological and/or sociological positioning.[5] Even though direct similarities can be used to generate a perceptual product space, construction usually begins with consumers rating existing brands (and, perhaps, an ideal or fictitious brand) independently on a set of attributes. Respondents are asked to rate their ideal brand so that the resulting perceptual space can be related to preference, if desired; that is, brands that are closer to the ideal brand are presumed to be preferred. Fictitious brands are often included to help interpret the resulting perceptual space; specifically, fictitious brands can be helpful when researchers interpret gaps in the perceptual space (if, of course, the fictitious brand occupies the gap), and they can be used to infer the relationship of brand alternatives that differ from the set of existing brands used to construct the product map. Typically, the scaling of each brand is done on either semantic differential scales,[6] bipolar-adjectives scales,[7] agree–disagree scales,[8] or anchored scales.[9] All of these scale types have been discussed and illustrated in Chapter 10.

Through **preference product maps** researchers attempt to identify how consumers use the perceived dimensions in making evaluations of a brand or in choosing among alternative brands. The axes of the product map in this case reflect those attributes most relevant from the standpoint of consumer preference; in other words, the product map represents the consumer's preference space. Preference data used to generate product maps usually are collected by stating direct comparisons that use a rank-order procedure (see Chapter 10). Essentially, each respondent would rank-order each brand in terms of preference; also, some variation of a paired comparison approach could be used. In the case of direct rank-order preference data, a nonmetric multidimensional scaling procedure is typically used to construct the product space (see Appendix 16A, Chapter 16). Specific methods for generating product maps are discussed further in Appendix 17A.

preference product maps
Attempts to position brands in the perceptual space in accordance with those product features or attributes that consumers view as most important in making evaluations of the brand or in choosing among alternative brands.

MARKET SEGMENTATION STUDIES

The term **market segment** refers to subgroups of consumers who respond to a given marketing-mix strategy in a similar manner; in other words, segments consist

market segment
Subgroups of consumers who respond to a given marketing-mix strategy in a similar manner.

---

[5]For further discussion, see A. D. Shocker and V. Srinivasan, "A Consumer-Based Methodology for the Identification of New Product Ideas," *Management Science*, February 1974, pp. 921–38; and A. D. Shocker and V. Srinivasan, "Multiattribute Approaches for Product Concept Evaluation and Generation: A Critical Review," *Journal of Marketing Research*, May 1979, pp. 159–80.

[6]For illustrative examples, see M. B. Holbrook and J. Huber, "Separating Perceptual Dimensions from Affective Overtones: An Application to Consumer Aesthetics," *Journal of Consumer Research*, March 1979, pp. 272–83; and J. Huber and M. B. Holbrook, "Using Attribute Ratings for Product Positioning: Some Distinctions among Compositional Approaches," *Journal of Marketing Research*, November 1979, pp. 507–16.

[7]For an illustrative example, see P. E. Green and V. Rao, *Applied Multidimensional Scaling* (New York: Holt, Rinehart & Winston, 1972).

[8]For an illustrative example, see J. R. Hauser and G. L. Urban, "A Normative Methodology for Modeling Consumer Response to Innovation," *Operations Research*, July–August 1977, pp. 579–619.

[9]For an illustrative example, see Yoram Wind, "A New Procedure for Concept Evaluation," *Journal of Marketing*, October 1973, pp. 2–11.

of subgroups of consumers who exhibit differing sensitivities to some marketing-mix element.[10] Although initially the contribution of segmentation analysis to marketing planning was to provide a framework for the analysis of existing data, today its role has expanded to provide a basis for identifying the data needed for strategy development and implementation. **Segmentation research** provides guidelines for a firm's marketing strategy and resource allocation among markets and products and, consequently, influences all marketing tactical plans and programs. By recognizing consumer heterogeneity, a firm can increase its profitability by segmenting its market.

segmentation research
Studies that provide guidelines for a firm's marketing strategy and resource allocation among markets and products.

Philosophy and Objectives

Segmentation research has been used to answer a wide variety of questions concerning market response to a firm's marketing strategies, that is, product changes, price changes, new product offerings, and the selection of target markets. Typical management questions that guide market segmentation studies involve such issues as

1. How do the evaluations of a set of new product concepts vary by different respondent groups—males versus females, users versus nonusers of the company's brand, light versus heavy users, and so on?

2. Are there different promotion sensitive segments for a new product concept, and if so, how do they differ with respect to product use, concept evaluations, attitudes, and demographic and psychographic profiles?

3. How do the target markets for a new product concept differ regarding the end benefits sought, product use characteristics, and other background characteristics?

From these management questions we see that there is an intimate relationship between product positioning and segmentation analysis. To effectively position a product to a specific target of consumers who share certain common characteristics (e.g., similar reactions to price, promotion, and the like) presumes that these subgroups of consumers have already been identified; in other words, the market has been segmented. In fact, it is reasonable to suggest that in order to develop effective marketing strategies, managers should employ the concept of segmentation in all studies.

a priori segmentation
Studies in which the basis for segmentation, such as use, brand loyalty, and product purchase, is specified in advance of the segmentation analysis.

Types of Market Segmentation Studies

Segmentation studies generally follow one of two types of approaches.[11]

1. *A priori segmentation.* In **a priori segmentation** designs the basis for segmentation (e.g., usage, brand loyalty, product purchase) is specified in

---

[10]A comprehensive, critical review of the theory, research, and practice of market segmentation can be found in Yoram Wind, "Issues and Advances in Segmentation Research," *Journal of Marketing Research*, August 1978, pp. 317–37.

[11]These distinctions, *a priori* and *post-hoc*, were suggested by P. E. Green, "A New Approach to Market Segmentation," *Business Horizons*, February 1977, pp. 61–73.

advance of the segmentation analysis. In other words, the segments are defined a priori and the analysis centers on profiling the various subgroups of consumers on the basis of product use characteristics, size, demographic variables, psychographics, and other relevant characteristics.

2. *Post-hoc segmentation.* In **post-hoc segmentation** designs segments are defined after the fact on the basis of some sort of clustering of respondents on a set of relevant characteristics (e.g., benefit sought, need, or attitudes). Once the segments have been formed, they are profiled on the basis of size, product use characteristics, and respondent background variables.

post-hoc segmentation Studies in which segments are defined after the fact on the basis of some sort of clustering of respondents on a set of relevant characteristics such as benefit sought, need, and attitudes.

In a priori segmentation studies the basis for segmentation must be specified in advance. Obviously, management's needs and knowledge of the market under study ultimately will determine what base will be used. Yoram Wind, an expert in the theory and practice of segmentation research, has listed several of his preferred bases for segmentation.[12]

- Benefits sought (in industrial markets, the criterion used is purchase decision).
- Product preference.
- Product purchase and use patterns.
- Brand loyalty and switching patterns.
- Reaction to new concepts (intention to buy, preference over current brand, and so on).
- Price sensitivity.
- Deal-proneness.
- Media use.
- Psychographic/lifestyle.
- Store loyalty and patronage.

The choice of descriptor variables to use for the purpose of profiling the segments is a more difficult question. First, there are an enormous number of descriptor variables from which to choose. Second, *actionable descriptor variables* should be used: The information on the discriminating descriptors can be used by management in developing the firm's marketing strategies. Third, there should be a relationship between the descriptors selected and the basis for segmentation in order for managers to identify segments with varying sensitivities to marketing-mix variables on the basis of demographic and other segment descriptors.

Research Design

The research design for a prototypical market segmentation study can be described in terms of the following seven stages:[13]

---

[12]Yoram Wind, "Issues and Advances in Segmentation Research," p. 320.
[13]Ibid, p. 321.

1. Selection (a priori) or determination (post-hoc) of the basis for segmentation.
2. Selection of a set of segment descriptors (including hypotheses on the possible link between these descriptors and the basis for segmentation).
3. Sample design—mostly stratified and occasionally a quota sample according to the various classes of the dependent variable.
4. Data collection.
5. Formation of the segments based on a sorting of respondents into categories.
6. Establishment of the (conditional) profile of the segments.
7. Translation of the findings about the segments' estimated size and profile into specific marketing strategies, including the selection of target segments and the design or modification of specific marketing strategies.

Note that with the exception of the fifth step, relating to the formation of the segments, and sometimes the third step, relating to the specific sample design used, the research designs for both a priori and post-hoc segmentation studies are the same.

Analysis Techniques

Most segmentation studies follow a two-step analysis procedure. In the first stage respondents are classified into segments. In the second stage the various segments are profiled in terms of key discriminatory variables.

Cluster Analysis. In a priori segmentation studies the delineation of clusters, or **cluster analysis,** is straightforward—respondents usually are sorted on the basis of the dependent variable (basis for segmentation). However, some thought should be given to the conceptual implications of the operational definition being used and the sensitivity of the resulting segments to this definition. For example, consider the frequently used segmentation base of brand loyalty and, specifically, the segments of brand-loyal users versus brand-switchers. An immediate question is how should the sample be divided? That is, what operational definition of brand loyalty should be used?

In post-hoc segmentation studies respondents must be allocated to the various segments in some way. The objective of most cluster analyses is to arrive at clusters of objects (i.e., people, brands, etc.) that display small within-segment variation relative to the between-segment variation. There are a large number of different clustering algorithms available. Two of the more conventional approaches are **hierarchical clustering** and **partitioning clustering.** Hierarchical clustering techniques perform successive fusions or divisions of the data. In this case, the allocation of an object to a segment is irrevocable. Once an object joins a segment it is never removed and fused with other objects that belong to some other segment.

Two major types of hierarchical clustering techniques are the **bottom-up approach** and the **top-down approach.** A bottom-up approach builds up clusters; at

---

cluster analysis
Commonly used technique for allocating respondents to segments where respondents are clustered on the basis of benefit sought, need, or other relevant characteristics and where the number and type of segments are determined by the clustering technique that is used.

hierarchical clustering
Techniques that allow successive fusion or divisions of the data. The allocation of an object to a segment is irrevocable.

partitioning clustering
Techniques that form segments on the basis of minimizing (or maximizing) some criterion, e.g., within-segment to between-segment variation. Objects can be reallocated.

bottom-up approach
Process of building up clusters—at the beginning, each respondent belongs to his or her own segment, and then segments are joined together on the basis of their similarity.

top-down approach
Process of breaking down clusters—at the beginning, all respondents belong to one segment, and then respondents are partitioned into two segments, then three segments, and so on until each respondent occupies his or her own segment.

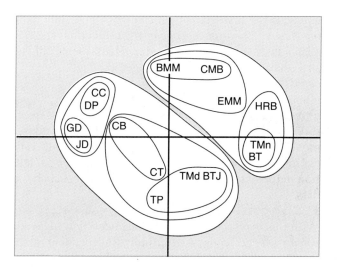

EXHIBIT 17–2
—
Complete-Link
Hierarchical
Clustering Solution
for the 15 Food
Items

Key:

1.	Toast pop-up	TP
2.	Buttered toast	BT
3.	English muffin and margarine	EMM
4.	Jelly donut	JD
5.	Cinnamon toast	CT
6.	Blueberry muffin and margarine	BMM
7.	Hard rolls and butter	HRB
8.	Toast and marmalade	TMd
9.	Buttered toast and jelly	BTJ
10.	Toast and margarine	TMn
11.	Cinnamon bun	CB
12.	Danish pastry	DP
13.	Glazed donut	GD
14.	Coffee cake	CC
15.	Corn muffin and butter	CMB

Source: R. E. Green and V. R. Rao, *Applied Multidimensional Scaling: A Comparison of Approaches and Algorithms* (New York: Holt, Rinehart & Winston, 1972), p. 31.

the beginning, each respondent belongs to his or her own segment, and then segments are joined together on the basis of their similarity. A top-down approach breaks down clusters; at the beginning, all respondents belong to one segment, and then respondents are partitioned into two segments, then three segments, and so on until each respondent occupies his or her own segment. Partitioning techniques form segments on the basis of minimizing (or maximizing) some criterion, for example, within-segment to between-segment variation. In contrast to hierarchical clustering techniques, partitioning techniques do not require that the allocation of an object be irrevocable; that is, objects may be reallocated if their initial assignments were, indeed, inadequate.

Exhibit 17–2 presents an illustration of hierarchical clustering applied to consumer ratings of 15 breakfast food items.[14] In the figure the innermost circles

[14]Green and Rao, *Applied Multidimensional Scaling.*

represent the first level of clustering; that is, buttered toast (BT) and toast and margarine (TMn) formed one of the initial (first-stage) segments. You will note at a later stage, hard rolls and butter (HRB) joined this segment. At the final stage all 15 breakfast food items join together.

Cluster Profiles.   Once the segments have been defined and respondents sorted into categories, the researcher focuses on profiling each segment in terms of its distinctive features. These profiles are called **cluster profiles.** The three most commonly used procedures for profiling segments are (1) simple cross tabulations, (2) multiple discriminant analysis, and (3) some variant of an **automatic interaction detection algorithm,** such as AID,[15] that searches for interactions in a set of data.

Cross tabulations are perhaps the simplest approach to profiling segments. With this approach the basis for segmentation (dependent variable) is cross classified with the segment descriptors (independent variables). Such tables can be used to make distinctive statements about the various segments. You will recall that we discussed and illustrated cross tabulations and methods for analysis in Chapters 14 and 15.

Multiple discriminant analysis has been frequently used in a segment profiling technique as well as in product positioning. In the case of standard discriminant analysis, the segments serve as the group factor. Segment descriptors are entered in a sequential or stepwise fashion and are assessed with respect to their discriminatory powers. The group centroids are used to position each group on the discriminant dimensions, and the correlation of each variable with the respective function is used as a means of interpreting the space.

AID-like algorithms have been successfully used in a large number of commercial applications. The standard AID procedure is restricted to dichotomous data (binary splits). Put simply, AID sequentially divides a total sample into mutually exclusive subgroups through a series of binary splits. Each split is determined by selecting a predictor variable and its categories that maximize the reduction in the unexplained variation in the dependent variable. The end result of this process is to have one group with a low criterion score (i.e., value of the dependent variable) and the other with a high criterion score. The process begins by considering, for each predictor variable in turn, the best split defined in terms of the ratio of B_c/T_c, where B_c is the between-groups sums of squares, T_c is the total sums of squares, and the subscript c is used to denote the criterion variable. Once the binary splits have been formed for each variable, the variable with the highest B_c/T_c is used to partition the total sample, and all other splits are discarded. Next each subgroup is treated as though it were a separate initial sample, and the process is repeated on that subgroup with the largest total sums of squares on the criterion variable. The process terminates if the B_c for that unsplit group having the largest T_c is less than some predetermined value, usually expressed as a percentage of the T_c for the entire sample.

cluster profiles
Profiling of each segment in terms of its distinctive features.

automatic interaction detection algorithm
Division of a total sample into mutually exclusive subgroups (segments) through a series of splits. Each split is determined by selecting a predictor variable and its categories that maximize the reduction in the unexplained variation in the dependent variable.

---

[15]J. A. Sonquist, *Multivariate Model Building* (Ann Arbor: Survey Research Center, 1970).

EXHIBIT 17–3   AID Analysis of Average Monthly Long-Distance Bill

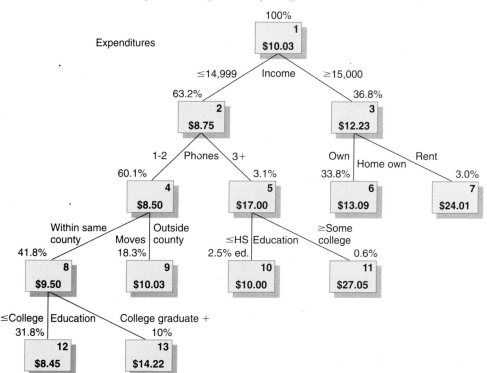

Source: W. R. Dillon and M. Goldstein, *Multivariate Analysis: Methods and Applications* (New York: John Wiley & Sons, 1984), p. 185.

To provide a specific illustration of how AID works consider Exhibit 17–3, which contains the tree developed from the AID analysis based on average monthly long-distance telephone charges (in dollars) and seven predictor variables. The figure can be read as follows: The entries outside of each box give the variable selected, its best split, and the percentage of the relevant sample—that is, of the previous split—belonging to each partition. The entry in the upper corner in each box numbers the stage in the splitting process. The dollar amount located in the center of each box is the average monthly long-distance telephone expenditure corresponding to the particular profile partition.

The process begins with family income. This variable is most important in the sense of producing the largest decrease in the unexplained variation in monthly long-distance telephone expenditures. The two segments generated at this stage relate to families with incomes less than $15,000 who expend, on the average, $8.75 per month, and those with incomes greater than $14,999 who expend $12.23. The segments' sizes are, respectively, 63.2 percent and 36.8 percent of the total sample. At the next stage each branch is considered separately. For those families that have income less than $15,000, the number of telephones (1 or 2 versus 3 or more) is split on, whereas for families whose income is in excess of

$14,999, home ownership (owns versus rent) is the splitting factor. Note that the partition segment sample percentages sum to the segment percentage of the immediately preceding partition (e.g., for the number of phones, 60.1 + 3.1 = 63.2). The algorithm proceeds in a similar fashion and selects that variable whose split produces the largest decrease in the unexplained variation in expenditures for a previously defined split. It appears that family income, number of telephones, home ownership, location of previous move, and head of household's education are the important predictors. These variables generate 12 distinct segments or clusters based on the best binary splitting of each.

As a final comment, note the asymmetry of the AID tree. Asymmetric trees must be indicative of higher order effects, that is, the presence of interactions. Typically, such nonadditive effects are investigated by a series of two-factor plots. For example, in the case of Exhibit 17–3 we might plot number of phones versus moves, number of phones versus head of household's education, and so on. Interaction effects are discussed further in Chapters 7 and 15.

Syndicated Services

We discussed syndicated data sources in Chapters 3 and 4. Specifically, in Chapter 3 we mentioned the Simmons Research Bureau and SRI International as sources of marketing-related information. Recently, several syndicated services that specifically provide information on target segments have become available.

PRIZM Neighborhood Lifestyle Clusters. The **PRIZM neighborhood lifestyle clusters** system assigns individuals to unique market segments on the basis of where the individual lives. The premise underlying the PRIZM system is that choice of neighborhood is the most basic consumer decision and one that ultimately reflects lifestyle choices. Census demographics coupled with other lifestyle factors form the basis of the PRIZM lifestyle clusters—neighborhoods with statistically similar demographics or lifestyle portraits form the clusters. PRIZM lifestyle clusters have been used for (1) explaining differences in behavior, responsiveness, and potential profitability; (2) targeting messages and offers; and (3) geographically locating prospects.

VALS. We discussed the VALS system in Chapter 3. The value and lifestyles program of SRI International divides Americans into nine types, identified by lifestyle, which are grouped into four categories on the basis of self-image, aspirations, and products used. Survivors and Sustainers are in the Need-Driven category, which accounts for 11 percent of the population; I-Am-Me's, Experientials, and the Societally Conscious are in the Inner-Directed category, 19 percent of the population; Belongers, Emulators, and Achievers in the Outer-Directed category, 68 percent of the population; and at the very top of the VALS hierarchy is the last type, the Integrateds, a mere 2 percent of the population. Exhibit 17–4 provides a more detailed description of each segment in terms of consumption patterns, media habits, and attitudes.

PRIZM neighborhood lifestyle clusters
Assigns individuals to unique market segments on the basis of where the individual lives; underlying premise is that choice of neighborhood is the most basic consumer decision and one that ultimately reflects lifestyle choices.

EXHIBIT 17–4
———
VAL Segment
Profiles

The Need Driven

Survivors

- Consumption patterns: Cigarettes; decaffeinated coffee; over-the-counter painkillers; small heater units.
- Media habits: Television game shows and soap operas; afternoon radio.
- Attitudes: Despairing; conservative; resigned.

Sustainers

- Consumption patterns: Beer; cold cereal; soft drinks; canned and prepackaged foods; cheap cameras.
- Media habits: Daytime television; radio news, talk shows, and ethnic programs; classified newspaper ads.
- Attitudes: Hopeful; resentful; not concerned with rules.

The Outer-Directed

Belongers

- Consumption patterns: American automobiles; garden equipment; canned vegetables.
- Media habits: Television soap operas; home magazines; country music.
- Attitudes: Conforming; unexperimental; church, family, and home oriented; patriotic.

Emulators

- Consumption patterns: Fast foods; cosmetics; weight-lifting equipment; prepared cocktail mixes.
- Media habits: Television adventure shows; progressive radio; automotive magazines.
- Attitudes: Ambitious; frustrated; envious.

Achievers

- Consumption patterns: Luxury cars; high-technology products; golfing; frozen entrees; wine; health and fitness gear.
- Media habits: Pay cable TV; business and sports magazines.
- Attitudes: Decisive; competitive; in search of fame and material success.

Inner-Directeds

I-Am-Me's

- Consumption patterns: Frozen pizza; corn chips; sheet music.
- Media habits: Television adventure shows; progressive radio; science and technology magazines.
- Attitudes: Spontaneous; receptive to new ideas, situations, and environments; flamboyant.

Experientials

- Consumption patterns: Yogurt; mineral water; foreign-made cars; foreign travel.
- Media habits: Little television viewing; adult rock and classical music; special-interest magazines.
- Attitudes: Idealistic; emotional; liberal; supportive of environmental protection.

Societally Conscious

- Consumption patterns: Small cars; tennis and hiking equipment; photography supplies; ethnic foods; natural cheese.
- Media habits: Public television; business and science magazines; radio news.
- Attitudes: Self-reliant; socially responsible; little faith in government; strong interest in the arts.

Integrateds

- Consumption patterns: Outdoor recreation; nonfiction books; imported products.
- Media habits: Little television viewing except for sports and documentaries; business, home, and special-interest magazines.
- Attitudes: Extremely self-aware; well adjusted; trusting; supportive of free enterprise.

Source: SRI International.

MARKET STRUCTURE STUDIES

Perceptual product maps provide insights about what products or brands are competitors, and so they can be used to define the boundaries of a market. Segmentation analysis provides insights into the reasons why a set of products or brands is competitive, and therefore, it can be used to explain a market. Neither procedure, however, provides information on the *magnitude* of competition among a set of products or brands. Procedures that attempt to measure the degree of substitutability between a set of competing products or brands fall under the umbrella of **market structure analysis.**

market structure analysis
The process of organizing a set of products or brands in terms of the degree of substitutability or competitiveness.

Philosophy and Objectives

The importance of accurately characterizing the structure of a market can be illustrated by examining Exhibit 17–5. The figure shows two alternative hypothetical structures presumed to characterize the instant coffee category. In part *a* the coffee brands are partitioned according to the attributes or features they possess. This type of partition is called form or attribute based. In part *b* the partitioning is according to brand, and consequently this type of partitioning is called brand based. The structures shown in the figures are called **hierarchical structures** because the brands are partitioned into several nested subsets. The representations are constructed in such a way that as one moves down the hierarchy the intensity of competition is presumed to increase. For example in part *a*, because Folgers and Maxwell House are partitioned at the lowest level of the hierarchy the presumption is that these two brands competed more fiercely against each other than either one does against, say, High Point. Another way of saying this is that according to part *a* we would expect more switching between Folgers and Maxwell House than, say, between Maxwell House and High Point.

hierarchial structure
Partitioning of brands into several nested subsets.

The two alternative hierarchies have very different implications. In one case (part *a*) consumers are presumed to first decide on the type of coffee to buy, either caffeinated or decaffeinated, and either regular or freeze dried. In the other case (part *b*) consumers are presumed to first decide on which brand of coffee to buy and then to make decisions concerning caffeination and processing. The competitive implications of these alternative representations are also markedly different. To illustrate consider the position of Proctor & Gamble (P&G), the manufacturers of High Point. If the coffee market is brand based (part *b*), then the absence of, say, a caffeinated regular brand does not hurt P&G's position in the market since, if such a variety were introduced, many of its customers would come from P&G's established brand, Tasters Choice. In other words, according to part *b*, any new product introduction would have acute cannibalistic effects. The situation is quite different if the coffee category is attribute based. Under the scenario depicted in part *a* of the figure, P&G could increase its share of market by introducing a caffeinated regular brand since this type of coffee would compete against Nescafe, Folgers, and Maxwell House, all of which are competitive brands.

EXHIBIT 17–5   A Hypothetical Illustration of the Product Hierarchy for the Instant Coffee Market

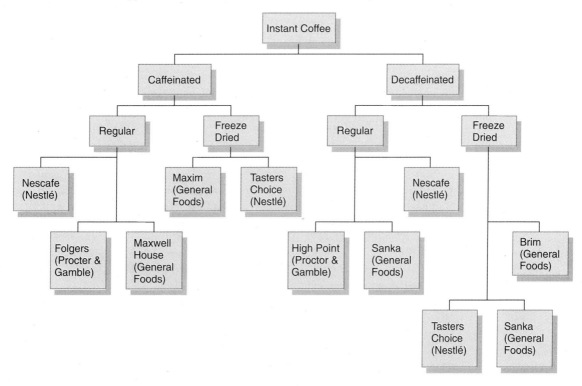

a. Attribute-based hierarchy

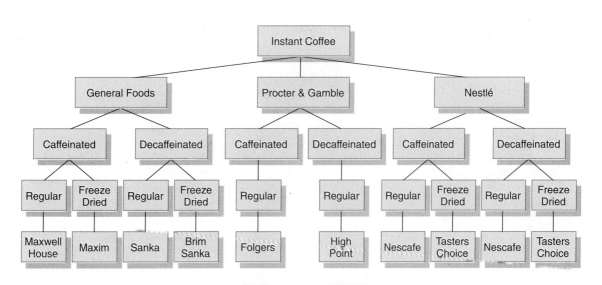

b. Brand-based hierarchy

Types of Market Structure Studies

Market structure studies can be classified according to (1) type of data used, (2) structure imposed, and (3) approach to analysis.

purchase or use behavior data
Information providing the most accurate indication of what people do or have done.

cross-price elasticity of demand
The percentage of change in demand for one product divided by the percentage change in price of the second product, assuming that all other factors affecting demand are constant.

brand switching
The probability of purchasing brand X, given that brand Y was purchased on the last purchase occasion.

judgmental data
Information generally based on perceptions or preference—may give better indications of future patterns of consumption.

decision sequence analysis
Process that uses protocols of consumer decision making that indicate the sequence in which various pieces of information (e.g., price or brand name) are employed to reach a final decision.

derived substitutability
Form of judgmental data collection where respondents indicate the degree to which a set of products or brands are substitutes.

Data Used.   Market structure procedures rely on either purchase or use behavior data or consumer judgmental data.

Purchase or use behavior data provide the most accurate indication of what people either do or have done. **Cross-price elasticity of demand** is a form of purchase/use data that measures the percentage of change in demand for one product divided by the percentage change in price of the second product—assuming that all other factors affecting demand are constant. A positive cross-price elasticity indicates substitutes, and a negative cross-price elasticity indicates complements. **Brand switching** is the probability of purchasing brand X, given that brand Y was purchased on the last purchase occasion. Brand switching is typically estimated on the basis of panel data. Panel data consist of a household's purchases of specific brands over some period of time. So-called purchase history strings are analyzed, and the frequency with which purchases of a given brand are preceded by purchases of a different brand are computed. The tacit assumption with this type of data is that respondents are more likely to switch between close substitutes than between distant ones, and consequently, brand switching incidences are indicative of brand substitutability.

Judgmental data are based on perceptions or preference and may give better indications of future patterns of consumption. **Decision sequence analysis** uses protocols of consumer decision making that indicate the sequence in which various pieces of information (e.g., price or brand name) are employed to reach a final decision. Typically, respondents are asked to verbalize what they are thinking as they make purchase decisions during the course of a shopping trip. The verbal account of their decision process is called a protocol. For *perceptual mapping*, similarity (dissimilarity) data are used to arrive at a geometric representation of the competitive nature of a market. When **derived substitutability** is used, respondents are asked to indicate, in some manner, the degree to which a set of products or brands are substitutes. These data can be collected by simple direct rating scales,[16] free responses,[17] or the dollar metric approach.[18]

Structure Imposed.   Market structure studies can be classified according to whether a hierarchical structure is imposed. We introduced an example of hierarchically structured markets in Exhibit 17–5. In such markets, the products or

---

[16]For an illustrative example, see Y. Wind, "The Perception of a Firm's Competitive Position," in *Behavioral Models for Market Analysis*, ed. F. M. Nicosia and Y. Wind (New York: Dryden Press), pp. 163–81.

[17]For an illustrative example, see P. E. Green, Y. Wind, and A. K. Jain, "Analyzing Free Response Data in Marketing Research," *Journal of Marketing Research*, February 1973, pp. 45–52.

[18]For an illustrative example, see E. A. Pessemier, *Product Management: Strategy and Organization* (Santa Barbara, Calif.: Wiley/Hamilton, 1977), pp. 203–54.

brands are sequentially partitioned into mutually exclusive and exhaustive subsets. The implicit assumption is that switching is more likely to occur at lower levels in the hierarchy than at higher levels. In other words, brands occupying subsets at lower levels in the hierarchy are presumably very similar to each other (i.e., they share certain features), as opposed to brands occupying other subsets higher up in the hierarchy; thus, at lower levels in the hierarchy the flow of switching is higher and the greater is the degree of competition between products or subsets of brands.

Approach to Analysis.   There are two general ways to proceed with a market structure analysis. We can assume that no prior knowledge of the structure of the market is known and proceed with the analysis in a purely **exploratory analysis** fashion; in such cases the data alone, in the form of household purchases or consumer judgments, provide the basis for the structure. In contrast to exploratory analysis, we can use prior knowledge of the presumed relationships among a set of products or brands to infer what the structure should look like. We can then use a method whereby we can restrict the system to be consistent with the hypothesized structure. In this sense, we are not relying solely on the data, but on a combination of what we actually observe in the marketplace and what we expect to observe based on our understanding of the product/service market under study. This type of an approach to market structure analysis is generally referred to as **confirmatory analysis** because through it we attempt to confirm or negate a hypothesized structure.

Methods for Investigating Structure

Many methods have been proposed for investigating the competitive structure of a product/service market. Even though it is not possible to discuss all of them, we describe three behavioral methods in Exhibits 17–6, 17–7, and 17–8. Each of these attempts to partition a market into competitive submarkets under the assumption that relatively high levels of switching among products or brands indicates close substitutes.

exploratory analysis
Type of analysis in which it is assumed that no prior knowledge of the structure of the market is known. In such cases, the data alone provide the basis for the structure that is uncovered.

confirmatory analysis
Approach that uses prior knowledge of the presumed relationships among a set of products or brands to infer what the structure should look like; also uses a method whereby we can restrict the parameters of the system so that they are consistent with the hypothesized structure.

EXHIBIT 17–6
—
Empirical Hendry System

empirical Hendry system
Method for investigating competitive structure where switching between competitive products is proportional to the product of market shares.

Premise:	Switching between competitive products is proportional to the product of market shares. The theoretical switching matrix is compared with the actual switching matrix. A proposed market partitioning is an adequate representation if switching within and among partitions is proportionate.
Data:	Brand-switching data.
Procedure:	1. Proposed market partitioning. 2. Calculate switching constants empirically within and across partitions. 3. Assess adequacy of proposed structure using goodness-of-fit tests

Source: M. U. Kalwani and D. G. Morrison, "A Parsimonious Description of the Hendry System," *Management Science,* January 1977, pp. 467–97.

EXHIBIT 17–7

——

Hierarchical
Clustering

Premise:	Consumers engage in a nonobservable hierarchical choice process. The lower the level in the hierarchy, where the "flow" of switching is higher, the greater the degree of competition between products or partitions.
Data:	Brand-switching data.
Procedure:	1. Set up a brand-switching matrix.
	2. Choose an approximate *proximity measure* (or similarity index) based on the flow of consumers between two products.
	3. Set up the resulting similarity matrix.
	4. Choose a clustering method.
	5. Cluster the proximity matrix.
	6. Test and interpret the solution.
	7. Compare different hierarchical structures for segment differences.

Source: R. R. Vithala and D. J. Sabavala, "Inference of Hierarchical Choice Processes from Panel Data," *Journal of Consumer Research,* June 1981, pp. 85–96.

EXHIBIT 17–8

——

Prodegy

prodegy
Method of investigating competitive structure in which consumers, faced with the deletion of a preferred product, will switch to a close competitor.

Premise:	Consumers, faced with the deletion of a preferred product, will switch to a close competitor. A proposed market structure is adequate if this "forced switching" within partitions is substantially greater than in unstructured markets.
Data:	Forced-choice data or brand-switching data.
Procedure:	1. Proposed market partitioning.
	2. Calculate difference in forced switching between structured and unstructured markets.
	3. Assess the adequacy of a proposed structure by using Z-test of differences in proportions.

Source: G. L. Urban, P. L. Johnson, and J. R. Hauser, "Testing Competitive Market Structures," *Marketing Science,* Spring 1984, pp. 83–112.

SUMMARY

This chapter has described various types of studies that attempt to provide information about the composition and structure of the competitive arena that a firm operates in. National market studies focus primarily on the changes that may have occurred in the competitive market over time. Strategic market studies are generally custom research products, and they focus on an indepth analysis of a product/service market. We considered three kinds of strategic market studies—*positioning studies*, through which an attempt to define market boundaries is made on the basis of consumer percep-

tions or preference; *market segmentation studies*, through which an attempt is made to identify segments of consumers who respond to marketing-mix variables in similar ways; and *market structure studies*, through which an attempt is made to investigate the extent of competition among a set of alternative brands. All of the studies discussed in this chapter can be used to formulate marketing strategies and to shape the course of subsequent marketing research activities relating to concept and product testing, package testing, advertising research, and test markets.

KEY CONCEPTS

strategic market studies

positioning studies

product maps

market segmentation studies

a priori segmentation

post-hoc segmentation

cluster analysis

cluster profiles

AID algorithm

market structure studies

REVIEW QUESTIONS

1. Discuss the role and importance of market studies in marketing research and, more generally, in developing marketing strategies.

2. Discuss the circumstances that would lead you to recommend that a strategic market study be undertaken.

3. As a recent addition to the marketing team of a major consumer package firm, you are asked to explain how product maps work.

4. Discuss the major research approaches to market segmentation.

5. Can the sellers of industrial and institutional goods and services also benefit from market segmentation and market structure studies? What suggestions can you offer for segmenting and structuring industrial markets?

METHODS USED TO GENERATE PRODUCT MAPS

Three major approaches have been used to generate product maps: multidimensional scaling (MDS), principal components analysis (PCA), and multiple discriminant analysis (MSA).

For discussion purposes, consider Table 17A–1, which presents the mean attribute ratings and standardized scores for each of four automobile brands. (We discussed how standardized scores are computed in Chapter 14.) The data were collected in a 1980 study in which 500 individuals rated the VW Rabbit, Plymouth Horizon/Omni, Chevrolet Chevette, and Honda Civic on five product characteristics. The attribute ratings were collected on nine-point rating scales. In the present context the standardized scores (which we will need in computing the location of a brand in the perceptual space) are obtained as follows: First, for each brand and attribute we compute the standard deviation of scores across all 500 respondents; next we subtract the average score for each brand on each attribute (see Table 17A–1) from each respondent's original rating, and we divide by the respective attribute's standard deviation.

Let us now turn our attention to the three common methods of creating product maps. Because these methods have been discussed in the Appendix to Chapter 16, the discussion will be brief.

TABLE 17A–1 Summary Measures

	Average Scores				
	Gas	Style	Reputation	Handling	Safety
Rabbit	7.66	5.02	6.97	6.51	5.75
Chevette	6.61	5.27	6.47	6.12	4.90
Horizon	6.57	5.54	5.35	5.61	4.71
Civic	7.50	5.21	6.02	6.16	4.47
	Standardized Scores				
	Gas	Style	Reputation	Handling	Safety
Rabbit	1.00	−1.12	1.11	1.11	1.18
Chevette	−0.83	0.05	0.39	0.05	0.31
Horizon	−0.90	1.30	−1.24	−1.32	−0.35
Civic	0.72	−0.23	−0.27	0.16	−1.18

Multidimensional scaling (MDS) can be used on direct comparison (rank-order) judgments regarding the similarities among a set of competing brands (non-metric MDS) or on derived similarities computed from respondents' rating of the brands on a set of product attributes (metric MDS). In either case, MDS creates a structure in which spatial proximities between brands are consistent with respondents' judgmental data on brand similarities or dissimilarities.

In the derived similarity approach, the first step is to compute the Euclidean distance between each pair of brands using the brand attribute ratings (see Chapter 16, Appendix 16A). Next, the Euclidean distances are submitted to an MDS procedure, and the dimensional solutions are examined. Exhibit 17A–1 shows a two-dimensional solution for the automobile data. You will note that the brands are spread out, and each automobile brand occupies one quadrant. Most notably, Rabbit is positioned to the far right of the origin, and Horizon is positioned to the far left. The uncovered dimensions and, specifically, the position of each brand in the space represent how the brands were perceived on the set of attributes. To interpret the space we can examine the correlation between a brand's rating on each attribute (gas economy, style, etc.) and its position on the two derived dimensions. In practice this is accomplished by simply regressing each of the five attribute (mean) ratings on the brand locations in the perceptual space; in other words, five regressions are run in which each attribute (mean rating) is the dependent variable and the brand coordinates are treated as independent variables. The association between the positions of the brands in the product map and each attribute is given by the standardized regression coefficients (beta weights). The standardized regression coefficients are given in Exhibit 17A–1. Thus reputation, handling, and safety are most associated with dimension 1, whereas dimension 2 reflects gas economy distinctions. Further technical details on MDS can be found in Chapter 16, Appendix 16A.

Principal components analysis (PCA) can also be used to uncover the dimensions underlying a product map. PCA uncovers dimensions that are linear combinations of the original attributes such that the uncovered dimensions account for as much variation in the original attribute ratings as possible. The first principal component, y_1, of the original attributes, $x_1, x_2, \ldots, x_p$, is that linear combination

$$y_1 = a_{11} x_1 + a_{21} x_2 + \ldots + a_{p1} x_p \qquad (17A–1)$$

of the attribute ratings whose sample variance

$$s_{y1}^2 = \sum_i \sum_j a_{i1} a_{j1} s_{ij} \qquad (17A–2)$$

is greatest; in other words, the first principal component (dimension) contains as much of the total information in all the p original attribute ratings as possible. Similarly, the second principal component, y_2, is the linear combination of the original attributes that account for the maximum amount of the remaining total variation not already accounted for by y_1. Further technical details regarding principal components were presented in Chapter 16, Appendix 16B.

Standardized regression coefficients dimension			
Attribute	1	2	R^2
(x_1) Gas economy	0.31	-0.95	0.81
(x_2) Style	0.74	-0.67	0.78
(x_3) Reputation	0.97	0.24	0.88
(x_4) Handling	0.95	0.31	0.89
(x_5) Safety	0.99	-0.14	0.91

loadings
Weights that give the correlation of the attribute with respect to the dimension.

In a prototypical product-map application using PCA, the analysis begins with the interattribute correlations computed across respondents and brands. The matrix of interattribute correlations is submitted to a PCA program that determines, among other things, the coefficients (that is, the a's) shown in Equation 17A–1. These weights, often called **loadings,** give the correlation of the attribute with the respective dimension. For the automobile data the loadings for the first two dimensions extracted from the (5 × 5) interattribute correlation matrix are shown on the side of Exhibit 17A–2. Consistent with the findings generated from using MDS, the first uncovered dimension reflects reputation, handling, and safety distinctions, whereas the second uncovered dimension is most associated with gas economy.

To position a particular automobile brand in the two-dimensional product space, we use Equation 17A–1 and the results shown in Table 17A–1 and the loadings. To illustrate, consider the Rabbit; substituting the respective loadings and standardized scores into Equation 17A–1 we have for dimension 1

$$y_1 = 0.54(1.0) + 0.67(-1.12) + 0.77(1.11) + 0.79(1.11) + 0.72(1.18) = 2.37$$

and for dimension 2

$$y_2 = 0.77(1.0) - 0.47(-1.12) + 0.08(1.11) + 0.40(1.11) - 0.27(1.18) = 1.11$$

Thus, the location of the Rabbit automobile in the perceptual product space is (2.37, 1.11). The positions of the other three brands of automobiles are given at the bottom of Exhibit 17A–2. The resulting perceptual product map is shown in this figure.

In the context of generating product maps, several features of PCA warrant some discussion. First, PCA that is based on interattribute correlations uncovers dimensions characterized by descriptive adjectives that mean the same thing to people; that is, PCA focuses on semantic meaning and, essentially, identifies groups of similar statements. Thus, one can say that PCA produces dimensions characterized by attributes that are seen as similar by respondents (i.e., people

		PCA loadings	
Attribute		y_1	y_2
(x_1) Gas economy		0.54	0.77
(x_2) Style		0.67	− 0.47
(x_3) Reputation		0.77	0.08
(x_4) Handling		0.79	0.04
(x_5) Safety		0.72	− 0.27

	Location of brands	
Automobile	*Dimension 1*	*Dimension 2*
Rabbit	2.37	1.11
Chevette	0.15	− 0.71
Horizon	− 1.86	− 1.36
Civic	− 0.70	0.97

EXHIBIT 17A–2

PCA Perceptual
Product Map

agree in their ratings). This means that the attributes that are most important in determining choice behavior could be overlooked if they were relatively independent of other attributes. Second, the importance of a dimension extracted by PCA with correlational input is determined by the number of attributes loading on the dimension and their perceived similarity—the more that are similar, the greater the apparent importance of the dimension. Thus, it is conceivable that the dimensions uncovered by PCA can be determined *in advance,* simply by determining how many statements about a given aspect of a brand (such as economy) will be rated by respondents.

Multiple discriminant analysis (MDA) is another approach to uncovering the dimensions underlying a product map. In the context of product-mapping applications, the brands serve as the groups. Discriminant analysis attempts to distinguish among a set of brands on the basis of a set of product attributes. Specifically, the objective in multiple discriminant analysis is to find axes (dimensions) that maximally separate the groups—that is, the axes maximize between-group to within-group variability. In the case of MDA the axes or dimensions that are uncovered represent linear combinations of the original attributes that best discriminate between the alternative brands. Letting z_i denote the ith discriminant function we have

$$z_i = b_0 + b_{1i}x_1 + b_{2i}x_2 + \ldots + b_{pi}x_p \qquad (17A\text{–}3)$$

where b_0 is a constant, and the $b_{1i}, b_{2i}, \ldots, b_{pi}$ are discriminant weights that reflect the importance of attribute p in the ith discriminant function. The number of **discriminant functions** retained define the dimensions of the perceptual product map; usually two or three discriminant functions are retained. The location of the brands in the perceptual product space is given by the mean rating on each discriminant function. These mean ratings, called **group centroids,** are obtained by entering average values on each attribute for each brand into each of the first two or three discriminant function equations in turn. Further technical details on discriminant analysis techniques were provided in Chapter 16, Appendix 16C.

multiple discriminant analysis (MDA)
Discriminant functions are linear combinations of the original attributes that best discriminate between the alternative brands.

discriminant functions
Axes or dimensions that in some sense account for brand differences.

group centroids
Mean ratings of each brand on each discriminant function.

EXHIBIT 17A–3   MDA Perceptual Product Map

	Discriminant function 1		Discriminant function 2	
Attribute	Weights	Correlations	Weights	Correlations
(x_1) Gas economy	– 0.43	– 0.15	0.93	0.68
(x_2) Style	0.66	0.21	0.25	– 0.002
(x_3) Reputation	– 0.75	– 0.65	– 0.72	– 0.42
(x_4) Handling	– 0.23	– 0.62	0.02	– 0.04
(x_5) Safety	0.10	0.42	– 0.29	– 0.27

	Location of brands	
Automobile	z_1	z_2
Rabbit	– 2.15	– 0.46
Chevette	0.11	– 1.13
Horizon	2.45	0.44
Civic	– 0.40	1.15

Dimension 2

Civic ●

Horizon ●

● Rabbit   Dimension 1

● Chevette

In MDA product-mapping applications the respondent × brand × attribute data are submitted to a discriminant analysis program, with the brands serving as the group factor. The **standardized discriminant function weights (the *b* coefficients)** indicate the importance of each attribute in distinguishing among the alternative brands. The standardized discriminant function weights for the four-automobile-brand/five-attribute data we have been discussing are shown on the side of Exhibit 17A–3. To interpret the dimensions the simple product moment correlations of each attribute with each dimension are also given. Note that the interpretation of each dimension is consistent with the previous analyses: Reputation, handling, and safety have the largest correlations with dimension 1, and gas economy has the largest correlation with dimension 2. To locate the brands in the perceptual product space we use Equation 17A–3 with the standardized weights and standardized scores shown in Table 17A–1. To illustrate, consider the Rabbit automobile; substituting the appropriate standardized weights and standardized scores into Equation 17A–3, we have for discriminant function 1

$$z_1 = - 0.43(1.00) + 0.66(-1.12) - 0.75(1.11)$$
$$- 0.23(1.11) + 0.10(1.18)$$
$$= - 2.15$$

And for discriminant function 2

$$z_2 = 0.93(1.00) + 0.25(-1.12) - 0.71(1.11)$$
$$+ 0.02(1.11) - 0.29(1.18)$$
$$= - 0.46$$

Thus, the location of the Rabbit automobile in the perceptual product space is $(-2.15, -0.46)$. The positions of the other three brands of automobiles are given on the side of Exhibit 17A–3. The resulting perceptual product map is shown in this figure.

In general, MDA will produce solutions that differ from those of either PCA or MDS. Differences in solutions are due to the fact that MDA takes into account the within-brand interattribute covariances, and the reduced space will be oriented to variables having relatively large between-brand to within-brand variation. Thus, compared with PCA and MDS, MDA will probably use fewer attributes; however, because the dimensions uncovered by MDA can be directly linked to attributes for which there exist large brand differences, the solution may actually prove more actionable in a managerial sense.

Concept and Product Testing

— Acquire an understanding of the importance of concept- and product-testing research.

— Describe the different types of concept tests.

— Define the purpose of procedures used in concept screening tests.

— Define the purpose of procedures used in concept evaluation tests.

— Discuss how conjoint analysis is used on concept/product development.

— Describe the role of product testing.

— Define the various types of product tests.

— Provide general guidelines concerning the appropriateness of monadic versus comparative product tests..

INTRODUCTION

In this chapter we provide a framework for understanding the practice of *concept* and *product* testing. The single most important determinant of market success is consumer acceptance of a firm's products. A consumer buys a product for its **end benefits,** that is, what the product offers in terms of satisfying the consumer's wants and needs, not simply what the physical product is. Concept- and product-testing procedures are directed at understanding consumers' perceptions of physical product characteristics, end benefits, and, consequently, the product's ultimate market acceptance. As such, concept and product tests play a necessary and integral role in developing effective marketing strategy.

CONCEPT TESTING: PHILOSOPHY AND OBJECTIVES

Put simply, a **concept** is an idea on its way to becoming a marketing strategy. A marketing strategy attempts to convince a target segment of consumers that a particular brand possesses those end benefits that they desire and presents evidence to support this claim. Concepts represent the essence of the product.

Thus, to be successful, concept testing must capture and effectively communicate this essence. Typically, concept tests are preceded by an **opportunity analysis** (usually contained within a market study—see Chapter 17), which identifies unfulfilled consumer wants and needs to ensure that the most salient product end benefits are communicated.

Concept testing provides a system for reshaping, redefining, and coalescing ideas to arrive at a basic concept for a product with greater vitality and potential for market acceptance. Specifically, concept tests are conducted to

1. Quantitatively assess the relative appeal of ideas or alternative product positionings that aim the product at different target segments by highlighting product features that are most desired by such segments of the population.
2. Provide necessary information for developing the product and product advertising.
3. Indicate segments of the population in which the appeal of the product is likely to be concentrated.

Procedures for concept testing vary greatly, depending on the stage of the research cycle. For example, concept testing can be used to screen new product ideas, to identify the most promising concepts. In this type of concept test, respondents are exposed to a **core benefit concept.** The core benefit concept focuses directly on the product's main end benefit, with little, if any, emphasis on secondary features. It is relatively emotionless, and its objective is not to persuade the consumer to buy the product. Exhibit 18–1 presents a core benefit concept. Alternatively, they can be used later in the prelaunch/test market phase to estimate ultimate consumer demand for the basic product concept before risking national rollout. In this type of concept test, respondents are exposed to a **positioning concept statement.** A positioning concept statement lists all of the product's end benefits as well as various secondary features; consequently, it is much longer than a core benefit concept, and it generally is several paragraphs long. In general, a positioning concept statement contains a photograph or illustration and it makes an attempt to persuade. Exhibit 18–2 (see page 560) presents a positioning concept statement. Finally, concept tests can be used after rollout of a product in established markets to investigate the level of consumer interest in a competitive new product concept in the prelaunch/test market phase or for line extensions of an existing brand. In this setting, the concept test could also identify the key appeal of the competitive entry and areas in which the established brand is particularly vulnerable.

end benefits
What the product offers in terms of satisfying the consumer's wants and needs.

concept
An idea aimed at satisfying consumer wants and needs.

opportunity analysis
Research to identify unfulfilled consumer wants and needs.

concept testing
A marketing research technique used to evaluate a concept's potential and ways of improving it.

core benefit concept
Focuses directly on product's main end benefit with little, if any, emphasis on secondary features.

positioning concept statement
Lists all the product's main end benefits and various secondary benefits.

**VASELINE INTENSIVE CARE LOTION MAKES
YOUR SKIN FEEL SOFT AND SMOOTH**

Treat your rough, dry skin with Vaseline Intensive Care Lotion. It causes your skin to heal fast and makes it smooth and soft.

Vaseline Intensive Care Lotion penetrates fast into your skin. And it doesn't feel greasy.

Source: David Schwartz, *Concept Testing* (New York: AMACOM, 1987), p. 6.

EXHIBIT 18–1
—
Vaseline Intensive Care Lotion Core Benefit Concept

EXHIBIT 18–2   Vaseline Intensive Care Lotion Positioning Concept

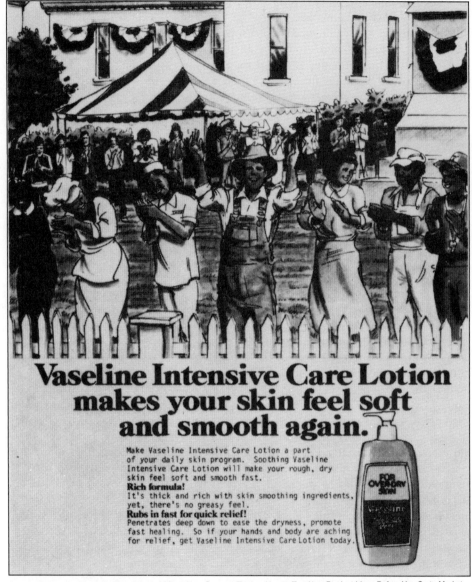

Vaseline Intensive Care Lotion makes your skin feel soft and smooth again.

Make Vaseline Intensive Care Lotion a part
of your daily skin program. Soothing Vaseline
Intensive Care Lotion will make your rough, dry
skin feel soft and smooth fast.
Rich formula!
It's thick and rich with skin smoothing ingredients,
yet, there's no greasy feel.
Rubs in fast for quick relief!
Penetrates deep down to ease the dryness, promote
fast healing. So if your hands and body are aching
for relief, get Vaseline Intensive Care Lotion today.

FOR OVER-DRY SKIN

Vaseline

Concept testing has proven effective for most kinds of products, excepting products that are radically innovative and that require significant changes in existing consumption patterns. Because such new products diffuse slowly through the population and require substantial commitment and behavioral change, a consumer's stated intentions with regard to them are likely to be highly unreliable. For example, before their introduction, it probably would have been difficult to

Category	Definitely Will Buy
Fragrance (no price)	9%
Detergents	12
Fragrance (with price)	18
Food	20
Cleaning products	28

TABLE 18–1
—
Average Purchase
Intent Scores in
Selected Categories

Source: David Schwartz, *Concept Testing* (New York: AMACOM, 1987), p. 46.

adequately assess the ultimate impact of personal computers, video games, pregnancy test kits, or other types of radically new technology.

TYPES OF CONCEPT TESTS

There are two broad categories of concept tests.

1. **Concept screening tests** identify and prioritize those ideas (out of a large number of concepts) with the greatest potential for further testing and development. The screening can be undertaken with respect to (1) many different new product ideas or (2) alternative end benefit incentives for the same new product idea. This type of concept testing is generally performed very early in the research cycle.

    concept screening tests *Concept tests for screening new product ideas or alternative end benefits for a single product idea.*

2. **Concept evaluation tests** gauge the level of consumer interest in a new product idea and determine the major strengths and weaknesses of the appeal. These tests are performed at various stages of the research cycle, that is, early in the prelaunch stage or just before a test market. Typically, however, they are performed after the process of initial screening and concept refinement.

    concept evaluation tests *Concept test designed to gauge consumer interest and determine strengths and weaknesses of the concept.*

Concept screening tests are designed to evaluate a set of ideas *before* significant resources are committed to their development. Most new-product ideas are not likely to meet with market acceptance. For example, consider Table 18–1, which provides average top box intent scores ("definitely buy") in several product categories. Thus, by employing effective concept-testing procedures, marketing research aids in making optimum use of research and development (R&D) laboratories as well as marketing budgets and management time.

CONCEPT SCREENING TESTS: IMPLEMENTATION

In concept screening tests, respondents are exposed to a series of many different new product concepts or alternative "benefit bundles" for the same product concept to (1) obtain a preliminary indication of market acceptance and (2) identify which ideas should be singled out for additional development and subsequent testing.

EXHIBIT 18–3
—
Project Proposal:
New Product
Concept Screening
Test

Brand:	New products.
Project:	Concept screening.
Background and Objectives:	The New York banking group has developed 12 new product ideas for investment products (services). The objectives of this research are to assess consumer interest in the concepts and to establish priorities for further development.
Research Method:	Concept testing will be conducted in four geographically dispersed, central location facilities within the New York metropolitan area.
	Each of the 12 concepts plus 1 retest control concept will be evaluated by a total of 100 men and 100 women with household incomes of at least $25,000. The following age quotas will be used for both male and female groups within the sample.
	18–34 = 50 percent 35–49 = 25 percent 50 & over = 25 percent
	Each respondent will evaluate a maximum of eight concepts. Order of presentation will be rotated throughout to avoid position bias.
	Because some of the concepts are in low-incidence product categories, user groups will be defined both broadly and narrowly in an attempt to asses potential among target audiences.
Information to Be Obtained:	This study will provide the following information to assist in concept evaluation: Investment ownership. Purchase interest (likelihood of subscription). Uniqueness of new service. Believability. Importance of main point. Demographics.
Action Standard:	In order to identify concepts warranting further development, top box purchase intent scores will be compared with the top box purchase intent scores achieved by the top 10 percent of the concepts tested in earlier concept screening studies. Rank order of purchase intent scores on the uniqueness, believability, and importance ratings will also be considered in the evaluation and prioritization of concepts for further development.
Material Requirements:	Fifty copies of each concept.
Cost:	The cost of this research will be $15,000 ± 10 percent
Timing:	This research will adhere to the following schedule:
	Fieldwork 1 week Top line 2 weeks Final report 3 weeks
Supplier:	Burke Marketing Research.

new product concept
screening test
*Concept screening tests
that focus on many new
product ideas.*

alternative buying
incentive concept
screening test
*Concept screening tests
that focus on alternative
end benefit incentives for
a single idea.*

When many new product ideas are involved, we refer to the procedure as a **new product concept screening test;** when the focus is on alternative end benefit incentives for a single idea, we refer to the procedure as an **alternative buying incentive concept screening test.** Exhibits 18–3 and 18–4 present prototypical marketing research proposals for these two procedures.

Brand:	Suave.
Project:	Hand lotion buying incentive test.
Background and Objectives:	The brand group is interested in assessing the potential of a large number of alternative strategies and claims in the hand lotion market. Accordingly, the objective of this research is to identify the key benefits of the hand lotion for incorporation in alternative concepts for subsequent testing.
Research Method:	Central location interviews will be conducted in four geographically dispersed markets with 200 adult women who are past-30-day hand lotion users. Age quotas will be

Age 18–34   45 percent
35–54   30 percent
55+   25 percent

	Respondents will be shown a series of benefit statements about hand lotion and asked to rate each in turn on purchase interest, uniqueness, believability, and importance. Order of presentation will be randomized in order to avoid position bias.
Information to Be Obtained:	— Category and brand use.
	— Purchase intention.
	— Purchase frequency (volume).
	— Uniqueness.
	— Believability.
	— Importance.
Action Standard:	— The themes that generate the highest percentage of top box purchase interest (percent saying "definitely would buy") will be incorporated into Suave advertising.
	— The statements that best communicate each theme, based on factor loading scores will be incorporated into Suave advertising.
Cost and Timing:	The cost of this research will be $10,000 ± 10 percent. The research will adhere to the following schedule

Fieldwork   1 week
Top line   2 weeks
Full tabulations   5 weeks
Final report   2 weeks

Supplier:	Leggett Lustig Firtle, Inc.

Procedures

Presentation of Concepts. In new product screening tests, the format used for presenting product descriptions (either core benefit concepts or positioning concept statements) to respondents is called a concept board. An illustrative **concept board** is presented in Exhibit 18–5 (see page 564). Essentially, only two elements are critical in the concept statement

1. Copy describing how the product works and its end benefits.
2. Some type of illustration, most often a simple line drawing, showing either the product or the product package.

concept board
Copy and possibly photograph or illustration that describes how the product works and its end benefits.

EXHIBIT 18–5   Illustative Concept Board

Lancia Introduces
Skillet Pizza

Now you can make real homemade pizza without using your oven.

With new SKILLET PIZZA, you can prepare a pizza that's fresher than the frozen variety and as delicious as any from a pizzeria—without turning on your oven.

Each SKILLET PIZZA package contains all the good ingredients you need, formulated to cook up into a perfect pizza in 20 minutes, in your skillet, on top of your stove. There are three flavors—cheese, pepperoni and sausage.

All come with a complete dough mix that only needs to have a half cup of cold water stirred in to form a dough that becomes a light crisp crust. No kneading. No waiting for dough to rise. And you can make the crust as thick or thin as you like.

There's a complete pizza sauce, too, rich and tomato-y, and to top it off in traditional style, a packet of shredded parmesan cheese is included in every package.

Directions are simple. Cook in your skillet, lid ajar, for 13 to 15 minutes. Uncover, cook another 3 to 5, and you have a beautiful golden thick crust pizza, to serve 4. LANCIA SKILLET PIZZA makes pizza the way your family loves it—without even turning on your oven.

The copy should be written simply without puffery and exaggeration. Photographs are generally not necessary for most product categories and tend to be expensive (exceptions are categories in which image plays an important part, e.g., cosmetics). The tendency is to also include price information, although in certain instances it may be omitted. When the name of the manufacturer adds real value to the new product concept, it should be explicitly stated.

Interviewing. Concept screening tests usually are conducted in a central location, although they also are conducted by telephone or mail. Typically, an intercept procedure in either a shopping mall, food store, or other high-traffic location is used. To judge consumer reaction in different markets, the interviewing can be divided among different cities. In new product concept screening tests the usual practice is to show each respondent no more than eight new product ideas, whereas when an alternative buying incentive concept screening test is used each respondent is exposed to a large number (at least 10 or 15, and possibly many more) of alternatives for the same product idea in order to screen to a smaller number for subsequent testing. Finally, it is preferable to expose each respondent to a variety of product ideas rather than to expose the same respondent to extremely similar concepts.

Focus groups are also frequently used to screen new product concepts (see Chapter 5); the groups are typically presented with five or six new concepts that provide the focus and orientation for discussion.

Questions Asked. In new product concept screening tests the most important questions to ask relate to

- Purchase intent.
- Purchase frequency (optional).
- Uniqueness of the idea.
- Believability of the idea.
- Importance of the (sales) message.

If an alternative buying incentive concept screening test is used, respondents are usually asked to rate the concepts, according to some sorting procedure, in terms of how interested they would be in purchasing the product. Other diagnostic questions typically relate to importance of the (sales) message, uniqueness, and believability.

Sampling Practices

In concept screening tests, nonprobability sampling procedures are used. Sample size determination is based on cost and conventional industry standards (see Table 8–2, Chapter 8).

Action Standard

A new product's top box (or top two box) intention score is the crucial factor determining whether the concept is singled out for further attention. This score is usually compared with some known normative data for the test category (e.g., 25 percent of the respondents in all food product concept tests say "definitely would buy.") Diagnostic questions pertaining to importance, believability, and uniqueness are examined with a view toward spotting weaknesses that, if corrected, might justify a concept's being recommended for subsequent testing.

In alternative buying incentive concept screening tests, the focus is on identifying (1) themes that generate the highest percentage of top box purchase intent scores and (2) statements that best communicate each theme. Other diagnostic questions pertaining to uniqueness, believability, and importance are used to identify strengths and weaknesses of each alternative buying incentive concept.

Analysis Approach

In both types of concept screening tests, the analysis centers on purchase intent scores. Standard ways of analyzing the purchase intent questions are to look at scores for either the top box ("definitely would buy") or the top two boxes ("definitely would buy" plus "probably would buy"), which is often referred to as the total positive interest score, across all of the rated concepts. Obviously, the objective of this analysis is to identify the proportion of potential buyers who have a strong interest in the product.

The diagnostic questions can be analyzed in a number of different ways. For example, the buying intent score and the unique score for each concept can be plotted. The quadrant of the grid in which each concept is located indicates the likelihood of ultimate market acceptance and the appropriate marketing strategy. To be more specific, each concept falls into one of the following four clusters:[1]

1. The me-too or generic products—characterized by concepts having high purchase intent scores but low product uniqueness scores. In order to be successful, a distinctive advantage must be created. Since the risks associated with products that are not really "new" are high, these concepts should be viewed with caution.

2. The winners—inhabited by concepts having high purchase intent scores and high product uniqueness scores. As such, these new product ideas have the greatest chance of meeting with market acceptance.

3. The long shots—characterized by concepts having low purchase intent scores and low product uniqueness scores. Unless the diagnostic data reveal specific correctable weaknesses, these product ideas should be eliminated from further consideration.

4. The fad or specialty products—inhabited by concepts having low purchase intent scores but high product uniqueness scores. These product ideas typically require high profit margins and are characterized by short product life cycles.

---

[1]Jeffrey L. Pope, *Practical Marketing Research* (New York: AMACOM, 1981), p. 138.

A typical approach in analyzing the results of alternative buying incentive concept tests is to cluster the various concept statements on the basis of their respective purchase intent scores to identify sets of concept statements having similar appeal. We want to identify subgroups of concept statements such that within a given subgroup the concept statements are *homogeneous* (small *within-cluster* variation), but across the subgroups the concept statements are *heterogeneous* (large *between-cluster* variation).

CONCEPT EVALUATION TESTS: IMPLEMENTATION

Typically, concept evaluation tests are conducted after initial screening and concept refinement. The purpose of a concept evaluation test is to

1. Assess market potential for each product (or product positioning).
2. Determine a product concept's strengths and weaknesses.
3. Provide an indication about the market segment in which each proposed product is likely to have the greatest acceptance.

Because concept evaluation tests involve a forecast of market potential, either in terms of share of market or unit/dollar volume, they are being used increasingly with slight modifications to help managers to decide whether to initiate a test market (see Chapter 21). Consequently, if we can determine prior to test marketing that a new product will not likely meet company objectives with respect to volume or share, the management team may decide to drop the product from further consideration and avoid the costs involved with test markets. In essence, concept evaluation tests are being used as a "simulated/pretest market" to acquire some perspective on how good the market is with a view toward determining which new product concepts should go into market testing. For this reason, we will discuss concept evaluation test services and specific forecasting techniques in Chapter 21, which considers test markets and simulated/pretest market (STM/PTM) applications. Exhibit 18–6 (see page 568) presents a prototypical concept evaluation test marketing research proposal. In this study, interest is focused on the relative strengths and weaknesses of each concept that is tested as well as each product's likely acceptance, although no forecasting of first-year sales is required.

Procedures

Presentation of Concepts. New product concepts can be presented to respondents in various ways. For example, concept boards, commercial advertisements, or actual product prototypes can be used. Because concepts have been previously screened and refined, the number of new product concepts or positionings being tested is typically small (two or three), and the product description formats tend to be more elaborate and, in some cases, reflect advertising copy scheduled to be used in actual market tests. In no case is a single concept tested in isolation. When a single concept is under study, either a second concept or a control concept should be included in the design. A control concept should be a product

EXHIBIT 18–6
—
Project Proposal:
Concept Evaluation
Test

Brand:	Sunshine.
Project:	Candy bar concept test.
Background and Objectives:	The brand group has developed three alternative positionings for the Sunshine product. The purpose of this research is to measure the relative appeal of the positionings and to identify market segments in which the product's appeal is likely to be concentrated.
Research Method:	A three-cell, monadic concept test will be conducted in geographically dispersed markets. Each concept will be exposed to 200 individuals who are past-30-day candy bar users. The following gender and age quotas, based on category volume, will apply to each cell:

Male = 45 percent   8–11 = 5 percent
Female = 55 percent   12–17 = 20 percent
                        18–34 = 35 percent
                        35–49 = 25 percent
                        50+ = 15 percent

Information to Be Obtained:	— Purchase intention.
	— Purchase frequency (volume/week).
	— Likes/dislikes.
	— Believability.
	— Uniqueness.
	— Overall rating.
	— Attribute ratings.
	— Importance of main benefit.
	— Other diagnostic questions.
	— Demographics.
Action Standard:	The positioning that generates the greatest top box purchase intention (percent saying "definitely would buy") will be recommended for further development.
Cost:	$22,500 ± 10 percent
Supplier:	Leggett Lustig Firtle, Inc.

that is available in the marketplace but that has low awareness levels among category users.

Interviewing. As in concept screening tests, interviews are typically conducted by intercept in a central location, but, again, interviewing could be conducted by mail or telephone, depending on budget constraints and study objectives. In order to identify the concept's target market, information on category and brand purchases should be obtained from respondents before they are exposed to the product description. Generally, a monadic design (Chapter 10) is used, that is, a separate group of respondents evaluates each alternative concept (or product positioning).

Questions Asked. After exposure to the product description the respondent is asked questions pertaining to

- Purchase intent.
- Purchase frequency (volume).
- Key benefit (open-ended question).
- Likes/dislikes (open-ended).
- Believability (open-ended).
- Uniqueness.
- Overall rating.
- Attribute ratings.
- Key benefit importance.
- Demographics.

Sampling Practices

In concept evaluation tests nonprobability sampling procedures are typically used. Interviews are usually completed on 200 respondents per concept. All respondents should be category users with specific age, sex, and user-group quotas, which usually are determined by total category volume contribution.

Action Standards

Action standards are generally explained in terms of top box (or top two box) purchase intent scores. If a sufficient number of concept evaluation tests have been completed, then category norms can be used. In cases in which a control concept has been used, the test concept should be recommended only if its purchase intent score is at least equal to that obtained by the control concept. The standard practice is to perform a test of the difference in purchase intent scores (i.e., either proportion saying "definitely would buy" or mean rating) for the test and control concepts at some prespecified confidence level (usually at least 80 percent). In cases in which interest centers on a forecast of first-year volume, volume predictions are compared with break-even levels and other category norms, if available.

Analysis Approach

Purchase intent scores are typically analyzed by use of conventional testing procedures. Tests of differences in proportions (for top box intent scores) or differences in means across alternative concepts or as compared with a control are accomplished with the use of testing procedures discussed in Chapter 15.

Data on uniqueness, believability, and end benefit importances are also analyzed to provide supporting diagnostic information. For example, quadrant analysis of end benefit importance scores and concept attribute ratings are often presented. You will recall that quadrant analysis was previously discussed in Chapter 14, Exhibit 18–7 (see page 570) presents a quadrant analysis conducted for a frozen-dinner product.[2] From the figure it is clear that the concept delivered a

---

[2]David Schwartz, *Concept Testing* (New York: AMACOM, 1987), p. 80.

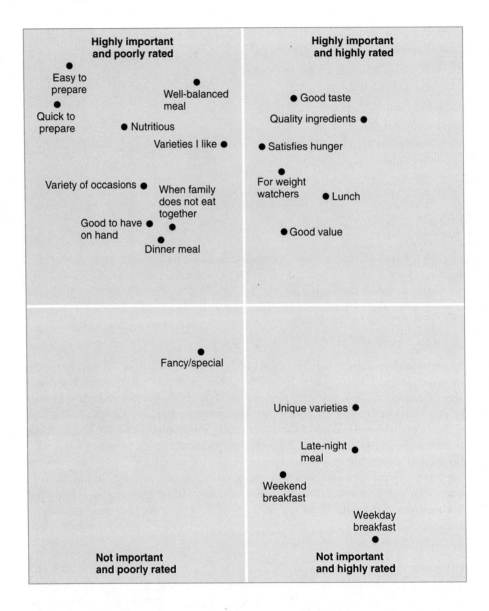

conjoint analysis
*An approach in which re-
spondents react to var-
ious products, brands,
and concepts, in terms of
overall preference, where
the various objects being
evaluated reflect a predetermined combination of
attributes in some sys-
tematic way.*

weak "convenience" message, which is an issue of high importance to the target
group. The concept adequately communicated end benefits relating to nutrition
and a well-balanced meal.

CONCEPT/PRODUCT DEVELOPMENT

A useful procedure for concept or product development is **conjoint analysis.** Conjoint analysis is particularly useful in concept and product testing when the potential set of relevant attributes that together define the new concept, product, or

service can be easily and realistically quantified. Typically, durable concepts, products (including industrial goods),[3] and services lend themselves to this approach to testing.

Overview

Put simply, conjoint analysis provides a way of modeling consumer preferences (or other reactions) for concepts, products, and services that are described in terms of bundles of attributes.

The first step in the execution of a conjoint study is to determine which attributes will be included in the study and what their levels will be. It is possible to predict preference only for products that can be described in terms of the attributes included in the study. The selection of attributes should be based on the following criteria:

1. They should capture the essence of any existing or potential products of interest.
2. They should differentiate among products.
3. The range of any quantitative attributes (such as price) should be broad enough to cover all anticipated specifications.

Several additional points are also worth noting. First, attribute definitions should be expressed in terminology from the respondent's point of view. Second, when soft (e.g., intangible or image) attributes are included, perceptual information should also be obtained. Third, it should be logically possible to present each level of each attribute with every level of every other attribute. Fourth, the attributes should represent independent dimensions of the product or service category. Finally, totally unacceptable attribute levels should not be included in the design because in principle it is assumed in the model that the presence of one attribute level can compensate for the absence (or undesirable) levels of some other attributes. If totally unacceptable attribute levels are used, this will not be the case. For example, if a respondent finds it totally unacceptable to pay a fee for using an automatic teller machine, then whenever this option (fee) is included in the profile description it does not matter what other features (attribute levels) are also present.

Conjoint analysis quantifies each individual's value system that is associated with the levels of the defining attributes. This is accomplished analytically by decomposing overall evaluations of a judiciously selected set of multiattribute products or services. The quantification process results in numbers called utilities, which represent that attribute's contribution to the overall evaluation.

A Specific Example. Suppose that a consumer package-goods company is concerned with consumer reactions to packaged soup mixes. Management interest centers on four attributes that are presumed to influence consumer preference

---

[3]For application of conjoint analysis to industrial goods, see F. Acito and T. P. Hustad, "Industrial Product Concept Testing," *Industrial Marketing Management*, 1981, pp. 67–73.

	Attribute (factor)	Description (level)
TABLE 18–2	Flavor	Onion
		Chicken noodle
Packaged Soup Attributes		Country vegetable
	Calories	80
		100
		140
	Salt-freeness	Yes
		No
	Price	1.19
		1.49

1. Flavor.
2. Calories (8 oz.).
3. Salt-freeness.
4. Price.

Under study are three alternative flavors, three alternative caloric levels, two alternatives involving salt-freeness, and two price alternatives. Table 18–2 describes the various alternatives. We will frequently refer to the attributes as *factors* and the specific values that they take on as *levels*; thus, we have 2 three-level factors and 2 two-level factors. There are in total $3 \times 3 \times 2 \times 2 = 36$ alternative product offerings. Table 18–3 describes each of the 36 product alternatives.

If conjoint analysis is used the respondent is asked to react to an alternative product in terms of an overall evaluation. The overall evaluation is generally a preference rating. For example, the respondent may be asked to rank the alternative products by overall preference, or the respondent may be asked to indicate his or her preference (from "least liked" to "most liked") for each alternative product on a nine-point scale. The last column in Table 18–3 shows one hypothetical respondent's actual rating of the 36 packaged soup alternatives, where the number 1 indicates "least liked" and the number 9 indicates "most liked." These data are used to compute the weight (i.e., the *utility*) of each attribute, which indicates how influential each is in shaping the consumer's overall evaluations.

Two basic data-collection procedures are used in conjoint analysis: the *trade-off procedure* and the *full-profile approach*. In the **trade-off procedure,** also commonly referred to as the *two-factor-at-a-time procedure*, the respondent is asked to consider two attributes at a time.[4] The respondent's task is to rank the various combinations of each pair of attribute descriptors from most preferred to· least preferred. Exhibit 18–8 (see page 574), part *a*, shows how this procedure is applied to consumer evaluations of packaged soup alternatives.

trade-off procedure
Technique where the respondent is asked to consider two attributes at a time—to rank the various combinations of each pair of attribute descriptors from most preferred to least preferred.

---

[4]R. M. Johnson, "Trade-Off Analysis of Consumer Values," *Journal of Marketing Research* 11 (1974), pp. 121–27.

Packaged Soup Alternative	Flavor	Calories	Salt-Freeness	Price	Rating*
1	Onion	80	Yes	$1.19	9
2	Onion	80	Yes	1.49	8
3	Onion	80	No	1.19	6
4	Onion	80	No	1.49	6
5	Onion	100	Yes	1.19	7
6	Onion	100	Yes	1.49	6
7	Onion	100	No	1.19	5
8	Onion	100	No	1.49	5
9	Onion	140	Yes	1.19	7
10	Onion	140	Yes	1.49	6
11	Onion	140	No	1.19	5
12	Onion	140	No	1.49	5
13	Chicken noodle	80	Yes	1.19	7
14	Chicken noodle	80	Yes	1.49	6
15	Chicken noodle	80	No	1.19	2
16	Chicken noodle	80	No	1.49	2
17	Chicken noodle	100	Yes	1.19	3
18	Chicken noodle	100	Yes	1.49	3
19	Chicken noodle	100	No	1.19	2
20	Chicken noodle	100	No	1.49	1
21	Chicken noodle	140	Yes	1.19	2
22	Chicken noodle	140	Yes	1.49	2
23	Chicken noodle	140	No	1.19	2
24	Chicken noodle	140	No	1.49	1
25	Country vegetable	80	Yes	1.19	9
26	Country vegetable	80	Yes	1.49	8
27	Country vegetable	80	No	1.19	7
28	Country vegetable	80	No	1.49	6
29	Country vegetable	100	Yes	1.19	8
30	Country vegetable	100	Yes	1.49	7
31	Country vegetable	100	No	1.19	6
32	Country vegetable	100	No	1.49	5
33	Country vegetable	140	Yes	1.19	6
34	Country vegetable	140	Yes	1.49	5
35	Country vegetable	140	No	1.19	5
36	Country vegetable	140	No	1.49	4

*1 = Least liked; 9 = Most liked.

TABLE 18–3

Packaged Soup Alternatives

The trade-off procedure simplifies both implementation and information processing. Because attribute descriptors are paired and presented two at a time, this approach is simple to apply, lends itself to mail questionnaire format, and reduces respondent information overload. However, the trade-off approach is not

EXHIBIT 18–8
—
Two Alternative
Data-Collection
Procedures

a. Two at a Time

What is more important to you? There are times when we have to give up one thing to get something else. We have a scale that will make it possible for you to tell us your preference in certain circumstances, for example, calories versus price. Please read the example below, which explains how the scale works, and then tell us the order of your preference by writing in the numbers from 1 to 6 for each of the six questions that follow the example.

Example: Calories versus Price

Procedure:
Simply write the number 1 in the combination that represents your first choice. In one of the remaining blank squares, write the number 2 for your second choice. Then write the number 3 for your third choice, and so on from 1 to 6.

Step 1

	Calories		
Price	80	100	140
$1.19	1		
$1.49			

Step 1 (Explanation)
You would rather pay the least ($1.19) and get the lowest caloric packaged soup alternative. Your first choice (1) is in the box as shown.

Step 2

	Calories		
Price	80	100	140
$1.19	1		
$1.49	2		

Step 2 (Explanation)
Your second choice is that you would rather pay $1.49 and get the lowest caloric packaged soup alternative.

Step 3

	Calories		
Price	80	100	140
$1.19	1	3	
$1.49	2		

Step 3 (Explanation)
Your third choice is that you would rather pay $1.19 and get the next lowest caloric packaged soup alternative.

Final judgments

	Calories		
Price	80	100	140
$1.19	1	3	5
$1.49	2	4	6

This shows a sample order of preference for all possible combinations. Of course, your preferences could be different.

EXHIBIT 18–8
—
(concluded)

b. Full Profile (Stimulus Card)

Flavor
        Onion
Calories
        80
Salt-freeness
        Yes
Price
        $1.19
Overall rating _____1_____

without limitations. First, rating descriptors two at a time can be confusing because if attributes tend to be correlated, which is a reasonable assumption in most cases, respondents may be unclear about what to assume about a particular descriptor that is not included in the pair being evaluated. For example, low-calorie packaged soup mixes may also apply to health/weight-conscious consumers because of their salt-freeness. Thus, in assigning a rank order to the pairing "80 calories and $1.19," the perceived relation between calories and salt-freeness could produce an evaluation that lacks clear meaning. Second, with this approach the respondent must make a relatively large number of (albeit simple) judgments. Even when procedures are used to reduce the number of two-way tables, the total number of judgments remain large. Third, respondents can easily adopt patterned responses, such as focusing on only one attribute before considering the other.[5] Fourth, this approach is particularly well suited to products whose essence can be sufficiently captured by a verbal description. If an important attribute is color, size, or shape, for example, then this approach may not be the best choice.

The alternative approach, the **full-profile procedure,** simultaneously presents the respondent with a complete set of attribute descriptors. A sample "stimulus card" for a packaged soup alternative is shown in Exhibit 18–8, part *b*. You will note that the stimulus card presents the respondent with a descriptor for each attribute that is included in the study. Respondents are asked to evaluate the product alternative, which is defined by the selected descriptors on the card.

The principal advantage of the full-profile approach is its realism. Respondents are forced to consider attributes simultaneously, as opposed to two at a time. This feature is particularly important when attributes are correlated; by defining the levels of each attribute, potential correlations between actual products or brands are taken into account. It has the disadvantage of making the respondent's task difficult because several attributes must be considered at once. Note that although the two-at-a-time approach provides only a set of rank orders, the full-profile

full-profile procedure Technique that simultaneously presents the respondent with a complete set of attribute descriptors. A stimulus card presents respondents with an attribute descriptor for each attribute included in the study; respondents are asked for an evaluation of the product alternative defined by the selected attribute descriptors appearing on the card.

---

[5] R. M. Johnson, "Beyond Conjoint Measurement: A Method of Pairwise Tradeoff Analysis," in *Advances in Consumer Research*, Vol. III, ed. B. B. Anderson, Proceedings of Association for Consumer Research, Sixth Annual Conference, 1976, pp. 353–58.

procedure can employ either a rank-order or rating (i.e., a nine-point, equal-appearing scale with, e.g., end labels "least liked" to "most liked") format.

Several additional issues warrant discussion. First, note that the number of two-way tables, in the case of the trade-off procedure, and the number of stimulus cards, in the case of the full-profile approach, can be greatly reduced by applying procedures that require the respondent to rate (or rank) far fewer combinations.[6] For example, in the case of a full-profile design that has as many as 256 distinct combinations, a respondent may be required to rate (or rank) as few as eight stimulus cards. However, if attributes are correlated by actual products or brands, such procedures can produce profiles that may be either unrealistic or even unbelievable. Second, the range of variation of attribute levels and interattribute correlation must be seriously considered. Larger ranges for attribute levels will, if all else is kept the same, improve the researcher's accuracy in estimating individual utilities, but large ranges in attributes may produce profiles that are not believable.

utility scale values
Ratings that indicate how influential each attribute level is in the consumer's overall evaluations.

There are various approaches to computing the **utility scale value** of each attribute. These utilities indicate how influential each attribute level is in shaping the consumer's overall evaluation. Depending on the procedure chosen, either the rank-ordered preference data or the preference rating data for each respondent constitutes the basic input. Individual utility scale values for each attribute level can be estimated at the individual or aggregate sample level; that is, for each respondent a set of attribute level utilities is estimated, and at the aggregate level utilities are estimated for the entire (or some portion of the entire) sample of respondents. In either case, the utility scale values for each attribute level are chosen so that when they are combined (added together), the total utility of each combination will correspond as closely as possible to the original rank orders or preference ratings.

As we indicated above, techniques for estimating utility scale values differ depending on whether the input data are assumed to be ordinal (rank order only) or interval (ratings). Among the methods that treat the preference data as at most ordinal scaled are MONANOVA,[7] PREFMAP,[8] Johnson's nonmetric trade-off procedure,[9] and LINMAP.[10] The most popular method when the preference data are assumed to be interval scaled is ordinary least-squares (OLS) regression,[11] which

---

[6]P. E. Green, "On the Design of Choice Experiments Involving Multifactor Alternatives," *Journal of Consumer Research* 1 (1974), pp. 61–68.

[7]J. B. Kruskal, "Analysis of Factorial Experiments by Estimating Monotone Transformations of the Data," *Journal of the Royal Statistical Society,* Series B, 27 (1965), pp. 251–63.

[8]J. D. Carroll, "Individual Differences in Multidimensional Scaling," in *Multidimensional Scaling: Theory and Applications in Behavioral Sciences*, Vol. I, ed. R. N. Shepard et al. (New York: Seminar Press, 1972), pp. 105–55.

[9]R. J. Johnson, "Varieties of Conjoint Measurement" (Working paper, Market Facts, Inc., Chicago, 1973).

[10]See V. Srinivasan and A. D. Shocker, "Linear Programming Techniques for Multidimensional Analysis of Preferences," *Psychometrika* 38 (1973), pp. 337–69; and V. Srinivasan and A. D. Shocker, "LINMAP Version IV—User's Manual" (Nashville, Tenn.: Vanderbilt University, 1981).

[11]J. Johnston, *Econometric Methods*, 2nd ed. (New York: McGraw-Hill, 1972).

we discussed in Chapter 16. The general consensus appears to be that these methods vary little in terms of their predictive validities.[12]

To derive utilities for the attributes requires that some sort of coding scheme quantifies the profiles that are evaluated. One relatively easy way to do this is to use what are called *dummy variables*. Dummy variables indicate the presence or absence of a particular attribute. More specifically, consider the following coding scheme. Let

$$D_1 = \begin{cases} 1, \text{ if the packaged soup alternative under evaluation is onion} \\ 0, \text{ if otherwise} \end{cases}$$

$$D_2 = \begin{cases} 1, \text{ if the packaged soup alternative under evaluation is chicken noodle} \\ 0, \text{ if otherwise} \end{cases}$$

$$D_3 = \begin{cases} 1, \text{ if the packaged soup alternative under evaluation is 80 calories} \\ 0, \text{ if otherwise} \end{cases}$$

$$D_4 = \begin{cases} 1, \text{ if the packaged soup alternative under evaluation is 100 calories} \\ 0, \text{ if otherwise} \end{cases}$$

$$D_5 = \begin{cases} 1, \text{ if the packaged soup alternative under evaluation is salt-free} \\ 0, \text{ if otherwise} \end{cases}$$

$$D_6 = \begin{cases} 1, \text{ if the packaged soup alternative under evaluation is priced at \$1.19} \\ 0, \text{ if otherwise} \end{cases}$$

For example, in the case of the first packaged soup alternative described in Table 18–3 we have

Packaged soup alternative 1:

- Onion.
- 80 calories.
- Salt-free.
- $1.19.

so that

$$D_1 = 1 \qquad D_4 = 0$$
$$D_2 = 0 \qquad D_5 = 1$$
$$D_3 = 1 \qquad D_6 = 1$$

In other words, this particular packaged soup alternative can be described by the string $(1,0,1,0,1,1)$. You have probably noted that we did not create a dummy variable for each level of an attribute. To avoid computational redundancies, we need only create $k - 1$

[12]See, for example, P. Cattin and D. R. Wittink, "A Monte-Carlo Study of Metric and Nonmetric Estimation Methods for Multiattribute Models" (Research paper No. 341, Graduate School of Business, Stanford University, 1976); and F. J. Carmone, P. E. Green, and A. K. Jain, "The Robustness of Conjoint Analysis: Some Monte Carlo Results," *Journal of Marketing Research* 15 (1978), pp. 300–303.

dummy variables for a variable having k levels.[13] Thus, we have defined two dummy variables for flavor (D_1 and D_2), two dummy variables for calories (D_3 and D_4), one dummy variable for salt-freeness (D_5), and one dummy variable for price (D_6).

Note also that the string $(0,0,0,0,0,0)$ corresponds to the packaged soup alternative:

- Country vegetable.
- 140 calories.
- Salt.
- $1.49.

The level of the attribute assigned to the value zero is called the *base category*, and it is completely arbitrary; in other words, results are not affected by which attribute level is assigned the zero value.

An estimated utility coefficient could be derived for each attribute level, based on the preference ratings and the dummy variables. Hypothetical utilities for the four packaged soup attributes are given in Table 18–4. According to these utilities, the least preferred packaged soup alternative would be

- Chicken noodle.
- 140 calories.
- Salt.
- $1.49.

Exhibit 18–9 shows a graphical representation.

Validation

One of the primary reasons researchers conduct a conjoint study is to be able to predict preference for products or services that have not been directly evaluated. Thus, some effort must be made to determine the predictive validity of the conjoint model developed. Ideally, the model's predictions would be compared against actual purchases. If this is not possible, then the model's predictions should be compared with respondent's preferences for products in a "hold-out" set. This requires a hold-out set of products that have been evaluated, in addition to those that have been used to estimate the utilities of the conjoint model. The objective

---

[13]To see why we need create only $k - 1$ dummy variables for an attribute having k levels, consider the following: The flavor attribute has three levels—onion, chicken noodle, and country vegetable. Let us specify one dummy variable for each level. Let the dummy variables be denoted by D_1, D_2, and D_3, where

$$D_1 = 1 \text{ if onion} \qquad D_2 = 1 \text{ if chicken noodle} \qquad D_3 = 1 \text{ if country vegetable}$$
$$0 \text{ if otherwise} \qquad 0 \text{ if otherwise} \qquad 0 \text{ if otherwise}$$

Consider now each flavor alternative and its corresponding dummy variable codes

	D_1	D_2	D_3
Onion	1	0	0
Chicken noodle	0	1	0
Country vegetable	0	0	1

The third dummy variable (D_3) is not needed because once we observe that $D_1 = 0$ and $D_2 = 0$, it must be that the packaged soup alternative is country vegetable (that is, D_3 must equal 1).

Attribute	Utility Coefficient
Flavor	
Onion	3.50
Chicken noodle	0
Country vegetable	3.66
Calories	
80	2.03
100	0.46
140	0
Salt-freeness	
Yes	1.84
No	0
Price	
$1.19	0.67
$1.49	0

TABLE 18–4
—
Utility Coefficients

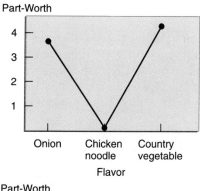

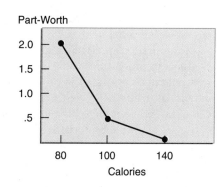

EXHIBIT 18–9
—
Graphical
Representation of
Utility Coefficients

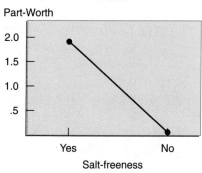

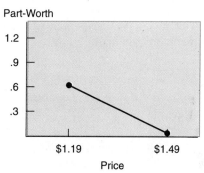

is to compare the model's predictions regarding those products with the actual evaluations. Two measures of predictive validity often used are (1) the percent of correct, first-choice predictions and (2) the median Spearman rank correlation (Chapter 16) between each individual's preference rankings and the model's predictions of those rankings. These measures provide some overall indication of how the model is doing.

Simulation Models

In conjoint analysis, simulating market share consists of determining what proportion of the respondents would choose each product or service in a fully specified set of products. This is accomplished by determining which product or products each respondent would choose and aggregating the results. The two most commonly used choice models are the first-choice and share-of-preference models.

In the **first-choice model** it is assumed that each individual always purchases the product for which he or she has the greatest utility. For example, for a consumer having the utility coefficients shown in Table 18–4 we would predict that he or she would purchase the

- Country vegetable
- 80 calories
- Salt-free
- $1.19

packaged soup alternative. This approach has been applied in situations where purchases are infrequent.

In the **share-of-preference model** it is assumed that each respondent purchases products in proportion to his or her utility for the products. With this procedure we would first compute the utility of each packaged soup alternative based on the individual utility coefficients. Next each respondent would be expected to purchase, say, product alternative j, in proportion to the utility of that product to the entire set of product alternatives; that is

$$P(\text{choose } j) = \frac{U(j)}{\sum\limits_{j=1}^{j} U(j)}$$

This model has been applied in situations in which the products are likely to be purchased frequently.

Market Simulations

Given the ability to predict relative preference and possibly purchase probability with the aid of the choice models just discussed, it is possible to simulate the consequences of (1) the introduction or removal of products and services from the marketplace and (2) modifications in the specifications of existing products or services, both one's own and competitors'.

Armed with this kind of information, it is possible to develop products that (1) maximize share, revenue, profits, and so on; (2) minimize the cannibalization of existing products or services; and (3) are targeted to specific groups of people. Strategies can also be developed to minimize the impact of changes in the competitors' products, and the degree of interest in a new product can be assessed.

---

first-choice model
Conjoint analysis model that assumes individuals always choose products for which they have greatest utility.

share-of-preference model
Conjoint analysis model that assumes individuals purchase products in proportion to their utility for the products.

To achieve these objectives, it is necessary to observe only the effect that variations in the specifications of products have on simulated shares. Because utilities are developed at the individual level, simulations can be performed at any level of aggregation. In addition, by cross tabulating predicted choice selections with respondent demographics, it can be determined who is buying what; by cross tabulating predicted choice selections between simulations, switching behavior can be studied. Finally, if the need arises, respondents can be weighted to reflect population characteristics, differential purchase frequency, or usage (see Chapter 14).

PRODUCT TESTING: PHILOSOPHY AND OBJECTIVES

Product tests attempt to answer one of the most basic of questions relating to the ultimate market acceptance of a product: "How does this product perform when evaluated by the consumer?" Performance can be evaluated in isolation, in a competitive frame, against its advertising, or against a formula variation. There is no better way to answer this question than to experience and use the product under real-life conditions. From product testing we learn what product is most acceptable to consumers. Product testing is particularly important in the consumer package-goods industries (food, health, and beauty aids; household products; etc.) where physical product improvements can quickly change market shares in a product category and where production/distribution of product prototypes is economically feasible.

Specifically, product tests are conducted for four purposes:

1. *Tests against the competition* seek to identify which of many alternative new formulas is best in terms of being most preferred or to measure the performance of the new product relative to other competitive products.

2. *Product improvement tests* attempt to determine whether an improved formula (or construction) should replace the current product.

3. *Cost-savings tests* attempt to determine whether a less expensive product should replace the current product.

4. *Concept-fit tests* attempt to determine which of several test-product variants most closely resembles what is being communicated by the "product sell."

TYPES OF PRODUCT TESTS

There are two broad types of product testing procedures:

1. **Monadic product tests** present the consumer with one product and ask for an evaluation of that product with no other specific product for comparison. Actually, the test product is rated and compared with all other similar products the consumer has ever used and, specifically, to the product currently being used.

2. **Comparison product tests** present the consumer with two or more products and ask for a comparison and rating of each. There are many different variations of comparison product tests. In **sequential monadic designs,** a

monadic product tests
Designs where a consumer evaluates only one product, having no other product for comparison.

comparison product tests
Designs where a consumer rates products by directly comparing two or more products.

sequential monadic designs
Comparison tests where a consumer rates one product and then is given a second product to rate independently.

protomonadic designs
Comparison tests where a consumer evaluates one product and then compares it with a second product.

paired comparison designs
Tests where a consumer directly compares two products.

repeat paired comparison designs
Tests where a respondent is given two or more sets of products to compare against each other at two different points in time.

round robin designs
Tests where a series of products is tested against each of the others.

triangle designs
Tests where a respondent is given two samples of one product and one sample of another and asked to identify the one that differs.

duo-trio designs
Tests where a respondent is given a standard product and asked to determine which of two other products is most similar.

discrimination/ difference designs
Tests where a respondent is asked if one product differs from others.

respondent tests one product, evaluates it, and is given a second product to evaluate independently. After the second product is (independently) rated, the respondent is asked to compare both products in terms of an overall evaluation. In **protomonadic designs,** a respondent tests one product, evaluates it, and is given a second product and compares the two. In **paired comparison designs,** a respondent is given two products to compare against each other. In **repeat paired comparison designs,** a respondent is given two or more sets of products to compare against each other at two different points in time. The objective is to determine whether the respondent chooses between them in the same way on more than one occasion. In **round robin designs,** each of a series of products is tested against each of the others, and the results are combined. In **triangle designs,** a respondent is given two blind samples of one product and one blind sample of another product and asked to identify the product that differs from the other two. In **duo-trio designs,** a respondent is given a "standard" product and asked to determine which of two other products matches it. Finally, in **discrimination/difference designs,** a respondent is asked to determine if one product differs from others.

The advantage of monadic testing is in its realism. In normal situations a respondent uses one product at a time and determines whether it is acceptable or unacceptable for repurchase. Monadic tests are designed specifically to test the qualities of the product itself—the fame of reference will be the product the respondent is currently using and all other products in the category. Because of this, the result of a monadic product test may be difficult to interpret, unless norms have been established; for example, what does it mean if 75 percent of the respondents rated the product's taste as "excellent"? In contrast, comparison tests, by their very nature, concentrate on the differences between the products being tested—the paired nature of the test makes comparison product tests more sensitive, if all else is kept the same, than monadic product tests; however, it is far more difficult to generalize to the universe of all products. Finally, comparison product tests may be impracticable in situations involving sensory (e.g., taste) evaluations. In such instances the use of one product may relieve the need of using the second product (as in a cough or antacid product test) or significantly alter the senses (as in a taste test).

PRODUCT TESTS: IMPLEMENTATION

Exhibit 18–10 presents a prototypical product test proposal.

Procedures

Presentation of Products.   A crucial issue in presenting the product to respondents is whether to disclose the brand and/or company name. In other words, should products be tested on a "blind" (no identification as to brand) or a "branded," "identified," "open" basis? **Blind testing** is undertaken when (1) new

blind testing
Tests where the brand name of the product is not disclosed during test.

EXHIBIT 18–10

Project Proposal:
Product Test

Brand:	New Products Hardy Soup.
Project:	Campbell's versus new Hardy Soup blind product test.
Background and Objectives:	R&D has developed a new Hardy Soup in two different flavors (chicken noodle and mushroom). Additionally, each flavor has been developed at two different flavor strengths. The brand groups have requested that research be conducted to determine (1) whether this product should be considered for introduction; (2) if so, if one or both flavors should be introduced; and (3) which flavor variation(s) would be preferred most by the consumer.
	The objective of this research will be to determine consumers' preferences for each flavor variation of the new product relative to Campbell's Chunky products.
Method:	There will be four cells. In each cell, a blind paired-product test will be conducted between a different flavor variation of the new product and the currently marketed Campbell's product, as follows:

- Campbell's Chunky Chicken Noodle versus Hardy's Chicken Noodle 1.
- Campbell's Chunky Chicken Noodle versus Hardy's Chicken Noodle 2.
- Campbell's Chunky Mushroom versus Hardy's Mushroom 1.
- Campbell's Chunky Mushroom versus Hardy's Mushroom 2.

	In each cell, there will be 200 past-30-day ready-to-serve soup user/purchasers.
	Respondents will be interviewed in a shopping mall and given both products to take home and try. Additionally, respondents must be positively disposed toward chicken noodle or mushroom flavors in order to be used in the test. Order of product trial will be rotated to minimize position bias. Telephone call backs will be made after one-week period.
Action Standard:	Each new soup flavor will be considered for introduction if one or more of its flavor variations achieves at least absolute parity with its Campbell's Chunky control.
	If for either flavor alternative more than one flavor level variation meets the action standard, the one that is preferred over Campbell's at the highest level of confidence will be recommended to be considered for introduction.
	A single sample *t*-test for paired comparison data (two-tail) will be used to test for significance.
Cost and Timing:	The cost of this study will be $32,000 ± 10 percent.
	The following schedule will be established:

Fieldwork	2 weeks
Top line	2 weeks
Final report	4 weeks

Research Firm:	Burke Marketing Research.

products are being tested where no brand name, packaging, or advertising has been developed as yet and (2) reactions to the "pure" product, apart from established image values, are desired. Note that the product test described in Exhibit 18–10 calls for a blind test because the brand group probably wants to see how consumers rate this product against the leading competitor (Campbell's Soups) without the outside influence of brand image or advertising.

branded testing
Test where brand name of product is disclosed during test.

Branded testing is usually undertaken when (1) measurement of the effects of the brand name, or brand image, on reactions to the products is required and (2) brand identification is so obvious, and its effect on ultimate market acceptance is so inevitable, that there is little point in conducting a blind test.

There are four basic principles to follow in preparing the product for testing. First, the test product should be representative of the product that will ultimately appear in the marketplace. Second, name and packaging materials should be as close as possible to those that will be used when the product goes to the market. Third, sensitivity to what is being tested is necessary; for example, if different formulas are being tested, then make sure all other factors (size, shape, color, etc.) are identical. Fourth, products should be labeled in a fashion that minimizes bias (e.g., avoid using letters or numbers that are obviously sequential).

Interviewing. Two research methods predominate in product-testing applications: (1) in-home placement and (2) central-location testing.

In-home product testing can be undertaken in a number of different ways. The interviewer may go from door to door to determine whether the respondent qualifies for the test; if the respondent qualifies, a product is left behind, and the interviewer will arrange a time to return when the respondent's reactions to the product will be recorded. In contrast, if the product test can be conducted quickly (typically the case in taste and smell tests), the interviewer may ask the respondent to test the product right on the spot. An increasingly frequent practice is to have the interviewer initiate contact via the telephone, and if the contacted respondent qualifies and is willing to cooperate the product is delivered by the interviewer or by mail. The respondent's reaction to the product is recorded, either through a personal interview or by telephone. Another variation of in-home placement is to interview respondents in shopping malls or other high-traffic locations and then give them the products to take home and use. Follow-ups can be scheduled either by personal interview or via telephone. Still yet another variation of in-home placement is to use a "mail panel" consisting of families who have previously agreed to test products. Products are delivered by mail, and therefore, the product tested must be suitable for mail shipment (see Chapter 6).

Central-location product testing has become very popular in recent years because in-home placement can be extremely expensive, especially with low-incidence product categories, in which the costs of screening and call-backs are expected to be substantial. If central-location testing is used, respondents are screened on location (or recruited by telephone) and invited to the testing location, usually a shopping mall or food store where the research company conducting the product test has rented space. Typically, food test products are prepared by home economists or trained kitchen personnel, and the respondent is invited to taste various samples of two or three of the products being tested; they usually are asked questions about each sample item. The major limitations of central-location testing is that the respondent does not get a chance to experience the product in his or her own kitchen and the information obtained does not reflect the opinions of the respondent's family. Clearly, for products where ease of preparation or application is important (e.g., cake mix and furniture polish) some sort of in-home testing is required.

A related issue involves the length of the product test; that is, how long should the test run? Obviously, the respondent should be given an ample opportunity to use the product as frequently as is desired and under realistic conditions. Generally, in-home tests last a minimum of one week. In certain situations, for example, in cases where the product is infrequently used, an **extended-use product test** is warranted; in this case, the respondent uses the product over a period of weeks or months. For example, it may be important to determine what kind of use or abuse the respondent will give the product over time (e.g., toys). Often, in the case of novelty products a **sales wave extended-use product test** is performed. If a sales wave product test is used, the respondent is given the opportunity to buy the product at intervals coinciding with the normal purchase cycle. This type of product test can (1) identify novelty products that are initially liked, but quickly wear out; (2) isolate target groups; (3) help in forecasting share of market or volume; and (4) identify specific problems.

extended-use product test
In-home test where respondent is given opportunity to use the product over a period of weeks.

sales wave extended-use product test
Respondent is given opportunity to buy the product at intervals coinciding with the normal purchase cycle.

Questions Asked. The types of questions asked will vary to some extent, depending on the interviewing method. In general, the most important questions to ask relate to

- ― Preference.
- ― Overall rating.
- ― Attribute ratings.
- ― Likes/dislikes.
- ― Advantages/disadvantages.
- ― Uniqueness.
- ― Frequency of use (if applicable).
- ― Who used the product (if applicable).
- ― When and how the product was used (if applicable).
- ― Use patterns (if applicable).

Sampling Practices

Once again nonprobability sampling designs are frequently used in product-testing applications. The typical approach is to specify age and sex quotas based on total category volume contribution. Standard minimum cell sizes for in-home use tests typically call for 100 to 200 respondents. In central-location tests the standard minimum cell size is typically 100 respondents, although simple test-versus-competitive-control studies are often conducted with as few as 50 respondents per cell.

Action Standards

The specific criteria for evaluating product tests depend on the stated purpose of the test. The following are action standards for three broad types of product tests:

Tests versus Competition.

1. New products as well as established products should achieve an overall preference difference that is statistically significant at the 90 percent level of confidence in each principal target group.
2. In copy-claim-support tests the test product must achieve significant preferences versus competition at the 95 percent confidence level for superiority claims and at least absolute parity (50 percent) for parity claims.

Product Improvement Tests.

1. We should recommend that the improved product replace the current product only if it achieves statistically equivalent preferences over the current product among brand users and significant preferences (90 percent) among nonusers (or vice versa, depending on the marketing objectives of the proposed product improvement).
2. In copy-claims-support tests, the improved product must achieve significantly higher preference scores than the old product at the 95 percent confidence level for superiority claims and at least absolute parity for parity claims.

Cost Savings Tests.

1. We should recommend that the less expensive product replace the current product only if it achieves parity among current users *and* nonusers of the brand. (Parity equals *not* losing to the current product at greater than some specified level of confidence.)

Analysis Approach

In product-testing applications interest centers on tests of mean differences and/or tests of proportions based on the key evaluative measures (e.g., overall rating or overall preferences). Guidance for research and development can be derived through an analysis of directional ratings in monadic designs (e.g., what percent of respondents felt that the level of sweetness was "too much," "not enough," or "just the right amount") and preference on specific attributes in paired designs.

SUMMARY

In this chapter we have considered two of the most important practices undertaken in marketing research—concept and product testing. We discussed and illustrated the basic types of concept screening, concept evaluation, and product tests. Through the use of hypothetical marketing research proposals, we have attempted to introduce the major issues involved in concept and product testing and to provide specific details on how concept and product tests are implemented.

KEY CONCEPTS

end benefits

concept

opportunity analysis

concept testing

core benefit concept

positioning concept statement

concept screening tests

concept evaluation tests

new-product concept screening test

alternative buying incentive concept screening test

concept board

conjoint analysis

trade-off procedure

full-profile procedure

utility scale values

first-choice model

share-of-preference model

monadic product tests

comparison product tests

sequential monadic designs

protomonadic designs

paired comparison designs

repeated paired comparison designs

round robin designs

triangle designs

duo-trio designs

discrimination/difference designs

blind testing

branded testing

extended-use product test

sales wave extended-use product test

REVIEW QUESTIONS

1. Discuss the differences between concept screening tests and concept evaluation tests.
2. Explain how conjoint analysis can be used in concept or product development. What are the critical issues in designing conjoint analysis concept or product tests?
3. Why are product tests conducted? Translate each of the reasons for conducting product tests into a number of specific types of product-testing applications.
4. Discuss the various types of product tests. For each of the following products or brands, which type of product test would you recommend and why?

 — New cold tablet.
 — Lancia Skillet Pizza.
 — Spaghetti in a jar.

5. Contrast in-home product tests with central-location product tests. For each of the following products or brands, determine whether you would suggest an in-home or central-location product test:

 — New cold tablet.
 — Lancia Skillet Pizza.
 — Spaghetti in a jar.

Name and Package Testing

— Describe how names are created and the primary approach to naming a
  product.
— Define the information typically collected in name testing studies.
— Describe how name tests are implemented.
— Define the basic functions that a package serves.
— Outline the reasons for conducting a package test study.
— Describe how package tests are implemented.

INTRODUCTION

The name of a new product and its package design are two integral components that influence ultimate market acceptance. With the advent of self-
service retail environments, name and package testing have become more
important during the last two decades: Consumer recognition and product
visibility are necessarily vital considerations in marketing any product. In
this chapter we discuss name and package testing research.

NAME TESTS

Names are important because of the information they convey; the name
of a product communicates both denotative and connotative meaning.
Denotative meaning refers to the literal, explicit meaning of a name.
Connotative meaning refers to the associations that the name provokes
beyond its literal, explicit meaning—in other words, the imagery that is associated with a brand name. Specifically, a brand name (1) identifies the product
to the consumer, retailer, distributor, and manufacturer and (2) differentiates
the product from competitive products and conveys physical and emotional
benefits.

   We don't mean to imply that a "good" name will save a bad product.
However, in these days of product "me-too-ism," a dull or otherwise inap-
propriate name can be a severe handicap even to a superior product.
Recognizing the value of a good name, many companies now make use

EXHIBIT 19–1
—
Name Calling

The Diehard
Value overwhelms metaphor: This is "the best adapted metaphor in the history of brand names," says Bachrach.

Anacin
Strong medicine: The brain doesn't think of pictures so much as of words. Using familiar language elements, or "morphemes," scientific-sounding Excedrin and Bufferin evoke strength. But competing Anacin is perceived negatively, due to its prefix meaning "not."

Nissan Sentra
No name is a good name: "Only recently have car names become rational," says Ira Bachrach, who has devised automobile names for several makers. For Nissan Motor, the message suggested by "Sentra" is safety. The public accepts the coined term to be a quality of the product. But good names aren't always names at all, for example, "240" works symbolically well for Mercedes-Benz, denoting cool efficiency.

Apple
The genesis of microcomputing: Apple was there first. The marketing challenge back then demanded a symbol of friendliness, trustworthiness, and simplicity—concepts, according to Ira Bachrach, of "nonspecific affect." Thus an innocuous fruit, irrelevant to technology, was appropriate. To Bachrach, it meant something that didn't screw up your utility bill.

Budweiser
A "Bud," not a "Budweiser": A name that becomes short, friendly, and familiar can make its way into the language.

Rainbow (Digital)
No pot of gold: After Apple, microcomputers became packaged goods that demanded specific messages. Thus, Bachrach feels, the amorphous "Rainbow" appeared far too late. Although commendably simple and easy, to the now-informed public it said "noncomputer." And it cast a sense of arbitrarily having been slapped on. "About as amateurish as you can get," observes Bachrach.

Source: Adapted from Robert A. Manis, "Name-Calling," *Inc. Magazine,* July 1984, pp. 67–74.

of commercial names experts. One such expert is Ira Bachrach, founder of NameLab, a commercial names factory. For $35,000 or so, Bachrach will assist you in naming your product entry. In Exhibit 19–1 Bachrach comments on the names of several products that you might recognize.

denotative meaning
The literal, explicit meaning of a name.

Philosophy and Objectives

Obviously, a name should be legible, pronounceable, memorable, and distinctive. However, the denotative and connotative meaning associated with a name should be consistent, and it should support the overall brand strategy plan and corporate direction. Once a name has been decided upon, all of the advertising, packaging, and promotional efforts are directed toward implanting that name in the minds and vocabulary of consumers. Thus, probably the last thing manufacturers want to do is to change the names of their products, although there have been exceptions, such as ESSO to EXXON and Datsun to Nissan.

connotative meaning
The associations that the name implies, beyond its literal, explicit meaning; the imagery associated with a brand name.

Name testing research is conducted for one or more of the following reasons:

1. To generate new name ideas.
2. To measure legibility and pronounceability.
3. To measure association with product category.

company names
Corporate names attached to the products they market.

explicit descriptive names
Names that are meant to describe the physical product.

line names
Names assigned to a variety of specific products that the company markets.

implicit imagery names
Names that do not literally describe the product but that implicitly and indirectly convey its characteristics.

created names
Names that do not have literal meaning with respect to the characteristics of a product; however, through advertising they may acquire indirect meaning that can reflect favorably on the product.

designer names
Names associated with leading figures of fashion design and lent to mass-marketed fashion and accessories.

4. To measure distinctiveness.

5. To measure relative ability to project strategy-supporting promises of product use and end benefits.

There are many different strategies in developing names for products. For example, some companies choose to give meaning to a meaningless name like "Kodak," whereas others choose names like "Rice Krispies," which literally describes the physical product. Approaches to naming a product include[1]

1. *Company names.* Libby, Scott Paper, General Mills, Pillsbury, and Kraft are all examples of companies that attach their corporate, or **company, names,** to the products they market. In contrast, other corporations such as General Foods and Procter & Gamble follow a strategy of using individual brand names for their products.

2. *Explicit descriptive names.* Minute Rice, Rice-A-Roni, Wheat Chex, and Light 'n Lively are examples of companies that use **explicit descriptive names** to describe the physical product.

3. *Line names.* **Line names** are assigned to a variety of specific products that the company markets. Betty Crocker, Green Giant, and Aunt Jemima are examples of line names.

4. *Implicit imagery names.* A common strategy is to use a name that does not literally describe the product, but implicitly and indirectly conveys characteristics about the product. Examples of **implicit imagery names** include Taster's Choice, Pampers, and Liquid Paper.

5. *Created names.* **Created names** do not have a literal meaning with respect to the characteristics of a product. However, through advertising they may acquire indirect meaning that can reflect favorably on the product. Examples of created names include Aim, Marlboro, Virginia Slims, and Scope.

6. *Designer names.* **Designer names** are associated with individuals who are leading figures of fashion design. They lend their names to mass-marketed fashion and accessories and in some cases even to unrelated products (e.g., automobiles). Examples include Bill Blass and Yves St. Laurent.

Procedures

There is no "right" way to choose a name. Only very general guidelines can be offered. To get some perspective on how names are given to products, consider Exhibit 19–2, which tells the story of Compaq, NameLab's biggest success.

A very general procedure for creating a list of new names is to (1) list objectives and benefits of the brand strategy and corporate direction statement; (2) list appropriate synonyms and antonyms; and (3) combine appropriate objectives and benefits with appropriate synonyms and antonyms to produce a list of "promising" words, prefixes, and suffixes. It is a good practice to never test a new name in

---

[1]Parts of the following discussion were adapted from Jeffrey Pope, *Practical Marketing Research* (New York: AMACOM, 1981), pp. 157–58.

EXHIBIT 19–2
—
Compaq

NameLab's most notable entry so far came in 1982 on behalf of a tiny startup that intended to sell portable computers. The founders, two engineers from Texas Instruments Inc., were content to name the company and its product after a local address, hence, Gateway Technology. The little machine presumably could be sold as Gateway, inasmuch as a computer is a "gateway" to some vague, but assuredly noble, end. To scientists, the connection seemed clever enough, but not to the company's prime investors, a partnership headed by Ben Rosen and L. J. Sevin. Justifiably concerned lest Gateway mean little to consumers, and even less to Wall Street, Rosen urged that NameLab be consulted. Enter Ira Bachrach, with his intensively linguistic and peculiarly totemic approach to naming things. Within a few weeks, Gateway was presented with several snappier choices, among them Cortex, Cognipak, and Suntek. Oh, yes—and Compaq.

No one can say for sure that the company might not have done equally well under the banners of Cognipac, Gateway, or even Tip-Top. Nonetheless, as Compaq, the corporation went on to sell $111 million worth of computers in 12 months, a U.S. record for first-year revenues. But this almost didn't come to pass, as a result of concern that the name might be challenged. In many of its particulars, trademark and service mark law is so vague, confusing, and regionalized that general counsel often prefers the discretion of another choice to the valor of stepping on toes, however unrelated. Gateway's attorneys felt that the proposed new trademark came too close to "Compac," a registered service mark of a transatlantic cable switching network owned by ITT Corporation, and asked that it be reconsidered. But with a public offering at stake, the board of directors sought a hot name, and Compaq it stayed. "If you ask lawyers, 'Should I go outside,' Bachrach complains good-humoredly, "they'll say, 'God, you could get run over!' "

An expert in marketing packaged goods from an earlier career in advertising, the 46-year-old Bachrach has discovered that the rules apply to nonpackaged-goods fields as well. To this discipline he also brings an approach to language developed in his graduate thesis that involves relationships among semantic fragments, by which he tried to win the George Bernard Shaw prize for developing an English phonetic alphabet. (Thuh pryez rhemaynz unwon evun toodae.) As a result, many NameLab creations enjoy multiple effects, sometimes via neologisms with implications that are hidden within ancient but evocative roots. To be sure, Compaq computers could easily have been called "Compacts," but with humdrum impact, weaker suggestiveness, and stage-sharing with cars and cosmetics.

The client had ordered up a word that would be memorable and at the same time "take command of the ideas of portableness"; something that would distinguish itself from all the other IBM personal computer compatibles. NameLab developed a table of basic word parts called "morphemes," of which 6,200 exist in English. An unabashed morpheme addict, Bachrach fashioned "Compaq" from two "messages," one of which indicated computer and communications and the other a small, integral object. The "com" part came easily. The "pac" followed with more difficulty, since its phonetic notation included endings in "k," "c," "ch," and, possibly, "q." NameLab considered all four of them. When the "q" hit, Bachrach gasped eureka. As a bonus to the assigned burden, "paq" also was affectively scientific, he reasoned, strongly hinting of "somebody trying to do something precisely and interestingly."

As a significant benefit, the "paq" suffix fits neatly into what could become a product family name: Printpaq, Datapaq, Wordpaq, and the like. Combining a corporate name with a product name results, by mere repetition, in consumer acceptance of substance and reliability. "By naming subsequent products '-paq,' " Bachrach reasons, "they get added free exposure. It doesn't cost them a dollar in advertising."

When Compaq's board of directors asked what would happen if the company wanted to produce larger systems under the restrictive "paq" concept, Bachrach explained that all good solutions are limited. The more general a solution is, he philosophized, the less effective, "Look, if it works," Bachrach told the board, "your name will become the dominant symbol for portable computers, like Xerox is the symbolic identity of copiers. If that happens and several years from now you want to introduce a megasupercomputer, you can always change your company name or use a model that doesn't have a 'paq.' In the meantime, you'll be crying all the way to the bank. A name that's any good," he lectures customers, "is scary. If it isn't, it's not going to accomplish very much."

Source: Robert A. Manis, "Name-Calling," *Inc. Magazine*, July 1984, pp. 67–74.

isolation. At least two alternatives should be tested for comparison. Note that reactions to a given name may be affected by the other names in the test; therefore, you should exercise extreme caution when comparing the results of one name test with those of another name test.

Name tests are generally conducted in a central location, either at a shopping mall or some other high-traffic location.

Interviewing Practices.   The format for presenting names to respondents is quite simple. Each new name is placed on a separate card, and the respondent is exposed to either the entire set of names (cards) or a limited set. Actually, the respondent is shown a concept statement containing one of the test names and a brief description of the product. If a brand strategy has been agreed upon, the product statement should be strategically oriented. The order of the names is rotated from respondent to respondent in order to dampen position-bias effects. After exposure to each name, the respondent typically is asked to read and pronounce the name and answer other questions.

<u>Questions Asked.</u>   Typically name tests collect information on:

1. *Legibility and pronounceability.* Respondents are asked to read and pronounce one new name at a time.

2. *Association.* Respondents are asked to associate the name with a product category. For example, typical questions are

   - "What type of product do you think this is?"
   - "Which one of the products on this card do you most associate with (*name*)? . . . Which others do you associate with it?"

3. *Distinctiveness.* Respondents may be asked to indicate the distinctiveness of the new name by being asked such questions as

   - "What brand(s) does this (*name*) most remind you of, and why?"
   - "Who do you think manufactured it, and why?"

4. *Imagery and end benefits.* Respondents are asked to use semantic differential scales to describe the new name/product. In such cases, the respondent will be shown a concept statement containing one of the test names and a brief description of the product. Note that product descriptors should (1) adequately cover all of the important end benefits, (2) focus on product-oriented issues like "crunchy" as opposed to name-oriented issues like "sounds good," and (3) be consistent with brand strategy and corporate direction statements. The set of scales also can be used for a competitive product or for a respondent's ideal brand.

Frequently the name given to a product is that of a celebrity (for example, "Krystle" perfume). In so-called designer or celebrity name studies, interest centers on

1. *Familiarity.* How familiar is the celebrity to the target segment?
2. *Appropriateness.* Respondents are asked to indicate the appropriateness of the celebrity and the product category.
3. *Imagery.* Respondents are asked to use semantic differentials to describe the imagery of the celebrity.

As an example, consider these issues with regard to Nike's use of Michael Jordan in selling their basketball shoes. The use of Michael Jordan is clearly consistent with all three criteria.

Sampling Practices

As we indicated, interviewing for a name test is usually conducted at a high-traffic, central location. Standard practice is to use a minimum of 100 category users per name variation and no less than 50 respondents for a subgroup analysis. Specific age and gender quotas also may be imposed, based on total category volume contribution or U.S. Census estimates.

Action Standards

Various criteria for name evaluation can be used. Performance criteria include

1. The relative importance of the various measurements.
2. The relative importance of the various descriptors and associations.
3. The resources available to develop a creative name, that is, to render a "meaningless" name "meaningful."

Although the specific criteria for name evaluation will vary, it is important to explain them clearly.

Approach to Analysis

Typically, the approach to analyzing the information collected in name tests is straightforward. First, new names are screened for their legibility and pronounceability. Names that respondents have difficulty reading or pronouncing are generally not candidates for further consideration. With respect to the association, distinctiveness, imagery, and end-benefits data, the typical approach is to use one- or two-tailed tests of proportions and means (see Chapter 15).

By way of summary, Exhibit 19–3 (see page 594) presents a prototypical marketing research proposal for a new test.

PACKAGE TESTS

The package design is one of the most important marketing components for a product. A package serves several basic functions.

1. It contains, protects, and dispenses the product.
2. It provides point-of-purchase advertising.

EXHIBIT 19-3
—
Marketing Research
Project Proposal:
Name Test

Brand:	Trident Candy.
Project:	Trident Sugarless Candy Name Test.
Background & Objectives:	The Brand Group has available five objective alternative names for the Trident Candy product. The objective of this test is to determine if any of the alternatives offer greater potential than the Trident name in terms of communicating the appropriate product category and conveying a favorable brand image.
Research Design:	A total of 300 respondents will be interviewed in a central location. All respondents will be past-30-day users of breath mints or hard candies. Age and gender specifications will be

Male	45%	Aged 8–11	20%
Female	55%	Aged 12–17	20%
		Aged 18–24	15%
		Aged 25–34	15%
		Aged 35–49	20%
		Aged 50+	10%

	Each respondent will be exposed to three of the six names (five test names and the Trident name), and will evaluate each name in terms of product associations. The respondent will be exposed to the remaining three names and will evaluate each in terms of brand image. Thus, each name will be evaluated by a total of 150 respondents. The purpose of exposing different names in the two phases of the interview is to separate the brand image ratings from the respondent's preconceptions about the names occurring in the initial product association section. The order of the names will be rotated from respondent to respondent in order to dampen position bias.
Information to Be Obtained:	This project will provide information on the degree of association with the product category on both aided and unaided bases and an image profile on each name tested on the semantic differential scales.
Action Standard:	The research group will recommend the name that generates the highest ratings on the critical attributes of (in order of importance):
	For me/Not for me. Tastes good/Does not taste good. Natural taste/Artificial taste. Sugarless/Contains sugar.
	and shows adequate association (50 percent very/somewhat appropriate) with the category.
Cost & Timing:	The cost for this research will be $25,200 (+ 10 percent contingency), and we will adhere to the following schedule:

Fieldwork	1½ weeks
Top line	1½ weeks
Final report	2 weeks

Selected Supplier:	Allen Marketing Research.

3. It serves as an attention getting device.

4. It provides a reminder to current users.

5. It is a source of information about directions, ingredients, and potential cautions.

	A Poor Package	A Good Package	Difference	
Visibility on the shelf	39%	59%	−20	TABLE 19–1
Interest in trial	13	48	−35	
Negative comments	81	31	−50	The Relevance
Looks appealing	28	82	−54	of Packaging for
Good value for the money	40	55	−15	a New Product
Attractive	3	30	−27	

Source: Elliot C. Young, "Judging a Product by Its Wrapper," *Progressive Grocer* (July 1985).

6. It provides a vehicle for announcing promotions and deals.
7. It promises physical and emotional end benefits.
8. It encourages purchase.

There are some very good reasons to focus on the efficacy of a package. The package is the piece of information that every consumer sees. In fact, it has been estimated that an average package in the supermarket generates approximately 15 billion exposures per year.[2] A number of facts about today's shoppers and the shopping environment also point to the importance of packaging and other point-of-purchase displays. For example,

1. Estimates indicate that the average supermarket contains over 17,000 items; of that amount, 2,300 new products are introduced each year.[3]
2. The average shopper is spending approximately 30 minutes during his or her normal shopping trip, which translates to 1,800 seconds in order to consider the 17,000 items.[4]
3. The 1978 Point of Purchase Institute/Du Pont Consumer Buying Habits Study documents that in-store decisions account for two-thirds of every dollar spent in the marketplace.[5]

Can packaging and point-of-purchase displays make a difference? Surely one simply has to look at the influence that packaging and point-of-purchase displays had on the success of such brands as L'eggs hosiery, Lite beer from Miller, Diet Rite Cola, O'Grady's, Janitor in a Drum, and Early Times Bourbon to realize that there is more to the product than its physical contents. Table 19–1 presents some comparative data on the relevance of packaging for a new product.

Put simply, an effective package[6]

− Is simple.
− Quickly communicates what the product is.
− Makes use of focal points.

---

[2]Elliot C. Young, "Packaging Research—Evaluating Consumer Reaction" (Strategic Packaging 1987 International Seminar, Toronto, September 1987),
[3]Ibid.
[4]Ibid.
[5]Elliot C. Young, "Judging a Package by Its Cover," *Madison Avenue* (August 1983).
[6]Young, "Packaging Research."

- Stands out from the competition.
- Makes selection within a product line easy.
- Has the right quality impression.
- Reflects the image of the product.

Philosophy and Objectives

Obviously, the package design must work; however, other aspects of the package must be tested as well. Most consumer goods package tests are conducted for the following purposes:

1. To assess the visibility of package alternatives, relative to one another and usually relative to a competitive brand.
2. To assess the ability of package alternatives to convey perceptions of physical and emotional end benefits.
3. To assess the believability of claims.
4. To assess the effectiveness of the package in stimulating trial.
5. To assess how functional the package is and whether there is any confusion concerning the label or instructions.

Procedures

The procedures involved in package testing research are a bit more involved than those used in name tests. Exposure to the package and measurement of its visibility and image must be carefully controlled. A package design should never be tested in isolation because a package alternative that may have high visibility scores when tested by itself can lose its impact when placed among competitive products; in addition, when testing packages designed for established products, the product's current package design should be included in the test as a control. Thus, for example, in a test of LifeSavers, other products found at the front end of stores (e.g., Tums, Rolaids, Trident, Certs, and Dentyne) should also be included in the test, even though some of these are in different product categories.

Control over exposure to package alternatives is sometimes accomplished by using slides and a tachistoscope (T-Scope). Slides allow greater control over exposure to the shelf space than if an actual display was used. The use of the T-Scope allows the researcher to control light intensity and exposure duration. Although package alternatives could be tested in actual store environments, either in test markets or in simulated test markets, this is rarely done. The substantial practical and cost considerations involved in producing the product in several different packages generally preclude this approach.

As we discussed in Chapter 5 there are some problems with using the T-Scope procedure. In the context of testing packaging and other point-of-purchase displays, the T-Scope has three primary deficiencies:

1. The time the researcher chooses to show each package is largely arbitrary. It is unimportant in package testing that package A communicates better than package B in one fifth of a second.

2. Familiar brands are generally identified faster. If the T-Scope procedure is used, new brands, therefore, are at a severe disadvantage.

3. For a product to win the T-Scope "contest," the designer simply must put the product logo in big, bold letters in the center of the package.

For these reasons some researchers have moved from the T-Scope procedure to what is called the *Find Test* (findability tests) when evaluating packaging. Findability tests are aimed at

1. Measuring the length of time a respondent searches for a product name to assess ease and time of find.

2. Providing initial exposures to measure the "impression retention" of a package.

3. Acquiring diagnostic information to assess what image the package conveys.

The rationale behind such a procedure is that a strong package should be easy to find, should convey a lasting impression, and should elicit an appropriate image. If a findability test is used, the shopper is asked to look at a cluttered in-store shelf scene and find specific products. Again, the assumption behind the test is that a package that can be found fastest is the most effective.

As we discussed in Chapter 5, eye-tracking methods do overcome some of the problems of using the T-Scope procedure. In this context, respondents would see close-up pictures of packages, including the test design, for a time period controlled by the respondent. Eye movements are recorded to the extent to which each element on the package (e.g., brand name, product type illustration, list of ingredients) is noted, the speed of noting, the sequence of viewing, the clarity of the copy, and the time spent. In the case of eye-tracking procedures, elements of a package that are quickly bypassed or totally overlooked can be easily identified.

Interviewing Practices.   Interviewing is usually conducted at high-traffic, central locations. Because slides are used to project pictures of the various package alternatives, the side must allow for total darkness (with the exception of a safety light), and it should include a partitioned-off interviewing area where respondents cannot overhear one another. The projector is usually placed 10 feet (and respondent 8 feet) from the viewing screen. Before exposure to a test slide, each respondent is shown a "dummy" slide so that they fully understand the procedure.

When the test begins, the respondent is exposed to one test variant that shows a picture of an alternative package among those of other products that appear in its normal environment; in other words, the test is monadic, and no respondent is exposed to more than one test variant. The pictures of the test variants are projected from standard 35-mm slides. The slides are constructed so that their longest dimension is on the horizontal, to depict an actual store environment. Pictures are taken against light-gray backgrounds to control for color effects. Typically, there are about 8 to 12 evenly distributed products per slide, and to minimize bias three random layouts of each test variant are used. Exhibit 19–4 (see page 598) shows a product-line extension package slide test for Eagle snacks.

EXHIBIT 19–4

Package Slide

Courtesy Anheuser-Busch Companies.

Respondents are exposed to each slide at four different intervals: $\frac{1}{8}$ second, $\frac{1}{4}$ second, $\frac{1}{2}$ second, and 1 second. After each exposure, the respondent indicates to the interviewer which brand he or she has seen. When imagery and end benefits data are needed, the respondent is escorted to a separate area and shown the product. The product can be displayed in a number of different formats; for example, the respondent can be shown a storyboard, the actual product, or a 35-mm slide.

Questions Asked.   Package tests typically focus on the following areas.

1. *Brand imagery.* Respondents are asked to describe, say, with semantic differential scales, their impressions of the product.
2. *Aesthetic appeal.* Does the respondent like the package? Is it pleasant to look at? Is it the kind of package that generates interest?
3. *Functional characteristics.* Respondents are asked to evaluate the functional aspects of the package. Does it prevent contamination or damage? Does it provide a convenient means of storing and dispensing the product?
4. *Likes and dislikes.* Generally open-ended questions that allow the respondent to express spontaneous reactions to the package and product.
5. *Purchase interest.* Questions designed to demonstrate degrees of commitment or resistance to trial.
6. *Product usage and demographics.* Respondents are asked to provide category usage data along with standard demographic information.

EXHIBIT 19–5
—

Marketing Research
Proposal:
Package Test

Brand:	Eagle snacks.
Project:	Eagle popcorn test.
Background & Objectives:	The brand group has three possible package designs for a new popcorn product that Eagle plans to roll out nationally. The objective of this test is to determine which package design is superior with regard to registering the Eagle Brand name, conveying end benefits that are associated with freshness and quality, and initiating trial.
Research Design:	A total of 450 respondents (150 per package alternative) category users will be recruited and interviewed at a central testing location. All respondents will have purchased popcorn in a supermarket for themselves or a member of their family within the past 30 days. Respondents will be seated at an eye-tracking recorder and will take a visual walk through a supermarket. Slides will include a series of in-store displays with one display showing the test package. Respondents will be asked to pick one of the packages. The respondent can take as much or as little time as needed with each slide. Eye tracking is recorded for each slide.
Information to Be Obtained:	Eye tracking will determine precisely which brands a shopper looks at in a display and in what order. It records how quickly each brand draws attention, the number of times a respondent looks at a particular package, and the total time the respondent spends with facings on the shelf. After exposure to the store slides, recall questions will be administered to determine how the package helps to register the brand name. In addition, questions focusing on
	1. Beliefs about product freshness and quality.
	2. Brand image.
	3. Aesthetic appeal.
	4. Purchase intent.
	will be asked.
Action Standard:	The brand group will recommend the package that
	1. Registers the highest brand recognition.
	2. Generates the highest top box scores on freshness and quality.
	3. Generates the highest top box intention scores.
Cost and Timing:	The cost for this research will be $32,500 (+ 10 percent contingency), and we will adhere to the following schedule:

Fieldwork	1½ weeks
Top line	1½ weeks
Final report	2 weeks

Selected Supplier:	Perception Research Services, Inc.

Sampling Practices

Interviewing for a package test is conducted at high-traffic, central locations. Standard practice is to use a minimum of 100 category users per test variant and no fewer than 50 respondents for a subgroup analysis. As in name testing, specific age and gender requirements may be established.

Action Standards

Various standards for package test evaluation can be used. Performance standards include

1. Whether the package must equal or have greater visibility than the current package designs or competitive packages.
2. Whether the package must equal or achieve better ratings on key attribute/ end benefit scale.
3. Whether visibility or image is to receive the greater weight in making the analysis.

Approach to Analysis

The analysis focuses on the visibility and image measures. As in name testing, visibility and image scores usually are tested across alternative package designs with test of proportions and means (see Chapter 15).

By way of summary, Exhibit 19–5 (see page 599) presents a prototypical marketing research proposal for a package test study.

SUMMARY

In this chapter we have discussed and illustrated the basic techniques and procedures used in name and package testing research. As we have indicated, name and package tests are extremely important marketing research activities because much of what is conveyed about a product is communicated through the product's name and package design.

KEY CONCEPTS

name tests	company names	line names	created names
denotative meaning	explicit descriptive names	implicit imagery names	package tests
connotative meaning			

REVIEW QUESTIONS

1. Discuss the primary approaches to naming a product.
2. Describe the key information that should be collected in a name test.
3. Describe the steps in conducting a name test.
4. Why is packaging an important consideration?
5. Describe the steps in conducting a package test. What issues should the researcher be particularly sensitive to?

Advertising Research Practices
Pretesting and Tracking

- Understand the many purposes that advertising serves.
- Define what is meant by advertising effectiveness.
- Describe and illustrate standard copy testing practices in the print and television media.
- Discuss the objectives of market tracking and market testing studies.
- Explain the procedures used in tracking and testing advertising campaigns.

INTRODUCTION

Advertising effectiveness is a crucial concern to most companies. Advertising serves multiple purposes: It provides information; it can generate favorable attitudes toward a brand; it can lead to favorable intentions to buy; it can cause an individual to buy a brand; and, as is typically the case with durable purchases, it can be used to rationalize a purchase.

Because advertising serves many purposes, measures of its effectiveness may take many different forms. The measures may be qualitative, quantitative, or a combination of both. They may be taken in a laboratory-like setting before a finished advertisement is ready. Alternatively, they may be taken on a finished advertisement either before the advertisement is placed in the media or at various times after it has been placed in the media. Thus, what is being measured, when the measurement is made, and which medium the advertisement is placed in determine the precise definition of effectiveness.

Most advertising research techniques focus on measuring the effectiveness of an ad in terms of awareness, communicability, and persuasiveness. Typical questions center on (see also Exhibit 20–1 on page 602).

- Whether the ad creates awareness.
- Whether the ad communicates the benefits of the product.
- Whether the ad creates a predisposition to purchase.

Although some people may argue that the ultimate goal of advertising is to increase sales, rarely is sales volume or market share directly used to measure the effectiveness of advertising. First, advertising is only one element in the

EXHIBIT 20–1

Questions Asked

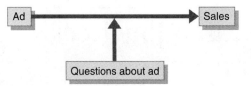

Do they:
- Notice it?
- Understand it?
- Get right image?
- Get involved?

Questions about brand
- Increased awareness?
- Improved/changed image?

Source: Gordon Brown, "Tracking Studies and Sales Effects" (Advertising Research Foundation, Key Issues Workshop on Advertising Tracking Studies, July 1984), p. 113.

overall marketing mix, and it is difficult, if not impossible, to unambiguously separate the effects of advertising from those of in-store promotions, distribution, shelf position, coupons, and so on. Second, in certain companies advertising budgets are fixed to sales volume; that is, advertising budgets are allocated as a fixed percentage of sales. In such cases, it may be impossible to isolate the effects of advertising because of the "chicken and egg" syndrome. Third, even when advertising does affect sales directly, there usually is a lag between when the ad is run and when the products are purchased, which makes measurement difficult. Fourth, the effects of competitive activities (e.g., new-product introductions, coupons, and the like) often cannot be separated from the effect of a given firm's advertising. Fifth, advertising has a cumulative effect so that attempts to isolate the effects of a single ad, especially for an established brand, can be very difficult.

THE ADVERTISING DECISION PROCESS

Measuring advertising performance, whether before or after it has been put into the marketplace, is often difficult. To better understand the problems that must be resolved let us first consider the process underlying advertising decisions.

Exhibit 20–2 presents a simple illustration of the decision process for advertising. Typically, the process begins with some sort of planning. As we discussed in Chapter 2, it is likely that the planning process will be guided, either explicitly or implicitly, by company or product strategies and objectives. Next, focus is directed toward developing advertising execution, or, as it is generally referred to, copy. This is the stage at which the advertising agency and its creative people are most important. Once executional copy has been developed, it is pretested prior to being used in the marketplace. As we discuss in the following sections, copy testing services vary greatly, depending on the medium in which the ad is placed. For this reason we will discuss copy testing services in the print and television media. Once the advertising campaign is launched, it is tracked and/or tested in the market-

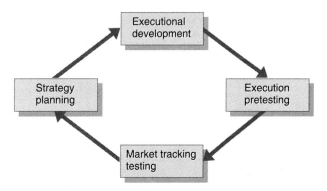

EXHIBIT 20-2
—
The Advertising
Decision Process

Source: James F. Donius, *Marketplace Measurement: Tracking and Testing Advertising and Other Marketing Effects* (New York: Association of National Advertisers, Inc., 1986), p. 2.

place. At this point we are concerned with whether the ad is performing well. In cases in which the ad is not performing up to expectations, the process comes full circle, that is, back to strategy and planning considerations.[1]

A SYSTEM FOR AD EVALUATION

The advertising decision process described above naturally leads to a system for evaluating advertisements. As depicted in Exhibit 20-3 (see page 604), the advertising evaluation system has several critical components.[2] Based on product positioning and advertising strategy considerations, the advertising is developed and pretested. However, it is important to realize that copy testing is only one of the elements. If a company's procedure for evaluating ads is to be useful, it must evaluate the effectiveness of the ad after it has been used in the marketplace. In other words, there must be some validation from the marketplace. As we will discuss shortly, this view of the role of market tracking as a validator for copy testing is an important distinction, and it can be the principal benefit of a tracking system.

Having recognized the need for both market tracking and copy testing, we can now turn our attention to current procedures used in both processes. In principle, these procedures can be undertaken directly by the advertiser, by the advertising agency, or by an independent, commercial marketing research supplier. Such commercial marketing research suppliers are used because they provide an independent, and presumably unbiased, means for which the advertiser and the advertising agency (who developed the ad) can evaluate the ad's effectiveness and marketplace performance.

In the following sections we provide an up-to-date discussion of three general types of advertising effectiveness studies: copy testing, market tracking, and market testing. Copy testing involves the pretesting of advertisements before they are

---

[1]This material has been discussed by James F. Donius, *Marketplace Measurement: Tracking and Testing Advertising and Other Marketing Effects* (New York: Association of National Advertisers, Inc., 1986), p. 1.

[2]Ibid., p. 2.

EXHIBIT 20–3

A System of
Advertising
Evaluation

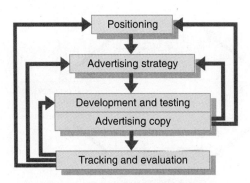

Source: James F. Donius, *Marketplace Measurement: Tracking and Testing Advertising and Other Marketing Effects* (New York: Association of National Advertisers, Inc., 1986), p. 3.

aired in the marketplace. Both market tracking and market testing involve the assessment of advertisements that are currently used in the marketplace. As we will discuss in the following paragraphs, the primary difference between these in-market testing systems is the degree to which the marketplace is disrupted when the testing is undertaken.

COPY TESTING: PRINT ADS

print ad tests
Attempts to assess the power of an ad placed in a magazine or newspaper to be remembered, to communicate, to affect attitudes, and, ultimately, to produce sales.

Print ad tests attempt to assess the power of an ad placed in a magazine or newspaper to be remembered, to communicate, to affect attitudes, and, ultimately, to produce sales. Even though in principle all print testing techniques focus on reactions to the ad, the impact of the ad on the perception of the product is also investigated. Exhibit 20–4 presents a prototypical marketing research proposal for a print ad test.

Philosophy and Objectives

Put simply, the objective of print ad tests is to make go/no-go decisions regarding the test advertisement. Print ad–testing procedures, which are typically applicable across all brands, provide comparative data that can be used as norms to judge proposed advertisements. For example, in the print ad test described in Exhibit 20–4, the new Soft Touch "Soft Drop" print ad will be compared with a past Soft Touch "Lulu" ad that was tested approximately six months earlier.

Research Design

The research design used in print testing depends on the shape and context in which the ad is presented to the respondent. Four basic types of research designs are described below.[3]

---

[3]The discussion in this section follows that of Holbert, et al., *Marketing Research for the Marketing and Advertising Executive* (New York: American Marketing Association, New York Chapter, Inc., 1981), chapter 10, pp. 196–99.

EXHIBIT 20–4

Print Ad Test:
Marketing Research
Project Proposed

Brand:	Soft Touch Hand Lotion.
Project:	"Soft Drop" print test.
Background and Objectives:	A new Soft Touch "Soft Drop" print ad has been developed and made available for testing. The Soft Touch "Lulu" ad was tested via the Mapes & Ross print copy test method. The purpose of this research is to determine the effectiveness of the Soft Drop ad in generating attention and purchase persuasion relative to the past Lulu ad.
Research Design:	The Mapes & Ross print test method will be used. The ad will appear in the May issue of *Good Housekeeping*. The sample will consist of 200 women, aged 18 to 65, who are regular readers of women's service magazines (*Family Circle, Good Housekeeping, Ladies' Home Journal, McCalls, Redbook, Woman's Day*), and have *not* read the *Good Housekeeping* test issue. The test issue will be placed with randomly selected women; and door-to-door interviews will be used. Each respondent will be asked to read the magazine as they normally would. When the test issue is placed, brand preferences for hand lotions, body lotions, and other product categories will be obtained (preprint exposure). The next day, respondents will be recontacted by telephone and will be asked to describe at least one article as proof of readership. Next, they will be asked the same brand preference questions that they were asked the day before (postprint exposure), and they will be asked to recall and describe six ads that appeared in the magazine, including the Soft Touch ad.

Information to Be Obtained:	Pre-exposure interview:
	
	  — Qualifying demographics.
	  — Brand preference (hand lotions, body lotions, and five additional product categories).
	
	Post-exposure interview:
	
	  — Brand preference (hand lotions, body lotions, and five additional product categories).
	  — Proven recall.
	  — Recall content.

Action Standard:	The Soft Drop copy approach will be recommended if it performs *significantly higher** than the Lulu ad on each of the following measures: Brand preference (pre-post) shift. Proven recall.
Cost & Timing:	The cost for this research will be $6,000 ± 10 percent. Time schedule for this research will be:

Fieldwork	1 week
Top line	2 weeks
Computer tabulations	2 weeks
Final report	1 week
Total	6 weeks

Research Supplier:	Dolan Research, Inc.

*Significant difference at the 90 percent or higher level of confidence.

single ad research design
Test where respondent is exposed to the test ad by itself; that is, the test ad is not shown with other ads, and it is not displayed in a magazine.

headline test
Design where the respondent is shown two or more headlines and is asked to indicate the one that is more interesting.

forced exposure tests
Design whereby pre- and post-exposure purchase preference questions are asked.

attitude shift ability
The difference between the percentage of the program audience who selected the test brand before viewing the ad or commercial and the percentage who selected it after viewing.

multiple ads/portfolio tests
Test in which respondent examines a portfolio of ads, one of which is the test ad.

dummy magazine tests
A realistic-looking test format using a dummy magazine that systematically varies the advertisements in such a way that some families receive a dummy magazine containing the test ad and other (matched) families receive a dummy magazine containing no ads at all.

Single Ad. In a **single ad research design** the respondent is exposed to the test ad by itself; that is, the test ad is not shown with other ads and is not displayed in a magazine. There are two approaches with this type of research design.

— *"Headline tests.* In **headline tests,** the focus is on the ad itself. Usually, the respondent is shown two or more headlines and is asked to indicate the one that is most interesting. After selecting the most interesting headline, the respondent is shown the corresponding ad and asked the usual diagnostics. The advantage of this research design is its approximation to reality; it is reasonable to expect that before a print ad is "seen," the headline must capture the person's attention.

— *Forced exposure tests.* In **forced exposure tests,** pre- and post-exposure purchase preference questions are asked. Before the respondent is exposed to the test ad, a purchase intention question is asked. After exposure to the test ad the respondent is again asked the purchase intention question and the top box (or top two box) percentages "pre" and "post" are compared. The difference in these percentages is said to reflect the ad's **attitude shift ability** (i.e., the ad's persuasiveness). Thus, this type of research design focuses on the ad's effect on perceptions of the product.

Multiple Ads. In **multiple ads** research design, commonly referred to as **portfolio tests,** an array of ads is prepared. In the portfolio, which resembles a book, each ad is presented on its own page. One of the ads in the portfolio is the test ad; some of the other ads are from the same product category, and some are from other product categories. The respondent is given the portfolio and asked to leaf through it. After the respondent examines the portfolio, it is taken away and an unaided-recall questioning period begins. In this case, interest centers on which brands the respondent recalls being advertised and specific information concerning the recalled ads. The test continues, and the respondent is exposed to the test ad again. The respondent is then asked about specific brand information contained in the ad and about its believability. The weakness of portfolio testing lies in its unrealistic settings and the forced (aided) question format feature of this method. On the positive side, it is inexpensive, quick, and can be easily interpreted if norms have been developed.

"Dummy Magazine" Tests. In **dummy magazine tests,** the effectiveness of the test ad is evaluated before the respondent realizes that he or she is participating in a copy test. Although there are several different ways to implement this design, a typical approach is to print a dummy magazine that looks realistic (i.e., contains articles, pictures, editorials, and so on) and systematically vary the advertisements in such a way that some families receive a dummy magazine containing the test ad(s) and other (matched) families receive a dummy magazine containing no ads. Several days after placing the dummy magazines in the respondent's home, the respondent is asked a "buffer" question relating to how he or she liked the magazine and product-centered rating questions relating to information presented in the test ads. The product-centered rating questions can be used to make comparisons (e.g., attitude shift scores) across the "exposed" and "unexposed" groups. Frequently, recall and comprehension questions are asked after the product ratings have been collected.

"Real Magazine" Tests.   In **real magazine tests,** interest centers on the magazine effect, that is, the context in which the ad appears. There are two popular varieties of real magazine testing studies.

- *Home placement.* In **home placement testing,** readers of a particular magazine are identified. The current issue of the magazine is given to the respondent one or two days before the issue is available to the general public. At the time of the placement, each respondent is informed about an intended telephone or personal call-back that will take place the following day so that they can answer more questions about the issue.

    In ad-centered home placement tests nothing is specifically said about the test ad. At the time of the call-back the respondent is simply asked to indicate all of the ads that were in the issue and specific information on what each ad contains (e.g., picture, headline, and so forth). Frequently, an aided question format is used in which the interviewer asks about the test ad, some other ad, or all ads that appear in the issue. In product-centered home placement tests, the procedure is the same, except that at the time of placement, the interviewer asks the respondent for purchase intention ratings. At call-back, the interviewer asks standard, unaided-recall questions, aided-recall questions, and diagnostic questions. At the end of the interview the purchase intention questions are asked again. The percentage difference between the "pre" (placement) interview and the "post" (call-back) interview intention scores for the test brand are used as a measure of effectiveness.

- *Starch scores.* In **Starch scores** research design, named after Daniel Starch, readers of specific magazines are located, and the interviewer determines whether each ad in the issue was remembered, whether the name of the brand or advertiser was read, and whether a substantial portion of the advertisement was read. Based on this information, the Starch service provides index scores and other normed data.

Questions Asked

As we indicated, the information collected in print ad tests usually relates to reactions to the ad or the effects the ad had on perceptions of the product. Typically, interest centers on four key measures.

1. *Recall.* **Recall** refers to a primary indicator of an ad's effectiveness, which is how many people remember having seen the test ad, both on an unaided and aided basis. Frequently, a **proven total recall** score is computed, which gives the percentage of respondents who correctly recalled specific copy or visual elements in the test ad. In addition, specific details about what each respondent saw are collected. Exhibit 20–5 (see page 608) shows

---

real magazine test
Test where interest centers on the "magazine" effect—that is, the context in which the ad appears.

home placement testing
Test where the current issue of a magazine is given to the respondent one or two days before the issue is available to the general public; at call-back time the respondent is asked to indicate all of the ads that were in the issue and specific information on what each ad contains.

Starch scores
Research design where readers of specific magazines are located, and the interviewer determines whether each ad in the issue was remembered, whether the name of the brand or advertiser was read, and whether a substantial portion of the advertisement was read.

recall
Measures of how many people remember having seen the test ad both on an unaided and aided basis.

proven total recall
Percentage of respondents in the program audience that correctly recalled copy or visual elements in the test ad or commercial.

EXHIBIT 20–5

———

Unaided and Aided
Question Formats for
a Print Ad Text

Unaided Questions

1a. Now, I'd like to change your attention to the ads that appeared in this magazine. Do you remember seeing any ads in this particular magazine for [*fill in product category form below*]? *If Yes:* What brand of _____ was advertised?

[*Note: Record respondent's answer exactly, as close to their pronunciation as possible, and/or any remark made on the name. Probe for specific name and type. Repeat for all product categories. Probe for mention of brands advertised in each category until the respondent cannot remember any more brands advertised in that category.*]

A. Pantyhose

( ) YES ( ) NO

Brand name *[Probe for as many brands as respondent can remember.]*

Brand name *[Probe for as many brands as respondent can remember.]*

Brand name *[Probe for as many brands as respondent can remember.]*

B. Toaster ovens

( ) YES ( ) NO

Brand name *[Probe for as many brands as respondent can remember.]*

Brand name *[Probe for as many brands as respondent can remember.]*

Brand name *[Probe for as many brands as respondent can remember.]*

C. Lotions for your body

( ) YES ( ) NO

Brand name *[Probe for as many brands as respondent can remember.]*

Brand name *[Probe for as many brands as respondent can remember.]*

Brand name *[Probe for as many brands as respondent can remember.]*

D. Cosmetics

( ) YES ( ) NO

Brand name *[Probe for as many brands as respondent can remember.]*

Brand name *[Probe for as many brands as respondent can remember.]*

Brand name *[Probe for as many brands as respondent can remember.]*

Aided Questions

1b. Next, I would like to read off the names of some of the ads in this issue. Please tell me whether or not you recall seeing them. Please say "yes" for each ad where you can actually recall some part of the illustration or the printing well enough to picture it in your mind. [*Read the ad list slowly. Give the respondent plenty of time to think about each ad. Remind her that we are only interested in the ads as they appeared in this particular issue.*]

			YES	NO
Start	1( )	L'eggs Sheer Elegance pantyhose	1( )	2( )
with	2(✓)	Proctor-Silex toaster oven	1( )	2( )
item	3( )	Johnson's baby lotion	1( )	2( )
checked	4( )	Merle Norman cosmetics	1( )	2( )

prototypical unaided and aided brand-recall question formats for the print ad test described in Exhibit 20–4.

2. *Recognition.* In **recognition,** interest typically centers on whether the respondent can recognize the name of the test brand. For example, a standard practice is to cut out the name of the brand, the package, or any other identifying feature, and then ask the respondent to indicate what the ad is for. Eye-movement copy testing services are essentially recognition tests because their purpose is to identify which parts of the ad the eye moved over.

3. *Diagnostics.* Standard **diagnostics** questions generally include measures of **believability** and **comprehension.** Was the main idea of the ad believable? Was there any information in the ad that you did not understand? Diagnostic testing also may include direct evaluation of the ad on bipolar adjective scales. This information is used to determine the percentage of respondents rating the ad as "clever," "dull," and so forth and can be compared with normed data, if available.

4. *Product perceptions.* **Product perceptions** questions relate to the ad's effect on perceptions and/or purchase intentions concerning the test brand. For product-centered print ad tests, a "pre" (placement) and "post" (call-back) procedure is used.

Sampling

Interviewing is usually conducted in several geographically dispersed markets, and a minimum of 150 respondents per advertisement is used. For subgroup analysis, no fewer than 50 respondents are typically used.

Action Standards

The action standards in prototypical print ad tests are specified in terms of the copy testing service's norms. For example, a typical action standard might say that the advertisement will be recommended if it generates proven total recall levels equal to or better than the norm and/or generates pre-post "Best or Better Brand" levels equal to or better than the norm. You will note that in the print ad test marketing research proposal presented in Exhibit 20–4, the action standard is specified with respect to the comparative-based Lulu ad.

Approach to Analysis

The analysis centers on proven recall and brand preference. Diagnostic measures are secondary.

COPY TESTING. TELEVISION COMMERCIALS

Television advertising is much more expensive than print advertising. For example, a 30-second airtime spot on the 1991 Super Bowl Program cost $850,000. Because of this, commercial copy testing services have become a big business. The number

recognition
A score that measures whether the respondent can recognize the name of the test brand.

diagnostics
Measures of believability and comprehension. Diagnostic testing may also include direct evaluation of the ad, perhaps on bipolar adjective scales.

comprehension/ believability
Percentage of respondents in the program audience that correctly understood/believed product claims that were communicated by the test commercial.

product perceptions
Questions relating to the ad's effect on perceptions and/or purchase intentions concerning the test brand.

of commercial copy testing services has grown dramatically during the past 20 years. Today, the number of techniques used to evaluate the effectiveness of television commercials is far too large to list. In this section we provide a general overview of testing procedures for television commercials.

Philosophy and Objectives

A television commercial can serve many different purposes. Ultimately it sells the product by conveying a specific appeal to an intended target audience. To accomplish this the television commercial must (1) attract attention, (2) register brand name and packaging, (3) communicate meaningful benefits, and (4) motivate purchase. Put simply, the testing of television commercials seeks to determine whether the commercial under study succeeds in doing what it is intended to do. To be more specific, the objectives of such tests are

1. To measure the commercial's intrusiveness—attention/recall.
2. To measure what is communicated—comprehension/believability.
3. To measure the impact of the commercial on purchase interest and brand attitudes.

You will note that the relative importance of each of these measures varies, depending on the type of commercial. For example, in the case of a new product introduction, intrusiveness and comprehension may be more important than attitude shift.

Research Design

off-air tests
Method for evaluating television commercials in which the testing takes place in a controlled environment that does not resemble the surroundings in which the individual usually views commercials.

on-air tests
Testing that takes place in realistic settings; respondents are asked their reactions to commercials that they have seen in their own homes, on their own television sets.

Methods for evaluating television commercials can be divided into two broad types: *off-air* and *on-air*. **Off-air tests** are artificial because the testing takes place in a controlled environment that does not resemble the surroundings in which the individual usually views commercials, that is, in one's home. Off-air tests are used to evaluate the commercial's communication effectiveness before it goes on the air. In contrast, **on-air tests** take place in realistic settings; respondents are asked their reactions to commercials that they have seen in their own home, on their own television sets. At the time of viewing the commercial, the respondent does not know that he or she will be questioned about what he or she saw.

Off-Air Tests.   These tests are designed to evaluate a commercial before it is aired in order to effect changes in the commercial that make it more effective. Off-air testing can take place almost anywhere—in theaters, in shopping malls, in mobile vans, or even in the person's home, using projectors that resemble television sets. Exhibit 20–6 presents a prototypical off-air marketing research proposal.

A popular setting for conducting *off-air* tests is in a theater. Respondents are invited to a local theater to view "pilots" of future television programs. Inserted into the program are several commercials. Before viewing the program each respondent is asked brand preference information about a number of product

EXHIBIT 20–6

Off-Air Test
Marketing Research
Project Proposal

Brand:	Colgate	
Project:	Copy Test "Midnight Delight."	
Background and Purpose:	A new commercial has been developed—"Midnight Delight." The brand group is interested in determining its effectiveness. The objectives of this study will be to determine	

  — Brand recall.
  — Copy recall.
  — Purchase intent shifts.
  — Comparison with previous copy testing results.

Research Method: This research will be conducted using central location mall facilities in Boston, Atlanta, Milwaukee, and San Francisco. Each commercial will viewed by 200 past-30-day toothpaste users as follows

		Age Group	Number of Respondents
Males	50%	8–11	30
Females	50%	12–17	50
		18–24	25
		25–34	25
		35–49	10
		50+	10
			150

Information to Be Obtained:

  — Brand recall.
  — Copy recall.
  — Pre- and post-purchase intentions.

Action Standard: This study, which is being done for information purposes, will be used in conjunction with previous copy testing results.

Cost and Timing: The cost for one commercial will be $6,500 ± 10 %. The following schedule will be established

Fieldwork	3 weeks
Top line	1 week
Final report	3 weeks
Total	7 weeks

Supplier: Leggett Lustig Firtle, Inc.

categories, including the test product category, under the pretense of a drawing in which the respondent will receive the product or cost of the product for which he or she has the strongest preference. After viewing the program (and commercials), respondents are again asked to express their brand preferences. A "pre-post" measure of effectiveness is used to evaluate the test commercial. The attitude shift effect is computed by taking the difference between the percentage of respondents who selected the test brand before viewing the commercial and the percentage who selected it after viewing the commercial. Attitude shift scores are compared with norms, that is, the results of past tests. Typically, comprehension and recall measures also are collected.

A different type of *off-air* copy testing service involves intercepting respondents as they enter food stores. In conveniently located trailers, respondents view a series

EXHIBIT 20–7

24-Hour-Recall
Marketing Research
Project Proposal

Brand:	Juicy Fruit.
Project:	"False Start" Burke on-air test.
Background and Objectives:	The William Wrigley Co. has requested a Burke on-air test for the new copy execution "False Start."
	The objective of this research is to measure the communication effectiveness of the False Start execution.
Research Method:	A sample of 150 past-30-day chewing gum users in the commercial audience will be interviewed. The air date is scheduled for the first Tuesday of the month in December, on "NYPD Blue." Interviewing will be conducted within five metro areas: Boston, Atlanta, Indianapolis, Dallas, and Phoenix.
Information to Be Obtained:	— Total commercial recall. — Copy recall. — Visual recall.
Action Standard:	The commercial will be considered acceptable in the areas of memorability and sales message communication if *a.* It generates 25 percent or better related recall score. *b.* At least 25 percent of the commercial audience remembers at least one sales message.
Timing and Cost:	Fieldwork First Tuesday in December Top line 1 week Final report 4 weeks The cost for this research will be $15,000 ± 10%.
Research Supplier:	Burke Marketing Research.

of commercials, one of which is the test commercial; as a reward the respondents are given a book of money-off coupons, one (or more) of which is for the test brand. A control group of respondents is used. They receive the book of coupons but do not view the commercials. The measure of commercial effectiveness used is the difference between the purchase incidence of respondents who viewed the commercials and those who did not.

On-Air Tests.   These tests are designed to evaluate a commercial after it has been placed on the air in order to assess whether the commercial does what it is supposed to do in a normal competitive environment. Two types of *on-air* testing can be distinguished: *on-air single exposure* tests and *on-air multiple* tests.

day-after recall
Single-exposure on-air technique where the test commercial is aired in several test cities; the next day, a sample of respondents who say they viewed the program on which the test commercial was telecast are interviewed.

One of the best known of the single exposure techniques is **day-after recall**. In the case of this technique, the test commercial is aired in several (three to four) test cities. The next day, a sample of respondents who say they viewed the program during which the test commercial was telecast are interviewed. Viewers of the program are questioned, on an unaided and aided basis, about whether they saw the commercial. If they did, they are asked what it said. These measures are compared with norms (e.g., recall scores for other products in the same or a similar category) in order to judge the relative effectiveness of the test commercial. Exhibit 20–7 presents an illustrative marketing research proposal for a day-after recall copy testing study.

Multiple-exposure techniques attempt to give a better indication of the test commercial's sales effectiveness. In this approach, the test commercial is aired in a test city (or cities) over time. Periodic on-air tests are conducted along with store audits of sales. Controlled cable test services have become very popular. Through this technique, one campaign is aired in homes in one city, or on side of town, or one side of a city block, and so on, and another campaign is aired in the homes of a matched sample. Thus, through repeated (over time) measures of recall and store audits for each group of viewers, the relative effectiveness of each campaign can be judged.

multiple-exposure technique
Technique where the test commercial is aired in a test city (or cities) over time; periodic on-air tests are conducted along with store audits of sales.

Questions Asked

Although the specific questions asked will depend on which commercial copy testing service is being used, there are a number of common measures collected in most television commercial tests. Several of these are

1. Proven total recall—percentage of respondents in the program audience who correctly recalled copy or visual elements in the test commercial.
2. Copy recall—percentage of respondents in the program audience who correctly recalled copy elements in the test commercial.
3. Visual recall—percentage of respondents in the program audience who correctly recalled visual elements in the test commercial.
4. Comprehension/believability—percentage of respondents in the program audience who correctly understood/believed product claims communicated in the test commercial.
5. Attitude shift—the difference between the percentage of the program audience who selected the test brand before viewing the commercial and the percentage who selected it after viewing the commercial.

It is important to note that specific questions are standardized for each copy testing service so that comparable norms can be developed.

Sampling

Sampling practices vary depending on the research design. In general, interviews are conducted with a minimum of 150 respondents per commercial, who are past-30-day users of the product category. If appropriate, age and gender quotas are based on category volume contribution. The specific test cities used will depend on which copy testing service is being used and whether the commercial is being tested on-air or off-air. Standard test cities will be discussed in Chapter 21.

Action Standards

The action standards in prototypical tests of television commercials are expressed in terms of copy testing service norms or with respect to a specific previous copy test. Each copy testing service has developed data banks on the effectiveness (e.g., recall, attitude shift) of ads across a large number of product categories. A commercial that achieved a proven recall score of 30 percent could be viewed as above average.

Approach to Analysis

Once again the analysis centers on recall and brand preference. As in print testing, diagnostic measures are secondary.

MARKET TRACKING[4]

As we indicated earlier, if a copy testing system is to be successful, it must include a method for later validation in the marketplace. Stated differently, in order for an effective pretesting system to be developed, at some point the advertisements that are given the "seal of approval" must be assessed in the natural environments in which they are aired.

Philosophy and Objectives

Among the phrases most often used to describe tracking are *periodic, benchmark, scorecard,* and *barometer.* All of these phrases reflect the notion that tracking provides a means for determining where a firm stands vis-à-vis the competition. In this regard, tracking serves two objectives. The first objective of tracking is to monitor the marketplace. **Market tracking studies** are often the principal source of data about category and brand-use patterns, demographic characteristics of users, consumer attitudes and predispositions, and brand awareness levels.

market tracking studies
Designed to determine where a firm stands vis-à-vis its competition by monitoring the marketplace and providing realistic performance benchmarks.

The second objective in market tracking, reassessment, is a natural outgrowth of monitoring. Tracking provides a follow-up or feedback role to management. By monitoring the marketplace it provides information on real-world performance, typically after exerting some degree of marketing force, thereby confronting managers with the results of their decisions. In essence, the strategic reassessment that market tracking affords allows managers to effectively set or develop measurable objectives. In other words, tracking provides realistic benchmarks by which the performance of real-world marketing campaigns can be evaluated.

Research Design

The first point to understand about market tracking is that it is relatively undisruptive; that is, market tracking does not deliberately introduce any alterations into the marketplace at the time of testing. A commercial is first aired, and over time, the marketplace is monitored regarding key measures that are designed to evaluate questions such as

---

[4]Much of the discussion on market tracking has been adapted from Donius, *Marketplace Measurement,* section III.

- How long should the commercial run?
- Have company objectives been achieved?
- Should strategies be reevaluated?
- Are brand awareness and other points made in the copy wearing out?

A number of design considerations can be made when implementing a market tracking study.

Cross-Category versus Within-Category. The most typical market tracking study considers a single category, or market frame, of reference. The reason for this is simple. By focusing on a single category, in-depth information about a brand's relative competitive position can be obtained. Cross-category designs allow an assessment of the relative performance of advertising across all categories. However, you will note that when cross-category tracking is undertaken, the information obtained for any given category is more limited.

Continuous versus Single Point-in-Time. By **continuous tracking** we mean taking readings (i.e., measurements) during the entire length of a campaign, as opposed to taking measurements at, say, two or three points in time. (Conventional tracking is usually undertaken every six months, and occasionally it is undertaken once a quarter.) A typical scenario might be: 100 interviews a week throughout the year, with 20 interviews per day. Even though in the United States single **point-in-time tracking** designs have been used with greater frequency than continuous designs, primarily because of their lower cost, evidence favors the continuous approach for several reasons. First, there appears to be no generally accepted way to decide on the periodicity of post-measurements. The amount spent, the pattern of spending and the nature of the advertising are just a few of the factors that influence the timing of when marketplace readings should be taken. Second, single point-in-time designs can provide misleading information. This is easily seen by examining Exhibit 20–8 (see page 616). The graph shows monthly awareness scores for brand X. Note that if a reading was taken in June and then in May, the conclusion would be that awareness increased by 40 percent. However, if the first reading was in December and the second in March, the conclusion would be that awareness decreased by 12 percent. Some 20 years ago AHF Marketing Research[5] took a more humorous stance on this same issue (see Exhibit 20–9 on page 617).

Panel versus Matched Samples. The basic issue here is whether to use a **longitudinal design** of the same respondents or a matched sample design, in which respondents are matched on a set of background characteristics— recall that we discussed matched samples in Chapter 7. Typically, longitudinal designs involve prerecruited diary or scanner panels that include detailed purchase records over time (diary panels and scanner services were discussed in Chapter 4). In the

continuous tracking
Studies in which measurements are taken during the entire length of a campaign.

point-in-time tracking
Studies in which measurements are taken at discrete points in time.

longitudinal design
Same respondents are questioned over time.

---

[5]AHF Marketing Research, "Their Way-Out Way," *Marketing Review,* 1973.

EXHIBIT 20–8

Spontaneous
Awareness

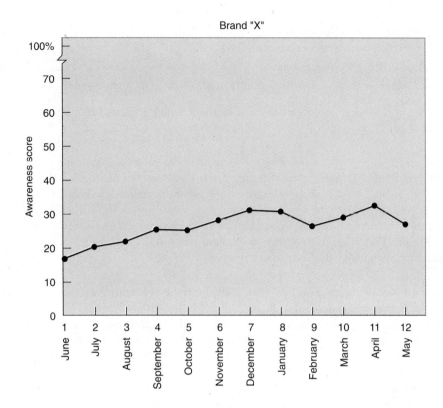

Brand "X"

context of market tracking, Haley and Gatty[6] discussed the advantages and disadvantages of these two approaches as well as a third approach. Longitudinal designs are more costly, and often they have lower completion rates. Perhaps the greatest disadvantage of the longitudinal design is the risk of conditioning; that is, by asking the same respondents the same questions, the responses can become conditioned, especially in the case of brand awareness and attitudes. Primarily for this reason, fresh samples, matched on selected demographic and usage variables, are often drawn in each wave. However, matched sample designs are generally inferior when it comes to conveying information about change. For example, consider Table 20–1, which provides hypothetical data on brand attitude for two interviews conducted with the same sample of respondents. Note that the totals for each interview are almost identical and similar to those that would have been obtained from a matched sample design with different respondents. However, the cells of the table provide insightful information that could not be obtained through the matched sample study. The longitudinal design allows us to define and, subsequently, to analyze change groups. (You will recall that in Chapter 15 we introduced a method of analyzing change tables like this.) To be more specific, we see that 15 percent of the respondents that held favorable brand attitudes

[6]Russell I. Haley and Ronald Gatty, "Monitoring Your Markets Continuously," *Harvard Business Review*, May–June 1968.

Their way.   # Our way.

EXHIBIT 20–9
—
AHF: "Their Way
Out"

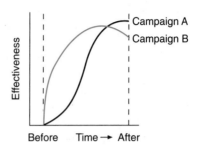

A lot of people in our business evaluate the effectiveness of advertising campaigns by doing a "before-after" test. They interview a sample of people, run the campaign and then interview another sample of people.

By running two campaigns in two groups of markets, they can compare the difference from "before" to "after" and tell which campaign is better.

We call this a "dumbbell" design (no pun intended).

Their way assumes that advertising builds in effectiveness like Campaign A.

But what happens if the campaign builds like B?

Their way wouldn't show how successful Campaign B was; in fact, it might look like a failure compared to A.

Our way is to consider alternative design possibilities. One such possibility is to measure the average height of the curve over the entire campaign rather than measuring it at two arbitrary points in time. It requires continuous readings over the entire length of the campaign, but out of it we get *total effects* and *wear-out*.

Think the problem through. That's our way.

Source: AHF Marketing Research, 20 West 33rd Street, New York, NY 10001.

TABLE 20–1

Brand Attitudes at
Two Points in Time

	Time 2		
Time 1	Favorable (%)	Unfavorable (%)	Total (%)
Favorable	50	15	65
Unfavorable	20	15	35
Total	70	30	100

changed, and 20 percent of the respondents that held unfavorable attitudes moved in the opposite direction.

A compromise design of some attractiveness combines aspects of the longitudinal and matched sample approaches. This design calls for reinterviewing a fixed percentage of the respondents contacted at the previous wave of interviewing and for obtaining interviews with a certain number of new respondents

Data Collection Methods. Generally, the type of design influences the method of data collection. For example, continuous tracking tends to be conducted on the telephone, most often with CATI systems. Point-in-time tracking is conducted by personal or telephone interviewing, and sometimes, although far less frequently, with prerecruited mail panels. One problem with mail interviewing relates to the awareness readings. In the case of a mail survey, a respondent can read ahead in the questionnaire and determine what brands the interviewer is most interested in.

We should add that a potentially growing format for market tracking will come from single-source data. You may recall from Chapter 4 that single-source syndicated services collect both viewing and purchase behavior, longitudinally, for the same household, Obviously, the advantage of single-source data is that we do not have to compare different samples, each with its own sampling error, since there is only one sampling error, which increases precision.

Questions Asked

The standard questions and the order of questions asked in prototypical market tracking studies refer to

- Brand and advertising awareness.
- Brand use.
- Brand purchase.
- Advertising recall.
- Likes/dislikes.
- Brand ratings.
- Other diagnostic questions.
- Classification questions.

Usually, the questions are standardized to ensure that the data collected are comparable from interview wave to interview wave.

The measurement of awareness deserves some special attention. An initial question concerns whether to use an aided or unaided format. The Opinion Research Corporation provides a helpful perspective.

> If a brand is in a fractioned, highly competitive market, or if it is new, aided awareness may be the most useful, sensitive measure for the brand. If, on the other hand, the brand is a household word, dominates its category and/or is in a highly advertised category with few competitors, spontaneous awareness is probably going to prove more sensitive and useful.[7]

Another potential problem is the lack of face validity of awareness measures. Typically, brand and advertising awareness are collected on both an aided and unaided basis and, as the following illustration indicates, total advertising awareness is often artificially inflated.[8] Consider Exhibit 20–10, which shows claimed national ad awareness for five brands. Note that the second-quarter awareness scores

---

[7]Opinion Research Corporation, "Caravan Trends Approach to Monitoring Marketing Efforts" (Unpublished working paper, 1985).

[8]Adapted from Donius, *Marketplace Measurement*.

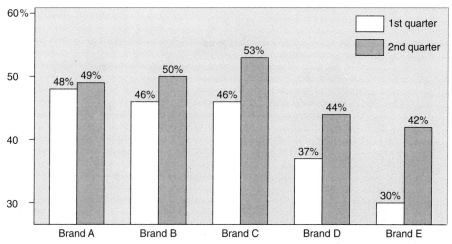

EXHIBIT 20–10
—
Claimed Ad
Awareness Nationally

Source: James F. Donius, *Marketplace Measurement: Tracking and Testing Advertising and Other Marketing Effects* (New York: Association of National Advertisers, Inc., 1986), p. 54.

are uniformly higher than their first-quarter counterparts. What is surprising is that these results were obtained in a period when brand B was not being advertised for almost a year. There are several possible explanations for the apparent "yea-saying," which include the fact that this brand was the first brand of its type in the category and it had a high degree of promotional activity. Brand and advertising-awareness levels should always be compared with marketplace advertising-expenditure levels.

A final issue concerns how to ask the awareness question. The type of question will determine the levels of memory that are being tapped. For example, consider questions concerning

- Highly specific advertising memories.
- More general advertisement memories.
- General advertising memories.

The general consensus today is that the reliability and meaningfulness of advertising awareness can be enhanced by asking questions concerning highly specific advertising memories as opposed to general advertising memories. The latter type of question often leads to overclaiming awareness, especially for television. Exhibit 20–11 (see page 620) provides several illustrations of different awareness question formats. Some authorities feel that version D leads to a minimum of overclaiming and maximum sensitivity to advertising changes.[9]

Sampling

Sample size requirements in national tracking studies are based on the various criteria discussed in Chapter 8. The standard minimum sample size in a national

---

[9]Arthur Juchens and Tony Twyman, "The Measurement of Advertising Awareness and Its Applications," *Journal of the Market Research Society* 14 (1984).

EXHIBIT 20–11
——
Awareness Question
Formats

Verson A

(i) Can you tell me the names of any brands of (product category) for which you have seen or heard any advertising recently? [*Probe: Any others?*]
(ii) Apart from these you have already mentioned, have you seen or heard any of these brands (show card already shown previously for brand awareness) advertised recently? [*Probe: Any others?*]
(iii) For each brand mentioned—where did you see or hear the advertising for _____?
Was it in newspapers, magazines, on television, poster, radio or elsewhere?

Version B

Have you seen or heard any advertising in the last month for any of the brands of _____
on this list?

Version C

(i) Have you seen or heard any advertising for _____in newspapers,
magazines, on cinema, on television, posters, or radio or anywhere?
(ii) If yes: Where have you seen or heard advertising for _____?

Version D

Can you remember any recent advertising for _____(go through brands one by one)

Source: Arthur Juchens and Tony Twyman, "The Measurement of Advertising Awareness and Its Applications," *Journal of the Market Research Society* 14 (1984).

market tracking study will be determined by the design issues discussed previously. Typically, the sample size is large enough to permit subgroup analysis (e.g., regional analysis). Category users are usually defined as consumers who have used a brand in the product category under study during a recent time period (e.g., the past 30 days). In the case of low incidence or seasonal products, a longer time frame is usually used.

If the basic sample does not produce the minimum number of respondents in a user group of interest, the sample is supplemented to ensure that sufficient respondents are obtained in the desired group. The supplemental sample is selected after the basic random sample has been completed. The procedures for selecting the supplemental sample should follow the same procedures used in selecting the primary sample.

Action Standards

In market tracking studies formal action standards are usually not stated. Action standards are not strictly applicable because in many instances the market tracking is conducted to revise or reformulate marketing strategies and to provide baselines to evaluate other marketing programs.

Approach to Analysis

In general terms, analysis focuses on differences in category incidence, brand awareness, use levels, and changes in these levels over time. In the case of continuous tracking, the typical approach is to cover the sampling points on a four-week

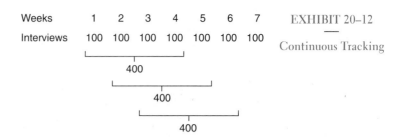

EXHIBIT 20–12

Continuous Tracking

cycle and to look at the data through a "rolling 4-weekly window." This is required because analysis of the weekly interviews generally provides too small a base. Exhibit 20–12 shows an illustration. Note that weeks 1 through 4 are added together and compared with weeks 2 through 5, 3 through 6, and so on. Generally, samples that number 400 are large enough for most measurements.

There are several specific types of analyses conducted in market tracking studies. In the following paragraphs, three specific types of applications are discussed.

Awareness and Advertising Spending. Much work in the United Kingdom has been directed toward investigating the relationship between awareness levels and advertising expenditures. Most notable is the work of Broadbent, who found that for a variety of brands and product categories there comes a point in time at which advertising awareness is predictable from the brand's advertising weight—but not just the most recent advertising weight.[10] *Advertising weight* is some measure of advertising effort, for example, gross rating points (GRP). The model developed is, in essence, a linear learning model, which recognizes that the effects of advertising decay exponentially. Awareness is a function of something called **adstock** plus a **base level** to which awareness would fall in the absence of advertising. *Adstock* is simply the effective weight of advertising that operates at the end of any particular time period. More specifically, it is that period's, say, GRPs plus appropriately decayed remnants of the GRPs in the earlier periods. If the proportion of advertising awareness carried over from one period to the next is t, the adstock at the end of period n is given by

$$\text{GRP}_n + t\text{GRP}_{n-1} + t^2\text{GRP}_{n-2} + t^3\text{GRP}_{n-3} + \ldots$$

adstock
Effective weight of advertising, operating at the end of any particular time period.

base level
The level that awareness would fall to in the absence of advertising.

Thus the model can be expressed as

$$\text{Awareness} = A + B(\text{Adstock})$$

where A is an intercept, a base level to which awareness would fall in the absence of advertising, and B is the slope of the relationship between adstock and awareness; that is, it gives the rate of increase in awareness due to a unit change in adstock. An alternative way to view the B is as an advertising efficiency measure. These relationships are shown in Exhibit 20–13 (see page 622).

[10]Simon Broadbent, "One Way TV Advertisements Work," *Journal of the Market Research Society* 21, no. 3 (1979).

EXHIBIT 20–13
—
Awareness and
Adstock

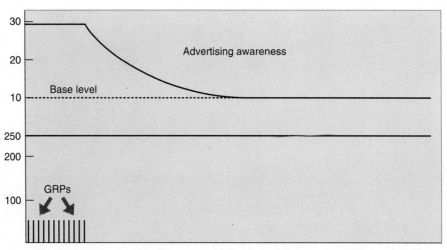

Source: Taken from Steven Coleman and Gordon Brown, "Advertising Tracking Studies and Sales Effects," *Journal of the Market Research Society* 25, no. 2 (1983).

Awareness and Recall.   Again, much of the research on the relationship between awareness and recall has been conducted in the United Kingdom. You will recall that measures focus on the respondent's ability to articulate the content of the advertising. Notwithstanding the criticism that recall measures are not relevant for advertisements that lack tangible, concrete elements and that have an emotional or mood orientation, Brown provides examples in which he uses recall and awareness to assess individual copy executions.[11] The procedure works as follows. After an advertising campaign has been launched, tracking begins. Every time people say they have seen a brand on TV recently, they are asked to describe it. Answers are recorded verbatim. The results are coded by matching the verbatim responses to the actual ads that are being aired so it is possible to determine which ad is being described. A graph (as shown in Exhibit 20–14) is prepared, which breaks out the proportion of people that describe each commercial. Exhibit 20–14 shows an illustrative application. Note that only a small proportion of the respondents ever described advertisement B. The situation became much worse when advertisement C came on the air because it displaced advertisement B from people's minds.

Awareness and Sales.   Coleman and Brown[12] recommended a procedure for investigating the relationship between awareness and sales for different copy executions. Their approach involves computing residual sales that are obtained by regressing sales on price changes, adstock, and the awareness index for a given brand over the time period of the study. Exhibit 20–15 provides an illustrative example for

[11]Gordon Brown, "Tracking Studies and Sales Effects" (Advertising Research Foundation, Key Issues Workshop on Advertising Tracking Studies, July 1984).

[12]Steven Coleman and Gordon Brown, "Advertising Tracking Studies and Sales Effects," *Journal of the Market Research Society* 25, no. 2 (1983).

EXHIBIT 20–14   Awareness and Recall

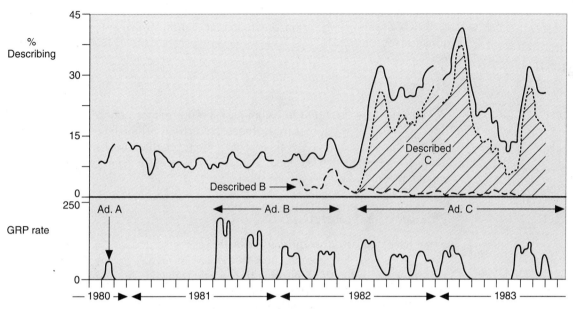

Source: Gordon Brown, "Tracking Studies and Sales Effects" (Advertising Research Foundation, Key Issues Workshop on Advertising Tracking Studies, July 1984).

Cadbury's Dairy Milk

EXHIBIT 20–15

Awareness and Sales

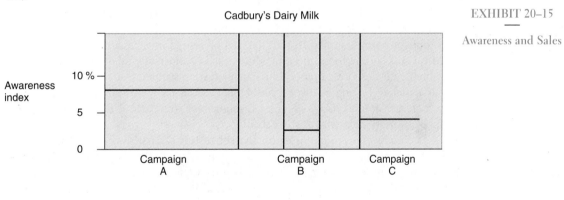

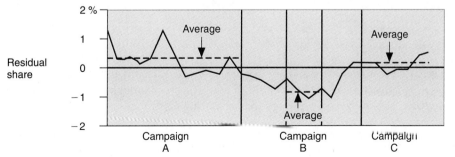

Source: Steven Coleman and Gordon Brown, "Advertising Tracking Studies and Sales Effects," *Journal of the Market Research Society* 25, no. 2 (1983).

Cadbury's Dairy Milk. Note it is rather clear that residual sales are correlated with the ability of the execution (campaign) to generate awareness.

By way of summary, Exhibit 20–16 presents a prototypical research proposal for a market tracking study.

MARKET TESTING[13]

We now turn our attention to techniques and procedures associated with market testing studies. As we discuss in the following section, although both market tracking and market testing are evaluative and intercept the advertising at the same point in time, namely when aired in the marketplace, there are important differences between these two types of studies.

Philosophy and Objectives

market testing
Studies designed to assess the impact of a change in a marketing-mix element

As we have discussed, one primary objective of market tracking is to monitor the marketplace regarding key measures. In the case of **market testing**, in contrast, we are less concerned with monitoring the natural goings on in the marketplace, but rather more concerned with assessing the impact of some change in a marketing-mix element. Testing represents a more overt action on the part of the advertiser because it involves a deliberate alteration of the marketplace. Consequently, market testing must be carefully planned so it can assess the effects of what has been manipulated while controlling for other possible confounds. If you think that this discussion sounds similar to the material presented in Chapter 7, you are correct. As we will see the tools and procedures used in experimental design are extremely valuable for designing *appropriate* market testing studies. Stated somewhat differently, market testing involves a *controlled experiment*. Finally, it should be pointed out that test marketing, which is discussed in some detail in Chapter 21, is a special variety of market testing study.

There are two primary uses for market testing.[14] First, market testing serves a control function because it allows managers to assess the consequences of an action (e.g., an advertising campaign) before implementing the same action on a larger scale. Second, market testing serves a predictive research function because it allows managers to determine whether an action should or should not be undertaken.

Research Design

The first point to understand about market testing is that it disrupts the marketplace because it involves manipulating a marketing-mix variable. In this discussion we focus on advertising, although market testing often focuses on other variables

---

[13]An excellent discussion of market testing can be found in Donius, *Marketplace Measurement*.

[14]A. Achenbaum, "Market Testing: Using the Marketplace as a Laboratory," in *Handbook of Marketing Research*, ed. Robert Ferber (New York: McGraw-Hill, 1974), pp. 4–31—4–54.

EXHIBIT 20–16

Market Tracking
Proposal

Brand:	Skweeky Kleen Bar Soap.
Project:	Bar Soap National Tracking Study.
Background & Purpose:	The Bar Soap Brand Group has requested that a continuous tracking study be conducted in 1994. This study will be a continuation of the 1993 tracking study.

The objectives of this study will be
1. To determine track changes in brand awareness and use since the introduction of new products.
2. To determine changes in volume contribution within the market.
3. To analyze consumer perceptions and to measure changes in those perceptions among various market segments.

Research Method:

The 1994 study will be conducted during the course of the year, and monthly waves of interviewing will begin in January. This monthly tracking system was also used in 1993.

As in previous studies, interviewing will be conducted by WATS telephone from a central location. Telephone numbers will be selected via strict probability methods from all working exchanges and numbers in the continental United States. Respondents will be randomly selected within households. A total of 2,400 past-30-day bar soap users will be interviewed (200 per month for the 12 months of January through December 1993).

The basic questionnaire will follow the format used in the 1993 study and will include the following question areas:

— Brand awareness (unaided and aided).

— Brand use (ever, past 30 days, most often).

— Number of bars used past 30 days.

— Brand ratings for brands ever used, but not past 30 days.

— Importance of product attributes.

— Other diagnostic question areas (to vary).

Timing and Cost:

Fieldwork will be conducted monthly, beginning in January. Top line reports on brand awareness and use will be provided monthly, whereas more complete reports will be reported quarterly and when all the interviews are completed. The specific timing will be

Interview Date	Number of Interviews	Timing of Monthly Top Lines	Timing of Quarterly Top Lines	Final Report
January	200	2/13	—	—
February	200	3/13	—	—
March	200	4/10	—	—
1st quarter	600	—	5/15	—
April	200	5/8	—	—
May	200	6/12	—	—
June	200	7/15	—	—
2nd quarter	600	—	8/14	—
July	200	8/11	—	—
August	200	9/11	—	—
September	200	10/12	—	—
3rd quarter	600	—	11/13	—
October	200	11/9	—	—
November	200	12/11	—	—
December	200	1/13	—	—
4th quarter	600	—	1/23	—
Total	2,400			3/25

The cost of this study will be $100,000 ± 10 percent.

Selected Supplier:	Burke Marketing Research.

such as promotion or the product. The crucial research design issue in market testing is how to conduct the test. To be more specific, the issue centers around designs that select a single geographic area to be extrapolated or pairs of areas that have been matched on one or more criteria (such as historical sales, brands available, area demographics) versus the utilization of controlled marketplace laboratory facilities, in which a single market is divided into test and control cells.

single market testing
Test involving a single market without control.

Single Market Testing.   **Single market testing** involves what the name implies. The test is introduced in a single market area, without any control. The typical approach to single market testing includes (1) selecting a test area, (2) fitting a regression model to historical sales data for the test area, (3) using the regression model to predict what future sales in the test area would be before introducing the test variable (e.g., a new advertising campaign), and (4) monitoring actual sales in the test area after introducing the test variable. There are three primary problems with this approach. First, the anticipated performance in the test area in the absence of the test variable is a function of how well the regression model fits historical data. Second, since actual sales in the absence of the test variable are not known, if the marketplace has actually changed, you have no information on what performance would have been in response to these marketplace changes in the absence of the test. Finally, as you will recall from Chapter 7, without a control there are other possible sources of variation that are not accounted for.

matched market testing
Test involving test and control stores/areas that are matched on key factors.

Matched Market Testing.   **Matched market testing** can be best described in terms of one of its most frequent applications, namely, media weight. The approach is as follows. First, control and test sets of markets are selected. In the case of an established brand, the control markets are assigned the current advertising weight level, whereas in the test markets, a higher level of advertising weight is assigned. In the case of a new product, two or more sets of markets are selected, and they are assigned different weight levels. The approach then calls for tracking through store audits, warehouse withdrawals, scanner panels, and so forth. Haley[15] pointed out several of the problems with this approach: (1) in general, it is costly; (2) it is easy for competitors to find out that a test is being conducted and to take action to invalidate the test (this is discussed in more detail in Chapter 22); (3) often there is considerable market-to-market variation in results, which typically renders conclusions ungeneralizable and makes predictions difficult; and (4) if the number of markets used is small, there is the risk of making errors in judgment (representative samples are just as necessary in this case as they are in other types of studies).

controlled store testing
Test involving matched panels of stores, from within a given market, from all stores in that market in which alternative testing treatments are assigned to the different panels of stores.

Controlled Store Testing.   **Controlled store testing** involves selecting matched panels of stores, generally from within a given market, from all stores in that market, and the alternative testing treatments are assigned to different panels of stores. Controlled store testing is more frequently undertaken in the case of promotion evaluation, as opposed to advertisements because it is easier to target

---

[15]Russell I. Haley, "Sales Effects of Media Weight," *Journal of Advertising Research*, June 1978.

specific promotional vehicles to specific stores within a market than it is to do the same for advertising. The efficacy of this design rests on the researcher's ability to effectively match stores. You will note from Chapter 7 that matching is a way to control for alternative sources of variation; however, if matching is used, it is presumed that we can identify these possible confounding sources. One legitimate concern that is raised regarding controlled store testing relates to the complexity of the marketplace. Or more precisely, can markets actually be matched?

In large measure, dissatisfaction with conventional market testing procedures has led to a new form of testing that is based on electronic scanners. Because we have discussed electronic scanner services in some detail in Chapter 4, our discussion here will be brief.

Marketplace Laboratories (Electronic Test Markets). A *laboratory* or **electronic test market** is any market in which there is control over the input of alternative advertising. In general, this is a single geographic area linked directly, on an individual household basis, to purchase and/or media data over time, typically measured by diary panels of scanner facilities. Often, electronic test markets are used for testing alternative copy execution, media weight, or both, and this would be for established as well as for new products. In order to have control of the input of alternative advertising, the electronic test markets use cable systems. Cable subscribers in the test area are recruited as panel members, and their purchases are scanned electronically. Based on panel information, households can be matched and assigned to cells that will receive different advertising executions via split-cable or targeted-cable systems. As we discussed in Chapter 4 and 21, a major issue with electronic test markets is their representativeness.

> electronic test markets
> *Any market in which there is control over the input of alternative advertising.*

Questions Asked

Although market testing studies address many of the same issues as tracking studies, the primary variable of interest is changes in sales. That is, interest centers on performance in the test stores after introduction of the treatment, as measured by the difference vis-à-vis the control stores or as measured against anticipated performance. Two fundamental measures relate to

1. Penetration—percent of households that buy.
2. Buying rate—volume per household that buy.

Sampling

Sampling in market testing studies involves issues that relate to how the test and/or control stores are selected; it also relates to the representativeness of the area itself if electronic test markets are used. We will defer a complete discussion of how to select test markets until Chapter 21, which considers the more general topic of test marketing. However, two points should be noted. When the number of markets considered is small and not dispersed, projection will be extremely risky. It is reasonable to expect that for matched market tests, projection error will decrease as the number of markets increases.

EXHIBIT 20–17

—

Market Testing
Proposal

Background:	Rising Bakers Company has been advertising Health-E Wheat Bread in the southwestern United States since 1986. This increased spending has led to sales gains in this area. As a result, marketing is considering expanding its advertising efforts into other regions. In 1994, advertising spending will be initiated in one market in each of the Piedmont and Central Sales Regions: Charlotte (North Carolina) and Columbus (Ohio), respectively. The basic plan provides for four weeks on air followed by four weeks off, over a six-month period beginning March/April, coupled with the introduction of at least one new flavor (to complete distribution of full product line):

Plan Summary

	Columbus	Charlotte
Advertising start	2/27	3/20
New flavors	Six Grains	Six Grains
	Oat Bran	Oat Bran
Introduction date	3/19	4/23

Purpose:	In order to evaluate the effectiveness of these programs (before expanding within region), management has requested that a tracking study be conducted. This (combined) tracking study will help to address the following key marketing questions:
	
	— What effect did each of the respective programs have on behavioral dynamics?
	
	  — Did it increase awareness of the Brand?
	
	  — How was purchase behavior affected?
	
	— Was Health-E's sales message communicated? (What impact did it have on brand imagery?)
	
	— Who is the target audience for the Brand?

Method:	Two (2) telephone tracking studies (with one "pre" and two "post" waves) will be conducted in the Piedmont and Central Sales Regions.
Sample:	A total of 1,200 (100 per market/wave) primary grocery shoppers, age 25 to 64, who have bought wheat bread in the past 30 days will be randomly selected and interviewed by telephone. Household telephone numbers will be selected via strict probability methods from all working exchanges and numbers within a sampled market. Three call-back attempts will be made in order to interview the desired individual. The following chart summarizes the sample design for the two studies:

Sample Design

Test	Pre	Post I	Post II	Total
Piedmont				
Charlotte	100	100	100	300
Piedmont control market	100	100	100	300
Central				
Columbus	100	100	100	300
Central control market	100	100	100	300
				Total 1,200

Questionnaire:	The questionnaire (about 20 to 25 minutes in length) will be designed to include, but not be limited to, the following information areas: — Brand awareness—unaided and aided.

EXHIBIT 20–17

(concluded)

— Advertising awareness—unaided and aided; source of advertising awareness.

— Copy recall (for brands seen advertising for).

— Brands/flavors purchased—ever, past 3 months, and past 30 days; number of loaves past 30 days; last time and time before last.

— Future purchase interest.

— Likes/dislikes (for Health-E and one key competitor among those aware—competitors rotated).

— Importance of specific product characteristics.

— Ratings on specific product characteristics (for Health-E and key competitor among those aware—same competitor as in likes/dislikes).

— Demographics.

Analysis: Computer tabulations will be provided after each wave of data collection (a total of six occasions).

In addition, a comprehensive written report *or* presentation will also be provided at the completion of each wave.

Cost: The study, as specified above, will cost $74,800 ± 10 percent to complete.

Timing: Scheduling for each wave of interviewing will be as follows:

Data collection	1 week
Top line/computer tables	1½ weeks
Final report	2 weeks
Total	4½ weeks

Selected Supplier: Evaluative Research, Inc.

Action Standards

Since in market testing studies the primary focus is the payoff of one alternative advertising execution over another or on the efficacy of heavy or increased advertising budgets, action standards are typically expressed in terms of finding statistically significant differences between test and control (or anticipated performance) and/or comparison with category norms. The action standards would be expressed with regard to penetration and buying rate.

Approach to Analysis

Analysis procedures generally involve statistical testing and the projection of test market results to the entire market. Projection of test market results is discussed in Chapter 21. Regarding statistical testing, the techniques and tools presented in Chapters 15 and 16 (e.g., *t*-test, regressional analysis) are frequently used to evaluate market testing results. One procedural issue in the analysis of results is the selection of the base period. The *base period* is that period of time against which measurements will be made, and, essentially, there are three choices: (1) the same period, one year ago; (2) the time period immediately preceding the test; and (3) the average over all pre-periods. The first option controls for seasonality, but necessitates a fair amount of back data and does not account for longer trend values.

The second option focuses on the time periods closest to the test, and presumably these have the most influence on what is observed during the testing, although with this approach seasonality is not controlled for. The third option gains the stability of more observations than a single period but assumes that averaging does not obscure differences that the one-year ago or most recent period comparisons would reveal.

By way of summary, Exhibit 20–17 (see page 628) presents a prototypical market testing proposal.

SUMMARY

This chapter has discussed advertising research practices, the many purposes that advertising serves, and what is meant by advertising effectiveness. During the course of this discussion, we came to realize that advertising effectiveness centers on measures such as awareness, communicability, and persuasion. A framework for understanding the advertising evaluation process was described, which emphasized the need to evaluate an advertisement or commercial both before and after it has been aired.

The bulk of the chapter was devoted to three general types of advertising effectiveness studies: copy testing, market tracking, and market testing. Copy testing involves the pretesting of advertisements before they are aired in the marketplace. Both market tracking and market testing involve the assessment of advertisements that are currently being used in the marketplace. As we discussed, the primary differences between in-market testing systems relates to the degree to which the marketplace is disrupted when the testing is undertaken.

KEY CONCEPTS

copy testing

print ad tests

single ad research design

headline test

forced exposure tests

multiple ads/portfolio tests

dummy magazine tests

real magazine tests

home placement testing

off-air tests

on-air tests

day-after recall (DAR)

multiple-exposure techniques

market tracking

cross-category versus within-category tracking

panel versus matched samples

continuous versus single point in time

adstock

market testing

controlled store tests

marketplace laboratories

REVIEW QUESTIONS

1. Discuss the issue of the effectiveness of advertisements.
2. Describe the basic types of research designs used in the copy testing print ad tests.
3. What information is usually collected in print ad tests?
4. Discuss the objectives of tests for television commercials. Does the importance of each objective

   vary with the type of commercial being tested?
5. Describe the basic types of research designs used in evaluating television commercials.
6. Discuss the distinctions between market tracking and market testing.
7. What are the crucial research design issues involved in market tracking and market testing?

Test Market Studies

— Describe the information provided by good test market programs.
— Define the basic steps in test market studies.
— Explain the procedures used in standard test market audits and controlled test market audits.
— Discuss and provide a comparative survey of simulated/pretest market services.

INTRODUCTION

Because of the highly competitive and risky nature of most product markets today, management is no longer simply responsible for making profits but also for maximizing the company's return on investment (ROI). New product introductions play a crucial role in determining a company's financial viability and they are, in fact, the lifeblood of most companies. And, according to all indications, management expects "new" products to contribute more to profits in the coming five years than they do at the present time.

Unfortunately, however, according to published data, about 80 percent of new packaged goods introduced fail, and approximately one-third of all nationally distributed new products are withdrawn from the market within one year after introduction. These failure estimates are even more alarming in light of the whole range of marketing research activities (e.g., concept tests and product tests) that occur prior to a national launch of a product. Data indicate that 65 percent of new product funds are spent on marginal or losing brands.[1] Because not all new product introductions will succeed, new product introductions must typically have projected ROI in the 30 to 40 percent range.

Test market services are designed to help marketing managers make the correct decision concerning new products and additions or revisions to existing product lines. The primary purpose of test market studies is to provide a real-world, in-market exposure for evaluating a product and its marketing program. By using a test market service the marketing manager has the ability to take a proposed national program with all of its separate elements and evaluate it in a

---

[1]Figures reported by Burke Marketing Services, Inc.

smaller, less expensive situation with a view toward determining whether the potential profit opportunity from rolling out the new product or line extension outweighs the potential risks. Good test market programs provide information on such factors as

- Market share of product and/or volume estimates.
- Who is buying the product, how often, and for what purpose.
- From where purchases are made, and at what price.
- What changes in strategy were made by the competition.
- What effect the new item has on already established lines.

Test markets are, however, not cheap. Average costs can run well over $2,000,000.

In addition to traditional test markets, this chapter also considers what are called simulated test marketing (STM) or pretest marketing (PTM). Simulated/ pretest marketing usually involves exposing a few hundred respondents to a commercial or storyboard for a proposed new product, giving them an opportunity to buy the product, and following up through telephone interviews with those who used the product to measure their reaction and repeat-purchase intention. Based on these data and other management-supplied information about specific marketing elements, market share and/or volume estimates are projected (i.e., forecasted). As we will see, a simulated test market saves time and money and has changed what is looked for in a test market.

Typically, test market results, whether real or simulated, involve a model used to forecast the new product's market share or volume at rollout. Standard forecasting methods will be discussed in Appendix 22A.

TO TEST OR NOT TO TEST?

Test marketing offers a firm two important benefits

1. It provides an opportunity to obtain a measure of a product's sales performance under reasonably natural market conditions. As a by-product, management can predict the product's likely national market share, and this forms the basis of the decision about whether to roll out the product nationally.
2. It provides an opportunity, prior to full distribution, for management to identify and correct product or marketing strategy weaknesses, which would be much more difficult and expensive to correct after national rollout.

Despite these benefits, certain issues should be considered before the decision to test the product is made. Test marketing has both direct and indirect costs. Direct costs of test marketing include product costs and marketing investment. Indirect costs involve (1) opportunity costs—revealing a new-product idea to a competitor, (2) exposure costs—the name of the company is exposed along with the brand, and (3) internal costs—diversion of employee time and activities (rarely quantified when the cost of the test market is estimated). In essence, whether to use a test market is a trade-off between reducing uncertainty by collecting additional information at considerable direct and indirect cost and immediately introducing the product nationally by avoiding any delays.

At least four major factors should be considered to determie the efficacy of test marketing:[2]

1. It is necessary to weigh the cost and risk of product failure against the profit and probability of success. If the costs and risks of product failure are low, a national launch should be considered. In contrast, high costs that are coupled with great uncertainty would favor the test market approach.

2. The difference in the scale of investment involved in the test versus national launch route has an important bearing on deciding whether to test. On one hand, if very little difference in manufacturing investment is called for whether a test or national launch is undertaken, then the investment risk favors the national launch approach. On the other hand, where plant investment for a national launch is considerable, but only slight for a test market, the investment risk favors the test launch approach.

3. Another factor is the likelihood and speed with which the competition will be able to copy your product and preempt part of your national or overseas market; where they have the technology, they will be developing their own versions of your product and marketing it, if given the opporunity to do so.

4. In addition to the investment in plant and machinery that may be involved, every new product launch is accompanied by a substantial marketing investment that varies with the scale of the launch. Typically, new product launches call for heavy advertising and promotional expenditure; they require the time, attention, and effort of a sales force; and they need shelf space in wholesale and retail outlets, sometimes obtained only at the expense of the space already given to the company's exising products. Moreover, if a new product fails such costs as rebating and reclaiming unwanted stock from customers must be incurred, along with the writeoff costs of dealing with unwanted and unusable materials and packaging. Management should also take into account the possible damage that a new product's failure can inflict on the company's reputation, which is a real, if not quantifiable, cost.

BASIC STEPS IN TEST MARKET STUDIES

Once a decision has been made to test a proposed new product or line extension, a number of basic steps should be followed to achieve the desired results with minimum use of time and money.[3] The basic steps outlined below should be followed in sequence, and no steps should be omitted.

---

[2]The following discussion was taken from N. D. Cadbury, "When, Where and How to Test Market," *Harvard Business Review*, May–June 1985, pp. 97–98.

[3]This section is based upon material found in *A Telling Look at the 27 Most Frequently Used Test Markets*, volume III (New York: New York Times Publishing Company, 1982).

Step 1: Define Objective

The first step in defining the objectives of a test market is to closely examine the product. The product that will be tested could be

1. A "me-too" product—essentially the same as the other brands that are currently available; for example, another women's hair removal shave cream, basically the same as a dozen others.
2. An improved product—an improvement over the brands that are currently available; for example, a women's hair removal shave cream with a new ingredient that prevents hair growth for up to two weeks.
3. A category extension—a "new" type of brand as compared with other brands that are currently available; for example, a women's hair removal shave cream that disposes of leg and arm hair without the need of a razor and has a "fresh" scent.
4. A "never-before" product—the product may be a totally new and unique product that is not currently available; for example, a new "pill" taken once every two weeks that retards the growth of arm and leg hair for up to 14 days.

Obviously, there is a relationship between the type of new product that will be tested and the risks and rewards associated with ultimate market failure or success. If, for example, the proposed new product entry is a me-too item, its introduction will require far less cost and time than if the product were a never-before item, which requires a much longer diffusion process.

Typical test market objectives are to project (forecast) such key market indicators as (1) dollar and unit sales volume and (2) dollar and unit shares. Frequently, these indicators are supplemented by forecasts of inventories and measure of shelf location, facings, price variation, promotion activity, and demographic factors. In effect, test markets measure what is happening in the marketplace at the retail level.

Step 2: Plan Strategy

Manufacturing and distribution decisions must be given immediate attention. Once management has decided how the proposed new-product entry will be manufactured, they should consider how it will be promoted in the marketplace. With a me-too product, advertising is crucial since—in large measure—positioning, strategy, and execution determine its market success or failure. On the other hand, with a never-before product, it is important to get the new entry into the hands of those individuals who will believe the veracity of the advertiser's claims and will have favorable evaluations. In this case, free samples and high-value cents-off coupons can prove to be effective inducements.

Media selection is another important part of developing an overall testing strategy. For example, if the national media plan for a new product includes magazines, the test market area must include a representative sampling of print so that the necessary projections can be made. Weekend magazines and TV guides that are published by local newspapers frequently serve as surrogates for national magazines in test markets. Newspapers are particularly effective for ads that require a large amount of explanatory information and for coupons that have short expiration dates. Newspapers also have relatively comprehensive reach in their specific geographic area. Finally, no test market area would be selected if it did not have at least three commercial TV stations and some cable TV viewers.

Step 3: Determine Methodology

After the objectives of the test and an appropriate strategy are determined, including a media plan, the next step is to determine the type of test market method that is consistent with the stated objectives; in other words, we must determine *how* the test will be conducted and *who* will do the actual testing and auditing. Test markets are a form of field experimentation. In test markets, management attempts to manipulate certain marketing elements while holding others constant in a real world environment. Consequently, the issues and methods discussed under experimental design in Chapter 7 are extremely important.

There are three general methods from which to choose. Each method described below will be discussed in greater detail in a later section of this chapter.

1. *The simulated/pretest market.* As we discussed earlier, **simulated/pretest markets** do not involve an actual test market, at least not in the traditional sense. Instead, various groups of preselected respondents are interviewed, monitored, and sampled about the new product; in addition, respondents may be exposed to various media messages in a controlled environment. The objective of simulated/pretest markets is to project (forecast) what the new product would do if it were rolled out nationally.

2. *The standard test market.* If the **standard test market** method were used, the company's sales force would be responsible for distributing the new product in the selected test market areas. Sales personnel would stock the shelves and would return at periodic intervals to restock and count movement of the product.

3. *The control test market.* If the **control test market** method were used, the entire test market project would be handled by an outside research company. The control method includes *mini-market* (or *forced distribution*) tests as well as smaller controlled store panels. The research company handling the test guarantees distribution of the new product in stores that represent a predetermined percentage of the market—hence, the term *controlled store panel.* They provide warehouse facilities and use their own field representatives to sell the product, and they are responsible for stocking shelves and counting the movement of the product. Because the guaranteed distribution allows marketing managers to begin advertising and promotion two weeks after a retailer agrees to stock the new product (instead of the usual 60 to 90 days it takes to go through regular distribution channels), faster readings are possible. Controlled store testing can be conducted by electronic or manual auditing. You will recall that we discussed electronic scanner services and traditional store audits in Chapter 4.

simulated/pretest market
Method whereby various groups of preselected respondents are interviewed, monitored, and sampled about the new product; in addition, respondents may be exposed to various media messages in a controlled environment.

standard test market
Method where the company's own sales force is responsible for distributing the new product in the selected test market areas. Sales force personnel would stock the shelves and return at periodic intervals to restock and count movement.

control test market
Method in which the entire test market project is handled by an outside research company.

Step 4: Select Markets

Where to test the proposed new product is obviously one of the most important questions facing the marketing manager. Exhibit 21–1 presents a list of recommended test markets. The clear trend in test markets has been to locate midsize cities that reflect national demographics. Test market overuse has not been a pressing concern. Most marketing professionals feel that as long as the testing is conducted properly (unobtrusively), the respondent will rarely know that he or she is involved in a test.

There appear to be four overriding factors to consider when selecting a test market

1. *Number of markets to use.* The more markets that can be used, the better because results will be more reliable and a greater number of variations can be tested. Geographically dispersed markets should be used whenever possible. When testing an existing product, the general approach is to use a matched market strategy, in which two markets are chosen for their similarities on several selection criteria, such as demography, geography, climate, category image, and competitive brand use.

2. *Size of markets to use.* Reliability and cost are the key here; selected markets should be large enough to give reliable results but not so large as to be prohibitively expensive. The standard practice is to use multimarkets, which are comparable in demographics, that collectively represent about 2 to 3 percent of the U.S. population. It is important to note that the larger the market, the greater the likelihood that the competition will gain knowledge of the test, and the more expensive the media buying.

3. *Markets with representative demographics.* Several criteria are important, for example, family size, age levels, income, buying habits, and so forth. If the new product will be rolled out nationally, the test market should come as close as possible to matching the demographic average of the nation. In general, the market environment should be consistent with the environment in which the new product will compete when it is rolled out.

4. *Markets that are isolated.* The test market should be relatively isolated in terms of media and physical distribution so as to minimize waste and to maximize security. **Spill-in** and **spill-out** are two components of isolation that are frequently examined. *Spill-in* refers to the amount of outside media that comes into a market. The accepted guideline is that if 30 to 40 percent of a market's population reads another city's newspaper and watches another city's TV station, there is too much spill-in. *Spill-out* refers to the amount of a test market's newspapers and TV being seen and read in distant cities: The 30 to 40 percent guideline is also used regarding spill-out. The concern with spill-out is that too much of the advertising effort is going into areas where the new product is not available. Finally, if markets are isolated there is a greater chance to keep the new product hidden from competitors; therefore, it will reduce the chance for competitors to **jam** the test market by reducing price, offering high-value coupons, and so on.

spill-in
The amount of outside media coming into a market.

spill-out
The amount of a test market's newspapers and TV that are being seen and read in distant cities.

jamming
Practice of reducing price, offering high-value coupons, and so on in order to disrupt a competitor's test market.

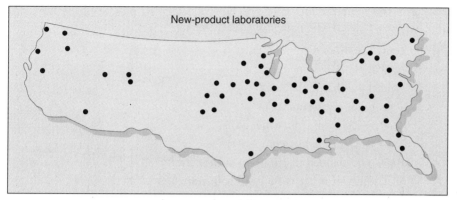

Dancer Fitzgerald Sample's preferred test markets

EXHIBIT 21–1

—

Recommended Test
Market Areas

Area	House-holds (000)	House-holds (%)	Area	House-holds (000)	House-holds (%)
1. Albany-Schenectady-Troy	498.9	0.53	26. Knoxville	406.1	0.43
			27. Little Rock	467.8	0.50
2. Atlanta	1,431.9	1.52	28. Louisville	534.1	0.57
3. Birmingham	521.6	0.55	29. Madison	285.3	0.30
4. Boise	161.2	0.17	30. Milwaukee	781.3	0.83
5. Buffalo	621.6	0.66	31. Minneapolis-St. Paul	1,369.6	1.45
6. Cedar Rapids-Waterloo-Dubuque	312.2	0.33	32. Nashville	715.9	0.76
7. Charlotte	750.2	0.80	33. New Orleans	647.4	0.69
8. Cincinnati	760.6	0.81	34. Oklahoma City	605.0	0.64
9. Cleveland	1,460.1	1.55	35. Omaha	366.7	0.39
10. Colorado Springs-Pueblo	241.4	0.26	36. Orlando-Daytona Beach-Melbourne	917.2	0.97
11. Columbus, OH	698.5	0.74	37. Peoria-Bloomington	226.8	0.24
12. Dayton	511.3	0.54	38. Phoenix	1,054.0	1.12
13. Denver	1,066.7	1.13	39. Pittsburgh	1,171.8	1.24
14. Des Moines	391.0	0.41	40. Portland, OR	845.5	0.90
15. Erie	155.9	0.17	41. Portland-Poland Spring	376.0	0.40
16. Evansville	268.8	0.29	42. Richmond	415.1	0.44
17. Ft. Wayne	237.1	0.25	43. Roanoke-Lynchburgh	380.4	0.40
18. Green Bay-Appleton	392.3	0.42	44. Rochester, NY	358.5	0.38
19. Greensboro-Winston Salem-High Point	526.6	0.56	45. Sacramento-Stockton	1,062.3	1.13
20. Greenville-Spartanburg-Asheville	657.7	0.70	46. St. Louis	1,125.0	1.19
			47. Salt Lake City	608.9	0.65
21. Harrisburg-York-Lancaster-Lebanon	576.3	0.61	48. Seattle-Tacoma	1,355.9	1.44
			49. South Bend-Elkhart	326.6	0.35
22. Houston	1,497.1	1.59	50. Spokane	332.4	0.35
23. Indianapolis	885.3	0.94	51. Syracuse	379.5	0.40
24. Jacksonville	478.5	0.51	52. Toledo	419.0	0.44
25. Kansas City	771.2	0.82	53. Tulsa	476.0	0.51
			54. Wichita-Hutchinson	435.7	0.46

Source: Saatchi & Saatchi Advertising.

If an electronic test market is used, the selection of the test markets can be
more problematic. First, selection of test markets is, by necessity, confined to cities
in which the electronic scanner equipment is in operation. Second, a company can
be "locked-out" of a possible test city because of a competitor who happens to be

testing in the same product category. The following list presents 10 criteria that should be considered when selecting a test market:

1. Representation as to population size.
2. Typical per-capita income.
3. Typical purchasing habits.
4. Stability of year-round sales.
5. Relative isolation from other cities.
6. Not easily jammed by competitors.
7. Typical of planned distribution outlets.
8. Availability of retailers that will cooperate.
9. Availability of media that will cooperate.
10. Availability of research and audit service companies.

Step 5: Execute the Plan

The key consideration in executing the test is to carry it out as a legitimate *test* and not to attempt to guarantee success. In this regard, there two tendencies to guard against. First, the marketing management team should not confuse attention with overattention. Overattention can cause the new product to do better in the test market than it would if it were rolled out nationally—it may be for this reason that only 40 percent of all new products that pass successfully through the testing stage are also successful nationally. Second, the marketing management team should not be overanxious regarding repeat-purchase incidence. Repeat purchase of a new product is critical to its eventual success. Frequently, the temptation is to abort a test when the first repeat-purchase cycle incidences look good. Whether good or bad, repeat-purchase rates should be examined very carefully to determine what may be the culprit (e.g., media mix, advertising, or the product) or what is leading to success (e.g., special deals or high-value coupons). In either event, the test should continue at least until the results begin to stabilize. NPD Research, Inc., has in the past used the following guidelines to evaluate repeat-purchase rates: 64 percent or more probably means success, 47 percent probably means "maybe," and a rate of 39 percent of less annually means failure.[4]

Step 6: Evaluate the Results

There are four critical areas to keep in mind when evaluating test market results.

1. *The awareness and attitude levels of consumers.* Key awareness information answers the questions: Do consumers know the product exists? Do consumers know what the product does? Do consumers know how much the product costs and where to get it? The awareness level will provide information on the effectiveness of the advertising. The attitude level, in

---

[4]Figures reported by NPD Research, Inc.

contrast, provides information on what consumers who have tried (or are aware of) the new product think about it.

2. *Purchase measures.* Another key factor in evaluating the test is trial-and-repeat purchase incidences. Purchase measures, particularly trial, indicate whether or not the advertising and promotion plan has worked.

3. *The effect on competition.* It is very important to monitor the actions of competitors during the test period. As we indicated, competitors can attempt to jam the test by offering sample products, price reductions, coupons, and the like.

4. *The effect on other products.* What product(s) the new product is taking sales from is particularly important. If most of the new product's sales are at the expense of one of the company's other established lines, there may not be any real market gain. This so-called cannibalization should be closely investigated.

5. *The next step.* After evaluating test market results, the marketing management team can move in one of the following directions:

   — Go back to the research and development department with an effort to improve the product.

   — Make a no-go decision; that is, abort the entire project.

   — Make a go decision; that is, give the green light to either launch the new project (or commission a test market, if evaluating the results from a simulated/pretest market).

SIMULATED/PRETEST MARKETING METHODS

During the 1970s and 1980s, simulated/pretest markets became increasingly popular. As we indicated earlier, simulated/pretest markets do not involve an actual test market. Instead, preselected individuals are interviewed, monitored, and sampled about the product. The prototypical procedure involves intercepting shoppers at a high-traffic location, sometimes prescreening them for category use, exposing the selected individuals to a commercial (or concept) for a proposed new product, giving them an opportunity to buy the new product in a real life or laboratory setting, and interviewing those who purchased the new product at a later date to ascertain their reaction and repeat-purchase intentions. Based on trial estimates, repeat-purchase data, and management-supplied data on advertising and distribution, the simulated/pretest market result is a projection of share and/or volume and repeat purchases of the product at rollout time.

The popularity of simulated/pretest markets can be traced to a number of factors. First, they are relatively fast—a full market evaluation can be finished in 12 to 16 weeks, depending on the service used. In contrast, test markets often run as long as one year. Second, they are confidential. The competition does not have the opportunity to jam the test. Third, compared with traditional test markets that can cost in excess of $2 million, they are relatively inexpensive, costing typically below $100,000, depending on the service. Finally, the validation evidence indicates that simulated/pretest markets can be quite accurate, with forecast errors generally less than 5 percent.[5] We will return to the issue of accuracy shortly.

Historical Perspective

The first simulated/pretest market was introduced by Yankelovich, Skelly and White, Inc., in 1968. This model, called LTM (Laboratory Test Market), was soon followed by a number of other models. Simulated/pretest markets should not be viewed as substitutes for test markets. From the results of a simulated/pretest market, management can better determine whether or not to proceed with a weak product and, consequently, save the time and money that would have been committed if a test market were conducted. In other words, simulated/pretest markets usually are used to determine whether it is worth the time, cost, and risk of performing a test market. When the decision is to use a test market, simulated/pretest markets also have changed what can be expected from the testing. Because the simulated/pretest market gives some indication of what can be expected, the test market can be designed to optimize the way in which the new product is priced, promoted, and distributed.

Another significant development in the history of simulated/pretest markets is their use very early on in the new product development process. Because the costs associated with the product development process increase at each step from raw idea to new product launch, today simulated/pretest markets are commonly used in the concept- and product-testing stages to get an early reading on sales potential. In this case, the objective is to quickly evaluate a new product's potential and to lower the risk involved in producing it.

A Comparative Review

Since the introduction of Yankelovich, Skelly and White's LTM model in 1968, a large number of other simulated/pretest market services have appeared. Today there are a number of simulated/pretest market models that are commercially available: ASSESSOR (M/A/R/C and Macro Strategies, Inc.); BASES (Burke Marketing Services); ESP (NPD); LITMUS (Blackburn and Clancy); DESIGNER (Novaction Inc.); and CRITERION (Custom Research, Inc.). Each service has its own distinct advantage and disadvantage. In deciding which service to use, the following factors should be considered: (1) cost, (2) time, (3) degree of confidentiality, (4) characteristics of the model, and (5) documentation of overall accuracy of forecasts.

Cost. The cost of conducting a simulated/pretest market will ultimately depend on the product and the corresponding category incidence rate, as well as on other specifics concerning how the test is conducted. In general, however, ASSESSOR is the most expensive of the simulated/pretest market models, and using it will

---

[5]See, for example, G. L. Urban and G. M. Katz, "Pre-Test-Market Models: Validation and Managerial Implications," *Journal of Marketing Research*, August 1983, pp. 221–34.

typcially cost in the $80,000 to $100,000 range, whereas BASES is the least expensive of the simulated/pretest market models, having typical costs in the $40,000 to $60,000 range.

Timing. The time needed to complete a simulated/pretest market will depend on the use-up rate for the new product being tested. Assuming a two-week use-up rate, the time needed from authorization of design to formal presentation typically runs from about 10 to 16 weeks.

Confidentiality. All market simulation services offer a degree of confidentiality not possible with any type of in-store testing because respondents are screened for security criteria before they are exposed to the advertising or to the product. Prerecruitment and product pick-up services provide additional security not possible in test marketing.

Model Characteristics. The services available for simulated/pretest marketing are, for the most part, based on different assumptions. The following provides several important characteristics:

1. The BASES model is designed to use the data generated by a general audience sample; that is, respondents need not be qualified in terms of product/brand usage. Thus, it is best suited to test (1) new products that address a general audience, (2) innovative new products, and (3) products for which category boundaries are unclear (e.g., snacks). BASES provides *volume* estimates.

2. In simulated/pretest market models that use purchase intent scales, the objective is to link the additudinal response (purchase intent) to purchase behavior (trial-and-repeat rate), adjusting for season, region, and advertising and promotion plans. Researchers generally agree, however, that there is some overstatement by consumers concerning purchase intentions. In other words, not all consumers who say they would buy a given product would actually buy it within a given period of time (e.g., a year). The critical element in interpreting the purchase intent is to calibrate the precise "rate of conversion" from this attitudinal response to behavioral measures. Historically, many conversion rates have been used. Four examples of conversion rates that are used by consumer packaged goods researchers in the United States are given in Table 21–1 (see page 642).

   Under scenario 1, purchase rates would be taken as 100 percent of the top box score on the purchase-intent measure. Under scenario 2, purchase rates would be computed by taking 52 percent of the top box purchase intentions plus 17 percent of the second top box purchase intentions plus 8 percent of the "might or might not buy" purchase intentions, and so on. In other words, under scenario 2, it is believed that 1 percent of the individuals who indicated that they "definitely would not buy" actually end up purchasing the product. As shown in Table 21–2 (see page 642), based on scenario 2 weights, the forecasted trial purchase level for the new product concept is 21.04 percent.

TABLE 21–1

Conversion Rate Examples

Purchase Intent	Scenario			
	1	2	3	4
Definitely would buy	100%	52%	100%	90%
Probably would buy	0	17	40	30
Might or might not buy	0	8	0	5
Probably would not buy	0	2	0	2.5
Definitely would not buy	0	1	0	2

Source: Y. Lynn et al., "New Product Analysis and Testing," in *Handbook of Business Problem Solving*, ed. K. J. Albert (New York: McGraw-Hill, 1980), pp. 4–13—4–27.

TABLE 21–2

Weighting Purchase–Intent Scores

Intent Scale	Simulated Test Result	Weights	Estimate of Potential Trial
Definitely buy	25%	0.52	13.00%
Probably buy	30	0.17	5.10
Might or might not buy	35	0.08	2.80
Probably not buy	7	0.02	0.14
Definitely not buy	3	0.01	—
Total	100		21.04

3. All of the simulated test market models adjust trial rate and repeat-purchase rate by marketing plans, that is, planned advertising spending and distribution levels. The following example illustrates the nature of the adjustment:

EXAMPLE

Estimated trial rate	10.7%
$\times$	$\times$
Total awareness (marketing plan)	50.0%
$\times$	$\times$
Percent distribution (marketing plan)	70.0%
=	
Net cumulative trial	3.8%
$\times$	$\times$
Estimated share of choice	28.5%
=	
Ongoing unit share	1.1%

Note that net cumulative trial is obtained by adjusting the estimated trial rate, which is obtained from, say, a concept-test purchase intention scale, by the scheduled advertising (awareness) and distribution weights. The advertising weight is generally fixed to the level of GRPs, whereas the distribution

	Number of Tests Conducted		Number of
Model	Claimed Number	Years Reported	Claimed Validations
ASSESSOR	450	1973–1982	44
BASES	1,500	1977–1983	152
ESP	86*	1982 only	30

*Cumulative total not known.

TABLE 21–3
—
Reported Number of
Tests and Validations
for Three Simulated/
Pretest Test Market
Models

weight is related to the anticipated ACV (all category volume) percentage. Estimated share of choices is determined from the repeat-purchase rate-estimated number of consumers who buy the product again (i.e., after trial).

4. ASSESSOR uses an attudinal measure to evaluate strength of repeat purchase and also to generate a brand *share* forecast independent of the trial-repeat model. In the ASSESSOR model, the "relevant" set of brands is determined by the respondent's "evoked set."

Overall Accuracy. Table 21–3 summarizes historical data on the reported number of tests conducted and actual validation cases by several of the simulated/pretest market models we have been discussing. In evaluating the overall accuracy of any of these services it is necessary to recognize the difficulties inherent in validating the market share/sales volume forecasts. For the most part, the marketing plans (i.e., total awareness, percent distribution) used as input into the forecasting models do not match the plan that is used in the new product introduction. Also, other factors that are not anticipated in the simulation may affect the new product's performance in the real world. Therefore, in order to validate a result, a forecast must be readjusted to match the real-world situation. This assumes, of course, that the client is willing to share this information with the simulation service; however, this is certainly not always the case. Further, there is a certain self-selection process that takes place because clients who are most pleased with the service are the ones most willing to offer validation information, which affects the ability of the validation data reported to be generalized. With these admonitions aside, note the following:

1. ASSESSOR, with 44 validations reported in the *Journal of Marketing Research*, August 1983, offers predictions that fall, on average, 0.8 share points from actual test market data, once the simulation has been adjusted for the real-world data. Approximately 70 percent of the predictions fall within 1.1 share points.

2. BASES (BASE II), with 152 validations reported as of 1982 (reflecting both test market and ADTEL validations), offers volume predictions that fall within 5 percent of actual first year volume, 35 percent of the time, and within 10 percent of the first year volume, 66 percent of the time, once the appropriate adjustments have been made.

3. ESP reports 30 validation cases. Over these cases volume prediction errors average ±9.9 percent, and they were within 10 percent of the first-year volume in 57 percent of the cases. Note, however, that validation data have not been published in a professional journal or been formally presented at a professional conference.

What could account for the inaccuracies in the simulated/pretest market models? First, some of the inaccuracy probably can be traced to new products that do not fit easily into established product categories; such introductions tend to confound market simulation models. Second, some of the variance surely can be traced to assumptions that are implicit to the idea of a simulation per se.

SUMMARY

This chapter has been devoted to the topic of test marketing. Simulated/pretest and test market studies are designed to provide varying extents of real-world, in-market exposure and evaluation of a product and its marketing program. Because of the risks associated with new-product introduction, simulated/pretest and test markets are likely to continue to be crucial elements in more effective marketing decisions.

KEY CONCEPTS

new-product failure rates

steps in test marketing

standard test market audits

controlled test market audits

test markets

simulated/pretest markets

REVIEW QUESTIONS

1. Discuss the reasons for conducting test markets.
2. What factors should be considered in determining the efficacy of test marketing?
3. Describe the steps in test market studies.
4. Why have simulated test market studies become popular?
5. Evaluate the three popular simulated test market models.

Marketing Decision Support Systems (MDSSs) and Forecasting Techniques

- Describe what an MDSS is.
- Explain the concept of a decision calculus.
- Discuss the essentials of an MDSS.
- Explain the specific benefits derived from using an MDSS.
- Illustrate those areas in which an MDSS can be particularly useful.
- Outline the issues involved in implementing MDSSs.
- Present several alternative forecasting methods.

INTRODUCTION

- "I need to see how much of each of my product lines has been sold in dollars, each month, for the year to date."
- "I need to rank my product lines by dollar sales this year."
- "I need to compare year-to-date advertising expenditures by media against budget targets, with variances expressed as a percentage."
- "I want to designate a target profit level, set some conditions such as price and a first-month sales volume, and determine what rate of sales growth is needed to reach the profit target; moreover, what are the implications of changing the base conditions?"

These activities illustrate applications that are well suited for **marketing decision support systems (MDSSs)**. What distinguishes the MDSS concept from other technologically based advances such as management information systems (MIS) and management science (MS) is its humanistic orientation. MIS touted the computer as the solution to management's problems; MS touted mathematical models and experts in "scientific" methods as the solution. MDSSs, in contrast, position the manager as the solution, equipped, of course, with the appropriate decision support technology. An MDSS improves the likelihood that a company will achieve its market objectives by amplifying the capabilities of the marketing manager; in particular, MDSS analysis enables marketing managers to identify the financial and volumetric impact of their marketing programs, derived, at least in part, from the bases of information collected through marketing research activities.

This chapter is devoted to a discussion of MDSS technology. Nearly all MDSSs use marketing research information; typically the marketing research department initiates the discussion and negotiation process that leads to the development of an MDSS. The purpose of this chapter is to illustrate how management expertise can be married to computer technology to provide a framework for making faster and more accurate marketing decisions. There are a great many different types of MDSSs; consequently, we will not be able to discuss all of the varieties here. Rather, our goal will be to discuss (1) the reasons for developing MDSSs, (2) the concept of a decision calculus, (3) the essentials of MDSSs, (4) the benefits and payoffs of using an MDSS, (5) areas in which MDSS can enhance decision making, and finally (6) the issues involved in implementation.

WHY AN MDSS?

The answer to this question is simple: competition! For better or worse, competitive environments incubate MDSSs. Because of the competitiveness of most markets, marketing researchers and managers find that they are not only making more decisions but also that the decisions must be made more quickly and with greater certainty. Coupled with the need to make quicker, more precise decisions is the proliferation of data. A common source of frustration is the knowledge that data that are relevant to the problem at hand exist somewhere in the organization but are not easily located, comprehended, formatted, or manipulated. MDSSs promise to provide key marketing managers and researchers with relevant information and the ability to work with it in order to enhance their decision making capabilities.

A pioneer in the development and dissemination of MDSSs is Professor John D. C. Little of the Sloan School of Management at the Massachusetts Institute of Technology. Little describes an MDSS as

> a coordinated collection of data, systems, tools, and techniques with supporting software and hardware by which an organization gathers and interprets relevant information from business and environment and turns it into a basis for marketing action.[1]

THE CONCEPT OF A DECISION CALCULUS

Decision calculus is a term invented by Little to describe MDSSs that represent an extension of a manager's ability to think about and analyze his or her operation.[2] Specifically, a decision calculus is defined as a model-based set of procedures for processing data and judgments to assist a manager in decision making.[3] According to Little, a decision calculus should be

---

[1] J. D. C. Little, "Decision Support Systems for Marketing Managers," *Journal of Marketing* 43 (Summer 1979), p. 11.

[2] This section is based on John D. C. Little, "Models and Managers: The Concept of a Decision Calculus," *Management Science*, April 1970, pp. B-466–B-485.

[3] Ibid., p. B-470.

1. *Simple.* Understanding can be increased by including only important information in a system. Only when it is demonstrated that detailed information can be understood and used by managers should it be included.
2. *Robust.* A system should not give bad answers; thus a structure should be imposed that inherently constrains answers to a meaningful range of values.
3. *Controllable.* A user should be able to make the system behave in a prescribed way. The user should fully understand how to set inputs to get almost any outputs. Parameters of the system should represent the operation as the manager sees it.
4. *Adaptive.* A system should be capable of being updated as new information becomes available.
5. *Complete.* A system should be able to handle a variety of different phenomena without becoming bogged down.
6. *Easy to use.* A system should allow a manager to change inputs easily and to obtain outputs quickly. Online, conversational input/output and personal computers make this a reality. Good online systems facilitate learning by providing user instructions and by allowing the user to get a feel for how the model works through direct experience.

In essence, then, a decision calculus orientation generates a system that brings the model to the manager and makes it a part of him or her.

THE ESSENTIALS OF AN MDSS

An essential element in an MDSS is a computer. However, contrary to what you might think, computers *cannot* automate complex decision making. Rather, their role is to help retrieve information quickly and to manipulate it creatively in order to enhance decision making capabilities. The key is to get relevant information to the manager as fast as he or she can use it. With this in mind, the following describes the important features of an MDSS.[4]

1. It is *computerized.* Computerization brings speed that allows managers to manipulate information in a variety of ways.
2. It is *interactive.* Online interactive systems provide the manager with menu-driven instructions and allow results to be generated on the spot. A computer programmer is not required, and the process is under the direct control of the manager; moreover, the manager need not wait for scheduled reports.
3. It is *flexible.* Flexibility means that the manager can sort, average, total, and manipulate the data in a variety of ways. It allows the manager to access and integrate data from a number of different sources.

---

[4]The following discussion has been adapted from Michael Dressler, Joquin Ives Brant, and Ronald Beall, Decision Support Systems: "What the Hot Marketing Tool of the '80s Offers You," *Industrial Marketing*, March 1983, pp. 51–60.

4. It is *discovery oriented.* A discovery orientation means that the manager can search for trends, identify problems, and ask new questions on the basis of the information provided.

5. It *minimizes the frustration quotient.* The system is easy to learn and use. Novice users, who are not particularly computer knowledgeable, should be able to use the system easily, initially selecting standard or "default" options so that they can immediately work with the basic system while gradually learning to exercise all of its options.

MDSSs have three essential features: databases, a user interface, and a library of analytical and modeling tools. Exhibit 22–1 depicts these essential characteristics. Note that the manager interfaces with the system through interactive instruction and display. The central database contains all of the information in the system. Typically, the practice is to "distribute" the MDSS; a network of microcomputers is linked to the control database, which is housed on a mainframe computer or minicomputer. This arrangement puts flexible computing power in the hands of managers, while the MIS group usually remains responsible for the update and integrity of the central database.

EXHIBIT 22–1

Decision Support System

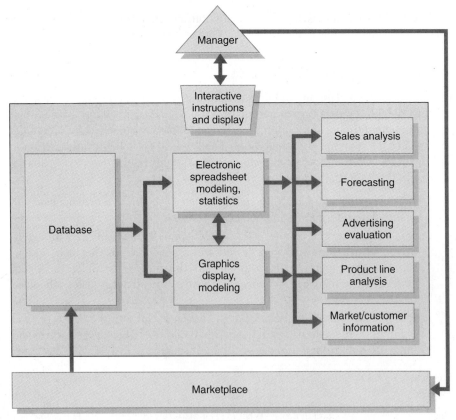

Source: Michael Dressler, Joquin Ives Brant, and Ronald Beall, *Industrial Marketing*, March 1983, p. 54.

The core of the MDSS is the **rational database manager.** The database manager provides the user with the ability to efficiently access and manipulate the data. The database manager program responds to commands from a user at the cathode ray tube (CRT) screen, extracts the correct information from the central database, and arranges it in a specified report format.

The selected data can be analyzed in a variety of ways. The analytical structure is generally organized in terms of subsystems, such as sales analysis, forecasting, advertising evaluation, product-line analysis, and market/customer information. The properly formatted data could be loaded into either an electronic spreadsheet, one of many different optimization models, a statistical package subroutine, or a graphics software subroutine. Electronic spreadsheets warrant some special comments because they probably represent the single greatest reason that managers have begun to use microcomputers routinely. Electronic spreadsheets appear as a large grid, similar to an accountant's worksheet, on which a manager can revise numbers. They are very useful for adjusting forecasts and for performing operations on a series of numbers; in addition, more sophisticated versions of spreadsheets have become available, offering such features as net present value and various forecasting models.

> **rational database manager**
> *A component of an MDSS that provides the user with the ability to efficiently access and manipulate the data.*

BENEFITS AND PAYOFFS

Proponents of the concept of an MDSS ascribe a number of specific benefits to it. Those frequently cited include the following:

- Increased staff efficiency—more work in less time.
- Increased managerial effectiveness—ability to focus on key issues.
- Increased response to change.
- Greater understanding of market dynamics.
- More extensive use of available data.
- More varied set of alternatives evaluated.
- Greater reliance on analytical methods.
- Development of a common basic database.
- Reliance on uniform analysis by various divisions.

Although this list of potential benefits is impressive, not all companies embrace MDSSs. An MDSS must overcome several barriers that we will discuss in regard to implementation.

One primary payoff of using MDSS is the ability to answer "what if" questions. Such sensitivity analysis is particularly useful for developing marketing strategy. For example, suppose a manager wants to adjust 12-month dollar sales-volume forecasts for several different brands for changes in price and units sold. Using spreadsheets and a model that relates units sold and price, the manager specifies alternative prices and instructs the computer to calculate units sold and dollar sales volume.

ENHANCED DECISION MAKING

Because of the potential for enhanced decision making and the diffusion of the personal computer, there has been a rapid proliferation of MDSS software. As we indicated earlier, MDSSs range from systems that provide data retrieval to those that do statistical analyses and complex modeling. In this section we describe several areas that lend themselves to MDSSs. Even though the systems that are described vary greatly, they all have in common the ability to enhance a manager's decision making capabilities.

Sales and Product Analysis

Sales and product analysis is a basic core feature of many MDSSs. Managers tend to be extremely interested in this application because of its critical role in decision making. Typically, an MDSS will allow the manager to see sales or unit volume by product broken down by sales representative and customer segment, by time period, geographical location, and so forth. The level of analysis will depend on the specificity of the company's database. Exhibit 22–2 presents several prototypical sales and product analyses obtained with the Acustar™ decision support system.[5]

Sales and Product Forecasting

Making forecasts is intrinsic to the management function. Many managers make forecasts on a routine basis, and, in many cases, the performance of the manager is in large measure determined by the accuracy of his or her forecasts.

There are many different forecasting methods. To some, forecasting means making "educated" guesses, whereas to others, forecasting involves the use of complex mathematical models and procedures.[6] For example, among *judgmental methods*, which are the least sophisticated of the forecasting techniques, are included:

sales force composite estimates
A method of forecasting based on the informed knowledge of the firm's sales force who provide estimates of future demand.

- **Sales force composite estimates,** which refers to forecasts based on the informed knowledge of the firm's sales force. Sales personnel provide estimates of future demand. This technique makes use of the relationship between a sales representative and his or her customers in order to develop accurate estimates about future trends. On the positive side, by participating in the forecasting process, the sales representative may have greater confidence in the derived sales quotas and, consequently, may be more motivated to achieve those quotas. This technique appears well suited to products that are fairly technical and subject to changing technology. On the negative side,

---

[5]ACUSTAR™ is distributed by TYMSHARE, Cupertino, California.

[6]For more details on various forecasting techniques, see John C. Chambers, Satinder K. Mullick, and Donald D. Smith, *An Executive's Guide to Forecasting* (New York: John Wiley & Sons, 1974); Spyros Makridakis and Steven C. Wheelwright, *Forecasting: Methods and Applications* (New York: John Wiley & Sons, 1978); Steven C. Wheelwright and Spyros Makridakis, *Forecasting Methods for Management*, 2nd ed. (New York: John Wiley & Sons, 1977); and Douglas Wood and Robert Fildes, *Forecasting for Business: Methods and Application* (New York: Longman Group, 1976).

EXHIBIT 22-2 Prototypical Sales and Product Analysis from Acustar™

SOURCE: FACTORY
CATEGORY: COFFEE
GEOGRAPHY: TOTAL U.S.

SALES PERFORMANCE UPDATE
BASIS: 5 MONTH SALES ENDING MAY 1982

PAGE: 1
DATE: 09/19/82
USER: JMH

K= THOUS.
M= MILL.

	LAST YR Y.T.D. SALES	CURRENT Y.T.D. SALES	INDEX CURRENT Y.T.D. VS YR AGO	Y.T.D. SALES FORECAST	INDEX CURRENT Y.T.D. VS FORECAST	TOTAL 1982 SALES FORECAST	SALES NEEDED TO MEET FORECAST	VOL LAST YR DURING REMAIN MONTHS	INDEX CURRENT TO GO VS YR AGO
TOTAL GENERAL COFFEE CO.	$66,871K	$91,175K	136	$89,267K	102	$227,759K	$136,584K	$160,888K	85
TOTAL IRISH HOST	$12,243K	$14,201K	116	$16,326K	87	$41,308K	$27,107K	$29,065K	93
IRISH HOST 4 OZ.	$4,883.9K	$5,564.8K	114	$6,000.0K	93	$16,211K	$10,646K	$11,327K	94
IRISH HOST 8 OZ.	$6,256.1K	$7,516.2K	120	$9,125.8K	82	$21,972K	$14,455K	$15,716K	92
IRISH HOST 12 OZ.	$1,102.9K	$1,120.0K	102	$1,200.1K	93	$3,125.4K	$2,005.4K	$2,022.6K	99
TOTAL ISLAND SUNSET	$37,271K	$55,525K	149	$51,421K	108	$128,446K	$72,921K	$91,175K	80
ISLAND SUNSET 4 OZ.	$8,802.2K	$10,758K	122	$11,014K	98	$26,854K	$16,096K	$18,052K	89
ISLAND SUNSET 8 OZ.	$17,288K	$24,949K	144	$23,948K	104	$59,232K	$34,283K	$41,944K	82
ISLAND SUNSET 12 OZ.	$11,181K	$19,819K	177	$16,460K	120	$42,360K	$22,542K	$31,180K	72
TOTAL PERFECT CHOICE	$17,357K	$21,449K	124	$21,521K	100	$58,005K	$36,556K	$40,649K	90
PERFECT CHOICE 4 OZ.	$5,031.7K	$4,845.4K	96	$5,892.5K	82	$14,236K	$9,390.5K	$9,204.1K	102
PERFECT CHOICE 8 OZ.	$9,502.9K	$12,504K	132	$11,938K	105	$33,345K	$20,841K	$23,842K	87
PERFECT CHOICE 12 OZ.	$2,822.0K	$4,100.3K	145	$3,690.7K	111	$10,424K	$6,324.2K	$7,602.5K	83

Update Sales Performance The status reports generated with Acustar offer a method of periodically reviewing market performance versus objectives. See how your brand is doing year-to-date (YTD). How does it compare with this year's forecast? What is the YTD percentage increase or decrease versus last year's sales?

EXHIBIT 22–2 (concluded)

SOURCE: SAMI+MAJERS
CATEGORY: COFFEE

IRISH HOST VS PRIVATE LABEL
REGIONAL PERFORMANCE COMPARISON

13 PD END PD+202 3/5/82

PAGE: 1
DATE: 09/19/82
USER: JMH

K = THOUS. M = MILL.	IRISH HOST				PRIVATE LABEL			
	AREA %CONTRIB TO TOTL DOLLARS	DOLLAR SHARE OF CATEGORY	AVERAGE PRICE PER POUND	SHARE OF CATEGORY WGTD VAL	AREA %CONTRIB TO TOTAL DOLLARS	DOLLAR SHARE OF CATEGORY	AVERAGE PRICE PER POUND	SHARE OF CATEGORY WGTD VAL
TOTAL U.S.	100.0%	14.2%	$0.92	12.3%	100.0%	9.1%	$0.67	4.7%
NORTHEAST	29.9%	20.2%	$0.89	11.6%	11.8%	5.1%	$0.67	1.1%
MID ATLANTIC	11.8%	20.2%	$0.88	18.6%	7.9%	8.7%	$0.66	8.5%
SOUTHEAST	9.3%	14.8%	$0.91	10.2%	8.6%	8.8%	$0.67	5.0%
MID SOUTH	2.7%	10.4%	$0.93	12.6%	6.3%	15.6%	$0.69	7.0%
CENTRAL	18.9%	17.8%	$0.93	12.2%	16.3%	9.8%	$0.65	4.9%
SOUTHWEST	6.6%	12.4%	$0.96	10.3%	11.6%	14.1%	$0.67	8.9%
NORTHWEST	6.0%	12.4%	$1.01	9.2%	9.2%	12.2%	$0.69	6.9%
SOUTH PACIFIC	11.7%	7.9%	$0.92	13.9%	20.2%	8.8%	$0.65	4.1%
NORTH PACIFIC	3.1%	6.0%	$0.98	8.8%	7.9%	9.7%	$0.68	3.4%

Compare Performance by Region Compare your brand with a competitor on a region-by-region basis. Answer questions like: Where and why are private-label brands performing better than my brand? What is my brand's average price per pound by region?

SOURCE: MAJERS + SAMI
CATEGORY: COFFEE
GEOGRAPHY: NEW ENGLAND

MAJOR BRANDS AREA TRENDS

K = THOUS.
M = MILL.

	PD#189 3/6 1981	PD#190 4/3 1981	PD#191 5/1 1981	PD#192 5/29 1981	PD#193 6/26 1981	PD#194 7/24 1981	PD#195 8/21 1981	PD#196 9/18 1981	PD#197 10/16 1981	PD#198 11/13 1981	PD#199 12/11 1981	PD#200 1/8 1982	CURRENT PD#201 2/5 1982	YR AGO PD#188 2/6 1981	52 WEEK PD#201 2/5 1982
ISLAND SUNSET															
1 PD UNIT SHARE	3.0%	3.0%	2.4%	2.4%	2.2%	2.2%	2.7%	2.8%	2.7%	2.6%	2.3%	1.8%	1.9%	2.8%	2.4%
1 PD PRICE/UNIT	$0.63	$0.64	$0.65	$0.65	$0.65	$0.65	$0.61	$0.60	$0.62	$0.64	$0.66	$0.70	$0.71	$0.63	$0.64
1 PD %WGTD VALUE	10.3%	5.7%	0.8%	7.2%	0.8%	0.0%	6.3%	1.0%	1.3%	0.6%	0.0%	0.0%	7.6%	10.0%	3.8%
IRISH HOST															
1 PD UNIT SHARE	7.5%	7.4%	7.2%	7.2%	7.1%	7.1%	6.8%	6.7%	6.8%	6.9%	7.0%	7.3%	7.2%	8.3%	7.1%
1 PD PRICE/UNIT	$0.65	$0.65	$0.65	$0.65	$0.67	$0.67	$0.67	$0.67	$0.67	$0.68	$0.69	$0.69	$0.69	$0.63	$0.67
1 PD %WGTD VALUE	0.0%	0.6%	6.0%	3.2%	0.9%	8.4%	0.9%	0.0%	0.0%	1.4%	0.7%	0.0%	0.8%	1.4%	1.5%
MOUNTAIN HIGHLANDS															
1 PD UNIT SHARE	6.4%	6.4%	6.4%	6.4%	7.2%	7.2%	7.0%	6.9%	6.5%	6.3%	6.4%	6.5%	6.5%	6.4%	6.6%
1 PD PRICE/UNIT	$0.73	$0.73	$0.74	$0.74	$0.77	$0.78	$0.78	$0.78	$0.79	$0.80	$0.80	$0.80	$0.80	$0.71	$0.77
1 PD %WGTD VALUE	0.0%	0.0%	0.0%	0.0%	2.7%	0.4%	0.0%	0.9%	0.4%	0.2%	0.0%	0.0%	0.0%	0.0%	0.4%

Review Trends Combine information from multiple data sources in one report to obtain a more complete picture of trends in your marketplace.

sales representatives are biased observers. Therefore, few companies use their estimates without some adjustments.

jury of expert opinion
A method of forecasting based on combining the views of key executives.

—   **Jury of expert opinion,** which refers to forecasts based on combining the views of key executives. The views of several key executives are combined to provide a more accurate forecast of future demand than would be possible with the use of a single estimator. Although this technique is used by all kinds of companies, it is more likely to be adopted by a consumer goods manufacturer or by a service firm than by an industrial marketer. The critical problems with the executive opinion approach are (1) too much weight is given to opinion, (2) executives' time is infringed upon, and (3) there is no optimal universally agreed-upon procedure for combining the individual (executives') forecasts.

Delphi method
A method of forecasting based on asking a group of experts for their best estimate of a future event, then processing and feeding back some of the information obtained, and then repeating the process; on the last set of responses, the median usually is chosen as the best estimate for the group.

—   **Delphi and related methods,** which refers to forecasts based on asking a group of experts for their best estimate of a future event, processing and feeding back some of the information, and repeating the process. After a number of cycles the estimate for the group is usually obtained by taking the median on the last set of responses. There are three key features to this approach: (1) *anonymous response,* in which opinions and assignments are obtained anonymously; (2) *interaction and controlled feedback,* in which systematic exercises are used to promote interaction with controlled feedback between rounds; and (3) *statistical group response,* where the estimate of group opinion is obtained by aggregating individual opinions at the final round.

Among the more sophisticated of the forecasting techniques are time-series and regression and econometric models.

time-series models
Methods that produce forecasts on the basis of the statistical analysis of past data that presumably incorporate enduring and identifiable causal relationships that will carry forward into the future.

—   **Time-series models** refer to methods that produce forecasts on the basis of statistical analysis of past data. These methods are based on the premise that past data incorporate enduring and identifiable causal relationships that will carry forward into the future. A large number of time-series models fall under the umbrella of what can be called smoothing techniques. The notion underlying smoothing techniques is that past data reflect some pattern in the values of the variable to be forecasted along with random fluctuations. By eliminating random fluctuations, smoothing techniques hope to identify the underlying pattern in the historical data. Because these models assume that very little is known about the underlying cause of demand and that the future will be similar to the past, they are most useful for short- or medium-term forecasts (usually less than one year). We will discuss and illustrate several time-series models in Appendix 22A.

regression and econometric model
Methods that produce forecasts based on expressing demand as a function of a certain number of deterministic factors.

—   **Regression and econometric models** refer to methods that produce forecasts based on expressing demand as a function of a certain number of deterministic factors. These models are not necessarily time dependent and therefore can be useful when making long-term forecasts. The development of a model that captures the structure between demand and its underlying causes should lead to a better understanding of the situation and improved accuracy. Appendix 22A discusses and illustrates how regression analysis is used in a forecasting context.

The features that the MDSSs bring to forecasting are speed and the ability to easily play "what if" games. With use of an MDSS the manager need not wait hours or days for the computer runs to be completed by other departments. In addition, forecasts can be updated quickly. Because of direct interaction with the MDSS, the manager can ask questions concerning different scenarios based on the information provided and his or her intuitive thinking about the future course of events. Exhibit 22–3 (see page 656) presents a prototypical forecasting system that illustrates the speed and flexibility that an MDSS brings to the forecasting task.

Advertising Readership

McGraw-Hill Research has developed an MDSS to assist in understanding the key elements that determine a print ad's effectiveness. McGraw's MDSS makes use of a relatively large database, incorporating over 4,000 advertisements appearing in 26 business publications studied by McGraw-Hill's AD SELL readership program. Each ad is coded for its various physical characteristics, and this information is "married" to the "steps to a sale" readership scores it receives. The readership scores and converted index numbers reported are normed by magazine and issue. The norming procedure employed allows advertisements from different magazines appearing in different issues to be compared. Exhibit 22–4 (see page 658) presents illustrative information from McGraw-Hills' MDSS program.

ASCID—Advertising Strategy and Copy Information Development

ASCID[7] is an MDSS that aids the manager in evaluating the efficacy of new brand advertising material. ASCID can be used in pretesting and post-evaluation environments. In a pretesting environment, ASCID can screen candidate advertisements and establish a rank ordering for the ability to "move" a referent brand to a desired position in the existing competitive space. In a post-evaluation setting, ASCID can determine the positioning/repositioning effectiveness of a particular copy. ASCID generates a perceptual product space. It accepts as input either direct or derived ratings. The process begins by generating the existing product space and then fits property vectors (if available). The research analyst, using data on the existing competitive environment, is asked to indicate the desired (or ideal) position that best matches brand/company objectives. The desired position reflects the displacement of the referent brand under the assumption that the proposed

---

[7]Further details on ASCID can be found in William R. Dillon, Teresa J. Domzal, and Thomas J Madden, "Evaluating Alternative Product Positioning Strategies," *Journal of Advertising Research* 26, no. 4 (August/September 1986), pp. 29–35.

EXHIBIT 22–3
—
MDSS Forecasting
System

```
Choose one:> forecast
forecasting methods

    1 Moving Averages (MAv)
    2 Double Moving Averages (DMAv)
    3 Exponential Smoothing (ExS)
    4 Double Exponential Smoothing (DExS)
    5 Regression

Choose one: MAv
Period to base Moving Average On:> 3
Enter data by year> 1976 28.2, 1977 31.6, 1978 30.5, 1979 31.8, 1980
34.2, 1981 36.3, 1982 39.3, 1983 41.7, 1984 50.0, 1985 46.8, 1986 43.7,
1987 52.1, 1988 63.3, 1989 69.9, 1990 72.3, 1991 76.0, 1992 76.1, 1993
78.0

What forecaster output(s) do you want?

    1 Graph (GRA)   1 Graph actual and predicted
    2 Report (REP)  1 Report actual, forecast, and change
    3 Adjust (ADJ)  1 Adjust the forecast
Choice: > 1
```

copy is successful in changing consumer perceptions. On the basis of postexposure rating (either direct or derived), the referent brand is then *repositioned in the existing competitive space*. Various positioning effectiveness measures are computed. The post-exposure reposition of the referent brand is accomplished in the *existing* competitive space. Exhibit 22–5 (see page 660) presents prototypical output from the ASCID MDSS.

Promotion Evaluation

An article appearing in *Marketing News* described the use of *K-PASA*, Kraft Promotion Analysis Self-Assessment.[8] The system provides brand managers with information on tonnage, share, promotion, and so forth. The system consists of a number of reports. Each report prompts the user for input values and has query capability and reporting, statistical, mathematical, financial, and graphical tools. Exhibit 22–6 (see page 661) shows a baseline application that compares what was sold by week with a base level of sales. By knowing when the promotion occurred, the manager can determine the incremental volume and profit received from each promotion. K-PASA provides quick information on the effects that promotion has on sales and volume. The information can then be divided among such factors as location, discount rate, and promotion period. Other system capabilities include profit and loss reports for each promotion and various options for specialized reports.

---

[8]"Modified Computer System Helps Kraft Make Plans," *Marketing News*, May 23, 1986, p. 31.

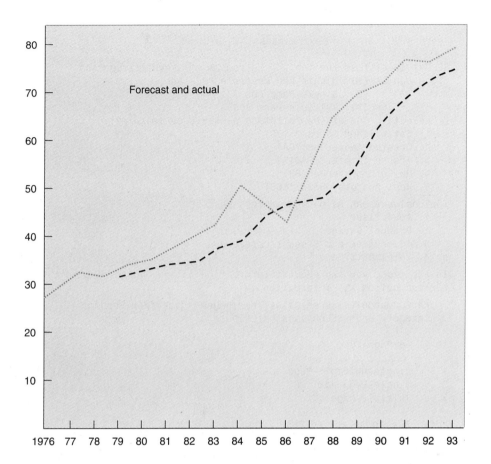

EXHIBIT 22-3

—

(*concluded*)

Advertising Budget Decisions (ADBUG)

The ADBUG MDSS models sales response to advertising.[9] Developed by John D. C. Little, the ADBUG MDSS models what is happening to the whole industry or product class of which a given brand is a part and what is happening to the brand's market share within the product class.

The ADBUG MDSS is quite easy to use. The basic equations defining the model are few in number while, at the same time, the structure allows the manager to consider the effects on share of advertising, copy and media effectiveness, product class seasonality and trend, share dynamics, and a variety of nonadvertising effects, such as promotion, competition, and price. Moreover, the system is designed to answer "what if" questions and to perform sensitivity analyses.

In order to calibrate a sales response to an advertising function, a number of working conditions must be assumed. Specifically, for a given time period, ADBUG MDSS assumes that

[9]The ADBUG MDSS is described in Little, *Management Science*, pp. B-466–B-485.

EXHIBIT 22–4
—
MDSS: Report

```
Press <CR> key for next screen:;

REPORT identifies the Top and Bottom X% of a publication ads,
which can be (1). Single and Multiple Page Ads,
              (2). Single-Page ads,
        or (3). Multiple-Page ads,
by selecting one of the following performance measures:
    1. Established Contact (EC)
    2. Created Awareness (CA)
    3. Arouse Interest (AI)
    4. Build Preference (BP)
    5. Kept Customer Sold (KCS).
The analysis can be performed for specific
    1. Advertiser
    2. Product Category
    3. Advertiser and Product Category
or 4. Total Data Base.
In addition, you can request information on each ad scoring in the
top and bottom X%. Information is:

    Performance Measures/Issue/Year/Page#/Advertiser/Product
    Category and ONE physical attribute.

ID     Ad Page Type
__     _____
1      Single/Multiple-Page ads
2      Single-Page ads
3      Multiple-Page ads

Enter ID# to select Ad Page Type: 1

ID     Performance Measure
__     _____
1      EC Establish Contact (attract attention)
2      CA Create Awareness (make prospect aware of something
       not known before)
```

1. With zero advertising, brand share will fall by a fixed amount; in other words, there is a floor on how much the share will fall from its initial value by the end of one time period.

2. With an extremely large advertising expenditure (say, something approaching saturation), brand share will increase by a fixed amount; in other words, there is a ceiling on how much the share will increase from its initial value by the end of one time period.

3. There is a level of advertising expenditure that will maintain the share at its initial level.

4. Based on data analysis or managerial expertise, it is possible to determine the effect on the share of a 50 percent increase in advertising expenditure over maintenance level.

EXHIBIT 22–4

(concluded)

```
3       AI Arouse Interest (cause action)
4       BP Build Preference
5       KCS Keep Customer Sold

Enter ID# to select Performance Measure: 1 Right (y/n)? y
ID              Function Type
__              _____
1               Advertiser
2               Product Category
3               Advertiser and Product Category
4               Total Data Base

Enter ID# to select Function Type: 4
Right (y/n)?   y

Enter the Top/Bottom X% that this report will be based on, e.g. 5
means 5%: 10 Right (y/n)? y

Input ad/sell data normalized by: issue/year
Mean Score Report ==> Ad Page Type: Single/Multiple-
                      Page ads
                   ==> 10% of EC with Total Data Base
          ID#   #Ads  EC     CA     AI     BP     KCS    Inq/#Ads
          ___   ____  ___    __     __     __     ___    _____
Top       1     15    96.9   36.4   56.7   60.0   91.1   0.0/0
Bottom    2     15    30.6   70.9   70.0   60.3   72.7   0.0/0

Enter ID# to select Item: 1 Right (y/n)? y

ID#    Item
___    _____
0      QUIT
1      Perform a T-test
2      Retrieve Ad Information
```

Source: McGraw-Hill Research.

Time delays are also taken into account. To incorporate time delays, the model defines

long run min = The level that share would eventually decay to in the absence of any advertising expenditures

persistence = The fraction of the difference between the share and *long run min* that is retained after decay

The advertising that goes into the response function in a given time period is determined from the following relation:

$$adv(t) = [\text{Media efficiency } (t)][\text{Copy effectiveness } (t)][\text{Advertising dollars } (t)]$$

The media efficiency index and the copy effectiveness index are assumed to have reference values of 1.0. If, for example, the brand manager thinks that the effi-

EXHIBIT 22–5   ASCID MDSS

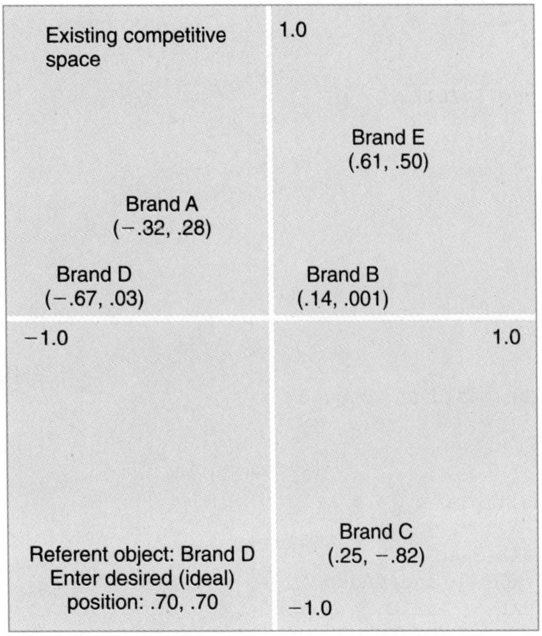

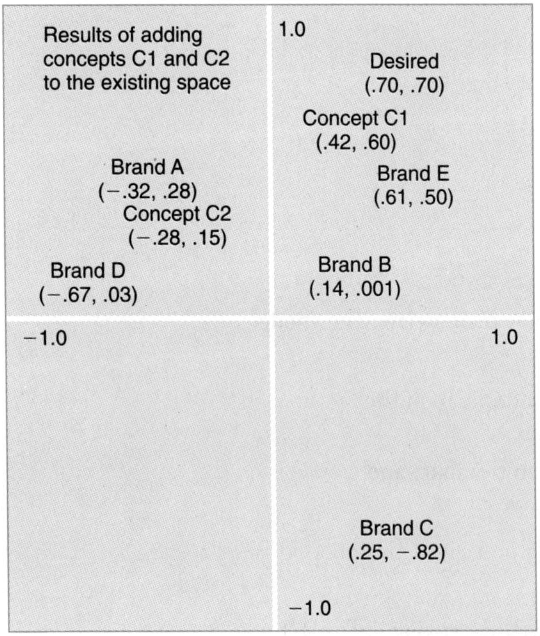

Existing competitive space

1.0

Brand E
(.61, .50)

Brand A
(−.32, .28)

Brand D
(−.67, .03)

Brand B
(.14, .001)

−1.0   1.0

Brand C
(.25, −.82)

Referent object: Brand D
Enter desired (ideal)
position: .70, .70

−1.0

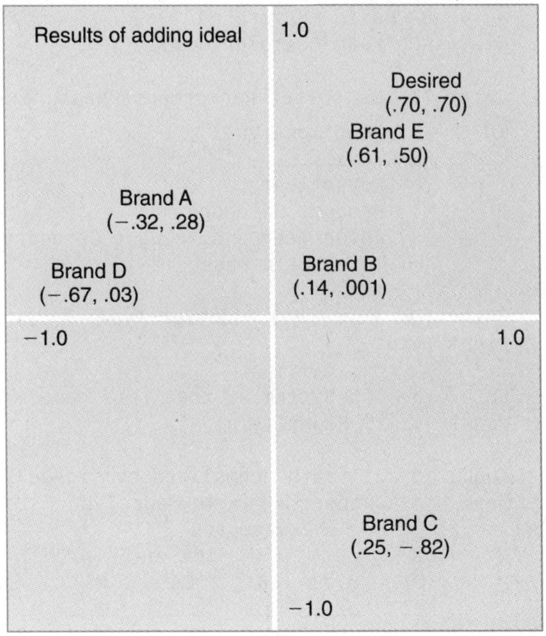

Results of adding ideal

1.0

Desired
(.70, .70)
Brand E
(.61, .50)

Brand A
(−.32, .28)

Brand D
(−.67, .03)

Brand B
(.14, .001)

−1.0   1.0

Brand C
(.25, −.82)

−1.0

Results of adding concepts C1 and C2 to the existing space

1.0

Desired
(.70, .70)

Concept C1
(.42, .60)

Brand A
(−.32, .28)
Concept C2
(−.28, .15)

Brand E
(.61, .50)

Brand D
(−.67, .03)

Brand B
(.14, .001)

−1.0   1.0

Brand C
(.25, −.82)

−1.0

Summary	Coordinates	Effectiveness index (%)
Brand D (Referent)	(−.67, .03)	– –
Desired (Ideal)	(.70, .70)	– –
Concept C1	(.42, .60)	198.5
Concept C2	(−.28, .15)	102.4

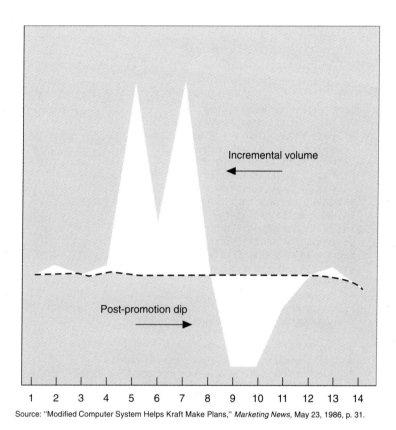

EXHIBIT 22–6

K-PASA

Source: "Modified Computer System Helps Kraft Make Plans," *Marketing News,* May 23, 1986, p. 31.

ciency of the media selected in a given time period will likely deliver above-average results, a value greater than 1.0 would be assigned. These indices can be determined subjectively or can be based on data on media costs, segment exposure incidences, copy testing results, and so forth. Other factors such as price promotion, package changes, product changes, competition, and the like also affect share and therefore should be either directly or indirectly incorporated into the system. An easy yet effective way to accomplish this is to introduce the concept of a *reference case,* which represents a set of values against which changes can be measured. The reference case includes a referenced time period, not one of the number time periods used in calculations but one set aside to serve as a standard. Thus, all time-varying effects, including media efficiency and copy effectiveness discussed above, are assigned a value in the reference period.

The final question that must be answered is, "How should advertising be changed to increase profits?" The cumulative contribution after advertising in the last period of the calculation provides the answer to this question. Specifically, a slope parameter for each time period is computed. The slope parameter gives

slope (t) = The change in cumulative contribution after advertising in the last period, per unit change in advertising dollars in time *t*

EXHIBIT 22–7
—
ADBUG MDSS

```
Run

Input with data statements? n
Number of periods (max 10)? 2

Reference case conditions
Mkt share at start of period? .087
Adv rate to maintain share (mm $/period)? 4
Mkt share at end of period
   If adv reduced to zero? .037
   If adv increased to saturation? .15
   If adv increased 20% over maintenance rate? .10
Mkt share in long run if adv reduced to zero? 0
Index of media efficiency? 1.2
Index of copy effectiveness? 1.2
Contribution profit (before adv. exp.)
Expressed in dollars/sales unit? 3.68
Average brand price ($/unit)? 10.7
Other data:
Mkt share in previous period? .080
Product sales rate at start of period (MM unit/period)? 78
Average price for product ($/unit)? 10.7

Budget horizon conditions
Consider response to product class advertising? n
Product has a seasonal or other non adv time effect? n
Brand share has a non adv time effect? n
Maintenance advtg varies? n
Media efficiency varies? y
Index of media efficiency for period
   1              ?  1.2
   2              ?  .9

Copy effectiveness varies? y
Index of copy effectiveness for period:
   1              ?  1.2
   2              ?  .1
Brand adv rate varies? n
Brand advertising (MM dollars)? 6.85

Action code: 1=output, 2= change, 3=stop

Action? 1
```

Period	Share pct units	Product Sales Units (MM)	Product Sales Dolrs (MM)	Brand sales Units (000)	Brand sales Dolrs (000)	Contr bef adv (000)	Brand adv dolrs (000)	Contr aft adv (000)	Cumul contr (000)	Slope CC$/$
1	11.95	78	835	9320	99726	34298	6850	27448	27448	2.05
2	5.11	78	835	3988	42671	14676	6850	7826	35274	−0.97

```
Action? 3
```

A positive slope indicates that advertising increases will be profitable; negative, unprofitable; and zero, indifferent.

Operation

The best way to see how the ADBUG MDSS operates would be by demonstration at a computer terminal. Short of this, we provide an example. The details are presented in Exhibit 22–7.

IMPLEMENTATION ISSUES

Much has been written on implementation of MDSSs.[10] Two issues critical to implementation are factors that affect adoption and implementation success.

Factors Affecting Adoption

Whether or not an organization embraces MDSSs is determined by a number of diverse factors. The following discussion takes into account several salient factors that can influence the likelihood of adoption.

Payoffs.   The payoffs of adopting an MDSS should be weighed against the cost. We have described several marketing decision areas that lend themselves nicely to MDSSs. If you recall, the payoff from these systems was quicker, improved decision making. Although, in our opinion, improved decision making that leads to increased profits should be the only payoff criterion considered, there are other possible reasons for building an MDSS—for example, (1) to change the decision making process, (2) to change the organization, (3) to establish a power base (a select group of MDSS users), (4) to gain attention within the firm, and (5) to challenge the "old line." In terms of costs, one must consider *time, money,* and *dissonance* (e.g., corporate inertia that produces resistance to change, coupled with frustration).

Organizational Structure.   The structure of an organization with respect to the stability of junior, middle, and top management, management interaction, and the degree of decentralization will affect the adoption of MDSS. In firms that are organized functionally and that have well-defined roles (jobs) and performance evaluation, it is more likely that the manager will have a personal stake in the adoption of any system that can enhance the quality of decision making.

---

[10]See, for example, Steven L. Alter, *Decision Support Systems: Current Practices and Continuing Challenges* (Reading, Mass.: Addison Wesley, 1980); Randall L. Schultz and Dennis P. Slevin, "Introduction: The Implementation Problem," in *The Implementation of Management Science,* ed. Robert Doktor, Randall L. Schultz, and Dennis P. Slevin (Amsterdam, Netherlands: North Holland, 1979), pp. 1–15; and Ralph H. Sprague and Eric D. Carlson, *Building Effective Decision Support Systems* (Englewood Cliffs, N.J.: Prentice Hall, 1982).

Corporate Culture. The prevailing norms, beliefs, and myths of each organization also determine how it views MDSSs. How competition is viewed, the toughness and competitiveness of its marketing and sales people, the philosophy concerning market expansion and innovation, and the attitude toward risk and decision making will all, to varying degrees, affect the likelihood of adoption.

Players. The quality of an organization's managers ultimately plays an important role in the adoption process. Their personal values (e.g., loyalty, hard work, and discipline) that are emphasized and their attitude toward teamwork also affect whether or not MDSS will be embraced.

Implementation Success

Implementation success means different things to different people. For some, implementation is successful when the manager has directly used the results derived from the MDSS in making a decision. Others believe that the fact that managers do not use the MDSS results directly is simply a sign that the manager is not losing responsibility or control. What is important is the manager-model-machine interaction because it invariably results, albeit indirectly, in a marriage of the MDSS output with the manager's own heuristic knowledge structure. Regardless of how you view implementation success, it is clear that the accent should be on improving the quality of decision making. Improvement implies change, but change alone does not guarantee improvement. An MDSS that improves decision making is "successfully implemented."

A general recommendation concerning implementation problems can be made. All of the available evidence indicates that there are likely to be fewer problems in MDSSs when the managers who must use the system are involved in the development of the system, that is, well before the final decision is made to implement it.

SUMMARY

In this chapter we have attempted to provide a brief introduction to MDSSs. We have concentrated on the practical issues involved in using an MDSS and have illustrated several different types of MDSSs. By now, you should understand the essentials of an MDSS, its payoffs and benefits, and the application areas in which it can be most useful, as well as how it fits into the marketing research function.

KEY CONCEPTS

MDSS	MDSS subsystems	sales force composite estimates	time-series models
decision calculus	MDSS benefits		regression and econometric models
MDSS essentials	judgment forecasting techniques	jury of expert opinion	
rational database manager		Delphi method	MDSS implementation

REVIEW QUESTIONS

1. Discuss the concept of a decision calculus and its importance to MDSS.
2. In designing an MDSS what considerations are important?
3. Describe the potential benefits derived from using an MDSS.
4. Discuss three application areas in which an MDSS could potentially prove useful.
5. Comment on the issues that should be considered when implementing an MDSS.

FORECASTING TECHNIQUES

OVERVIEW

The forecasting techniques described in this appendix are primarily smoothing techniques—that is, moving averages and exponential smoothing. In addition, we present a brief example of how regression analysis can be used as a forecasting technique. Our discussion of smoothing techniques parallels the presentation in Chapter 3 of Wheelwright and Makridakis's book, *Forecasting Methods for Management*, which we recommend for the interested reader.[1]

Smoothing techniques use a series of historical data to predict or forecast the value for some future event of the series. For example, if we were interested in forecasting the level of sales for next year we would use the value of sales for some historical period (say the last 10 years) to obtain the forecasted value.

The basic notion inherent in smoothing methods is that there is some pattern to the series of data and that this pattern will continue in the future; consequently, past events are drawn upon to predict or forecast future events. The accuracy of the forecast with smoothing techniques depends primarily on (1) the cohesiveness of the series of historical data and (2) how far in the future the forecast is made. Before we present the smoothing methods, let's first take a brief look at these two conditions.

When we use smoothing methods for forecasting, we are assuming that there is some pattern to the data and that each data point in the historical series represents that underlying pattern plus some random fluctuation.[2] Smoothing methods attempt to remove the random fluctuations from the data and base the forecast on the underlying pattern. When the series of data is primarily characterized by random fluctuation there exists little pattern to the data and consequently our forecasts will be based more on randomness than on pattern. Hence, we should not be surprised if our forecast does not predict the future value very well.

The second element that can affect the forecast is how far into the future we want to predict. We must remember that we are basing the forecast of the future events (forecasted value) on past events. Hence, we are assuming that the environment that produced the past events will exist in the future.

---

[1]Steven C. Wheelwright and Spyros Makridakis, *Forecasting Methods for Management*, 2nd ed. (New York: Wiley & Sons, 1977).

[2]Ibid., p. 30.

Moving Averages

The method of moving averages uses the average of some specified historical period to forecast the value of a future period. For example, if we use a three-period moving average, then the future period $(t + 1)$ forecast would be the average of the last three data points in the historical series. That is, if we had annual sales data for the historical period 1980 to 1992, and we wanted to forecast sales for the period 1993, the forecast would be the average sales value for the periods 1990, 1991, and 1992. A five-year moving average forecast would use the last five years.

Table 22A–1 contains revenue data for Tootsie Roll, Inc., for the period 1966 to 1983. We use these data to explicate the method of moving averages. Table 22A–2 (see page 668) presents the forecasted values for a three- and five-period (in this case, years) moving average.

Double Moving Averages

This method of forecasting is an extension of the moving average method. The procedure is the same; however, the values used to provide the estimates are the values calculated for the simple moving averages. The estimates resulting from a double moving average for the Tootsie Roll data are presented in Table 22A–3 (see page 668).

When the historical data are characterized by an increasing trend, as with the data shown in Table 22A–1, moving average estimates are always below the actual data. You will note from Table 22A–3 that the single moving average estimates are

Year	Revenues (millions)
1966	28.2
1967	31.6
1968	30.5
1969	31.8
1970	34.2
1971	36.3
1972	39.3
1973	41.7
1974	50.0
1975	46.8
1976	43.7
1977	52.1
1978	63.3
1979	69.6
1980	72.3
1981	76.0
1982	76.1
1983	78.0

TABLE 22A–1

Revenue Values for Tootsie Roll, Inc., 1966–1983

TABLE 22A–2

—

Simple Moving
Averages, 1966–1983

Year	Actual Value	Forecast 3 Years	Forecast 5 Years
1966	28.2	—	—
1967	31.6	—	—
1968	30.5	—	—
1969	31.8	30.1	—
1970	34.2	31.3	—
1971	36.3	32.17	31.26
1972	39.3	34.10	32.88
1973	41.7	36.60	34.42
1974	50.0	39.10	36.66
1975	46.8	43.67	40.30
1976	43.7	46.17	42.82
1977	52.1	46.83	44.30
1978	63.3	47.53	46.86
1979	69.6	53.03	51.18
1980	72.3	61.67	55.10
1981	76.0	68.40	60.20
1982	76.1	72.63	66.66
1983	78.0	74.80	71.46
		76.7	74.4

TABLE 22A–3

—

Double Moving
Averages, 1966–1983

Year	Actual Value	Forecast 3-Year Single Moving Average	Forecast 3-Year Double Moving Average
1966	28.2	—	—
1967	31.6	—	—
1968	30.5	—	—
1969	31.8	30.1	—
1970	34.2	31.31	—
1971	36.3	32.17	31.19
1972	39.3	34.10	32.52
1973	41.7	36.60	34.29
1974	50.0	39.10	36.60
1975	46.8	43.67	39.79
1976	43.7	46.17	42.98
1977	52.1	46.83	45.56
1978	63.3	47.53	46.84
1979	69.6	53.03	49.13
1980	72.3	61.67	54.08
1981	76.0	68.40	61.03
1982	76.1	72.63	67.57
1983	78.0	74.80	71.94

	(1)	(2)	(3)			
	Actual	**Single Moving Average**	**Double Moving Average**	**A**	**B**	F''_{t+1}
1966	28.2	—	—			
1967	31.6	—	—			
1968	30.5	—	—			
1969	31.8	30.10	—			
1970	34.2	31.30	—			
1971	36.3	32.17	31.19	33.15	0.98	34.13
1972	39.3	34.10	32.52	35.68	1.58	37.26
1973	41.7	36.60	34.29	38.91	2.31	41.22
1974	50.0	39.10	36.60	41.60	2.50	44.10
1975	46.8	43.67	39.79	47.55	3.88	51.43
1976	43.7	46.17	42.98	49.36	3.19	52.55
1977	52.1	46.83	45.56	48.10	1.27	49.37
1978	63.3	47.53	46.84	48.22	0.69	48.91
1979	69.6	53.03	49.13	56.93	3.90	60.83
1980	72.3	61.67	54.08	69.26	7.59	76.85
1981	76.0	68.40	61.03	75.77	7.37	83.14
1982	76.1	72.63	67.57	77.69	5.06	82.75
1983	78.0	74.80	71.94	77.66	2.86	80.52

TABLE 22A–4

Double Moving Averages Forecasts, 1966–1983

consistently below the actual data; for example, 31.8 versus 30.1, 34.2 versus 31.31, 36.3 versus 32.17. In addition, the double moving average estimates are always below the single moving average estimates. To prepare forecasts we use both the single and double moving average estimates. First, we must calculate two factors, A and B. Letting S'_{t+1} be the estimate derived from the single moving averages, S''_{t+1} be the estimate derived from double moving averages, and n be the number of years used to calculate the moving average, the factors A and B are[3]

$$A = 2S'_{t+1} - S''_{t+1} \qquad (22A\text{–}1)$$

and

$$B = \frac{2}{n-1}(S'_{t+1} - S''_{t+1}) \qquad (22A\text{–}2)$$

The forecasted value is

$$F''_{t+P} = A + BP$$

where P equals the number of time periods in the future we wish to forecast. The calculations for the forecasts using both single and double moving averages are provided in Table 22A–4.

---

[3]Ibid., p. 43.

Exponential Smoothing

A major limitation to the method of moving averages is that the years used to compute the estimates are given equal weights and any previous years are given zero weights. For example, the estimate for 1993 would be, with a three-year moving average, one-third of each of the three preceding years; all years prior to 1990 would receive a zero weight in the estimation of the forecast for 1993.

Intuitively, we would expect future events to be most similar to the most recent historical events; consequently, we would like to develop forecasts whereby the most recent events receive more weight than less recent events. The method of exponential smoothing allows us to apply differential weighting.

Letting F_{t+1} be the forecast for the period $t + 1$ (i.e., the next period), the formula for exponential smoothing can be written as

$$F_{t+1} = F_t + \alpha(S_t - F_t) \qquad (22A\text{–}3)$$

where

$$F_t = \text{Forecast for the } t^{\text{th}}, \text{ or last period}$$
$$S_t = \text{Actual value for the } t^{\text{th}}, \text{ or last period}$$
$$\alpha = \text{Smoothing constant, which is equal to } \frac{1}{n}$$

Additional insight into the smoothing constant α can be gleaned by rewriting Equation 22A–3 as

$$F_{t+1} = \frac{1}{n}S_t + \left(1 - \frac{1}{n}\right)F_t \qquad (22A\text{–}4)$$

Now, n represents the number of past years upon which we wish to base our forecast; hence, the fewer the number of past years we base our forecast on, the more the weight given to the most recent observations.

To illustrate the method of exponential smoothing, we again use the data shown in Table 22A–1 for values of α equal to 0.2 and 0.5. These estimates are shown in Table 22A–5.

When $\alpha = 0.5$ we are placing more weight on the most recent observation than when $\alpha = 0.2$. Note the difference between the forecasts for years 1975 and 1977 for $\alpha = 0.2$ and $\alpha = 0.5$. In 1974 there was a considerable jump in revenues from the past period, 1973 (50.0 versus 41.7). When $\alpha = 0.5$, which does weight the discrepancy more heavily, the forecast for 1975 is considerably closer to the actual value than when $\alpha = 0.2$.

Additionally, look at the forecast for 1977. In 1976 the level of revenues actually fell from the previous year (43.7 versus 46.8). When $\alpha = 0.5$ the forecast for 1977 reflected this change, and the forecasted value was less than the forecasted value for 1976. However, when $\alpha = 0.2$ the forecasted value is greater than the previously forecasted value.

Year	Actual Value	Forecast F_{t+1}	
		$\alpha = 0.2$	$\alpha = 0.5$
1966	28.2	—	—
1967	31.6	28.20	28.20
1968	30.5	28.90	29.90
1969	31.8	29.22	30.20
1970	34.2	29.74	31.00
1971	36.3	30.63	32.60
1972	39.3	31.76	34.45
1973	41.7	33.27	36.88
1974	50.0	35.00	39.29
1975	46.8	38.00	44.65
1976	43.7	39.76	45.73
1977	52.1	40.55	44.72
1978	63.3	42.86	48.41
1979	69.6	46.95	55.86
1980	72.3	51.48	62.73
1981	76.0	55.64	67.52
1982	76.1	59.71	71.76
1983	78.0	62.98	73.93
		65.98	75.97

TABLE 22A–5

Single Exponential Smoothing for $\alpha = 0.2$ and 0.5, 1966–1983

Double Exponential Smoothing

From Table 22A–5 we can see that the estimates produced by simple exponential smoothing, like moving averages, are consistently below the actual values. This will always be the case when the actual values are characterized by an increasing trend. To refine our estimate, we use double exponential smoothing. As we will see momentarily, the estimates from double exponential smoothing will also be consistently below the simple exponential smoothing estimates.

The basic method of double exponential smoothing is analogous to the method of double moving averages. That is, we exponentially smooth the already smoothed estimates and use the difference between the two to produce a better estimate of the actual values when there exists a linear trend to the data.

Letting α equal $1/n$, Equation 22A–4 can be rewritten as

$$F_{t+1} = \alpha S_t + (1 - \alpha)F_t \qquad (22A\text{–}5)$$

where

S_t = The actual value for period t
F_t = The forecasted value for period t

The formula for double exponential smoothing is

$$F''_{t+1} = \alpha F'_{t+1} + (1 - \alpha)F''_t \qquad (22A-6)$$

where

F''_{t+1} = The double exponentially smoothed estimate for period $t + 1$
F'_{t+1} = The single exponentially smoothed estimate for period $t + 1$
F''_t = The double exponentially smoothed estimate for period t
α = The smoothing constant

Note that

$$F'_{t+1} = \alpha F_t + (1 - \alpha)F'_t \qquad (22A-7)$$

The forecasted value F_{t+P} is

$$F_{t+P} = A + BP \qquad (22A-8)$$

where

$$A = 2F'_{t+1} - F''_{t+1} \qquad (22A-9)$$

and

$$B = \frac{\alpha}{1 - \alpha}(F'_{t+1} - F''_{t+1}) \qquad (22A-10)$$

F_{t+P} = The double exponentially smoothed forecast for the pth period
P = The number of periods in the future we wish to forecast

Table 22A–6 presents the estimates from the double exponential smoothing method.

Evaluating Smoothing Techniques

In our presentation of moving averages and exponential smoothing we arbitrarily chose values for the period of moving averages, or α. In practice these values are typically determined by choosing a number of different values and comparing the accuracy of the forecasts that are derived. For example, we might choose values of α equal to 0.2, 0.25, 0.3, 0.35, . . ., 0.95 and then calculate estimates of sales for each α level. To assess the accuracy we compare the discrepancy between the actual value and the predicted value.

One measure commonly used to compare the accuracy of the forecasted values is the mean absolute error, which is calculated as

$$\left[\sum_{t=1}^{T} \frac{|S_t - F_t|}{S_t} \right] \Big/ T \qquad (22A-11)$$

where

S_t = The actual value.
F_t = The forecast value.

Year	Actual Value	S_t'	S_t''	A	B	Forecast ($\alpha = .5$) F_{t+1}	TABLE 22A–6
1966	28.2	—	—	—	—	—	Double Exponential Smoothing Forecast, 1966–1983
1967	31.6	28.2	28.2	28.2	0.00	—	
1968	30.5	29.9	29.05	30.75	0.85	31.6	
1969	31.8	30.2	29.28	30.77	0.57	31.34	
1970	34.2	31.0	30.14	31.68	0.68	32.36	
1971	36.3	32.6	31.37	33.74	1.14	33.88	
1972	39.3	34.5	32.94	36.06	1.56	37.62	
1973	41.7	36.9	34.92	38.88	1.98	40.86	
1974	50.0	39.3	37.11	41.49	2.19	43.68	
1975	46.8	44.7	40.90	48.50	3.80	52.30	
1976	43.7	45.7	43.30	48.10	2.40	50.50	
1977	52.1	44.7	44.00	45.40	0.70	46.10	
1978	63.3	48.4	46.20	50.60	2.20	52.80	
1979	69.6	55.9	51.05	60.75	4.85	65.60	
1980	72.3	62.7	56.88	68.52	5.82	74.34	
1981	76.0	67.5	62.19	72.81	5.31	78.12	
1982	76.1	71.8	67.00	76.60	4.80	81.40	
1983	78.0	73.9	70.45	77.35	3.45	80.80	

Earlier we described smoothing techniques as methods that use a series of historical data to ascertain any underlying patterns in the data. If the historical series is in fact characterized by an underlying pattern, the more time periods we use the more likely we are to discover this underlying pattern. That is, we will smooth out the random fluctuations. For this reason, we typically take only the mean absolute error for the last 10 or 15 periods.

In practice the job of the forecaster is simplified by computer software that will rapidly calculate the mean absolute error (or some other accuracy measure) for different values of α and provide the value of α for which mean absolute error is minimized.

Forecasting with Regression

In Chapter 16 we described regression analysis as a statistical method for describing the linear relationship between two (or more) variables. In addition, we showed how regression analysis can be used to forecast values of $y(\hat{y})$, given some value of x. In this case, the values of x would simply be a linear trend representing the different years—that is, 1966 = 1, 1967 = 2, . , 1983 = 18. The dependent variable would be the values of revenues for the different years.

Regressing revenues on the time periods yields the following equation:

$$\hat{y}_t = 19.44 + 3.23(x_t) \tag{22A–12}$$

Table 22A–7 presents the forecasted values of revenue for the Tootsie Roll data contained in Table 22A–1 using regression analysis.

TABLE 22A–7
—
Regression Forecasts, 1966–1983

Year	Actual Value	Forecast
1966	28.2	22.67
1967	31.6	25.90
1968	30.5	29.13
1969	31.8	32.36
1970	34.2	35.59
1971	36.3	38.82
1972	39.3	42.05
1973	41.7	45.28
1974	50.0	48.51
1975	46.8	51.74
1976	43.7	54.97
1977	52.1	58.20
1978	63.3	61.43
1979	69.6	64.66
1980	72.3	67.89
1981	76.0	71.12
1982	76.1	74.35
1983	78.0	77.58

CASE STUDIES FOR PART VI

CASE 1
More Marketers Tap Employees to Star in Ads

By Kevin Goldman

When Sprint wanted to jazz up its image and restore its competitive edge in the long-distance phone market, it hired sassy and classy actress Candice Bergen. When rival MCI Communications wanted to do the same, it tapped Lisa Mikkelson and Wilma Knox.

Who?

Like a growing number of advertisers, MCI is shunning the glamorpusses and the stuffy, heavily compensated chief executive officers who populated ads in the free-spending 1980s. (Remember Lee Iacocca?) Increasingly, worker bees—from the laborer on the loading dock to the stiff behind the counter at a fast-food diner—are the stars of television commercials. Ads for McDonald's hamburgers and Subway sandwiches, Nynex phone service and United Parcel Service, General Motors' Saturn automobiles and even strait-laced Shearson Lehman Brothers shun buttoned-down executives in favor of testimonials from employees and customers.

There was a time when struggling actors portrayed so-called consumers. While companies still are employing actors for commercials, they are increasingly using actual employees to personalize their products.

Marketers and Madison Avenue executives say the reason for the growth is so simple it sounds like an ad slogan: Real people have real credibility. Corporate executives are now perceived as being out of touch with the masses and are under attack for excessive salaries; take a look at how many have been given the gate by their own boards in the past year. Now they are getting booted out of ad campaigns, as well.

Enter Lisa Mikkelson and Wilma Knox. They are actual MCI operators, and in MCI spots they promote a free month of long-distance service for new subscrib-

ers. The ad, produced by ad agency Messner Vetere Berger McNamee Schmetterer, is one of a series of four spots in which MCI gathered hundreds of employees in a gigantic MCI phone center based in Phoenix, Arizona, to be videotaped while handling calls.

Another commercial shows some 800 MCI operators celebrating the sign-up of the ten-millionth customer. It is a surreal scene as dozens of MCI employees grin into one of five cameras and say, "Being a part of history is exciting," or "We're a part of history today," and then they whoop, holler, exchange high-fives, and toss confetti as an oversized tote board ticks off to the magic number.

"This is wall-to-wall real," says Barry Vetere, a partner in MCI's ad agency. "This approach was perfect since MCI is in a people-contact industry. We wanted to put a face on the company."

Vetere says no lines were scripted. Instead, employees were preinterviewed and then were asked to repeat some of their remarks on camera. Flubs were also recorded. In fact, MCI is planning to release a spot within the next two weeks that begins with a voiceover saying, "People call us all the time and ask whether those are real MCI employees. Well, they're not actors." Then, MCI's own version of bloopers and blunders is shown.

Such an approach "humanizes a large, faceless corporation," says Ellen G. Gartrell, the director of the center for sales, advertising, and marketing history at Duke University. "This is an emotional appeal in advertising. It's a way to use middle-of-the-road people instead of executives in ivory towers."

Even when executives pop up in ads these days, it rarely is a regal appearance in luxurious surroundings. For instance, Charles Lazarus, the chairman of Toys "R" Us, appears in an American Express ad, leaning back and chatting lazily about kids. Danny Meyer, the owner of New York's tiny Union Square Cafe, is also featured in ads for the credit-card company discussing using leftovers to feed the homeless. And the guy who

675

runs 1-800-FLOWERS appears in an ad showing a tacky ersatz talk show championing the delivery service.

"Real people are another device to get people to pay more attention to the commercial and to break through the clutter," says Gartrell. "If people can see themselves in a commercial, as opposed to someone they might not identify with, perhaps the ads will be more effective. It's a way to get in touch with the consumer."

Breaking through the clutter is exactly what ad agency Hal Riney & Partners' Chicago office proposed to Subway Associates, the chain of sandwich stores based in Milford, Connecticut. Instead of a glitzy ad campaign that may be more comfortable on, say, MTV, the agency came up with a series of spots that would be more at home on the Family Channel: just plain folks at their workstations in the yellow and white cateries, all chatting up their expertise as sandwich artists.

The agency held screen tests at Subway locations for budding stars nationwide. But Subway, unlike MCI, was not taking any chances. It scripted everything. "Then they had to memorize," says Dick Pilchen, Subway's vice president for marketing. "Employees are the best spokespeople."

Consumers, says Mr. Pilchen, have come to know that when a celebrity endorses a product, it is usually the money that is the motivation and not the star's actual love for the merchandise. "When you interview actual employees, you get a sense of how the company is run, instead of just propping up the chairman," he adds.

United Parcel Service took the worker ethic a step further. Instead of featuring the shipper's own rank and file, ad agency Ammirati & Puris shot a series of jarring, grainy profiles in hand-held-camera style to focus on real UPS customers: a he-man on the loading dock, clerks in the mailroom, a secretary who doesn't deign to get her boss's coffee.

The acting fee for the employees do not exactly break the bank. Most times, they receive $414.25 a day, which is Screen Actors Guild scale, even though, naturally, they are not SAG members. (The one-time appearance makes them eligible to join SAG, however, if they fall in love with the camera.) Most of the commercials in the various campaigns were shot in three days or less.

MCI did not pay all of its 800 employees who appeared in the celebration commercial. It only paid those who actually spoke on camera, while the others performed their jobs as the cameras rolled.

Predictably, the trend to use actual employees does not thrill the Screen Actors Guild. "We want actors to do this work," says John Sucke, executive director of SAG's New York branch. "An actor makes a better presentation than any employee. Our people are real, too," he complains.

Finding those employees who can "perform" in front of a camera "wasn't easy," concedes Bernie Bloomfield, managing director of marketing communications at Nynex, which has been running six spots showing workers on the job, including a woman who repairs pay phones and a cellular-phone salesman.

Nynex contacted supervisors for recommendations of the best and brightest and looked over 300 employees for the first six commercial profiles. When they were finally chosen, a camera crew from Nynex's agency, WPP Group's Ogilvy & Mather, simply followed the individuals and recorded conversations.

"A lot went into the editing," Mr. Bloomfield says.

So one Nynex spot dutifully records the gushy remarks of a repairman named Dominick Ventola, who has been based in New York's South Bronx for 22 years: "I get real quick satisfaction on giving people a dial tone." It's a line few self-respecting copywriters would dare put to paper and one that a star spokeswoman like Candice Bergen might have trouble pulling off.

Case Question

Develop a marketing research proposal to test the claims regarding the use of celebrities versus "real people."

Source: *The Wall Street Journal*, February 22, 1993, p. B–1.

CASE 2
Ore-Ida Dishes Up New Potato Products

By Gabriella Stern

The king of the potato patch smells danger.

Ore-Ida, a unit of H. J. Heinz Company, dominates frozen potatoes, with more than 50 percent of the market. Lately, though, it has been threatened by consumers moving away from french fries and by innovations from makers of rival products such as J. R. Simplot Company's MicroMagic microwavable frozen fries and Northern Star Company's Simply Potatoes cooked, refrigerated mashed potatoes. As a counterpunch, Ore-Ida is introducing two new products—frozen mashed potatoes and a new fast-food-style french fry.

Ore-Ida, which is based in Boise, Idaho, was jolted from complacency a few years ago when Universal Foods Corporation, Milwaukee, rolled out frozen curly fries and seasoned batter-dipped fries—items Ore-Ida did not offer.

Frozen potatoes are an approximately $2.3 billion business (wholesale and retail combined) in the United States where, according to the National Potato Board, the average person gobbles 131 pounds of potatoes—fresh, frozen, or otherwise—each year and prefers them baked or fried, and mostly the latter.

Overall, the market for frozen potatoes declined 3.5 percent, based on supermarket sales in the latest 52 weeks ended November 29, 1992, according to Information Resources Inc.'s InfoScan service. The big loser was fried potatoes. Sales of fried potatoes, although still the largest selling category, dropped 5.1 percent, to $657 million, in the 52-week period, in part as health-conscious Americans try to limit fried foods in their diets. By contrast, sales of nonfried potatoes rose 5.1 percent in the period, to $133.1 million.

"We had too long a cycle of new-product development and capital investment," says Pat Kinney, Ore-Ida vice president of sales. "We weren't as reactive to the market, especially to new products, as we should have been." In recent years, however, the Heinz unit halved the lead time on new products and in 1990 introduced competing curly and battered fries in quick succession.

But this winter marks Ore-Ida's biggest, most expensive new-product rollout since the launch of Tater Tots in 1953. The company is advertising its new Fast Fries as tasting like french fries from fast-food outlets and its frozen mashed potatoes as tasting close to home-cooked.

Ore-Ida is pouring $30 million into marketing Fast Fries. The product, which the company says fared well in test markets, is an oven-baked, shoestring french fry whose light oily coating gives it a buttery flavor, which also seems to help it stay crisp. Fast Fries are already in many supermarkets nationwide. A national TV ad campaign kicks off this month, as does a direct-mail coupon campaign.

But some wonder whether the new fry will fly, considering competition with faster, microwave versions. "Do Fast Fries bring anything new to the party? Is it a step back in terms of convenience?" wonders Timothy S. Ramey, an analyst with C. J. Lawrence.

Ore-Ida says it is targeting consumers who have been disappointed by traditional oven-baked and microwavable fries and who do not want to spend the money or time on takeout fries at the nearest McDonald's. The company boasts that Fast Fries have half the fat of fast-food fries: seven grams of fat per three-ounce serving. That is still more fat than Ore-Ida Classic Cut fries, which have four grams of fat per serving, notes Cincinnati-based food consultant Tracy Duckworth.

Ore-Ida makes some microwavable frozen potatoes—Crinkle Cuts, Tater Tots, and hash browns. "They're good products, but they're not great," says Gary Laney, Ore-Ida new-products manager, adding that they are "mushier" than they should be. Ore-Ida is trying to improve the products, he says.

Ore-Ida's biggest competition comes from private-label frozen potatoes, which hold the number 2 spot in the supermarket. Private-label concerns thrive particularly during potato gluts when plummeting prices allow them to undercut Ore-Ida's premium prices even more than usual. At such times, "We can offer equal quality and better value," says a spokesman for Topco Associates Inc., Chicago, whose frozen potatoes carry various labels, including Food Club, Top Frost, Mega, Maxi, and Valu Time.

"Ore-Ida's market share hasn't grown over the last several years because of continued cheap potatoes and private labels," says Ramey, the analyst (see Table 1). Although Ore-Ida sales suffered when potatoes were overly abundant from September 1991 to June 1992, the supply has since stabilized, Ore-Ida says.

Case Questions

1. Develop a complete research agenda that will identify whether or not Ore-Ida should introduce the "fast-food-style french fry."

2. For each study specified in your research agenda, describe what information you expect from the study and how it will be used.

Source: *The Wall Street Journal*, January 14, 1993, p. B–1.

CASE 3
P&G Planning a Fresh Face for Max Factor

By Valerie Reitman

Proctor & Gamble (P&G) is overhauling its mature Max Factor makeup line and plans to launch the new cosmetics in its first simultaneous worldwide product introduction in May 1993.

TABLE 1
—
Top Frozen
Fried-Potato Brands*

	Sales (millions)	Percent Change from Year Earlier	Percent Share of Category
Ore-Ida	$380.4	−2.5%	57.9%
Private Label	155.1	−5.2	23.6
Inland Valley	34.1	−31.8	5.2
J. R. Simplot A Grade	21.7	−7.1	3.3
McCain	13.3	−4.4	2.0
Simply Potatoes	11.3	2.4	1.7

*Based on sales in supermarkets during the 52 weeks ended November 29, 1992.
Source: Information Resources, Inc.

The Max Factor line, which was acquired by P&G for $1.06 billion from Revlon Inc. last year, will feature more elegant styling and a substantially larger number of eyeshadow and blush colors. New eyeshadows, blushes, and lipsticks will be out in the spring followed by new foundations, face powders, and mascaras in 1994. The new products and advertising for Max Factor will feature similar style, image, and color palette across the world, including Europe and Asia, which generate most of Max Factor's revenue.

With its global launch, the Cincinnati-based consumer products company hopes to copy the success of prestige brands Clinique and Chanel, says industry consultant Allan Mottus. Clinique, made by Estee Lauder, is recognized worldwide for its blue-green packaging, while Chanel Inc.'s products are renowned for their classic black compacts. Lower priced cosmetics sold at chain stores or in European pharmacies, which are Max Factor outlets, are largely tailored to each country and often made by local manufacturers.

P&G, which gets about half of its $29.4 billion a year in sales from international operations, is attempting to unify and consolidate many of its marketing and advertising expenses for brands marketed in several countries. For example, its Ariel detergent is sold throughout Europe, and its Pert Plus shampoo is marketed worldwide. But Max Factor International will be its first simultaneous global product introduction, P&G says.

Currently, Max Factor products sold in the United States are substantially different from those sold in Europe and Japan. For example, its Japanese line consists primarily of skin-care products sold through department stores, some at prices well over $100. With the new products, P&G will promote more color cosmetics, such as eyeshadow and blush, trying to expand on Japanese women's interest in moisturizers and cleansers. It faces other hurdles with the new line, even in countries where Max Factor is strong. In the United Kingdom, there is fierce competition from private-label cosmetics, along with a weak economy. And in the rest of Europe, "Max Factor has no critical mass," says Mottus. In Germany and Switzerland, P&G may be able to build on its Betrix cosmetics line, acquired from Revlon along with Max Factor, but in France, Cosmair Inc.'s L'Oreal is king.

With the new line, P&G is also trying to regain market share lost in the $2.1 billion U.S. mass-merchandise cosmetics market to two rivals that have already revamped their lines, Revlon and L'Oreal. P&G also plans to change its store displays to allow more flexibility in moving items on racks. The additional elegance will come at a price, however; prices will likely rise 8 to 10 percent above current Max Factor prices.

P&G made a false start earlier this year by revamping some Max Factor products, which now may need another makeover. Max Factor's Shadow Sweep blush, introduced last summer in a thin blue opaque plastic case, will now have a thicker, dark blue case with a pushbutton latch or spring-open lid like the rest of the new line's compacts. "One thing about Proctor, if they don't get it right the first time, they do it over again," said cosmetic consultant Suzanne Grayson. New lipsticks will feature click-close caps and will turn more easily.

Two large cosmetics retailers, which have seen some of the new products, were impressed. "The final product will be first class, with a very European styling," said Ben Kovalsky, president of the 44-store Cosmetic Center based in Savage, Maryland. Patty Klein, vice president of marketing at F&M Distributors, a chain of 117 health and beauty aid stores, said, "There's a tremendous expansion of eye shadow and blush colors." That should help the store compete better with department store brands such as Estee Lauder, which generally carry more colors. With new packaging similar to that offered by competitor Maybelline Inc., Max Factor customers will be better able to see new eye shadow colors.

Meanwhile, P&G is still struggling to resolve production and distribution snags, which retailers say have cost it market share. While national market share figures for 1992 were not available, Revlon and L'Oreal have gained share at Cosmetics Center and F&M Distributors stores, according to those chains. "They still can't meet what we need," said Kovalsky, and, as a result, P&G and the chain are losing "hundreds of thousands of dollars in sales." Max Factor sales at F&M Distributors remained flat in 1992, while Revlon's sales soared 35 percent, and L'Oreal's jumped 20 percent, Klein said.

Case Questions

1. What research products would you recommend to the management team planning strategy for the worldwide introduction?

2. How will cultural factors affect the research methodology?

Source: *The Wall Street Journal,* December 29, 1992, p. B–1.

CASE 4
Research—A Potent Factor in Reaching the "Macho Market"

By Frank Tobolski

"Macho marketing" is the trend to watch for in the 1990s.

In one of the many current dialects of marketing—be it lifestyles, psychographics, megatrends, demographics, etc.—each and every market segment deserves a name.

From the 1980s emerged the yuppie segment and its subgroups, the dinks (double income, no kids) and the dimps (double income, multiple progeny), for example. Not to be short-sold in an era where companies have targeted marketing to females, the "macho market" is flexing its muscles.

Macho marketing refers to the consumer segment, not the marketers themselves. It's no longer just the age of the emerging female; there's another side of the coin that adds up to big dollars.

At a time when men's roles are changing, more and more consumer product companies want to gear their packaging design, as well as the products themselves, toward men.

Quite correctly, marketing in the last two decades has focused on the expanding women's role in the workplace and the marketplace. This type of marketing remains important, but consumer buying today is continually becoming more segmented, fractionalized, and pluralistic.

Males, single and married, are making more purchasing decisions—particularly in the grocery stores—than ever before. This trend of men in nontraditional roles should not be underestimated. It's altering definitions of products, how they are used and designed, and how packaging connects with the new liberated male segment.

More and more organizations—the Food Marketing Institute, Cunningham and Walsh, Campbell Soup Company, and Factline among them—have identified male market segment behaviors and the related opportunities.

We've been studying the characteristics needed for products and packaging to succeed with this new all-male macho consumer segment, and discovered the following:

— Approximately 40 percent of shoppers in the supermarket are men.
— About one-third of men do major food shopping alone, and another 25 percent shop regularly with their wives.
— Some 80 percent of men do fill-in shopping in a month's period.
— Almost 50 percent of men prepare complete meals for their families.

Men now account for about 40 percent of the food-shopping dollars. Not too long ago, women spent 80 percent or more.

Social scientists claim that, over time, men are being "reconditioned" for their broadened roles and augmenting their purchasing characteristics in line with the new norms. They are now co-breadwinners as they squeeze the Charmin and literally bring home the bacon.

In many instances, they are the family. Today, approximately 38 percent of men between the marrying ages of 25 and 29 have remained single. In 1970, only about 19 percent of the males in the same age group were still unmarried. These changing roles press men to make more buying decisions for the family, but very often in their own male-oriented terms.

Many components and elements of the marketing mix trigger the male purchasing decision. In fact, this new and growing segment may help in the renewal of the hypermarket.

Hypermarkets often have 200,000 square feet of selling space and offer convenient, one-stop shopping. Groceries, laundry, snacks, home repair, maybe even a haircut, all are available at the hypermarket.

But, whether in regular grocery stores, warehouse outlets, or hypermarkets, packaging and display are key to the perception of the product and its benefits.

Packaging must efficiently communicate the most essential product information and imagery pertinent to its target-market segments. The package must work harder to reach its male targets and, in many cases, appeal to females as well. Research, therefore, is an essential element in developing competitive package/product design as well as innovative positioning.

Macho packaging needs shelf impact, more "easy finding power" to help male shoppers save even more time. The male is looking to undercut the average American's 27-minute stay in the grocery story. He tends to operate with a finite shopping list for his myopic mission to purchase specific items and then move out.

Our research indicates that the male shopper, in general, is looking for bold, linear packaging without superfluous clutter, such as coupons, detailed nutritional information, or recipes. And clear symbols of identity are necessary to create brand awareness and future recognition loyalty.

Some of our research indicates that men tend to purchase based on the images communicated through packaging rather than being influenced by specific product information.

Marketers working with package designers and consumer researchers can hone in on this opportunity by:

- Fine-tuning existing products/packages using diagnostic research for creative direction.

- Recycling, restaging, and introducing new brands and products.

- Updating brands and product images with new, contemporary packaging structures and graphics.

- Refreshing sales promotions and point-of-purchase displays.

- Tracking follow-ups with additional fine-tuning.

When my company consulted on the restaging effort for Kraft's Pourable Salad Dressings, we focused on maintaining the product's valuable equity while strengthening its appeal in the emergent male shopper segment.

We categorized the strategy as "1, 2, 3"—(1) brand/product, (2) benefits, and (3) application. The man wants to know what the product is, what it does, and how to use it.

This information impact is quite different from earlier shelf impact strategies, where the main objective was to shout the package off the shelf. The new Kraft Salad Dressing bottle shape and label graphics are seen as more masculine if not totally "macho." It draws male attention not only because it's easily seen but also because it's congruent with male values.

Our research also has shown that males have been a significant factor in the "microwave movement," which has revolutionized the supermarket freezer case.

By 1990, it's estimated that microwave ovens will be in at least 80 percent of American households. Microwave ovens now outnumber home dishwashers, VCRs, and even toaster ovens.

Packaging will continue to need creative design (graphics and structure) and consumer market research (communication and imagery) to confirm a product's positioning and acceptance for a target market.

Research helps the design consultant and the marketer understand the one known constant—things are always changing. Next time you're at the grocery store, just ask any man.

Case Question

Assume you are a marketing research analyst at Kraft. As part of your responsibilities develop a research proposal to test the new "1, 2, 3" package.

Source: Reprinted from *Marketing News*, September 26, 1988, published by the American Marketing Association.

CASE 5
Students' Preferences for Apartment Complexes

J. Smyrl had been in the building business for over 25 years, and for the first time was contemplating the de-

EXHIBIT 1
—
Salient Attributes

Location
   Less than a 5-minute drive from campus.
   Between a 5- and 15-minute drive from campus.
   Greater than a 15-minute drive from campus.

Bedrooms
   One bedroom.
   Two bedrooms.
   Three bedrooms.

Neighborhood
   Safe/nice neighborhood.
   Unsafe/unnice neighborhood.

Age of complex
   New (less than 7 years old).
   Old (7 or more years).

Apartment features
   Dishwasher/garbage disposal/laundry in unit.
   No dishwasher/no garbage disposal/no laundry in unit.

Complex amenities
   Pool/tennis courts/club house.
   No pool/no tennis courts/no club house.

velopment of some property for himself. He investigated the local housing market and, based on vacancy rates, determined there was potential for an apartment complex specifically designed for students. In an attempt to build a complex most desirable to students, he was interested in what attributes students valued the most when selecting an apartment. Consequently, he decided to talk with a local marketing research supplier.

The research supplier suggested the first step would be to conduct some focus group interviews to determine the attributes most important to students when selecting an apartment complex. The focus group identified six salient characteristics of apartments important to the student population with respect to selecting an apartment complex: location, number of bedrooms, type of neighborhood, age of the complex, apartment features, and complex amenities.

Smyrl was interested in the results from the focus group, but he indicated that determining just how important each of these characteristics is would be the most helpful. For example, he said, "I can build a complex with or without a swimming pool, tennis courts, and other amenities, and I am sure the students would be happy to have them; however, the question is just how much value is gained by including versus not including them?" The project manager suggested a follow-up study with the students using a conjoint analysis

approach would provide Smyrl with the necessary information. He said the results of the conjoint study would determine exactly how much utility was associated with each level of the six salient attributes identified by the focus groups. Smyrl gave the project manager the okay to do the conjoint study.

The project manager conducted a second focus group study to determine the relevant levels of the six attributes. The attributes and the levels of the attributes are shown in Exhibit 1.

The appropriate fractional factorial design indicated that 16 stimulus cards were necessary. Exhibit 2 presents the design, along with the dummy variable coding. A sample of 54 students was used to collect the data. To be an eligible subject, a student had to have been involved in the selection decision of an apartment in the last six months. Table 1 presents the ranking of the 16 stimulus cards by the sample of students. To estimate the part-worth utilities these rankings were regressed, using ordinary least-squares, on eight dummy variables representing the six attributes. Exhibit 2 provides a reference for the dummy variables and the attribute levels. Ordinary least-square regression was used to estimate the part-worth utilities for each level of the attributes. Table 2 presents the estimates of the coefficients for each subject. It must be remembered that the stimulus cards were ranked from 1 to 16, with 1 being the most preferred; hence, the larger the coefficient the less the utility.

Case Question

Based on the information in Table 2 what would you recommend to Mr. Smyrl?

EXHIBIT 2

Fractional Factorial Design

Stimulus Card	Attribute							
	1		2		3	4	5	6
1	0	0	0	0	0	0	0	0
2	1	0	0	0	1	1	0	0
3	0	1	0	0	1	0	1	1
4	1	0	0	0	0	1	1	1
5	1	0	1	0	1	0	0	1
6	0	0	1	0	0	1	0	1
7	1	0	1	0	0	0	1	0
8	0	1	1	0	1	1	1	0
9	0	1	0	1	0	1	0	0
10	1	0	0	1	1	0	0	0
11	0	0	0	1	1	1	1	1
12	1	0	0	1	0	0	1	1
13	1	0	1	0	1	1	0	1
14	0	1	1	0	0	0	0	1
15	1	0	1	0	0	1	1	0
16	0	0	1	0	1	0	1	0

Attribute 1: Location
0   0 = Less than a 5-minute drive from campus
1   0 = Between a 5- and 15-minute drive from campus
0   1 = Greater than a 15-minute drive from campus

Attribute 2: Bedrooms
0   0 = One bedroom
1   0 = Two bedrooms
0   1 = Three bedrooms

Attribute 3: Neighborhood
0 = Safe/nice neighborhood
1 = Unsafe/unnice neighborhood

Attribute 4: Age of complex
0 = New (less than 7 years old)
1 = Old (7 or more years)

Attribute 5: Apartment features
0 = Dishwasher/garbage disposal/laundry in unit
1 = No dishwasher/no garbage disposal/no laundry in unit

Attribute 6: Complex amenities
0 = Pool/tennis courts/club house
1 = No pool/no tennis courts/no club house

TABLE 1   Rankings of Stimulus Cards

Subject	1	2	3	4	5	6	7	8	9	10	11	12	13	14	15	16
												Ranking of Card				
001	02	10	16	06	08	01	03	15	14	07	12	04	09	13	05	11
002	03	14	10	09	05	02	15	06	07	11	08	12	04	01	16	13
003	01	13	15	06	10	02	05	16	04	09	14	07	11	03	08	12
004	01	09	16	06	14	04	03	13	05	08	12	07	11	15	02	10
005	01	14	11	05	15	02	03	12	07	09	13	04	10	08	06	16
006	13	14	15	16	10	07	08	12	01	03	04	02	09	05	06	11
007	06	05	14	03	08	07	12	13	16	09	11	02	01	10	04	15
008	16	15	14	13	06	04	02	08	03	05	12	10	07	01	09	11
009	01	10	16	08	13	06	02	11	04	12	15	07	14	05	03	09
010	13	08	06	14	05	10	15	03	12	04	01	11	02	09	16	07
011	01	13	15	04	10	06	03	14	07	16	12	02	09	08	05	11
012	01	11	16	06	12	02	04	15	08	13	09	03	14	07	05	10
013	02	12	16	08	13	03	05	14	01	10	15	07	11	04	06	09
014	01	06	15	08	13	02	03	16	05	11	12	04	10	14	07	09
015	01	07	08	04	11	02	03	16	13	14	12	09	15	06	05	10
016	01	10	15	08	13	02	05	12	04	09	16	07	14	03	06	11
017	08	13	12	09	15	11	02	05	01	06	16	10	14	04	03	07
018	04	12	16	15	07	03	09	10	02	05	14	13	06	01	08	11
019	01	11	16	08	10	03	05	14	04	09	15	07	12	02	06	13
020	01	14	13	03	12	02	04	11	08	10	09	06	16	07	05	15
021	01	11	13	07	10	03	04	14	05	09	15	08	16	02	06	12
022	01	13	12	06	08	04	02	15	07	10	16	11	14	03	05	09
023	01	09	13	08	12	03	04	16	02	10	14	07	11	05	06	15
024	01	11	16	08	09	02	06	15	14	12	04	07	10	13	05	03
025	04	12	16	08	11	03	07	14	01	09	13	05	10	02	06	15
026	02	14	16	11	13	01	07	15	09	12	04	06	05	10	08	03
027	01	09	14	05	10	02	06	15	04	12	16	08	11	03	07	13
028	04	16	03	08	12	11	07	15	10	02	06	09	13	05	14	01
029	01	03	04	02	06	05	07	09	13	14	16	15	11	08	12	10
030	08	09	16	07	11	04	02	13	03	12	15	06	10	01	05	14
031	04	12	16	08	10	03	06	15	01	09	13	05	11	02	07	14
032	01	13	09	05	14	02	06	10	03	15	11	07	16	04	08	12
033	03	10	16	05	15	01	07	14	08	09	13	06	11	02	04	12
034	04	12	16	08	13	07	01	11	02	09	14	05	15	06	03	10
035	01	02	16	15	07	06	10	12	03	05	13	14	08	04	11	09
036	04	11	15	09	10	03	07	13	01	05	16	06	14	02	08	12
037	01	04	12	13	14	02	06	11	15	03	09	10	05	16	08	07
038	01	14	16	08	12	04	02	10	05	13	15	07	11	06	03	09
039	02	11	13	16	09	01	03	15	04	08	14	06	10	07	05	12
040	01	13	16	06	10	02	03	15	12	09	08	05	14	11	04	07
041	01	05	13	16	11	09	02	10	04	06	14	15	12	07	03	08
042	01	13	11	05	10	02	03	15	07	09	16	08	14	04	06	12
043	01	09	05	10	06	02	13	14	08	15	11	03	16	04	07	12
044	01	12	16	04	13	02	03	15	07	11	10	06	14	08	05	09
045	02	12	16	08	09	03	05	15	01	10	14	06	11	04	07	13
046	01	06	14	15	10	08	03	11	02	05	13	16	09	07	04	12
047	02	11	15	09	05	10	01	16	04	12	14	06	07	03	08	13
048	01	09	15	07	10	06	03	13	02	11	16	08	14	05	04	12
049	04	11	13	12	08	01	02	14	15	09	06	10	07	16	05	03
050	03	14	16	15	10	01	02	13	08	11	12	07	04	06	05	09
051	04	14	12	08	10	02	07	16	03	09	13	05	15	01	06	11
052	01	10	14	09	08	05	03	13	04	15	10	07	12	02	06	11
053	05	12	16	06	11	01	03	15	08	13	09	02	14	07	04	10
054	01	11	14	08	10	02	06	16	04	09	15	05	12	03	07	13

TABLE 2   Part-Worth Utility Estimates

Subject	β_0	β_1	β_2	β_3	β_4	β_5	β_6	β_7	β_8	R_2
1	2.88	0.00	8.00	−0.38	0.75	5.00	1.00	1.00	0.25	0.89
2	6.38	4.25	−0.50	−1.25	0.50	0.75	−0.50	5.25	−4.25	0.81
3	0.88	1.38	2.25	−0.38	−0.25	8.00	1.50	3.75	0.00	0.98
4	1.63	0.75	5.50	1.00	0.00	6.25	−1.50	0.25	4.25	0.94
5	2.88	0.25	1.50	1.25	0.50	8.00	0.25	0.50	0.00	0.79
6	12.63	−0.25	−0.50	−6.00	−12.00	2.50	0.25	1.50	0.00	0.95
7	9.00	−4.25	3.50	1.75	2.50	2.00	−2.00	1.50	−3.00	0.76
8	13.88	−2.38	−4.25	−8.50	−7.00	2.50	0.75	2.75	−0.25	0.86
9	1.25	0.88	1.25	−0.88	0.75	8.00	0.75	0.75	4.00	0.99
10	14.38	1.63	−0.25	−1.88	−3.25	−8.00	−0.50	1.25	−2.50	0.95
11	3.50	0.25	3.50	0.00	1.00	8.00	0.50	−0.50	−0.50	0.87
12	1.13	3.00	6.00	0.13	−0.25	8.00	0.50	0.00	0.25	0.99
13	1.38	1.75	1.50	−1.38	−1.25	8.00	0.50	3.00	2.25	0.96
14	0.25	1.75	6.50	1.75	0.50	6.00	−0.50	1.50	2.50	0.83
15	−0.88	2.25	4.50	3.50	7.00	6.25	1.50	−0.25	−0.25	0.89
16	0.25	1.50	1.00	−0.25	0.50	8.00	1.00	3.00	2.50	0.97
17	7.13	−1.50	−5.00	−2.88	−2.25	5.00	1.00	−1.00	5.75	0.93
18	5.00	1.38	−0.75	−4.88	−3.25	3.25	0.50	7.00	1.75	0.97
19	1.25	0.50	1.00	−0.88	−0.25	8.00	1.25	4.00	1.25	0.99
20	2.25	2.00	3.00	1.25	0.50	8.00	0.00	−0.50	0.00	0.83
21	0.00	1.13	0.75	0.38	1.25	8.00	2.25	2.75	1.50	0.95
22	0.13	1.13	1.75	−0.50	3.00	7.25	3.00	2.00	1.50	0.92
23	0.88	0.13	0.75	1.25	0.50	8.00	0.25	3.75	1.25	0.95
24	1.75	6.00	12.00	−1.13	0.25	3.00	0.25	−1.00	0.25	0.98
25	4.38	−0.25	−0.50	−1.50	−3.00	8.00	−0.25	4.00	0.00	0.99
26	3.13	7.00	10.00	−3.00	−3.00	3.50	−0.25	0.50	−0.50	0.86
27	0.50	0.50	1.00	1.13	2.75	8.00	0.25	4.00	0.25	0.99
28	2.38	4.63	2.75	2.00	−1.00	0.00	6.25	−1.25	−0.25	0.73
29	0.25	0.75	0.50	6.00	12.00	1.25	0.75	1.75	−0.25	0.91
30	6.50	−2.50	−2.00	−2.50	−1.00	8.00	−0.50	2.50	0.50	0.94
31	3.75	0.00	0.00	−1.50	−3.00	8.00	0.50	4.00	0.00	0.99
32	1.00	4.00	0.00	2.00	2.00	8.00	0.00	0.00	0.00	0.98
33	2.25	1.13	2.75	−0.25	0.50	8.00	−0.50	2.25	0.25	0.87
34	3.75	−0.50	0.00	−1.75	−2.50	8.00	1.00	0.00	4.00	0.99
35	0.63	1.75	1.50	−0.13	0.25	1.00	0.50	8.00	3.75	0.96
36	2.50	0.00	−1.00	−1.13	−2.75	7.00	1.75	4.50	1.75	0.94
37	1.63	3.13	8.75	1.13	1.75	−0.75	−0.25	2.00	3.25	0.67
38	2.63	1.50	2.00	−2.63	0.25	8.00	0.50	0.50	2.75	0.96
39	2.25	1.25	2.50	−2.75	−2.50	6.00	2.00	4.00	2.00	0.81
40	1.25	3.50	9.00	−0.75	−0.50	6.00	1.50	−1.00	1.00	0.97
41	1.00	0.75	0.50	−1.00	1.00	2.75	1.25	3.25	7.25	0.89
42	0.25	0.75	1.50	0.75	2.50	8.00	2.50	2.00	0.50	0.93
43	1.13	3.38	1.25	3.00	3.00	5.00	2.25	1.75	−2.75	0.66
44	0.50	3.00	6.00	0.38	0.25	8.00	0.25	0.00	1.25	0.98
45	2.25	0.50	1.00	−1.13	−1.75	8.00	0.75	4.00	0.75	0.98
46	2.00	0.00	0.00	−1.00	0.00	3.00	0.00	5.00	6.00	0.84
47	4.13	−2.38	−0.25	−1.38	−0.25	6.25	2.75	3.50	0.25	0.77
48	1.00	−0.50	0.00	0.38	1.25	8.00	0.75	2.50	3.25	0.97
49	4.00	4.50	11.00	−3.00	0.00	0.75	0.75	−0.75	1.25	0.87
50	4.88	2.25	4.50	−5.75	−2.50	5.25	1.00	2.75	0.75	0.83
51	2.38	1.75	0.50	−1.00	−2.00	8.00	2.25	2.50	−0.50	0.94
52	1.50	0.50	0.00	−1.00	2.00	7.75	1.75	2.75	1.25	0.92
53	4.00	1.88	5.25	−1.63	−1.75	8.00	0.25	−0.75	−0.50	0.96
54	0.75	0.75	1.50	0.13	−0.25	8.00	1.75	4.00	0.25	0.99

REPORT PREPARATION AND ETHICAL ISSUES

This part of the book addresses two issues at the heart of the marketing research process: report preparation and ethical issues. In Chapter 23, we present suggestions for writing and orally presenting the results of a research project. The written and oral presentation are the culmination of months of work involved in any marketing research study. They are the "final product" of the study. As such they must be handled in an effective and professional manner.

Chapter 24 presents various ethical concerns that need to be acknowledged or taken into account at various stages in the research process. From planning and execution to interpretation, there are many critical issues that must be handled in an ethical way in order to preserve the integrity of the research effort, the client, and the researcher.

Presenting the Research

— Explain the issues involved in communicating the research findings to management.
— Discuss the general guidelines for writing the research project.
— Explain the organization of the research project.
— Illustrate how the data should be presented.
— Discuss the general guidelines for the oral presentation.
— Illustrate the use of visual aids.

INTRODUCTION

Marketing researchers do not work for themselves. The results of their research must be effectively communicated to company managers. As we have seen, there are some interesting ways to communicate research results.

Research results are usually provided to managers in an oral presentation and a formal written research report. The report and presentation are important for three reasons. First, the research report is tangible evidence of the research project—after the study has been completed and a decision is made, there is very little physical evidence of the resources in time, money, and effort that went into the project. Second, the written report and oral presentation are typically the only aspect of a study that many marketing executives are exposed to—management's evaluation of the research project rests on how well this information is communicated. Third, the effectiveness and usefulness of the material contained in the written report are critical in determining whether that particular supplier will be used in the future.

Every research firm has its own style, and each person writes differently. Nevertheless, there are some basic principles for writing a clear research report and for making a good oral presentation. The principles we discuss in this chapter provide a perspective on style that can help you to communicate the critical essence of your marketing research study.

WRITTEN REPORT

We have said that the written report is critical because (1) it is the basis upon which decisions are made, (2) it serves as a historical record, and (3) it is critical in determining whether the supplier will get future research projects. Preparing a research project involves more than writing, which is the last step in the process. Before writing can take place, the results of the research project must be fully understood and some thought given to how the results are best presented. Thus, preparing a research report involves three steps: *understanding*, *organizing*, and *writing*.

Usually, the marketing research supplier will review the data and discuss specific requirements with a marketing person from the sponsoring firm. This "meeting" can be by telephone or in person. The first step is to outline the major findings and to arrange them in order of priority. All report requirements are clearly explicated at this time. The meeting confirms specific dates for the report to be delivered and for other data, if requested, to be available.

The marketing research supplier is responsible for report writing. What the client (sponsoring firm) wants is a well-analyzed, tersely written report. Typically, either the marketing research analyst or another marketing executive at the sponsoring firm will be responsible for the final editing and for writing the "Marketing Implications and Recommendations" section. Whether you write research reports at a supplier house, are a marketing research analyst who must edit and write specific sections of the research report, or are a brand manager or other marketing executive who must react to and use the information communicated in written research reports, there are several aspects of report writing that you should be aware of.

General Guidelines

The guidelines you would follow in writing any report or research paper should be followed when you write a marketing research report.

Think of Your Audience. Marketing researchers are primarily involved in planning and conducting marketing research studies. Marketing managers use the results of a study to make decisions, and it is they who must understand the report. Don't be overly technical or use too much jargon; in other words, the tone and content of the research report must be appropriate for the audience that will read it.

Understand the Results and Draw Conclusions. The marketing managers who read the report will expect to see interpretive conclusions about the information presented in the research report. Thus, before you write, you must have an overall understanding about what the results mean, and you must be able to describe the results in a few sentences. Simply reiterating facts that are presented in tables and exhibits won't do.

Be Complete yet Concise. A written report should be complete in the sense that it stands by itself and needs no additional clarification. Remember that for the majority of people who read the report it will be their only exposure to the project. On the other hand, the report must be concise: It must focus on the critical

EXHIBIT 23–1
———
Report Format

The organization of the written research report essentially follows the format used in developing the research proposal. The following outline is the suggested format for writing the research report:

I.   Title page.
II. Table of contents.
III. Introduction.
    A.   Background and objectives.
    B.   Methodology
        — Sample.
        — Procedure.
        — Questionnaire.
    C.   Action standards.
IV. Management summary.
    A.   Key findings.
    B.   Conclusions.
    C.   Marketing implications and recommendations.
V. Detailed findings.
    A.   Evaluative measures.
    B.   Diagnostic measures.
    C.   Profile composites.
IV. Appendices.
    A.   Questionnaire.
    B.   Field materials.
    C.   Statistical output (supporting tables not included in body).

elements of the project, leaving out minor issues and findings. The "Background and Objectives" section of the proposal provides a guideline for deciding what is important and what is not.

Report Format

The organization of the written report essentially follows the format used in developing the research proposal. Exhibit 23–1 presents a typical organizational structure.

Title Page.   The title page should contain

1. A title that accurately conveys the essence of the study.
2. The date.
3. The agency (typically, a marketing research supplier) submitting the report.
4. The organization that has sponsored the study.
5. The names of those persons who should receive the written report.

Table of Contents.   The table of contents lists

1. The sequence of topics covered in the report, along with page references.
2. The various tables and exhibits contained in the report, along with page references.

Introduction. The introduction section of the report gives details on the research project regarding (1) background and objectives, (2) methodology, and (3) action standards. This section closely follows the research proposal, except that any technical jargon that might have been used in the research proposal should be translated into everyday terms. This section tells the reader why the study was conducted, how it was conducted, and how the results were evaluated.

Management Summary. The management summary is perhaps the most important component of the written report because many managers who are designated to receive the report will read only this section. For this reason, the management summary must be clear and concise. It presents findings, accompanied by interpretive conclusions. The conclusions should answer research questions derived from the study objectives, and they should be supported by study findings. Exhibit 23–2 provides a prototypical management summary.

Detailed Findings. The detailed findings section provides information about key measures collected in the study. Typically, findings are reported for (1) **evaluative measures** such as purchase intent, which help answer the question, "What happened?"; (2) **diagnostic measures** such as likes/dislikes and attribute ratings, which help answer the question, "Why did it happen?"; and, finally, (3) **profile composites,** of heavy users, for instance, which help answer the question, "To whom did it happen?" In all cases, detailed findings are reported in order of importance with the unaided-question format results reported first, followed by the aided-question format results. This section, which usually is written by the sponsoring firm, specifically focuses on the marketing problem at hand and, more importantly, uses the research findings and conclusions to provide alternative actions that can potentially solve the problem.

Appendices. The appendix, or appendices, contains information that will not be of primary interest to all readers of the research report. The sampling plan, copies of the questionnaire, details on the interviewing procedures and general field instructions, and in-depth statistical tables generally are relegated to the appendix.

Presenting the Data

Easy-to-understand tables and graphics will greatly enhance the accessibility of the written research report. All tables and figures that appear in the report should contain (1) an identification number to permit easy reference; (2) a title that conveys the contents of the table; and (3) table banner heads (column labels), table stub heads (row labels), and **legends,** which define specific elements in the exhibit. Tables should be labeled consistently and appear in a logical, meaningful order for the reader. For example, the column of data that shows the "control" product in a five-cell product test should be placed either first or last so that the reader can readily compare the four "test" products to it. A table that summarizes data that

---

evaluative measures
Research findings that help answer the question, "What happened?"

diagnostic measures
Like/dislike and attribute ratings that help answer the question, "Why did it happen?"

profile composites
Research findings that answer the question, "To whom did it happen?"

legends
Explanations of specific elements in a figure.

EXHIBIT 23–2

—

Management
Summary

The revised edition of the Westbank Access Account commercial, "Money Crazed II," performs somewhat better than its predecessor, "Money Crazed." Money Crazed II generates greater brand-name recognition on an unaided basis (while performing at parity on total recall) and communicates a broader spectrum of benefits (combined accounts, banking ease, higher interest rates, fee savings) than the earlier version (convenient access and check-bouncing protection). Both versions are seen as relevant, creating positive attitudes toward Westbank, entertaining, and realistic, while being deficient in news value area and for generating purchase motivation.

— Money Crazed II is at least as intrusive as Money Crazed. Although no differences emerge between the two ads for total recall (with nearly 9 in 10 viewers recalling the Westbank Access Account brand name), the revised execution (Money Crazed II) achieves levels of unaided brand-name recall (64 percent) that are significantly higher than levels realized for the original Money Crazed execution (50 percent).

— Although Money Crazed II is not an improvement over Money Crazed, the executional device is still prominent in communication playback (40 percent mention at least one executional element in Money Crazed II, 52 percent for Money Crazed). Most important, nearly 7 in 10 Money Crazed II viewers and better than half of all Money Crazed viewers recall some services. Key areas of playback for each execution are outlined below.

Money Crazed	Money Crazed II
24-hour banking	Checking/savings in one account
Easy access to money	Interest rates (high/er)
Checks won't bounce	Transferring money
Get cash fast	Fee savings

Responses to the bank service recall and main point questions were quite similar to those cited above.

— Consumers evaluated the Westbank Access Account ad on a series of viewer response profile characteristics in order to yield information on entertainment value, empathy, confusion, familiarity, relevance, and brand reinforcement. Money Crazed II is rated at parity on most items vis-à-vis Money Crazed, although Money Crazed was described as more entertaining and realistic, and it provided a message individuals could identify with.

On the positive side, both executions were relevant, reinforcing favorable brand attitudes, providing entertainment value, and presenting their respective messages in a realistic manner. Also, both commercials were judged as weak in providing news value and a message that bank customers would identify with.

— Interest in opening a Westbank Access Account (after exposure to the ad) is relatively low, and both versions performed at parity on this measure: 44 percent of Money Crazed viewers said that they "definitely/probably would open an Access Account," whereas 41 percent of Money Crazed II respondents made the same assertion.

are multidimensional (likes/dislikes, attribute ratings, usage occasions) should be ordered so that the characteristic that has the highest frequency of response appears first.

Exhibit 23-3 (see page 692) displays typical illustrations of how data can be presented in tabular and graphic form. Three commonly used graphic presentations are shown: the pie chart, the bar chart, and the line chart. (You will recall that we have already discussed graphic representations of data in Chapter 14.)

EXHIBIT 23–3   Three Commonly Used Graphic Presentations: The Pie Chart, the Bar Chart, and the Line Chart

Part A: Market shares by region

	Region			
Brand	North	South	East	West
A	.10	.35	.12	.30
B	.15	.25	.18	.05
C	.30	.08	.35	.11
D	.20	.12	.10	.14
E	.25	.20	.25	.40

Part B: Market shares by region (pie chart)

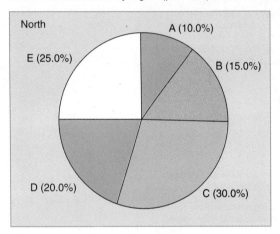

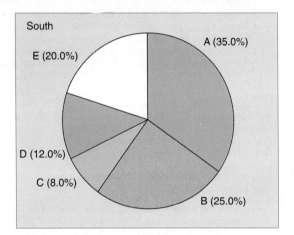

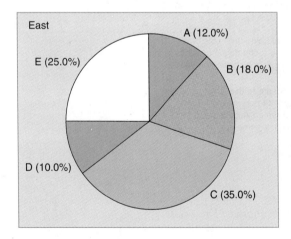

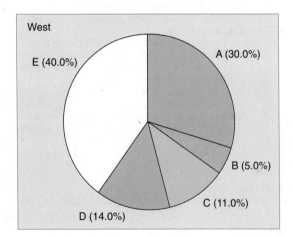

EXHIBIT 23–3   *(continued)*

Part C. Market shares by region (bar chart)

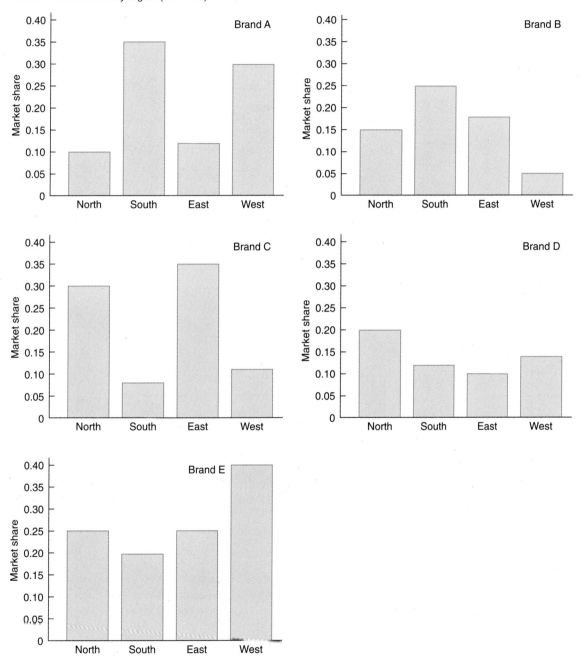

EXHIBIT 23–3   *(continued)*

Part D. Market shares by region (bar chart)

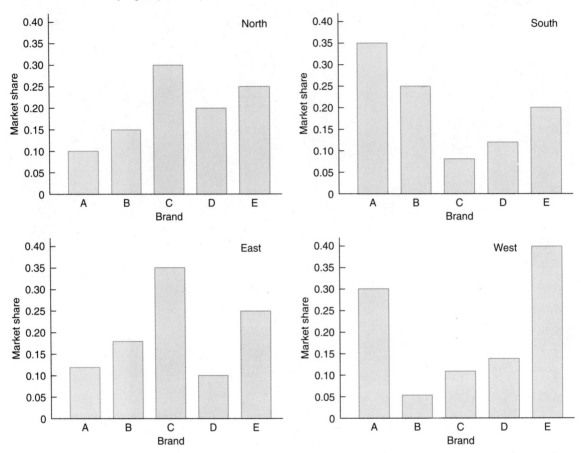

Pie Chart.   A pie chart is a circle divided into sections, where the size of each section corresponds to a portion of the total. Part B of Exhibit 23–3 displays the market-share data, given in part A of the figure, in the form of four pie charts. Note that each section of each pie reflects a brand's market share in the respective region.

Bar Chart.   A bar chart displays data in the form of vertical (or horizontal) bars, where the length of each bar reflects the magnitude of the variable of interest. Parts C and D of Exhibit 23–3 display two types of bar charts for the market-share data given in part A.

Line Chart.   A line chart is a graph. Part E of Exhibit 23–3 presents a line chart for the market-share data given in part A. Line charts are superior to bar charts when (1) the data involve a long time period; (2) several series are involved; (3)

EXHIBIT 23–3   *(concluded)*

Part E. Market shares by region (line chart)

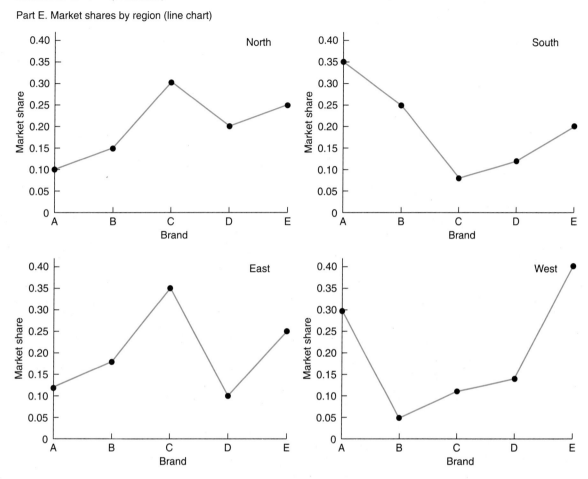

the emphasis is on the movement rather than the actual amount; (4) trends of frequency distribution are presented; (5) a multiple-amount scale is used; or (6) estimates, forecasts, interpolation, or extrapolation will be shown.

ORAL PRESENTATION

In many instances, the oral presentation is as important in determining how the overall project is received as the written report. It provides the management team with opportunities to ask questions and to have points clarified; most importantly, it allows managers to think aloud about their interpretations of the research findings. Typically, major projects require a series of informal oral reports as well as a formal oral presentation given at the conclusion of the study. The concluding oral presentation by the sponsoring firm can take place before or after the written research report has been distributed.

1. **The "So-What" Test**

   What are three benefits to my listeners?

2. **Attention-Getting Opening**

   What will grab my listeners' attention and focus their interest on my topic?

3. **Two Experiences, Brief Stories, or Examples**

   What personal or business-related experiences support my key points?

4. **Quote(s)**

   What did somebody else say that is relevant to my topic or situation?

5. **Analogies**

   How can I compare my ideas with examples that are familiar to my audience? What about: Statistical comparisons? Humorous stories? Metaphors? Future projections—"what ifs"—? Can I use vivid descriptions that are easily visualized?

6. **Pictures in My Visual Aids**

   How can I help my audience to picture and to remember the situation?

7. **Strong Closing**

   A day, a week, a month from now, what do I want my listeners to *do*? What do I want them to *remember*? To *know*? What lasting *feeling* do I want them to *feel*? If all they remember is my last statement, *what counts most*?

Source: Decker Communications, Inc. (San Francisco, 1982).

Support your *point of view.*

Give only what listeners *need to know.*

Discuss information in *bite-size pieces.*

Remember, visual means *visual* (not just letters and numbers).

Apply *big, bold and brilliant.*

Always *appropriate.*

Use *rule of threes* (maximum of six).

Don't *read* (look at visual, then talk to listeners).

Source: Decker Communications, Inc. (San Francisco, 1982).

General Guidelines

The general guidelines for written reports apply equally well to oral presentations. In addition, the following suggestions may prove useful:

1. Prepare a written script or detailed outline for the presentation.
2. Begin the presentation with a discussion of the background of the study, the research objectives, and the method used.
3. Make extensive use of visual aids.
4. Practice the presentation several times in front of a live audience.
5. Check audiovisual equipment thoroughly before the presentation.

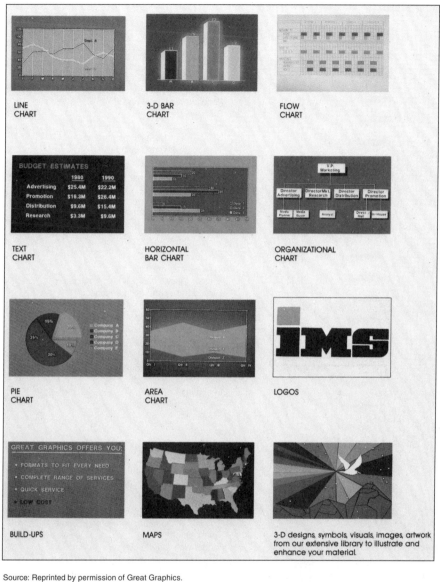

EXHIBIT 23–6
—
35-mm Slide Formats
for Oral
Presentations

Source: Reprinted by permission of Great Graphics.

Exhibit 23–4 presents guidelines by Decker Communications, Inc., a consulting firm that specializes in giving seminars about effective communication techniques.

Visual Aids

Visual aids are critical to the oral presentation. Exhibit 23–5 lists several considerations in the use of visual aids.

EXHIBIT 23–7   Visual Aids: Pros and Cons and Do's and Don'ts

Flip Charts—Best for Smaller, More Informal Groups

Pro: Quick and easy to prepare.
          Inexpensive.
          Easy to use.
          Flexible.
          Interactive with group.

Con: Limited audience size.
          Limited control.
          Quality is limited or costly.
          Bulky to carry.

Techniques: *Do:*
                Consider visibility/readability.
                Prepare in advance, fill in data.
                Speak to listeners, *not chart!*
                Pencil notes lightly on side.
                Remove after use.
                Use color.
                Use to record sensitive questions.
                Turn page to reach conclusion.

                Don't:
                Put too much information/detail on.
                Talk to the chart.
                Play with marking pen or pointer.
                Write too small or too light.

Overhead Projector—Most Versatile

Pro: Quick and easy.
          Fully lit room.
          You can turn it on and off.
          Face your listeners.
          Portable.
          Almost any size group.
          Use overlays.
          Inexpensive.
          Easy last-minute changes.

Con: Limited full-color effect.
          Poor photo projection.
          Screen placement.
          Sometimes it is less professional.

Techniques: *Do:*
                Use revelation.
                Turn light on and off.
                Have a friend change transparencies.
                Locate transparency in advance.
                Use pencil as a pointer.
                Place screen in corner.
                Make notes on frame.
                Use overlay technique.

                Don't:
                Put too much information/detail on the screen.
                Talk to machine.
                Leave light on.
                Be married to machine.

Slides—Best for Formal, Structured Speeches

Pro: Excellent visual effect.
          Directed light.
          Very professional.
          Colorful and creative.
          Portable.
          Any size group.
          Easily reproducible.

Con: Lack of control (canned).
          Limited eye contact (lose eye contact).
          Lead time required (last-minute changes difficult).
          Cost factors.

Techniques: *Do:*
                Keep a light on *you.*
                Reveal one line at a time.
                Show in six-slide segments.
                Show five seconds per slide.
                Dry run for sequence.

                Don't:
                Think that slides are your presentation—*You are!*
                Read slides.
                Fidget with remote control.
                Beware . . . early morning or after lunch.

Source: Decker Communications, Inc. (San Francisco, 1982).

Overhead projector acetates, graphic poster boards, and 35-mm slides can be effective for communicating the research findings. Exhibit 23–6 (see page 697) presents several different 35-mm slide formats. Today, visual aids like the ones shown in Exhibit 23–6 can be constructed on a personal computer by using computer-graphics software packages.

By way of summary, Exhibit 23–7 provides pros and cons and do's and don'ts of using flip charts, overheads, and slides.

SUMMARY

The written report and the oral presentation are the culmination of the months of work involved in any marketing research study. They are the final product of the study, not an incidental by-product. Both the written report and the oral presentation must be prepared with care and attention to detail. They should follow the general guidelines that apply to any report or presentation in the social sciences. Elements that are specific to a marketing research report, moreover, require special attention; the management summary is an example. Good reports and presentations will get the attention they deserve, and most likely they will get more business for the supplier. In conclusion, remember to:

— Think of your audience.
— Be concise, yet complete.
— Understand the results and draw conclusions.
— Begin an oral presentation with a discussion of the study, the research objectives, and the methodology used.
— Use visual aids appropriately.

KEY CONCEPTS

research report   management summary   oral presentation   visual aids
report format

REVIEW QUESTIONS

1. What general guidelines would you follow in writing a research report and in preparing an oral presentation?

2. In Chapter 16 you performed several different types of hypothesis tests. For review questions 2–5 in that chapter, recast your results in language that a manager would easily understand.

3. Comment on the statement: "Although visual aids are critical to the oral presentation, it doesn't matter whether one uses flip charts, an overhead projector, or slides."

4. Go through *The Wall Street Journal*, or other business publication such as *Business Week* or *Fortune*, and pick out three graphic illustrations. For each graphic illustration determine what type of chart or graphic presentation is being used and discuss its positive and negative features.

5. The table on page 700 provides information on the operating income of Exxon Inc.
   a. Develop a visual aid to present Exxon's quarterly gross profit.
   b. Develop a visual aid that would compare the change in net income to the change in net sales.
   c. Develop a visual aid that would present information on how expenses change over the six quarters.

	Quarterly Income (000) Fiscal Quarter Ending					
	06/30/91	03/31/91	09/30/90	06/30/90	03/31/90	09/30/89
Net sales	$26,982,000	$30,193,000	$28,826,000	$25,669,000	$26,383,000	$23,432,000
Cost of goods	14,129,000	15,578,000	15,683,000	13,389,000	11,424,000	12,287,000
Gross profit	12,853,000	14,615,000	13,143,000	12,280,000	14,959,000	11,145,000
R&D expenditures	193,000	185,000	261,000	212,000	190,000	211,000
Selling, general, and administrative expenses	9,750,000	9,947,000	9,734,000	8,864,000	11,161,000	7,730,000
Income before depreciation and amortization	2,910,000	4,483,000	3,148,000	3,204,000	3,608,000	3,204,000
Depreciation and amortization	1,188,000	1,205,000	1,185,000	1,323,000	1,286,000	1,205,000
Nonoperating income	285,000	492,000	191,000	309,000	330,000	225,000
Interest expense	173,000	248,000	240,000	321,000	391,000	373,000
Income before tax	1,834,000	3,522,000	1,914,000	1,869,000	2,261,000	1,851,000
Provision for income taxes	662,000	1,181,000	781,000	769,000	910,000	667,000
Minority interest (income)	47,000	101,000	58,000	n.a.	71,000	74,000
Net income before extraordinary items	1,125,000	2,240,000	1,075,000	1,100,000	1,280,000	1,110,000
Net income	$ 1,125,000	$ 2,240,000	$ 1,075,000	$ 1,100,000	$ 1,280,000	$ 1,110,000

n.a. = Not available.

Ethical Issues

- — Define ethics.
- — Discuss the factors leading to business ethics.
- — Discuss ethics in marketing research.
- — Discuss ethical issues relating to respondents, clients, and the general public.
- — Present a behavioral decision model of ethical/unethical decisions.
- — Present possible solutions to control current unethical marketing research practices.

INTRODUCTION

This final chapter broaches the subject of ethics in general terms, then focuses on the ethical and unethical practices of marketing research. Following a general definition of ethics—specifically ethics in business situations—a model depicting the internal and external influences on the decision to behave in an ethical or an unethical manner is presented and discussed. The chapter then addresses the concerns of ethical/unethical marketing research practices from the perspective of customers, clients, and the general public. The chapter closes with some recommendations for ensuring ethical practices in marketing research.

ETHICS DEFINED

Throughout history many scholars have devoted their time to the development of a theory of ethics. Some have advocated a normative perspective in which the theorists construct moral standards and codes that one ought to follow. Other scholars have followed an empirical-based perspective of ethics, which attempts to describe and explain how individuals actually behave in an ethical situation.

A major preoccupation of many ethical theories has been an attempt at providing a universal definition of ethics. After reviewing many definitions of ethics, John Tsalikis and David Fritzsche concluded that the term ethics is often considered synonymous with morals. And, therefore, ethics refers to the study of moral conduct.[1]

In a major study, Phillip Lewis reviewed 158 textbooks and 50 articles on business ethics from the period 1961 to 1981.[2] In addition, a survey was randomly distributed to 359 blue-collar workers and white-collar executives. The survey simply asked, "What is your definition of business ethics?" Based on the results of the study, four concepts emerged as integral to a definition of business ethics:

1. Rules, standards, codes, or principles.
2. Morally right behavior.
3. Truthfulness.
4. Specific situations.

Lewis noted that in addition to the four concepts, business ethics also may be defined in terms of the following:[3]

1. Focus on social responsibility.
2. Emphasis on honesty and fairness.
3. Emphasis on the Golden Rule.
4. Values that are in accord with common behavior or with one's religious beliefs.
5. Obligations, responsibilities, and rights toward conscientious work or enlightened self-interest.
6. Philosophy of what is good and bad.
7. Ability to clarify the issues in decision making.
8. Focus on one's individual conscience and/or legal system.
9. System or theory of justice questioning the quality of one's relationships.
10. Relationship of means to ends.
11. Concern for integrity, what ought to be, habit, logic, and/or principles of Aristotle.
12. Emphasis on virtue, leadership, character, confidentiality, judgment of others, placing God first, situationalness, temporalness, and publicness.

As defined by Lewis, "Business ethics is moral rules, standards, codes, or principles which provide guidelines for right and truthful behavior in specific situations."[4]

ETHICS IN MARKETING RESEARCH

As early as 1962, Leo Bogart identified four possible ethical/unethical situations in marketing research:[5]

---

[1]John Tsalikis and David J. Fritzsche, "Business Ethics: A Literature Review with a Focus on Marketing Ethics," *Journal of Business Ethics* (1989), pp. 695–743.

[2]Phillip V. Lewis, "Defining 'Business Ethics': Like Nailing Jello to a Wall," *Journal of Business Ethics* 4 (1985), pp. 377–83.

[3]Ibid., p. 382.

[4]Ibid, p. 382.

[5]Leo Bogart, "The Researcher's Dilemma," *Journal of Marketing* (1962), pp. 6–11.

- The extent of the researcher's honesty in doing what he or she purports to do.
- The manipulation of research techniques in order to produce desired findings.
- The propriety of business judgment exercised in undertaking research (e.g., when a client chooses to define a problem in terms the researcher cannot accept).
- The forthright relationship of the researcher to those interviewed regarding the study's true purpose and sponsorship.

These situations are still prevalent today and highlight the potential ethical/unethical practices and dilemmas between the researcher and (1) the research respondent, (2) the researcher's client, and (3) the general public. The constituencies are discussed in the sections that follow.

Research Respondents

Marketing researchers must have integrity. After all, they expect respondents to be willing participants who honestly and accurately respond to their questions. Presumably, respondents agree to provide information because they believe it is a valuable commodity and that the exercise is in their best interest. However, they are entitled to expect marketing researchers to respect their rights.

Alice Tybout and Gerald Zaltman introduced what they called the respondent's bill of rights.[6] These rights included the

- Right to choose. There should be no forced compliance.
- Right to safety. If confidentiality is promised, then respondents must remain anonymous; that is, they are not identified with their responses.
- Right to be informed. Respondents should be debriefed at the end of the study, especially if an experimental manipulation is used.

Whereas Tybout and Zaltman focused primarily on experimental research,[7] Kenneth Schneider discussed ethical issues with respect to respondents in both survey and experimental research.[8] His ethical/unethical issues centered on respondent abuse concerning:

1. Deceptive/fraudulent practices—for example, fake sponsorship or not keeping responses anonymous.
2. Lack of consideration for subjects—for example, poorly conducted surveys or failure to debrief.

---

[6]Alice M. Tybout and Gerald Zaltman, "Ethics in Marketing Research: Their Practical Relevance," *Journal of Marketing Research* (1974), pp 357–68.

[7]For a comment on the general ability of Tybout and Zaltman, see Robert L. Day, "A Comment on Ethics in Marketing Research," *Journal of Marketing Research* (1975), pp. 232–33.

[8]Kenneth C. Schneider, "Subject and Respondent Abuse in Marketing Research," *MSU Business Topics* 25, pp. 13–20.

An Ad Agency Goes to Court in Boston

A David and Goliath courtroom fight is starting in Boston, and the outcome could shake the loyalty some advertisers have to their agencies.

At issue is how aggressively an agency can promote its past experience for a competitor when going after a potential new client.

Apart from advertiser concerns regarding the ability of agencies to keep proprietary information confidential, the Boston case also is raising questions about the procedures agencies have to protect such information.

The issue may get a full airing, courtesy of Rossin Greenberg Seronick & Hill, a $26 million agency that is about to countersue Lotus Development Corporation, a $200 million computer software marketer.

Cambridge, Massachusetts–based Lotus sued the agency earlier this month, after software rival Microsoft Corporation, Redmond, Washington, forwarded a copy of a flier it had received from Boston-based RGS&H, which was pitching the $10 million-plus Microsoft business.

The court granted Lotus a temporary restraining order barring RHS&H from revealing any trade secrets, effectively barring the agency from pitching the Microsoft or any other Lotus competitors' account.

The flier sent to Microsoft said: "You probably haven't thought about talking to an agency in Boston. . . . But since we know your competition's plans, isn't it worth taking a flier?

"The reason we know so much about Lotus is that some of our newest employees just spent the past year and a half working on the Lotus business at another agency.

"So they are intimately acquainted with Lotus' thoughts about Microsoft and their plans to deal with the introduction of [Microsoft] Excel."

Rob Lebow, Microsoft director of corporate communications and the coordinator of its agency review, said he was "horrified" by the RGS&H flier.

"And I'm no choirboy," Mr. Lebow added.

RGS&H President Neal Hill said he will wait to determine what kind of countercharges to file until after a December 23 hearing in Suffolk Superior Court, when Lotus presents its case. He acknowledged, however, that a protracted—and costly—legal battle could effectively close down the agency.

3. Invasion of privacy—for example, undisclosed one-way mirrors or projective techniques.

Client Concerns

In terms of suppliers servicing clients, there also are a number of ethical considerations. Marketing research suppliers, for example, must ensure that information about their clients remains confidential. Suppliers often have access to confidential client information about specific projects. Consider, for example, the relationship between advertisers and their agency.

Lotus contends it is protecting its proprietary corporate information by enforcing a confidentiality clause in its contract with its agency, Leonard Monahan Sabaye, Providence, Rhode Island.

"If a client fires an agency, in my view it's perfectly appropriate for an agency to go after a client in the same category, and the quicker the better," said Jack Bowen, chairman-CEO, D'Arcy Masius Benton & Bowles, New York.

But, he adds, it is "despicable" for an agency to try to sell confidential information about the old client to the new one.

Many shops have informal policies governing exchange of proprietary information.

Other agencies say ethical considerations and ordinary judgment determine how and when to capitalize on prior experience in a category.

"When we have confidential information for a client and they resign us or we resign them, it's still confidential as far as I'm concerned," said Marvin Sloves, chairman-CEO of Scali, McCabe, Sloves, New York.

"The general rule is to protect clients," said John McNamara, president-chief operating officer of McCann-Erickson Worldwide, New York.

"There's a thin line between experience and first-hand, recent knowledge (of a competitor's business). I can't imagine a new-business presentation in which the agency didn't introduce people who worked on the prospect's kind of business," McNamara said.

He said some agency/client contracts call for a period of time in which the agency cannot do business with a competitor.

"After a brief period of time, the kind of information an agency might have, about new strategies or campaigns about to break, becomes unusable," he said.

Young & Rubicam's "conduct of business policy" is issued to new employees and covers privileged information from both clients and prospects, said R. John Cooper, executive VP-general counsel.

Cooper said an agency would not want to betray a prospect's trust because, even if the agency did not get the business this time, it might want to get it sometime in the future.

Besides, trading on other companies' secrets would irritate an agency's current client, he said.

"It would be like cutting off your nose to spite your face," Cooper said.

Source: Cleveland Horton, "Ethics at Issue in Lotus Case," *Advertising Age*, December 21, 1987, p. 6.

Marketing research suppliers also are ethically obligated to provide unbiased designs and honest and objective fieldwork, whether results confirm or contradict their client's expectations about the outcome of a study. Finally, marketing researchers are ethically obligated to not pirate research designs and other relevant information that is obtained, say, through requests for proposals, as these are seldom legally protected. (See From the World of Research 24–1.)

The General Public

Even though marketing research practices are grounded in social science methodology and statistics that are based on well-established guidelines and principles, the collection of information has a subjective element because it is vulnerable to distortion both by the people who have the responsibility of collecting and disseminating the information and by those who provide the answers. The possibility of distortion raises ethical questions.

Consequently, the outcome of the research may affect the general public. Errant practices of marketing research suppliers and other practitioners can have harmful effects on consumers, clients, and the general public.

From the general public's point of view, there are a number of practices that can lead to deception. Two examples, the pseudo poll and result misrepresentation, are on the rise.

Pseudo poll

"We're conducting a survey," reads the letter from XYZ Survey Research Company.

The "survey," which will be sent to 50 million homes, is a questionnaire asking for respondents' preferences for consumer products and their names, addresses, telephone numbers, occupations, and family income. For the respondents' cooperation, the sponsoring company offers them free samples and discounts from consumer products companies.

What the material *does not* say is that the personal information will be compiled onto data tapes and sold to marketers to help them promote their products.

Pseudo polls use the public's willingness to be surveyed in order to accomplish something other than survey research. It is a misrepresentation to the consumer when a selling or marketing activity uses the forms, language, and aura of survey research to mask the real nature of the activity. Selling under the guise of marketing research is known in the industry as *sugging*. In 1982, 15 percent of the people surveyed in a study tracking trends in the marketing research industry said that they had been exposed to a sales pitch disguised as a survey. By 1988, 22 percent reported that they had been sugged.[9]

Result misrepresentation

A local television news program asked whether or not the United States should provide additional funding for space exploration. Sixty-eight thousand viewers called in their opinion by using a "900" number. Of those, 59 percent wanted additional funding. This result is in marked contrast to the results of another survey, also reported on the program, indicating that over 60 percent of the sample opposed additional support.

Result misrepresentation frequently occurs with call-in, write-in, or other forms of volunteer surveys in which the researcher has no control over who participates in a study. People participating in the poll conducted by the local telephone news program may not be representative of the entire community. The reason for the disparate results is simply that different groups of people responded to the two surveys. A "survey" where the respondents can self-select is not a legitimate survey because it is unlikely to be representative of the population at large, no matter how many people respond. Misrepresentation occurs when self-selected survey results are reported as "true" about anyone other than those who have responded.

---

[9]Randall Rothenberg, "Surveys Proliferate but Answers Dwindle," *New York Times*, October 5, 1990, p. D4.

EXHIBIT 24–1

Errant Marketing
Research Practices

— A person answers a few questions only to find him or herself suddenly eligible to buy a specific product or service. This misuse of the survey approach as a "blind" for sales canvassing is by no means new, and it shows no sign of abating.

— Questionnaires about products and brands are sent to households, and response is encouraged by the offer of free product samples to respondents. The listing firms compile their information by implying to the prospective customer that he or she has been interviewed in an opinion or market study. Although the components of questionnaires vary by sponsor, in each case respondents are asked to specify their name, addresses, and telephone numbers. Presumably, to the individual, these data are requested in order to provide the respondent with an incentive. However, the consumer is not told that the company conducting the survey is in business other than research. A brochure for one of these consumer database companies describes their business as the "the reporting of name, address, phone number, demographics, and results to client-customized questions" to potential clients such as "advertising agencies, distributors, wholesalers," and others.

— A telemarketing company uses "surveys" to promote services offered to broadcasters. Contacts occur during audience measurement periods. According to the company's literature, hundreds of thousands of computerized telephone calls are placed that not only promote a specific broadcast but also poll audience opinions about program subject matter. Here, the "poll" is used to raise broadcast audience ratings.

— Because marketing principles have been applied to nonprofit organizations and political candidates, the survey approach has been misused to generate donations. The incentives for response are the opportunities to provide information, to receive a report of findings, and, at the same time, to contribute financially to an association or to a candidate.

— Newspaper questionnaires are frequently printed as an insert or as part of the paper. In these polls, readers are asked to express their opinions by completing the questionnaire and sending it to the paper; results of the poll are often reported in a later issue. A varation is the use of insert questionnaires by public officials in their newsletters to their constituents; the results of these polls also are reported to the public in a later newsletter.

— Automated polling devices are often placed in recreation centers, retail outlets, airports, and other locations that have substantial pedestrian traffic. The hardware typically includes a computer, a monitor screen, and a keyboard. Through graphics, music, taped messages, and other techniques, passers-by are attracted to these devices, which invite participation in a self-administered survey. The results of "polls" using this equipment have appeared in hundreds of newspapers.

Source: "Phony or Misleading Polls," Advertising Research Foundation, *ARF Position Paper,* September 1986.

Exhibit 24–1 provides additional illustrations of errant marketing research practices that lead to consumer deception and mistrust.

Errant marketing research practices have serious implications for the general public and public policymakers. Among other consequences, unethical practices can:

1. Impair legitimate research activities by diminishing the public's willingness to participate in survey research. This affects response rates, statistical reliability, and, ultimately, response quality.

2. Distort the policymakers' perceptions of public opinion and business-related issues. Dangerous feedback can result if policymakers misread consumer sentiment because of invalid research procedures.

EXHIBIT 24–2   Behavior Model of Ethical/Unethical Decision Making

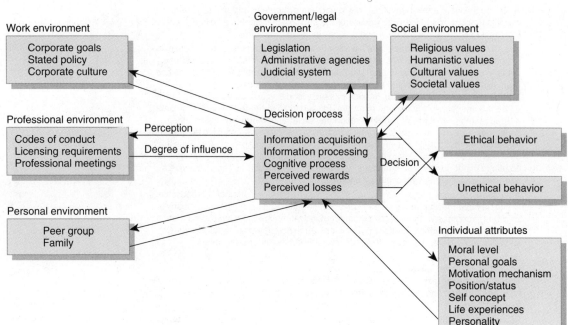

Source: Adapted from Michael Boomer, Clarence Grato, Jerry Gravander, and Mark Tuttle, "A Behavioral Model of Ethical and Unethical Decision Making," *Journal of Business Ethics* 6 (1987), p. 266.

3. Lessen the public's ability to distinguish valid from invalid research findings. Even valid polls with inconsistent results may render the public indifferent to, confused about, or distrustful of what they read, see, or hear from survey research. Phony polls do worse, as they result in miseducation.

A Model of Ethical/Unethical Decisions

The model depicted in Exhibit 24–2 describes the various influences that can affect the cognitive process, resulting in the decision to behave ethically or unethically in a given situation.[10] Individual characteristics such as goals, morals, and self-concept that constitute the individual's life experiences and personality interact with external influences such as the work environment as well as legal and social environments. This highlights the fact that the interpretation as to whether the decision was ethical or unethical is influenced by a variety of factors, many of which are outside the control of the individual.

---

[10]For an in-depth discussion of the model shown in Exhibit 24–2, see Michael Boomer, Clarence Grato, Jerry Gravander, and Mark Tuttle, "A Behavioral Model of Ethical and Unethical Decision Making," *Journal of Business Ethics* 6 (1987), pp. 265–80.

ORGANIZATIONAL PERSPECTIVES

The organization to which managers belong is an important determinant of their perspectives on ethics. Organization norms play a crucial role in the practice or acceptance of ethical or unethical behavior. In other words, the current set of norms that pervade an organization determine what is or is not appropriate behavior. Because members of an organization, or for that matter a department, are known to share organizational values and beliefs, existing company norms, whether stated or implicit, determine the ethical environment and guide the thoughts and actions of decision makers.

Other factors can influence managers' adherence to ethical practices. There is evidence to suggest that referent and significant others play a role in determining ethical or unethical behavior.[11] The terms *referent* and *significant others* simply identify those individuals that serve as a reference for executives when making decisions. Peers and top managers often assume the role of referent or significant others. Evidence also indicates that job demands are an important factor.

Job demands are particularly relevant when comparing marketing research jobs with marketing management jobs. Research jobs, in general, require greater adherence to rules and standards as they relate to scientific methods of inquiry and data collection, while marketing management jobs are more likely to be evaluated in terms of profit and loss. A recent survey designed to elicit marketing professionals' opinions about ethical issues in marketing research asked a group of marketing researchers and marketing executives to indicate their approval/disapproval of the action(s) of the marketing research director in 11 different scenarios relating to different marketing research practices.[12] The results (see Exhibit 24–3 on page 710) showed marked differences in the opinions of marketing researchers and marketing executives. In particular, executives have higher disapproval rates than researchers concerning the use of ultraviolet ink (item 1), one-way mirrors (item 2), advertising and product misuses (item 4), and the provision of potentially damaging information (item 6). On the other hand, marketing researchers have higher disapproval rates than executives concerning possible conflict of interest (item 3) and sharing information with trade associations (item 5).

Solutions

The problems generated by errant marketing research practices are complex, and they are not easily solved. One way to curb abuses is to establish guidelines and regulations to educate, ensure consistency, and protect. Historically, such

---

[11]See, for example, O. C. Ferrell and Larry G. Gresham, "A Contingency Framework for Understanding Ethical Decision-Making in Marketing," *Journal of Marketing* 49 (Summer 1985), pp. 87–96; and Linda Klebe Trevino, "Ethical Decision Making in Organizations: A Person-Situation Interactionist Model," *Academy of Management Review* 11 (July 1986), pp. 601–17.

[12]Ishmael P. Akaah and Edward A. Riordan, "Judgments of Marketing Professionals about Ethical Issues in Marketing Research: A Replication and Extension," *Journal of Marketing Research*, February 1989, pp. 112–20.

EXHIBIT 24–3   Comparison of Responses to the Ethical Scenarios (items)

	Percentage of Disapprovals*	
Scenario (item)	Marketing Researchers Present Study (*n* = 205)	Marketing Executives Present Study (*n* = 215)
Confidentiality		
1. Use of ultraviolet ink. A project director went to the marketing research director's office and requested permission to use an ultraviolet ink to precode a questionnaire for a mail survey. The project director pointed out that although the cover letter promised confidentiality, respondent identification was needed to permit adequate cross tabulations of the data. The marketing research director gave approval.	57	69
2. One-way mirrors. One of the products of X company is brassieres. Recently, the company has been having difficulty making decisions on a new product line. Information was critically needed regarding how women put on their brassieres. The marketing research director therefore designed a study in which two local stores agreed to put one-way mirrors in the foundations of their dressing rooms. Observers behind these mirrors successfully gathered the necessary information.	94	97
Conflict of interest		
3. Possible conflict of interest. A marketing testing firm to which X company gives most of its business recently went public. The marketing research director of X company had been looking for a good investment and proceeded to buy some $20,000 of their stock. The firm continues as X company's leading supplier for testing.	54	44
4. Advertising and product misuse. A recent study showed that several customers of X company were misusing product B. Although this posed no danger, customers were wasting their money by using too much of the product at a time. But, yesterday, the marketing research director saw final comps/sketches on product B's new ad campaign, which not only ignored the problem of misuse but actually seemed to encourage it. The marketing research director quietly referred the advertising manager to the research results, well known to all of the people involved with product B's advertising, but did nothing beyond that.	39	55
Social issues		
5. General trade data to center-city group. The marketing research department of X company frequently makes extensive studies of their retail customers. A federally supported minority group working to get a shopping center in their residential area wanted to know if they could have access to this trade information. Since the marketing research director has always refused to share this information with trade organizations, the request was declined.	13	10

*To simplify the table, only disapproval rates ("disapprove somewhat" or "disapprove") are reported.

Source: Ishmael P. Akaah and Edward A. Riordan, "Judgments of Marketing Professionals about Ethical Issues in Marketing Research: A Replication and Extension," *Journal of Marketing Research,* February 1989, pp. 112–20.

EXHIBIT 24–3   *(concluded)*

	Percentage of Disapprovals*	
Scenario (item)	Marketing Researchers Present Study (*n* = 205)	Marketing Executives Present Study (*n* = 215)
6. NMAC request for recent price study. The National Marketing Advisory Council (formed of top marketing executives and marketing educators to advise the U.S. Commerce Department) has a task force studying inner-city prices. The head of this study group recently called to ask if they could have a copy of a recent X company study that showed that inner-city appliance prices are significantly higher than in suburban areas. Since X company sells appliances to these inner-city merchants, the marketing research director felt compelled to refuse the request.	20	26

standards and regulations have been established by the federal government or by the industry.[13]

Government Regulation.   The Federal Trade Commission (FTC) has considered the unethical or illegal use of research. Specifically, Section 5 of the FTC Act declares unfair or deceptive acts to be unlawful. The FTC considers the use of research as a sales ploy to be deceptive, and it has ruled in this manner in several court cases. It is clear that the FTC considers using research as a "door opener" illegal.

The Federal Communications Commission (FCC) has addressed the practice of misrepresenting results. The FCC recognizes the threat associated with the reporting of results of phone-in polls in its Public Notice to Licensees, which states:

> Broadcast facilities should not report the results of polls they have conducted without making clear to the public the nature of the poll, and specifically that the poll does not purport to be conducted upon a scientific basis where, in fact, it is not so based.

Local communities, states, and Congress also have considered legislation. The recent advent of electronic interviewing techniques has led to proposals for the regulation of this type of interviewing as well as proposals for the regulation of telemarketing.

Industry Standards.   Industry standards that guide and regulate the practice of marketing research exist because they serve several important functions. First, a code of ethics provides objective criteria upon which to judge the behavior of the profession. Second, a professional code of ethics provides a potential counter-

---

[13]The following discussion is taken from "Phony or Misleading Polls," Advertising Research Foundation, *ARF Position Paper*, September 1986.

From the World
of Research
—
24–2

Right to Privacy Issue Pits Consumers Against Marketers, Researchers

Big Brother is no longer watching you. He's accessing you.

Just about anyone in any facet of sales and marketing with a computer and a checkbook can not only buy names of consumers but also information regarding everything from their finances to their favorite flavors. Whether or not consumers pop up as part of a marketing research study or, more often, a telemarketing campaign is beyond their control.

The question is whether the marketing research, telemarketing, and direct marketing communities infringe on each other to the point that their own self-regulating policies are insufficient to provide comfortable levels of consumer privacy.

"Where it becomes an issue," said Larry Chiagouris, senior vice president and director of strategic planning at the Bozell ad agency in New York, "is where people don't know that when they buy a car, subscribe to a magazine, respond to an 800 (telephone) number solicitation, etc., their name goes into a file. Marketing professionals sell those names to other professionals."

It has become an accepted way of doing business, and "there's nothing wrong with that," he said. "We never give a name that's been generated under research to a direct marketing organization."

Despite his assertion, and similar ones from his peers, Chiagouris and his colleagues know that the public holds somewhat different perceptions.

And the public seems to have a friend in the government, at least with the privacy issue.

Bonnie Guiton, director of the U.S. Office of Consumer Affairs and special adviser to President Bush on the matter, told a congressional subcommittee last month that the 1970 Fair Credit Reporting Act (FCRA) is no longer sufficient to guarantee respect for consumer privacy, at least not in regard to "the business community's need to base credit and other business decisions on adequate and relevant information."

She hinted at changes in the FCRA or new laws altogether.

Consumers, she told the subcommittee, "would be surprised to learn that financial information they generally regarded as confidential is used as a criterion to put them on lists that are subsequently sold to marketers for a myriad of uses," despite what she described as "the efforts of dedicated consumer educators," such as the Your Opinion Counts (YOC) Public Education Program.

"Consumers need to understand all the methods companies use to get their names, addresses, and telephone numbers with or without their permission," Guiton added.

Source: Howard Schlossberg, *Marketing News*, October 23, 1989, pp. 1, 19. Used with permission.

balance to interests within a company that may attempt to compromise an individual's integrity. Third, a professional code of ethics provides guidelines to companies that may not have the resources to develop their own code.

A number of industry groups in the marketing research field have developed codes of ethics to guide researchers. Among the industry groups with published codes of ethics are the American Marketing Association (AMA), the American Association for Public Opinion Research (AAPOR), the Marketing Research Association (MRA), and the Council of American Survey Research Organizations

(CASRO). Although each set of guidelines is somewhat different, they are in consensus regarding many marketing research practices. For example, the various codes agree on (1) the respondent's right to privacy, (2) the respondent's right to anonymity, and (3) the public's right to know how a survey was conducted at the time the results are reported. (See From the World of Research 24–2.)

SUMMARY

In this chapter we discussed a variety of ethical issues facing the marketing researcher. We began by presenting factors that are integral to the definition of ethics. To define ethics we must incorporate (1) rules, standards, codes, or principles; (2) morally right behavior; and (3) truthfulness in specific situations. Consequently, unethical actions minimally violate one or all of these factors. The marketing researcher must consider these factors when interacting with clients and with the respondents that provide the data. In addition, marketing researchers must consider the results and effects of their decisions on the general public.

The chapter closed with a discussion of organizational perspectives and sanctions for ethical/unethical behavior and some recommended solutions to control errant marketing research practices.

KEY CONCEPTS

definition of business ethics

ethical situations in marketing research

ethical concerns of respondents

ethical concerns of clients

ethical concerns of the public

CASE STUDIES FOR
PART VII

CASE 1
Consumers' Attitudes and Perceptions toward Seafood when Eating Out—Report Phase

Case Studies for Parts II, IV, and V examined various data on consumers' attitudes and perceptions toward nontraditional fish consumption when eating out. This case study presents additional information in Tables 1 through 4 and Exhibits 1 through 11.

Case Question
Prepare an oral report scheduled for 20 minutes making use of the relevant information presented here, as well as in Parts II, IV, and V.

TABLE 1		n	Sample (%)	Population (%)
Sample and Population Profiles	Sex			
	Male	553	29.0	48
	Female	1,376	71.0	52
	Age			
	Less than 29	301	15.6	48
	30 to 39	510	26.4	14
	40 to 49	387	20.1	10
	50 to 59	346	17.9	11
	Greater than 60	386	20.0	18
	Household income			
	Less than 15,000	160	11.3	42
	15,000 to 24,999	240	16.9	27
	25,000 to 34,999	341	24.0	16
	35,000 to 49,999	338	23.8	9
	Greater than 50,000	341	24.0	5
	Race			
	Caucasian	1,827	94.7	96
	Hispanic	5	0.3	4
	Black	13	0.7	(nonwhite)
	Religion			
	Catholic	937	54.2	45
	Non-Catholic	792	45.8	55
	Hometown residence			
	Coastal areas	1,160	60.5	53
	Noncoastal areas	757	39.5	47

Source: This material was graciously provided by Dr. Robert C. Lewis, Department of Hotel Administration, University of Massachusetts.

Behaviors
Eating out frequency per month

			95% CI
Luncheon	Mean	6.06	5.77 to 6.36
	SD	5.87	
Dinner	Mean	5.30	5.10 to 5.51
	SD	4.40	

Frequency of ordering fish per month

Luncheon	Mean	3.06	2.88 to 3.24
	SD	2.93	
Dinner	Mean	3.22	3.08 to 3.36
	SD	2.78	

Attitudes
Scale: (1) Strongly disagree to (5) Strongly agree

	Mean	Standard Deviation	Strongly Disagree (1 & 2)	Strongly Agree (4 & 5)
Enjoy going to restaurants	4.39	0.87	3%	84%
Think about nutrition	3.15	1.33	32	43
Think about calories	2.78	1.37	42	32
For special occasions only	2.29	1.32	61	20
Concerned about price	3.37	1.25	22	48
Enjoy different restaurants	4.25	0.96	6	81
Try entrees never had before	3.12	1.28	32	39
Order what I don't eat at home	4.30	1.04	6	82

TABLE 2
—
Behaviors and Attitudes toward Eating Out

A. Awareness and trial

	Never Heard of	Heard of, Never Tried	Eaten, Did Not Like	Eaten, Liked
Butterfish	56.5%	26.3%	2.1%	11.1%
Dogfish	41.8	49.8	2.0	2.3
Hake	33.8	43.5	4.8	13.4
Eel	4.8	64.6	11.3	15.5
Skate	25.5	58.4	3.6	8.3
Tilefish	63.3	26.6	1.4	4.4
Herring	2.0	30.8	22.5	41.4
Mackerel	1.1	18.1	26.7	51.4
Monkfish	39.8	36.1	4.0	15.3
Pollock	7.4	24.7	13.2	50.9
Squid	5.0	44.0	17.0	29.9
Whiting	26.5	35.4	2.9	28.0
Cusk	46.3	33.0	3.6	12.9

TABLE 3
—
Familiarity with Nontraditional Fish*

TABLE 3
———
(concluded)

B. Experience of triers

	Liked	Not Liked
Butterfish	84%	16%
Hake	74	26
Skate	70	30
Tilefish	76	24
Monkfish	79	21
Whiting	82	18
Cusk	78	22
Dogfish	54	46
Eel	58	42
Herring	65	35
Mackerel	66	34
Pollock	79	21
Squid	64	36

*Percentages do not add to 100% due to missing responses.

TABLE 4
———
Influences in
Not Trying
Nontraditional Fish*

A. Mean and standard deviation

Variable	Mean	Standard Deviation
Name of fish	2.69	1.55
Risk of not liking	3.36	1.42
Unfamiliarity	3.36	1.40
Expected taste	3.60	1.30
Past experience	3.55	1.45
Trust in restaurant	3.58	1.40
Image of the fish	3.33	1.46
Social behavior of the fish	2.30	1.48

B. Percent of respondents

Variable	Not influential (1 & 2)	Very influential (4 & 5)
Name of fish	49%	34%
Risk of not liking	28	50
Unfamiliarity	28	51
Expected taste	19	58
Past experience	24	57
Trust in restaurant	22	60
Image of the fish	28	51
Social behavior of fish	60	23

*Scale: (1) Not at all influential to (5) Extremely influential.

EXHIBIT 1   Butterfish

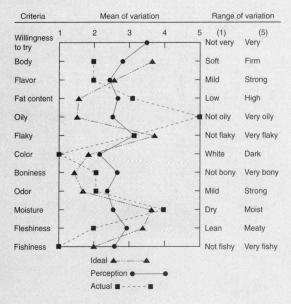

EXHIBIT 2   Hake

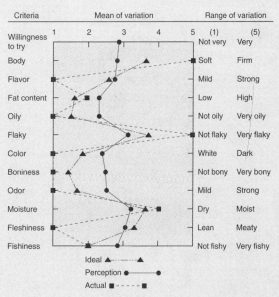

EXHIBIT 3   Mackerel

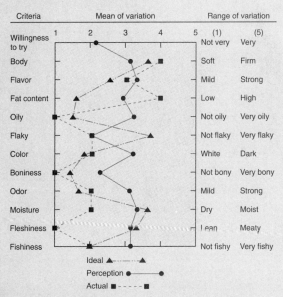

EXHIBIT 4   Monkfish

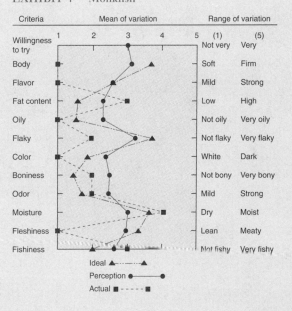

EXHIBIT 5   Squid

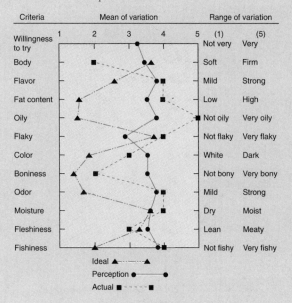

EXHIBIT 6   Pollock

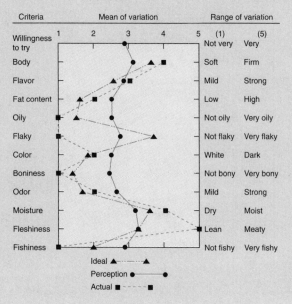

EXHIBIT 7   Whiting

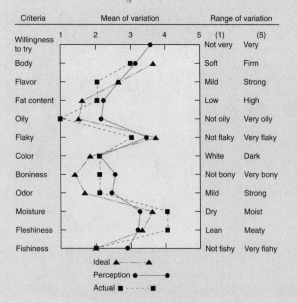

EXHIBIT 8   Skate

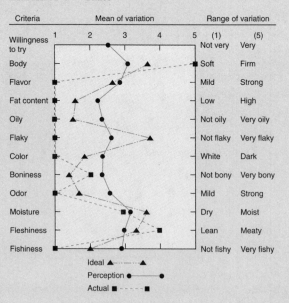

EXHIBIT 9   Eel

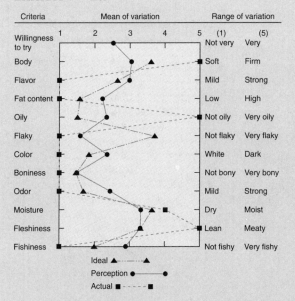

EXHIBIT 10   Cusk

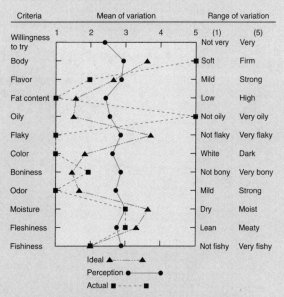

EXHIBIT 11   Tilefish

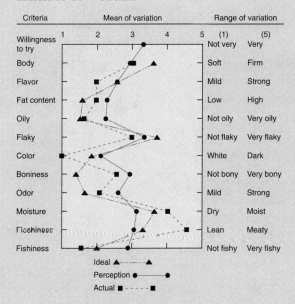

CASE 2
Leading Researchers Invite Criticism— And They Get It

ST. PETERSBURG, FLA.—Pollsters are taking notice of critics who say self-serving marketing research and an explosion of political polls get too much attention.

"It hasn't been hard to find people in the research business who readily concede there's a lot of junk masquerading as studies these days," said Cynthia Crossen, who investigated the survey industry for *The Wall Street Journal.* "Of course, it's always the other guy."

Instead of polls being a quest for truth, "many today are little more than vehicles for pitching a product or opinion," Crossen said in a speech at the annual meeting of the American Association for Public Opinion Research.

Christopher Hitchens, Washington editor of *Harper's Magazine,* said polls no longer just measure public opinion, but influence it.

Leading pollsters invited this criticism and listened intently because their profession is perpetually at the mercy of the kindness of strangers: More people than ever are unwilling to take time to answer surveys.

"We need to face the problem squarely and solve it," Norman Bradburn, director of the National Opinion Research Center, said in a speech marking the end of his term as president of the pollsters' professional association.

James Beninger, a University of Southern California professor who invited Crossen and Hitchens, said public confidence in surveys will erode if people feel they are being spoon-fed cooked data, even if the numbers are pulled from legitimate polls.

Likening such partial results to campaign sound bites, Stanford University professor Herbert Clark dubbed them "poll bites."

As examples of self-serving polls, Crossen cited a study sponsored by Chrysler that found test-drivers preferred Chryslers to Toyotas, and one sponsored by the paper-bag industry that found shoppers prefer paper bags.

Other junk polls are based on tiny samples or self-selected groups or have loaded questions, pollsters say.

Crossen said editors push reporters to get statistics, even from sloppy studies. Even more troubling, she said, reporters and editors promise good, uncritical play for studies promised as exclusives.

Sheldon Gawaiser, a polling consultant for both marketers and the media, said it is the reporter's responsibility to treat an advocacy poll critically.

"If you got any other information from someone who has a vested interest, you're going to treat that information differently than if you get it from a subject that's independent," Gawaiser said.

Harry O'Neill, vice chairman of the Roper Organization, said a few reporters have learned to differentiate between good polls and bad, but many have not. It is the polling company's responsibility to make sure an advocacy group releases its data completely and accurately, "but once the media get hold of it, that's where my control ends," he said.

The New York Times's survey director, former Princeton University professor Michael Kaguy, said his department screens polls before they are cited in stories. Other major media organizations also have in-house experts, but they regularly swap stories about bad polls that got by them.

Hitchens said political reporters have an especially "overwarm" relationship with pollsters, sometimes paying more attention to polls than candidates.

"Their shoe leather can remain intact Gucci. They can punch up a few numbers on the screen and say they have taken the temperature of the nation," Hitchens said. "The same can be said for politicians."

He says polls are so influential that people who used to be opinion makers now swap the latest poll findings rather than talking about issues. "There is a danger of surrogate democracy taking place in a political vacuum," he said.

Case Question

A number of industry groups have specified criteria that constitute ethical from unethical practices. Assume that Mr. Kagoy of *The New York Times* has asked you to create guidelines for discriminating between ethical and unethical polls. Prepare this set of guidelines.

Source: *Marketing News,* June 22, 1992, p 5. Used with permission.

Statistical Appendix

TABLE 1 Random Number Table

Line/Col.	(1)	(2)	(3)	(4)	(5)	(6)	(7)	(8)	(9)	(10)	(11)	(12)	(13)	(14)
1	10480	15011	01536	02011	81647	91646	69179	14194	62590	36207	20969	99570	91291	90700
2	22368	46573	25595	85393	30995	89198	27982	53402	93965	34095	52666	19174	39615	99505
3	24130	48390	22527	97265	76393	64809	15179	24830	49340	32081	30680	19655	63348	58629
4	42167	93093	06243	61680	07856	16376	39440	53537	71341	57004	00849	74917	97758	16379
5	37570	39975	81837	16656	06121	91782	60468	81305	49684	60072	14110	06927	01263	54613
6	77921	06907	11008	42751	27756	53498	18602	70659	90655	15053	21916	81825	44394	42880
7	99562	72905	56420	69994	98872	31016	71194	18738	44013	48840	63213	21069	10634	12952
8	96301	91977	05463	07972	18876	20922	94595	56869	69014	60045	18425	84903	42508	32307
9	89579	14342	63661	10281	17453	18103	57740	84378	25331	12568	58678	44947	05585	56941
10	85475	36857	53342	53988	53060	59533	38867	62300	08158	17983	16439	11458	18593	64952
11	28918	69578	88231	33276	70997	79936	56865	05859	90106	31595	01547	85590	91610	78188
12	63553	40961	48235	03427	49626	69445	18663	72695	52180	20847	12234	90511	33703	90322
13	09429	93969	52636	92737	88974	33488	36320	17617	30015	08272	84115	27156	30613	74952
14	10365	61129	87529	85689	48237	52267	67689	93394	01511	26358	85104	20285	29975	89868
15	07119	97336	71048	08178	77233	13916	47564	81056	97735	85977	29372	74461	28551	90707
16	51085	12765	51821	51259	77452	16308	60756	92144	49442	53900	70960	63990	75601	40719
17	02368	21382	52404	60268	89368	19885	55322	44819	01188	65255	64835	44919	05944	55157
18	01011	54092	33362	94904	31273	04146	18594	29852	71685	85030	51132	01915	92747	64951
19	52162	53916	46369	58586	23216	14513	83149	98736	23495	64350	94738	17752	35156	35749
20	07056	97628	33787	09998	42698	06691	76988	13602	51851	46104	88916	19509	25625	58104
21	48663	91245	85828	14346	09172	30163	90229	04734	59193	22178	30421	61666	99904	32812
22	54164	58492	22421	74103	47070	25306	76468	26384	58151	06646	21524	15227	96909	44592
23	32639	32363	05597	24200	13363	38005	94342	28728	35806	06912	17012	64161	18296	22851
24	29334	27001	87637	87308	58731	00256	45834	15398	46557	41135	10307	07684	36188	18510
25	02488	33062	28834	07351	19731	92420	60952	61280	50001	67658	32586	86679	50720	94953
26	81525	72295	04839	96423	24878	82651	66566	14778	76797	14780	13300	87074	79666	95725
27	29676	20591	68086	26432	46901	20849	89768	81536	86645	12659	92259	57102	80428	25280
28	00742	57392	39064	66432	84673	40027	32832	61362	98947	96067	64760	64584	96096	98253
29	05366	04213	25669	26422	44407	44048	37937	63904	45766	66134	75470	66520	34693	90449
30	91921	26418	64117	94305	26766	25940	39972	22209	71500	64568	91402	42416	07844	69618
31	00582	04711	87917	77341	42206	35126	74087	99547	81817	42607	43808	76655	62028	76630
32	00725	69884	62797	56170	86324	88072	76222	36086	84637	93161	76038	65855	77919	88006
33	69011	65795	95876	55293	18988	27354	26575	08625	40801	59920	29841	80150	12777	48501
34	25976	57948	29888	88604	67917	48708	18912	82271	65424	69774	33611	54262	85963	03547
35	09763	83473	73577	12908	30883	18317	28290	35797	05998	41688	34952	37888	38917	88050
36	91567	42595	27958	30134	04024	86385	29880	99730	55536	84855	29088	09250	79656	73211
37	17955	56349	90999	49127	20044	59931	06115	20542	18059	02008	73708	83517	36103	42791
38	46503	18584	18845	49618	02304	51038	20655	58727	28168	15475	56942	53389	20562	87338
39	92157	89634	94824	78171	84610	82834	09922	25417	44137	48413	25555	21246	35509	20468
40	14577	62765	35605	81263	39667	47358	56873	56307	61607	49518	89656	20103	77490	18062
41	98427	07523	33362	64270	01638	92477	66969	98420	04880	45585	46565	04102	16880	45709
42	34914	63976	88720	82765	34476	17032	87589	40836	32427	70002	70663	88863	77775	69348
43	70060	28277	39475	46473	23219	53416	94970	25832	69975	94884	19661	72828	00102	66794

TABLE 1   *(concluded)*

44	53976	54914	06990	67245	68350	82948	11398	42878	80287	88267	47363	46634	06541	97809
45	76072	29515	40980	07391	58745	25774	22987	80059	39911	96189	41151	14222	60697	59583
46	90725	52210	83974	29992	65831	38857	50490	83765	55657	14361	31720	57375	56228	41546
47	64364	67412	33339	31926	14883	24413	59744	92351	97473	89286	35931	04110	23726	51900
48	08962	00358	31662	25388	61642	34072	81249	35648	56891	69352	48373	45578	78547	81788
49	95012	68379	93526	70765	10592	04542	76463	54328	02349	17247	28865	14777	62730	92277
50	15664	10493	20492	38301	91132	21999	59516	81652	27195	48223	46751	22923	32261	85653
51	16408	81899	04153	53381	79401	21438	83035	92350	36693	31238	59649	91754	72772	02338
52	18629	81953	05520	91962	04739	13092	97662	24822	94730	06496	35090	04822	86774	98289
53	73115	35101	47498	87637	99016	71060	88824	71013	18735	20286	23153	72924	35165	43040
54	57491	16703	23167	49323	45021	33132	12544	41035	80780	45393	44812	12515	98931	91202
55	30405	83946	23792	14422	15059	45799	22716	19792	09983	74353	68668	30429	70735	25499
56	16631	35006	85900	98275	32388	52390	16815	69293	82732	38480	73817	32523	41961	44437
57	96773	20206	42559	78985	05300	22164	24369	54224	35083	19687	11052	91491	60383	19746
58	38935	64202	14349	82674	66523	44133	00697	35552	35970	19124	63318	29686	03387	59846
59	31624	76384	17403	53363	44167	64486	64758	75366	76554	31601	12614	33072	60332	92325
60	78919	19474	23632	27889	47914	02584	37680	20801	72152	39339	34806	08930	85001	87820
61	03931	33309	57047	74211	63445	17361	62825	39908	05607	91284	68833	25570	38818	46920
62	74426	33278	43972	10119	89917	15665	52872	73823	73144	88662	88970	74492	51805	99378
63	09066	00903	20795	95452	92648	45454	69552	88815	16553	51125	79375	97596	16296	66092
64	42238	12426	87025	14267	20979	04508	64535	31355	86064	29472	47689	05974	52468	16834
65	16153	08002	26504	41744	81959	65642	74240	56302	00033	67107	77510	70625	28725	34191
66	21457	40742	29820	96783	29400	21840	15035	34537	33310	06116	95240	15957	16572	06004
67	21581	57802	02050	89728	17937	37621	47075	42080	97403	48626	68995	43805	33386	21597
68	55612	78095	83197	33732	05810	24813	86902	60397	16489	03264	88525	42786	05269	92532
69	44657	66999	99324	51281	84463	60563	79312	93454	68876	25471	93911	25650	12682	73572
70	91340	84979	46949	81973	37949	61023	43997	15263	80644	43942	89203	71795	99533	50501
71	91227	21199	31935	27022	84067	05462	35216	14486	29891	68607	41867	14951	91696	85065
72	50001	38140	66321	19924	72163	09538	12151	06878	91903	18749	34405	56087	82790	70925
73	65390	05224	72958	28609	81406	39147	25549	48542	42627	45233	57202	94617	23772	07896
74	27504	96131	83944	41575	10573	03619	64482	73923	36152	05184	94142	25299	84387	34925
75	37169	94851	39117	89632	00959	16487	65536	49071	39782	17095	02330	74301	00275	48280
76	11508	70225	51111	38351	19444	66499	71945	05422	13442	78675	84031	66938	93654	59894
77	37449	30362	06694	54690	04052	53115	62757	95348	78662	11163	81651	50245	34971	52924
78	46515	70331	85922	38329	57015	15765	97161	17869	45349	61796	66345	81073	49106	79860
79	30986	81223	42416	58353	21532	30502	32305	86482	05174	07901	54339	58861	74818	46942
80	63798	64995	46583	09785	44160	78128	83991	42865	92520	83531	80377	35909	81250	54238
81	82486	84846	99254	67632	43218	50076	21361	64816	51202	88124	41870	52689	51275	83556
82	21885	32906	92431	09060	64297	51674	64126	62570	26123	05155	59194	52799	28225	85762
83	60336	98782	07408	53458	13564	59089	26445	29789	85205	41001	12535	12133	14645	23541
84	43937	46891	24010	25560	86355	33941	25786	54990	71899	15475	95434	98227	21824	19535
85	97656	63175	89303	16275	07100	92063	21942	18611	47348	20203	18534	03862	78095	50136
86	03299	01221	05418	38982	55758	92237	26759	86367	21216	98442	08303	56613	91511	75928
87	79626	06486	03574	17668	07785	76020	79924	25651	83325	88428	85076	72811	22717	50585
88	85636	68335	47539	03129	65651	11977	02510	26113	99447	68645	34327	15152	55230	93448
89	18039	14367	61337	06177	12143	46609	32989	74014	64708	00533	35398	58408	13261	47908
90	08362	15656	60627	36478	65648	16764	53412	09013	07832	41574	17639	82163	60859	75567
91	79556	29068	04142	16268	15387	12856	66227	38358	22478	73373	88732	09443	82558	05250
92	92608	82674	27072	32534	17075	27698	98204	63863	11951	34648	88022	56148	34925	57031
93	23982	25835	40055	67006	12293	02753	14827	23235	35071	99704	37543	11601	35503	85171
94	09915	96306	05908	97901	28395	14186	00821	80703	70426	75647	76310	88717	37890	40129
95	59037	33300	26695	62247	69927	76123	50842	43834	86654	70959	79725	93872	28117	19233
96	42488	78077	69882	61657	34136	79180	97526	43092	04098	73571	80799	76536	71255	64239
97	46764	86273	63003	93017	31204	36692	40202	35275	57306	55543	53203	18098	47625	88684
98	03237	45430	55417	63282	90816	17349	88298	90183	36600	78406	06216	95787	42579	90730
99	86591	81482	52667	61582	14972	90053	89534	76036	49199	43716	97548	04379	46370	28672
100	38534	01715	94964	87288	65680	43772	39560	12918	80537	62738	19636	51132	25739	56947

Source: Abridged from *Handbook of Tables for Probability and Statistics*, second edition, edited by William H. Beyer (Cleveland: The Chemical Rubber Company, 1968). Reproduced by permission of the publishers, The Chemical Rubber Company.

TABLE 2   Cumulative Standard Unit Normal Distribution

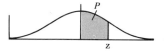

Values of P corresponding to Z for the normal curve. Z is the standard variable. The value of P for $-Z$ equals one minus the value of P for $+Z$, e.g., the P for -1.62 equals $1 - .9474 = .0526$.

Z	.00	.01	.02	.03	.04	.05	.06	.07	.08	.09
0	.5000	.5040	.5080	.5120	.5160	.5199	.5239	.5279	.5319	.5359
.1	.5398	.5438	.5478	.5517	.5557	.5596	.5636	.5675	.5714	.5753
.2	.5793	.5832	.5871	.5910	.5948	.5987	.6026	.6064	.6103	.6141
.3	.6179	.6217	.6255	.6293	.6331	.6368	.6406	.6443	.6480	.6517
.4	.6554	.6591	.6628	.6664	.6700	.6736	.6772	.6808	.6844	.6879
.5	.6915	.6950	.6985	.7019	.7054	.7088	.7123	.7157	.7190	.7224
.6	.7257	.7291	.7324	.7357	.7389	.7422	.7454	.7486	.7517	.7549
.7	.7580	.7611	.7642	.7673	.7704	.7734	.7764	.7794	.7823	.7852
.8	.7881	.7910	.7939	.7967	.7995	.8023	.8051	.8078	.8106	.8133
.9	.8159	.8186	.8212	.8238	.8264	.8289	.8315	.8340	.8365	.8389
1.0	.8413	.8438	.8461	.8485	.8508	.8531	.8554	.8577	.8599	.8621
1.1	.8643	.8665	.8686	.8708	.8729	.8749	.8770	.8790	.8810	.8830
1.2	.8849	.8869	.8888	.8907	.8925	.8944	.8962	.8980	.8997	.9015
1.3	.9032	.9049	.9066	.9082	.9099	.9115	.9131	.9147	.9162	.9177
1.4	.9192	.9207	.9222	.9236	.9251	.9265	.9279	.9292	.9306	.9319
1.5	.9332	.9345	.9357	.9370	.9382	.9394	.9406	.9418	.9429	.9441
1.6	.9452	.9463	.9474	.9484	.9495	.9505	.9515	.9525	.9535	.9545
1.7	.9554	.9564	.9573	.9582	.9591	.9599	.9608	.9616	.9625	.9633
1.8	.9641	.9649	.9656	.9664	.9671	.9678	.9686	.9693	.9699	.9706
1.9	.9713	.9719	.9726	.9732	.9738	.9744	.9750	.9756	.9761	.9767
2.0	.9772	.9778	.9783	.9788	.9793	.9798	.9803	.9808	.9812	.9817
2.1	.9821	.9826	.9830	.9834	.9838	.9842	.9846	.9850	.9854	.9857
2.2	.9861	.9864	.9868	.9871	.9875	.9878	.9881	.9884	.9887	.9890
2.3	.9893	.9896	.9898	.9901	.9904	.9906	.9909	.9911	.9913	.9916
2.4	.9918	.9920	.9922	.9925	.9927	.9929	.9931	.9932	.9934	.9936
2.5	.9938	.9940	.9941	.9943	.9945	.9946	.9948	.9949	.9951	.9952
2.6	.9953	.9955	.9956	.9957	.9959	.9960	.9961	.9962	.9963	.9964
2.7	.9965	.9966	.9967	.9968	.9969	.9970	.9971	.9972	.9973	.9974
2.8	.9974	.9975	.9976	.9977	.9977	.9978	.9979	.9979	.9980	.9981
2.9	.9981	.9982	.9982	.9983	.9984	.9984	.9985	.9985	.9986	.9986
3.0	.9987	.9987	.9987	.9988	.9988	.9989	.9989	.9989	.9990	.9990
3.1	.9990	.9991	.9991	.9991	.9992	.9992	.9992	.9992	.9993	.9993
3.2	.9993	.9993	.9994	.9994	.9994	.9994	.9994	.9995	.9995	.9995
3.3	.9995	.9995	.9995	.9996	.9996	.9996	.9996	.9996	.9996	.9997
3.4	.9997	.9997	.9997	.9997	.9997	.9997	.9997	.9997	.9997	.9998

Source: Taken with permission from Paul E. Green: *Analyzing Multivariate Data* (Hinsdale, Illinois: The Dryden Press, 1978).

TABLE 3   Upper Percentiles of the *t* Distribution

v^*	.75	.90	.95	$1 - \alpha$ .975	.99	.995	.9995
1	1.000	3.078	6.314	12.706	31.821	63.657	636.619
2	.816	1.886	2.920	4.303	6.965	9.925	31.598
3	.765	1.638	2.353	3.182	4.541	5.841	12.941
4	.741	1.533	2.132	2.776	3.747	4.604	8.610
5	.727	1.476	2.015	2.571	3.365	4.032	6.859
6	.718	1.440	1.943	2.447	3.143	3.707	5.959
7	.711	1.415	1.895	2.365	2.998	3.499	5.405
8	.706	1.397	1.860	2.306	2.896	3.355	5.041
9	.703	1.383	1.833	2.262	2.821	3.250	4.781
10	.700	1.372	1.812	2.228	2.764	3.169	4.587
11	.697	1.363	1.796	2.201	2.718	3.106	4.437
12	.695	1.356	1.782	2.179	2.681	3.055	4.318
13	.694	1.350	1.771	2.160	2.650	3.012	4.221
14	.692	1.345	1.761	2.145	2.624	2.977	4.140
15	.691	1.341	1.753	2.131	2.602	2.947	4.073
16	.690	1.337	1.746	2.120	2.583	2.921	4.015
17	.689	1.333	1.740	2.110	2.567	2.898	3.965
18	.688	1.330	1.734	2.101	2.552	2.878	3.922
19	.688	1.328	1.729	2.093	2.339	2.861	3.883
20	.687	1.325	1.725	2.086	2.528	2.845	3.850
21	.686	1.323	1.721	2.080	2.518	2.831	3.819
22	.686	1.321	1.717	2.074	2.508	2.819	3.792
23	.685	1.319	1.714	2.069	2.500	2.807	3.767
24	.685	1.318	1.711	2.064	2.492	2.797	3.745
25	.684	1.316	1.708	2.060	2.485	2.787	3.725
26	.684	1.315	1.706	2.056	2.479	2.779	3.707
27	.684	1.314	1.703	2.052	2.473	2.771	3.690
28	.683	1.313	1.701	2.048	2.467	2.763	3.674
29	.683	1.311	1.699	2.045	2.462	2.756	3.659
30	.683	1.310	1.697	2.042	2.457	2.750	3.646
40	.681	1.303	1.684	2.021	2.423	2.704	3.551
60	.679	1.296	1.671	2.000	2.390	2.660	3.460
120	.677	1.289	1.658	1.980	2.358	2.617	3.373
∞	.674	1.282	1.645	1.960	2.326	2.576	3.291

*v = Degrees of freedom.

Source: Taken with permission from Table III of R. A. Fisher and F. Yates: *Statistical Tables for Biological, Agricultural, and Medical Research*, published by Oliver & Boyd Ltd., Edinburgh, 1963.

TABLE 4   Selected Percentiles of the χ^2 Distribution

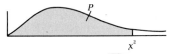

v^*	$\chi^2_{.005}$	$\chi^2_{.01}$	$\chi^2_{.025}$	$\chi^2_{.05}$	$\chi^2_{.10}$	$\chi^2_{.90}$	$\chi^2_{.95}$	$\chi^2_{.975}$	$\chi^2_{.99}$	$\chi^2_{.995}$
1	.000039	.00016	.00098	.0039	.0158	2.71	3.84	5.02	6.63	7.88
2	.0100	.0201	.0506	.1026	.2107	4.61	5.99	7.38	9.21	10.60
3	.0717	.115	.216	.352	.584	6.25	7.81	9.35	11.34	12.84
4	.207	.297	.484	.711	1.064	7.78	9.49	11.14	13.28	14.86
5	.412	.554	.831	1.15	1.61	9.24	11.07	12.83	15.09	16.75
6	.676	.872	1.24	1.64	2.20	10.64	12.59	14.45	16.81	18.55
7	.989	1.24	1.69	2.17	2.83	12.02	14.07	16.01	18.48	20.28
8	1.34	1.65	2.18	2.73	3.49	13.36	15.51	17.53	20.09	21.96
9	1.73	2.09	2.70	3.33	4.17	14.68	16.92	19.02	21.67	23.59
10	2.16	2.56	3.25	3.94	4.87	15.99	18.31	20.48	23.21	25.19
11	2.60	3.05	3.82	4.57	5.58	17.28	19.68	21.92	24.73	26.76
12	3.07	3.57	4.40	5.23	6.30	18.55	21.03	23.34	26.22	28.30
13	3.57	4.11	5.01	5.89	7.04	19.81	22.36	24.74	27.69	29.82
14	4.07	4.66	5.63	6.57	7.79	21.06	23.68	26.12	29.14	31.32
15	4.60	5.23	6.26	7.26	8.55	22.31	25.00	27.49	30.58	32.80
16	5.14	5.81	6.91	7.96	9.31	23.54	26.30	28.85	32.00	34.27
18	6.26	7.01	8.23	9.39	10.86	25.99	28.87	31.53	34.81	37.16
20	7.43	8.26	9.59	10.85	12.44	28.41	31.41	34.17	37.57	40.00
24	9.89	10.86	12.40	13.85	15.66	33.20	36.42	39.36	42.98	45.56
30	13.79	14.95	16.79	18.49	20.60	40.26	43.77	46.98	50.89	53.67
40	20.71	22.16	24.43	26.51	29.05	51.81	55.76	59.34	63.69	66.77
60	35.53	37.48	40.48	43.19	46.46	74.40	79.08	83.30	88.38	91.95
120	83.85	86.92	91.58	95.70	100.62	140.23	146.57	152.21	158.95	163.64

*v = Degrees of freedom.

Source: Adapted with permission from *Introduction to Statistical Analysis*, 2nd ed., by W. J. Dixon and F. J. Massey, Jr., McGraw-Hill Book Company, Inc., 1957.

TABLE 5   Selected Percentiles of the F Distribution

$F_{.90(v_1, v_2)}$ $\alpha = 0.1$

v_1^* / v_2^{**}	1	2	3	4	5	6	7	8	9	10	12	15	20	24	30	40	60	120	∞
1	39.86	49.50	53.59	55.83	57.24	58.20	58.91	59.44	59.86	60.19	60.71	61.22	61.74	62.00	62.26	62.53	62.79	63.06	63.33
2	8.53	9.00	9.16	9.24	9.29	9.33	9.35	9.37	9.38	9.39	9.41	9.42	9.44	9.45	9.46	9.47	9.47	9.48	9.49
3	5.54	5.46	5.39	5.34	5.31	5.28	5.27	5.25	5.24	5.23	5.22	5.20	5.18	5.18	5.17	5.16	5.15	5.14	5.13
4	4.54	4.32	4.19	4.11	4.05	4.01	3.98	3.95	3.94	3.92	3.90	3.87	3.84	3.83	3.82	3.80	3.79	3.78	3.76
5	4.06	3.78	3.62	3.52	3.45	3.40	3.37	3.34	3.32	3.30	3.27	3.24	3.21	3.19	3.17	3.16	3.14	3.12	3.10
6	3.78	3.46	3.29	3.18	3.11	3.05	3.01	2.98	2.96	2.94	2.90	2.87	2.84	2.82	2.80	2.78	2.76	2.74	2.72
7	3.59	3.26	3.07	2.96	2.88	2.83	2.78	2.75	2.72	2.70	2.67	2.63	2.59	2.58	2.56	2.54	2.51	2.49	2.47
8	3.46	3.11	2.92	2.81	2.73	2.67	2.62	2.59	2.56	2.50	2.50	2.46	2.42	2.40	2.38	2.36	2.34	2.32	2.29
9	3.36	3.01	2.81	2.69	2.61	2.55	2.51	2.47	2.44	2.42	2.38	2.34	2.30	2.28	2.25	2.23	2.21	2.18	2.16
10	3.29	2.92	2.73	2.61	2.52	2.46	2.41	2.38	2.35	2.32	2.28	2.24	2.20	2.18	2.16	2.13	2.11	2.08	2.06
11	3.23	2.86	2.66	2.54	2.45	2.39	2.34	2.30	2.27	2.25	2.21	2.17	2.12	2.10	2.08	2.05	2.03	2.00	1.97
12	3.18	2.81	2.61	2.48	2.39	2.33	2.28	2.24	2.21	2.19	2.15	2.10	2.06	2.04	2.01	1.99	1.96	1.93	1.90
13	3.14	2.76	2.56	2.43	2.35	2.28	2.23	2.20	2.16	2.14	2.10	2.05	2.01	1.98	1.96	1.93	1.90	1.88	1.85
14	3.10	2.73	2.52	2.39	2.31	2.24	2.19	2.15	2.12	2.10	2.05	2.01	1.96	1.94	1.91	1.89	1.86	1.83	1.80
15	3.07	2.70	2.49	2.36	2.27	2.21	2.16	2.12	2.09	2.06	2.02	1.97	1.92	1.90	1.87	1.85	1.82	1.79	1.76
16	3.05	2.67	2.46	2.33	2.24	2.18	2.13	2.09	2.06	2.03	1.99	1.94	1.89	1.87	1.84	1.81	1.78	1.75	1.72
17	3.03	2.64	2.44	2.31	2.22	2.15	2.10	2.06	2.03	2.00	1.96	1.91	1.86	1.84	1.81	1.78	1.75	1.72	1.69
18	3.01	2.62	2.42	2.29	2.20	2.13	2.08	2.04	2.00	1.98	1.93	1.89	1.84	1.81	1.78	1.75	1.72	1.69	1.66
19	2.99	2.61	2.40	2.27	2.18	2.11	2.06	2.02	1.98	1.96	1.91	1.86	1.81	1.79	1.76	1.73	1.70	1.67	1.63
20	2.97	2.59	2.38	2.25	2.16	2.09	2.04	2.00	1.96	1.94	1.89	1.84	1.79	1.77	1.74	1.71	1.68	1.64	1.61
21	2.96	2.57	2.36	2.23	2.14	2.08	2.02	1.98	1.95	1.92	1.87	1.83	1.78	1.75	1.72	1.69	1.66	1.62	1.59
22	2.95	2.56	2.35	2.22	2.13	2.06	2.01	1.97	1.93	1.90	1.86	1.81	1.76	1.73	1.70	1.67	1.64	1.60	1.57
23	2.94	2.55	2.34	2.21	2.11	2.05	1.99	1.95	1.92	1.89	1.84	1.80	1.74	1.72	1.69	1.66	1.62	1.59	1.55
24	2.93	2.54	2.33	2.19	2.10	2.04	1.98	1.94	1.91	1.88	1.83	1.78	1.73	1.70	1.67	1.64	1.61	1.57	1.53
25	2.92	2.53	2.32	2.18	2.09	2.02	1.97	1.93	1.89	1.87	1.82	1.77	1.72	1.69	1.66	1.63	1.59	1.56	1.52
26	2.91	2.52	2.31	2.17	2.08	2.01	1.96	1.92	1.88	1.86	1.81	1.76	1.71	1.68	1.65	1.61	1.58	1.54	1.50
27	2.90	2.51	2.30	2.17	2.07	2.00	1.95	1.91	1.87	1.85	1.80	1.75	1.70	1.67	1.64	1.60	1.57	1.53	1.49
28	2.89	2.50	2.29	2.16	2.06	2.00	1.94	1.90	1.87	1.84	1.79	1.74	1.69	1.66	1.63	1.59	1.56	1.52	1.48
29	2.89	2.50	2.28	2.15	2.06	1.99	1.93	1.89	1.86	1.83	1.78	1.73	1.68	1.65	1.62	1.58	1.55	1.51	1.47
30	2.88	2.49	2.28	2.14	2.05	1.98	1.93	1.88	1.85	1.82	1.77	1.72	1.67	1.64	1.61	1.57	1.54	1.50	1.46
40	2.84	2.44	2.23	2.09	2.00	1.93	1.87	1.83	1.79	1.76	1.71	1.66	1.61	1.57	1.54	1.51	1.47	1.42	1.38
60	2.79	2.39	2.18	2.04	1.95	1.87	1.82	1.77	1.74	1.71	1.66	1.60	1.54	1.51	1.48	1.44	1.40	1.35	1.29
120	2.75	2.35	2.13	1.99	1.90	1.82	1.77	1.72	1.68	1.65	1.60	1.55	1.48	1.45	1.41	1.37	1.32	1.26	1.19
∞	2.71	2.30	2.08	1.94	1.85	1.77	1.72	1.67	1.63	1.60	1.55	1.49	1.42	1.38	1.34	1.30	1.24	1.17	1.00

$F_{.95(v_1, v_2)}$ $\alpha = 0.05$

v_2 \\ v_1	1	2	3	4	5	6	7	8	9	10	12	15	20	24	30	40	60	120	∞
1	161.40	199.50	215.70	224.60	230.20	234.00	236.80	238.90	240.50	241.90	243.90	245.90	248.00	249.1	250.10	251.10	252.20	253.30	254.30
2	18.51	19.00	19.16	19.25	19.30	19.33	19.35	19.37	19.38	19.40	19.41	19.43	19.45	19.45	19.46	19.47	19.48	19.49	19.50
3	10.13	9.55	9.28	9.12	9.01	8.94	8.89	8.85	8.81	8.79	8.74	8.70	8.66	8.64	8.62	8.59	8.57	8.55	8.53
4	7.71	6.94	6.59	6.39	6.26	6.16	6.09	6.04	6.00	5.96	5.91	5.86	5.80	5.77	5.75	5.72	5.69	5.66	5.63
5	6.61	5.79	5.41	5.19	5.05	4.95	4.88	4.82	4.77	4.74	4.68	4.62	4.56	4.53	4.50	4.46	4.43	4.40	4.36
6	5.99	5.14	4.76	4.53	4.39	4.28	4.21	4.15	4.10	4.06	4.00	3.94	3.87	3.84	3.81	3.77	3.74	3.70	3.67
7	5.59	4.74	4.35	4.12	3.97	3.87	3.79	3.73	3.68	3.64	3.57	3.51	3.44	3.41	3.38	3.34	3.30	3.27	3.23
8	5.32	4.46	4.07	3.84	3.69	3.58	3.50	3.44	3.39	3.35	3.28	3.22	3.15	3.12	3.08	3.04	3.01	2.97	2.93
9	5.12	4.26	3.86	3.63	3.48	3.37	3.29	3.23	3.18	3.14	3.07	3.01	2.94	2.90	2.86	2.83	2.79	2.75	2.71
10	4.96	4.10	3.71	3.48	3.33	3.22	3.14	3.07	3.02	2.98	2.91	2.85	2.77	2.74	2.70	2.66	2.62	2.58	2.54
11	4.84	3.98	3.59	3.36	3.20	3.09	3.01	2.95	2.90	2.85	2.79	2.72	2.65	2.61	2.57	2.53	2.49	2.45	2.40
12	4.75	3.89	3.49	3.26	3.11	3.00	2.91	2.85	2.80	2.75	2.69	2.62	2.54	2.51	2.47	2.43	2.38	2.34	2.30
13	4.67	3.81	3.41	3.18	3.03	2.92	2.83	2.77	2.71	2.67	2.60	2.53	2.46	2.42	2.38	2.34	2.30	2.25	2.21
14	4.60	3.74	3.34	3.11	2.96	2.85	2.76	2.70	2.65	2.60	2.53	2.46	2.39	2.35	2.31	2.27	2.22	2.18	2.13
15	4.54	3.68	3.29	3.06	2.90	2.79	2.71	2.64	2.59	2.54	2.48	2.40	2.33	2.29	2.25	2.20	2.16	2.11	2.07
16	4.49	3.63	3.24	3.01	2.85	2.74	2.66	2.59	2.54	2.49	2.42	2.35	2.28	2.24	2.19	2.15	2.11	2.06	2.01
17	4.45	3.59	3.20	2.96	2.81	2.70	2.61	2.55	2.49	2.45	2.38	2.31	2.23	2.19	2.15	2.10	2.06	2.01	1.96
18	4.41	3.55	3.16	2.93	2.77	2.66	2.58	2.51	2.46	2.41	2.34	2.27	2.19	2.15	2.11	2.06	2.02	1.97	1.92
19	4.38	3.52	3.13	2.90	2.74	2.63	2.54	2.48	2.42	2.38	2.31	2.23	2.16	2.11	2.07	2.03	1.98	1.93	1.88
20	4.35	3.49	3.10	2.87	2.71	2.60	2.51	2.45	2.39	2.35	2.28	2.20	2.12	2.08	2.04	1.99	1.95	1.90	1.84
21	4.32	3.47	3.07	2.84	2.68	2.57	2.49	2.42	2.37	2.32	2.25	2.18	2.10	2.05	2.01	1.96	1.92	1.87	1.81
22	4.30	3.44	3.05	2.82	2.66	2.55	2.46	2.40	2.34	2.30	2.23	2.15	2.07	2.03	1.98	1.94	1.89	1.84	1.78
23	4.28	3.42	3.03	2.80	2.64	2.53	2.44	2.37	2.32	2.27	2.20	2.13	2.05	2.01	1.96	1.91	1.86	1.81	1.76
24	4.26	3.40	3.01	2.78	2.62	2.51	2.42	2.36	2.30	2.25	2.18	2.11	2.03	1.98	1.94	1.89	1.84	1.79	1.73
25	4.24	3.39	2.99	2.76	2.60	2.49	2.40	2.34	2.28	2.24	2.16	2.09	2.01	1.96	1.92	1.87	1.82	1.77	1.71
26	4.23	3.37	2.98	2.74	2.59	2.47	2.39	2.32	2.27	2.22	2.15	2.07	1.99	1.95	1.90	1.85	1.80	1.75	1.69
27	4.21	3.35	2.96	2.73	2.57	2.46	2.37	2.31	2.25	2.20	2.13	2.06	1.97	1.93	1.88	1.84	1.79	1.73	1.67
28	4.20	3.34	2.95	2.71	2.56	2.45	2.36	2.29	2.24	2.19	2.12	2.04	1.96	1.91	1.87	1.82	1.77	1.71	1.65
29	4.18	3.33	2.93	2.70	2.55	2.43	2.35	2.28	2.22	2.18	2.10	2.03	1.94	1.90	1.85	1.81	1.75	1.70	1.64
30	4.17	3.32	2.92	2.69	2.53	2.42	2.33	2.27	2.21	2.16	2.09	2.01	1.93	1.89	1.84	1.79	1.74	1.68	1.62
40	4.08	3.23	2.84	2.61	2.45	2.34	2.25	2.18	2.12	2.08	2.00	1.92	1.84	1.79	1.74	1.69	1.64	1.58	1.51
60	4.00	3.15	2.76	2.53	2.37	2.25	2.17	2.10	2.04	1.99	1.92	1.84	1.75	1.70	1.65	1.59	1.53	1.47	1.39
120	3.92	3.07	2.68	2.45	2.29	2.17	2.09	2.02	1.96	1.91	1.83	1.75	1.66	1.61	1.55	1.50	1.43	1.35	1.25
∞	3.84	3.00	2.60	2.37	2.21	2.10	2.01	1.94	1.88	1.83	1.75	1.67	1.57	1.52	1.46	1.39	1.32	1.22	1.00

*v_1 = Degrees of freedom for numerator. **v_2 = Degrees of freedom for denominator.

TABLE 5 (concluded)

$F_{.975(v_1, v_2)}$ $\alpha = 0.025$

v_2 \ v_1	1	2	3	4	5	6	7	8	9	10	12	15	20	24	30	40	60	120	∞
1	647.8	799.5	864.2	899.6	921.8	937.1	948.2	956.7	963.3	968.6	976.7	984.9	993.1	997.2	1001	1006	1010	1014	1018
2	38.51	39.00	39.17	39.25	39.30	39.33	39.36	39.37	39.39	39.40	39.41	39.43	39.45	39.46	39.46	39.47	39.48	39.49	39.50
3	17.44	16.04	15.44	15.10	14.88	14.73	14.62	14.54	14.47	14.42	14.34	14.25	14.17	14.12	14.08	14.04	13.99	13.95	13.90
4	12.22	10.65	9.98	9.60	9.36	9.20	9.07	8.98	8.90	8.84	8.75	8.66	8.56	8.51	8.46	8.41	8.36	8.31	8.26
5	10.01	8.43	7.76	7.39	7.15	6.98	6.85	6.76	6.68	6.62	6.52	6.43	6.33	6.28	6.23	6.18	6.12	6.07	6.02
6	8.81	7.26	6.60	6.23	5.99	5.82	5.70	5.60	5.52	5.46	5.37	5.27	5.17	5.12	5.07	5.01	4.96	4.90	4.85
7	8.07	6.54	5.89	5.52	5.29	5.12	4.99	4.90	4.82	4.76	4.67	4.57	4.47	4.42	4.36	4.31	4.25	4.20	4.14
8	7.57	6.06	5.42	5.05	4.82	4.65	4.53	4.43	4.36	4.30	4.20	4.10	4.00	3.95	3.89	3.84	3.78	3.73	3.67
9	7.21	5.71	5.08	4.72	4.48	4.32	4.20	4.10	4.03	3.96	3.87	3.77	3.67	3.61	3.56	3.51	3.45	3.39	3.33
10	6.94	5.46	4.83	4.47	4.24	4.07	3.95	3.85	3.78	3.72	3.62	3.52	3.42	3.37	3.31	3.26	3.20	3.14	3.08
11	6.72	5.26	4.63	4.28	4.04	3.88	3.76	3.66	3.59	3.53	3.43	3.33	3.23	3.17	3.12	3.06	3.00	2.94	2.88
12	6.55	5.10	4.47	4.12	3.89	3.73	3.61	3.51	3.44	3.37	3.28	3.18	3.07	3.02	2.96	2.91	2.85	2.79	2.72
13	6.41	4.97	4.35	4.00	3.77	3.60	3.48	3.39	3.31	3.25	3.15	3.05	2.95	2.89	2.84	2.78	2.72	2.66	2.60
14	6.30	4.86	4.24	3.89	3.66	3.50	3.38	3.29	3.21	3.15	3.05	2.95	2.84	2.79	2.73	2.67	2.61	2.55	2.49
15	6.20	4.77	4.15	3.80	3.58	3.41	3.29	3.20	3.12	3.06	2.96	2.86	2.76	2.70	2.64	2.59	2.52	2.46	2.40
16	6.12	4.69	4.08	3.73	3.50	3.34	3.22	3.12	3.05	2.99	2.89	2.79	2.68	2.63	2.57	2.51	2.45	2.38	2.32
17	6.04	4.62	4.01	3.66	3.44	3.28	3.16	3.06	2.98	2.92	2.82	2.72	2.62	2.56	2.50	2.44	2.38	2.32	2.25
18	5.98	4.56	3.95	3.61	3.38	3.22	3.10	3.01	2.93	2.87	2.77	2.67	2.56	2.50	2.44	2.38	2.32	2.26	2.19
19	5.92	4.51	3.90	3.56	3.33	3.17	3.05	2.96	2.88	2.82	2.72	2.62	2.51	2.45	2.39	2.33	2.27	2.20	2.13
20	5.87	4.46	3.86	3.51	3.29	3.13	3.01	2.91	2.84	2.77	2.68	2.57	2.46	2.41	2.35	2.29	2.22	2.16	2.09
21	5.83	4.42	3.82	3.48	3.25	3.09	2.97	2.87	2.80	2.73	2.64	2.53	2.42	2.37	2.31	2.25	2.18	2.11	2.04
22	5.79	4.38	3.78	3.44	3.22	3.05	2.93	2.84	2.76	2.70	2.60	2.50	2.39	2.33	2.27	2.21	2.14	2.08	2.00
23	5.75	4.35	3.75	3.41	3.18	3.02	2.90	2.81	2.73	2.67	2.57	2.47	2.36	2.30	2.24	2.18	2.11	2.04	1.97
24	5.72	4.32	3.72	3.38	3.15	2.99	2.87	2.78	2.70	2.64	2.54	2.44	2.33	2.27	2.21	2.15	2.08	2.01	1.94
25	5.69	4.29	3.69	3.35	3.13	2.97	2.85	2.75	2.68	2.61	2.51	2.41	2.30	2.24	2.18	2.12	2.05	1.98	1.91
26	5.66	4.27	3.67	3.33	3.10	2.94	2.82	2.73	2.65	2.59	2.49	2.39	2.28	2.22	2.16	2.09	2.03	1.95	1.88
27	5.63	4.24	3.65	3.31	3.08	2.92	2.80	2.71	2.63	2.57	2.47	2.36	2.25	2.19	2.13	2.07	2.00	1.93	1.85
28	5.61	4.22	3.63	3.29	3.06	2.90	2.78	2.69	2.61	2.55	2.45	2.34	2.23	2.17	2.11	2.05	1.98	1.91	1.83
29	5.59	4.20	3.61	3.27	3.04	2.88	2.76	2.67	2.59	2.53	2.43	2.32	2.21	2.15	2.09	2.03	1.96	1.89	1.81
30	5.57	4.18	3.59	3.25	3.03	2.87	2.75	2.65	2.57	2.51	2.41	2.31	2.20	2.14	2.07	2.01	1.94	1.87	1.79
40	5.42	4.05	3.46	3.13	2.90	2.74	2.62	2.53	2.45	2.39	2.29	2.18	2.07	2.01	1.94	1.88	1.80	1.72	1.64
60	5.29	3.93	3.34	3.01	2.79	2.63	2.51	2.41	2.33	2.27	2.17	2.06	1.94	1.88	1.82	1.74	1.67	1.58	1.48
120	5.15	3.80	3.23	2.89	2.67	2.52	2.39	2.30	2.22	2.16	2.05	1.94	1.82	1.76	1.69	1.61	1.53	1.43	1.31
∞	5.02	3.69	3.12	2.79	2.57	2.41	2.29	2.19	2.11	2.05	1.94	1.83	1.71	1.64	1.57	1.48	1.39	1.27	1.00

$F_{.99(v_1,v_2)}$ $\alpha = 0.01$

v_2 \\ v_1	1	2	3	4	5	6	7	8	9	10	12	15	20	24	30	40	60	120	∞
1	4052	4999.5	5403	5625	5764	5859	5928	5982	6022	6056	6106	6157	6209	6235	6261	6287	6313	6339	6366
2	98.50	99.00	99.17	99.25	99.30	99.33	99.36	99.37	99.39	99.40	99.42	99.43	99.45	99.46	99.47	99.47	99.48	99.49	99.50
3	34.12	30.82	29.46	28.71	28.24	27.91	27.67	27.49	27.35	27.23	27.05	26.87	26.69	26.60	26.50	26.41	26.32	26.22	26.13
4	21.20	18.00	16.69	15.98	15.52	15.21	14.98	14.80	14.66	14.55	14.37	14.20	14.02	13.93	13.84	13.75	13.65	13.56	13.46
5	16.26	13.27	12.06	11.39	10.97	10.67	10.46	10.29	10.16	10.05	9.89	9.72	9.55	9.47	9.38	9.29	9.20	9.11	9.02
6	13.75	10.92	9.78	9.15	8.75	8.47	8.26	8.10	7.98	7.87	7.72	7.56	7.40	7.31	7.23	7.14	7.06	6.97	6.88
7	12.25	9.55	8.45	7.85	7.46	7.19	6.99	6.84	6.72	6.62	6.47	6.31	6.16	6.07	5.99	5.91	5.82	5.74	5.65
8	11.26	8.65	7.59	7.01	6.63	6.37	6.18	6.03	5.91	5.81	5.67	5.52	5.36	5.28	5.20	5.12	5.03	4.95	4.86
9	10.56	8.02	6.99	6.42	6.06	5.80	5.61	5.47	5.35	5.26	5.11	4.96	4.81	4.73	4.65	4.57	4.48	4.40	4.31
10	10.04	7.56	6.55	5.99	5.64	5.39	5.20	5.06	4.94	4.85	4.71	4.56	4.41	4.33	4.25	4.17	4.08	4.00	3.91
11	9.65	7.21	6.22	5.67	5.32	5.07	4.89	4.74	4.63	4.54	4.40	4.25	4.10	4.02	3.94	3.86	3.78	3.69	3.60
12	9.33	6.93	5.95	5.41	5.06	4.82	4.64	4.50	4.39	4.30	4.16	4.01	3.86	3.78	3.70	3.62	3.54	3.45	3.36
13	9.07	6.70	5.74	5.21	4.86	4.62	4.44	4.30	4.19	4.10	3.96	3.82	3.66	3.59	3.51	3.43	3.34	3.25	3.17
14	8.86	6.51	5.56	5.04	4.69	4.46	4.28	4.14	4.03	3.94	3.80	3.66	3.51	3.43	3.35	3.27	3.18	3.09	3.00
15	8.68	6.36	5.42	4.89	4.56	4.32	4.14	4.00	3.89	3.80	3.67	3.52	3.37	3.29	3.21	3.13	3.05	2.96	2.87
16	8.53	6.23	5.29	4.77	4.44	4.20	4.03	3.89	3.78	3.69	3.55	3.41	3.26	3.18	3.10	3.02	2.93	2.84	2.75
17	8.40	6.11	5.18	4.67	4.34	4.10	3.93	3.79	3.68	3.59	3.46	3.31	3.16	3.08	3.00	2.92	2.83	2.75	2.65
18	8.29	6.01	5.09	4.58	4.25	4.01	3.84	3.71	3.60	3.51	3.37	3.23	3.08	3.00	2.92	2.84	2.75	2.66	2.57
19	8.18	5.93	5.01	4.50	4.17	3.94	3.77	3.63	3.52	3.43	3.30	3.15	3.00	2.92	2.84	2.76	2.67	2.58	2.49
20	8.10	5.85	4.94	4.43	4.10	3.87	3.70	3.56	3.46	3.37	3.23	3.09	2.94	2.86	2.78	2.69	2.61	2.52	2.42
21	8.02	5.78	4.87	4.37	4.04	3.81	3.64	3.51	3.40	3.31	3.17	3.03	2.88	2.80	2.72	2.64	2.55	2.46	2.36
22	7.95	5.72	4.82	4.31	3.99	3.76	3.59	3.45	3.35	3.26	3.12	2.98	2.83	2.75	2.67	2.58	2.50	2.40	2.31
23	7.88	5.66	4.76	4.26	3.94	3.71	3.54	3.41	3.30	3.21	3.07	2.93	2.78	2.70	2.62	2.54	2.45	2.35	2.26
24	7.82	5.61	4.72	4.22	3.90	3.67	3.50	3.36	3.26	3.17	3.03	2.89	2.74	2.66	2.58	2.49	2.40	2.31	2.21
25	7.77	5.57	4.68	4.18	3.85	3.63	3.46	3.32	3.22	3.13	2.99	2.85	2.70	2.62	2.54	2.45	2.36	2.27	2.17
26	7.72	5.53	4.64	4.14	3.82	3.59	3.42	3.29	3.18	3.09	2.96	2.81	2.66	2.58	2.50	2.42	2.33	2.23	2.13
27	7.68	5.49	4.60	4.11	3.78	3.56	3.39	3.26	3.15	3.06	2.93	2.78	2.63	2.55	2.47	2.38	2.29	2.20	2.10
28	7.64	5.45	4.57	4.07	3.75	3.53	3.36	3.23	3.12	3.03	2.90	2.75	2.60	2.52	2.44	2.35	2.26	2.17	2.06
29	7.60	5.42	4.54	4.04	3.73	3.50	3.33	3.20	3.09	3.00	2.87	2.73	2.57	2.49	2.41	2.33	2.23	2.14	2.03
30	7.56	5.39	4.51	4.02	3.70	3.47	3.30	3.17	3.07	2.98	2.84	2.70	2.55	2.47	2.39	2.30	2.21	2.11	2.01
40	7.31	5.18	4.31	3.83	3.51	3.29	3.12	2.99	2.89	2.80	2.66	2.52	2.37	2.29	2.20	2.11	2.02	1.92	1.80
60	7.08	4.98	4.13	3.65	3.34	3.12	2.95	2.82	2.72	2.63	2.50	2.35	2.20	2.12	2.03	1.94	1.84	1.73	1.60
120	6.85	4.79	3.95	3.48	3.17	2.96	2.79	2.66	2.56	2.47	2.34	2.19	2.03	1.95	1.86	1.76	1.66	1.53	1.38
∞	6.63	4.61	3.78	3.32	3.02	2.80	2.64	2.51	2.41	2.32	2.18	2.04	1.88	1.79	1.70	1.59	1.47	1.32	1.00

Source: Adapted with permission from *Biometrika Tables for Statisticians*, Vol. I, 2nd ed., edited by E. S. Pearson and H. O. Hartley, Cambridge University Press, 1958.

Glossary

a posteriori comparisons Techniques used to determine which of the means are statistically different once the null hypothesis is rejected.

a priori segmentation Studies in which the basis for segmentation, such as use, brand loyalty, and product purchase, is specified in advance of the segmentation analysis.

acquiescence bias Tendency to agree or disagree with all statements.

action standards A basis for defining the performance criterion that will be used in evaluating the results of a marketing research study.

actionable descriptor variables Information on the discriminating descriptors that can be used by management in developing the firm's marketing strategies.

adstock Effective weight of advertising, operating at the end of any particular time period.

affect A person's feelings toward an object. Feelings denote the person's overall evaluation (like/dislike, goodness/badness) of an object.

affect referral Model based on consumers forming holistic images of the various alternatives, and the consumer chooses the best alternative from the set of products/brands available. The consumer choice is driven by one's overall impression and little or no cognitive processing of attribute-based beliefs is required.

after-only design Experiment that exposes respondents to a single treatment condition followed by a post-exposure measurement.

after-only with control design Experiment where a control group is added to the standard after-only design to control for extraneous sources of bias.

aided questions Questions that provide clues that will potentially help the respondent recall more accurately.

aided recall Respondents are asked if they remember a commercial for the brand being tested.

alpha (α) level The likelihood of committing Type I error.

alternative buying incentive concept screening test Concept screening tests that focus on alternative end-benefit incentives for a single idea.

alternative form reliability Method of calculating reliability; the same subjects are measured at two different times, usually two weeks apart, with two scales designed to be similar in content but not so similar that the scores on the scale administered first affect the scores on the scale administered after two weeks have elapsed.

alternative hypothesis A competing hypothesis to the null.

analysis of covariance (ANCOVA) A means of statistical control where the effects of the confounding variable on the dependent variable are removed by a statistical adjustment of the dependent variable's mean value within each treatment condition.

analysis of variance (ANOVA) A way to test hypotheses of no differences among means for more than two independent samples. ANOVA is applicable whenever we have interval measurement on k independent groups.

The Arbitron County Coverage Report Report that measures audiences in every county in the continental United States.

Arbitron Information on Demand (AID) An interactive computer-based system that provides the basis for Arbitron custom reports for clients.

Arbitron Marketing Research A customized research service offered by Arbitron.

attitude A learned predisposition to respond in a consistently favorable or unfavorable manner with respect to a given object.

attitude shift ability The difference between the percentage of the program audience who selected the test brand before viewing the ad or commercial and the percentage who selected it after viewing.

audit A formal examination and verification of either how much of a product has sold at the store level (retail audit) or how much of a product has been withdrawn from warehouses and delivered to retailers (warehouse withdrawal audits).

automatic interaction detection algorithm Division of a total sample into mutually exclusive subgroups (segments) through a series of splits. Each split is determined by selecting a predictor variable and its categories that maximize the reduction in the unexplained variation in the dependent variable.

balanced scale Scale using an equal number of favorable and unfavorable categories.

banner The variables that span the columns of the cross tabulation; generally represents the subgroups being used in the analysis.

base level The level that awareness would fall to in the absence of advertising.

Bayesian decision analysis Process that bases the decision on how large a sample to draw on both the expected value of the information obtained by the sample and the cost of taking the sample.

before-after design Experiment where a measurement is taken from respondents before they receive the experimental treatment condition; the experimental treatment is then introduced, and post-treatment measurement is taken.

before-after with control design Experiment that adds a control group to the basic before-after design; the control group is never exposed to the experimental treatment.

behavioral intentions A person's intentions to perform a specific behavior with regard to an object.

between-group variation Between-group differences in scores for groups that were exposed to different treatments—represents "explained" variation.

bibliographic databases Computerized files that contain citations to journal articles, government documents, technical reports, market-research studies, newspaper articles, dissertations, patents, and so on.

blind guessing Using informed intuition to determine how many units to sample.

blind testing Tests where the brand name of the product is not disclosed during test.

bottom-up approach Process of building up clusters—at the beginning, each respondent belongs to his or her own segment, and then segments are joined together on the basis of their similarity.

box and whisker plots A graphic technique that provides information about central tendency, variability, and shape of distribution.

brand switching The probability of purchasing brand X, given that brand Y was purchased on the last purchase occasion.

branded testing Test where brand name of product is disclosed during test.

buying power index (BPI) A weighted index that converts three basic elements—population, effective buying income, and retail sales—into a measurement of a market's ability to buy; expressed as a percentage of U.S. potential.

cartoon completion test Projective technique that presents respondents with a cartoon of a particular situation and asks them to suggest the dialogue that one cartoon character might make in response to the comment(s) of another cartoon character.

case The unit of analysis for the study.

casewise deletion Strategy for missing responses where any case, respondent, is removed if any of his or her responses are identified as missing.

casuality Relationship where a change in one variable produces a change in another variable. One variable affects, influences, or determines some other variable.

cell matching Sample balancing procedure that involves adjusting each cell individually to match the corresponding population frequency.

census A complete enumeration of the prespecified group.

check-in procedure Initial step in data processing; involves a check of all questionnaires for completeness and interviewing quality and a count of usable questionnaires by required quota and/or use groups as per study design.

chi-square test statistic Measure of the goodness of fit between the numbers observed in the sample and the numbers we should have seen in the sample, given the null hypothesis is true.

classification variable Variable used to place each population element into a particular subpopulation.

cleaning A check of all internal consistencies, all possible codes, and all impossible punches.

cluster analysis Commonly used technique for allocating respondents to segments where respondents are clustered on the basis of benefit sought, need, or other relevant characteristics and where the number and type of segments are determined by the clustering technique that is used.

cluster profiles Profiling of each segment in terms of its distinctive features.

cluster sampling Design whereby a sample of clusters is first selected and then a decision on which sampling units to include in the sample is made.

clusters Groups or collections of sampling units.

code sheets Forms that give instructions to the coders about how each question will be handled.

coding Assignment of a numerical value (code) or alphanumerical symbol to represent a specific response to a specific question along with the column position that the designated code or symbol will occupy on a data record.

coefficient of determination (r^2) The ratio of explained to total variation.

coefficient of variation (C_y) A measure of relative dispersion given by dividing the population mean by its (true) standard deviation.

cognitions A person's knowledge, opinions, beliefs, and thoughts about the object.

company names Corporate names attached to the products they market.

comparative scaling (nonmetric scaling) Scaling process in which the subject is asked to compare a set of stimulus objects directly against one another.

comparison product tests Designs where a consumer rates products by directly comparing two or more products.

compensatory models Models based on weighting, either through an adding or averaging combinatorial rule, attribute-based information concerning the alternative product/brands under consideration such that the presence of one or more attributes can compensate for the absence of other attributes.

completely randomized factorial designs Generic name for class of designs where each level of a particular treatment is crossed with each level of another treatment.

compositional models Models that focus on the relationship between evaluative judgments and subjective attribute perceptions.

comprehension/believability Percentage of respondents in the program audience that correctly understood/believed product claims that were communicated by the test commercial.

computer-assisted telephone interviewing (CATI) Survey systems involving a computerized survey instrument. The survey questionnaire is entered into the memory of a large mainframe computer, into a small microprocessor, or even into a personal computer. The interviewer reads the questions from the CRT screen and records the respondent's answers directly into the computer memory banks by using the terminal keyboard or special touch- or light-sensitive screens.

concept An idea aimed at satisfying consumer wants and needs.

concept board Illustration and copy describing how the product works with its end benefits.

concept/construct Names given to characteristics that we wish to measure.

concept evaluation tests Concept tests for screening new-product ideas or alternative end benefits for a single product idea.

concept tests Collection of information on purchase intentions, likes/dislikes, and attribute ratings in order to measure the relative appeal of ideas or alternative

positioning and to provide direction for the development of the product and the product advertising.

concomitant variation The degree to which a variable (x) thought to be a cause covaries with a variable (y) thought to be an effect.

conditional rank-order scale Procedure that takes each object in turn as a standard for comparison. Each respondent is asked to rank the remaining objects in order of their similarity to this standard.

confidence interval Range into which the true population value of the characteristic being measured will fall, assuming a given level of certainty.

confirmatory analysis Approach that uses prior knowledge of the presumed relationships among a set of products or brands to infer what the structure should look like; also a method whereby we can restrict the parameters of the system so that they are consistent with the hypothesized structure.

confounds or confounding variables Extraneous causal factors (variables) that can possibly affect the dependent variable and, therefore, must be controlled.

conjoint analysis Decompositional approach in which respondents react to various products, brands, and concepts in terms of overall preference, where the various objects being evaluated reflect a predetermined combination of attributes in some systematic way.

connotative meaning The associations that the name implies, beyond its literal, explicit meaning; the imagery associated with a brand name.

constant sum scale Procedure whereby respondents are instructed to allocate a number of points or chips among alternatives according to some criterion—for example, preference, importance, and so on.

constitutive definition Specifications for the domain of the construct of interest so as to distinguish it from other similar but different constructs.

construct validity Determination of whether the independent and dependent variables in a study adequately represent the intended theoretical constructs.

content validity Indication of the representativeness of the content of a measurement scale; focuses on whether the scale items adequately cover the entire domain of the construct under study.

continuous rating scale (graphic rating scale) Procedure that instructs the respondent to assign a rating by placing a marker at the appropriate position on a line that best describes the object under study.

continuous tracking Studies in which measurements are taken during the entire length of a campaign.

control test market Method in which the entire test market project is handled by an outside research company.

controlled store testing   Audit in which the supplier takes over warehousing and distribution of test product as well as total control of test variables within the market under examination—in addition to the basic task of measuring product sales.

convenience sampling   Studies in which respondent participation is voluntary or that leaves the selection of sampling units primarily up to the interviewer.

convergent validity   Indication of the extent to which measurement scales designed to measure the same construct are related.

copy recall   Percentage of respondents in the program audience that correctly recalled copy elements in the test commercial.

copy testing   Generic term for advertising effectiveness studies.

covariation   A systematic relationship between the level of one variable and the level of some other variable.

CPM (cost-per-thousand)   Cost-efficiency calculation that represents a television program's ability to deliver the largest target audience at the smallest cost.

Cramer's contingency coefficient (V)   Measure of the degree of association between nominal variables, which is appropriate for any size contingency table.

created names   Names that do not have literal meaning with respect to the characteristics of a product; however, through advertising they may acquire indirect meaning that can reflect favorably on the product.

creation   Situation whereby a respondent recalls an event that did not actually occur.

criterion of internal consistency   An individual item satisfies the criterion of internal consistency if the item score significantly correlates with the attitude score.

criterion or dependent variable   The variable to be predicted.

criterion validity (predictive validity)   Indication of whether the measurement scale behaves as expected in relation to other constructs.

Cronbach's alpha   Mean reliability coefficient calculated from all possible split-half partitions of a measurement scale.

cross-price elasticity of demand   The percentage of change in demand for one product divided by the percentage change in price of the second product, assuming that all other factors affecting demand are constant.

cross-sectional surveys   Collection of informative data from a number of different respondents at a single point in time.

cross tabulation   Common method for describing frequency distributions of two variables simultaneously.

customized research services   Tailor-made, one-of-a-kind studies.

customer markets   The markets that the firm serves. They are made up of consumers who desire the same set of end benefits from the products they consume in specific usage contexts.

day-after recall (DAR)   Single-exposure on-air technique where the test commercial is aired in several test cities; the next day, a sample of respondents who say they viewed the program on which the test commercial was telecast are interviewed.

debriefing   Procedure of asking respondents to explain their answers, to state the meaning of each question, and to describe any problems they had with answering or completing the questionnaire.

decision calculus   A model-based set of procedures for processing data and managerial judgments designed to assist a manager in decision making.

decision sequence analysis   Process that uses protocols of consumer decision making that indicate the sequence in which various pieces of information (e.g., price or brand name) are employed to reach a final decision.

decompositional models   Models that use overall evaluative judgments instead of set criteria to make inferences about product/brand attributes that presumably were themselves used to form those overall evaluative judgments.

Delphi method   A method of forecasting based on asking a group of experts for their best estimate of a future event, then processing and feeding back some of the information obtained, and then repeating the process; on the last set of responses, the median usually is chosen as the best estimate for the group.

demand artifacts   Those aspects of the experiment that cause respondents to perceive, interpret, and act upon what is believed to be the expected or desired behavior.

dendogram   A tree-like structure that shows which clusters were joined or partitioned at each step.

denotative meaning   The literal, explicit meaning of a name.

dependent variable   The response measure under study in an experiment whose value is determined by the independent variable.

depth interview ("one-on-one")   Sessions in which free association and hidden sources of feelings are discussed, generally through a very loose, unstructured question guide, and administered by a highly skilled interviewer. It attempts to uncover underlying motivations, prejudice, attitudes toward sensitive issues, etc.

derived similarities   Similarity data constructed or derived from the respondent's ratings of each stimulus on a set of verbal descriptors. The respondent is presented with each object and asked to evaluate it on a number of adjectives.

derived substitutability   Form of judgmental data collection where respondents indicate the degree to which a set of products or brands are substitutes.

description   Collecting basic descriptive data on the company, competitors, customers, served markets, and other aspects of the external environment.

designer names   Names associated with leading figures of fashion design and lent to mass-marketed fashion and accessories.

diagnostic measures   Like/dislike and attribute ratings that help answer the question, "Why did it happen?"

diagnostics   Measures of believability and comprehension. Diagnostic testing also may include direct evaluation of the ad, perhaps on bipolar adjective scales.

diary panels   Samples of households that have agreed to provide specific information regularly over an extended period of time. Respondents in a diary panel are asked to record specific behaviors as they occur, as opposed to merely responding to a series of questions.

direct "cold" mail surveys   Surveys in which questionnaires are sent to a "cold" group of individuals who have not previously agreed to participate in the study.

direct or positive association   Relationship where, as the value of one variable increases (decreases), there is a tendency for the value of the other variable to increase (decrease).

direct similarities   The case where respondents are presented with object pairs and asked to judge their similarity.

directory-based sampling designs   Sample where telephone numbers are selected from the directory in some prescribed way.

directory databases   Computerized files composed of information about individuals, organizations, and services.

discriminant functions   Axes or dimensions that in some sense account for brand differences.

discriminant validity   Indication of extent to which the measurement scale is novel.

discrimination/difference designs   Tests where a respondent is asked if one product differs from others.

discussion guide   Agenda that establishes the plan of the focus group interview, including the topics to be covered and sometimes the time allocated to each topic.

disproportional or optimal allocation   Double weighting scheme where the number of sample elements taken from a given stratum is proportional to the relative size of the stratum and the standard deviation of the distribution of the characteristic under consideration among all elements in the stratum.

dollar metric scale (graded pair comparison)   Scale that extends the paired comparison method by asking respondents to indicate which brand is preferred and how much they are willing to pay to acquire their preferred brand.

double-barreled questions   Questions in which two opinions are joined together.

dummy magazine tests   A realistic looking format using a dummy magazine that systematically varies the advertisements in such a way that some families receive a dummy magazine containing the test ad and other (matched) families receive a dummy magazine containing no ads at all.

duo-trio designs   Test where a respondent is given a standard product and asked to determine which of two other products is most similar.

editing process   Review of the questionnaires for maximum accuracy and precision.

electronic scanner services   Services that record information on *actual* purchase behavior, as opposed to human reported behavior, through electronic optical checkout devices.

electronic test markets   Any market in which there is control over the input of alternative advertising.

emic instrument   An instrument constructed for investigating a construct in a specific culture.

empirical Hendry system   Method for investigating competitive structure where switching between competitive products is proportional to the product of market shares.

end benefits   What the product offers in terms of satisfying the consumer's wants and needs.

error component   Those factors that cause the person's observed scale score to differ from the person's true score.

estimation of effects   Method of handling nonresponse error by linking nonresponse rates to nonresponse effects; to estimate the effects of nonresponse, nonresponse size is linked to estimates of differences between respondents and nonrespondents.

ethnography   The systematic recording of human cultures.

etic instrument   An instrument that can be used in different cultures to provide direct comparisons of the same variable across nations.

evaluation Judging the success of what has been done or the likelihood of future success

evaluative measures Research findings that help answer the question, "What happened?"

experimental design Research concept where the researcher has direct control over at least one independent variable and manipulates at least one independent variable.

experimental effect Impact of the treatment conditions on the dependent variable. Each treatment condition's effect indicates the influence of that condition on the dependent variable.

explanation An attempt to either describe the conditions under which an event varies or to identify its antecedents, causes, or effects so as to understand the event under study.

explicit descriptive names Names that are meant to describe the physical product.

exploratory analysis Type of analysis in which it is assumed that no prior knowledge of the structure of the market is known. In such cases, the data alone provide the basis for the structure that is uncovered.

extended-use product test In-home test where respondent is given opportunity to use the product over a period of weeks.

external secondary data Data available outside the organization from libraries and syndicated services.

external validity Determination of whether the research findings of a study (cause-and-effect relationships) can be generalized to and across populations of persons, settings, and times.

field experimental environments Natural settings; experiments undertaken in the environment in which the behavior under study would likely occur.

filter question A question that is asked to determine which branching question, if any, will be asked.

finite population correction factor (fpc) Correction for overestimation of the estimated variance (standard deviation) of a population parameter (such as a mean, or proportion) when the target sample represents 10 to 20 percent or more of the target population.

first-choice model Conjoint analysis model that assumes individuals always choose products for which they have greatest utility.

focus-group interview Interview in which the interviewer listens to a group of individuals, who belong to the appropriate target market, talk about an important marketing issue.

follow-ups Ways of contacting the respondent periodically after the initial contact.

foot-in-the door technique Method of reducing nonresponse involves first getting respondents to complete relatively short, simple questionnaire and then, at some later time, asking them to complete a larger questionnaire on the same general topic.

forced exposure tests Design whereby pre-and post-exposure purchase-preference questions are asked.

forced itemized rating scale Procedure in which a respondent indicates a response on a scale, even though he or she may have "no opinion" or "no knowledge" about the question.

frequency distribution The number of respondents who chose each alternative answer as well as the percentage and cumulative percentage of respondents who answer.

full-profile procedure Technique that simultaneously presents the respondent with a complete set of attribute descriptors. A stimulus card presents respondents with an attribute descriptor for each attribute included in the study; respondents are asked for an evaluation of the product alternative defined by the selected attribute descriptors appearing on the card.

full-service suppliers External parties that perform all aspects of a research project.

full-text databases Computerized files containing the complete text of the source documents that make up the database.

funnel sequence The procedure of asking the most general (or unrestricted) question about the topic under study first, followed by successively more restricted questions.

gap Difference between the operational population and the target population.

graduated buying power indexes Indexes that correlate product potential and buying power of households with low income, moderate income, or high income.

gross incidence Product-category use incidence for the entire population.

group centroids Mean ratings of each brand on each discriminant function.

headline test Design where the respondent is shown two or more headlines and is asked to indicate the one that is most interesting.

hierarchical clustering Techniques that allow successive fusion or divisions of the data. The allocation of an object to a segment is irrevocable.

hierarchical structure Partitioning of brands into several nested subsets.

history Threat to internal validity; refers to those specific events that occur simultaneously with the experiment, but that have not been controlled for.

home placement Test where the current issue of a magazine is given to the respondent one or two days before the issue is available to the general public; at call-back time the respondent is asked to indicate all of the ads that were in the issue and specific information on what each ad contains.

homoscedasticity In the population the variance of the variable being tested is the same in all samples.

hypothesis An assumption or guess the researcher or manager has about some characteristic of the population being sampled.

implicit imagery names Names that do not literally describe the product but implicitly and indirectly convey its characteristics.

imputation Approach that imputes nonresponses to specific questions on an entire questionnaire on the basis of a set of characteristics available for both respondents and nonrespondents.

imputed response Approach to missing responses where the respondent's answers to other questions asked are used to impute or deduce an appropriate response to the missing question.

independent consultants Individuals with unique and specialized marketing skills hired for research projects by the client or the research supplier.

independent samples The measurement of the variable of interest in one sample in no way affects the measurement of the variable in the other sample.

independent variable A factor in an experiment over which the experimenter has some control; if the experimenter manipulates its value, this is expected to have some effect on the dependent variable.

industry standards Those rules of thumb, developed from experience, that have become standard industry guidelines for determining how large a sample to draw.

instrumentation Threat to internal validity; refers to changes in the calibration of the measurement instrument or in the observers or scorers themselves.

interactive effects of selection bias Threat to external validity; situation where the improper selection of respondents interacts with experimental treatment conditions to produce misleading and unrepresentative results.

internal consistency reliability Method of calculating reliability; the item scores obtained from administering the scale are in some way split in half and the resulting half scores are correlated. Large correlations between split-halves indicate high internal consistency.

internal secondary data Data available within the organization—for example, accounting records, management decision support systems, and sales records.

internal validity Determination of whether the experimental manipulation actually produced the differences observed in the dependent variable.

interquartile range Difference between the 75th and 25th percentile.

interval data Measurements that allow us to tell how far apart two or more objects are with respect to the attribute and consequently to compare the difference between the numbers assigned. Because the interval data lack a natural or absolute origin, the absolute magnitude of the numbers cannot be compared.

inverse or negative association Relationship where, as the value of one variable increases (decreases), the value of the other variable decreases (increases).

inverted-funnel sequence Sequence inverted in the sense that the questioning begins with specific questions and concludes with the respondent answering the general question.

item analysis Procedure for checking scale items to ensure that Likert's criterion of internal consistency is satisfied.

item-to-item correlations A measure of internal consistency in which each item is correlated with the total score obtained from summing the entire set of items used in computing the attitude score.

itemized (closed-ended) questions Format in which the respondent is provided with numbers and/or predetermined descriptions and is asked to select the one that best describes his or her feelings.

itemized rating scale The respondent is provided with a scale having numbers and/or brief descriptions associated with each category and is asked to select one of the limited number of categories, ordered in terms of scale position, that best describes the object under study.

jamming Practice of reducing price, offering high-value coupons, and so on in order to disrupt a competitor's test market.

judgmental data Information generally based on perceptions or preference—may give better indications of future patterns of consumption.

judgmental sampling Studies in which respondents are selected because it is expected that they are representative of the population of interest and/or meet the specific needs of the research study.

jury of expert opinion A method of forecasting based on combining the views of key executives.

laboratory experimental environment Research environment constructed solely for the experiment. The experimenter has *direct control* over most, if not all, of the crucial factors that might possibly affect the experimental outcome.

latent theoretical construct   Construct that is not directly observable.

leaving them blank   Procedure whereby missing data are recorded as blanks.

legends   Explanations of specific elements in a figure.

Likert scales   Scaling technique where a large number of items that are statements of beliefs or intentions are generated. Each item is judged according to whether it reflects a favorable or unfavorable attitude toward the object in question. Respondents are then asked to rate the attitude object on each scale item in terms of a five-point category-labeled scale.

limited-service suppliers   External parties that specialize in only one or just a few aspects of a research project.

line marking   Similarity judgments recorded by making a mark on a 5-inch line anchored by the phrases "exactly the same" and "completely different."

line marking/continuous rating noncomparative scale   Procedure that instructs the respondent to assign a rating by placing a market at the appropriate position on a line that best describes the object under study. There is no explicit standard for comparison.

line names   Names assigned to a variety of specific products that the company markets.

loaded questions   Questions that suggest what the answer should be or indicate the researcher's position on the issue under study.

loadings   Weights that give the correlation of the attribute with respect to the dimension.

local field services   Outside party used by market research suppliers to collect interviews.

longitudinal design   Same respondents are questioned over time.

longitudinal surveys   Questioning of the same or different respondent at different points in time.

magnitude estimation   Scale in which respondents assign numbers to objects, brands, attitude statements, and the like so that ratios between the assigned numbers reflect ratios among the objects on the criterion being scaled.

mail diary services   General term for services involving a sample of respondents who have agreed to provide information such as media exposure and purchase behavior on a regular basis over an extended period of time.

mail surveys   Data-collection method that involves sending out a fairly structured questionnaire to a sample of respondents.

mall-intercept personal survey   Survey method using a central-location test facility at a shopping mall; respondents are intercepted while they are shopping.

manipulation   Setting the levels of an independent variable to test a specific cause-and-effect relationship.

marginal matching   Sample balancing procedure that involves matching the sample to control population or census on each of the variables separately.

mark-sensed questionnaire   Format that requires answers to be recorded with a special pencil in an area coded specifically for that answer and which can be read by a machine.

market penetration studies   Collection of information on such measures as awareness, trial, and past-30-day usage, where the objective is usually to track brand awareness, purchase, and usage levels.

market segment   Subgroups of consumers who respond to a given marketing-mix strategy in a similar manner.

market structure analysis   The process of organizing a set of products or brands in terms of the degree of substitutability or competitiveness.

market studies   Marketing research studies designed to provide information about the composition and structure of a product market.

market testing   Studies designed to assess the impact of a change in a marketing-mix element.

market tracking studies   Designed to determine where a firm stands vis-à-vis its competition by monitoring the marketplace and providing realistic performance benchmarks.

marketing decision support system (MDSS)   Computer-based procedures and methods that regularly generate, store, analyze, and disseminate relevant marketing information.

marketing research   The systematic gathering, recording, processing, and analyzing of marketing data, which—when interpreted—will help the marketing executive to uncover opportunities and to reduce risks in decision making.

marketing research suppliers   The primary data gatherers and analysts who executive studies and/or take ultimate responsibility for all technical aspects of a research project.

matched market test   Test involving test and control stores/areas that are matched on key factors.

matching   Involves matching respondents on one or several background characteristics or other factors before assigning them to treatment conditions.

maturation   Threat to internal validity; refers to changes in biology or psychology of the respondent that occur over time and can affect the dependent variable irrespective of the treatment conditions.

mean   The average value

mean response   Approach to missing responses that involves replacing a missing response with a constant—the mean, median, or mode response to the question, depending on the measurement scale used.

measurement   Process of assigning numbers to objects to represent quantities of attributes.

measurement/operational definitions   Specifications as to how unobservable constructs are related to their observable counterparts; that is, the procedure that provides a correspondence between the concept and the real world.

measurement levels   Measurements that can be distinguished according to the underlying assumptions regarding the correspondence of numbers assigned to the properties of objects and the meaningfulness of performing mathematical operations on the numbers.

median   Value halfway between the highest and lowest values.

mode   Most frequently occurring response.

monadic products tests   Designs where a consumer evaluates only one product, having no other product for comparison.

mortality   Threat to internal validity; refers to the differential loss (refusal to continue in the experiment) of respondents from the treatment condition groups.

multicollinearity   Correlation among independent variables. Multicollinearity causes problems in interpreting the individual regression coefficients because the values are affected by the amount of association between the independent variables themselves.

multidimensional scaling (MDS)   Scaling technique that attempts to uncover how consumers perceive the relationships among products or brands by identifying the relevant dimensions along which products or brands are compared. MDS is a mathematical tool that enables us to represent the proximities between objects spatially as in a map.

multiple ads/portfolio tests   Test in which respondent examines a portfolio of ads, one of which is the test ad.

multiple discriminant analysis (MDA)   Discriminant functions are linear combinations of the original attributes that best discriminate between the alternate brands.

multiple-exposure techniques   Technique where the test commercial is aired in a test city (or cities) over time; periodic on-air tests are conducted along with store audits of sales.

multiple-item formats   Attitude scaling techniques that ask the respondent to respond to several (usually many) items that are statements of beliefs, feelings, and/or intentions.

multiple regression model   Model that considers the general case of more than one independent variable.

mutual exclusivity   Condition in which the response choices to a question do not overlap with one another.

national market studies   Studies concerned with monitoring changes in the marketplace over time. The information collected includes category and basic-use patterns and customer demographic and psychographic data.

negative association   Relationship where high (low) values of one variable are associated with low (high) values of another variable.

net incidence   The factored-down gross incidence that includes all target population qualifications.

nets   Basic category headings.

new product concept screening test   Concept screening tests that focus on many new product ideas.

no or zero association   A situation in which there is no systematic relationship between the level of one variable and the level of another variable.

nominal data   Measurement in which the numbers assigned allow us to place an object in one and only one of a set of mutually exclusively and collectively exhaustive classes with no implied ordering.

noncomparative scaling (monadic scaling)   Scaling method whereby the respondent is asked to evaluate each object on a scale independently of the other objects being investigated.

nondirectory sampling designs   Telephone survey samples that do not make direct use of telephone directories. Instead, numbers are prescriptively added to working exchanges (also called prefixes).

nonequivalent before-after with control quasi design   Experimental design similar to the before-after with control design except not utilizing a random assignment rule. Respondents are first matched on one or a set of relevant background factors to produce two groups of matched pairs and then one group receives the experimental treatment.

nonexperimental designs/ex post facto   Research that entails no manipulation. The effect outcome is observed and then an attempt is made to find the "causal factor" that indicates why the effect occurred.

nonprobability samples   Form of sampling where there is no way of determining exactly what the chance is of selecting any particular element or sampling unit into the sample.

nonresponse error   Error that occurs because not all of the respondents included in the sample respond; in other words, with nonresponse, the mean true value (on the variable of interest) of these sample respondents who do respond may be different from the entire sample's true mean value (on the variable of interest).

nonsampling error Degree to which the mean observed value (on the variable of interest) for the respondents of a particular sample agree with the mean true value for the particular sample of respondents (on the variable of interest).

normal equations/ordinary least-squares Formulas that produce a regression line such that Σe^2_i is minimized.

NTI-NAD (Nielsen Television Index, National Audience Demographics) A report combining viewing and audience characteristics used to identify a program (or programs) that will potentially reach the most appropriate and largest target audience.

null hypothesis The hypothesis that is tested.

numeric databases Computerized files that contain original survey data such as time-series data.

observational methods Observation of behavior, directly or indirectly, by human or mechanical methods.

off-air tests Method for evaluating television commercials in which the testing takes place in a controlled environment that does not resemble the surroundings in which the individual usually views commercials.

omission Interviewing condition that occurs when a respondent cannot recall that an event has occurred.

on-air tests Testing that takes place in realistic settings; respondents are asked their reactions to commercials that they have seen in their own homes, on their own television sets.

one-sample proportion test Test of the hypothesis that a proportion is equal to some prespecified value.

one-tail hypothesis test Test used when the alternative hypothesis is directional—the entire region of rejection is in one tail of the distribution.

online vendors Intermediaries used to access databases rather than going directly to the database producer.

open-ended questions Questions that allow the respondent to choose any response deemed appropriate, within the limits implied by the question.

operational population The sampling frame that is used.

opportunity analysis Research to identify unfulfilled consumer wants and needs.

optical scanning Direct machine reading of numerical values or alphanumeric codes and transcription onto cards, magnetic tape, or disk.

order bias Condition whereby brands receive different ratings depending on whether they were shown first, second, third, etc.

ordinal data Measurements in which the response alternatives define an ordered sequence so that the choice listed first is less (greater) than the second, the second less (greater) than the third, and so forth. The numbers assigned do not reflect the magnitude of an attribute possessed by an object.

overall model test (*F*-test) Determination of whether the multiple correlation coefficient is statistically significant.

overregistration Condition that occurs when a sampling frame consists of sampling units in the target population plus additional units as well.

package testing A system for assessing the visibility of package alternatives, relative to one another and usually to a competitive brand, and the ability of package alternatives to convey product end-use benefits.

paired comparison designs Tests where a consumer directly compares two products.

paired comparison scale Scale that presents the respondent with two objects at a time and asks the respondent to select one of the two according to some criterion.

pairwise deletion Strategy for missing responses that involves using all of the available nonmissing data for each calculation.

partitioning clustering Techniques that form segments on the basis of minimizing (or maximizing) some criterion, e.g., within-segment to between-segment variation. Objects can be reallocated.

Pearson product moment correlation Measure of the linear association between interval or ratio-scaled variables.

perceptual product maps Spatial representations that show the relative positions of a set of products on a set of evaluative dimensions.

personal in-home survey Survey that involves asking questions of a sample of respondents face-to-face in their homes.

physical control An attempt to hold constant the value or level of the extraneous variable.

point-biserial correlation coefficient Coefficient that measures the association between a dichotomous variable and an interval-scale variable.

point-in-time tracking Studies in which measurements are taken at discrete points in time.

positioning A system for determining how to set the mix elements of product, price, promotion, and distribution so as to maximize appeal of a product to a particular target population.

positioning studies   Attempts to portray the interrelationships among a set of brands in terms of consumers' perceptions and preferences for these brands.

positive association   Relationship where high (low) values of one variable are associated with high (low) values of another variable.

post-hoc segmentation   Studies in which segments are defined after the fact on the basis of some sort of clustering of respondents on a set of relevant characteristics such as benefit sought, need, attitudes, and the like.

postcoding   Coding specifications designated after the questionnaires have been returned from the field.

power of the test $(1 - \beta)$ The probability of making a correct decision of rejecting the null hypothesis (HO:) when, in fact, it is false.

precision   Level of uncertainty about the characteristics of the construct being measured.

precoding   Procedure of assigning a code number to every possible response to an open-ended question.

precommercialization stage   Developmental stage of a product, characterized by much marketing research activity designed to ensure that the launched product will be successful in matching or exceeding management's performance objectives.

prediction   The attempt to make statements about future events on the basis of the effects of past, current, or proposed events.

predictor or independent variable   The variable upon which the prediction is based.

preference product maps   Attempts to position brands in the perceptual space in accordance with those product features or attributes that consumers view as most important in making evaluations of the brand or in choosing among alternative brands.

prescription   Selecting a course of action based on the objectives of the study and identifying relevant alternatives and their likely consequences.

pretest markets   A system for providing management with information on the likely share or volume a new product will capture prior to conducting a test market.

primary data   Data collected for a specific research need; they are customized and require specialized collection procedures.

primary sampling units (PSUs)   Clusters used at the first stage of sampling.

principal components analysis (PCA)   A popular approach to factor analysis; uncovers dimensions that are linear combinations of the original attributes such that

the uncovered dimensions account for as much variation in the original attribute ratings as possible.

print ad tests   Attempts to assess the power of an ad placed in a magazine or newspaper to be remembered, to communicate, to affect attitudes, and, ultimately, to produce sales.

prior notification   Method of reducing nonresponse that involves sending potential respondents an advance letter to notify them of the impending telephone or personal contact.

PRIZM neighborhood lifestyle clusters   Assigns individuals to unique market segments on the basis of where the individual lives; underlying premise is that choice of neighborhood is the most basic consumer decision and one that ultimately reflects lifestyle choices.

probability proportional to size (PPS) sampling   Design in which clusters are sampled at the first stage with probability proportional to the number of sampling units in the cluster.

probability sampling designs   Samples drawn in such a way that each member of the population has a known, nonzero chance of being selected.

prodegy   Method of investigating competitive structure in which consumers, faced with the deletion of a preferred product, will switch to a close competitor.

product maps   Space which represents the perceived relationships among a set of brands; the spatial distance between any two brands represents the degree to which they are perceived as being similar in terms of relevant attributes or preferences.

product perceptions   Questions relating to the ad's effect on perceptions and/or purchase intentions concerning the test brand.

product/service market   The set of products/services that can be substituted for each other within those use situations where similar benefits are sought and the customers for whom such usages are relevant.

product target AID   A microcomputer that categorizes television viewers by their purchasing patterns.

profile composites   Research findings that answer the question, "To whom did it happen?"

project proposal   A research written description of the key research design factors that define the proposed study.

projective techniques   A class of techniques which presume that respondents cannot or will not communicate their feelings and beliefs directly; provides a structured question format in which respondents can respond indirectly by projecting their own feelings and beliefs into the situation while they interpret the behavior of others.

proportional allocation   Sampling design guaranteeing that stratified random sampling will be at least as efficient as SRS. The number of elements selected from a stratum is directly proportional to the size of the stratum.

protocol analysis   Procedure in which the respondent "thinks aloud" while completing the questionnaire.

protomonadic designs   Comparison tests where a consumer evaluates one product and then compares it with a second product.

proven total recall   Percentage of respondents in the program audience that correctly recalled copy or visual elements in the test ad or commercial.

proximities   Any set of numbers that express the amount of similarity or difference between pairs of objects.

purchase-intent scales   Procedure attempting to measure a respondent's interest in a brand or product.

purchase or use behavior data   Information providing the most accurate indication of what people do or have done.

Q-sort scales   Rank-order procedure in which objects are sorted into piles based on similarity with respect to some criterion.

qualitative research methods   Techniques involving small numbers of respondents who provide descriptive information about their thoughts and feelings that are not easily projected to the whole population.

quantitative research methods   Techniques involving relatively large numbers of respondents, which are designed to generate information that can be projected to the whole population.

quasi-experimental designs   Experimental designs in which the researcher is unable to achieve complete control over the scheduling of the treatments or cannot randomly assign respondents to experimental treatment conditions.

quota sampling   Design that involves selecting specific numbers of respondents who possess certain characteristics known, or presumed to affect, the subject of the research study.

radio and television AID   Analysis of a station's audience by selected demographics, specific geography, or nonstandard time periods.

random-digit directory sample designs   Samples of numbers drawn from the directory, usually by a systematic procedure. Selected numbers are modified to allow all unlisted numbers a chance for inclusion.

random sampling error   Error caused because selected sample is an imperfect representation of the overall population; therefore, the true mean value for the particular sample of respondents (on the variable of interest) differs from the true mean value for the overall population (on the variable of interest).

random sources of error   Denoted by X_R, component made up of transient personal factors that affect the observed scale score in different ways each time the test is administered.

randomization   Process by which respondents are randomly assigned (e.g., pulling a respondent's name out of a hat) to treatment conditions for the purpose of controlling extraneous factors in an experimental setting.

range   Difference between largest and smallest values of distribution.

rank-order scale   Scale in which respondents are presented with several objects simultaneously and requested to "order" or "rank" them.

rating   The percent of all households that have at least one television set viewing a program for at least 6 minutes out of every 15 minutes that the program is telecast.

ratio data   Measurements that have the same properties as interval scales, but which also have a natural or absolute origin.

rational database manager   A component of an MDSS that provides the user with the ability to efficiently access and manipulate the data.

reactive or interactive effects of testing   Threat to external validity that occurs when a pre-exposure measurement increases or decreases the respondent's sensitivity or responsiveness to the experimental treatment conditions and thus leads to unrepresentative results.

real-magazine tests   Test where interest centers on the "magazine" effect—that is, the context in which the ad appears.

realistic research environment   Situation similar to the normal situation in which the behavior under study would naturally occur.

recall   Measures of how many people remember having seen the test ad both on an unaided and aided basis.

recognition   A score that measures whether respondent can recognize the name of the test brand.

record   A string of coded data in a machine-readable format.

refusal conversion (persuasion)   Method of reducing nonresponse; skilled interviewers reduce the proportion of refusals by not accepting a refusal to a request for cooperation without making an additional plea.

region of rejection   A cut point often referred to as a critical value; if the value of the test statistic falls to the right or the left of this critical value, we reject the null hypothesis.

regression analysis   Procedure that determines how much of the variation in the dependent variable can be explained by the independent variable.

regression and econometric model   Methods that produce forecasts based on expressing demand as a function of a certain number of deterministic factors.

regression line   A line fitted to the data that in some sense best captures the functional relationship.

related samples   The measurement of the variable of interest in one sample can affect the measurement of the variable in some other sample.

relative tolerance level (r)   The difference between the estimate and its unknown true population value expressed as a percentage.

reliability   The extent to which measures are free from random error and yield consistent results.

reliability coefficient   Measure that indicates the amount of systematic variation, relative to the total observed scale variation.

repeat paired comparison designs   Tests where a respondent is given two or more sets of products to compare against each other at two different points in time.

replacement   Approach to reducing nonresponse; included in the survey are the addresses (or telephone numbers) of nonrespondents from an earlier survey that used similar sampling procedures. When a response is obtained in the current survey, the interviewer replaces the nonresponse address with an address for a nonresponse in a previous study.

repositioning   A strategy that defines a new role (new users or uses) for an aging product in the marketplace.

research cycle   Research activities in distinct stages matched to the unique needs of the product during each stage of its life cycle (prelaunch, rollout, and established markets).

residual   An error term representing the difference between the actual and predicted values of the dependent variable.

response error   Error that occurs because respondents (who do respond) may give inaccurate answers, or a respondent's answers may be misrecorded.

response rates   The total number of respondents sent questionnaires who complete and return them, expressed as a percentage.

round robin designs   Test where a series of products is tested against each of the others.

sales force composite estimates   A method of forecasting based on the informed knowledge of the firm's sales force who provide estimates of future demand.

sales wave extended-use product test   Respondent is given opportunity to buy the product at intervals coinciding with the normal purchase cycle.

sample   A subset of the target population from which information is gathered to estimate something about the population.

sample balancing   Procedure by which the sample is weighted to match the general population on specific characteristics before tabulating other variables to estimate their population distribution.

sampling   Identification of a group of individuals or households (or institutions or objects) who (that) can be reached by mail, telephone, or in person, and who (that) possess the information relevant to solving the marketing problem at hand.

sampling frame   An explicit list of individuals or households that are eligible for inclusion in the sample.

sampling interval   Computed by taking n/N together with r, the first chosen element to be included in the sample, determines which elements will be included in the sample.

sampling units   The elements that make up the population.

sampling variable   Variable that represents the characteristic of the population that we wish to estimate.

scale transformations   Procedures for transforming data by one of a number of simple arithmetic operations to make comparisons across respondents and/or scale items.

scatter diagram   A bivariate plot of two variables.

secondary data   Data that have been collected for another project and have already been published. Sources can be in-house or external.

secondary sampling units (SSUs)   Sampling units selected at the second stage of sampling.

segmentation research   Studies that provide guidelines for a firm's marketing strategy and resource allocation among markets and products.

segmentation studies   Attempts to identify subgroups of consumers who will respond to a given marketing-mix configuration in a similar manner.

selection bias   Threat to internal validity; refers to the improper assignments of respondents to treatment conditions.

self-administered CRT interview An interviewing method where the respondent sits at a computer terminal and answers the questionnaire by using a keyboard and a screen.

self-perception theory Theory proposing that individuals come to know their attitudes through interpreting the causes of their behavior. To the extent that one's behavior is attributed to internal causes and not to circumstantial pressures, a positive attitude toward the behavior develops, and these attitudes, or self-perceptions, exert a direct influence on subsequent behavior.

semantic differential scale Semantic scale utilizing bipolar adjectives as end points.

semantic scale Procedure where respondents describe their feelings on a rating scale with end points or categories associated with labels having semantic meaning.

sentence completion Projective technique whereby respondents are asked to complete a number of incomplete sentences with the first word or phrase that comes to mind.

sequential monadic designs Comparison tests where a consumer rates one product and then is given a second product to rate independently.

share The percent of households with a television set and who are tuned to a specific program at a specific time.

share-of-preference model Conjoint analysis model that assumes individuals purchase products in proportion to their utility for the products.

simple one-stage cluster sampling One-step design in which first stage clusters are selected by SRS, and within each selected cluster all sampling units are chosen.

simple random sampling (SRS) Design guaranteeing that every sample of a given size as well as every individual in the target population has an equal chance of being selected.

simple two-stage cluster sampling Design in which the clusters at the first stage are selected by SRS; at the second stage the sampling units are selected probabilistically by SRS from each sample cluster so that with clusters of equal size the same fraction of sampling units is drawn from each sample cluster.

simple weighting Procedures that attempt to remove nonresponse bias by assigning weight to the data that in some sense account for nonresponse.

simulated test market Method whereby various groups of preselected respondents are interviewed, monitored, and sampled about the new product; in addition, respondents may be exposed to various media messages in a controlled environment.

single ad research design Test where respondent is exposed to the test ad by itself; that is, the test ad is not shown with other ads, and it is not displayed in a magazine.

single-item formats Scaling technique that involves asking the respondent to make a judgment about the object in question.

single market test Test involving a single market without control.

single-stage cluster sample One-step design where, once the sample of clusters is selected, every sampling unit within each of the selected clusters is included in the sample.

situation analysis Taking stock of where you have been, where you are now, and where you are likely to end up if current trends persist.

skewed distribution Distribution where one tail is fat, while the other is thin.

snowball design Sample formed by having each respondent, after being interviewed, identify others who belong to the target population of interest.

sorting Procedure that involves presenting the respondent with the total stimulus set and asking him or her to sort the set into groups of like objects.

Spearman's rank-order correlation coefficient Measure of linear association between variables that have ordinal scale properties.

spill-in The amount of outside media coming into a market.

spill-out The amount of a test market's newspapers and TV that are being seen and read in distant cities.

split-halves Scale items split in terms of odd- and even-numbered items or randomly.

spurious association Inappropriate causal interpretation of an observed association.

standard deviation Index of variability in the same measurement units used to calculate the mean.

standard error ($s_{\bar{y}}$) Indication of the reliability of an estimate of a population parameter; it is computed by dividing the standard deviation of the sample estimate by the square root of the sample size.

standard test market Method where the company's own sales force is responsible for distributing the new product in the selected test-market areas. Sales force personnel would stock the shelves and return at periodic intervals to restock and count movement.

standardized discriminant function weights (the *b* coefficients)   Measures of the importance of each attribute in distinguishing among the alternative brands.

standardized research services   Studies conducted for different clients but always in the same way.

stapel scale   Procedure using a single criterion or key word and instructing the respondent to rate the object on a scale.

Starch scores   Research design where readers of specific magazines are located, and the interviewer determines whether each ad in the issue was remembered, whether the name of the brand or advertiser that was read, and whether a substantial portion of the advertisement was read.

statistical conclusion validity   Involves drawing inferences about whether two variables covary.

statistical hypothesis test   Test that determines the probability of observing a sample mean of $\overline{X}$ if indeed the population mean (or hypothesized mean) is μ.

statistical test of each regression coefficient   Determination of significance of each regression coefficient separately.

statistically significant finding   Indication that our notions (hypotheses) about a population are likely, given the sample evidence.

storage instantaneous audimeter   Instrument that continuously monitors and records television viewing in terms of when the set was turned on, what channels were viewed, and for how long.

store audits   Studies that monitor performance in the marketplace among dollar and unit sales/share, distribution/out of stock, inventory, price, promotional activity, and feature ads.

strategic market studies   Studies that focus on in-depth analysis of a specific product/service market; they fall under the umbrella of customer research and are tailored to address specific marketing issues and/or problems.

stratified sampling   Design that involves partitioning the entire population of elements into subpopulations, called strata, and then selecting elements separately from each subpopulation.

structure studies   Attempts to define the competitive relationships within a product/service market.

structured interview   Method of interviewing where the questions are completely predetermined.

stub   Delineates the response formats that will be used in the cross tabulation. Stubs make up the rows of the cross tabulation.

substitutions   Methods of handling nonresponse; nonresponses are replaced with other substitute respondents who are expected to respond.

surrogate situations   Use of experimental settings, test units, and/or treatment conditions that differ from those to be encountered in the actual setting that the researcher is interested in.

survey   A method of gathering information from a number of individuals (the respondents, who collectively form a sample) in order to learn something about a larger target population from which the sample was drawn.

symmetric distribution   Distribution where values on either side of the center of the distribution are the same.

syndicated research services   Market research suppliers who collect data on a regular basis with standardized procedures. The data are sold to different clients.

systematic sampling   Design whereby the target sample is generated by picking an arbitrary starting point (in a list) and then picking every *n*th element in succession from a list.

systematic sources of error   Denoted by X_s, component made up of stable characteristics that affect the observed scale score in the same way each time the test is administered.

tab houses   Outside suppliers that perform tabulating work and other analyses when neither the client nor the marketing research supplier has the necessary computing resources.

target AID   Categorization of audiences by lifestyle, purchasing habits, and economic standing.

target population   Set of people, products, firms, markets, etc., that contain the information that is of interest to the researcher.

telephone surveys   Survey that involves phoning a sample of respondents drawn from an eligible population and asking them a series of questions.

telescoping   Condition that occurs when a respondent either compresses time or remembers an event as occurring more recently than it actually occurred.

test markets   A system that allows the marketing manager to evaluate the proposed national marketing program in a smaller, less expensive situation with a view toward determining whether the potential profit opportunity from rolling out the new product or line extension outweighs the potential risks.

testing   Threat to internal validity; refers to the consequences of taking before-and-after exposure measurements on respondents.

test-retest reliability Method for calculating reliability; respondents are administered identical sets of scale items at two different times under similar conditions. The reliability coefficient is computed by correlating the scores obtained from the two administrations.

thematic apperception test (TAT) Projective technique presenting respondents with a series of pictures or cartoons in which consumers and products are the primary topic of attention.

third person/role playing Projective technique that presents respondents with a verbal or visual situation and asks them to relate the feelings and beliefs of a third person to the situation, rather than to directly express their own feelings and beliefs about the situation.

time-series models Methods that produce forecasts on the basis of the statistical analysis of past data that presumably incorporate enduring and identifiable causal relationships that will carry forward into the future.

time-series quasi design Experiment that involves periodic measurements on some group or individual, introduction of an experimental manipulation, and subsequent periodic measurement.

tolerance level The allowable difference permitted between the estimate and its known true population value.

top-box purchase intention scores The percentage of respondents who indicate they "definitely" would buy.

top-down approach Process of breaking down clusters—at the beginning, all respondents belong to one segment, and then respondents are partitioned into two segments, then three segments, and so on until each respondent occupies his or her own segment.

top-line reports Highlights of the study's results given to the marketing executive before all of the data have been tabulated.

total survey error The difference between the overall population's true mean value (on the variable of interest) and the mean observed value (of the variable of interest) obtained from the particular sample of respondents.

total variation Sum of between variation plus within variation.

tracking System for measuring the key sales components of customer awareness and trial-and-repeat purchases.

trade-off procedures Technique where the respondent is asked to consider two attributes at a time to rank the various combinations of each pair of attribute descriptors from a most preferred to least preferred.

treatment Term for that independent variable that has been manipulated.

triangle designs Tests where a respondent is given two samples of one product and one sample of another and asked to identify the one that differs.

true score Component part of a person's observed score that reflects the person's actual score on the construct of interest.

true-score model A person's (true) specific attitude toward buying and using the brand, denoted by X_T.

two-factor after-only with control design Experiment differing from the after-only with control group designs by having more than one independent variable.

two-independent-sample test Test whether the observed proportion (mean) in one sample is equal to the observed proportion (mean) in another sample.

two-tail hypothesis test Test used when the alternative hypothesis is nondirectional—the region of rejection is in both tails of the distribution.

Type I error Situation occurring when the null hypothesis is in fact true, but is nevertheless rejected on the basis of the sample data.

Type II or beta (β) error Situation occurring when we fail to reject the null hypothesis ($HO:$) when in fact the alternative ($HA:$) is true.

unaided questions Questions that do not provide any clues to the answer.

unaided recall Respondents are asked if they remember seeing a commercial for a product in the product category of interest.

unbalanced scale Scale using an unequal number of unfavorable scale categories.

underregistration Condition that occurs when a sampling frame contains fewer sampling units than the target population.

unfinished scenario story completion Projective technique whereby respondents complete the end of a story or supply the motive for why one or more actors in a story behaved as they did.

unstructured interview Method of interviewing where questions are not completely predetermined and the interviewer is free to probe for all details and underlying feelings.

utility scale values Ratings that indicate how influential each attribute level is in the consumer's overall evaluations.

validation Procedure where between 10 and 20 percent of all respondents "reportedly" interviewed are recontacted by telephone and asked a few questions to verify that the interview did in fact take place.

validity   Refers to the best approximation to truth or falsity of a proposition, including propositions concerning cause-and-effect relationships.

variable (re)specification   Transformation of data that creates new variables and/or collapses the categories of existing variables in order to respecify a variable into a form consistent with the aims of the study.

verification   Procedures aimed at ensuring that data from the original questionnaires have been accurately transcribed.

visual recall   Percentage of respondents in the program audience that correctly recalled visual elements in the test commercial.

within-group variation   Within-group sum of squares; reflects differences in scores for respondents in the same group—represents "unexplained" variation.

word association   Projective technique whereby respondents are presented with a list of words, one at a time, and asked to indicate what word comes immediately to mind.

Name Index

Subject Index